Quantitative Risk and Portfolio Management

A comprehensive modern introduction to risk and portfolio management for quantitatively adept advanced undergraduate and beginning graduate students who will become practitioners in the field of quantitative finance. With a focus on real-world application, but providing a background in academic theory, this text builds a firm foundation of rigorous but practical knowledge. Extensive live data and Python code are provided, allowing a thorough understanding of how to manage risk and portfolios in practice. With its detailed examination of how mathematical techniques are applied to finance, this is the ideal textbook for giving students with a background in engineering, mathematics, or physics a route into the field of quantitative finance.

Kenneth J. Winston is a Lecturer in Economics at the California Institute of Technology and an Adjunct Professor of Mathematics at New York University. Having trained as a combinatorist at MIT, he moved into the field of quantitative finance, creating algorithms for equity and option investment strategies. He worked as a Chief Risk Officer at Western Asset Management and Morgan Stanley, and is a founder of the Buy Side Risk Managers Forum. Winston won the 2006 Roger Murray Award at the Institute for Quantitative Research in Finance and is a co-editor of *The Oxford Handbook of Quantitative Asset Management* (Oxford University Press, 2014).

"This is the book I wish I had had when I started my career in quantitative finance twenty years ago. It is written with the rigor of an academic, the insight of an experienced practitioner, and the didactic style of an empathetic and engaging teacher. Winston connects with his readers through insightful and entertaining discussions of historical background and of how actual financial markets behave or misbehave. At the same time, he provides rigorous but crystal clear and unhurried explanations of technical concepts. His choice of topics reflects current practice. A practitioner will find much to learn and enjoy in this book. A student who masters this material will be well prepared for a career in quantitative finance."

Colm O'Cinneide, *Franklin Templeton Investments*

"Ken Winston has created a concise, valuable reference for the quantitatively minded that, in addition to describing our standard approaches for asset pricing and risk management, shows how these tools can and must be extended to reflect the more complicated risks we actually face."

David Germany, *Pitzer College*

"This book is a remarkable combination of finance theory, mathematics, and practice. The development of finance theory is deep enough to challenge the most advanced students, yet it is full of applications. The author's long history of developing risk models is evident in every chapter. The book belongs in the curricula of the best graduate programs in finance and economics."

Charles Trzcinka, *Indiana University*

"Few people are as qualified as Ken Winston to provide an academically disciplined practitioner view of how to manage and profit from investment risk-taking. Trained as a mathematician, Ken was the chief risk officer for some of the world's largest investment managers. Successful risk managers must have excellent quantitative and people skills, and Ken has both. The value of quantitative skill is evident in a game of numbers. People skills are necessary to communicate and successfully enforce limits on managers who too often dream of unachievable profits. Ken drew on both sets of skills to produce this innovative book, already well tested in his classrooms at Cal Tech and NYU. It is an essential read for all aspiring investment managers."

Larry Harris, *University of Southern California*

"This is the book that I wish I had been able to have when I switched from applied math/ engineering to applied finance more than thirty years ago. In essence, the book fills a very important void: how to approach financial engineering problems from the practitioner's viewpoint. A must-have for risk managers and investment professionals."

Arturo Cifuentes, *Chile Sovereign Fund*

Quantitative Risk and Portfolio Management

Theory and Practice

Kenneth J. Winston

California Institute of Technology

Shaftesbury Road, Cambridge CB2 8EA, United Kingdom

One Liberty Plaza, 20th Floor, New York, NY 10006, USA

477 Williamstown Road, Port Melbourne, VIC 3207, Australia

314–321, 3rd Floor, Plot 3, Splendor Forum, Jasola District Centre, New Delhi – 110025, India

103 Penang Road, #05–06/07, Visioncrest Commercial, Singapore 238467

Cambridge University Press is part of Cambridge University Press & Assessment, a department of the University of Cambridge.

We share the University's mission to contribute to society through the pursuit of education, learning and research at the highest international levels of excellence.

www.cambridge.org
Information on this title: www.cambridge.org/highereducation/isbn/9781009209045

DOI: 10.1017/9781009209090

First published 2024

Printed in the United Kingdom by TJ Books Limited, Padstow, Cornwall, 2024

A catalogue record for this publication is available from the British Library

Library of Congress Cataloging-in-Publication Data
Names: Winston, Kenneth James, author.
Title: Quantitative risk and portfolio management : theory and practice /
   Kenneth J. Winston, California Institute of Technology.
Description: Cambridge, United Kingdom ; New York, NY : Cambridge
   University Press, 2023. | Includes bibliographical references and index.
Identifiers: LCCN 2022055743 (print) | LCCN 2022055744 (ebook) |
   ISBN 9781009209045 (hardback) | ISBN 9781009209076 (paperback) |
   ISBN 9781009209090 (epub)
Subjects: LCSH: Portfolio management–Mathematical models. | Financial risk
   management–Mathematical models.
Classification: LCC HG4529.5 .W566 2023 (print) | LCC HG4529.5 (ebook) |
   DDC 332.6–dc23/eng/20221201
LC record available at https://lccn.loc.gov/2022055743
LC ebook record available at https://lccn.loc.gov/2022055744

ISBN 978-1-009-20904-5 Hardback

Additional resources for this publication at www.cambridge.org/winston

Contents

List of Images

List of Figures

Preface

Humans have far longer planning horizons than other species. We alone have the desire and ability to ponder multiple hypothetical versions of a decades-away future. Dolphins demonstrate self-awareness, problem-solving, innovation, and teaching skills but there aren't any dolphins with living wills.[1]

Some situations admit only a very narrow range of outcomes, so there is little subtlety needed to consider how they might unfold over a planning horizon. Other situations have possible consequences that differ dramatically. A wide spread of potential ways in which the future can unfold is called **risk**, which is one of the two central subjects of this book.

In particular, we'll explore financial risk. The financial system is a place-holder for human effort; it directs and transports human effort, its inputs, and its outputs across time and space. But no one can know now exactly which efforts will pay off in the future: again, that's risk.

There are many mechanisms for reacting to, and planning for, financial risk:

- Beneath a veneer of technology, financial markets are as subject to primitive emotional behaviors as any other high-stakes human activity. Hardwired pathways in our brains trigger hot-blooded reactions to short-term risky situations. Panic, for example, can kick in when some of the possible outcomes include great harm. Financial panics occur regularly when market participants lose faith en masse in all or part of the financial system.
- But we humans are also capable of cool-headed sorting through multiple possible long-term outcomes. This allows us to form plans – like living wills – that can last many years and involve many other individuals.
- Quantitative methods even allow the search for risky optimal planning to transcend biology.

The word "transcend" in the last point is aspirational. Quantitative methods span a spectrum from intuitively approachable closed-form formulas, through complex human-specified algorithms, to fully artificial intelligence. Certainly these methods are *not* biology: they are implemented on computers. But they

---

1 Whale and Dolphin Conservation. "How Intelligent Are Whales and Dolphins?" Website. https://us.whales.org/whales-dolphins/how-intelligent-are-whales-and-dolphins/; Mayo Clinic. "Living Wills and Advance Directives for Medical Decisions." www.mayoclinic.org/healthy-lifestyle/consumer-health/in-depth/living-wills/art-20046303.

show only intermittent ability to *transcend* biology – that is, human intuition. No one could write a serious paper titled "The Unreasonable Effectiveness of Mathematics in Quantitative Finance."[2]

Thus, a continuing theme in this book will be the need to mix intuition with quantitative rigor. At the beginning of Chapter 2 we review a litany of cautionary sayings that warn that truth in economics and finance is a moving target. It's a good idea not to fall in love with formulas or algorithms: their constancy is suspect. And it's still better not to fall in love with one's intuitive hunches: they're even more fickle. We'll show the quantitative methods that can work together with intuition to help gain an understanding of the future in a way that we hope does transcend biology alone.

Human emotion was assumed away in early economics and finance treatments: people were assumed to act as if they were computers running optimizations. Even the proponents of this view knew it wasn't true, but it was hoped that individual irrationalities canceled out and the overall market was rational, maybe even Gaussian. But the thinking we'll discuss in this book assumes that market moods shift over time. No parameter is fixed forever: ultimately, everything is time-varying. We will discuss time-varying estimation methods that have shown good out-of-sample predictive power.

The second main subject of this book is the management of **portfolios**, which are collections of risky ventures. The mechanisms for dealing with uncertainty change dramatically when multiple risky situations are in play: the range of outcomes can be narrowed by balancing efforts.

For example, Tainter (1990, p. 173), discussing the Maya – but more generally all complex societies, noted

> In environments characterized by high topographic diversity, where food procurement systems with different productivity cycles exist in close proximity, it is common to alleviate resource fluctuations by developing regional systems of economic symbiosis ... a local group can insure itself against lean times by converting temporary surpluses into reciprocal obligations that are called in during times of scarcity.

The diversification of the food portfolio practiced by the Maya was intended to narrow the range of future outcomes by removing starvation from the list of possibilities.

While a portfolio is by definition a collection of risky ventures, it is more than a muddle of individual shiny objects. Modern investors can take chances on ventures without knowing exactly which ones will succeed as long as they are confident that enough ventures will succeed to give them a good overall return. This is more than a financial gimmick: it's a sensible way of organizing

---

2 [Wigner 1960].

cooperative productive behavior. In the absence of knowledge of what exactly will succeed, some need to fail so that others can make progress.

The possibility of losing all one's money concentrates the mind almost as wonderfully as the possibility of an interruption in the food supply. That concentration tends to make the required return on a single risky venture high, as less-than-heroic investors demand combat pay to leave their barracks and join the battle. Prices can go up or down as investors get less or more skittish; or they can go up or down as fundamental information improves or degrades an asset's future prospects. Disentangling investor risk preferences from investor assessments of future prospects is difficult. Decades-long academic work in this area shows a glimmer of practical fruit but is still in the early stages in real-world applications.

Risk preference is particularly important in a portfolio context, as overall market sentiment tends to shift like human moods do. In a pessimistic market, risk premia tend to widen in lockstep, increasing correlations and weakening the diversification benefit of portfolios.

In fact, the time-varying nature of virtually all financial parameters leads to fat tails: historical patterns work until, violently, they don't. Thus, studying tail behavior is an important part of risk and portfolio management. In this book, we'll discuss simple Gaussian models, but we'll also discuss distributions and time series approaches that attempt to deal with the one-in-a-billion shocks that actually happen every five years or so in financial markets.

The quantitative finance field encompasses two almost wholly disjoint subfields: "hard quant" and "soft quant" (equivalently, "heavy quant" and "light quant"). The hard/heavy discipline brings to bear techniques from mathematics and physics; practitioners often hold PhDs in quantitative fields and apply their craft to understanding exotic financial instruments. The soft/light discipline uses techniques from social sciences, primarily regressions and machine learning, to find patterns of behavior inductively.

Despite the mildly disparaging "soft/light" terminology, neither discipline has a monopoly on truth or brilliance. The weakness of hard/heavy is its reliance on axioms that cannot possibly be true; strong results mainly come from strong assumptions. The weakness of soft/light is its reliance on techniques that cannot possibly be proven false, as they are designed to fit past data.

But over years, a body of elegant work has been done that transcends – there, I've said it – the limitations of each subfield. The aim of this book is to present a coherent picture of the progress that has been made on the foundations of quantitative risk and portfolio management.

Reader Competencies

In the author's experience as a practitioner and as an educator, a solid majority of people learning about and working in the field of quantitative finance do not have degrees in quantitative finance or economics. Instead, backgrounds in fields like engineering, computer and data science, physics, and mathematics are common. This book is aimed at the quantitatively adept student at the late undergraduate or graduate level. No previous knowledge of economics or finance is assumed, but facility with mathematics and statistics is essential.

This book gives quantitatively adept students a comprehensive introduction to the body of knowledge required to be a working "quant," that is, a practitioner of quantitative finance. Both the soft/light and hard/heavy quant subfields described above are covered. Thus, the reader should be comfortable with (or able to get comfortable with) both probability theory (heavier) and regression (lighter). We discuss simple stochastic processes, but no previous knowledge is required.

Quants can suffer from overspecialization. That's a pitfall for new quants; it's like an actor being typecast. An actor who specializes too soon might be doomed to always be the sympathetic friend who gives wise and funny advice to the star before getting out of the way. As a quant, you may find yourself slotted as the person spending all day thinking about double-knockout inflation-linked catastrophe bonds. You may be called in for a brief stint on the stage when decision makers want a little information about double-knockout inflation-linked catastrophe bonds, but you won't be one of those decision makers if you overspecialize.

The frontier of quant knowledge is not a single place: rather, it is a widely separated group of places. For example, we discuss options in several contexts, but certainly a number of separate full classes in options are required before the student can think of doing professional work with options. We discuss error-limiting portfolio construction techniques like Black–Litterman and resampled efficient frontiers, but further education is required to approach mastery. The aim of this book is to get you to where you can see a number of frontiers from where you stand so that you can decide which one or ones you want to visit.

The book was originally written in Jupyter notebook form, with mixed text and Python[3] code segments. In the text version of the book, the code segments have been moved to a Code Appendix. The Code Segments are numbered so the reader can refer to them to see how figures and results were generated.

In addition, Cambridge University Press hosts the runnable code segments on cambridge.org/9781009209090/chx, where $x = 1, 2, \ldots, 12$ corresponding to the book's 12 chapters. Readers may wish to read the online code while reading the text: the code can be run and variables examined to gain a better understanding of the material.

---

3 Python™. Website. www.python.org/.

Problem sets and review questions have been included in the online material under URLs that look like cambridge.org/9781009209090/pbx, where $x = 1, 2, \ldots, 12$.

Problem sets consist of questions of varying difficulty: some are pure theory questions while others involve Python coding and data. I have generally allowed unlimited "open book" access for these problems.

Each chapter also has review questions that are considerably easier than the full problems, but that are intended to be given "closed book" so students and/or instructors can see what material has been internalized.

At the time of writing, a popular index puts Python as the most popular computer language in the world.[4] This is puzzling as there is little about the language that would cause a computer scientist to release oxytocin. But it gets the job done and serves as a repository for a vast number of probability, statistics, optimization, machine learning, and other relevant packages. Many students who have taken the classes that formed the basis of this book were more fluent in Python than they were in their native English. If you aren't already fluent, you should want to be in order to use this book.

Outside of academia (and even mostly inside of academia), there is no area of quantitative finance that doesn't require diving headfirst into data and algorithms. Data are messy. Some of the code segments contain workarounds where the sources have known problems. If you feel that you should be above such mundane earthly concerns, this book is not for you.

Many code segments retrieve data from free sites. I have tried to use government and academic sources where possible. In some cases, sites maintained by industry groups like SIFMA[5] have been used.

Chapter Outline

We start **Chapter 1** by thinking about the nature of risk. Some people use the word "risk" to mean a hazard or a danger, but in a financial context it usually makes more sense to think of risk as an endeavor with a wide range of outcomes, some good and some bad. Portfolio management involves forging ahead when there are chances of bad outcomes, not removing every possibility of bad outcomes.

Frank Knight, an early twentieth-century economist, thought through the various aspects of financial risk in his book *Risk, Uncertainty, and Profit*. His approach still resonates in the early twenty-first century, and we discuss it. His approach used what we would call today a finite probability space.

---

4 Tiobe. "TIOBE Index for October 2022." www.tiobe.com/tiobe-index/.
5 SIFMA. Website. www.sifma.org/.

We then ask readers to record their intuitive responses to some hypothetical risky situations. After reviewing some basic economics, capital markets, and probability theory terminology, we build up the mechanism of Von Neumann–Morgenstern utility theory. In particular, the idea of risk preference – usually but not always risk aversion – is a key contribution of utility theory. We then use the theoretical framework to revisit the reader's intuitive responses to risky situations. We note that there are many paradoxes and counterexamples to pure utility theory, so it's best used as a way to guide intuition rather than as a natural law.

In **Chapter 2** we look at metrics for risk. First, we caution the reader with several well-known "laws of no laws": maxims that warn against overreliance on precise metrics. Mathematical laws that describe the physical world generally don't change the behavior of the physical world: they just describe it. But economic participants do change their behavior because once they know that others are relying on a law, they try to game that law.

We proceed nonetheless to describe some precise metrics. Our view is that they are still useful as long as the user is aware of the possibility of behavior shifts. Common risk-adjusted reward measures are also discussed. We show that Artzner, Delbaen, Eber, and Heath's definition of coherent risk and its relatives give a good framework for assessing the quality of a prospective risk measure.

We then note that risk preferences are embodied in prices. Together with the assumption of no-arbitrage, this brings us to state-price securities and the difference between the risk-neutral probability space and the physical probability space. We conclude Chapter 2 with an examination of stochastic discount factors and the Ross Recovery Theorem, which is an approach to determining market assessments of physical risk from prices. Some trading methods have been proposed based on Ross Recovery, but other work shows that the recovered probabilities are unrealistic. Thus, practical applications of this heavily trodden academic ground remain elusive.

Chapter 3 concerns fixed-income modeling. We first note the three different definitions of the time value of money – nominal, real, and inflation – and show that any or all of them can be positive or negative. Thus, discounting future sure amounts of money to the present can actually involve both increases and decreases.

The generic pricing equation for any financial arrangement says that today's price equals the sum of the discounted values of future expected cash flows. Different conventions for discounting are shown.

We illustrate the basics of default-free lending and borrowing by working through an example using a US Treasury bond. Pricing, duration, and convexity are shown in general. Closed-form formulas for a bullet bond priced with a flat curve are also worked out. We show that a first-order approximation to price changes using just duration is reasonable in a small neighborhood of the current discount rate, and a second-order approximation bringing in convexity is better. But a large enough move in the discount rate will degrade the quality of even the second-order approximation.

Moving away from the assumption of a flat curve, we look at different types of yield curves. We show that level, slope, and twist explain the vast majority of yield curve behavior. Key rates and smoothing techniques like Nelson–Siegel also allow important elements of yield curve behavior to be captured in a few variables.

After introducing implied forward curves and reviewing stochastic process terminology, we look at short-rate models of the term structure of interest rates. We examine some of the features of the original Vasicek model, and then work through a Hull–White model applied to the current US Treasury curve. Finally, we show other short-rate models including some that are in current use.

Chapter 4 focuses on equity modeling, starting with Markowitz's efficient frontier approach. Formulas for the equality-constrained frontier are developed and an example using currency data is worked out. We also discuss the inequality-constrained frontier, the relationship between the efficient frontier and utility functions, capital market line, and benchmark-relative frontiers. We note that there is a big gap between efficient frontier theory and practical reality so (as with utility functions) this approach is best used as a way to guide intuition rather than as a natural law.

After a review of Bayes's Rule, we look at some Bayesian approaches to mitigating some of the implementation problems with efficient frontier theory. Shrinkage estimators like James–Stein and Ledoit–Wolf are covered. We also cover some statistical tests like Hotelling, Levene, and Box's M that can be used to test how well shrinkage estimators are working out of sample.

We close Chapter 4 with investigations of two widely used methods – Jorion's resampling approach and Black–Litterman – that are intended to alleviate problems of errors in parameter estimation for efficient frontier calculation.

Chapter 5 is an overview of convex optimization that is used to form portfolios and to fit model parameters to data. Fortunately, the most commonly arising optimization problems in quantitative finance have convex objective functions and convex constraints, so the vastly more efficient procedures that can be brought to bear under convexity can be used. The aim of this chapter is to provide the reader with enough convex optimization expertise that he or she will be able to use some of the many excellent available optimization packages on practical problems, especially portfolio construction problems.

After reviewing optimization terminology, we discuss some of the key properties of convex functions that make optimizing them so much easier. We then look at unconstrained optimization methods including finding pseudo-inverses, gradient descent, and Newton's Method.

The more realistic approach of constrained optimization is then covered, starting with the familiar Lagrange multipliers approach and expanding to Lagrange duality. That leads to a discussion of the Karush–Kuhn–Tucker conditions and strong duality. We then talk about barrier methods to encode inequality constraints in the objective function, and work an example of a barrier method problem. Finally, we redo a portfolio optimization problem from Chapter 4 using a convex optimization package.

While Chapter 4 showed the power of portfolio diversification to lower risk without changing the average reward, **Chapter 6** shows that there are limits to the benefits of diversification. There are factors that affect all, or many, assets that can't be diversified away just by adding more assets. Determining these factors can help estimate future behaviors of portfolios.

At the beginning of Chapter 6, we discuss the Efficient Market Hypothesis ("EMH"), the academic theory that all available information is contained in stock market prices. This once-popular theory has been used in practice to justify passive investing in which an investor just participates in a market without seeking to beat it. Current beliefs about market efficiency are more nuanced.

The EMH gave rise to simple academic models like the Capital Asset Pricing Model (CAPM) and the Fama–French five-factor model. We then develop the Arbitrage Pricing Theory, both in Ross's original exact form and in Huberman's form allowing for idiosyncratic behavior. These models, especially the five-factor model, are widely used in academia but are not used much by practitioners forming investable portfolios.

Practitioners do use commercial factor models generally based on company-specific factors such as those originally used by Rosenberg and Marathe in 1976. A number of vendors provide factor model data and software that are heavily used by practitioners forming equity and fixed-income portfolios; these data are based on information about assets like the size of the underlying company and its industry group(s). Practitioners also use models based on principal components analysis of covariance matrices, that is, finding their eigensystems and principal eigenvectors. Some hybrid models combining company-specific information and principal components are also in use.

Chapter 7 is an exploration of probability distributions relevant to mathematical finance. It starts with a review of the Central Limit Theorem, which is a powerful force muscling distributions of natural phenomena into becoming Gaussian (normal). But it is only a weak force in mathematical finance, where histograms often look roughly bell-shaped but are actually spectacularly fat-tailed. Various methods of checking normality – Q-Q and P-P plots and Jarque–Bera – are shown to fail dramatically when applied to financial data. Theorems don't fail but their assumptions might; we note that it is the assumption of independence that is often violated in finance.

If normal distributions don't fit financial data, what does? We look at Student's T distributions, which are close to normal but have fatter tails, much like empirical financial data. A better although slightly less closed-form approach is a mixture of normals, which also seems like a plausible first-order model of market regime changes.

In the 1960s, Benoit Mandelbrot analyzed cotton prices and concluded that they couldn't possibly be normally distributed. He looked for the Central Limit Theorem assumption that failed to apply and concluded that finite variance was the culprit. That's not the mainstream belief now – as noted, failure of independence is now more widely thought to be the guilty party – but Mandelbrot's approach still commands a minority following. We explore the family of distributions that Mandelbrot suggested, Lévy α-stable distributions. The normal distribution is part of the family, but other than distributions that are very close to normal, we find that the stable family is too extreme to represent realistic surviving markets.

While the normal distribution is the limiting distribution for averages of suitably well-behaved distributions, the generalized extreme value ("GEV") distributions are limits for maxima of suitably well-behaved distributions. We look at GEV distributions and the related GPD (Generalized Pareto Distribution) family that describes tail distributions. These distributions are not as intuitive as normal distributions, but are much better at guiding human intuition through extreme situations.

Chapter 8 is about simulation, scenarios, and stress testing. Simulation is used when it is difficult or impossible to develop a closed-form formula for the sample space of a portfolio or instrument's rates of return. For example, the holdings in a portfolio might be priced with complex nonlinear functions of variables like key rates (Chapter 3) or factors (Chapter 6). The interactions between these nonlinear functions could be difficult to predict, so a simulation can be run where multiple values of the input variables are generated and fed through the pricing functions to produce a finite sample space whose characteristics can be computed.

Historical simulation is used when there is no need or no desire to impose a model on the distribution of input variables; the historical simulation simply uses the empirical distribution of past values as inputs to the pricing functions. We also show delta-normal simulations where input variables are assumed to follow multivariate normal distributions and portfolios are priced based on first-order dependencies (deltas) on these input variables. While we know from Chapter 7 that multivariate normal distributions are poor descriptors of financial variables, delta-normal is a way to get a quick first-order understanding of outcomes because Euler decomposition of contributions can be used. Higher-order understandings can be obtained with more terms: we show a delta-gamma-theta simulation that adds second-order (gamma) and time dependencies.

We discuss Markov Chain Monte Carlo methods that use random sampling in a way that is intended to enrich the predictive validity of the sample. We describe the widely used Metropolis–Hastings Algorithm that is used for efficient sampling of states when there is a known state transition matrix. We further describe the Gibbs Sampler, which among other things is useful for filling in the most likely values of missing observations.

Scenarios and stress testing are hybrid approaches that use both qualitative and quantitative insights; these methods can be used to supplement the shortcomings of delta-normal assumptions. We explain that in stress testing, the analyst chooses one or a small number of input variables – like the average level of interest rates – and reprices a portfolio after applying an enormous shock to that variable. For example, a 200-basis point (bps) shock might be applied to interest rates. Scenarios are more elaborate versions of stress testing where an analyst chooses a highly unlikely financial story to investigate: for example, a disorderly breakup of the European Union. Reflecting this story in movements in input variables is an art, but then rigorously applying these movements to pricing functions for instruments in a portfolio can give the analyst some intuitive insight.

In Chapter 7, we noted that the failure of the Central Limit Theorem to apply to most financial data is due to a failure of the independence assumption. Understanding the nature of dependence, then, might lead to a better understanding of financial distributions. **Chapter 9** looks at methods to capture the time-varying nature of volatility, that is, how volatility in one time period may depend on volatility in previous time periods.

The chapter starts by showing that the long-term patterns of volatility in the US stock market can't be explained by sampling variation. There are clearly regimes, like human moods, in the stock market.

We then review options terminology because of the tight connection between volatility and options prices. We expect that many readers of this book will have taken a standalone options class; we give a brief background so that all readers can follow our use of options formulas. Options markets are naturally markets for volatility, along with more explicit volatility instruments like variance swaps and VIX® futures and options.

The shapes of implied volatility skews are clues that the Black–Scholes assumption of lognormality is incorrect. We pursue this idea through the Breeden–Litzenberger risk-neutral recovery of an underlying distribution from options prices. That allows us to complete Chapter 2's description of the Ross Recovery Theorem's real-world density recovery process. Stochastic and local volatility models are shown, along with a brief description of the standard SABR (Stochastic Alpha, Beta, Rho) model. We show the replicating portfolio used by the Cboe to compute VIX® in a distribution-agnostic way.

We then give a brief review of time series terminology on the way to describing Auto-Regressive Conditional Heteroskedasticity (ARCH) and Generalized Auto-Regressive Conditional Heteroskedasticity (GARCH) models.

We fit a GARCH(1,1) model to US stock market data and show that the de-GARCHed time series has lower kurtosis, moving part of the way to the goal of a "no surprise" stationary time series. We conclude the chapter with a review of some variants of ARCH and GARCH, mentioning the Merton model of corporate structure as a brief, and possibly incorrect, justification for asymmetric time series models.

In **Chapter 10**, we focus on relationships between assets. We start with a review of standard Pearson and Spearman correlations. We then discuss conditional versus unconditional correlations. We show that time-varying patterns between correlation pairs of regional stock market indices cannot be due to sampling noise.

We discuss the relationship between correlations and the overall economy. We note that highly correlated economies like Saudi Arabia's limit the opportunities for diversification – a fact the Saudis are most focused on changing. In a diversified economy like the USA, lower pairwise correlations are available. However, correlations tend to rise in bad times as previously different ventures become more driven by a general slowdown than by their individual properties. We note that in the USA, stocks and bonds have been negatively correlated since the late 1990s, but there is no guarantee that this will continue forever.

There isn't a general way to get an option-implied correlation between a pair of stocks, but we do show a way to get an average option-implied correlation between a pair of stocks in an index with traded options. This is the methodology used by the Cboe for the COR3M series that we display. The series clearly shows the effects of the Global Financial Crisis of 2007–2009 in increasing average pairwise correlations.

We then turn to copula functions as a more general way to describe relationships than correlations. We give a simplified example of the Li copula approach to collateralized debt obligations (CDOs), indicating the problems that ensued when this model was in wide practice.

The remainder of the chapter focuses on methods to estimate correlation matrices. The simplest is historical estimation with various types of weighting schemes. We show that constant conditional correlation is not a good model, as even after deGARCHing component time series, correlations are clearly nonstationary. Dynamic conditional correlation models like an integrated model, a mean-reverting model, and an asymmetric model are shown and applied to regional stock market index correlations. We end with a discussion and application of Engel's MacGyver method.

Chapter 11 concerns credit modeling. While Chapter 3 analyzed lending arrangements with sure cash flows, Chapter 11 looks at lending where there is a possibility that the borrower will be unable or unwilling to repay the lender. Borrowing and lending are two of the oldest financial activities: we note that in the absence of information networks, the fear of default led lenders to avoid borrowers that they did not know. That generally put a cap on economic growth, but the development of information networks like notaries in France allowed wider interactions and spurred growth.

Currently, vast amounts of data are available on individuals and businesses. In particular, credit rating agencies collect data on corporate and sovereign bond issuers and produce creditworthiness scores that investors rely on. We examine the categories that ratings agencies use and show how the qualitative assessments that they make lead to excellent ordinal rankings for probabilities of default, but also time-varying cardinal measures. We show that investment-grade bonds have very low frequencies of default, even during the Great Depression of the 1930s.

We note that sovereign (government) borrowers have different criteria and behaviors than corporate borrowers. Some governments, like Argentina, default regularly but are still able to return to the capital markets and borrow again. Overall, the default frequencies for governments are not very different by rating than the default frequencies for corporations.

We then discuss the credit spread premium puzzle: the fact that compensation for default and the risk of default seems too high. Various explanations have been advanced for this premium, but the puzzle remains. We revisit the Merton model and work examples showing that structural models badly underpredict credit spreads for all but the riskiest bonds. We further explore the commercial KMV model, which addresses some of the practical features missing from the pure Merton model. We describe a power function that balances Type I and Type II error; this can be used to assess the quality of credit rating methods.

We show that credit spreads have had reliable negative correlations with risk-free rates for decades (excluding the 1930s), and have positive correlation with volatility (VIX®) as structural models predict.

We then upgrade definitions of duration and convexity to cover credit spreads and other variables, defining effective duration, spread duration, and effective convexity. We describe factor models used to form credit portfolios and discuss the DTS (duration times spread) and ASD (adjusted spread duration) approaches.

Practical models like Altman's Z-scores, reduced form and hybrid models are covered. We discuss a multi-factor model of correlated defaults that is used to evaluate CDOs. We also show tree models to recover risk-neutral probabilities of default. We finish the chapter with a discussion of credit default swaps.

In **Chapter 12**, we look at five different motivations for hedging, together with associated techniques and relevant instruments.

The first motivation is unbundling. We give an example of a French investor whose base currency is euros wanting to invest in the US company Tesla denominated in dollars. The French investor may want the risks of Tesla, but not of dollar/euro. Hedging with currency forwards is only partly effective if it isn't updated frequently. A quanto option would be more effective but, since quantos are bespoke instruments, possibly not available.

The second motivation for hedging is franchise preservation. We give an example of a company importing US wine into France (which we acknowledge is purely hypothetical); the company can go bankrupt on a big enough strengthening of the dollar versus the euro. Currency hedging could be used, but a structural diversification of the company into a US subsidiary importing French wine (less hypothetical) as well as the original French unit importing US wine is more naturally hedged. However, this introduces Siegel's Paradox, which we discuss.

We discuss Modigliani–Miller reasoning, which in its purest form would argue against franchise preservation hedging. In practice, the friction of bankruptcy focuses the mind of most corporations. But we note that franchise preservation hedging involves gaming among competitors.

Bank franchise preservation hedging is a matter of necessity. We cite Diamond and Dybvig, showing that bank runs can only be prevented by government intervention, like a deposit insurance program. Leaving aside runs, the natural asset–liability mismatch in banks between short-term liabilities and long-term assets can be hedged with interest rate swaps, which we discuss. We note that pension plans are a natural counterparty to banks in interest rate swaps, but that pension plans are subject to longevity risk, which we also discuss.

The third type of hedging is for illiquidity. We note that some assets, like commercial real estate, are difficult to transact. Illiquidity hedging might involve transacting in a similar but more liquid instrument to raise or lower exposure. For example, the CMBX (commercial mortgage-backed securities) credit default swap based on commercial mortgages is easy to buy and sell. An investor wanting to raise or lower general exposure to commercial real estate might use the CMBX index as a liquidity hedge. However, this can introduce basis risk, where the illiquid item being hedged could move in the same direction as the hedge, making matters worse.

The fourth category is distribution reshaping hedging. The simplest example is adding cash or leverage to a portfolio to decrease or increase exposures linearly, making the outcome distribution less or more volatile. Futures are often used for delta-one (linear) distribution reshaping.

Other distribution reshaping techniques involve options, which can be fine-tuned to move around parts of outcome distributions. We review several of the more popular techniques. We then display a table of simple option Greeks, and indicate how option dealers hedge overall portfolios by adjusting overall Greeks. We finish this part with a discussion of fixed-income options used to reshape distributions of fixed-income portfolios.

The fifth reason for hedging is for convexity. We note that in some cases there can be rapid nonlinear movements in markets, and trying to trade through such markets to hedge these movements can be procyclical. We use the example of mortgage convexity hedging. We develop a simplified formula for swaption pricing and show how swaptions can be used to alleviate mortgage convexity exposure.

Acknowledgments

I'd like first to acknowledge my students at Caltech and at NYU. Their curiosity, creativity, and enthusiasm provided endless inspiration. While most were graduate students with strong quantitative backgrounds (in fields like mathematics, physics, computer science, and engineering), some were undergraduates and some came from fields less common to quantitative finance like meteorology and biology.

Whatever the background, I was always pleased to see unconventional approaches to material that I thought was straightforward being taken by students who weren't burdened by knowing what traditionally had been the right answer. The other students and I benefitted from these unconstrained thinkers.

My teaching assistants at Caltech and NYU, mostly former students, were also great to work with. I gradually became aware that many of them were holding sessions where they patiently explained what I really meant, only in clearer language.

Many people were kind enough to provide suggestions, assistance, readings, and guidance. I'd especially like to mention (in alphabetic order) Irina Bogacheva, Justin Bois, Kim Border, Peter Bossaerts, Arturo Cifuentes, Jaksa Cvitanic, Peg DiOrio, Charles Fishkin, David Germany, Bob Gingrich, Larry Harris, Thomas Hewett, Mark Kritzman, Tom Kwong, Vadim Martynov, Colm O'Cinneade, Houman Owhadi, Ramesh Pandey, Eugene Park, Daniel Sandberg, Bernd Scherer, Ivor Schucking, Charles Trzcinka, and Xiaotian (Jim) Zhang.

Finally in sequence but first in importance I'd like to thank my wife Jackie for her demure and quiet forbearance . . . sorry, wrong universe. Actually I would like to thank her for firmly bringing joy to my life.

1 What Is Risk?

Risk is **lack of information about the future.** A situation is risky if it has widely varying possible outcomes and there's no way to determine with high confidence which outcome will occur. A riskless or risk-free situation is one whose future is known exactly.

We humans yield to no species in our ability to worry, so there is a tendency to focus on whether or not negative outcomes might impend. Indeed, most definitions of the noun "risk" stress the downside: for example, *the possibility of loss, injury, or other adverse or unwelcome circumstance* is the first of several definitions of risk in the *Oxford English Dictionary.*[1] This is a gloomy strain of the more general definition above: a magnitude 8 earthquake is not a risk because we lack information about whether it will be enjoyable. It is a risk because we lack information about whether this unequivocally unpleasant thing will happen.

Expressing your love for the first time to another person involves *the possibility of loss, injury, or other adverse or unwelcome circumstance*: the other person may reject you.[2] So why do people override their pounding pulses and stammer out their feelings? It is because the unknown future also includes positive outcomes: the other person may return your affection.[3] Declaring your feelings is a risky situation, but you do so because you hope that a good outcome will occur.

The *Oxford English Dictionary* encompasses positive outcomes in an alternative definition of risk: *A person or thing regarded as likely to produce a good or bad outcome in a particular respect. Ex.: "The key to their success is information: on-the-ground knowledge of who is a good credit risk."* The phrase "good credit risk" in the example indicates that the good outcome (getting paid back after extending credit) was considered more likely due to on-the-ground knowledge.

1 Oed.com, September 2022. "risk, n." *Oxford English Dictionary.* www.oed.com/view/Entry/166306.
2 Madeline Holcombe and Giulia McDonnell, "A Confession of Love Ended in a Professor Attacking Her Friend with a Fire Poker, Police Say." CNN, January 7, 2020. www.cnn.com/2020/01/07/us/mount-holyoke-professor-attack/index.html.
3 [Shakespeare 1597], Act II, Scene II.

The philosopher Karl Popper noted that for scientific theories,

> Confirmations should only count if they are the result of **risky predictions**; that is to say, if, unenlightened by the theory in question, we should have expected an event which was incompatible with the theory – an event which would have refuted the theory.[4]

Popper thus captures the essence of this type of risk: a momentous choice about the future has to be made. A scientist has to make a risky prediction (emphasis added above) that can be proved right or wrong; a lender has to decide whether or not making a loan will probably result in repayment; a lover has to choose speech or silence.

So in practice there are two kinds of risks:

- **perils**, where there are no positive outcomes. There is only (a) nothing happens; or (b) bad things happen. Earthquakes, fires, floods, hurricanes, and other natural disasters are risks in this sense.
- **ventures**, where there are both positive and negative outcomes. Investments – such as making loans – are risks in this sense.

Perils are managed by avoidance (stay out of earthquake zones); fortification (build strong structures); and backstops (have emergency services and a pool of money ready to deal with the inevitable damage).

Ventures require a more subtle approach, because both positive and negative outcomes have to be weighed against each other. Should I make a conjecture;[5] extend credit; or declare my love? These are tough questions.

1.1 Frank Knight's Formulation

In 1921, Frank Knight – then an Associate Professor of Economics at the University of Iowa; later the influential head of the University of Chicago's economics department – wrote *Risk, Uncertainty, and Profit*.[6]

Knight delved into the philosophical nature of knowledge itself, but eventually got down to a very pragmatic list of ways in which we can organize our knowledge (or lack thereof) about the future (pp. 224–225):

1. **A priori probability**. ... [O]n the same logical plane as the laws of mathematics.
2. **Statistical probability**. Empirical evaluation of the frequency of association between predicates.
3. **Estimates**. [T]here is *no valid basis of any kind* for classifying instances.

---

4 [Popper 1962].
5 [Kim and Pittel 2000].
6 [Knight 1921].

An example of something with a priori probability is the throw of a perfect die. As Knight says, "the mathematician can easily calculate the probability that any proposed distribution of results will come out of any given number of throws." That doesn't help anyone know which face will come up on the next throw of the die; probability theory is silent on that subject. But a priori probability is vocal about the fact that betting even money on the same face coming up 50 times in a row is a bad idea when the die is fair.

A little less information about the future attaches to Knight's second category, *statistical probability*. An example here might be the chance that a 40-year-old male dies in the next year. Life insurance companies have gathered extensive statistics about mortality rates among 40-year-old males. As long as they have a sufficiently large pool of insureds, they can make a reasonable guess as to what to charge for insuring a 40-year-old male life. But there is no *a priori* mathematical model as there is with the throw of a die.

The final category has the least information. Here intuition must be used. Will my beloved return my affection if I declare it? There is no mathematical model, so the first category doesn't apply. Very few people have had the opportunity to build large databases of outcomes of their previous declarations of love, so the second category doesn't apply either. The terrified lover is left only with hunches.

Knight condenses his three categories into two with this more succinct statement (p. 233):

> To preserve the distinction which has been drawn … between the measurable uncertainty and an unmeasurable one, we may use the term "risk" to designate the former and the term "uncertainty" for the latter.

1.2 Finite Probability Spaces

At about the same time that Frank Knight was developing his ideas, the foundations of modern probability theory were being constructed by people like Émile Borel, Henri Lebesgue, and Andrey Kolmogorov. But Knight's formulation is amenable to a simple finite treatment.

For his "risk" (measurable) category, he assumed a finite number of future outcomes $s_1, \ldots, s_n$ and a known set of associated probabilities $p_1, \ldots, p_n$ (where $\sum_{i=1}^{n} p_i = 1$ and each $p_i \geq 0$). In the more general language of probability theory, $\{s_1, \ldots, s_n\}$ is the **sample space**, often denoted Ω.

Some probabilists treat finite and discrete probability spaces as the poor cousins of continuous probability spaces. But as Carlo Rovelli notes,

> Continuity is only a mathematical technique for approximating very finely grained things. The world is subtly discrete, not continuous.[7]

---

7 [Rovelli 2018], Chapter 5, p. 84.

It may be mathematically convenient to smooth out the world so that, for example, derivatives can be taken. But in fact Knight's "simple" finite formulation is sufficient to describe all states of the world that could arise in finance, or more generally in human experience.

An American roulette wheel is subject to what is now called **Knightian Risk**. Such a wheel has 38 outcomes (s_i = the ball falls in the slot numbered i for $i = 1, \ldots, 36$; s_{37} = the ball falls in the slot labeled 0; and s_{38} = the ball falls in the slot labeled 00). So the roulette sample space is

$$\Omega_{roulette} = \{s_1, \ldots, s_{38}\} = \{1, \ldots, 36, 0, 00\}. \tag{1.1}$$

Every slot is equally likely, so $p_i = \frac{1}{38}$ for $i = 1, \ldots, 38$.

Casinos make money on their roulette wheels, just as they do at their dice tables. In both cases, bettors can wager on *events*, which are combinations of outcomes. For example, in American roulette a bettor can place a bet on "even," which pays off if the future outcome lies in the event

$$E = \{s_2, s_4, \ldots, s_{36}\}. \tag{1.2}$$

Note that neither s_{37} nor s_{38} (neither 0 nor double-0) is contained in E. So the sum of the probabilities associated with the event E is only $\frac{18}{38} \approx 47.4\%$

If you bet on even and it occurs, you get two dollars for every dollar you bet. If even doesn't occur you lose the money you bet and you get nothing. The expected value of a dollar bet is $\frac{18}{38} * 2 + \frac{20}{38} * 0 = 18/19$, meaning the casino expects to make 5.2 cents for every dollar bet on the even event. Put another way, the casino charges a 5.2 percent fee per 4 minutes[8] to provide the entertainment of betting on the even event.

Knightian Risk is amenable to simple probabilistic calculations like this.

Perhaps the most common mistake made in financial mathematics is to forget that modeling the world of finance with Knightian Risk is a tactic, not a law.

1.3 Knightian Uncertainty

Within the broad umbrella of risk = lack of information about the future, Knight identified a more difficult type: what he called "unmeasurable," and what economists now call Knightian Uncertainty.

Knightian Uncertainty means either

- The sample space $\Omega = \{s_1, \ldots, s_n\}$ is known, but the associated probabilities $p_1, \ldots, p_n$ are not; or
- The sample space Ω is not known.

---

8 Roulette Life, "How Long Does It Take to Spin 100 Times in to a BM Casino (Average)?," post dated June 15, 2015, by user kav. www.roulettelife.com/index.php?topic=358.0.

Declaring love is a situation where the outcomes are (broadly) known: acceptance or rejection. But there is *no valid basis of any kind* to arrive at accurate probabilities.

Keynes (1937, p. 213) gave examples of Knightian Uncertainty:

> By "uncertain" knowledge, let me explain, I do not mean merely to distinguish what is known for certain from what is only probable. The game of roulette is not subject, in this sense, to uncertainty.... The sense in which I am using the term is that in which the prospect of a European war is uncertain, or the price of copper and the rate of interest twenty years hence, or the obsolescence of a new invention, or the position of private wealth owners in the social system in 1970. About these matters there is no scientific basis on which to form any calculable probability whatsoever.

In Keynes's examples, the outcomes of whether there will be "a European war" are known: yes or no. But the "prospect" (probability) is not. Or more precisely, in 1937 the probability *was* not; now we know there was a European (in fact, World) war. But in 1937 some future states of the world contained a European war and some didn't. Eventually (by September 3, 1939, when France and Britain declared war on Germany[9]) there were no longer any future states of the world that didn't have a European war in them.

Even deeper uncertainty attached to his last example, "the position of private wealth owners in the social system in 1970" – a date 33 years in the future from the time of his writing. Neither all the outcomes nor all the probabilities were known. Keynes was concerned about whether socialism, capitalism, or communism would prevail, but those broad groupings didn't constitute a precise and exhaustive listing of the outcomes, let alone guide the choice of associated probabilities.

We can be quite certain that if the upper-crust Keynes had tried to list the possible outcomes for "the position of private wealth owners in the social system in 1970," he would not have included the eventual reality. By then, a kind of socialist-tinged capitalism would be in place and one of the larger private wealth owners would be a 30-year-old commoner from Liverpool – John Lennon of the Beatles.[10] Such open-ended outcomes defy the tidy enumeration required for Knightian Risk to obtain.

The financial world is a world of Knightian Uncertainty, not of Knightian Risk.

Despite the fuzziness of Knightian Uncertainty, decisions have to be made. Freezing and doing nothing is a choice. This is the idea behind Pascal's Wager:[11] "Il faut parier." You have to make a bet: even not deciding is deciding.

---

9 History.com editors, 2009. "World War II," Section 2, Outbreak of World War II (1939). Online article. www.history.com/topics/world-war-ii/world-war-ii-history#section_2.

10 Biography.com editors, Original Published Date April 2, 2014; Last Updated April 14, 2021. "John Lennon: Biography." Online article. www.biography.com/musician/john-lennon.

11 [Hájek 2022].

In many cases, quantitative finance makes a first approach to problems by assuming that they can be described by Knightian Risk. However, we must never forget that this is an approximation, a guide, a forensic tool to help frame our thinking and intuition as we make decisions about an uncertain future.

1.4 Making Risky Decisions

All the focus on classifying what may happen in the future is done so that decisions can be made about what to do now: Set the payoffs on a roulette wheel; price a life insurance policy; determine an interest rate for a loan to a good credit risk; declare love or pine away, mute.

In this chapter, we'll describe a framework for thinking about how risky decisions are made. The framework will reflect the intuitively obvious fact that there are very few purely right or wrong answers; in many situations, personal preferences for safety versus risk play an important role.

For now, consider the following questions about what you might do in the risky situations described below. There aren't any tricks of logic you need to worry about: just answer what seems right to you.

1.4.1 Reader Poll 1: St. Petersburg Paradox

The **St. Petersburg Paradox** was posed by Nicolas Bernoulli in 1713. One resolution of the paradox was proposed by his cousin Daniel Bernoulli, who worked on the problem while he was a mathematics professor in St. Petersburg. D. Bernoulli's solution was published in 1738, although he probably wrote it around 1728.

N. Bernoulli asked how much someone should pay to enter a doubling lottery. In N. Bernoulli's lottery, a coin is tossed. If it comes up heads, the participant gets \$2 and the lottery is over. If it comes up tails, it is tossed a second time. If it then comes up heads, the participant gets \$4 and the lottery is over. Otherwise there's a third toss with an \$8 payoff if heads, and so forth, doubling the payoff every time. The lottery continues until the first head comes up. If the head comes up on the ith toss, the payoff is $\$2^i$.

N. Bernoulli pointed out that the expected value is infinite, since the probability of the lottery ending on the ith toss is 2^{-i}. One might (anachronistically, since Knight was two hundred years in the future) label this Knightian Risk or a priori probability, and evaluate all the outcomes and all the probabilities to find that the expected value to the participant of entering the lottery is:

$$\sum_{i=1}^{\infty} 2^{-i}2^i = \sum_{i=1}^{\infty} 1 = \infty.$$

The lottery is risky – you don't know which toss of the coin will be the first heads – but unequivocally positive: you will get at least $2 if you enter it. So it seems sensible that you would pay at least $2 to enter, since you'll get that half the time, and more than that the other half of the time. But it seems just as sensible that you would not pay infinity, or even a very large portion of your personal wealth, to enter this lottery.

We'll analyze this in more detail, but for now answer intuitively: *How much would you pay to enter this lottery?*

Make a note of your answer – call it A_{pete}. We'll come back to it later.

1.4.2 Reader Poll 2: The Generous Billionaires

You are walking down the street and you run into John D. Rockefeller and Andrew Carnegie (Image 1.1), both of whom have a net worth well over $100 billion.

"Hello," Rockefeller says, "We've decided to be generous to the next person we see, and that's you! But we have a disagreement about how to dispense our generosity. So we need you to decide between the following two offers."

Carnegie says, "My offer is very simple. I'm just going to give you this check for $500,000,000."

Rockefeller says, "But my offer is more interesting. I'm going to toss a fair coin – 50 percent chance of either heads or tails. If it comes up heads, I'll give you $1,000,000,000. But if it comes up tails, I'll give you nothing."

(a)   (b)

Image 1.1 (a) John D. Rockefeller, (b) Andrew Carnegie. Source: (a) FPG/Archives Photos/Getty Images. (b) Hulton Archive/Stringer/Getty Images.

You must choose only one. Decide whether you want to take Carnegie's offer (sure thing) or Rockefeller's offer (coin toss).

Make a note of your answer (Rockefeller or Carnegie) – call it $A_{generous}$. We'll come back to it later.

Changing Generosity

If you chose Carnegie's offer (the check for $500,000,000):

Assume that Rockefeller's offer ($1,000,000,000 or 0 depending on coin toss) remains unchanged, but that Carnegie is only offering a check for $400,000,000. Would you still take the check? What about a check for $200,000,000? What about $100,000,000? At some point you will switch: presumably if Carnegie's offer is only $0.01, you'll take Rockefeller's coin toss instead. So where's your switching point, that is, what amount of sure check from Carnegie will put you just on the edge between that check and Rockefeller's billion-or-zero coin toss? Make a note of this number – call it A_{switch}.

If you chose Rockefeller's offer (billion-or-zero coin toss):

Assume that Rockefeller's offer remains unchanged, but that Carnegie offers a sure check for $1,000,000,000. At that point you are always better off with Carnegie, so presumably you would take Carnegie's offer over Rockefeller. So somewhere on the way up between a Carnegie offer of $500,000,000 and a Carnegie offer of $1,000,000,000 you switched from Rockefeller to Carnegie. What is your switching point? Make a note of this number – call it A_{switch}.

1.4.3 Reader Poll 3: The Probabilistic Thug

You are walking down a dark street when you run into a thug pointing a gun at you (Image 1.2).

"Hello," the thug says, "Because I am a thug, I am going to do something that one might characterize as unequivocally negative.

"I'm going to give you a choice. In Option A, I will break one of your fingers."

"Ouch," you say.

"But I'm going to give you another choice. In Option B, I will toss a fair coin. If it comes up heads, you can leave unharmed. But if it comes up tails, I will break two of your fingers on the same hand."

Which would you choose?

Image 1.2 Probabilistic thug. Source: Flying Colours Ltd./Digital Vision/Getty Images.

Make a note of this number – call it A_{thug}. We'll come back to it later.

1.5 Basic Economics Terminology

While many of the concepts in this book were formulated by people who won Nobel Prizes in economics,[12] this isn't an economics book and an economics background isn't necessary to understand it. Here we'll give a brief background on some of the rudimentary economics terms that we'll use.

Let's start with a definition: **Economics is the study of how people allocate resources under uncertainty.** Resources include human effort, the results of human effort, and natural resources like water. Uncertainty here comprises both Knightian Risk and Knightian Uncertainty.

The sample spaces we will study will generally encompass a range of allocations of effort and resources. We will be focused on characterizing and dealing with the uncertainty of which allocations will be desirable and which allocations will be undesirable. That is, we will be concerned with the risks of allocation.

The allocation problem studied in economics is essentially a problem of human cooperation. Suppose there were only two people in the world: one a farmer and the other a hunter. The farmer alone may fail to survive a year in which the crop is infested by insects; the hunter alone may fail to survive a year in which game migrates elsewhere. But by pooling their efforts, they might survive on apples in a year when the crop is good and the hunting is bad. Next

---

12 Alfred Nobel, who died in 1896, didn't include economics in his list of prizeworthy fields. "In 1968, Sveriges Riksbank (Sweden's central bank) established the Sveriges Riksbank Prize in Economic Sciences in Memory of Alfred Nobel." (`www.nobelprize.org/prizes/facts/nobel-prize-facts/`). All the Nobel Prizes cited in this book are of this type.

year perhaps the apple crop will be bad, but since they cooperated, the hunter will still be alive to bring in enough wild boar meat so they can both survive. By cooperating and diversifying their efforts, they can better deal with the unknowns of the future food supply.

Diversification is central to the risk and portfolio management techniques that will be discussed in this book. Indeed, diversification is central to all of economics and human organization: it does far less good to allocate redundant resources than to allocate nonoverlapping resources. We saw this same idea in Joseph Tainter's observation about the Mayan food supply diversification techniques cited in the Preface.

Current world population is about 8 billion.[13] Human efforts have branched out far beyond farming and hunting. How is it decided which things should get done and which things shouldn't, and who should do what? How can the efforts of 8 billion people be choreographed?

While conspiracy theorists[14] believe otherwise, in fact there is no choreographer. There is no global central decision-making authority that allocates the efforts of the 8 billion people in the world. On the other hand, it is not the case that each person is entirely free to decide what to do. Certainly not in totalitarian countries where a central authority dictates behavior, but not even in countries that are nominally free. The world has a spectrum of systems to allocate human effort ranging from highly centrally planned to highly distributed.

While allocation systems vary widely in different parts of the world, virtually every economic system uses money as some part of the allocation process. If I wanted to become a professional opera singer, in most parts of the world there would be nothing preventing me from giving a recital where I promise to hit all nine high Cs in the aria "Pour mon âme"[15] from Donizetti's *La fille du régiment*. But since I have a terrible singing voice and wouldn't be able to hit a single one of them, no one would pay to attend my recital. If I devoted my efforts to giving recitals to which no one came, I would not have enough money for food, shelter, or clothing. Through (the lack of) money, I would receive the signal that I have to reallocate my efforts to something more useful and less painful to others.

Money isn't the only factor in allocation. If someone offers you a large amount of money to commit a crime, it is to be hoped that primarily ethics and secondarily fear of arrest will cause you to decline. So personal preferences and a moral, legal, and regulatory framework usually also play a big role in the allocation of effort.

13 U.S. and World Population Clock, September 30, 2022. www.census.gov/popclock/.

14 Conspiracy Theory: "a belief that some covert but influential agency (typically political in motivation and oppressive in intent) is responsible for an unexplained event." Under "conspiracy, n," OED Online. September 2022. Oxford University Press. www.oed.com/view/Entry/39766.

15 Anthony Tommasini, "Review: A Tenor Reaches 18 High Cs at the Metropolitan Opera," *The New York Times*, February 8, 2019. www.nytimes.com/2019/02/08/arts/music/review-metropolitan-opera-donizetti-fille-camarena.html.

To see how money directs effort and resources, consider the following four functions through which it acts:

Most simply, money is first a **medium of exchange**. In the two-person economy we imagined the farmer and the hunter exchanging apples and boar meat. But suppose you are a farmer in a larger economy: exchange and barter are far less efficient than selling apples for cash to (say) a professional online gamer who stops by your orchard, and then using the cash to buy boar meat from a butcher who is miles away from your apples. Money streamlines the process of exchanging the results of people's productive efforts.

The second use of money is as a **store of value**. If you happen to be a great farmer and singlehandedly grow enough apples to feed 100 people for a year, you can convert the apples into money by selling them to many people. You can then use the money at a later time. For example, when you are too old to operate a farm, you will still be able to pay younger farmers and hunters to supply you with apples and boar meat. You have converted your very productive 100-people-year effort into money and stored it for the future.

This ability to translate productive effort across time represents a spectacular advance in human cooperation. You were very successful growing apples – but that was 40 years ago. Your apples are long gone. But you can still get a young person to go out and get meat for you. That's because the young person trusts the money – the hunter can use your money to get someone else to do something for her, like programming a boar-finding app. Money is intersubjective: as long as everyone believes they can use it to get other humans to give them valuable efforts and resources at different times and places, it works.

A related use of money is as a **unit of account**, where money is used to keep track of economic activity and balances. When we said above that the farmer grew enough apples to feed 100 people for a year, we were trying to give a sense of the volume of his output. But that's not a very precise amount – was it enough to feed 100 very large sumo wrestlers, or 100 very small horse racing jockeys? It would have been less vague to describe the farmer's output as (say) $300,000 worth of apples.

Economists from Adam Smith to Ludwig von Mises to F. A. Hayek have argued that the ability to communicate information through prices is what allows the human race to function at its high level of coordination. This lofty assessment was expressed eloquently by Hayek (1945, pp. 519–520), where he explains

> The economic problem of society is ... a problem of the utilization of knowledge not given to anyone in its totality. ... This problem can be solved, and in fact is being solved, by the price system.

By the "price system," Hayek meant the fact that relative values of productive (or produced) items can be communicated by prices. Hayek points out that a manufacturer using tin as an input doesn't need to be an expert on how the tin is produced; the manufacturer only needs to know that tin is a lot cheaper to use than (say) aluminum. This is a bit overstated, as a temporary price advantage (due, say, to an aluminum mine shutting down for brief repairs) is different from a permanent price advantage. While the user of tin may not need to be an expert metallurgist, some knowledge beyond price is desirable. Still, price communicates volumes.

On the other hand, the value of money can change over time; we'll show various ways in which this can happen in the discussion around Figure 3.1 in Chapter 3. Purchasing power adjustments might need to be made. Still, the use of money as a unit of account brings clarity to the activities of individuals like the farmer, to the activities of companies, to cities, and to nations. Money's unit of account function also allows unlike assets to be aggregated into a balance sheet showing the overall value of an enterprise.

This unit of account function of money also allows economists to make quantitative models of human economic activity, either in Knight's a priori or his statistical probability category.

Utility functions, which we'll study below, are part of an a priori probability model that gives specific formulas for human decision making. For example, a casino's study of the amount of money lost by an average customer is a statistical model that might help it decide whether to hire more croupiers.

1.6 Basic Capital Markets Terminology

The fourth function of money is as **financial capital**. Generally, **capital** is an item that increases the effectiveness of human effort or natural resources. It could be a tool, like a backhoe to help the apple farmer dig up his field. It could be a municipality's public transport system, built to facilitate the flow of people and goods. Capital can even be **human capital** – say, a professional opera singer's talent and years of training that make him a better singer than, certainly, me.

In modern economies, many people have gotten beyond hand-to-mouth existence. They have money beyond what is needed to satisfy their current – and maybe even their future – wants. They can begin to use the money to gain control of resources and to direct the productive efforts of other people. When money is used in this way – to facilitate the production of something, rather than for current or future consumption – it falls under our definition of capital.

For example, we imagined a farmer who had done well enough growing apples to buy meat not only now, but in his retirement years in the future. But beyond this, the farmer might have an idea for a better way to get meat: create a cattle ranch rather than hunt for it. Ranching domesticated cattle is vastly more efficient than hunting for wild animals. If the farmer has enough money after satisfying his present and future wants, he might start a cattle ranch and pay some other people to run the ranch for him. He hasn't quit his day job growing apples; he has invested money but not his direct productive effort in the ranch.

Economists have argued for centuries over what exactly constitutes capital and who should benefit from it. At one end of the spectrum, capital's "economic value merely represents the power of one class to appropriate the earnings of another."[16] This kind of thinking leads to the banning or heavy restriction of private ownership of capital.

The other end of the spectrum is simply called **capitalism**. There, the ownership of capital by private individuals is thought to foster innovation and progress. For example, our farmer is highly incentivized to come up with his cattle ranch idea and make sure that it works, since his money is at stake. So according to a capitalist, rather than appropriating his ranch employees' earnings, the farmer is creating jobs for them and increasing food production efficiency. That benefits everyone, except maybe the farmer's boar-hunting friend, who is put out of business by the new ranch technology. One hopes she can get one of the many new jobs created at the ranch.

Neither pure idea works in practice: both the banning of private ownership of capital and laissez-faire (literally "let them do" [whatever they want to do]) capitalism have been tried. Ironically, they both seem to lead to a similar result – the untenable concentration of power in the hands of a few. An old Soviet joke (sometimes attributed to the economist J. Kenneth Galbraith) says "Under capitalism, man exploits man. Under communism, it's just the opposite."

Most economic systems in the world today consist of some form of regulated capitalism, aiming to get the benefits that come with private ownership of capital (motivation, innovation, and efficiency), while avoiding the pitfalls (concentration of power in the hands of a few plutocrats).

Returning to the ranch-owning farmer: he might be initially successful with his cattle ranch but he might decide that he could make an even bigger, even more efficient, ranch if he had more money than he personally can raise. He might estimate that the ranch is currently worth $100,000, all of which he owns. But if he could get another $25,000 to buy more grazing land and cattle sheds, he thinks the value of the ranch will be even more than $125,000. So – noticing that the online gamer who keeps buying his apples appears to be prosperous – he might ask her if she's interested in owning a 20 percent portion of the ranch company in exchange for her investing $25,000 of new capital. If all goes well, the new $25,000 does indeed make the ranch better and it becomes worth (say) $200,000 overall. The farmer's share is now worth $160,000; the gamer's, $40,000. The farmer and the gamer have converted their skills in producing apples and winning games – together with a good idea about meat production – into even more money.

---

16 [George 1879], Chapter 2.

Just as money's medium of exchange function allowed more efficient allocation of human effort than barter or direct exchange, there are more efficient ways of allocating capital than a farmer having a one-on-one talk with a gamer. A **security** is a claim on ownership of something. In the case of the ranch, the farmer initially owned all the stock in the ranch company; **stock** is a security that is a claim on ownership of a company. A **share** is a unit of stock; the total number of shares representing all of the ownership of a company can vary. For example at this writing the ownership of the world's largest company by revenue, Walmart, is divided into 2.8 billion shares.[17]

Security markets allow more efficient exchange of capital. Instead of having to find a specific investor and make a one-off exchange of shares for money, the cattle ranch entrepreneur could list shares of his ranch company on a **stock exchange** and potentially have millions of investors from all over the world evaluating his company's prospects and deciding whether to direct capital to it.

Other securities include **commodity contracts**, which are claims on ownership of natural resources, and **bonds**, which are claims on specific monies that are expected to be generated by an activity in the future.

An investor in a company's stock participates along with the other stockholders in the company's success or failure. An investor in a company's bonds receives specific amounts at specific dates if the company is able to pay them, but doesn't receive anything over the agreed-on amounts if the company does well.

In securities markets, you can use your stored human effort to direct the efforts of others. If the collective decisions made by everyone buying and selling securities are wise, then the productive efforts of much of the human race will be directed efficiently and the world will prosper and progress. If not, there will be a situation like the Great Depression of the 1920s and 1930s or the Great Recession of 2008 and after. Former Federal Reserve Governor Frederick Mishkin summed this up by saying

> the financial system [is] the brain of the economy.... It acts as a coordinating mechanism that allocates capital, the lifeblood of economic activity, to its most productive uses by businesses and households. If capital goes to the wrong uses or does not flow at all, the economy will operate inefficiently, and ultimately economic growth will be low. No work ethic can compensate for a misallocation of capital and the resulting failure to invest in the most profitable ventures. Hard work will not be productive unless it is accompanied by the right amount and kinds of capital.[18]

This book focuses on quantitative models for the risks inherent in investing in securities, particularly portfolios of securities. But we should never forget that

---

17 Walmart, Inc, Common Stock. September 30, 2022. www.nasdaq.com/symbol/wmt/stock-report.
18 [Mishkin 2006].

securities are just placeholders for human effort and natural resources. All the mathematical models we will discuss ultimately need to have a sensible effect on the allocation of human effort and natural resources.

1.7 Basic Probability Terminology

It's assumed that you are familiar with probability theory. (If you're not, Durrett 2013 is a good probability textbook.) This section is not meant to be a course in probability, but rather is a clarification of the terminology that will be used in this book. At the end of this section, we will have built up enough terminology so we can try to apply a standard concept in probability to your Generous Billionaires choice.

Probability theory starts with a **sample space** Ω that is the set of all things that can happen, that is, all outcomes. For example, Ω might be the set $\Omega_{roulette}$ of 38 American roulette outcomes defined in (1.1) above.

An **event** is a subset of the sample space, such as $\{2, 4, \ldots, 36\}$ representing the "even" event as in (1.2). The sample space can be continuous. In order to make both countable and uncountable sample spaces work sensibly, probability theorists insist that the set of all events be a **sigma-algebra** (denoted σ-algebra). A σ-algebra on Ω is a collection of subsets of Ω that (a) includes the empty set; (b) is closed under complement; and (c) is closed under countable union and intersection. The pair (Ω, S) is called a **measurable space** when S is a σ-algebra of Ω; S contains the **measurable subsets** of Ω.

A **probability measure** p on a measurable space (Ω, S) maps S into the unit interval $[0, 1]$ and satisfies $p(\emptyset) = 0$ ($\emptyset$ means the null set), $p(\Omega) = 1$, and

$$p\left(\bigcup_i E_i\right) = \sum_i p_i, \qquad (1.3)$$

where the E_i are a countable collection of pairwise disjoint events in S. A **probability space** is the triple (Ω, S, p) of sample space, associated σ-algebra, and associated probability measure. The probability $p(E)$ of an event $E \in S$ is the event's **unconditional probability**. The probability of event A given that another event B happened is called event A's **conditional probability**.

For example, if you throw an unweighted six-sided die, you know before looking that the probability that the number two came up is $1/6$. But suppose you throw the die and I look at the result before you do. I might tell you that an even number came up and ask you for the probability that the number was two. You now know the probability is $1/3$, not $1/6$.

Formally, the **conditional probability** of event E, given that event F has occurred, is written $p(E \mid F)$, and by definition equals

$$p(E \mid F) = \frac{p(E \cap F)}{p(F)}. \qquad (1.4)$$

In the example above, F was the event that an even number came up ($p(F) = 1/2$) and event E was the number two coming up; ($p(E) = p(E \cap F) = 1/6$). So $p(E \mid F) = \frac{1/6}{1/2} = \frac{1}{3}$.

If (a) the sample space Ω is finite or countably infinite, and (b) the σ-algebra is the power set of Ω, then the probability measure is a **probability mass function** p that assigns a value $p(\omega)$ to each $\omega \in \Omega$, where $\sum_{\omega \in \Omega} p(\omega) = 1$. If (a) is true but not (b), then there are one or more probability mass functions that are compatible with the probability measure.

For example, suppose Ω consists of the six outcomes of the throw of a single die, and $S = \{\emptyset, \{1\}, \{2, 3, 4, 5, 6\}, \Omega\}$. A probability measure that assigns $\frac{1}{6}$ to the event $\{1\}$ and $\frac{5}{6}$ to the event $\{2, 3, 4, 5, 6\}$ is compatible with the usual mass function that assigns $\frac{1}{6}$ to each outcome. It is also compatible with a mass function that assigns $\frac{1}{6}$ to each of $1, 2, 3, 4$; assigns $\frac{1}{3}$ to 5; and zero to 6.

However, for most practical applications, when Ω is countable, then the σ-algebra is simply the power set of Ω. When the sample space is not countable, the probability measure p will be defined on elements of the σ-algebra but not necessarily on individual outcomes.

For our purposes, a **random variable** X is a function that maps Ω into the real numbers $\mathbb{R}$, where Ω is the sample space of a probability space (Ω, S, p). The intuition is easiest for a **discrete random variable** where Ω is countable and S is the power set of Ω; in that case, we can look at the values of the random variable on each outcome.

For example, Ω might be a set of people taking a Mathematical Finance 300 class; S the power set of Ω; and the probability mass function $p(\omega) = 1/n$ where n is the number of people in Ω. The random variable $X(\omega)$ might be the score of person ω on ω's Math Finance 300 final exam. We could then write an expression like $Pr(X > 90)$ to mean $p(\{\omega \mid X(\omega) > 90\}) = \sum_{X(\omega) > 90} p(\omega)$. $Pr(X > 90)$ tells us the probability that a person taking Math Finance 300 scored over 90 on the final exam.

A random variable is an example of a **measurable function**. That means the function's domain is the sample space Ω of a probability space (Ω, S, p), and its range is the sample space A of a measurable space (A, B). Further, if $s = \{\omega \mid X(\omega) \in b\}$, then $s \in S$ whenever $b \in B$; that is, if the range is measurable, so is the domain. Note that "measurable" has different meanings for domain and range.

For our purposes, the range sample space A will either be finite, countable, the real numbers $\mathbb{R}$, or an interval on the real line. Usually, B is either the power set of A, or the **Borel algebra** of A (the smallest σ-algebra containing all of its open sets).

The **probability distribution** associated with a random variable X (Pr_X or just Pr when the association is clear) is defined as the function

$$Pr(X \in b) = p(\{\omega \mid X(\omega) \in b\}) \text{ when } b \in B.$$

For example, $X(\omega)$ might be the logarithm of the price of an asset in economic scenario ω, and the b we're interested in might be the interval $(-\infty, 5]$ indicating we want to know the probability that the log-price is less than or equal to 5. In that case, we might use a notation like $Pr(X \leq 5)$.

$Pr(X \leq x)$ is called a **cumulative distribution function (cdf)** for the random variable X, and is often also denoted $F(x)$ (or $F_X(x)$ if we want to be explicit about the underlying random variable). Because of the properties of probability measures, $F(x)$ is a nondecreasing function ranging from 0 to 1 over its domain, which is the real numbers or some subset of the real numbers.

If $F(x)$ is differentiable, then its derivative $\mathrm{pdf}(x) = F'(x)$ is called the **probability density function (pdf)** of the random variable X. (Notation like $\mathrm{pdf}_X(x)$ can be used if it isn't clear what random variable X underlies the distribution.) When X takes on only a countable number of values, then as noted above $\mathrm{pdf}(x)$ is a probability mass function giving the probability that the discrete value x will be observed.

A **characteristic function** is another way to express a probability distribution. If X is a random variable, then its characteristic function $\varphi_X(t)$ is:

$$\varphi_X(t) = \int e^{itx} dF_X(x) = \int e^{itx} f_X(x) dx,$$

where $F_X(x)$ and $f_X(x)$ are, respectively, the cdf and pdf of the probability distribution and i is the imaginary unit. Thus, the characteristic function is the Fourier transform of the pdf. If the pdf is symmetric about zero, then the characteristic function is real-valued; otherwise, it can be complex. The pdf can be recovered from the inverse Fourier transform:

$$f_X(t) = \frac{1}{2\pi} \int e^{-itx} \varphi_X(x) dx.$$

The most widely used probability distributions include the uniform distribution $F(x) = x$, where $0 \leq x \leq 1$, and the normal distribution $\mathrm{pdf}(x) = \frac{1}{\sqrt{2\pi}} \exp(-x^2/2)$.

The **expectation operator** $\mathbb{E}[]$ gives the average value of a function of a random variable over the random variable's probability distribution. More formally,

$$\mathbb{E}[f(X)] = \int f(x)\mathrm{pdf}(x)dx = \int f(x)dF(x). \tag{1.5}$$

Note that the distribution over which the expectation is taken is often not explicitly stated in the $\mathbb{E}[]$ notation. If it's not clear by context which $\mathrm{pdf}(x)$ or $F(x)$ is being used, a superscript or a subscript is attached to $\mathbb{E}$.

The **average or mean value** $\mathbb{E}[X] = \int x \cdot \mathrm{pdf}(x)dx = \int xdF(x)$ is also called the **first moment** of the distribution and is often denoted as $\overline{X}$. Often the Greek letter μ ("mu") is used for the mean, that is, $\mu_X = \overline{X}$, or just $\mu = \overline{X}$ when the context is clear.

Another metric that captures a central value of a distribution is its **median**, often denoted by the Greek letter v ("nu"):

$$v_X = m \text{ such that } \int_{-\infty}^{m} \mathrm{pdf}_X(x)dx = \int_{m}^{\infty} \mathrm{pdf}_X(x)dx = \frac{1}{2}. \qquad (1.6)$$

That is, the median is the point where it's equally likely that a point of the distribution will be to its left or to its right on the real line. Equation (1.6) works for continuous distributions; for discrete distributions, some interpolation may be needed.

The ith **(central) moment** of the distribution is

$$m_i = \mathbb{E}[(X - \mu)^i] = \int (x - \mu)^i \mathrm{pdf}(x)dx, \qquad (1.7)$$

where $\mu = \overline{X}$ is the mean of the distribution.

The second moment, called **variance**,[19] is sometimes written $Var(X)$. Here $Var(X) = m_2 = \mathbb{E}[(X - \mu)^2] = \int (x - \mu)^2 \mathrm{pdf}(x)dx$. The square root of variance is called **standard deviation**; usually when people refer to the **volatility** of a distribution, they mean its standard deviation. Often the Greek letter σ is used for standard deviation, that is, $Var(X) = \sigma^2$ or $\sigma^2(X)$.

Skewness or skew is the scaled third central moment, $s = m_3/\sigma^3$. If the distribution is symmetric about its mean, then its skewness is zero. There is some ambiguity about the definition of skewness, with some authors looking at the difference between a distribution's mean and its median, all divided by standard deviation. This is (a) not the definition we will use; and (b) not equivalent to our (third-moment-based) definition. The general concept is similar – zero skew means some kind of symmetry; positive skew means a distribution that tends to stretch out more to the right than to the left. But the two definitions can differ on specific distributions.

While any number of moments of a distribution can be computed, most distributions that are of practical use can be specified by their first four moments. The scaled fourth moment (m_4/σ^4) is called **kurtosis**. Kurtosis is a unitless quantity that is often compared to the kurtosis of a normal distribution for context. The term **excess kurtosis** is often used, meaning kurtosis minus three, since three is the kurtosis of a normal distribution. In fact, kurtosis is so often reported relative to a normal distribution that sometimes writers say "kurtosis" when they mean "excess kurtosis," which of course can be rather confusing. We will try to set context when we use this term. A distribution with positive excess kurtosis is called **leptokurtic** or **fat-tailed**, meaning it has more probability

---

19 The word "variance" is used by accountants to mean "difference"; for example, if the corporate budget was $100Mn and the company spent $110Mn, the accounting variance is −$10Mn. In financial contexts with nonquantitative audiences, it's best to be clear whether accounting variance or statistical variance is being used.

attached to unusual observations than a normal distribution. A distribution with zero excess kurtosis is **mesokurtic**, and a **thin-tailed** distribution with negative excess kurtosis is called **platykurtic**.

A random variable X **first order stochastically dominates** another random variable Y if $F_Y(x) \geq F_X(x)$ for all scalars x. (There are other kinds of stochastic dominance, but if we say just "stochastic dominance," we will mean first order.) A standard result is: X stochastically dominates Y if and only if $\mathbb{E}[f(X)] \geq \mathbb{E}[f(Y)]$ for all nondecreasing functions f, where the expectation is defined. In particular stochastic dominance of X over Y implies $\mathbb{E}[X] \geq \mathbb{E}[Y]$, although this implication does not work in the other direction.

An even more overwhelming form of dominance is called **statewise dominance**, where $X(\omega) \geq Y(\omega)$ for all $\omega \in \Omega$, Ω the sample space. **Strict statewise dominance** occurs when there is statewise dominance and at least one ω, where $X(\omega) > Y(\omega)$. If X and Y represent financial variables like rates of return, strict statewise dominance is unlikely to occur because an arbitrageur would simultaneously buy X and sell Y. That would cost nothing but would be at least break-even, and possibly profitable, in all future states of the world. We'll discuss arbitrage more fully in Chapter 2.

Intuitively, X stochastically dominates Y when Y has more probability associated with low outcomes than X does. Eventually, both cumulative distribution functions must get to their highest values – the value 1. But Y is always in more of a hurry to get to 1 than X, meaning Y is always more likely to have a low (disappointing) result than X.

Does that help us make the Generous Billionaires choice? If X was the sure check for $\$500,000,000$ and Y was the coin toss for $\$1,000,000,000$ or zero, then neither was stochastically dominant. X's cumulative distribution function looks like $F_X(x) = 0$ for $x < 500,000,000$ and $F_X(x) = 1$ otherwise; Y's cdf looks like $F_Y(x) = 0$ for $x < 0$; $F_Y(x) = \frac{1}{2}$ for $0 \leq x < 1,000,000,000$; and $F_Y(x) = 1$ for $x \geq 1,000,000,000$. So $F_Y(x) > F_X(x)$ between 0 and 500,000,000, but then the inequality goes the other way between 500,000,000 and 1,000,000,000.

If the sure check was for $\$1,000,000,000$ (Z), then Z would stochastically dominate the coin toss Y. In fact, this Z *statewise dominates* Y; Z is better than (or equal to) Y in every future state of the world. Certainly any sentient decision maker would prefer a statewise dominant random variable.

Suppose the Generous Billionaires have only one coin between them and they both make offers referencing a toss of that coin. Andrew Carnegie offers to give you $\$100,000,000$ if the coin comes up tails, and nothing if it comes up heads (random variable W). John D. Rockefeller makes his same offer – nothing if the coin comes up tails, $\$1,000,000,000$ if heads (random variable Y). Y stochastically dominates W, but it doesn't statewise dominate. Still, no matter what attitude you have toward risk and reward, you should prefer the stochastically dominant offer – since the future states are arbitrary, the stochastically dominant offer will be statewise dominant in a reordering of states.

So unfortunately, these observations don't help with the original Generous Billionaires choice, since the original offers were designed so that there wasn't stochastic dominance. To frame choices where there isn't clear dominance, an additional mechanism is needed.

1.8 Utility Theory

Utility theory is a disciplined way to assess trade-offs between risk and reward. This will be our first exploration of a mathematical framework that attempts to describe and predict human financial behavior.

The concept appears to have been invented by Gabriel Cramer in 1728.[20] He is most well known for Cramer's Rule for solving systems of linear equations. Writing to N. Bernoulli, he summed it up as follows:

> the mathematicians estimate money in proportion to its quantity, and men of good sense in proportion to the usage that they may make of it.

Cramer favored a square root function for utility. In other words, $25 is not 25 times as useful as $1; it is only 5 times as useful.

Applying Cramer's square root utility function to the St. Petersburg lottery shows its expected (Cramer) utility rather than its expected value. A win of 2^i only has "usage" or utility of $2^{i/2}$, so summing probabilities times utilities gives:

$$\sum_{i=1}^{\infty} 2^{-i}(2^i)^{\frac{1}{2}} = \sum_{i=1}^{\infty} 2^{-i/2} = \frac{2^{-1/2}}{1 - 2^{-1/2}} = \sqrt{2} + 1 \approx 2.41.$$

Thus entering the St. Petersburg lottery has the same usefulness as you would get from $(\sqrt{2} + 1)^2 = 5.83$ sure dollars. So (assuming usefulness is assessed with a square root utility function), the St. Petersburg lottery is worth the same as $5.83, not infinity. If your A_{pete} from the reader poll above was close to $5.83, then you may have been (probably not consciously) using a square root utility function.

Daniel Bernoulli (1738, p. 24) pursued the idea further, stating

> The determination of the value of an item must not be based on the price, but rather on the utility it yields.... There is no doubt that a gain of one thousand ducats[21] is more significant to the pauper than to a rich man though both gain the same amount.

Daniel Bernoulli expressed two fundamental ideas in the quote above. His first idea echoes Cramer's observation of ten years earlier. In the same paper,

---

20 [Cramer 1728].

21 The Austrian Mint (www.muenzeoesterreich.at/eng/Produkte/1-Ducat) makes modern restrikes of gold ducats. Based on gold content (which hasn't changed much since Bernoulli's time), we can guess that Bernoulli's "one thousand ducats" is the equivalent of around $200,000 today.

Bernoulli suggested a logarithmic utility function that is still widely used; this seems to capture preferences more realistically than Cramer's square root function, which is more aggressive.

With a logarithmic utility function, the usefulness of $\$2^i$ is i. Without loss of generality base-2 logarithms can be used here; any other base just applies a constant scale factor that cancels out when comparing utilities to make decisions. So the expected logarithmic utility is:

$$\sum_{i=1}^{\infty} 2^{-i} i = 2.$$

The sure amount that has a log-2-utility of 2 is $2^2 = \$4$. This amount tends to be the most popular with bidders for the St. Petersburg lottery; if your A_{pete} from Section 1.4.2 was $\$4$, then you may have been (probably not consciously) using a logarithmic utility function.

So both Cramer and Bernoulli "solved" the St. Petersburg Paradox by explaining through a utility function why people would not bid infinity to enter it.

But Bernoulli's second sentence quoted above introduces a new idea: that the game would likely not be seen in isolation – it would have to be evaluated in the context of the gambler's entire wealth, so the true answer is more complicated. Suppose the Generous Billionaires hadn't been so generous and had only offered a choice between (a) a sure check for $\$0.50$ and (b) a coin toss for $\$1.00$ or zero. Probably neither amount of the diminished choice is significant compared to your usual spending patterns, so you might take the coin toss just because $\$1.00$ is a little more noticeable than $\$0.50$. So, as Bernoulli noted, context matters.

While Cramer and Daniel Bernoulli were convincing when they explained why no one bids infinity for the St. Petersburg Paradox, they omitted a simpler and more practical consideration that was eventually pointed out by Cramer in a 1728 personal communication to N. Bernoulli. According to the bank Credit Suisse,[22] at the end of 2021 the recognizable wealth of all the people in the world was $\$464$ trillion. That's about 2 to the 49th power.

So even if the world agreed to pool its wealth to pay you (if necessary) in the St. Petersburg lottery, the payoff would be capped at about 2^{49}, meaning that the terms after $i = 49$ have a finite sum. In reality, the economic agent offering you the St. Petersburg lottery is not the entire world, so the cap starts quite a bit earlier than $i = 49$. Thus the supposed infinite expected value of the St. Petersburg Paradox does not arise from any lottery that could be played in practice.

22 Credit Suisse Research Institute, "Global Wealth Report 2022." www.credit-suisse.com/media/assets/corporate/docs/about-us/research/publications/global-wealth-report-2022-en.pdf. p. 5.

1.8.1   Von Neumann–Morgenstern Utility Theory

In 1944, utility theory was formalized into a mathematical discipline by John von Neumann and Oskar Morgenstern ("VNM"). VNM established a full axiomatic system around the general intuition of utility theory in *Theory of Games and Economic Behavior*.[23]

As we saw above, a utility function can describe some behaviors reasonably. But it's implausible to think that economic agents are continually computing utility functions as they make choices. (An economic agent takes economic actions and is generally a person, a group of people, a company or other organization, a government, or an algorithm.) But it's certainly true that economic agents have preferences: they might prefer billionaire offer 1 to billionaire offer 2. So it's not implausible to assume that economic agents can express a preference between pairs of probability distributions assigning probabilities to different levels of wealth. More generally, agents can express preferences between probability distributions that include non-monetary outcomes ("I declare my love and things go well"; "I prove P=NP";[24] etc.).

VNM (1953) analyzed preferences by starting with a finite, discrete formulation – essentially the same as the formulation of Knightian Risk. They assumed:

1. There is a situation we wish to evaluate with n mutually exclusive outcomes of interest, which we can denote by $s_1, s_2, \ldots, s_n$.
   (a) A very simple setup might be the toss of a coin, with two possible outcomes – heads (s_1) or tails (s_2). When the outcomes map to monetary amounts, VNM called them "prizes."
   (b) Going to the other extreme, a maximally complex setup would be to enumerate all the future states of the universe. Note there is only a finite number of configurations that can be taken on in a finite amount of space over a finite amount of time; physical reality is discrete in that sense.[25] Thus the sample space of economic outcomes on the planet Earth (and, say, a billion light-years' vicinity) for the next billion or so years is finite. As we noted when discussing Knightian Risk, modeling economics and finance with continuous mathematics is a convenience – for example, it is helpful to be able to take derivatives of functions – but it is not reality, which is finite. Thus there is nothing intrinsically continuous about economic reality and the discrete VNM framework is sufficient.

---

23 [VNM 1953].

24 Stephen Cook, "The P vs. NP Problem," Clay Mathematics Institute. www.claymath.org/sites/default/files/pvsnp.pdf.

25 It has been estimated that a cubic meter of space can take on at most 10 to the 10 to the 70 configurations ([Cain 2015]). It may never be known whether the universe is finite, but that is not relevant for the economic reality of the human race on the planet Earth over a finite time period. This is the gist of Rovelli's previously cited comment that the world is "subtly discrete" (2018).

2. There is a set of probabilities associated with future outcomes: that is, a vector of nonnegative real numbers $p_1, p_2, \ldots, p_n$ that sum to one where p_i is the probability of outcome s_i occurring. VNM used the term *lottery* to denote a set of probabilities.

    (a) This is a discrete probability measure.

3. An economic agent makes choices between lotteries (probability vectors) with a preference relation.

For example, there might be three outcomes: s_1 = you receive \$0; s_2 = you receive \$500,000,000; and s_3 = you receive \$1,000,000,000. You may be asked to decide between two probability vectors, $p_1 = (0, 1, 0)$ and $p_2 = (.5, 0, .5)$.

So, p_1 means you definitely receive \$500,000,000, while p_2 means you have a 50-50 chance of getting either \$1,000,000,000 or nothing. This is a reframing of your Generous Billionaires choice.

More generally, let s be the n-vector whose entries contain all possible future outcomes. Define $\Delta(s)$ as the set of all lotteries on s – that is, the set of all probability n-vectors p where $p^\mathsf{T} u = 1$ and all elements of p are nonnegative. In this book when u is a vector, it is a vector of all ones with dimension determined by context. T denotes transpose. So $p^\mathsf{T} u$ is the dot product of p and u.

Clearly $\Delta(s)$ is convex – if $p_1, p_2 \in \Delta(s)$, then for any $0 \leq \alpha \leq 1$, $\alpha p_1 + (1 - \alpha) p_2 \in \Delta(s)$ must hold. Note that s hasn't actually been used in the definition of $\Delta(s)$, so any vector of n outcomes has the same set of lotteries, namely, the segment of the hyperplane $p^\mathsf{T} u = 1$, each $p_i \geq 0$, in n-space $\mathbb{R}^n$. It will, however, be convenient to keep in mind a set of outcomes s when looking at $\Delta(s)$.

A ranking between lotteries in $\Delta(s)$ is a binary relation $\succeq$ where $\succeq \subseteq \Delta(s) \times \Delta(s)$. For two lotteries $p, q \in \Delta(s)$, we write $p \succeq q$ if p is preferred to or equivalent to q. (Equivalence is denoted by $\equiv$ and means both $p \succeq q$ and $q \succeq p$.) $p \succ q$ means that $p \succeq q$, but it is not true that $q \succeq p$.

The agent's decision process is encoded in the $\succeq$ function. Therefore, we need to determine the properties of such preference functions.

1.8.2 VNM Axioms and Theorem

VNM[26] required that certain axioms apply to preference functions, arguing that these axioms were simply expressions of rationality. The first set of requirements (translated into modern terminology) indicated that preference functions are now what are called *total preorders*,[27] satisfying these axioms:

1. *Transitivity.* For $p, q, r \in \Delta(s)$, $p \succeq q$ and $q \succeq r$ means $p \succeq r$.
2. *Connex.* For $p, q \in \Delta(s)$, either $p \succeq q$ or $q \succeq p$ or both; if both are true, then we say $p \equiv q$.

26 [VNM 1953], p. 26.
27 [Stanley 1997], p. 297.

A third property, *reflexivity* ($p \succeq p$ so $p \equiv p$), follows from those two.

These axioms indicate that an economic agent has one of three mutually exclusive opinions about every pair p and q of lotteries: either p is strictly preferred to q; q is strictly preferred to p; or p and q are equivalent. A lottery is equivalent to itself, but there can be other lotteries that are not the same but are equivalent. The existence of unequal equivalence is the difference between a total preorder and a total order. Transitivity means there are no circular preferences; if I like chocolate better than vanilla and vanilla better than strawberry, then I like chocolate better than strawberry.

While humans aren't always rational, it can generally be assumed that departures from these axioms will be quickly corrected. VNM adopted two other axioms that are sensible but not as basic as the first three. We've updated the language and format from their original presentation:

3. *Independence.* If $p, q, r \in \Delta(s)$ with $p \succ q$ and $\alpha \in (0, 1)$, then $\alpha p + (1 - \alpha) r \succ \alpha q + (1 - \alpha) r$.

Intuition: if p is preferred to q, that preference remains unchanged when we mix in a piece of a third lottery r. If I like chocolate better than strawberry, then – no matter how I feel about vanilla – I like (a mixture of chocolate and vanilla) better than (the same mixture of strawberry and vanilla).

While this is not horribly implausible, it is also not as basic a guide to rational behavior as the previous axioms. It is certainly possible that there could be interactions between items that would alter the results. To get powerful results, VNM had to make powerful assumptions: in this case, they assumed that lotteries are independent of each other and there are no such interactions.

The last VNM axiom is even stronger:

4. *Continuity.* If $p, q, r \in \Delta(s)$ with $p \succ q \succ r$, then there is a scalar $\alpha \in (0, 1)$ such that $\alpha p + (1 - \alpha) r \equiv q$.

Intuition: If we have three ordered lotteries, we can create a linear mixture of the worst one (r) and the best one (p) that is equivalent to the one in the middle (q). So if I prefer chocolate to vanilla, and I prefer vanilla to strawberry, then there is some mixture of chocolate and strawberry that I like the same as vanilla.

This property requires that preferences don't just jump from one level to another, but vary smoothly between (for example) strawberry and chocolate without skipping over the vanilla satisfaction level. Like the independence axiom, this is not implausible but is also not entirely fundamental. I might hate the taste of mixtures and dislike even the smallest adulteration of my beloved chocolate, so there is no combination that gets me to the same satisfaction level as vanilla.

The two strong VNM axioms are not implausible: they basically enforce a kind of linearity of preference when combining lotteries. Eventually, the strength of these axioms gets the theory into trouble: we'll show later that at some point going down this path departs from reasonably describing choices that most people make. But for now and to a first order, these axioms seem to give a sensible description of how people make economic choices. A preference function seems much more intuitive than a utility function. But VNM[28] proved that utility functions and preference functions lead to the same results.

> **VNM Theorem** *An economic agent has a preference function $\succeq$ satisfying the four VNM axioms if and only if the agent has a associated utility function U : $\Delta(s) \to \mathbb{R}$, where for any $p, q \in \Delta(s)$, $p \succeq q$ if and only if $U(p) \geq U(q)$.*

More precisely, let $\Delta(s)$ be a convex subset of $\mathbb{R}^n$. Let $\succeq$ be a binary relation on $\Delta(s)$. Then $\succeq$ satisfies the four axioms above if and only if there is a function $U : \Delta(s) \to \mathbb{R}$ such that:

(a)   U represents $\succeq$ (i.e. $\forall p, q \in \Delta(s), p \succeq q \iff U(p) \geq U(q)$);
(b)   U is affine (i.e. $\forall p, q \in \Delta(s), \alpha \in [0,1], U(\alpha p + (1 - \alpha)q) = \alpha U(p) + (1 - \alpha)U(q)$).

Further, U is unique up to a positive linear transformation: If $V : \Delta(s) \to \mathbb{R}$ also satisfies (a) and (b), then there are $b, c \in \mathbb{R}$ (where $b > 0$) such that $V = bU + c$.

The proof of the VNM theorem is quite long, although not particularly hard. We'll give a flavor of the proof but not the whole thing. The first thing VNM note is:

> **Lemma** *If $p, q \in \Delta(s)$ with $p \succ q$, and $\alpha > \beta \in [0,1]$, then $\alpha p + (1 - \alpha)q \succ \beta p + (1 - \beta)q$.*

Proof of Lemma: Define $\gamma = \frac{\beta}{\alpha}$; γ is in the unit interval. Since $p \succ q$, the independence axiom says $\alpha p + (1 - \alpha)q \succ \alpha q + (1 - \alpha)q = q$. Let $r = \alpha p + (1 - \alpha)q$; we can apply the independence axiom to $r \succ q$ by adding some (more) r to both sides: $(1 - \gamma)r + \gamma r \succeq (1 - \gamma)q + \gamma r$. Collecting terms, the RHS is $\beta p + (1 - \beta)q$ and the LHS is $r = \alpha p + (1 - \alpha)q$, proving the lemma. ∎

Continuing along these lines, they prove that the map from the unit interval to linear combinations $\alpha p + (1 - \alpha)q$ is one-to-one, monotone, and onto $\{r \mid p \succeq r \succeq q\}$. They then break down lotteries into combinations of 100 percent lotteries, that is, they let x_i be the lottery that gives outcome s_i with 100 percent probability. Without loss of generality, we can assume the lotteries are ordered so that $x_n \succeq x_{n-1} \succeq \cdots \succeq x_1$. Start construction of the utility function U by defining $U(x_1) = 0$ and $U(x_n) = 1$, unless $x_n \equiv x_1$ in which case the trivial utility function $U(x) = 0$ for all lotteries x works.

From the continuity axiom we know that there is an α_i so that $\alpha_i x_n + (1 - \alpha_i)x_1 \equiv x_i$ for any $1 \leq i \leq n$. They set $U(x_i) = \alpha_i$. The 100 percent lotteries then become the basis for all the other lotteries, since a general lottery x

---

28 [VNM 1953], Appendix A.1 pp. 617ff.

is an n-vector of probabilities $x = (p_1, \ldots, p_n)$; we define $U(x) = \sum p_i \alpha_i$. The axioms and observations like the Lemma allow them to prove that this utility function encodes preference order.

So in fact VNM not only proved that there is a utility function U that operates on lotteries and encodes preference order: they also proved (as the construction of U shows) that we can just have utility functions that operate on outcomes (which are probably monetary amounts). So if $p = (p_1, ..., p_n)$ is a lottery in $\Delta(s)$, a VNM preference function can be encoded as $\sum_{i=1}^{n} p_i u(s_i)$. We use the small-u notation to indicate a function that operates on outcomes, while the big-U notation indicates a function that operates on lotteries.

1.8.3 Risk Preferences

A special kind of outcome set is monetary, where each outcome state s_i maps to an amount of money. We noted above in that case, VNM called the outcomes **prizes**. A utility function on prizes maps real numbers to real numbers.

So in utility terms, your original meeting with the billionaires had three possible prizes: s_1=you receive \$0; s_2=you receive \$500Mn; and s_3=you receive \$1Bn.

We asked about the preference between two lotteries $p_1 = (0, 1, 0)$ and $p_2 = (.5, 0, .5)$. p_1 is a sure thing: you definitely receive \$500Mn. Risk is lack of knowledge about future outcomes of an action, but you know exactly what will happen with p_1. So there is no risk in p_1.

On the other hand, p_2 is a risky lottery. The poll above asked whether $p_1 \succ p_2$. We now know (assuming the VNM Theorem holds) that it can be answered by looking at whether

$$\sum_{i=1}^{3} p_1(i) u(s_i) > \sum_{i=1}^{3} p_2(i) u(s_i).$$

This is equivalent to asking if $u(500Mn) > \frac{1}{2} u(0) + \frac{1}{2} u(1Bn)$.

Given the VNM equivalence, a more universal notation can be used when outcomes are If p is a lottery, write $\mathbb{E}_p[X]$ to mean the expected value of the random variable X that maps the sample space $\Omega = \{1, 2, \ldots, n\}$ to amounts $\{s_1, \ldots, s_n\}$ under the probability measure (mass function) p:

$$\mathbb{E}_p[X] = \sum p_i X(i) = \sum p_i s_i. \tag{1.8}$$

For the St. Petersburg lottery, this quantity was infinite. For the risky billionaire coin toss, this quantity was \$500Mn.

Equation (1.8) is a scalar monetary amount, so if there is a utility function that operates on monetary amounts, it can be applied to (1.8): $u(\mathbb{E}_p[X])$ is the utility of definitely receiving the expected value of the lottery p.

On the other hand, the utility of the risky lottery can be evaluated with the expression:

$$\mathbb{E}_p[u(X)] = \sum p_i u(X(i)) = \sum p_i u(s_i). \tag{1.9}$$

The difference is the order in which we apply probabilities and utilities – if expected value is taken first, then a sure thing is created, after which its utility is evaluated. If utility is applied first, then there are a variety of outcomes with different utilities whose probability-weighted expectation is taken.

We can characterize attitudes toward risk as follows. For nonsure p's:

- **Risk aversion**: $u(\mathbb{E}_p[X]) > \mathbb{E}_p[u(X)]$
- **Risk indifference or neutrality**: $u(\mathbb{E}_p[X]) = \mathbb{E}_p[u(X)]$
- **Risk seeking**: $u(\mathbb{E}_p[X]) < \mathbb{E}_p[u(X)]$

In your Generous Billionaires meeting, $\mathbb{E}_{p_2}[X] = \$500\text{Mn}$, so we asked about the relationship between $u(500Mn) = u(\mathbb{E}_{p_2}[X])$ and $\mathbb{E}_{p_2}[u(X)]$ (the utility of taking the risk of the coin toss); in other words, we asked whether you were risk averse, neutral, or risk seeking.

If your $A_{generous}$ choice was for the sure check, then you are risk averse. Most people in fact are risk averse. This seems to be a deep evolutionary tendency; in fact, even other species demonstrate risk aversion. Chen, Lakshminarayanan, and Santos (2006) set up a token-based economy for capuchin monkeys, and found that – once they understood the idea of token-based money – monkeys preferred to spend on definite rewards (one apple slice, say) than random rewards (a variable number of apple slices).

More accurately, most people (and primates) demonstrate *upside risk aversion*. Your Probabilistic Thug choice A_{thug} was probably for the coin toss, figuring that you had a 50 percent chance of escaping unharmed. While having two broken fingers is worse than having one broken finger, it probably isn't twice as bad. In other words, the negative utility grows more slowly than risk-neutral/linear, just like positive utility. This probably made you **downside risk seeking**. Since the utility of any number of broken fingers is negative, and assuming the utility of nothing happening (no broken fingers) is zero, your decision probably looked like $-.5|u_2| > -|u_1|$, or $|u_2| < 2|u_1|$ (with obvious, if morbid, notation).

Recall that a function f is **concave** if $f(ax + (1 - a)y) \geq af(x) + (1 - a)f(y)$ for all a in $[0, 1]$ (mnemonic: "inside the cave is better," where the cave is the set of parentheses that surrounds the argument of the function). If the inequality goes the other way, the function is **convex**; if both sides are equal, the function is **affine**. When a function f is twice differentiable, it is concave, affine, or convex according to whether the second derivative f'' is negative, zero, or positive.

It is not hard to see the following:

Proposition *A utility function u on prizes is risk averse on all lotteries if and only if it is strictly concave; is risk indifferent on all lotteries iff affine; and risk seeking on all lotteries iff strictly convex.*

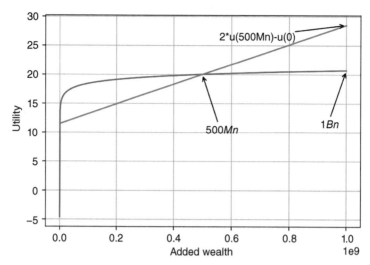

Figure 1.1 Concave upside utility.

This indicates that utility functions might reverse shape on the downside, since as we've seen, behavior might be downside risk seeking.

Figure 1.1 above (generated by Code Segment 1.1) shows a concave (logarithmic) utility function in blue. If it starts raining from the top of the graph down to the bottom of the graph, a concave utility function will shed water. The figure shows utility in the range of the Generous Billionaires amounts for someone with starting wealth $100,000. The utility of $1Bn is only about 3.5 percent higher than the utility of $500Mn. This small increase makes the agent risk averse; the utility at $1Bn would have to be twice the utility at $500Mn minus the utility of zero (shown at the top of the orange line) to make up for the 50 percent chance of getting nothing.

Similarly, Figure 1.2 below (generated by Code Segment 1.2) shows a convex (negative logarithmic) utility function in blue based on number of fingers broken by the Probabilistic Thug. The upside-down logarithm is now convex (holds water), reflecting the idea that two broken fingers is not twice as bad as one broken finger.

Let Ω be a finite sample space and let X be a random variable that gives a monetary amount $X(\omega)$ when the state of the world is $\omega \in \Omega$. Let p be a lottery, that is, a set of probabilities $p(\omega) > 0$ with $\sum_{\omega \in \Omega} p(\omega) = 1$. Let u be a utility function that operates on monetary amounts (prizes). Then the **certainty equivalent** of prizes X under lottery p is the number m such that:

$$u(m) = \mathbb{E}_p[u(X)]. \tag{1.10}$$

Thus, m is the sure prize that the utility function values equally with the risky set of outcomes X with probabilities p. The amount A_{switch} you recorded in the billionaire choice problem was your certainty equivalent of the billion dollar coin toss.

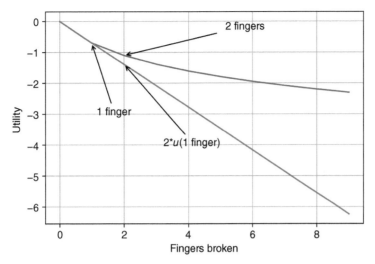

Figure 1.2 Convex downside utility.

For most sensible, purely financial situations, a fifth axiom of utility functions on prizes holds: people never prefer less money to more. The fact that people are sometimes philanthropic is not a counterexample, since the outcome set that takes philanthropy into account includes nonmonetary outcomes comprising different levels of social satisfaction. If the only outcomes are monetary, it is reasonably safe to assume more is preferred to less, and therefore utility functions on prizes are nondecreasing. For a scalar utility function u, this means u's first derivative is non-negative: $u'(x) \geq 0$.

This leads to another

Proposition *Suppose the outcome set consists of an interval of the real line and u is a continuous utility function on this interval. Then every lottery p has at least one certainty equivalent. If u is strictly increasing, then p has at most one certainty equivalent.*

For well-behaved utility functions, the degree of risk aversion can be captured with Pratt's **coefficient of absolute risk aversion** (1964), which is minus the second derivative divided by the first derivative of a (twice continuously differentiable strictly increasing) utility function:

$$\text{Coeff}_{abs}(u,x) = -\frac{u''(x)}{u'(x)}. \tag{1.11}$$

One way to understand the coefficient of absolute risk aversion is in a certainty-equivalent context as in (1.10). Let x be an agent's current wealth and let z be a zero-mean lottery. Then (1.10) can be rewritten as

$$u(x - c) = \mathbb{E}_p[u(x + z)].$$

Here c is the amount that needs to be deducted from current wealth to induce the risk-averse agent to take risk. (c will be negative if the agent is risk seeking.) The LHS can be approximated by a Taylor series for u about x: $u(x - c) \approx u(x) - c \cdot u'(x)$. Another Taylor series for u about x on the RHS gives $\mathbb{E}_p[u(x + z)] \approx u(x) + \mathbb{E}_p[z]u'(x) + \frac{1}{2}\mathbb{E}_p[z^2]u''(x) = u(x) + \frac{1}{2}\sigma_z^2 u''(x)$, where σ_z^2 is the variance of z. Equating the two Taylor approximations gives:

$$c \approx \frac{1}{2}\sigma_z^2 \operatorname{Coeff}_{abs}(u, x).$$

The risk-aversion deduction c is the product of a term that describes the riskiness of the gamble (σ_z^2) times the agent's risk aversion at the current level of wealth $\operatorname{Coeff}_{abs}(u, x)$.

Similarly, the **coefficient of relative risk aversion** is $\operatorname{Coeff}_{rel}(u, x) = \operatorname{Coeff}_{abs}(u, x) \cdot x$. Relative risk aversion is expressed as a percentage of wealth, rather than as absolute monetary amounts.

For example, Gabriel Cramer's utility function was $u(x) = \sqrt{x}$. So $u'(x) = \frac{1}{2\sqrt{x}}$, and $u''(x) = -\frac{1}{4x^{3/2}}$, giving an absolute risk aversion of $\frac{1}{2x}$. For positive arguments x, this indicates the square root's absolute risk aversion is positive – that is, the square root is risk averse.

The square root's relative risk aversion is ½, a constant. This means that the square root function belongs to the CRRA (Constant Relative Risk Aversion) class of utility functions. CARA (Constant Absolute Risk Aversion) is another important class.

Intuitively, a more risk-averse agent should be reluctant to take some risks that a less risk-averse agent would plunge into. This leads to the

> **Definition** Given two utility functions u and v and a random variable X mapping state indices to prizes, u *is more risk averse than* v if, for every lottery p and sure amount m, where $\mathbb{E}_p[u(X)] \geq u(m)$, then $\mathbb{E}_p[v(X)] \geq v(m)$, while there exists a lottery q and a sure amount k such that $\mathbb{E}_q[v(X)] \geq v(k)$ but $\mathbb{E}_q[u(X)] < u(k)$.

This definition says if u is "willing" to take the risk on p, then v is too, but there is some q, where v is "willing" to take the risk but u isn't. This intuitive concept of degree of willingness to take gambles ties in to the numerical coefficient (1.11) in the way one would hope:

> **Theorem (Pratt)** *If u and v are increasing utility functions, u is more risk averse than v if and only if u's coefficient of absolute risk aversion is higher than v's.*

Suppose there is a binary lottery: it takes 0 with 50 percent probability, takes \$10 with 50 percent probability. This is a losing lottery, so participants will demand compensation to enter it. If a participant has a utility function u and starting wealth is w, then the indifference point c – the minimum amount that participant will demand to be paid to enter this losing lottery – is:

$$u(w) = .5 * u(w + c) + .5 * u(w + c - 10).$$

- If the indifference point c is the same for all wealth levels w, then u is **CARA (Constant Absolute Risk Aversion)**.
- If c is increasing in w, then u is **IARA (Increasing Absolute Risk Aversion)**.
- If c is decreasing in w, then u is **DARA (Decreasing Absolute Risk Aversion)**. Most people act as if their utility function is DARA, which was Daniel Bernoulli's insight back in 1738.

Imagine another binary lottery: it takes 0 with 50 percent probability, and takes 10 percent of the participant's wealth with 50 percent probability. Let f be the fraction of a participant's existing wealth w that the participant will demand to be paid in order to be indifferent to entering this lottery. Then the indifference fraction f is:

$$u(w) = .5u(w(1+f)) + .5u(w(1+f-.1)).$$

- If f is the same for all wealth levels w, then u is **CRRA (Constant Relative Risk Aversion)**.
- If f is increasing in w, then u is **IRRA (Increasing Relative Risk Aversion)**.
- If f is decreasing in w, then u is **DRRA (Decreasing Relative Risk Aversion)**. Most people act as if their utility function is CRRA.

In fact, many economists assume that utility functions are CRRA, which (after solving the differential equation $-\frac{u''(x)}{u'(x)} \cdot x = k$) gives a utility function of the form $u(x) = ax^{1-k} + b$, usually standardized to $u(x) = \frac{x^{1-k}-1}{1-k}$, where k is the degree of relative risk aversion. Many economists have attempted to infer a societal k, that is, an average degree of relative risk aversion across a population such as participants in the US stock market. Tödter (2008) used 77 years of US stock market data from 1926–2002, solving

$$\sum_{t=1}^{77} \pi_t (1 + rf_t)^{1-k} = \sum_{t=1}^{77} \pi_t (1 + rm_t)^{1-k}$$

for k, where rf_t is the risk-free rate in year t; rm_t is the return on the US stock market in year t, and a uniform distribution $\pi_t = \frac{1}{77}$ $\forall t$ is assumed. Tödter finds an average $k = 3.5$, but with a wide $[1.4, 7.1]$ 95% confidence interval.

Generally economists find that most plausible utility functions fall in the **HARA** class **(Hyperbolic Absolute Risk Aversion)**. A utility function u is HARA if its **coefficient of absolute risk tolerance** $-\frac{u'(x)}{u''(x)}$ is a linear function of the form $ax + b$. Note the coefficient of absolute risk tolerance is the reciprocal of the coefficient of absolute risk aversion.

A HARA function with $a = 0$ is CARA, and with $b = 0$ is CRRA. If $a \neq 0$ and $a \neq 1$, then $u(x) = (a-1)^{-1}(ax+b)^{(a-1)/a}$ up to an affine transformation.

1.8.4 Drawbacks of Utility Theory

The mathematical scaffolding built on utility theory is powerful; surely all this cleverness must be a great guide to how people make economic decisions. If we knew each person's utility function, couldn't we set about maximizing utility globally and move toward economic optimality for the human race?

Unfortunately not. Almost as soon as utility theory was proposed, inconsistencies between utility theory and common sense started becoming apparent. Utility remains a powerful concept and a good first-order guide to economic decision making. But it buckles under even mild pressure, departing from what people actually do. One point of departure is the overstrong set of assumptions about what constitutes rational decision making: while necessary to reason mathematically, some of these assumptions are debatable. Another point of departure comes from humans' stubborn insistence on being irrational.

There is an entire industry based in significant part on the failure of utility theory to capture individual preferences: it's called **wealth management**. Wealth managers advise individuals on how to achieve their financial goals. A related field is **robo-investing**, where an individual's data and preferences are collected by an automated process. Decisions in the robo-investing process are then made algorithmically.

Neither human nor robot advisers typically assume that their advisees' preferences can be described by a utility function. Pan and Statman (2012, p. 54) described some typical drawbacks:

- "Each investor has a multitude of risk tolerances.... For example, an investor might have low risk tolerance in a retirement mental account, populating it with bonds or Treasury bills, while at the same time have high risk tolerance in a 'get rich' mental account, populating it with aggressive growth funds or even lottery tickets."
- "Investors' risk tolerance varies by circumstances and associated emotions." Investors are subject to mood swings, displaying exuberance and higher risk tolerance in overheated markets and fear and lower risk tolerance in crashing markets.
- "Foresight is different from hindsight, and the risk tolerance of investors, assessed in foresight, is likely different than the risk tolerance of investors assessed in hindsight." Some investors will tend to look backward and will want to change their investments radically based on perceived missed opportunities or just bad results in the past, while others will maintain forward-looking preferences.

The interplay of emotions, changing life circumstances, recent events, and rational investing goals is impossible to capture in a single static utility function. But the explosion of hard-to-calibrate parameters that would come with multiple time-varying utility functions robs the utility function framework of predictive power. If I say $y = x^k$ but I have to keep adjusting k because actually $y = e^x$, I haven't said anything.

There are internal inconsistencies even within the utility function framework. Consider Daniel Bernoulli's framework: logarithmic utility dependent on current wealth w. If an economic actor's current w is low enough, utility theory predicts that the actor will not take **any** gamble beyond that wealth level.

For example, if someone's current wealth is $w = \$100$, and she is offered a coin toss where tails means she loses \$101 and heads means she wins \$1,000,000,000,000, logarithmic utility says she will decline the gamble since

$$\frac{1}{2} \ln(100 - 101) + \frac{1}{2} \ln\left(100 + 10^{12}\right) = -\infty < \ln(100).$$

In fact there is no finite amount of money on the "win" side of the coin toss that will induce such an economic actor to take the gamble. But that's absurd: of course anyone who is close to destitute would not mind being totally destitute, or even owing a little, in order to have a chance at a trillion dollars.

This particular example can be patched up by flooring the argument to the logarithm. But Rabin's Paradox (due to Matthew Rabin [2000, p. 1281]) indicates this isn't just a technical problem with the logarithm: there's a fundamental problem that is difficult to fix. Rabin proves a theorem that states that:

> within the expected-utility model, anything but virtual risk-neutrality over modest stakes implies manifestly unrealistic risk aversion over large stakes. This theorem is entirely "nonparametric," assuming nothing about the utility function except concavity.

Rabin (2000, p. 1282) shows inconsistencies like this:

> Suppose that, from any initial wealth level, a person turns down gambles where she loses \$100 or gains \$110, each with 50 percent probability. Then she will turn down 50–50 bets of losing \$1,000 or gaining *any* sum of money.

This is similar to the observation about a person with low wealth and a logarithmic utility function, but it applies to any concave (risk-averse) utility function. The conclusion from Rabin's theorem is that it's difficult to calibrate a utility function to make reasonable decisions over both modest amounts and large amounts.

There is also the possibility of **background noise**. It is rare that economic agents are presented in isolation with a decision like the St. Petersburg Paradox, or the Generous Billionaires, or the Probabilistic Thug. In business or life decisions, risks of changes in the general economic or personal environment may be as large or larger than the risk of success or failure of a particular venture. In fact, Pomatto, Strack, and Tamuz (2020) have shown that if there are two random variables X and Y with $\mathbb{E}[X] > \mathbb{E}[Y]$, then there must exist a zero-mean background noise random variable Z independent of X and Y so that $X + Z$ stochastically dominates $Y + Z$. Thus the right kind of background noise can obliterate any risk considerations that might go into a decision between X and Y.

For example, suppose X is the Generous Billionaires coin toss ($1Bn on heads and zero on tails), and Y is a sure check for $400Mn. Then $\mathbb{E}[X] > \mathbb{E}[Y]$, but as we've seen risk aversion will cause many people to choose Y anyway. However, let Z cost $250Mn on heads and pay $250Mn on tails. Then $X + Z$ pays $750Mn and $250Mn on heads and tails, respectively. This stochastically dominates $Y + Z$ which pays $150Mn and $650Mn on heads and tails, respectively. Thus any minimally rational economic agent will prefer $X + Z$ to $Y + Z$, so the presence of the background noise Z has befuddled any risk preference the agent had.[29]

Another inconsistency is called the **Allais problem**, described by Maurice Allais in 1953. Allais would win the Sveriges Riksbank Prize in Economic Sciences in Memory of Alfred Nobel in 1988.[30] As slightly modified and simplified by fellow (2002) Nobel Prize–winner Daniel Kahneman,[31] the Allais problem envisions two choices:

Choice 1: (a) 61 percent chance to win $520,000 or (b) 63% chance to win $500,000.

Choice 2: (a) 98 percent chance to win $520,000 or (b) 100% chance to win $500,000.

Most people choose 1a and 2b. But if 1a is preferred to 1b, we must have:

$$.61u(520) + .39u(0) > .63u(500) + .37u(0),$$

where $u(x)$ means the utility of gaining x thousand dollars. Thus,

$$.61(u(520) - u(500)) > .02(u(500) - u(0)).$$

Assuming only that the utility function u is sensible (more is preferred to less, $u' > 0$), both sides of this last inequality are positive.

Preferring the certain 2b to the highly probable 2a means:

$$u(500) > .98u(520) + .02u(0) > 0,$$

29 For this simple example, the background noise Z is not independent, but the general result ensures that independent background noise Z can be found. In the general result, risk preference is not being altered through diversification of the original choices X and Y.

30 Nobelprize.org. Maurice Allais: Facts. Website. www.nobelprize.org/prizes/economic-sciences/1988/allais/facts/.

31 Nobelprize.org. Daniel Kahneman: Facts. Website. www.nobelprize.org/prizes/economic-sciences/2002/kahneman/facts/.

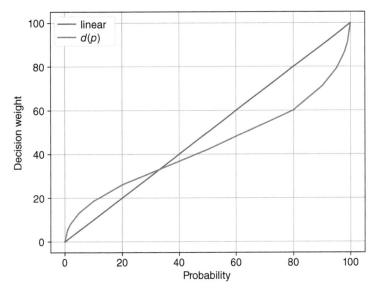

Figure 1.3 Kahneman's empirical decision weights $d(p)$.

which gives:

$$.02(u(500) - u(0)) > .98(u(520) - u(500)).$$

Thus, for any sensible utility function, $1a \succ 1b$ and $2b \succ 2a$ are incompatible.

One way to address the Allais problem is to assume that people are systematically irrational in the way they perceive probabilities. This is a key tenet of the **Prospect Theory** put forward by Kahneman and Tversky (1979). Prospect Theory is in turn part of the field of **behavioral economics**, which uses both psychological theory and empirical observations to back the idea that humans are not only irrational, but are reliably irrational when making economic decisions.

More precisely, let $d(p)$ be a monotone increasing distortion function applied to probabilities (the unit interval $[0, 1]$), where $d(0) = 0$ and $d(1) = 1$ but d is nonlinear in between. If people are acting on $d(probability)$ rather than on the stated probability, it can explain why someone would choose 1a and 2b in the Allais problem. Kahneman (2011) gives some experimentally determined estimates of $d(p)$ for gains, and notes that the estimates for losses are very similar.[32] These are shown expressed in percentage units in Figure 1.3 (generated by Code Segment 1.3).

Note d increases rapidly just above 0 showing the **possibility effect** (people overvalue small possibilities of events happening), and increases rapidly again between 90 and 100 percent, showing the **certainty effect** (people overvalue guarantees versus mere high likelihood). Both effects can be gamed by dispassionate adversaries, even without knowledge of an economic actor's utility function.

---

32 [Kahneman 2011], Chapter 29, Table 4.

These drawbacks tell us not to rely too heavily on utility theory alone. In general, financial and economic modeling cannot replace human intuition, but it can inform it and be informed by it. When taken together with common sense, utility theory can be a powerful tool to help understand decision making in the presence of risk.

For Code Segments in this chapter, see the Code Appendix starting on p. 440. For executable code, visit www.cambridge.org/9781009209090/ch1

For problem sets for this chapter, visit www.cambridge.org/ 9781009209090/ch1_problems

2 Risk Metrics

If risk is *lack of information about the future*, and measurement is *the act of determining a quantity with precision*, then the phrase **risk measurement** is at war with itself. It is only possible to measure Knightian Risk, where all the outcomes and all their probabilities are known a priori. Thus a casino can *measure* the risk that a lucky bettor will win a million dollars at roulette.

But real-world economic activity cannot be fully described by Knightian Risk, so risk in financial markets cannot really be measured. It can only be *estimated*. At best, there might be extensive empirical experience with a relevant quantity, along with a strong rational basis for certain kinds of behaviors, that allow the analyst to estimate risk with a high degree of confidence. At worst, a situation might fall into the abyss of Knight's lowest category where "there is no valid basis of any kind" to classify risks.

Estimating **risk metrics** is a worthwhile activity: it imparts discipline and transparency to the process of analyzing risk. Discipline and transparency in turn allow the metrics, and the process of estimating them, to improve over time. However, the usual caution applies: false precision needs to be counterbalanced by common sense.

One of the oldest risk metrics is volatility: the more a quantity varies, the less sure we are about its future. We will discuss this metric here and in Chapters 4 and 9. We'll also discuss Value at Risk, a metric widely used by some financial market participants, along with related metrics. We'll discuss coherent risk measures, also intended for use by financial market participants.

We'll then discuss pricing kernels, also known as stochastic discount factors and intertemporal marginal rates of substitution. Pricing kernels are not widely used by financial market participants, but are a central paradigm for economists. We'll discuss some recent work that has improved the testability of stochastic discount factor theory, although widespread practitioner use of the theory remains elusive.

2.1 Caveat Laws

Many commentators have captured the problem with the phrase "risk measurement," or indeed any "measurement" of economic or financial parameters: when patterns begin to emerge in measurements made of markets and economies, the participants in those markets and economies see the patterns and change their behaviors, changing the patterns.

An early version of this sentiment is **Goodhart's Law**, named after British economist Charles Goodhart's statement in 1974:[1]

> When a measure becomes a target, it ceases to be a good measure. |

Goodhart was talking about Frank Knight's second category of risk – statistical probability – in the context of public policy targets set by the Bank of England,[2] the central bank of the United Kingdom. As soon as economic actors know that there is a target, they will alter their behavior so that (for example) events that only happened 1 percent of the time in the past now happen more often.

Goodhart's Law was extended by Daníelsson (2002, p. 1276) to say:

> A risk model breaks down when used for its regulatory purposes. |

Daníelsson (2002, p. 1274) pointed out that some people assume in error that:

> ... the role of the risk forecaster is akin to a meteorologist's job, who can forecast the weather, but not influence it. [But] if risk measurements influence people's behavior, it is inappropriate to assume market prices follow an independent stochastic process.

Similarly, most economists are keenly aware of the Nobel Laureate Robert Lucas's[3] version of the idea, called the **Lucas Critique**. Lucas (1976) claimed that econometric models – once again, essentially Knight's statistical probability – can be used only for short-term forecasting and not to make economic policy decisions because:

> ... the features which lead to success in short-term forecasting are unrelated to quantitative policy evaluation, that the major econometric models are (well) designed to perform the former task only, and that simulations using these models can, in principle, provide no useful information as to the actual consequences of alternative economic policies.[4]

To continue Daníelsson's meteorologist analogy, Lucas says that examining past economic patterns may help to predict the weather for the short term, but it doesn't tell you how to change the weather.

These cautionary statements are daunting; if nothing works, then why bother? An answer can be obtained by thinking about these two statements:

1. All humans are giraffes, except the ones who aren't.
2. All humans have five fingers on each hand, except the ones who don't.

1 Charles Goodhart cited in [Strathern 1997], p. 108.
2 Bank of England, "Our History." www.bankofengland.co.uk/about/history.
3 Nobelprize.org. Robert E. Lucas Jr.: Biographical. Website. www.nobelprize.org/prizes/economic-sciences/1995/lucas/biographical.
4 [Lucas 1976], p. 20.

Image 2.1 Twelve-fingered man. Source: Anadolu Agency/Getty Images.

Both statements are true, but the first one is only vacuously true: everyone falls into the exception category. But as an approximation to human fingerness, five is pretty good: there aren't that many exceptions. For many practical purposes – for example, for a glove manufacturer setting up a mold for its glove-making machine – it suffices to say that humans have five fingers on each hand. However if someone were to bet a billion dollars that every human has five fingers on each hand, polydactyl people[5] would arrive to disprove the hypothesis and collect the billion dollars (Image 2.1).

The statistician George Box managed to extract an optimistic take on the inevitable fallibility of human attempts to capture the world in numbers (1976). His point can be summarized as:

All models are wrong, but some are useful. |

His anti-law is now widely cited, sometimes with frustration and sometimes with hope. Our rendering of this common theme is:

All laws in quantitative finance have counterexamples, except this one. |

2.1.1 Portfolio Insurance

To illustrate the caveats we've just seen, we'll consider the **portfolio insurance** strategy. This is a method that purports to allow an investor to participate in up-moves in markets while avoiding down-moves. While this sounds delightful,

---

5 Medlineplus.gov. "Polydactyly." `https://medlineplus.gov/ency/article/003176.htm`

portfolio insurance has been implicated in the US stock market crash of October 19, 1987: that day's 22.6 percent drop in the Dow Jones Industrial Average was the worst ever.

The original idea of portfolio insurance is from Rubinstein and Leland (1981). The basic portfolio insurance strategy consists of maintaining a mix of stocks and bonds, and adjusting the proportion so that more stock is bought (sold) after the stock market has gone up (down) relative to bonds. Leland and Rubenstein, along with John O'Brien, formed a company (Leland O'Brien Rubenstein Associates, "LOR") that offered this strategy to institutional investor clients such as pension and endowment funds. LOR became quite successful, managing tens of billions of dollars.

A simplified version, called constant proportion portfolio insurance ("CPPI"), is due to Black and Perold (1992). CPPI works like this:

1. Choose a protection time period T and a leverage ratio λ. Set $t = T$. Suppose an amount 100 is to be invested. Set $P(t) = 100$.
2. Compute the current floor value $F(t)$ of risk-free bonds that will be worth 100 at time t in the future. For example, if $t = 5$ years and the 5-year risk-free rate is 4.56%, $F(5) = 80$.
3. Allocate $\min(\lambda(P(t) - F(t)), P(t))$ to stock and the rest to bonds. For example, if $\lambda = 3$, $P(t) = 100$, and $F(t) = 80$, allocate 60 to stock and 40 to bonds.
4. At regular intervals, update t (how much time is remaining until the original protection time period is reached) and the current value of the stock-bond portfolio $P(t)$. When $t = 0$, stop. Otherwise, go back to Step 2.

Continuing the example, suppose that one year has passed so that remaining $t = 4$, and that no rebalancing (Step 3) has been done since inception. Suppose that $F(4) = 84$. That means the bond portion of the portfolio is worth $40 * \frac{84}{80} = 42$. Suppose the stock portion of the portfolio has gone from 60 to 70. Then the portfolio is worth $P(4) = 70 + 42 = 112$. Step 3 says to allocate $3(112 - 84) = 84$ to stock. Thus, the CPPI manager would buy $84 - 70 = 14$ more stock and sell 14 of bonds, leaving $42 - 14 = 28$ in bonds.

While different forms of portfolio insurance have different formulas, this illustrates the basic nature of portfolio insurance. If the stock market does well, then the portfolio's value $P(t)$ will be larger than the floor value $F(t)$. As the cushion $P(t) - F(t)$ gets larger, more and more risk is taken by allocating more and more to stock. As the cushion shrinks, less risk is taken. If things go poorly enough, there will be no cushion and the portfolio will be 100 percent invested in bonds. Once that happens, there is no possibility of buying stock again until the protection period ends.

In this way, the CPPI method tries to keep the value of the portfolio above $F(t)$ with time t remaining, aiming to have at least 100 at the end of the protection period. That's the "insurance" part, although there isn't really an insurance company or a guarantee. If the stock market gaps sharply downward before a Step 3 reallocation can be done, there might not be 100 at the end. Otherwise, the CPPI portfolio hopes to enjoy the upside of a stock allocation by investing the over-floor amount in the stock market. The larger the leverage ratio λ, the more aggressive the method is in deploying the over-floor amount to stocks.

This means that the method buys more stock after stocks have done well and sells stock after stocks have done poorly. This reveals the **procyclical** nature of portfolio insurance: it wants to keep going in the same direction that the market went. If a procyclical strategy is followed by enough market participants, the market can become a runaway train either on the upside or the downside as buying (selling) begets more buying (selling).

The popularity of LOR and other portfolio insurance methods grew during the 1980s. By October 19, 1987, tens of billions of dollars were moving procyclically. Portfolio insurance became what is called a **crowded trade**: a large enough part of the market that it affected the market, creating a negative feedback loop. In Ruder (1988, p. 7), then Securities and Exchange Commission chair David Ruder said that "great selling pressure [was] exacerbated on October 19th and 20th by large stock and futures sales by institutions pursuing a variety of arbitrage and portfolio insurance strategies."

While other postmortems have assigned varying degrees of culpability to portfolio insurance, all analyses agree that there was a stampede on October 19, 1987, as market participants panicked:

> Given the uncertainty, investors apparently sought to sell and close out their positions. With the dearth of reliable information, herd behavior reportedly became common. Robert Shiller surveyed market participants promptly after the crash and many conveyed to him that, on the day of the crash, they were reacting more to the price movements than to any particular news.[6]

Daníelsson's meteorologist anti-analogy is apt here: portfolio insurance and other procyclical strategies assume that the participants are mere observers. If that is true, then it can be shown theoretically that a CPPI strategy is similar to buying some bonds and a call option, which is equivalent to buying some stock and a put option (insurance).

In order for that theoretical finding to hold, the act of following a portfolio insurance strategy should not cause herd behavior. But it does: under enough stress, following the allocation formula affects the allocation formula. If there are enough participants doing similar procyclical strategies,[7] they will cause herd behavior even among those not pursuing those strategies as market participants

---

6 [Carlson 2007], p. 17.
7 The author managed a CPPI portfolio in the early 2000s. I was keenly aware of the procyclical trap, but by the early 2000s very few market participants were engaged in this strategy so the risk of 1987-type herding was low.

"[react] more to the price movements than to any particular news." A market where participants are reacting only to price movements is unmoored from external reality such as the financial health of the economy or of the companies traded in the market.

The mathematics of finance and economics can be beautiful and deep, and resulting metrics can be appealingly precise, but they are not really binding as they would be in mathematics or physics. There are always exceptions, some of them engendered by the very act of stating the "theorem" or "law." A liberal application of common sense is needed to see whether or not we are inadvertently encouraging searches for polydactyly or procyclical strategies. But if results and metrics are seen as guides to intuition rather than irrevocable laws, they can be quite useful.

2.2 Volatility

Neuroscientists using functional magnetic resonance imaging (fMRI) have found that human (and other species, such as macaque monkey) brains seem to have built-in systems to monitor and update volatility estimates. Bossaerts (2018, p. 1) summarized the state of the art as of December 2018:

> Learning signals that have been identified in neural activation within aIns [anterior insula] appear to be related to risk and surprise. That is, neural signals correlate with the size of prediction errors (PEs), i.e., the un-signed PE (it is always non-negative) (Fouragnan et al., 2017, 2018). aIns neural signals encode the anticipated size of upcoming PEs, which means that they track risk. When uncertainty materializes, aIns neural signals encode surprise, i.e., the extent to which the size of the PE is greater or less than anticipated (Preuschoff et al., 2008).

Behrens, Woolrich, Walton, et al. (2007, p. 1214) did experiments using a game where subjects needed to estimate both averages and volatilities to do better. They found

> ...that human subjects assess volatility in an optimal manner and adjust decision-making accordingly. This optimal estimate of volatility is reflected in the fMRI signal in the anterior cingulate cortex (ACC) when each trial outcome is observed. When a new piece of information is witnessed, activity levels reflect its salience for predicting future outcomes.

We noted that the word "volatility" usually means standard deviation:

$$\sigma = \sqrt{\mathbb{E}\left[(x - \mathbb{E}[x])^2\right]}.$$

This is a natural number to quantify *lack of information about the future*; the bigger the standard deviation of (say) changes in a value, the bigger the chance that the future value will be far away from the present value (plus the average

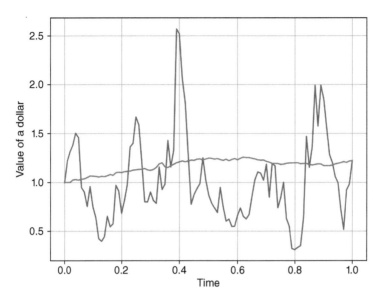

Figure 2.1 High versus low volatility: same returns.

change). A related quantity that is used in some of the neuroscience investigations is **mean absolute deviation**, that is,

$$MAD = \mathbb{E}\big[\big|x - \mathbb{E}[x]\big|\big]. \tag{2.1}$$

For a normal distribution, $MAD = \sqrt{\frac{2}{\pi}}\sigma$. Standard deviation generally gives more weight to outliers than MAD.

Functional magnetic resonance imaging tests are not needed to demonstrate the instinctive assessment of volatility; you can immediately see it. Consider the two time series randomly generated in Figure 2.1 (generated by Code Segment 2.1). The horizontal axis is time, and the vertical axis represents the time-varying value of an original dollar invested at time zero.

Here standard deviation has been used for volatility; the blue time series in Figure 2.1 was generated with 30 times the standard deviation of the orange time series. They have been forced to end up in the same place – the starting dollar at time period 0 grows to \$1.22 at time period 1. But if you were asked to predict where each time series would be at future time period 2, you would instinctively have much more confidence predicting that the low-volatility orange time series would continue to grow at about the same pace between period 1 and period 2 as it did between period 0 and period 1. It would be very difficult to make any prediction about where the blue series would be at time period 2.

Sometimes **downside semi-variance** or its square root, **downside semi-standard-deviation** is used:

$$\sigma^2_{down} = \frac{\int_{-\infty}^{\mu}(x - \mu)^2 \cdot dF(x)}{F(\mu)}. \tag{2.2}$$

Here μ is the mean of the distribution. Some writers have favored σ_{down} on the basis of a supposed indifference to "upside risk." If risk is peril, then this might make sense: the focus would mainly be on the bad outcomes.

However, if risk is venture, then the justification for using σ_{down} is less obvious. For example, consider the following two distributions, each with the four equally likely outcomes shown:

- Distribution A: $-5\%, -2\%, 3.5\%, 3.5\%$
- Distribution B: $-5\%, -2\%, 0.1\%, 6.9\%$

These both average zero and have the same downside semi-variance. Distribution B has a higher overall variance, reflecting the bigger range of upside possibilities. If we care about the upside – which we do when we are engaged in venture portfolio management rather than peril portfolio management – the overall variance is more informative.

Some practitioners use **interquartile range** as a risk measure. If F is a cdf, then its interquartile range is:

$$IQR(F) = F^{-1}(.75) - F^{-1}(.25).$$

More generally, the **inter-p-tile range** is:

$$IR(p,F) = F^{-1}(1-p) - F^{-1}(p). \tag{2.3}$$

Ranges fit nicely with the intuition of risk as lack of information about the future, because smaller ranges mean more is known and bigger ranges mean less is known. For example the interdecile range $IR(.1, F)$ gives the length of the 80% confidence interval about the median. Ranges are also easy to compute for both empirical and theoretical distributions.

Ultimately probability distributions can be arbitrarily complex so compressing all the information in the cdf $F(x)$ into a single number is not going to work. We can try to optimize the amount of information we get from a single scalar metric – some are better than others depending on the context – but ultimately multiple metrics are needed.

2.3 VaR, ES, cVaR, and Spectral Measures

A natural question to ask when making a risky investment is: how bad can things get?

The problem with this question is that there's no limit to the range of possibilities. Whatever terrible situation we can imagine can usually be one-upped by an even more terrible one. At some point we descend into absurdity,[8] speculating perhaps that evil aliens with hopelessly superior technology land on

---

8 "Worst thing that could happen." https://xkcd.com/2261/.

Earth and destroy all human life. This grisly scenario is so unrealistic that there's nothing we could or should do about it. Such extreme speculation is not a guide to actions we should take now.

A more interesting question is: how bad are the things that can realistically happen that we might have a chance of planning for and doing something about? This seems more down to earth, but we need to know what "realistically" means.

A measure called **Value at Risk** (or VaR[9]) was created to answer the question "How bad can things get *realistically*?" It's now widely used and, in some cases, required by financial regulators[10] to be computed and acted on.

VaR is simply a percentile of a probability distribution of a financial quantity of interest. The quantity is usually one of the following:

- *P&L* (profit&loss, that is, change in wealth from the current wealth); or
- *Rate of return* or just *return* of wealth; that's ending wealth divided by beginning wealth, all minus one; or
- *Log-return*, which is the logarithm of one plus the rate of return.

All of these quantities can in general take on both positive and negative values. Value at Risk is concerned with how much can be lost, so the convention is to reverse the sign in a way we'll describe below, giving bigger positive numbers for bigger losses.[11]

Let X be the random variable giving the future value of whichever one of the quantities above is being analyzed, and let $F_t(x)$ be the cumulative distribution function (cdf) of X's value at some time t in the future. The Value at Risk (VaR) over time $t > 0$ with probability $0 \leq p \leq 1$ is:

$$VaR_t(p) = -\inf\{x \mid F_t(x) = Pr(X \leq x) \geq 1 - p\}. \qquad (2.4)$$

If X's cdf F_t is continuous, then the calculation simplifies to:

$$VaR_t(p) = -F_t^{-1}(1-p); \qquad VaR_t(p) = x \iff \int_{-\infty}^{-x} f_t(y)dy = 1 - p, \qquad (2.5)$$

where $f_t(y)$ is the probability density function of the distribution.

In words, we say that $VaR_t(p)$ is the ***t*-year p Value at Risk**. t could also be denominated in other time units like days, and might be left implicit if it is specified elsewhere.

For example, if a bank wants to estimate how bad things can get in its trading operations, the random variable of interest might be Δw, the change (P&L) in its

---

9 The abbreviation VaR is case-sensitive: usually "Var" means statistical variance (the square of standard deviation), while "VaR" means value at risk.

10 Federal Reserve System. Part 225, Appendix E: Capital Adequacy Guidelines for Bank Holding Companies: Market Risk Measure. www.govinfo.gov/content/pkg/CFR-2012-title12-vol3/pdf/CFR-2012-title12-vol3-part225-appE.pdf.

11 If the quantity being analyzed is always positive by definition – for example, an amount of wealth rather than a change in the amount of wealth – then the sign-reversing conventions shown in this section are not used.

trading capital w by the end of tomorrow's trading day. The one-day 99% VaR for its trading operations would be the (positive) loss amount that was expected to exceed $-\Delta w$, 99 days out of 100. So if the one-day 99% VaR is \$50,000,000, then the bank expects to lose less than \$50,000,000 on all but one out of 100 trading days.

Here's a problem with VaR: suppose a trader at the \$50,000,000 one-day 99% VaR bank has established a strategy where every day, she sells \$100,000 worth of options that have only a 1-in-200 chance of paying off. If the options don't pay off, the bank will keep the \$100,000, but if they do pay off, the bank will owe \$1,000,000,000. The 99% VaR calculation does not "see" the 99.5% quantile where the options strategy pays off (i.e. loses); it only sees the \$100,000 profits and deems the trade riskless. The VaR of the trade would actually be negative. But the chance that the bank owes a billion dollars is $1 - .995^n$, where n is the number of days the strategy is employed; in about six months, there will be a greater than 50% chance that the bank will owe a billion dollars, possibly wiping out its trading capital.

By drawing a line at 99%, the bank encouraged behavior just on the other side of the 99% threshold. This is an example of the caveat laws we saw above. The bank in the example tried to define "how bad can things get *realistically*" to exclude far-fetched scenarios like alien invasions. But as soon as that definition was in place, economic actors were encouraged to engage in behavior that was now deemed far-fetched but that wasn't actually at alien-invasion levels of absurdity.

We will see that there are better measures than VaR, but any measure is subject to gaming. Further, if more market participants engage in strategies that are just on the other side of the line, their aggregate behavior changes the probabilities so their strategies might no longer be just on the other side of the line. Other techniques, like scenario analysis and stress testing (Chapter 8), are needed to complement VaR-type measures.

One way to take into account behavior beyond the VaR threshold $1 - p$ was put forward by Acerbi and Tasche (2001). They defined **Expected Shortfall** as an average of the "bad" VaRs:

$$ES(p) = \frac{1}{1-p} \int_p^1 VaR(z)dz. \tag{2.6}$$

Another approach to analyzing beyond-VaR behavior is to find the expected value conditional on the outcome being in the VaR tail of the distribution. This is called **cVaR, or conditional Value at Risk** (Rockafellar and Uryasev 2000).

$$cVaR(p) = -\mathbb{E}[X|X \le -VaR(p)] = \frac{-1}{F\left(-VaR(p)\right)} \int_{-\infty}^{-VaR(p)} yf(y)dy. \tag{2.7}$$

The $1 - p$ standardization factor on the right of (2.6) equals the $F(-VaR(p))$ standardization factor on the right of (2.7) when the cdf F is continuous. However, if F is not continuous then it might be true that $F(-VaR(p)) > 1 - p$, as the inf in (2.4) might be forced to select a point away from the desired cutoff $1 - p$. In any case, these standardization factors scale the probability density functions so they integrate to one in the tail. For ES, the pdf is uniform, while for cVaR the pdf is the pdf of the random variable X.

When F is differentiable, the change of variable $1 - z = F(y)$ in the definition of $ES(p)$ makes it equal to $cVaR(p)$.

Acerbi (2002) defined a family of extensions to Expected Shortfall he called **spectral measures of risk.** Let $w(x)$ be an increasing weight function whose domain is the interval $[0, 1]$ and whose range is the nonnegative real numbers. So $w'(x) \geq 0$ and $\int_0^1 w(x)dx = 1$. Then the spectral measure based on w is

$$SRM(w) = \int_0^1 VaR(x)w(x)dx. \qquad (2.8)$$

When $w(x) = 0$ for $x < p$ and $w(x) = \frac{1}{1-p}$ for $x \geq p$, $SRM(w) = ES(p)$. Spectral measures outside of Expected Shortfall are not widely used at this writing. They might come into play when an analyst wants a transition to the risk-critical area that is less jumpy than Expected Shortfall.

For a normal distribution, cVaR equals ES because the cdf is differentiable. If $Norm^{-1}(z)$ is the inverse standard normal function (so that $z = \frac{1}{\sqrt{2\pi}} \int_{-\infty}^{Norm^{-1}(z)} \exp(\frac{-x^2}{2})dx$), then the p-Value-at-Risk of a normal distribution with mean μ and variance σ^2 is

$$VaR_{Norm}(p) = -(\mu + \sigma Norm^{-1}(1 - p)). \qquad (2.9)$$

So the normal cVaR is

$$cVaR_{Norm}(p) = -\mu + \frac{-1}{1 - p} \frac{1}{\sigma \sqrt{2\pi}} \int_{-\infty}^{-v} y \exp\left(\frac{-y^2}{2\sigma^2}\right) dy$$

$$= -\mu + \frac{\sigma}{(1 - p)\sqrt{2\pi}} \exp\left(\frac{-v^2}{2\sigma^2}\right), \qquad (2.10)$$

where $v = VaR_{Norm}(p)$ for brevity.

2.3.1 VaR Measures with Discrete Distributions

Discrete distributions can sometimes cause problems with evaluations of VaR, ES and cVaR. VaR is essentially the inverse of the cumulative distribution function, but that inverse can be bumpy when it's applied to a finite distribution. This is more of a technical problem than a substantive one: if there are a large but finite number of points in the distribution being analyzed then edge effects are small. If there are so few points in the distribution that edge cases are significant, then the confidence interval about an estimate of VaR (or ES or cVaR) is probably so wide that it's meaningless.

Consider for example a process that has three outcomes:

- With probability .5%, loses 100;
- With probability 2%, loses 50;
- With probability 97.5%, gains 1.

The pdf f is a mass function; $f(-100) = .005$; $f(-50) = .02$; and $f(1) = .975$. That means the cdf F has:

$$F(x) = \begin{cases} 0, & \text{if } x < -100, \\ .005, & \text{if } -100 \leq x < -50, \\ .025, & \text{if } -50 \leq x < 1, \text{ and} \\ 1, & \text{if } x \geq 1. \end{cases}$$

Equation (2.4) says that:

$$VaR(p) = \begin{cases} 100, & \text{if } 99.5\% \leq p, \\ 50, & \text{if } 97.5\% \leq p < 99.5\%, \text{ and} \\ -1, & \text{if } p \leq 97.5\%. \end{cases}$$

Let's calculate 99% ES and 99% cVaR for this distribution. $VaR(99\%) = 50$.

- For ES, the $VaR(z)$ in the integral (2.6) is equal to 100 half the time and equal to 50 the other half of the time, so $ES(99\%) = 75$.
- For cVaR, the integral in (2.7) becomes a sum of two terms. At the value -100, the probability mass is .005, so the contribution is $-.5$. At the value -50, the probability mass is .02, so the contribution is -1. Therefore, the sum is -1.5. The standardization factor $F(VaR(99\%)) = F(50) = .025$. With the sign reversal, $cVaR(99\%) = 1.5/.025 = 60$.

Thus, ES and cVaR don't agree here. The difference came about because the distribution had discontinuous probability jumps.

But as the number of observations goes up, the edge cases caused by discontinuities become less and less important. Some kind of interpolation or extrapolation around probability mass points can be applied to smooth the distribution, assuming that the smoothed process does not irrevocably depart from the underlying process.

Figure 2.2 (generated by Code Segment 2.2) generates 1,000 random numbers and computes the sample 99% VaR – the number at the first percentile of the distribution. A useful convention when analyzing sample distributions consisting of n points is to assume that the ith point is the $\frac{i}{n+1}$ percentile of the distribution, thereby allowing for more extreme values at either end than the ones that have been observed so far. So the first percentile of the 1,000 numbers is a little bigger than the tenth smallest observation (i.e. the loss is a little less).

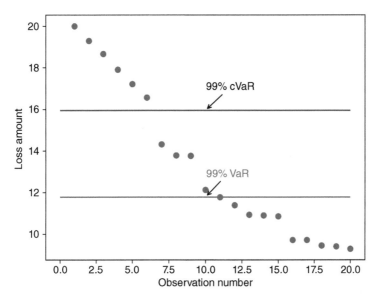

Figure 2.2 Worst 20 losses out of 1,000.

The code also computes the average of the observations that are less than 99% VaR and displays that average (red line) as cVaR.

Because the distribution is finite, there are edge issues, although they're minor. We show two ways of dealing with the edge issues in Code Segment 2.2 in the Code Appendix. In addition to Figure 2.2, Code Segment 2.2 computes the following quantities:

```
99% VaR is  11.781890699024686
99% cVaR is  15.949993320207135
99% interpolated VaR is  12.12450571944469
99% interpolated cVaR is  16.3625655225223
```

There are small differences between the VaR/cVaR defined above, and VaR/cVaR obtained from straight-line interpolating between probability masses.

Comparing the sample statistics with the formula values under the (counterfactual) assumption of normality results in the following quantities calculated by Code Segment 2.3:

```
99% Sample VaR is  11.781890699024686
99% Normal VaR is  7.5958778057456735
99% Sample cVaR is  15.949993320207135
99% Normal cVaR is  8.43350174708078
```

The random sample has worse empirical VaR and much worse cVaR than a normal distribution. We will see in Chapter 7 that this is not unusual.

2.4 Risk-Adjusted Reward Measures

Chapter 1's Terrified Lover would, in our scenario, only achieve a good result by taking a risk. Similarly Chapter 1's Hyperproductive Farmer took a risk by starting a cattle ranch. A natural question for each to ask is: Is it worth it to take the risk?

We emphatically disavow the idea that there are metrics that might apply to the Terrified Lover. But we've just seen a number of risk metrics that do apply to financial situations. A natural answer to the question "Is it worth it?" is to look at the ratio of reward gained to risk taken. This can be done in retrospect using historical data, or forward-looking data if there is a model of future outcomes.

One of the most widely used ratios is the **Sharpe Ratio**, named after William Sharpe,[12] one of the co-winners of the 1990 Sveriges Riksbank Prize in Economic Sciences in Memory of Alfred Nobel. Sharpe is currently an emeritus professor of finance at the Graduate School of Business, Stanford University.[13]

Sharpe (1994) pointed out that he originally named the measure the "reward-to-variability ratio," but others attached his name to it. Sharpe Ratios are used both as backward-looking empirical measures and as forward-looking expectation measures. As a backward-looking measure, the Sharpe Ratio is

$$SR_a(x) = \frac{AvgRet(x) - RF_a}{StdDev(x - RF)}. \tag{2.11}$$

Here $AvgRet(x)$ is the average period-by-period rate of return of an investment x and $StdDev(x)$ is its standard deviation over the same periodicity. RF_a is the average per-period risk-free rate – e.g. the interest rate on a completely safe bank account. We'll discuss the risk-free rate in more detail in the next section. The standard deviation calculation is actually the standard deviation of excess returns, that is, period-by-period differences between the investment's return and the risk-free rate.

Most Sharpe Ratios are quoted in annual periodicity by multiplying by the square root of the number of periods per year; for example, a Sharpe Ratio using monthly data is multiplied by $\sqrt{12}$.

In practice, (2.11) is often replaced with a variant:

$$SR_g(x) = \frac{GeomRet(x) - RF_g}{StdDev(x)}. \tag{2.12}$$

Here, $GeomRet(x)$ is the periodic geometric (compound) return of the investment and RF_g is the periodic geometric (compound) return of a risk-free instrument. Thus, a two-period investment x having returns $+5\%$ in the

---

12 Nobelprize.org. William F. Sharpe: Biographical. Website. www.nobelprize.org/prizes/economic-sciences/1990/sharpe/biographical.

13 Stanford Graduate School of Business. Faculty Profile: William F. Sharpe. Website. www.gsb.stanford.edu/faculty-research/faculty/william-f-sharpe.

first period and -5% in the second period would have $AvgRet(x) = 0$ and $GeomRet(x) = \sqrt{1.05 * .95} - 1 = -12.51$bps (a basis point or "bp" is one one-hundredth of a percent). Geometric mean return is always less than (or equal to, if there is no variance) the arithmetic mean return, so $SR_g(x) \le SR_a(x)$. $SR_g(X)$ is not the authoritative (i.e. Sharpe's) definition of the Sharpe Ratio, but the reader should be aware that less rigorous calculations might use it rather than $SR_a(x)$, thereby biasing the ratio downward.

Another frequent departure from Sharpe's definition is a failure to use the standard deviation of excess (over risk-free) returns in the denominator. Some calculations simply take the standard deviation of returns without subtracting the risk-free rate. Usually the variability of the risk-free rate is quite small compared to the variability of the investment. A failure to remove the risk-free rate will probably bias standard deviation upward and hence bias the Sharpe Ratio downward.

Both SR_a or SR_g can be converted to forward-looking measures if investment x's returns have an associated probability distribution from which expectations of the relevant quantities can be computed.

The **Treynor Ratio** is named for Jack Treynor,[14] one of the founders of quantitative investment management. Treynor (1965) used the same numerator as the Sharpe Ratio, but the risk measure in the denominator is $Cov(x - RF, m - RF)/Var(m - RF)$, where m is the overall market in which the investments are being made. For example, m might be the Standard & Poor's 500 Index[15] if the relevant market is the US stock market. Here Cov means covariance, either empirically from historical performance data or modeled from forward-looking expectations. ("Var" as usual means variance.) We will see in Chapter 6 that this denominator, popularly called "beta," is an important measure of market risk.

Jensen's Alpha is due to Michael Jensen,[16] currently an emeritus professor at Harvard Business School. Jensen noted (1967, p. 389),

> The concept of portfolio "performance" has at least two distinct dimensions:
>
> 1. The ability of the portfolio manager or security analyst to increase returns on the portfolio through successful prediction of future security prices; and
> 2. The ability of the portfolio manager to minimize (through "efficient" diversification) the amount of "insurable risk" born [sic] by the holders of the portfolio.

14 The Institute for Quantitative Research in Finance. About Jack Treynor. Website. www.q-group.org/jack-treynor-prize/.

15 S&P Dow Jones Indices. S&P 500® Overview. Website. www.spglobal.com/spdji/en/indices/equity/sp-500/#overview.

16 Harvard Business School. Michael C. Jensen. Website. www.hbs.edu/faculty/Pages/profile.aspx?facId=6484.

Jensen assumed that his item 2 was risk arising from exposure to the market from which the portfolio was chosen. His model is:

$$x - RF = \alpha + \beta(m - RF) + \epsilon.$$

Here x represents an investment portfolio; RF the risk-free rate; and m the market from which the portfolio x is selected. When this approach is used as a backward-looking performance measure over T time periods, the inputs x, RF, and m are T-vectors of rates of return and α and β are the scalars that minimize $\epsilon^{\mathsf{T}}\epsilon$; that is, α and β are regression coefficients. The β here gives the exposure to market risk and is similar to the denominator in the Treynor Ratio. The outperformance – item 1 in Jensen's list – is given by α.

The **Modigliani and Modigliani** (or M^2) measure was developed by the late Franco Modigliani[17] and his granddaughter Leah Modigliani. Franco Modigliani won the 1985 Sveriges Riksbank Prize in Economic Sciences in Memory of Alfred Nobel. Leah Modigliani is a market strategist.[18]

Modigliani and Modigliani (1997) define their measure in a few equivalent ways. One way is

$$M^2(x,b) = SR_a(x) \cdot StdDev(b) + RF. \qquad (2.13)$$

Here b is a benchmark investment: it may be the same as the m (market) in Jensen's measure, or may be a more specific benchmark such as an index of small growth-oriented companies. $StdDev(b)$ is the standard deviation of b's excess returns over the risk-free investment's returns. Another way to write the M^2 measure is:

$$M^2(x,b) = AvgRet(x)\frac{StdDev(b)}{StdDev(x)} + RF\left(1 - \frac{StdDev(b)}{StdDev(x)}\right).$$

The more volatile x is, the less weight is placed on its return and the more weight is placed on the risk-free instrument. The idea is that good returns that may be in $AvgRet(x)$ need to be penalized if they were obtained by taking undue risk. On the other hand, if x takes less risk than its benchmark, the returns it achieved get scaled up. Thus, higher-than-benchmark risk is penalized and lower-than-benchmark risk is rewarded.

The **Sortino Ratio**, due to Sortino and Price (1994), does not use risk-free rates or benchmarks as points of comparison. Instead, it assumes that the investor

---

17 Nobelprize.org. Franco Modigliani: Biographical. Website. www.nobelprize.org/prizes/economic-sciences/1985/modigliani/biographical.
18 Julia Hanna, "Highly Recommended: Leah Modigliani." Harvard Business School Alumni. Website. www.alumni.hbs.edu/stories/Pages/story-bulletin.aspx?num=5207.

has a target rate T that she or he wants to attain; Sortino calls this the "minimal acceptable return." The ratio is:

$$Srt(x, T) = \frac{AvgRet(x) - T}{\sqrt{\frac{1}{F(T)} \int_{-\infty}^{T} (T-r)^2 f(r) dr}}. \tag{2.14}$$

Here, $f(r)$ is the probability density function (either empirical or modeled) for the investment's returns. The denominator of (2.14) is therefore the same as downside semistandard deviation (2.2), but with a cutoff at T rather than at the mean μ.

The **Omega Ratio** is due to Keating and Shadwick (2002); they originally called it "gamma" rather than "omega." Like Sortino, they contemplate a target rate T and integrate over a distribution:

$$\Omega(x, T) = \frac{\int_{T}^{\infty} (1 - F(r)) dr}{\int_{-\infty}^{T} F(r) dr}. \tag{2.15}$$

Here $F(r)$ is the cumulative distribution function of asset x's returns.

Using integration by parts, the denominator in (2.15) can be rewritten:

$$\int_{-\infty}^{T} F(r) dr = TF(T) - \mathbb{E}[x\delta(x \leq T)].$$

Here the δ function is 1 if its argument is true and 0 otherwise. The numerator can be rewritten:

$$\int_{T}^{\infty} (1 - F(r)) dr = -T(1 - F(T)) + \mathbb{E}[x\delta(x \geq T)]$$

$$= TF(T) - T + \mathbb{E}[x] - \mathbb{E}[x\delta(x \leq T)].$$

Note:

$$TF(T) - \mathbb{E}[x\delta(x \leq T)] = \mathbb{E}[(T-x)^+],$$

where the $^+$ operator returns the argument $(T-x)$ if the argument is positive and returns zero otherwise. So we can rewrite (2.15) as:

$$\Omega(x, T) = \frac{\mathbb{E}[x] - T}{\mathbb{E}[(T-x)^+]} + 1.$$

From this we can see that the Omega Ratio rewards (in the numerator) expected returns over the target T, and penalizes (in the denominator) the expectation of the shortfall in returns under the target.

2.5 Coherent Risk

In the late 1990s and thereafter, four co-authors Artzner, Delbaen, Eber, and Heath ("ADEH") postulated a series of mathematical axioms that, they claimed, any reasonable ("coherent") measure of financial risk should have. ADEH (2001) were trying to avoid damaging situations like the trader's option strategy described in Section 2.3.

ADEH's definition of risk is more accounting oriented than the essentially probabilistic Knight definitions. For ADEH, risk is how much cash has to be put into a portfolio to make it acceptable. An "acceptable" portfolio is one that passes regulatory or other hurdles. So to ADEH, risk is a peril – the chance of having an unacceptable portfolio – and the metric for risk is the size of the monetary fortification you need to build to protect yourself from the peril.

For example, if your portfolio contains Section 2.3's options trading strategy, losing a billion dollars would probably be unacceptable. Maybe "acceptable" means never having less than $100,000,000$. If you added $1,100,000,000$ in cash to that portfolio, you'd eliminate the possibility of ending up below the threshold, making the portfolio (or at least that part of the portfolio) acceptable. The ADEH-type risk of the portfolio might then be $1.1 billion.

More formally, ADEH defined a **risk measure** as a mapping from a random variable X to the real numbers. X could be an amount of money; a change in an amount of money; or a rate of return. The sample space Ω (which ADEH assume is finite) encompasses all relevant economic conditions one period forward.

ADEH assumed there is a single risk-free instrument R_f, sometimes called a **money market account** or just **cash**. R_f is an investment that will always be worth one unit of currency one period in the future, no matter what state the world is in at that time. In practice, R_f is a loan to a completely reliable institution like a very solid government or bank. We'll learn more about the time value of money in Chapter 3, but for now note that money in the future is not the same as money now, so R_f is not necessarily worth one unit of currency now. If the completely reliable institution is paying a rate of interest r_f per period, R_f will be worth $\frac{1}{1+r_f}$ now.

ADEH (2001) put forward four axioms that sensible risk measures ρ must satisfy.

- Axiom T (**Translation Invariance**): $\rho(X + \alpha R_f) = \rho(X) - \alpha$. This says we can decrease our risk by adding cash to our portfolio. ADEH point out that this means $\rho(X + \rho(X)R_f) = 0$, that is, $\rho(X)$ is the amount of cash that will eliminate risk.
- Axiom S (**Subadditivity**): $\rho(X + Y) \leq \rho(X) + \rho(Y)$. This says diversification helps, or at least doesn't hurt, to reduce risk. ADEH note that if this were not true, entities (trading desks, banks, companies, portfolios) would be encouraged to split up into pieces to give the appearance of having less risk.
- Axiom PH (**Positive Homogeneity**): If $\lambda \geq 0$, then $\rho(\lambda X) = \lambda \rho(X)$. We know from Axiom S that $\rho(nX) \leq n\rho(X)$. This says that equality holds, and fills

in between the integers. In effect, this ignores liquidity risk,[19] which ADEH acknowledge; they are focused on whether an amount of money is sufficient or not.

- Axiom M (**Monotonicity**): If $X \leq Y$, then $\rho(Y) \leq \rho(X)$. Here, $X \leq Y$ means that the random variable Y stochastically[20] dominates the random variable X. So this axiom says that having more money is less risky than having less money.

A risk measure satisfying these four axioms is called **coherent**.

To see whether you've understood coherent risk, see if you can resolve the following puzzle:

> Suppose X is a random variable that gives us more money than we have now under any circumstances, say, $X(0) = 0$, where 0 is the current time, and $X(1) = 2$ or $X(1) = 4$ with equal probability at time 1 in the future. Let $Y = 2X$. Axiom PH says $\rho(Y) = 2\rho(X)$. But Axiom M says $\rho(Y) \leq \rho(X)$. How can both statements be true?

The axioms of subadditivity and positive homogeneity are sometimes replaced by a single, weaker axiom:

- Axiom C (**Convexity**): If $1 \geq \lambda \geq 0$, then $\rho(\lambda X + (1 - \lambda)Y) \leq \lambda\rho(X) + (1 - \lambda)\rho(Y)$.

A risk measure satisfying translation invariance, convexity, and monotonicity is called a **convex risk measure**.

We've already seen an unfortunate failing of the VaR measure: it fails to detect rare but disastrous events that are below the probability threshold. But ADEH (2001) give another example that shows that VaR isn't convex, so it certainly isn't coherent.

Suppose there are two digital options on a stock. The first one, A, costs h at time 0 and pays 1,000 at time 1 if the value of the stock is over some H, and 0 otherwise. The second digital option, B, costs l (lowercase L) at time 0 and pays 1,000 at time 1 if the value of the stock is under some L, and 0 otherwise. Here $L < H$.

The payoff profile of buying both A and B: you get 1,000 if the stock ends up under L or over H, and nothing in between. Suppose we choose L and H so

---

19 Liquidity risk is the uncertainty about whether you will be able to turn an asset into cash, or cash into an asset, on a desired time frame at its assumed market price. If you own shares of Apple Computer, you can easily sell them at very little discount from whatever the latest quote was. If you want to sell your house tomorrow, you won't be able to do it at the appraised price. Apple Shares are highly liquid; houses are not. See Chapter 12, where we discuss liquidity hedging.

20 ADEH use the notation $X \leq Y$, which is ambiguous for random variables. My guess from their discussion is that they meant statewise dominance, but stochastic dominance is less stringent and works just as well in the axiomatization.

that $Pr(Stock < L) = Pr(Stock > H) = 80$bps. A is a lottery ticket that pays off 1,000 with probability 80bps, and zero the rest of the time. Its expected value is 8, and any risk-averse utility function is going to value it less than 8. Even a risk-loving but reasonable utility function will value it closer to 8 than to 1,000, and similarly for option B.

Assume without loss of generality that the risk-free instrument R_f is worth 1 today (i.e. the risk-free rate is 0). Then there is no time value of money to worry about and the 99% money VaR of writing (going short) 2 A's is $-2h$, because 99.2% of the time the option does not pay off and you pocket $2h$ from writing the options. Having positive money is negative value at risk. Similarly the 99% money VaR of writing two B's is $-2l$.

However, suppose you write one A and one B. The middle ground between L and H – the place where neither pays off – has $100\% - .8\% - .8\% = 98.4\%$ probability. There is a 1.6% chance the stock will end up either very low (less than L, where B pays off) or very high (greater than H, where A pays off). The 99% money VaR of writing one A and one B is $1,000 - l - h$, a (large) positive=bad number.

So this is another example of VaR not seeing concentrated risk. One A and one B is a better-diversified portfolio than two A's. In effect the VaR measure encourages its users to double up on their low-probability bets (or triple up or quadruple up ...).

You can't hide problems in the tail with Expected Shortfall/cVaR/spectral risk measures – they get averaged in. ES/cVaR/SRM do the right thing in the digital options example. Acerbi (2002) showed that spectral risk measures are coherent, so Expected Shortfall (and therefore cVaR when there is a differentiable cdf F) is also coherent. In January 2011 (about 13 years after ADEH's first version), Basel (2011, p. 2) noted:

> VaR has become a standard risk measure in finance. Notwithstanding its widespread use, it has been criticised in the literature for lacking subadditivity. ... The most popular alternative to VaR is expected shortfall, which is subadditive. It is slowly gaining popularity among financial risk managers.

In fact, at this writing, most financial institutions still report only VaR to shareholders and regulators. When ES is used, it is often used internally.

2.6 Risk-Averse Prices

Most people are risk averse and won't pay expected or average value for risky propositions. This was most apparent with the St. Petersburg lottery (Section 1.4.1) whose expected value was infinite in its pure form, or perhaps around $48 when taking into account the finite wealth of the world. Bidding for this lottery usually centers on $4, consistent with a risk-averse logarithmic utility function.

This risk aversion carries over into securities markets. We don't have to fantasize about meeting Generous Billionaires: a little more realistically, we can suppose there is a company with a similar payoff pattern.

Assume that Beyond Vegetables is a startup company developing a potential blockbuster process to change beef into kale. Beyond Vegetables will be worth $1 billion one year from now if its testing phase is successful, and nothing if not. Suppose further that analysts agree that there is a probability p that testing will succeed and a probability $1 - p$ that it won't.

Beyond Vegetables issues 1 billion shares, that is, each share represents ownership of one one-billionth of the company. For people with risk-neutral utility functions, a share is worth p now (assuming for now there is no time value of money). But we know that investors don't have risk-neutral utility functions: they are generally risk averse.

For example, someone whose current wealth is w and who has a logarithmic utility function might be considering an investment of a fraction f of her total wealth in Beyond Vegetables. The security will be worth $1 per share if it's successful. If it's currently valued at q per share, then its payoff factor on success is $1/q$ per share. The point of indifference between investing in this security and doing nothing is:

$$p \cdot \ln(w(1 - f + f/q)) + (1 - p) \cdot \ln(w(1 - f)) = \ln(w). \qquad (2.16)$$

That gives:

$$q = \frac{f}{(1 - f)^{1 - 1/p} - (1 - f)}. \qquad (2.17)$$

Applying L'Hôpital's Rule to (2.17) shows that when $f = 0$, the investor is willing to pay $q = p$ per share, that is, the price based on the security's expected value. In other words, if the investment is negligible to the investor, she is risk neutral. But as $f \to 1$, the risk of the investment becomes more and more of a concern, so the price q the investor is willing to pay approaches zero; that is, the payoff factor $1/q$ required to convince the investor to take the risk approaches infinity.

Code Segment 2.4 generates Figure 2.3, which shows isoprobability lines where each line shows the indifference price per share q for a fixed p at differing fractions of wealth f.

The maximum share price on each isoprobability curve in Figure 2.3 is p, the probability of success. But the price q that investors are willing to pay drops as the fraction of wealth at risk gets higher and higher, because investors demand a premium to take the risk. Eventually with log-utility they just won't pay anything.

Different potential investors will have different levels of starting wealth, so their places on the X-axis of Figure 2.3 will vary. In practice, no one has definitive knowledge of the probability of success p, so different investors will have different ideas about where to be on the Y-axis of Figure 2.3. Some or all

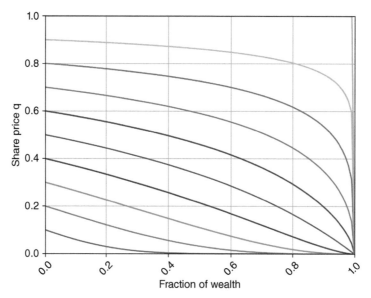

Figure 2.3 Isoprobability (constant p) curves.

potential investors may not have log-utility functions. In fact, they may not even act as if they have utility functions. There is some evidence that certain kinds of securities even elicit risk-loving rather than risk-averse preferences.

All these complications are rather discouraging. Nonetheless, securities do manage to trade. Market participants come to a price they would be willing to pay (if they are potential buyers) or receive (if they are potential sellers) based on their combined thoughts about probability of success and risk preference. If the highest-price buyer has a price that is above or equal to the lowest-price seller, then a transaction will take place at a **market-clearing price** q that matches up overlapping buyers and sellers. These buyers and sellers are cleared from the market since their wishes are fulfilled.

2.7 No-Arbitrage

Let's use "W" (for "win") to denote a share of Beyond Vegetables; W's price is q. And suppose that there exists a complementary security "L" (for "lose") that pays \$1 if the beef-to-kale transmogrification process fails, and \$0 if it succeeds. A portfolio consisting of one W and one L will be worth \$1 one year from now no matter what happens.

While W alone or L alone are risky securities – we don't know at the present time whether they will pay off or not – the combination W + L is risk free. We know exactly what will happen to W + L in the future: no matter which outcome is realized, W + L will be worth \$1. That's the same as the risk-free instrument R_f. If the value of $W + L$ today is less than the value of R_f today, then we would buy $W + L$ and sell R_f (the equivalent of borrowing money). That would net a positive amount $W + L - R_f$ today and always be worth nothing in the future, so we would be able to pocket free money by doing this. If the value of $W + L$ today is greater than the value of R_f today, we'd reverse signs on the transaction and pocket free money.

A fundamental principle in markets is that there shouldn't be opportunities to make free money. If an investor can take on a position that costs nothing, and its value in at least one future state of the world is strictly positive while its value in no future state of the world is negative (i.e. the investor never owes money), then that's free money. Or equivalently, if taking on a position has a strictly negative cost (i.e. taking on the position gives money to the investor in the present time) while in all future states of the world the position's value is nonnegative, then that's free money.

Such a free money position is called a **(risk-free) arbitrage**, and the assumed lack of such opportunities is called **no-arbitrage**. There can actually be risk in a risk-free arbitrage; there can be uncertainty about exactly how much free money the arbitrage will produce. A risk-free arbitrage is actually a **peril-free arbitrage**; there is no danger of losing money. But the "risk-free" label is universally used.

A slightly narrower version of the no-arbitrage idea is the **Law of One Price**, which says that the same item can't have two different prices in two different markets at the same time. If it did, an arbitrageur could buy the item where it is cheaper and sell it where it is dearer, creating a riskless arbitrage.

2.7.1 Limits of Arbitrage

However, in practice arbitrages can and do exist. A particularly shocking example occurred on April 20, 2020, when the price of oil went negative (according to the US Energy Information Administration) to as low as −$40.32 per barrel.[21] The oil market was already disrupted due to lingering effects of a Russian–Saudi oil price war, lack of demand due to the COVID-19 economic slowdown, and lack of storage facilities.

These fundamental oil market drivers interacted badly with the technicalities of financial contracts to cause negative financial market prices, with contemporaneous analysis from the US Energy Information Administration (U.S. EIA 2020) suggesting:

> ...that the phenomenon of negative [oil] prices could be confined to the financial market, with few physical market participants paying negative prices. The positive pricing of other crude oil benchmarks ... suggest that the recent [negative] price action was predominantly driven by the timing of the May 2020 contract expiration.

21 [U.S. EIA 2020].

Vigilant investors will quickly see such anomalies and take advantage of them: the price of oil did return to a positive number within a day. The very act of taking advantage of arbitrages will eventually make them disappear, since the arbitrageur will exert pressure on prices in the right direction by buying too-cheap assets and selling too-expensive assets.

It is also possible for less sensational arbitrages to exist over longer time periods. Most obviously, there may be costs or other annoyances involved in taking advantage of the arbitrage. For example, in theory it appears that the price of .995 fine gold in New York should be the same as .995 fine gold in London. If the price of gold in New York is less than the price of gold in London, then the Law of One Price implies that an arbitrageur could buy gold in New York and sell it in London.

But as a practical matter gold dealers would charge a commission for the purchase in New York and the sale in London, and it would cost something to transport the gold from New York to London. Further, the transportation would take a little time, during which the price could change, so the arbitrage wouldn't be riskless. There might be taxes in one or both locations. There might be regulatory restrictions on importing or exporting gold. There might be costs to store the gold in a secure warehoues during the pendancy of the transaction. (Indeed, extreme storage costs were a large factor in the negative price of oil on April 20, 2020.)

There might be **counterparty risk**: the arbitrageur pays the New York dealer to deliver gold, but the dealer then goes bankrupt and fails to deliver the gold. Similarly, the arbitrageur might deliver the gold to the London dealer but the dealer then goes bankrupt and fails to pay. Even if the arbitrageur manages to retain or get back its money or gold when the dealer fails, there's still a problem (called **execution risk**) because the transactions no longer offset each other. For example, based on the assumption that it had obtained gold from the now-failed New York dealer, the arbitrageur may have entered into an obligation to deliver gold to the London dealer. In that case, the arbitrageur would have to obtain the gold very quickly somewhere else, possibly at a much higher price.

More subtly, taking advantage of an arbitrage requires the temporary use of money that can be needed elsewhere, especially during market disruptions when arbitrages are most apparent. Therefore, using money has a cost, known as the **cost of capital**.

The various impediments to pure theoretical arbitrage are collectively known as **Limits of Arbitrage** (Shleifer and Vishny 2012).

2.7.2   Short Sales and Short Squeezes

Section 2.7 contained the claim "If the value of $W + L$ today is greater than the value of R_f today, we'd reverse signs on the transaction and pocket free money."

This statement assumed that negative positions in the W and L securities could be easily established. A negative position in an asset is called a **short**, and of course a positive position is called a **long**.

Most theoretical work assumes that a short position can be taken simply by deploying the minus key on a keyboard. In practice, however, the process of establishing and maintaining short positions (called **short selling**) has many peculiarities that make it more problematic than establishing positive positions. We'll explore these features as a cautionary tale about the gap between the theory and the practice of arbitrage.

In practice, an investor establishes a short position in a security by borrowing it. (If there are derivatives markets in the security, there may be other ways to establish short positions; for now, we'll just focus on short selling of primary securities.)

To establish a negative position in W (the stock of Beyond Vegetables), an investor must find (through a broker) someone who owns W and who is willing to lend it. The borrowing investor agrees to give back a share of W to the lending owner whenever the owner demands. The shares of a company are divided into a small number of classes whose members are indistinguishable from each other (i.e. they are fungible), so the investor doesn't have to earmark the particular share that was borrowed to be given back to the lending owner. Any share of the same class will suffice for repayment.

After obtaining a borrowed W, the investor sells it on the open market for cash. Let's suppose the investor gets $0.50 when W is sold. After the sale, the investor has created a short position in Beyond Vegetables because a share is owed to the owner. The investor also has $0.50 in cash.

The short seller has applied negative pressure (through the sale of W) on Beyond Vegetables' stock price, causing the price to reflect a slightly more negative view of Beyond Vegetables' future prospects than before the short sale. Of course, pessimistic views could also be reflected in the price simply because buyers avoid the stock. But short sellers can speed up the rate at which negative sentiment is impounded into prices.

This function has long been derided at length by long investors, especially company insiders who naturally would prefer to avoid negative sentiments affecting their stock prices. For example, Elon Musk, the founder of Tesla, tweeted (2021):

> u can't sell houses u don't own, u can't sell cars u don't own, but u *can* sell stock u don't own!? this is bs – shorting is a scam legal only for vestigial reasons.

Mr. Musk is engaged here in a practice at least as old as short selling called "talking one's book," that is, trying to convince other investors to take one's position, thereby enhancing its value. In this case, Mr. Musk was trying to prevent other investors from taking an opposite position.

But, properly used, short selling can improve price discovery and market efficiency. Since the idea of turning beef into kale is in fact idiotically inefficient absent a fundamental change in energy conservation laws, the activity of a short seller in Beyond Vegetables moves prices in the right direction. Further, short selling can help eliminate inconsistencies between markets.

Thus, when the rest of the world realizes that turning beef into kale is uneconomical and Beyond Vegetables fails, the short-selling investor will benefit. When the price falls, the investor can buy a share of W on the open market for close to zero. That share of W is then given back to the original owner, extinguishing the investor's short position. The short seller's net profit in this case is close to $0.50, minus some costs we'll note below.

While buying a positive asset like W produces a positively skewed distribution, selling it short produces a negatively skewed distribution. Suppose that Beyond Vegetables researchers stumble across a heretofore undiscovered quantum tunneling effect that makes the idea of turning beef into kale fabulously more profitable than anyone expected, and the price of Beyond Vegetables skyrockets to $10 a share. The short-selling investor is now looking at a big loss: after closing out the short position by buying back a share, the investor has lost $9.50 on an position that had a maximum gain of $0.50.

During the time the short investor owes the share to the original owner, the investor must pay borrowing fees to the owner and to the broker. If the stock pays dividends, the short seller must pay the dividend amounts to the owner. Typically, short-sale arrangements are terminated on the initiative of the short seller, but in fact the owner can demand the stock back on very short notice at any time. For example, if the owner decides to sell the stock, a demand will be made for return of the borrowed shares.

In addition, the broker arranging the short sale will not wait until the owed share is worth $10 to check whether the short-selling investor has enough money to buy it back. Short sellers must maintain **margin** (a cash account that the broker can seize) of (typically) 150%. So in our example, when the investor first borrows the stock and sells it for $0.50, the investor must leave the $0.50 proceeds in the margin account and deposit another $0.25 in cash. As the price moves, the broker will demand that the investor adjust the margin position (a **margin call**). If the investor can't come up with newly required margin cash, the broker may use the existing margin cash to buy back the owed stock, closing out the position.

Engleberg, Reed, and Ringgenberg (2018, p. 755) summed this up by saying

> Short selling is a risky business. Short sellers must identify mispriced securities, borrow shares in the equity lending market, post collateral, and pay a loan fee each day until the position closes. In addition to the standard risks that many traders face, such as margin calls and regulatory changes, short sellers also face the risk of loan recalls and the risk of changing loan fees.

Thus it's clear that short selling has annoyances (borrowing fees, dividends, margin maintenance, the usual transactions costs of buying and selling shares) that make the practice more frictive than the theory.

Engleberg, Reed, and Ringgenberg (2018) further identified dynamic risks associated with short selling. They noted that some stocks have greater uncertainty about future loan fees and availability than others. An increase in loan fees and a decrease in shares that can be borrowed can be a problem for short sellers, creating a noticeable short-selling risk premium (i.e. lower future returns due to lack of appropriate short selling).

A particular form of short-selling risk that can elevate the drawbacks of short selling from annoying to catastrophic is a **short squeeze**. Short squeezing is the practice of deliberately driving up share prices, typically when there is a large aggregate short position in the stock, in order to force short sellers to buy back the shares they owe at disadvantageous prices. The initial higher stock price in a squeeze forces some short sellers to close out their positions to avoid further losses; other short sellers may not be able to meet their margin calls and may have their short positions forcibly closed out by their brokers. Further upward pressure on stock prices is then provided by the short sellers buying back shares, leading (the squeezer hopes) to a strong upward spike in prices.

Historical examples of short squeezes are not themselves in short supply. Allen, Litov, and Mei (2006, pp. 682–683) give this example:

> Allan Ryan, known in the early twentieth century as a speculator good at the art of squeezing short sellers, had bought a controlling interest in the Stutz Motor Company of America, Inc. At the beginning of 1920, its price had risen steadily from $100 to $134. Ryan was told that short sellers had taken action thinking that the price had risen too high. Among the short sellers were some prominent members of the stock exchange. To counter the bears, Ryan borrowed substantial amounts to buy additional shares. At first, despite Ryan's heavy purchase, the price went down, since the short-selling pressure was considerable. But then the price increased in late March, reaching $391. Towards the end of March, short sellers were selling stock that had to be borrowed from Ryan, since he had almost all floating shares.

Trading in Stutz Motor was eventually suspended due to irregular price movements. A market-clearing price of $550 was agreed by mediation.

A more recent example of a short squeeze was the stock of Gamestop, Inc. (symbol GME). While the information technologies in the Stutz and Gamestop eras were very different, there are many similarities.

Gamestop, Inc.[22] is a retailer of video games. Much of Gamestop's business involves the sale of games and other items in physical format through

---

22 Gamestop Corporate Fact Sheet. `https://news.gamestop.com/static-files/a07563a1-de5d-43d0-bb11-d6bfd309dacd`.

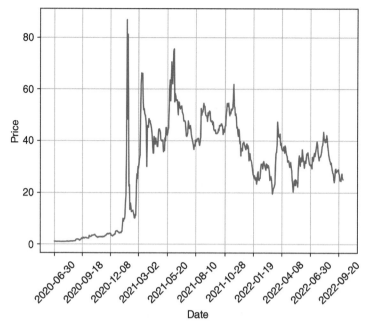

Figure 2.4 GME short squeeze.

brick-and-mortar stores. While Gamestop does provide streaming platforms, it was in decline and lost money during 2020 due in part to the rise of streaming technology. Short sellers, reportedly mostly hedge funds, took notice and began massively shorting GME. For much of the first quarter of 2020, GME short positions were around 100 percent of the floating (publicly trading) shares;[23] by late 2020 around 140 percent of GME was shorted.[24]

In 2020, Wall Street Bets[25] subreddit began discussing GME and its heavy short positions. The group mobilized thousands of small investors to buy GME, hoping to squeeze the shorts. The ensuing market disruption was spectacular, as the price of GME lost all contact with the actual business prospects of Gamestop, as shown in Figure 2.4 (generated by Code Segment 2.5).

During the GME disruption, parts of the financial system became strained because GME prices, unmoored from the fundamental reality of Gamestop's business, fluctuated so wildly. As noted above, short selling is implemented via borrowing. At the same time, many buyers of GME bought on margin: that is, they borrowed cash to buy shares of GME. Thus, big swings in any

---

23 Marketbeat: GameStop – GME Short Interest Ratio & Short Volume. April 3, 2020. `www.marketbeat.com/stocks/NYSE/GME/short-interest/`.

24 When a short seller initiates its short position by selling a borrowed share in the open market, there is nothing identifying that share as a borrowed share. Thus, the buyer of that share can lend it out again to another short seller. That rehypothecation makes it possible to have over 100 percent of shares sold short.

25 Reddit.com. wallstreetbets. Website. `www.reddit.com/r/wallstreetbets/`

direction could expose lenders (of stock or of cash) to increasing chances of not getting repaid. Broker-dealers and clearinghouses scrambled to raise margin (cash collateral) from clients to buffer themselves against the possibility of defaults by those clients, and trading in GME was halted on some platforms.

A narrative often heard during short squeezes is that short sellers represent the Wall Street Establishment, while the squeezers represent feisty entrepreneurs and Main Street ordinary folks. Thus the reference to the shorts being "prominent members of the stock exchange" in the 1920 Stutz squeeze. Speaking of the short squeeze on the supermarket chain Piggly Wiggly in 1923, Pringle (2021) said:

> As with GameStop ..., Piggly Wiggly was being sold short by several big Wall Street investment firms. This aroused an unexpected popular backlash, stirred by resentment of "city slickers" getting rich off the "yaps," or little guys. So there was a sense of triumph when investors fought back and put the squeeze on the shorts. "New York investors," crowed one newspaper, "made to pay through the nose."

In fact, the Piggly Wiggly short squeeze was orchestrated by Clarence Saunders, the multimillionaire founder and president of Piggly Wiggly. Mr. Saunders could be called the Elon Musk of his day: he invented the self-serve supermarket concept. Previously, shoppers had waited while clerks retrieved items from shelves. Mr. Saunders also apparently shared Mr. Musk's feelings about short selling.

The populist narrative remains a useful part of the short squeezer's talking-the-book toolkit. In 2021, the Gamestop squeezers were cheered on by a shout-out from US Representative Ro Khanna (2021), who prepended a modern technology garnish to the century-old short squeeze narrative:

> However, this entire [Gamestop] episode has demonstrated the power of technology to democratize access to American financial institutions, ultimately giving far more people a say in our economic structures. This also showed how the cards are stacked against the little guy in favor of billionaire Wall Street Traders.

It's important to recall that overall economic welfare is enhanced when a stock market is a forum for discovering prices that reflect the likely future prospects of the companies that trade in the market. That helps to direct resources to efficient projects and away from inefficient ones. Gamestop, along with other "meme stocks," now trades on crowd sentiment rather than on economic efficiency.

Gamestop was a loss-making enterprise during 2020 with dubious prospects for significant future profits just before the runup shown in Figure 2.4. Billions of dollars of capital that could have been directed to more productive enterprises changed hands due to GME trading. Despite a century of legal, regulatory, and technological advances, the stock market's price discovery function failed just as badly for GME in 2021 as it did for Stutz Motor Company of America in 1920.

2.7.3 No-Arbitrage Formulation

Market imperfections like short squeezes and negative oil prices can bankrupt the unwary. But it's hard to write down simple equations that anticipate the effects of subreddit discussions.[26]

Thus most theoretical work assumes that no arbitrage opportunities are available. In most markets, this is approximately correct: the New York gold price might be a little different from the London gold price and it wouldn't be worth the cost of closing the gap. But if there's a big enough price difference then someone will arbitrage it away, or at least down. For more dramatic departures from no-arbitrage such as negative oil prices, the practitioner simply has to keep a sharp eye out.

A general mathematical formulation of the no-arbitrage principle is the following: For any linear combination $a_1x_1 + \cdots + a_nx_n$ of securities $x_1, \ldots, x_n$ where the current price of the combination is zero, then either (a) the price of the combination must be zero in all future states of the world; or (b) there must be at least one future state with a strictly positive price and at least one future state with a strictly negative price.

2.8 State Prices and Risk-Neutral Probabilities

Absent the discovery of a new quantum tunneling effect, the outcomes of Beyond Vegetables were couched in starkly binary terms – either it succeeded fully and $W(L)$ was worth \$1 (\$0) a share, or it failed fully and $W(L)$ was worth \$0 (\$1) a share. That means these securities are examples of what economists call **state-price securities** or **Arrow–Debreu contingent claims**. In financial markets, they are called **binary (or digital) options**, such as the ones used in ADEH's example of the problems with VaR regarding coherent risk (2001). Such securities are indicator variables: they pay \$1 contingent on the occurrence of some outcome (e.g. beef-to-kale success) and nothing if that outcome doesn't happen.

---

26 While it's hard to anticipate how many market participants will participate in a short squeeze, it's not hard to see that a massively shorted stock like GME is ripe for this activity. In the USA and other jurisdictions, there are rules intended to slow downward pressure on prices from shorting like those in Securities and Exchange Commission (2010), but there are generally no limits on what percentages of a company can be shorted. The other limits to arbitrage – transactions costs, taxes, fees, regulations. . . – are similarly hard to capture in simple formulas.

Let q be the multiplier such that the price of the win security W equals qR_f today, where R_f is the current price of the risk-free instrument that will be worth $1 in the future period. From no-arbitrage and the assumption of a binary set of outcomes, it follows that the price of the failure security L must equal $(1 - q)R_f$ today.

Note that the assumption of risk preferences affecting security prices becomes more subtle under the combination of the no-arbitrage and binary outcome assumptions: both W and L are risky securities and, in isolation, would each be priced to reflect risk aversion similar perhaps to (2.17). But together they must add to a risk-free price to avoid arbitrage. Thus risk preference must average away over the combination of W and L.

So $\{q, 1 - q\}$ are said to form a **risk-neutral probability measure** for the two-outcome space {Beyond Vegetables success, Beyond Vegetables failure}. The term "risk-neutral" in this context means "derived from observed state prices under the counterfactual assumption that market participants are risk neutral."

Generalizing the two-outcome example, assume the following:

- A one-period world with a present (time 0) period and a future period;
- All possible outcomes that have nonzero probability of occurring in the future period are contained in a finite sample space Ω, but which $\omega \in \Omega$ will occur in the future period is not known in the present;
- For every $\omega \in \Omega$, there is an ω state price security that can be bought or sold in the current period for a price $q_0(\omega)$. The ω-state price security will pay $1 in the future period if state ω occurs, and $0 otherwise;
- No-arbitrage.

Under these assumptions, if any $q_0(\omega) \leq 0$, then purchasing the claim on ω would be a riskless arbitrage, so we can assume $q_0(\omega) > 0 \; \forall \omega \in \Omega$. The assumptions also indicate that in the future period, exactly one of the state price securities will be worth one; all the others will be worthless. Thus, if the sample space is finite, as in the Knightian or Von Neumann–Morgenstern framework, it follows that $\sum_{\xi \in \Omega} q_0(\xi) = R_f = \frac{1}{1+r_f}$. The probability mass function $q(\omega) \equiv \frac{q_0(\omega)}{\sum_{\xi \in \Omega} q_0(\xi)} = (1 + r_f)q_0(\omega)$ is the desired risk-neutral probability measure under the assumptions above.

As noted above in the two-outcome case, the combination of assumptions (complete set of state price securities, no-arbitrage) means that risk preferences affecting state price variables will average to zero across the complete set. If some of the q's have prices that are lowered due to risk aversion, other q's must have heightened prices so that the sum of all the q's is one.

The assumption of a finite sample space is not actually necessary. Clearly, everything noted above works for a countably infinite sample space. Further, discrete state prices can be generalized to continuous state price densities when the outcome space is an interval on the real line representing quantities like monetary amounts, rates of return, log-returns, or interest rates. Let $Q_0(x)$ be a cumulative state price function that pays \$1 if the outcome is less than or equal to x, and \$0 otherwise. If Q_0 is differentiable, then $q_0(x) = Q'_0(x)$ is the state price density function. As in the finite case, an adjustment for the time value of money must be applied to the current functions to make them probability densities and cumulative distribution functions; in continuous situations it is customary to use the adjustment $\exp(r_f)$ rather than $1+r_f$. So $Q(x) = \exp(r_f)Q_0(x)$ is a cdf and $q(x) = \exp(r_f)q_0(x)$ is a pdf with the appropriate properties, assuming no-arbitrage.

Thus, under the assumptions above, a risk-neutral probability measure Q can be constructed by observing the market prices of the state price securities and adjusting by the risk-free rate.

2.9 Stochastic Discount Factors

Today's price of the Beyond Vegetables "win" security W, which we called qR_f, does not tell us the market consensus probability that Beyond Vegetables will succeed. qR_f is contaminated by the aggregate attitude to risk, and perhaps other factors like needs for liquidity. If we were able to poll every market participant, we might find out what we'll call p, the aggregate assessment of Beyond Vegetables' success. But that's impractical, so p, called the **real-world probability** or **natural probability**, remains unobservable. However, economists have built up an elaborate mechanism that attempts to translate between risk-neutral and real-world probabilities.

The language here can be misleading. We've already pointed out that "risk-neutral" probabilities are based on market attitudes, which are anything but risk neutral. The terms – "real-world" or "natural" probability – can also be misleading. Financial markets, as we have noted, are not generally subject to Knightian Risk. So the real real-world probabilities of events remain unknowable in advance. "Real-world" and "natural" probabilities are the unobservable market consensus *opinions* of these quantities, not the even more unobservable facts.

It follows under the assumptions listed in the previous section that the sum of all state prices equals the time-zero value of the risk-free instrument. That is, $\sum_{\omega\in\Omega} q_0(\omega) = \frac{1}{1+r_f}$ when using discrete discounting, or $\exp(-r_f)$ when using continuous discounting; we'll explore these different conventions in Chapter 3.

Let X be a random variable giving future-period prices of a particular security; that is, X maps future states ω into an interval of the real line representing prices of the security we can also call X. When the sample space Ω is finite, the current (time 0) price of X can be written as:

$$Price(0,X) = \sum_{\omega\in\Omega} X(\omega)q_0(\omega) = \left(\sum_{\xi\in\Omega} q_0(\xi)\right)\left(\sum_{\omega\in\Omega} X(\omega)\frac{q_0(\omega)}{\sum_{\xi\in\Omega} q_0(\xi)}\right)$$

$$= \frac{1}{1+r_f}\mathbb{E}_Q[X], \tag{2.18}$$

where $q_0(\omega)$ is the time-zero state price of outcome ω, so the risk-neutral probability mass is $q(\omega) = \frac{q_0(\omega)}{\sum_{\xi \in \Omega} q_0(\xi)}$.

The continuous version of (2.18) for Ω an interval of the real line is:

$$Price(0,X) = \int_{\omega \in \Omega} X(\omega)dQ_0(\omega) = \left(\int_{\xi \in \Omega} dQ_0(\xi) \right) \left(\int_{\omega \in \Omega} X(\omega) \frac{dQ_0(\omega)}{\int_{\xi \in \Omega} dQ_0(\xi)} \right)$$

$$= \exp(-r_f)\mathbb{E}_Q[X] \tag{2.19}$$

for the current (time-zero) price of X, where $Q_0(\omega)$ is the current price of a security that pays \$1 if the outcome is less than or equal to ω and \$0 otherwise. Let the derivative of $Q_0(\omega)$ be denoted $q_0(\omega) \equiv \frac{dQ_0(\omega)}{d\omega}$. The risk-neutral cdf is $Q(\omega) \equiv \frac{Q_0(\omega)}{\int_{\xi \in \Omega} dQ_0(\xi)}$.

In keeping with the shift from discrete to continuous, we shifted the discounting convention from the factor $\frac{1}{1+r_f}$ used in (2.18) to the factor $\exp(-r_f)$ used in (2.19). The risk-neutral pdf (probability density function) is $q(\omega) \equiv Q'(\omega) = \frac{q_0(\omega)}{\int_{\xi \in \Omega} dQ_0(\xi)}$.

Let $r_X \equiv X/Price(0,X) - 1$ be the **rate of return** of the investment X, and let $R_X \equiv 1 + r_X$ be X's **return relative**. Multiplying both sides of (2.18) by $\frac{1+r_f}{Price(0,X)}$ gives $1 + r_f = \mathbb{E}_Q[1 + r_X]$. Note the one inside the expectation is a future one, not a current one, so $\mathbb{E}_Q[1] = 1$. Therefore,

$$r_f = \mathbb{E}_Q[r_X]. \tag{2.20}$$

Making the analogous adjustment to (2.19) gives a similar result in the continuous case, with $\exp(r_f) - 1$ on the LHS. Equation (2.20) is an intuitive feature of the risk-neutral measure under no-arbitrage with a complete set of state-price securities: all risky and risk-free expected returns are the same.

Let $P(\omega)$ and $p(\omega)$ be the real-world cdf and pdf corresponding to $Q(\omega)$ and $q(\omega)$, respectively. For example, in the finite case $p(\omega)$ is the market consensus probability that outcome ω will occur. Then we can define the expected value of a security X under the P probability measure as:

$$\mathbb{E}_P[X] = \left. \begin{cases} \sum p(\omega)X(\omega) & \text{discrete} \\ \int X(\omega)p(\omega)d\omega & \text{continuous} \end{cases} \right\}. \tag{2.21}$$

Define a random variable:

$$\varphi(\omega) = \frac{q_0(\omega)}{p(\omega)}. \tag{2.22}$$

This definition is valid for both the discrete case (using probability mass functions) and the continuous case (using the density functions defined above). The random variable φ is called a **pricing kernel** or **stochastic discount factor** (**"SDF"**).

Time discounting allows us to take a riskless amount of cash in the future and say what it is worth today. Stochastic discounting (the SDF) allows us to do the same for a risky amount of cash in the future; it combines time discounting and risk preference discounting into a single quantity. Thus, with no-arbitrage we can say

$$\mathbb{E}_P[\varphi X] = R_f \mathbb{E}_Q[X] \implies Price(0,X) = \mathbb{E}_P[\varphi X]. \tag{2.23}$$

Technically, the stochastic discount factor is the Radon–Nikodym derivative of the cdf Q with respect to the natural probability distribution P (adjusted for time discounting).

Pukthuanthong and Roll (2015, pp. 1–2) (hereafter "PR") noted that in academia "the Stochastic Discount Factor (SDF) has become a dominant paradigm in … asset pricing research." But SDF's are not widely used in financial practice, because – as PR also noted – "the empirical success of SDF theory is less apparent."

There are some empirically testable hypotheses that arise from SDF theory. To find these testable hypotheses, we start with some simple properties of an SDF φ under the assumptions of the previous section.

Setting $X = 1$ in (2.23) shows that:

$$\mathbb{E}_P[\varphi] = R_f. \tag{2.24}$$

That is, the expected value of the stochastic discount factor is: the non-stochastic discount factor.

Dividing both sides of (2.23) by $Price(0,X)$ gives:

$$\mathbb{E}_P[\varphi R_X] = 1. \tag{2.25}$$

That is, the product of the SDF with any return relative has expected value equal to one.

Let $e_X \equiv R_X - \frac{1}{R_f}$ be the excess rate of return of the investment X over the risk-free rate. If investors are generally risk-averse, then $\mathbb{E}_P[e_X] \geq 0$ since it is the expected difference between investing in a risky security (X) and a security that is always worth 1 in the future state. Note too that (2.24) and (2.25) show that:

$$\mathbb{E}_P[\varphi e_X] = \mathbb{E}_P[\varphi R_X] - \frac{1}{R_f}\mathbb{E}_P[\varphi] = 0. \tag{2.26}$$

That is, the product of the SDF with any excess return has expected value equal to zero.

Starting with the definition of covariance, we have:

$$cov_P(\varphi, e_X) \equiv \mathbb{E}_P[(\varphi - \mathbb{E}_P[\varphi])(e_X - \mathbb{E}_P[e_X])]$$
$$= \mathbb{E}_P[\varphi e_X] - \mathbb{E}_P[\varphi]\mathbb{E}_P[e_X] = -\mathbb{E}_P[\varphi]\mathbb{E}_P[e_X] \tag{2.27}$$

using (2.26).

Decomposing the LHS of (2.27) into correlation and standard deviation, we have:

$$corr(\varphi, e_X)\sigma(\varphi)\sigma(e_X) = -\mathbb{E}_P[\varphi]\mathbb{E}_P[e_X]. \tag{2.28}$$

Correlations range from -1 to $+1$, so (using (2.24)) we have Hansen and Jagannathan's **Hansen–Jagannathan bound** (1991):

$$R_f \left| \frac{\mathbb{E}_P[e_X]}{\sigma(e_X)} \right| \leq \sigma(\varphi). \tag{2.29}$$

The ratio on the LHS of (2.29) is the Sharpe Ratio of a particular security X. But the expression on the RHS of (2.29) is a single marketwide number – the standard deviation of the stochastic discount factor – which must therefore be greater than the largest discounted absolute value Sharpe Ratio in the market. Thus, the Hansen–Jagannathan bound gives an idea of how volatile the SDF should be.

There have been many empirical tests of SDF theory. Generally, the results have been lukewarm failures to reject an SDF hypothesis. These tests have not shown the precision necessary to select individual assets, which would be required for use by financial market participants.

An investigation by Araújo and Issler (2011) found an average discount of 2.97 percent, that is, the realized value of $\mathbb{E}_P[\varphi] = \exp(-2.97\%)$, which is reasonable. Araujo and Issler further found that large capitalization stocks behaved in a way that was consistent with SDF theory, but small capitalization stocks did not.

Equation (2.25) tells us that the expected value of the product of the SDF and any return relative $R_{X,t}$ of security X during time period t is one. But the SDF is a scalar random variable so it can only have one realization, while in period t there are many different return relatives $R_{X,t}$ because there are many different securities X. So the realized product of the SDF and any given return relative is probably not equal to one; only the average is required to equal one.

PR investigated the differences between the expectation (one) and the realization of φX for a given security X over many time periods. They extended (2.25) to:

$$\varphi_t R_{X,t} = \mathbb{E}_{P,t-1}[\varphi_t R_{X,t}] + \epsilon_{X,t} = 1 + \epsilon_{X,t} \tag{2.30}$$

where φ_t is the realization of the SDF in time period t and $\epsilon_{X,t}$ is the "surprise"; the difference between the expectation and the realization. If SDF theory is correct, the surprises should diversify away so that $\overline{\epsilon_X} = \frac{1}{T}\sum_{t=1}^{T}\epsilon_{X,t}$ approaches zero over enough time periods.

To test whether this happens, PR construct an empirical SDF from rates of return. Suppose there are n securities and T time periods, and let R be the $T \times n$ matrix whose (t, i) entry is the rate of return relative of security i in time period t.

Let Φ be the T-vector of empirical SDF's in each time period, and let u be the unit n-vector of all ones. Then:

$$\frac{1}{T}R^{\mathsf{T}}\Phi \approx u. \tag{2.31}$$

The key hypothesis in (2.31) is that each time period has the same SDF for all n securities. Left-multiplying (2.31) by R and inverting gives:

$$\Phi \approx T(RR^{\mathsf{T}})^{-1}Ru. \tag{2.32}$$

This can only be done if $n \geq T$ and RR^{T} is nonsingular, but there are thousands of securities available to test, so this isn't a difficult constraint.

Note that the eigenvalues of the $T \times T$ matrix RR^{T} are (except possibly for some zeroes) the same as the eigenvalues of the $n \times n$ matrix $R^{\mathsf{T}}R$, since:

$$RR^{\mathsf{T}}e = \lambda e \implies R^{\mathsf{T}}RR^{\mathsf{T}}e = \lambda R^{\mathsf{T}}e \implies (R^{\mathsf{T}}R)f = \lambda f.$$

That is, an eigenvalue λ of RR^{T} with associated eigenvector e is an eigenvalue of $R^{\mathsf{T}}R$ with associated eigenvector $f = R^{\mathsf{T}}e$. This means that the eigenvalue patterns observed for covariance matrices $R^{\mathsf{T}}R$ will also be seen in the matrix used to find SDFs. We will discuss these patterns in Section 6.5 later in this book, but for now note that there tends to be a small number of dominant eigenvalues. Thus the space spanned by SDFs will also be effectively low-dimensional compared to n and T.

Among other things, the estimate (2.32) can be used to test the Hansen–Jagannathan bound (2.29). Equation (2.32) can be used to compute:

$$\hat{\sigma}(\varphi) = \sqrt{\frac{1}{T}\Phi^{\mathsf{T}}\Phi - \overline{\Phi}^2} \tag{2.33}$$

purely from observed historical rates of return. Previous work by Welch (2000) leads to an estimate of .44 for a high Sharpe Ratio. Multiplying .44 times $\mathbb{E}[\varphi] = \overline{\Phi}$ doesn't change much because the multiplier is close to one, both in theory and empirically. PR find that the SDF volatility computed from (2.33) is "comfortably" higher than the $\approx .44$ lower bound.

PR then use the estimate of Φ from (2.32) to form average surprises $\overline{\epsilon_X}$, and then apply statistical tests to see if the average surprise becomes small. They conclude that for large enough n, the hypothesis of a common SDF embodied in (2.32) cannot be rejected.

2.10 The Ross Recovery Theorem

The risk-neutral probability measure is a construct that allows economists to investigate broad indicators of societal tendencies like risk aversion. But we can't tell what the market thinks is the probability that Beyond Vegetables will succeed if we are given the risk-neutral probability of Beyond Vegetables' success.

Stephen Ross (2013) addressed this problem in "The Recovery Theorem." Of course, disentangling real-world probabilities from aggregate risk preferences is impossible without making some assumptions, since both are present in observed prices. Ross's assumptions are strong, like those of utility theory. Like utility theory, the assumptions are probably not a bad start. But also like utility theory, these assumptions depart from empirical reality.

2.10.1 Ross Recovery: Key Assumptions

Ross (2013) starts with a modification of (2.18), where there was a state-price security $q_0(\omega)$ that paid \$1 if the world transitioned from the current state to the state ω one period forward. Assume a process that keeps moving through states over time, so at any time it would be at one of the states $\omega_i \in \Omega$, and then would transition in the next time period to some other state $\omega_j \in \Omega$. That context gives rise to the idea of transition-oriented state price securities $q_0(\omega_i, \omega_j)$ with a \$1 payoff if the world moves from state $\omega_i \in \Omega$ to $\omega_j \in \Omega$ over a unit time period.

> Assumption 1: **Calendar Independence.** Neither $q_0(\omega_i, \omega_j)$ nor as-yet-unknown real-world transition probability $p(\omega_i, \omega_j)$ is a function of the calendar time. They both give single-period transition probabilities starting from any calendar time. A transition from ω_i to ω_j over a period of one week in the year 2040 has the same state price and real-world probability as a transition from ω_i to ω_j over a period of one week in the year 2050.

Under this assumption a transition-based pricing kernel (SDF) is:

$$\varphi(\omega_i, \omega_j) = \frac{q_0(\omega_i, \omega_j)}{p(\omega_i, \omega_j)}. \tag{2.34}$$

Calendar independence is a strong assumption – in fact it's clearly not true. The hope is that some time-averaged transition probability is informative.

Another strong assumption is:

> Assumption 2: **Transition Independence**. The SDF has the following form:
>
> $$\varphi(\omega_i, \omega_j) = \delta \frac{h(\omega_j)}{h(\omega_i)}, \tag{2.35}$$
>
> where δ is a positive scalar and h is a positive function of the states.

Assumption 2 is motivated by the idea of a **representative utility-maximizing investor**. In the real world, there are many financial market participants with many behavioral patterns that are not necessarily captured by utility functions. Some investigations assume that all the different behaviors of all the different participants in a state-price security market can be averaged into a single representative investor who has a Von Neumann–Morgenstern utility function that she tries to maximize. This is a heroic leap that surely doesn't reflect empirical reality, but it does provide mathematical tractability and perhaps some high-level intuitive guidance.

Suppose the representative investor is making decisions during state i about allocating her budget to buying state price securities that pay off in the next time period. We'll discuss portfolio optimization in depth in Chapters 4 and 5, but for now note that we can capture the investor's decision in the following optimization problem:

$$\text{maximize}_{a_0,\ldots,a_n} \quad u(a_0) + f\sum_{j=1}^{n} p(\omega_i, \omega_j)u(a_j)$$

$$\text{subject to} \quad a_0 + \sum_{j=1}^{n} q_0(\omega_i, \omega_j)a_j = 1. \tag{2.36}$$

Here

- a_j $(j = 1,\ldots,n)$ is the amount the investor allocates to buying the state price security that will pay off if state j is the next state;
- a_0 is the amount used at the current time in the current state i;
- We have standardized the investor's wealth to be 1;
- f is the one-period discount factor;
- $u()$ is the investor's utility function;
- $p(\omega_i, \omega_j)$ is the investor's belief about the actual (not risk-neutral) probability that the state of the world will transition from ω_i now to ω_j one period from now.

Equation (2.36) is a Lagrange multipliers problem with solution

$$u'(a_0) = \lambda$$

$$fp(\omega_i, \omega_j)u'(a_j) = \lambda q_0(\omega_i, \omega_j).$$

So

$$\varphi(\omega_i, \omega_j) \equiv \frac{q_0(\omega_i, \omega_j)}{p(\omega_i, \omega_j)} = f\frac{u'(a_j)}{u'(a_0)} = \delta\frac{u'(a_j)}{u'(a_i)}.$$

For the last equality, set $\delta = f\frac{u'(a_i)}{u'(a_0)}$ where δ is as in (2.35). Under the further assumption that the δ defined this way is a constant not dependent on the starting state, this is the same as (2.35) when the h function is the derivative of the utility function of the representative investor.

However assumption (2.35) is motivated, when it holds then (2.34) can be rewritten as:

$$q(\omega_i, \omega_j) = \delta\frac{h(\omega_j)}{h(\omega_i)}p(\omega_i, \omega_j). \tag{2.37}$$

2.10.2 Ross Recovery: Matrix Calculations

Equation (2.37) can be put into matrix form. Define the following quantities:

- $n = |\Omega|$, the number of possible states;
- Q, the $n \times n$ matrix with unit-period state-price-security-derived probabilities $q(\omega_i, \omega_j)$ in the (i, j) position;
- D, the unknown $n \times n$ diagonal matrix with $h(\omega_i)$ in the ith diagonal position;
- P, the unknown $n \times n$ matrix with the real-world (natural) probability $p(\omega_i, \omega_j)$ in the (i, j) position.

Then (2.37) is equivalent to:

$$DQ = \delta PD. \tag{2.38}$$

Solving for the unknown natural probabilities P gives:

$$P = \frac{1}{\delta} DQD^{-1}. \tag{2.39}$$

Since all the outcomes in the sample space Ω are in the rows of P, it must be true that P is a row-stochastic matrix, that is, that:

$$Pu = u, \tag{2.40}$$

where u is the unit n-vector of all ones. This just says that whatever state the world is currently in (corresponding to a row of P), there is a 100 percent chance that the world transitions to one of the other states in Ω. Together with (2.39), this shows that $z = D^{-1}u$ is an eigenvector of Q with associated eigenvalue δ:

$$Qz = \delta z. \tag{2.41}$$

Ross (2013) assumes that Q is irreducible: an $n \times n$ nonnegative matrix A is irreducible if, for every $0 \leq i, j \leq n$, there is some $0 \leq k(i, j) \leq n$ where the (i, j) entry of $A^{k(i,j)}$ is strictly positive. Thus, Q is nonnegative because it consists of probabilities recovered from state price securities that can't sell for negative prices. It seems plausible that there will eventually be some positive-probability path between any two states i and j, that is, there should be some (possibly large) k such that the k-step transition probability matrix Q^k has a nonzero (i, j) entry. So this assumption is not as strong as Assumptions 1 and 2 above.

Irreducibility allows the Perron–Frobenius Theorem to be invoked. Perron–Frobenius[27] says that Q has a single largest positive eigenvalue, and its associated eigenvector z is strictly positive (or strictly negative, but then $-z$ is strictly positive). Moreover, z is the only strictly positive eigenvector.

---

27 The use of Perron–Frobenius theory in this context seems to have originated with [Backus, Gregory, and Zin 1989]. For a general mathematical treatment of Perron–Frobenius, see e.g. [Meyer 2000].

This closes the gap between the number of equations and the number of unknowns. The procedure is, thus: Figure out Q from observed prices and then compute Q's eigensystem. Find the largest positive real eigenvalue; that has to be the unknown discount factor δ. The associated all-positive eigenvector equals $D^{-1}u$, so the ith entry of the associated eigenvector is $1/h(\omega_i)$. There are no other candidates to solve (2.41) among the eigensystem because none of the other eigenvectors is all positive. Thus, by invoking Perron–Frobenius, Ross (2013) is able to fill in the $n + 1$ unknowns (δ and the $h(\omega)$'s) on the RHS of (2.39).

Generally the state-price securities necessary to fill in the risk-neutral transition matrix Q only exist in economic theory. But in some real-world cases there is an observable market for state prices. Section 9.3.1 later in this book describes the Breeden–Litzenberger process to derive state probability mass functions (and hence state prices) from options markets. This options-based process applies when the state space Ω consists of price levels: for example, the states could enumerate possible prices of a stock like TSLA, with $\omega_1 = 0$, $\omega_2 = \$1, \ldots, \omega_n = \$n$.

For now, it suffices to know that risk-neutral probabilities $qq(c,j,t)$ of a security's transitioning from its current price level ω_c to any of the price levels $\omega_1, \omega_2, \ldots, \omega_n$ at time t from now can be computed by observing the current prices of options on that security. There must be a robust set of traded option contracts maturing at time t for this to work: even so, some interpolation will be needed between times and states. Recall that the Calendar Independence assumption applied to a single period; so qq relates to q through the equality $qq(c,j,1) = q(\omega_c, \omega_j)$.

Thus, we can define another matrix QQ_c whose (j,t) entry consists of the quantity $qq(c,j,t)$. We will suppose that QQ_c is obtainable by observing options prices using the Breeden–Litenberger process that we'll see in Section 9.3.1.

The problem is that QQ_c only supplies one row of Q: the cth row where ω_c is the current state. This is not enough to compute a stochastic discount factor: more input information needs to be acquired. There are two approaches, both of which use the time argument of qq to produce needed data.

2.10.3 Computing the SDF: Ross's Method

The first approach (from Ross 2013) iterates from the overlap between the desired single-period risk-neutral transition matrix Q and the observable QQ_c. As we noted, the vectors marked in red below are the same:

$$Q = \begin{bmatrix} \vdots & \ddots & \vdots \\ q(c,1) & \cdots & q(c,n) \\ \vdots & \ddots & \vdots \end{bmatrix},$$

$$QQ_c = \begin{bmatrix} qq(c,1,1) & \cdots & qq(c,1,n) \\ \vdots & \cdots & \vdots \\ qq(c,n,1) & \cdots & qq(c,n,n) \end{bmatrix}.$$

The rest of Q can be bootstrapped by noting that going from state c now to state i at time t means the state of the world went from c now to some state j at time $t-1$, and then did a one-period transition from state j to state i. Summing over all the intermediate states gives:

$$qq(c,i,t) = \sum_{j=1}^{n} qq(c,j,t-1)q(\omega_j, \omega_i).$$

In other words, the (i,t) entry of the known matrix QQ_c is the dot product of:

- column i of the as-yet-unknown $n \times n$ matrix Q; and
- column $t-1$ of QQ_c.

At time zero (now), the state is definitely c, so the vector δ_c of all zeroes except for a 1 in the c place represents the probabilities at time zero.

Putting the points of the previous two paragraphs together in a matrix equation gives:

$$QQ_c = Q^\mathsf{T} \times (\delta_c \mid QQ_c(1, n-1)), \tag{2.42}$$

where $QQ_c(1, n-1)$ consists of the first $n-1$ columns of QQ_c and "$\delta_c \mid$" means the column vector δ_c is prepended. In words, (2.42) moves periods 0 through $n-1$ on the RHS to periods 1 through n on the LHS.

Solving for Q^T gives:

$$Q^\mathsf{T} = QQ_c(\delta_c \mid QQ_c(1, n-1))^{-1}.$$

This retrieves the entire risk-neutral one-period state transition matrix from the risk-neutral probabilities extracted from multiple time periods. From there Ross (2013) uses the largest eigenvalue of Q and its associated eigenvector to fill in the matrix equations of the previous section, obtaining the SDF and the natural probability transition matrix P.

2.10.4 Computing the SDF: Jackwerth and Menner's Method

A second approach to computing the SDF comes from Jackwerth and Menner (2020). They note that raising the single-period transition matrix Q to the tth power gives the t-period transition matrix. In our notation: $Q^t(i,j) = qq(i,j,t)$.

That means that all the columns of QQ_c are informative: the t column of QQ_c equals the c (current state) row of Q^t.

Multiplying both sides of (2.41) by Q^{t-1} and iterating gives $Q^t z = \delta^t z$. Thus,

$$\sum_{j=1}^{n} qq(c,j,t) z_j = \delta^t z_c. \tag{2.43}$$

Letting t vary from 1 to n gives n equations in the n unknowns z_j / z_c ($j \neq c$) and δ.

Jackwerth and Menner (2020) note that simply solving the equations can violate "reasonable economic constraints," so they solve an optimization problem that imposes constraints:

$$\underset{\frac{z_j}{z_c}, \delta}{\text{minimize}} \quad \sum_{t=1}^{n} \left(\sum_{j=1}^{n} qq(c,j,t) \frac{z_j}{z_c} - \delta^t \right)^2$$

$$\text{subject to} \quad \frac{z_j}{z_c} > 0, 1 > \delta > 0. \tag{2.44}$$

This approach solves directly for the SDF and the factor δ but does not fill in the entire single-period risk-neutral transition matrix Q. Only the current-period probability mass function $q(\omega_c, \omega_j)$ ($j = 1, \ldots, n$) is observed. But together with the SDF and factor that are the outputs of (2.44), having the current-period PMF q allows the current-period real-world PMF p to be computed. Given the nature of the problem solved in (2.44), $\sum_{j=1}^{n} p(\omega_c, \omega_j)$ may not equal one, so the p's may need to be rescaled so they add to one.

2.10.5   Ross Recovery Theorem: Empirical Problems

Finding an SDF allows empirical tests of predictions like Hansen–Jagannathan, equation (2.29), to be performed. Further, the Recovery Theorem gave rise to the hope that trading strategies based on recovered probabilities could be developed.

For example, Audrino, Huitema, and Ludwig (2015) used a neural network approach to fill in Q from observed options prices. They then investigated trading strategies based on the Ross-recovered moments of the distribution of S&P 500 returns. They found that such trading strategies performed better than strategies based on the moments of the risk-neutral distribution.

Martin and Ross (2019) applied recovery techniques to find the SDF for the fixed-income market. They showed that under the calendar independence assumption, rates of return on a perpetual bond directly reveal the SDF for bonds, so an options market is not necessary. They explored the differences between perpetual bonds and long but finite maturity bonds, finding that it is possible for very slow convergence to exist, making their work impractical to implement. Subsequent empirical tests by Qin, Linetsky, and Lie (2018) cast doubt on a key requirement (the growth optimality of the long bond), making it less likely that the Martin–Ross assumptions hold in the real world.

The general findings of empirical tests of Ross Recovery have been negative: the strong assumptions (calendar and transition independence) do not appear to hold in the data.

Jackwerth and Menner (2020) arrived at several negative findings:

> We reject this hypothesis [that future returns are really drawn from Ross-Recovered distributions] strongly using four different density tests. ... Further, we show that the means and variances of the recovered physical distributions cannot predict future returns and realized variances. Also, Ross recovery does not produce downward-sloping SDFs (as one would expect given risk-averse preferences) but rather ones that are riddled with local minima and maxima.

Jackwerth and Menner (2020) found that the Ross (2013) method for computation of calendar-independent risk-neutral transition probabilities from observable option prices is problematic, even before trying to recover natural probabilities. They needed to impose many conditions to force the $q(\omega_i, \omega_j)$ to make some sort of economic sense:

1. They look at rolling averages of transition probabilities rather than single-period results in order to smooth out transitory irregularities in the recovered distribution;
2. They have to force the transition probabilities to be positive;
3. They have to force implied risk-free rates $\sum_j q_0(\omega_i, \omega_j)$ into a reasonable interval; otherwise they get implied risk-free rates as low as -98% and as high as 576%;
4. They have to force the transition probabilities to be unimodal, that is, they must force $q(\omega_i, \omega_j) > q(\omega_i, \omega_k)$ where the distance between ω_k and ω_i is greater than the distance between ω_j and ω_i.

Further departures from empirical reality arise when the SDF is computed by either the Ross (2013) or Jackwerth and Menner (2020) method. Jackwerth and Menner (2020) test whether out-of-sample returns of the Standard & Poor's 500 US stock index could be drawn from the real-world probability mass functions (PMFs) that result from either recovery process. These recovered real-world PMFs fail every statistical test of distribution similarity that Jackwerth and Menner subject them to.

They do, however, find two simple approaches that work much better than Ross Recovery. One is to assume a representative investor with a specified power utility function with coefficient 3, that is,

$$u(x) = \frac{1 - x^{-2}}{2}.$$

That gives $u'(x) = x^{-3}$, so the h function in (2.37) is just $h(\omega_i) = \frac{1}{\omega_i^3}$ and the SDF is:

$$\varphi(\omega_i, \omega_j) = \delta \left(\frac{\omega_i}{\omega_j} \right)^3.$$

Jackwerth and Menner (2020) apply this SDF to the PMF obtained from the current state, that is, to the one row of Q that overlaps with QQ_c and thus is immediately observable. They find that the resulting real-world distribution agrees much more closely with the shape of the out-of-sample realized distribution of returns than the Ross Recovery–based distribution does.

Jackwerth and Menner (2020) also look at whether past historical return distributions look like future realized return distributions, and find that they do even better than the power utility representative investor, that is, they score higher on statistical tests of whether out-of-sample realized returns could be drawn from the distribution.

This is a low bar to clear, so the indictment of the extensive theoretical structure behind natural distribution recovery is severe. The state of the art is therefore similar to the circles-within-circles theory of planetary motion that prevailed before Johannes Kepler. A circle is a rough approximation to empirical planetary motion, but one that clearly fails under scrutiny. Kepler's elliptical model replaced circles and prevailed for three hundred years until it was surpassed by general relativity. Mathematical finance is still in the circles stage, but the very empirical failure of Ross's recovery work may open the door to the equivalent of the elliptical model.

For Code Segments in this chapter, see the Code Appendix starting on p. 440. For executable code, visit www.cambridge.org/9781009209090/ch2

For problem sets for this chapter, visit www.cambridge.org/ 9781009209090/ch2_problems

3 Fixed-Income Modeling

Fixed-income (UK **Fixed-interest**) investing is based on the translation of future money to present money via borrowing arrangements. A lender has a long (positive) position in future money (including any interest and principal payments) and a short (negative) position in present money. The interest rate that the lender receives reflects among other things the tradeoff of future money for present money.

J. Wellington Wimpy,[1] a character in 1930's *Popeye* cartoons, was famous for saying, "I'll gladly pay you Tuesday for a hamburger today." Mr. Wimpy apparently did not contemplate paying interest, and was unequivocal on where he stood on the future versus present money issue: he liked present money (the cost of the hamburger now) better than future money (Tuesday's repayment).

This is a popular idea: an amount of money now must be worth more than the same amount of money in the future, because one of the things you can do with money now is nothing. You can just wait for the future, and then do any of the things you could do with future money. So the set of things you can do with present money is a superset of the things you can do with money in the future, and therefore money in the future is worth less than money now.

Unfortunately, popular ideas are not necessarily valid; this commonsense argument in favor of present money is wrong. It is possible that the purchasing power of money will increase over time so what you can buy with $100 today is less than what you will be able to buy with $100 a year from now. In that case, you can do more with money in the future than you can do with money today. This is *deflation*, which is rare but does sometimes happen, usually during bad economic times. Code Segment 3.1 retrieves data from FRED, the database maintained by the Federal Reserve of St. Louis (part of the US central banking system). Code Segment 3.1 then uses that data to generate Figure 3.1, which shows wholesale prices from 1914 to 1968.

---

1 Popeye.fandom.com. 'J. Wellington Wimpy.' Website. https://popeye.fandom.com/wiki/J._Wellington_Wimpy.

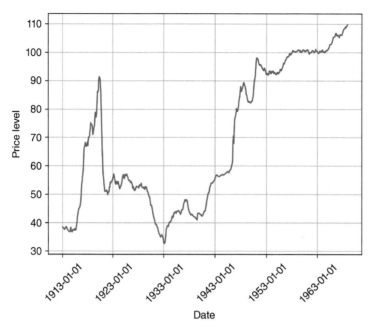

Figure 3.1 US wholesale prices.

3.1 Real, Inflation, and Nominal Rates

In May of 1920, it cost $91.5 to buy the same things that would later (in February of 1933) cost only $32.7. So if "now" was May of 1920, and "the future" was February of 1933, then "money in the future" was going to be worth almost three times as much as "money now." Your ability to buy things would have grown at a compound rate of about 8.4 percent a year during this period; that is, you would have been rewarded at that rate for being patient and postponing your purchases until later.

Mr. Wimpy's proposal of a hamburger today in exchange for payment in the future was probably made in cartoons written in the early 1930s and was a bad financial move in that deflationary period, since he would be borrowing the price of a hamburger today and paying it back with more valuable future money. Actually, the running joke in *Popeye* cartoons was that Mr. Wimpy was a deadbeat: he was unlikely to ever pay back the cost of the hamburger. That's credit risk, which we'll explore in Chapter 11. In this chapter, we'll only be concerned with the time value of money in the absence of uncertainty about whether or when it will be repaid.

The **inflation** (or, if negative, **deflation**) rate is the annual rate of decay in the ability of money to purchase a constant basket of goods and services. We saw in Figure 3.1 a period where the inflation rate was about -8.4% (=deflation rate about 8.4%), at least for wholesale goods.

Another important rate used to translate between money now and money in the future is the **default-free rate**, which is the rate you get paid to lend money with 100% chance of getting paid back fully and on time; so by definition there is no possibility of default (which is *not* getting paid back fully and on time). Equivalently,[2] it is the rate you pay to borrow if you are a default-free borrower. This is the same concept as the **risk-free rate** introduced in Chapter 2.

If you want to know today's value of a dollar received (say) one year in the future, consider making a one-year loan today of $\$\frac{1}{1+r}$ to a default-free borrower, where r is the risk-free or default-free rate, for example, 3% per year. You will receive a dollar one year from now. So the value of the dollar a year from now is $\$\frac{1}{1+r}$ today, e.g. about \$.9709 if the risk-free rate is 3%.

If you lend money with no adjustment for inflation, then the lending rate is called a **nominal rate**. There are arrangements where inflation adjustments are made: for example, the US Treasury issues Treasury Inflation Protected Securities ("TIPS")[3] that pay more when there is inflation and less when there isn't. Such securities are said to pay a **real rate**, that is, a rate that reflects only the time value of money after keeping purchasing power constant.

The real rate plus the inflation rate equal the nominal rate.[4] If there were no inflation or deflation, then the do-more-with-money-now argument at the beginning of this chapter would seem to be compelling. So one would think that the real rate, which removes inflation, must always be positive.

Figure 3.2, generated by Code Segment 3.2, shows the yield to maturity on constant-maturity 5-year TIPS, that is, the 5-year real rate. Figure 3.2 shows that 5-year real rates were continuously negative in the USA from March 2011 through September 2014, after March 2020 in response the COVID-19 pandemic, and also for shorter periods. At times, investors who were thinking of saving money (by making a loan to the US government for five years) estimated that they would lose over 1 percent a year in purchasing power by doing so. So although the argument for positive real rates seems to be compelling, it isn't.

However, an even more compelling argument can be made for positive nominal default-free rates. If the nominal rate is negative, you'll get back less money than you started with if you make a loan to a default-free borrower. The cure is obvious: don't lend. Just keep the money in a safe deposit box during the period you would have loaned it; then at least you'll have the same amount and not less in the future.

---

2 There may be different default-free borrowing and lending rates. To keep things simple, we'll assume they're the same.
3 Treasury Direct®. "Treasury Inflation-Protected Securities (TIPS)." Website. `www.treasurydirect.gov/marketable-securities/tips/`.
4 The relationship between the rates is: (1+nominal) = (1+real)(1+E[inflation]), where E[] is the current expectation of inflation. This is called the Fisher equation after economist Irving Fisher. Over small periods of time, the cross-term is negligible.

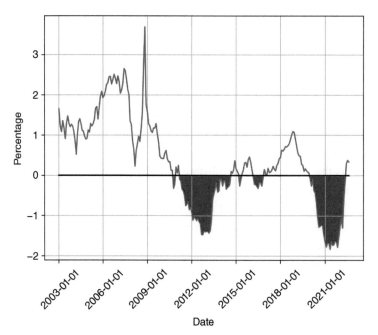

Figure 3.2 Five-year US real rates, 2003-01 to 2022-08.

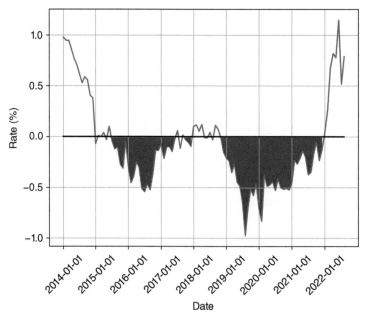

Figure 3.3 Swiss 10-year nominal rates, 2014-02 to 2022-08.

Thus, one might think, we should never see negative nominal rates because no one would lend at such rates.

The Swiss government is considered a default-free borrower. Figure 3.3 (generated by Code Segment 3.3) shows Swiss nominal rates starting in 2014.

3.2 Discounting

Figure 3.3 shows that at times, investors gave the Swiss government CHF 100, knowing that in ten years they would only get back about CHF 95. Other countries (Germany and Japan, for example) have also had negative nominal rates.

Why didn't these investors keep the money in a safe deposit box and get back CHF 100 in ten years rather than CHF 95? Some investors did do this, but it's hard to pay bills with money in a safe deposit box. Assets that are part of the global electronic financial system – like Swiss government bonds held in a custodian bank – can be used easily by pushing a button to convert them to something else. Also, for institutions with hundreds of millions, or billions, of Swiss francs, safe deposit boxes aren't a practical option. And safe deposit boxes (or warehouses with armed guards, for larger investors) cost money too. Investors interested in finding a safe and convenient place for their Swiss francs were willing to pay the Swiss government a storage fee.

So inflation, real, and nominal rates can all be negative. Despite this, it is customary to speak of **discounting** future money to the present to reflect future money's supposedly diminished value compared to present money. In fact, inflation, real and nominal rates are usually positive so discounting is usually the right thing to do. The relatively few periods of negative rates can be handled with negative discounting, which is linguistically confusing but mathematically straightforward.

The rate (usually per year) at which future money is discounted to make it equal to present money is called the **discount rate**, and the associated multiplicative factor applied to sums of future money is called the **discount factor**. Usually, the discount rate applied to sure future money is the same as, or very close to, the default-free nominal rate.

There are many different discounting conventions for transforming an annual discount rate r over a time period t denominated in years into a multiplicative factor. For now, we will use the **discrete discount factor** $(1 + r)^{-t}$. Another convention is the **k-period discrete discount factor** of $(1 + r/k)^{-kt}$ when flows are observed k times a year, that is, $k = 12$ for monthly discounting. In the limit as $k \to \infty$, this becomes the **continuous discount factor** $\exp(-rt)$. Among the many other discounting conventions is **Actual/360**, which is $(1 + r/360)^{-365t}$; this is an even higher discount than continuous.

We will sometimes use the continuous factor when it is mathematically convenient. It's simply a change of variable:

$$r_{continuous} = k \ln(1 + r_{discrete}/k);$$

$$r_{discrete} = k(\exp(r_{continuous}/k) - 1).$$

In this chapter, we're not going to differentiate between the components of the nominal rate; we'll essentially assume that real=nominal and we won't delve into the effects of inflation.

The rate at which future sure money is discounted is a description of one of the most fundamental human choices: consume now versus save for later. Investors looking at negative real rates in the red sections of Figure 3.2 were seeing a discouraging environment for saving money for the future by loaning it to a default-free borrower (the US Treasury). That encouraged spending rather than saving, thereby speeding up the economy. High real rates encourage saving over spending.

In most modern economies, a key agent trying to encourage a desired level of spending versus saving is a government institution called the **central bank**, which has the power to create or destroy money. Using this power, the central bank can force risk-free rates down using a variety of techniques: one technique is to drive the price of risk-free instruments up (thereby driving interest rates down) by buying these instruments using money it has created. Consumption then becomes relatively more attractive than saving and the economy is encouraged to speed up. In the other direction a central bank can drive rates up using such techniques in reverse, encouraging less consumption so the economy slows down. In the USA the central bank is called the *Federal Reserve*.[5]

Curiously, investing at the risk-free rate is not risk-free. The next section explores this apparent paradox.

3.3 The Risk in the Risk-Free Rate

Certain government ("sovereign") borrowers – among them the US Treasury,[6] the Norwegian Ministry of Finance,[7] the German Federal Ministry of Finance,[8] the Monetary Authority of Singapore,[9] the New Zealand Debt Management Office[10] – are currently considered to pose no peril of default. If you lend these sovereigns money, short of an alien invasion you'll get all the interest payments they promised you, when they promised them, and you'll get all your original principal back when they said they would pay it back to you.

Thus to observe a risk-free or default-free rate, you can look at the rate paid by a default-free sovereign. These rates are not all the same, since they are in different currencies. The USA pays in dollars; Norway in krone; Germany in

5 Board of Governors of the Federal Reserve System. "About the Fed." Website. www.federalreserve.gov/aboutthefed.htm.
6 U.S. Department of the Treasury. "Role of the Treasury." Website. https://home.treasury.gov/about/general-information/role-of-the-treasury.
7 Government.no. "Ministry of Finance." www.regjeringen.no/en/dep/fin/id216/.
8 Bundesrepublik Deutschland Finanzagentur GmbH. "Federal Securities." Website. www.deutsche-finanzagentur.de/en/federal-securities/types-of-federal-securities/overview-federal-securities.
9 Monetary Authority of Singapore. "Bonds and Bills." Website. www.mas.gov.sg/bonds-and-bills.
10 Te Tai Ōhanga: The Treasury. "New Zealand Debt Management." Website. https://debtmanagement.treasury.govt.nz/.

Image 3.1 US Treasury bond. Source: `https://sites.google.com/site/financialportfoliowg/treasury-bond`.

euros. That leads to additional complications. Let's just stick with the USA in dollars for now.

If you loan $1,000,000 to the US government at 7 5/8% per year for (say) 30 years, the usual convention is that you get 60 payments of $38,125 (one every 6 months for 30 years), and a repayment of the $1,000,000 loan amount (called "principal") in 30 years. To show how serious it was about repaying you, the US Treasury used to give you an impressive certificate like the one in Image 3.1.

Generally, a **bond** is a legally enforceable agreement between a borrower – in this case, the US Treasury – and a lender. Image 3.1 is a "bearer bond," which indicates that the person who physically possesses the certificate gets the payments described above.

The practice of issuing physical certificates is now archaic in the USA,[11] but when it was common, some of the certificates would have detachable coupons. The coupons would need to be clipped off and sent in to the issuer (the US Treasury, in this case) each six months in order to get the payment, say, the $38,125 semiannual payment that would actually be associated with a 7 5/8% bond with $1,000,000 principal.

Now virtually all bonds are issued electronically. But the terminology persists – a "coupon" bond is one that pays regular, fixed-interest payments in addition to a final repayment of principal. More precisely, such a bond is a

---

11 As of August 31, 2022, total US debt outstanding was $30.936 trillion. Legacy bearer (physical) debt was $87 million – roundoff error in the total. From "Debt Position and Activity Report," August 31, 2022. `www.treasurydirect.gov/govt/reports/pd/pd_debtposactrpt.htm`.

non-callable coupon bond or a **bullet bond**, meaning the issuer pays you back all the principal at the end (30 years in the example) and can't force you to take an early repayment of principal. A **callable** bond gives the issuer the right to pay you back early if it so desires.

An even simpler arrangement is a **zero-coupon bond** where there is only one payment at the end. For example, a 30-year 7 5/8% zero-coupon bond (sometimes called just a "zero") might start with you loaning the US Treasury $\frac{\$1,000,000}{1.07625^{30}} = \$110,308$ now. Then nothing would happen for 30 years. Then you would receive $\$1,000,000$ from the US Treasury.

Suppose you have purchased the non-callable coupon bond described above (that is, you've loaned $1 million to the US Treasury for 30 years) – except for ease of calculation let's assume the interest rate is a round 7%. Let's also suppose for ease of calculation that you just receive one annual interest payment of $70,000 rather than the usual semiannual payments.

Think about the time one year after buying the bond, when you have just received an electronic credit of $70,000 in your bank account. Since exactly one year has passed, you now have a 29-year-maturity bond. Suppose further that the US Treasury has just issued a separate new bond with 29 years maturity. This is a thought experiment; the US Treasury only issues bonds at certain standard maturities and 29 years isn't one of those standard maturities. The only real way to get a 29-year bond from the US Treasury is to buy a 30-year bond and wait one year.

But in our thought experiment, the US Treasury has just issued a new 29-year bond with an 8% coupon. The new bond is called the **on-the-run** bond and the old bond is called an **off-the-run** or **seasoned** bond. Clearly, you'd rather receive $80,000 a year from the on-the-run than $70,000 a year from the off-the-run for the next 29 years. They'll both pay the same principal at the end. So you call your bank or brokerage firm and tell them to sell the seasoned bond you own and buy the on-the-run.

Of course what you will find is that you will not get par (par=100 cents on the dollar that you originally loaned to the US Treasury) when you sell your seasoned bond. If you did, there would be an arbitrage; buy the on-the-run and sell the off-the-run and receive $10,000 a year for no investment. So you will have to sell your seasoned bond for a discount. The discount will (within transaction costs) equalize the values of the on-the-run and the off-the-run bonds so there is no arbitrage available.

There is a lot of so-called fixed-income mathematics that can be brought to bear – there are in fact entire textbooks just on that subject. Much fixed-income mathematics is really fixed-income accounting that keeps track of cash flows. We'll do just enough to explain what might happen to your 7% bond. But you can already see the risk in the "risk-free" rate: the value of one of the safest investments in the world has dropped due to a change in interest rates.

3.4 Basic Fixed-Income Mathematics

A **cash flow** is just an exchange of money between parties. If you are one of the parties, then a positive cash flow to you means you receive money from someone else; a negative cash flow means you pay money to someone else. A generic financial arrangement contemplates one party receiving or paying future cash flows from/to another party. The cash flows are $c_1, c_2, \ldots, c_n$ at times $t_1 \le t_2, \cdots \le t_n$ in the future.

So, the simplified 7% Treasury non-call coupon bond had at its inception (time 0):

$$c_1 = -1,000,000; c_2 = \cdots = c_{31} = 70,000; \ c_{32} = 1,000,000;$$

$$t_i = i - 1 (i = 1, \ldots, 31); \ t_{32} = 30. \tag{3.1}$$

Equation (3.1) describes a **fixed-income** instrument; the cash flows are known constants at time zero. In full generality, any of these quantities (the cash flows c_j and the times t_k) can be random variables. If the issuing entity is not default free, then we might not get some of the interest payments, or might only get them partially, or might get them late. It is similar with the final repayment of principal. Or there could be a formula for the payments: they could depend on a benchmark whose future value is not known today, like SOFR, the Secured Overnight Financing Rate used in the multi-trillion-dollar interest rate swap market.[12] Or there could be optionality in the bond, where the issuer has the right to pay back early if interest rates go down and the issuer wants to retire high-rate debt and replace it with lower-rate debt. (This is called "prepayment risk.") Some instruments contain options the other way, where the lender gets to put the bond back to the issuer if the lender wishes.

In fact, the term "fixed income" is ambiguous, since fixed-income instruments don't have to be fixed (i.e. have nonstochastic cash flows) nor do they have to provide income. But generally the distinguishing characteristic of fixed-income instruments is that their cash flows are contractually planned, while equity instruments do not have planned cash flows.

In most of this chapter, we are just assuming away the possible stochastic nature of future cash flows. We are assuming that the c_j's and t_k's are constants known at time 0 when the bond is first issued.

But as we've pointed out, the bond is still not risk free: money now is not the same as money later. The discount rate that translates future cash flows into today's value depends on prevailing default-free interest rates at the time.

---

12 Interest Rate Swaps are discussed in Chapter 12. Federal Reserve Bank of New York. "Secured Overnight Financing Rate Data." Website. `https://apps.newyorkfed.org/markets/autorates/sofr`.

So where's the risk? In a Knightian Risk sense, we know all of the outcomes (there is only one outcome: 30 payments of $70,000 every year, and one payment of $1,000,000 in 30 years) and all their probabilities (100%).

The risk is that *the risk-free rate changes*.

3.4.1 Generic Pricing Equation

The general expression for the price at time t of a generic instrument with cash flows $c_1, c_2, \ldots, c_n$ at times $t \le t_1 \le t_2, \ldots, \le t_n$ in the future is:

$$P_t = \sum_{i=1}^{n} \frac{\mathbb{E}_t[c_i]}{(1 + r_{i,t})^{t_i - t}}. \tag{3.2}$$

$\mathbb{E}_t[x]$ is the expectation at time t of the future cash flow x; in this chapter, all the cash flows will be constants, so $\mathbb{E}[x] = x$. The $r_{i,t}$ are discount rates for the appropriate times – that is, the rates we think (at time t) we should discount the cash flow c_i on this instrument that will occur $t_i - t$ years in the future.

One way to look at (3.2) is as a pricing equation, where the P_t on the left-hand side is the only unknown. To start, we'll simplify by assuming a common known discount rate r_t, that is, $r_{i,t} = r_t$ for all i.

A particularly simple expression results from applying a common discount rate r_t to a simplified, generic $100 principal Treasury bond with regularly spaced payments of c every year and a maturity T years after time t. Define $y_t = (1 + r_t)^{-1}$; then (3.2) can be rewritten as

$$P_t(r_t) = \sum_{i=1}^{T} cy_t^i + 100y_t^T = cy_t \frac{1 - y_t^T}{1 - y_t} + 100y_t^T. \tag{3.3}$$

Another way to look at (3.2) is backward: that is, P_t may be an observable price in a market. In that case, if future cash flows c_i and timings t_i are known, the discount factors $r_{i,t}$ become the unknowns to be found. If there is only one instrument's price P_t to be observed, then only one unknown can be found. In that case, it's customary to assume again that all $r_{i,t}$ have a common value r_t, and solve for it. That r_t is called the **internal rate of return** of the instrument (abbreviated "IRR" or "IROR") and sometimes the **yield**[13] of the instrument.

We considered above what could happen to a bond with a 7% coupon. We supposed that after a year there was a new on-the-run bond with a higher interest rate than the original 7%, causing the seasoned bond's price to go down. But if interest rates had gone down from 7%, the seasoned bond would have been worth

---

13 While "internal rate of return" is a well-defined term, "yield" is not: there are many different types of yield. Generally, if we just use the term "yield" without further elaboration, we mean internal rate of return. However, even that term is ambiguous as it depends on the discounting convention. For example, if an internal rate of return is computed using a k-period discount factor (Section 3.2) for $k \ne 1$ (especially $k = 2$), it is called a `bond-equivalent yield`.

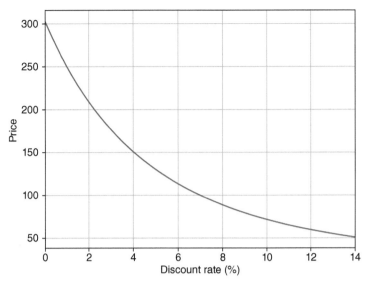

Figure 3.4 Seasoned 29-year 7% coupon bond price.

more, since \$70,000 payments every year would then be more attractive than the new bond's terms. The price of the 7% bond with 29 years left as a function of the new interest rate is shown in Figure 3.4 (which uses (3.3)), generated in Code Segment 3.4.

3.4.2 Price Changes as Rates Change

For the 7% bond at its inception time $t = 0$, we know $P_0 = 100$ because that's what we paid for it (i.e. that's what we loaned to the US Treasury), thereby establishing the market price. You can verify that putting $r_0 = .07$ $\left(y_0 = \frac{1}{1.07}\right)$ in (3.3) with a $c = 7$ coupon gives $P_0 = 100$.

Figure 3.4 shows P_1, the price of the seasoned bond after one year has passed, by applying (3.3) with $c = 7$ and $T = 29$ and with r_1's varying along the X-axis. At $r_1 = 8\%$, $P_1 = \$88.84$. Of course, if prevailing interest rates had dropped, we would have gained: for example, if the new 29-year bond paid 6%, our seasoned 7% coupon bond would be worth \$113.59.

Note that as the prevailing interest rate changed by 1% up or down, the price of the seasoned bond went down or up by somewhere around 12%. It is natural to want to find the relationship between changes in prevailing interest rates and the price of a bond – this could translate interest rate moves directly into price moves. If the discount rates in (3.2) were the same for all cash flows ($r_{i,t} = r$ for all i), and the cash flows and times were known constants, we could expand around the current rate r_t in a Taylor series, taking derivatives with respect to r:

$$P_t(r) = P_t(r_t) + P_t'(r_t)(r - r_t) + \frac{1}{2}P_t''(r_t)(r - r_t)^2 + \cdots + . \qquad (3.4)$$

Or, writing this in terms of percentage changes with obvious notation:

$$\frac{\Delta P_t(r)}{P_t(r_t)} = \frac{P'_t(r_t)}{P_t(r_t)}(\Delta r) + \frac{1}{2}\frac{P''_t(r_t)}{P_t(r_t)}(\Delta r)^2 + \cdots + . \qquad (3.5)$$

If there is a common discount rate r_t and $\mathbb{E}[c_i]$ is not a function of r_t, then taking the first and second derivatives of (3.2) with respect to r_t and using $y_t = 1/(1 + r_t)$ gives:

$$P'_t(r_t) = -y_t \sum_{i=1}^{n}(t_i - t)\mathbb{E}[c_i]y_t^{t_i-t} \text{ and } P''_t(r_t) = y_t^2 \sum_{i=1}^{n}(t_i - t)^2\mathbb{E}[c_i]y_t^{t_i-t} - y_t P'_t.$$

$$(3.6)$$

The first derivative shown in (3.6) is a multiple of the weighted average of the times at which we will receive the cash flows: Let $w_i = \frac{\mathbb{E}[c_i]y_t^{t_i-t}}{P_t}$; note $\sum w_i = 1$. Let $s = \frac{-1}{y_t P_t}$. Then $s \cdot P'_t = \sum w_i(t_i - t)$.

The concept of finding the average time at which we will receive cash flows was introduced by Macaulay (1938). Macaulay pointed out that maturity (for example, 29 years in Figure 3.3) was not necessarily the most important time-related characteristic of an instrument with known cash flows (that is, a bond). To take an extreme example, suppose a bond pays two cash flows: $99.99 in one year and $0.01 in thirty years. That bond is for all practical purposes a one-year bond, not a thirty-year bond. Macaulay introduced a new term:

> Let us use the word "duration" to signify the essence of the time element in a loan. (p. 44)

Macaulay's suggestion was to use $-\frac{P'_t}{y_t P_t}$ as the "essence" of the time element; today we call that **Macaulay duration**. Without the y_t in the denominator (i.e. just $-\frac{P'_t}{P_t}$), the expression defines **modified duration**.

For the simplified Treasury bond example in (3.3), the derivative has a closed form. For Macaulay duration before normalizing by dividing by price, we have (using $y_t = 1/(1 + r_t)$, $y'_t = -y_t^2$):

$$\frac{-P'_t(r_t)}{y_t} = \frac{cy_t}{(1 - y_t)^2}\left((1 - y_t^T) - T(1 - y_t)y_t^T\right) + 100Ty_t^T. \qquad (3.7)$$

When the original 7% bond was issued at par ($P_0 = 100$), parameters were $c = 7$, $T = 30$. The discount rate was $r_0 = 7\%$ as established by this bond. Putting these numbers into the right-hand side of (3.7) shows the Macaulay duration of the new 30-year bond is 13.3 years. This is dramatically shorter than the 30-year maturity. Generally, a newly issued 30-year par bond has Macaulay durations that drop off rapidly as the coupon payment increases and more of the discounted cash flows are pushed closer to the present.

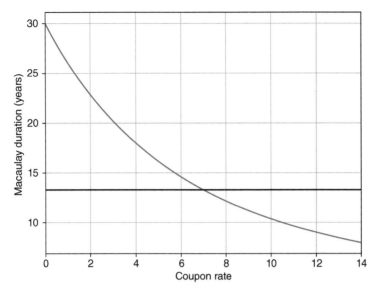

Figure 3.5 New 30-year bond duration.

3.4.3 Duration Calculations; Convexity

Figure 3.5 (generated by Code Segment 3.5) shows that the only coupon rate at which duration=maturity is zero; that is, only a zero-coupon bond has full duration. Intuitively that's because there's only one cash flow at T=maturity, which is 30 years in the figure. So in that case the only possible average time to maturity is T. You can also see this by dividing (3.7) by (3.3) with c=0.

Otherwise in Figure 3.5 durations are lower than 30 years as more of the weighted average cash flows come earlier as the coupons get higher.

The black line in Figure 3.5 shows the Macaulay duration of a bond maturing in 30 years, paying 7% coupons with a discount rate of 7%; it's $\frac{-P_t'(7\%)}{yP_t(7\%)} \approx 13.3$ years. So in some sense, a bond maturing in 30 years and paying an annual 7% coupon acts like a zero coupon bond maturing in 13.3 years.

Let's work through the calculations to get a sense of how the prices move. Suppose there is an instantaneous rise of rates from 7% to 7.01%.

- Plugging in $c = 7$, $r_t = .0701$, $T = 30$ to (3.3) gives 99.87603. The difference between the original price of 100 (par) and this new price is $\Delta P_t = -.124$. So the left-hand side of (3.5) is $\Delta P_t(7.01\%)/P_t(7\%) = \Delta P_t(7.01\%)/100 = -.124\%$ for the 7% coupon bond.
- Thus, 13.3 (actually 13.27767) years is (3.7) divided by (3.3) with $c = 7$, $r_t = .07$, $T = 30$. For a zero-coupon bond with this maturity, its starting price is $\frac{100}{1.07^{13.27767}} = 40.72413$. Recalculating the price at $r = 7.01\%$, we get $\frac{100}{1.0701^{13.27767}} = 40.67363$, a difference of $\Delta P_t = -.050501$. So for the zero-coupon bond, $\Delta P_t(7.01\%)/P_t(7\%) = -.050501/40.72413 = -.124\%$.

In both cases, there's a $-.124\%$ change in response to a .01% rise in rates. Note that the Macaulay duration divided by $y_t = 1.07$ is the modified duration; 13.3 divided by 1.07 is 12.4. Multiplying (minus) that times $\Delta r = .01\%$ gives the $-.124\%$ changes we have seen in both bonds. That's because they have the same durations.

So the math works! To a first approximation, the 13.3-year zero is like the 30-year 7% coupon bond. Unless the prices were exactly as stated by the formulas above, there's an arbitrage by going long the 30-year 7% coupon bond and shorting $100 worth of 13.3-year zero-coupon bonds, or the opposite. For small changes in rates, the two of them should offset each other. But this is only a local arbitrage in the neighborhood of $r = 7\%$; for larger moves in rates, they'll start to behave very differently.

For example, if the discount rate instantaneously goes to zero – which is not at all local to 7% – the price of the coupon bond will go to $310. (That's 30 cash flows of $7 plus $100 principal repayment, none of it discounted.) But the price of the zero will go to $100, times $100/40.72413$ (i.e. $100 worth of zeroes at the original price). The difference is $64.45, or minus that if we established the trade in the other direction. So there is still quite a bit of risk in this trade and it's only an arbitrage locally.

A better approximation of price changes brings in the second term of the Taylor series in (3.5). This term $\frac{P''_t}{P_t}$ is called **convexity**. A close inspection of (3.6) reveals that as long as the cash flows are positive constants, convexity is positive. This is good: it gives an upward curl to prices as interest rates change. That upward curl was seen in Figure 3.3 because the pricing function shown there was convex:

$$P_t(\lambda x + (1 - \lambda)y) \le \lambda P_t(x) + (1 - \lambda)P_t(y),$$

where P_t is given by (3.3).

Numerically, at 7% the bond is at par ($P_t = 100$); at 10%, it drops to $P_t = 71.9$, while at 4%, it rises to $P_t = 151$. Both 10% and 4% are $|\Delta r| = 3\%$ away from the current rate of 7%. The first-order approximation based on modified duration would indicate the price move should be $3 \times 12.4 = \$37.2$ – that is a drop to $62.8 (at 10%) and a rise to $137.2 (at 4%). In both cases, the actual price was better. That's the upward "smile" of positive convexity.

Positive convexity is a bonus; if things change, there are better-than-linear results. In fact, there was even a hedge fund called Convexity Capital Management: the name signaled a hope for such better-than-linear results.[14]

Negative convexity (concavity) can occur when the bondholder has given away options: the cash flows are still positive but they aren't constant. For example, in many cases bonds issued by corporations are callable, meaning that

---

14 The fund, which opened in 2005, closed in 2019. [Orr 2019].

the issuer can pay early. So say you bought a callable 30-year 7% coupon bond from the pharmaceutical company Johnson & Johnson,[15] that is, you loaned J&J $100. If a year later prevailing interest rates dropped to 5%, you might be contemplating how to spend your profits because (3.3) says the bond is now worth $130.28. However, (3.3) assumes (incorrectly in this case) fixed cash flows; in fact at that point J&J would probably opt to give you back only your original $100 and borrow $100 from someone else at the new lower rate of 5%. The fact that J&J (rather than you) has the option to control the timing of payback is disadvantageous to you, since you are now stuck with the problem of reinvesting your $100 exactly at a time when interest rates are lower. If interest rates had gone higher, J&J would not have opted to pay you back early. Depending on how much optionality you, the bondholder, have given away, you could see a horrifying downward curl in the price graph.

Taking the derivative of (3.7) (and rearranging the extra $-1/y_t$ term) gives the unnormalized convexity. Note that the convexity of a zero is $T(T+1)y_t^2$.

$$P_t''(r_t) = \frac{cy_t^3}{(1-y_t)^3}\left(2 - (T+1)(T+2)y_t^T + 2T(T+2)y_t^{T+1} - T(T+1)y_t^{T+2}\right)$$
$$+ 100T(T+1)y_t^{T+2}. \tag{3.8}$$

Figure 3.6 (generated by Code Segment 3.6) shows first-order (duration only) and second-order (duration plus convexity) approximations to the simplified 30-year 7% coupon bond as rates change.

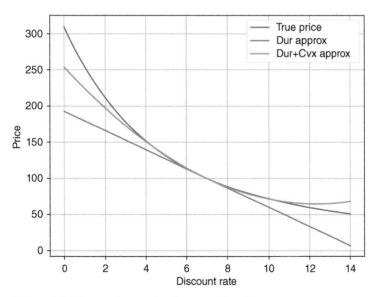

Figure 3.6 First- and second-order approximations.

15 Johnson & Johnson. "About Johnson & Johnson." Website. www.jnj.com/about-jnj.

3.4.4 Approximations and Basis Risk

Figure 3.6 shows the prices of the 30-year 7% coupon bond (Y-axis) as the discount rate (X-axis) changes. The green line is the 2-term Taylor series from (3.4); the blue line is the actual discounted set of cash flows from (3.3); orange is the 1-term Taylor from (3.4). The duration/convexity approximation works well in a much bigger neighborhood around 7% than the linear duration-only approximation.

So a default-free bond's duration is the main determinant of its behavior, and duration ties individual bonds to the behavior of the overall market (and the overall economy) through the prevailing level of interest rates. The idea of having a first-order approximation is not a bad one. It seems plausible that the major source of uncertainty in a bond's price is an indicator of the relative values of consumption now (encouraged by low interest rates) versus consumption later (encouraged by high interest rates), as represented by the general level of interest rates.

If life were this simple, the financial industry would not need legions of quantitative analysts to figure things out. There are two sources of divergence from first-order approximations. One is just having more terms in the Taylor series, which we've seen is helpful. But there are diminishing returns to the effort of expanding the Taylor series out further and further. For most practical purposes, only two terms of the Taylor series are used. Beyond that, it's usually best to use a full pricing function.

A bigger source of uncertainty not explained by the duration relationship is what's sometimes called "basis risk." This is the shorthand for the fact that sources of risk are multidimensional. We've assumed away most complications in our analysis so far, but in fact many factors can arise that affect the variables in the fundamental instrument description (3.1).

Even bonds issued by the same issuer – say, the US Treasury – can have different behaviors. For example, a close look at the language on the bond in Image 3.1 reveals that it had a five-year cleanup period at the end of its life (from 2002 to 2007) when it was callable by the US Treasury. As we've noted, that can cause negative, or at least less positive, convexity. That, in turn, will cause the price, duration, and convexity to differ from the simple formulas.

We also noted that there are on-the-run (newly issued) and off-the-run (seasoned) bonds. Generally, there is a premium for on-the-run bonds; they get more attention and therefore are easier to buy and sell than equivalent off-the-run bonds.

Those are a few reasons why even very similar bonds from the same issuer can have prices that differ from the formulas. When we bring in other issuers – even issuers considered default free – even more factors cause differences.

A very common method in fixed-income portfolio management is to look at a "portfolio duration," which is the weighted average of the durations of the individual bonds in the portfolio. Unfortunately, this first-order figure can be confusing, if not downright misleading. Other sources of risk in a portfolio will have relationships with the discount rate used to find duration. For example, during bad economic times the premium for on-the-run bonds generally increases because there's an even bigger desire for liquidity. At the same time, interest rates might be falling because the central bank might be trying to stimulate economic activity by lowering interest rates. Thus, portfolios of on-the-run bonds will react differently to interest rate drops than portfolios of off-the-run bonds, even if they have the same durations. In other economic environments, however, the relationships might shift. We will see in later chapters how to take into account multidimensional sources of risk.

3.5 Yield Curves

Prevailing interest rates paid by certain issuers or groups of issuers such as:

- the US Treasury
- US "GSEs" (Government-Sponsored Enterprises) like FNMA (Federal National Mortgage Association)[16]
- the Japanese government[17]
- the German government[18]
- the Chinese government inside mainland China ("onshore")[19]
- the Chinese government in Hong Kong ("offshore"), known as "Dim Sum" bonds[20]
- investment-grade European corporations[21]
- very shaky (CCC-rated) companies with a high chance of bankruptcy[22]
- state and local governments in the USA[23]
- securitized credit card receivables[24]

---

16 Fannie Mae. "Debt Securities." Website. www.fanniemae.com/portal/funding-the-market/debt/index.html.
17 Ministry of Finance, Japan. "Japanese Government Bonds." www.mof.go.jp/english/jgbs/.
18 Bundesrepublik Deutschland Finanzagentur GmbH. "Bund Fact Sheet." Website. www.deutsche-finanzagentur.de/fileadmin/user_upload/Institutionelle-investoren/auktionen/bund_fact_sheet.pdf.
19 [Samouilhan 2021].
20 [Lockett and Leng 2022].
21 S&P Dow Jones Indices. "S&P Eurozone Investment Grade Corporate Bond Index." Website. https://us.spindices.com/indices/fixed-income/sp-eurozone-investment-grade-corporate-bond-index.
22 Fred.stlouisfed.org, "ICE BofA CCC & Lower U.S. High Yield Effective Yield." Website. https://fred.stlouisfed.org/series/BAMLH0A3HYCEY.
23 S&P Dow Jones Indices. "S&P Municipal Bond Index." Website. https://us.spindices.com/indices/fixed-income/sp-municipal-bond-index.
24 [Furletti 2022].

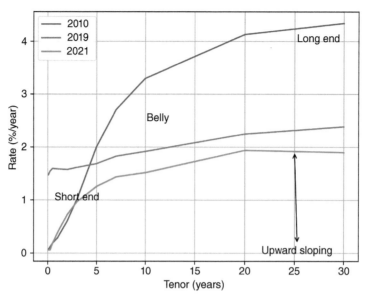

Figure 3.7 US yearend Treasury curves.

- bonds with payoffs related to the intensity of hurricanes in Florida ("cat bonds,"[25] where "cat" means catastrophe) ...

are gathered regularly into datasets called **yield curves.**

For simplicity in our previous analysis, we assumed that $r_t = r_{i,t}$ for all i; that is, the discount rate was the same at all maturities. (This is called a **flat curve.**) That's rarely true.

A yield curve graph has time to maturity on the X-axis, and an interest rate on the Y-axis. Code Segment 3.7 generates Figure 3.7, which graphs the US Treasury yield curve at the ends of the years shown. Code Segment 3.7 also prints the rates in the most recent yearend curve:

```
Most recent yearend curve (2021-12-31)
1MO 0.06
3MO 0.06
6MO 0.19
1 0.39
2 0.73
3 0.97
5 1.26
7 1.44
10 1.52
20 1.94
30 1.9
```

25 NAIC Center for Insurance Policy and Research. "Catastrophe Bonds." Website. https:// content.naic.org/cipr-topics/catastrophe-bonds.

Features of Yield Curves

Figure 3.7 shows that rates for **short-term** loans (often considered to be less than 2 years[26]) are called the **short end** of the curve. The US Treasury calls its borrowings in this maturity range bills.[27] The middle (or, more viscerally, the **belly**) of the yield curve (which we consider to be 2 to 15 years) comprises rates for **intermediate-term** loans, which the US Treasury calls notes.[28] **Long-term** loans (which we consider to be 15 years or more) are in the **long end** of the curve; the US Treasury calls these bonds.[29] In previous sections we have used the term "bond" to generally refer to a lending agreement of any length, but these terms are more precise. These are often abbreviated to T-bill, T-note, and T-bond.

The 2010 and 2021 curves in Figure 3.7 are atypical in that short-term interest rates on the left side of the curve are practically zero. These were results of the Global Financial Crisis ("GFC") of 2007–2009 and of the COVID-19 pandemic starting in 2020. Both saw economic activity slow dramatically. As we've noted above, the central bank can encourage present economic activity by forcing risk-free rates lower. From December 2008 to December 2015, the US Federal Reserve pushed short-term rates to the lowest possible positive notch (.25%). In December 2015, the economy was deemed healthy enough so that maximal encouragement of current spending was no longer needed, and the Fed began raising its targets for short-term rates. But in March 2020, short-term rates were again slashed to near zero in response to the COVID-19 pandemic.

The US Treasury curves in Figure 3.7 were upward-sloping – the longer the maturity, the higher the yield. That is generally an indicator that the bond market thinks there will be economic growth, or at least inflation, in the future. In late 2010, the 10 year minus 1 year slope was near the all-time steeps,[30] indicating a bond market belief that the economic future would be more robust, or at least more inflationary, than the present.

An animated version of US yield curves going back to the late 1990s has been called "five minutes to a complete understanding of recent US economic history." This is a bit of an exaggeration, but it is quite informative to see how yield curves reshape and move up and down over time. Major events like the US Federal reserve interventions after the 2008 and COVID-19 crises

---

26 There isn't any universal definition of the maturity ranges that comprise short, intermediate, and long. For example, we consider the boundary between short and intermediate to be two years, but some authors say the boundary between short and intermediate is at three years.

27 Treasury Direct®. "Treasury Bills." Website. `www.treasurydirect.gov/indiv/products/prod_tbills_glance.htm`.

28 Treasury Direct®. "Treasury Notes." Website. `www.treasurydirect.gov/indiv/products/prod_tnotes_glance.htm`.

29 Treasury Direct®. "Treasury Bonds." Website. `www.treasurydirect.gov/indiv/products/prod_tbonds_glance.htm`.

30 The all-time-high 1–10 steepness was 3.53% on April 5, 2010. By the end of 2011, the 1–10 steepness had fallen to 1.77%.

are clearly visible. Touch the "animate" button at `https://stockcharts.com/freecharts/yieldcurve.php`.

Figure 3.7 just used straight-line interpolation between data points supplied by the Treasury, but the Treasury itself uses a smoothing algorithm so that there is a continuous yield function $y(m)$, where m is the maturity. Historically a quasi-cubic hermite spline function was used, but on December 6, 2021, the Treasury shifted to a monotone convex method:[31]

> The [Monotone Convex] method begins with secondary market prices converted to yields and used to bootstrap the instantaneous forward rates at the input maturity points so that these instruments are sequentially priced without error. The initial step is followed by a monotone convex interpolation performed on forward rates midway between the input points to construct the entire interest rate curve. This fitting minimizes the price error on the initial price input points, resulting in a true par curve.

As of December 31, 2021, there were 83 US Treasury bills, 324 Treasury notes, and 209 US Treasury bonds classified as "marketable" outstanding.[32] (There were also 128 TIPS issues and 24 floating-rate notes with coupons that change based on the most recent 3-month T-bill rate.) While this is a large number, many of these issues are seasoned. The Treasury prefers not to use seasoned bonds for yield curve construction. So, for example, there might not be any actual newly issued 15-year maturity Treasury bond whose observable price would determine a 15-year yield for the Treasury's curve. Instead, there might be 10-year and 20-year on-the-run issues to observe, and the Treasury would use a spline algorithm fitted to the 10- and 20-year rates to infer a 15-year rate.

3.5.2 Zero Curves and Par Curves

To explain the reference to a **par curve** in the quote above from the US Treasury, we'll start with the far more sensible concept of a **zero curve**, sometimes called a **spot curve**. Suppose there were 360 zero-coupon bonds issued by the US Treasury, maturing 1 month from now, 2 months from now, ..., 30 years from now. In that case, we could take the 360 observations $z_t = (100/Z_t)^{12/t} - 1$, where Z_t is the current price of the zero that will pay \$100, t months in the future. Each z_t would be the market's annualized discount rate for cash flows scheduled to occur at time $t/12$ years in the future. Since in practice not all 360 observations exist, a smoothing algorithm can be used to fill in the curve between actual observations.

31 U.S. Department of the Treasury. "Yield Curve Methodology Change Information Sheet." Website. `https://home.treasury.gov/policy-issues/financing-the-government/yield-curve-methodology-change-information-sheet`.

32 U.S. Treasury Monthly Statement of the Public Debt. "Detail of Treasury Securities Outstanding." December 31, 2021. Website. `https://fiscaldata.treasury.gov/datasets/monthly-statement-public-debt/detail-of-treasury-securities-outstanding`.

Such a spot curve could be used as a discount curve, and it would have the power of arbitrage behind it. If some other default-free instrument had US dollar cash flows that were not being discounted at rates z_t, then an arbitrage portfolio could be formed. For example, if the instrument was too cheap according to the zero curve, then the arbitrage would buy the instrument and sell zero-coupon bonds in amounts matching the instrument's cash flows and flow times. This would be (to within the practical limits of arbitrage, including costs and other frictions) a riskless arbitrage.

Fortunately for the US taxpayer, the US Treasury does not borrow so often that there are always 360 perfectly spaced zero-coupon bonds to observe over the next 30 years. Sometimes "strips" can be used – a dealer (or sometimes the Treasury itself[33]) buys a coupon Treasury bond and then issues two certificates based on that bond: a "PO" (principal-only) certificate that entitles the holder to just the final principal repayment and an "IO" (interest-only) certificate that entitles the holder to just the coupon payments. The PO is equivalent to a zero-coupon bond and its traded price can be used to get zero rates.

However, even after taking into account these synthetic instruments, zeroes are not as heavily traded or as widely available in different maturities as are coupon bonds. So a process called **bootstrapping** is used to infer a zero curve from yields (internal rates of return) on coupon-paying bonds.

To illustrate bootstrapping, suppose that instead of 360 zero-coupon bonds maturing every month for the next 30 years, there are 360 coupon-paying bonds with the same maturities and monthly coupons. First, consider the coupon bond maturing in one month: it has no cash flows between now and maturity. The combination of the coupon payment c_1 and the principal payment 100 at maturity is indistinguishable[34] from a single payment of $100 + c_1$ at maturity. Thus this bond is effectively a zero-coupon bond. If the bond is currently priced at P_1, the annualized one-month point on the bootstrapped zero curve is $z_1 = ((100 + c_1)/P_1)^{12} - 1$.

Next, consider the two-month maturity coupon-paying bond. For this instrument there's a coupon c_2 one month from now, and another coupon c_2 (along with a principal repayment of $100) two months from now. This bond has some currently observable price P_2 in the market. So the generic pricing equation (3.2) can be used to find z_2:

$$z_2 = \left(\frac{100 + c_2}{P_2 - \frac{c_2}{(1+z_1)^{1/12}}} \right)^{12/2} - 1. \tag{3.9}$$

33 Treasury Direct®. "Separate Trading of Registered Interest and Principal of Securities (STRIPS)." Website. www.treasurydirect.gov/marketable-securities/strips/.

34 Coupons and principal may be treated differently for tax purposes, but an adjustment can be made to account for this.

Everything on the RHS of (3.9) is known, giving the LHS which is the pure discount rate z_2 for cash flows occurring at 2 months and at no other time. An entire spot curve can be derived by continuing this process, deriving each z_t from the par curve and the previously derived set of $\{z_1, \ldots, z_{t-1}\}$. The cash flows don't usually line up as nicely as in our example, but with smooth interpolation techniques a spot curve can be reasonably filled in.

The assumption behind an internal rate of return calculation such as (3.3) is that all cash flows associated with an instrument are discounted at the same rate. That would mean that cash received 10 years from now as a coupon payment on a 20-year bond gets discounted differently from cash received 10 years from now as the final return of principal on a 10-year bond. That could lead to arbitrages.

On the other hand, the bootstrap process – or direct observation of zeroes, if available – forms a more consistent zero curve. Each time period gets its own discount rate.

The par curve is probably a legacy of pre-computer days.[35] When a bond is priced at par (price=principal amount), then its coupon rate is the same as its internal rate of return. Today it's trivial to compute an IRR with an iterative process, but before computers, it wasn't. So if there is a representative set of bonds priced at (or close to) par, a yield curve can be constructed just by observing their coupons. While such par curves are easy to construct, they suffer from the inconsistency in IRRs pointed out above.

Despite this inconsistency, par curves are still widely used, probably due to historical inertia. To make up for the dearth of bonds pricing at par, a process is used to create virtual coupon-paying bonds using a zero curve. For every time T (say, every 6 months for 30 years), a virtual coupon-paying bond is constructed, one that pays a constant coupon $c_T/2$ every 6 months for T years, with a final payment of 100 at maturity at T. The cash flows on this bond are discounted to the present using the (bootstrapped) zero curve. Then the coupon rate c_T is iteratively adjusted until the price of the bond is par ($100). The rates c_T form the par curve.

If a real coupon bond whose market price was close to $100 was used in the bootstrapping process to form the zero curve, then – assuming the process didn't interpolate too much – the real bond's coupon rate should be consistent with the virtual par curve's rates. Virtual par curves are often used as a reporting convention because many participants in the fixed-income markets are used to thinking in par curve terms.

---

35 Interest rates have been recorded for a long time: "Old Sumerian documents, circa 3000 B.C., reveal . . . loans of grain by volume and loans of metal by weight. Often these loans carried interest." [Homer and Sylla 2005], p. 17.

3.5.3 Types of Yield Curves

There are many kinds of interest rate curves in common use:

- Yield curves obtained from internal rates of return required to match market-observed prices of bonds, usually coupon paying;
- Zero or spot curves of yields of zero-coupon bonds, or of artificial zero-coupon bonds created from the bootstrap process shown above;
- Discount curves – the rates used to discount cash flows at various times in the future to bring them back to the present; usually these are the same as zero or spot rates;
- Forward curves – the future rates implied by today's curve; these will be discussed below;
- Short-rate curves – instantaneous forward rates; that is, the 5-year point on the short-rate curve is the annualized rate from 5 years to 5 years plus one microsecond from now; these will be discussed below.
- Par curves – coupon rates required to make a hypothetical coupon-paying bond price at par (100) if each of its cash flows is discounted at the rates implied by a zero curve. A par curve can also be a yield curve (IRRs formed from observed prices) of bonds pricing close to par – that's actually what the US Treasury uses.

Current fixed-income analytic software often inputs a par curve but then bootstraps it internally to a spot curve before using the rates to discount cash flows. This is strange since the par curve had to be constructed from the spot curve in the first place. Further, durations are sometimes defined with respect to a par curve, leading to discrepancies, like 25-year maturity bonds with 25.5-year durations.

3.5.4 Yield Curves and Economic Conditions

The rate curves in Figure 3.7 were all upward sloping – longer maturities meant higher rates (i.e. if $y(m)$ is the function giving the yield for maturity m in one of these curves, then $y'(m) \geq 0$). But this isn't always true. Figure 3.8 (generated by Code Segment 3.8) shows the US Treasury yield curve on January 2, 2001.

This curve is downward sloping ("inverted") from 0–5 years and then mostly flat to about 15 years. In particular, the 10-year rate is lower than rates up to about 1 year. This unusual curve shape in January 2001 was followed by an economic recession in March of 2001.

In fact, the relationship between inverted curves and subsequent recessions is very strong. Figure 3.9 (generated by Code Segment 3.9) shows "steepness," which is defined here as the difference between the 10-year Treasury rate and the 3-month Treasury rate. There are many parts of the curve that can be examined for slope, but this is a fairly common one.

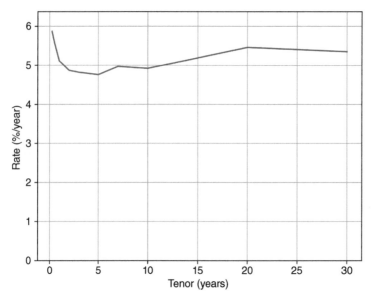

Figure 3.8 US Treasury curve, 2001-01-02.

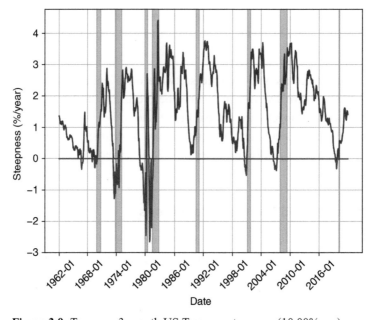

Figure 3.9 Ten-year, 3-month US Treasury steepness (10.00%neg).

The gray-shaded areas in Figure 3.9 are business contractions as defined by the National Bureau of Economic Research.[36] Each shaded area is preceded by an inverted curve (negative steepness). These data are monthly: even the 1990

---

36 National Bureau of Economic Research. "US Business Cycle Expansions and Contractions." Website. `www.nber.org/cycles/cyclesmain.html`.

recession was preceded by an inverted curve when taking into account intramonth data. There is one false positive, or perhaps just an early warning, in the 1960s.

Kessel (1971) noted – using US data from the 1920s to the 1960s – that term structure moves with the business cycle. This idea was refined by Campbell Harvey in his 1986 PhD thesis (written up in a 1988 journal article) and subsequently:[37] he showed that inverted real yield curves were excellent predictors of real recessions. The decades since 1986 have provided an excellent out-of-sample test of the inverted-curve prediction hypothesis, which has acquitted itself brilliantly.

Harvey and others saw the inversion of the yield curve as an accurate sentiment indicator:

- The US Treasury 10-year bond is considered the safest and most liquid asset in the world. When investors fear a crisis or recession, there is a flight to the safety of this bond, driving 10-year rates down.
- At the same time that investors may be fearing future bad times, the central bank may be fearing an unsustainable overheated economy. Usually the central bank raises short-term rates to cool things down in this situation, inverting the curve even more.
- The capital moved into bonds is not being put at risk in developing new software, new pharmaceuticals, new factories, exacerbating (or even causing) a slowdown in the economy.

In fact, as Figure 3.9 shows, the inverted-curve predictor has been near-perfect, which has made it something of a self-fulfilling prophecy.

3.5.5 Rolldown and Key Rate Durations

Figure 3.9 shows that since 1980, the US rate curve was usually upward sloping (10-year rate greater than 1-year rate), but about 10% of the time it was not. As pointed out above, recessions have been reliably preceded by the steepness dipping below zero, that is, inverted curves.

So it's fortunate that US rate curves have been upward sloping about 90% of the time. Upward slope allows a nice feature called **rolldown**. Suppose an investor buys a 10-year bond today and – as is usually the case with an upward-sloping curve – 7-year rates are lower than 10-year rates. What happens to the price of the investor's bond in 3 years? While of course lots of things could happen to change the yield curve in those 3 years, if nothing happens then the bond will be discounted at a lower rate in 3 years than it is now. Since lower discount rates mean higher prices, the tendency will be for the price of the bond to rise.

---

37 [Harvey 1988]. Harvey has written extensively on term structure and the economy over the course of his career. For a summary of his work in this area, see http://people.duke.edu/~charvey/research_term_structure.htm.

There are different conventions for quantifying the rolldown effect, but one common metric is $y'(T) \cdot P \cdot T$, where y' is the slope of the yield curve at the bond's time to maturity T, and P is the bond's price. For example consider the year-end 2010 curve in Figure 3.7. The 10-year rate was 3.3% and the 7-year rate was 2.71%. Using simple linear interpolation, the slope at 10 years was $(3.3\% - 2.71\%)/3 = 20\text{bps}$ per year. (A basis point or "bp" is one one-hundredth of a percent.) If a 10-year bond was priced at $90, then its annual rolldown would be 20 bps/year times $90 ties 10 years, or $1.80. Of course, as Figure 3.7 shows, the curve is constantly undergoing reshaping, so rolldown is only an instantaneous expectation.

So far, then, we have seen two big economic risk factors that are reflected in the shape of the yield curve:

- The overall level of the yield curve is an indicator of the economy's trade-off between present consumption and future consumption; and
- The slope of the yield curve is an indicator of an expectation of growth or slowdown in the future.

We estimated some of the risk that variations in the present consumption/future consumption factor (as reflected in the overall level of rates) pose to a bond's price by computing the bond's duration. We could take that process further and use **key rate durations**, which are a sensitivity to the change in a particular part of the yield curve. So instead of having to assume $r_{i,t} = r_t$ for all i in (3.2), we could just take derivatives of price with respect to each $r_{i,t}$ separately. A bond with no cash flows at or near 7 years would have zero 7-year key rate duration, but if it had cash flows at 8 years, then there would be some response to changes in the 8-year rate and the 8-year key rate duration would be nonzero.

How much precision in key rate durations is too much? The two big economic risk factors noted above cause at least two degrees of freedom in movements of yield curves. On the other hand, if we take 30 key rate durations from 30 points on the yield curve, we might be trying to squeeze too much information out of the yield curve.

Litterman and Scheinkman (1991) pointed out that duration and convexity exposures assume a single, constant interest rate and seek to determine a bond's sensitivity to it. However, they note that rates at different maturities can move differently, perhaps even in opposite directions.

Litterman and Scheinkman (1991) note that there appear to be the three main determinants of the shape of the yield curve noted above:

- Level: This is the general level of interest rates, where all rates go up or down by the same amount.
- Steepness or slope: This is how rapidly the yield curve goes up (or down) from short rates to longer rates.

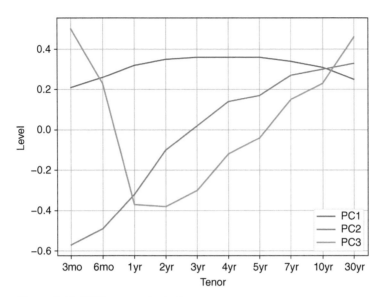

Figure 3.10 UST curve principal components.

- Curvature or twist: This is a butterfly shape that occurs between short-, medium-, and long-term rates.

It is possible to take a time series of interest rates at different maturities and form a covariance matrix between them. Principal components analysis (Section 6.5 in Chapter 6) can then be applied. For most yield curves (US Treasury, other sovereigns, other types of bonds), the first three components explain over 90 percent of the variation in the covariance matrix. The eigenvectors associated with the largest eigenvalues have weights that agree with the level, steepness, and curvature interpretation. The eigenvalues are far larger than random matrix theory would suggest.

The data in Code Segment 3.10 are taken from Frye (2005) and are based on US Treasury rates for 1,543 days from 1989 and 1995. Code Segment 3.10 uses these data to produce Figure 3.10, which clearly shows a roughly straight line for PC1, an increasing line for PC2, and a twist for PC3. These are consistent with the intuitive explanations.

3.5.6 Interpolation and Smoothing Techniques

We've noted that smoothing techniques are used to create continuous curves. The US Treasury uses a monotone convex spline method. This matches beginning and end points and tangents at each knot point; the knot points are mainly those maturities where the Treasury was able to observe an on-the-run bond's price.

Another approach that is less highly fitted was pioneered by Nelson and Siegel (1987). If $r(0,f)$ is the smoothed yield (r = rate) for a zero-coupon bond starting now (time $t = 0$) and going to some final maturity time $t = f$ in the future, then Nelson–Siegel's smoothed version of $r(0,f)$ is:

$$r(0,f) = \beta_0 + \beta_1 \frac{\tau}{f}\left(1 - \exp\left(-\frac{f}{\tau}\right)\right) + \beta_2 \frac{\tau}{f}\left(1 - \exp\left(-\frac{f}{\tau}\right)\left(1 + \frac{f}{\tau}\right)\right).$$
(3.10)

While later examples of this class of smoothing techniques use more parameters, the Nelson–Siegel version uses the four parameters $\beta_0, \beta_1, \beta_2,$ and τ, which can be fitted to observed input yields $y_1, \ldots, y_k$ at maturity times $t_1, \ldots, t_k$ to provide in most cases a good fit.

The expression (3.10) is a linear combination of three functions that capture the level, slope, and twist factors observed by Litterman and Scheinkman. Let $t = \frac{f}{\tau}$ be the scaled tenor. Then:

- Level is a constant function of scaled tenor t;
- Slope is the function $\frac{1-\exp(-t)}{t}$; and
- Twist is the function $\frac{1-\exp(-t)(1+t)}{t}$.

Figure 3.11 (generated by Code Segment 3.11) shows these three component functions. Up to scaling and translation, they look very similar to the three components shown in Figure 3.10.

The Nelson–Siegel curve is simply β_0 times level, plus β_1 times slope, plus β_2 times twist. Intuitively:

- As $f \to \infty$, all terms except for β_0 approach zero, so β_0 is the yield level at the long end of the curve.

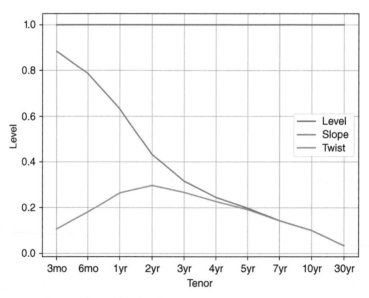

Figure 3.11 Nelson–Siegel components.

- As $f \to 0$, $r(0,f)$ approaches $\beta_0 + \beta_1$, so β_1 is the opposite of the slope between the level of the curve at the short (instantaneous) end and the level of the curve at the long end.
- β_2 determines yield levels in the middle (belly) of the curve.
- τ controls how fast the levels transition from short end to belly to long end.

Diebold and Li (2006) used a Nelson–Siegel framework to predict future US Treasury rates. They noted that the limited number of parameters in the Nelson–Siegel approach was similar in spirit to the three usual factors (level, slope, curvature), for example, in Litterman–Scheinkman. Using time series techniques, Diebold and Li fitted time-varying parameters to the Nelson–Siegel model and showed that six-month-ahead and one-year-ahead forecasts of interest rates were generally better than competing forecasting methods.

3.6 Implied Forward Curves

Fixed-income investors are concerned about the possible ranges of future interest rates. We've seen that interest rates at different maturities are neither all the same nor completely unrelated. The original simplifying assumption that $r_{i,t} = r_t$ for all i in (3.2) was good to gain initial intuition, but not realistic: 30-year interest rates are clearly quite different from 1-year interest rates.

On the other hand, yield curves are not just databases listing observations of unrelated instruments. We've seen that there are only about three significant principal components in a covariance matrix of interest rates, so there are strong connections between rates at different maturities. And, as Figure 3.5 showed, the shape of the yield curve (including its average level) can be different at different times.

In order to have a good model of the probability distribution of future prices of fixed-income instruments, we need to have a good model of the probability distributions of yield curves as they evolve into the future.

To find such models, we'll start by introducing the notation $r(s,f)$ for the yield on a zero-coupon bond starting at time s in the future (or present if $s = 0$) and maturing at time $f \geq s$. Rates that look like $r(0,f)$ are called **spot rates**. They are known now or "on the spot." (This is confusing since as we saw above, a "spot curve" is the same as a zero curve, so the word "spot" has two different meanings that have to be resolved by context.) Rates that look like $r(s,f)$ where $s > 0$ are called **forward rates** and are not known today.

Forward rates are in full generality stochastic. However, the current yield curve contains a prediction of what the yield curve will be in the future. This prediction is similar to the risk-neutral market expectation of the price of Beyond Vegetables; it contains a mash-up of expected values and compensation for the risk that reinvestment in a future bond will not be at the anticipated rate.

To compute the implied forward curve, let $Z(0,f) = \frac{1}{(1+r(0,f))^f}$ (discrete) or $Z(0,f) = \exp(-r(0,f) \cdot f)$ (continuous) be the currently observable cost of a zero-coupon bond bought now and maturing at 1 at time f in the future. Let $Z(s,f)$ be the currently unknown cost of a zero bought at time s in the future and maturing at 1 at time f in the future. Its cost will be $\frac{1}{(1+r(s,f))^{f-s}}$ (discrete) or $\exp(-r(s,f) \cdot (f-s))$ (continuous).

Consider the following actions:

1. Buy a fraction $Z(0,1) \cdot Z(1,2)$ of a zero now and maturing one year from now. When that matures, it will be worth $Z(1,2)$.
2. Invest that amount $Z(1,2)$ in what will then be the current one-year zero, whose rate today is denoted $r(1,2)$. When that matures, it will be worth 1.

Equivalently,

3. Invest $Z(0,2)$ in a two-year zero now. That will also give 1 two years from now.

Thus, the implied price for a one-year zero one year from now is $Z(1,2) = Z(0,2)/Z(0,1)$. In general, we have (using the discrete convention):

$$Z(s,f) = \frac{1}{(1+r(s,f))^{f-s}} = \frac{Z(0,f)}{Z(0,s)} = \frac{\frac{1}{(1+r(0,f))^f}}{\frac{1}{(1+r(0,s))^s}}, \tag{3.11}$$

$$r(s,f) = \frac{(1+r(0,f))^{\frac{f}{f-s}}}{(1+r(0,s))^{\frac{s}{f-s}}} - 1. \tag{3.12}$$

Or, using the continuous convention:

$$Z(s,f) = \exp(-r(s,f)(f-s)) = \frac{Z(0,f)}{Z(0,s)} = \frac{\exp(-r(0,f)f)}{\exp(-r(0,s)s)}, \tag{3.13}$$

$$r(s,f) = r(0,f)\frac{f}{f-s} - r(0,s)\frac{s}{f-s}. \tag{3.14}$$

For the rest of this chapter, it will be more convenient to use continuous discounting $\exp(-rt)$ rather than discrete discounting $(1+r)^{-t}$.

In a risk-neutral world, the implied $r(s,f)$ would simply be the aggregate market estimate of what the $(f-s)$-maturity rate will be, s years from now. Market participants who thought the implied rate was too low – that is, the time-zero implied price of $Z(s,f)$ was too high – would sell short a bond maturing at time f at a price of $Z(0,f)$, and buy $Z(0,s)Z(s,f)$ bonds maturing at time s, for net zero expenditure. At time s in the future, their long position would be worth $Z(s,f)$, but if they were right they would then be able to buy a zero maturing at time f for less than that, netting a profit. Investors with the opposite belief would do the opposite. Through these actions, the current prices of zeroes would match the aggregate belief as to what $r(s,f)$ will be, s years from now.

This is called the **expectations hypothesis**: the idea that the implied forward curve reflects expectations of future rates. But we're not in a risk-neutral world. Investors will demand compensation for the reinvestment risk; that is, there will be a range of outcomes s years from now if they set up the offsetting trades in actions 1 and 2 versus action 3 above. The time-zero implied rate $r(s,f)$ may turn out to be either lower or higher than expected.

While the implied forward curve given by (3.14) is not the result of a riskless arbitrage, it is still a useful object as it shows a risk-adjusted market expectation of the future. As we noted, smoothing techniques are applied to the finite number of observations on actual curves to make a continuous yield function, which in our notation here is $r(0,f)$. Then (3.14) is applied for a given value of s to form the "s forward curve."[38] For example, we can compute the one-month, one-quarter, one-year, and so on implied forward curves.

Before we proceed to model the evolution of yield curves, we'll set down some stochastic process terminology.

3.7 Stochastic Process Terminology

A *stochastic process* is a sequence of indexed random variables $\{x_t\}$, together with a rule for the evolution of the process as the index t (usually time) increases. A common kind of stochastic process is a **diffusion**:

$$dx_t = \alpha dt + \sigma d\beta_t. \tag{3.15}$$

To gain intuition, it is helpful to think of (3.15) as an algorithm running over small finite time increments, which says:

> Start at the current time $t = 0$ with a known value x_0. To generate $x_{t+dt} - x_t = dx_t$ (where dt is a small time increment), generate a random number $d\beta_t$; scale that random number by σ; and add α times the time interval dt.

In the limit, dt can go to zero and this becomes a continuous process. In finance, x_t might be an interest rate or the logarithm of a price. Without the random term, (3.15) would be a simple differential equation whose solution is $x_t = \alpha t + x_0$. So α indicates how much the process drifts up or down over time.

But the other term introduces a random process $d\beta_t$. The term "diffusion" used to describe (3.15) means that $d\beta_t$ is a **white noise process**. That means that there is an underlying cdf $F(x)$ that has mean zero and variance equal to dt; often but not necessarily this is a normal distribution. In a white noise process, (a) each $d\beta_t$ (for all t) is distributed according to the common cdf $F(x)$; and (b) for $s \neq t$, $\mathbb{E}[d\beta_s d\beta_t] = 0$, that is, different time periods are uncorrelated. In most cases, it is further assumed that different time periods are independent, that is, that

---

38 Our definition of an s-forward curve is the set of $r(s,f)$ where $f \geq s$. Another convention (which we will not use) is that the x-forward curve is the set of $r(s, s+x)$ for some fixed term x.

the joint distribution $F_{s,t}(x,y)$ of $d\beta_s$ and $d\beta_t$ for $s \neq t$ are equal to $F_s(x)F_t(y)$. When independence holds in addition to a common cdf, the process is said to be **independent and identically distributed ("i.i.d.")**.

The idea here is to assume that news from the world that affects financial variables is a form of Knightian Risk: we don't necessarily know what the next piece of news will be but we know that the way it affects our variable (price, interest rates, etc.) is described by the distribution of $d\beta$. So without knowing the next thing that's going to happen, we assume that we do know the range of things that can happen and their probabilities.

More generally, the parameters of the stochastic process (3.15) can be functions:

$$dx = \alpha(t,x)dt + \sigma(t,x)d\beta. \qquad (3.16)$$

(Here we have dropped the "t" subscripts on x and β; they are usually kept implicit if the meaning is clear from context.) $d\beta$ is a white noise process.

For example, a widely used process looks at the evolution of percentage changes in price rather than the price itself, so $\alpha(t,x) = \alpha \cdot x$ and $\sigma(t,x) = \sigma \cdot x$ (where the standalone α and σ are scalar constants), giving:

$$\frac{dx}{x} = \alpha dt + \sigma d\beta. \qquad (3.17)$$

Thus, if $x_t = 100$ and $x_{t+dt} = 101$, the LHS is 1%.

Let x be a process following (3.16) and let f be a twice-differentiable function. Then the chain rule and a Taylor series expansion to two terms says:

$$df(t,x) = \frac{\partial f}{\partial t}dt + \frac{\partial f}{\partial x}dx + \frac{1}{2}\frac{\partial^2 f}{\partial x^2}dx^2 + \frac{\partial^2 f}{\partial t \partial x}dtdx + \frac{1}{2}\frac{\partial^2 f}{\partial t^2}dt^2. \qquad (3.18)$$

Terms of the order of dt^2 and $dt \cdot d\beta$ are vanishingly small, and in a white noise process by definition $(d\beta)^2 = dt$. So we can rearrange (3.18) to say

$$df(t,x) = \left(\frac{\partial f}{\partial t} + \alpha(t,x)\frac{\partial f}{\partial x} + \frac{\sigma^2(t,x)}{2}\frac{\partial^2 f}{\partial x^2}\right)dt + \sigma(t,x)\frac{\partial f}{\partial x}d\beta. \qquad (3.19)$$

Equation (3.19) is known as Itô's Lemma,[39] and is often used in mathematical finance.

The most common use of Itô's Lemma in finance is with (3.17). Let $f(x) = \ln(x)$. Then the derivative of f with respect to time t is 0 since there aren't any t terms in f. The first derivative with respect to x is $1/x$, and the second derivative is $-1/x^2$.

---

39 [Protter 2005], p. 81. Protter, along with most other stochastic processes texts, presents an integral version of "Itô's formula." Taking derivatives of the integral formula produces the form shown in (3.19).

Putting those terms into (3.19) shows that if (3.17) holds; then $d\ln(x) = \left(\alpha - \frac{\sigma^2}{2}\right)dt + \sigma d\beta$. This has the nice property that the coefficients on the RHS are constants. Equation (3.17) is called a **lognormal process** or a **geometric Brownian motion** when $d\beta$ samples from a normal distribution. Most securities are *positive assets*; that is, the worst that can happen if you have a long position in the security is that you can lose your whole investment; you won't owe money by virtue of a long position in the security. Lognormal processes are attractive models for positive assets because the worst that can happen to the logarithm is that it's $-\infty$, which corresponds to a zero value of x.

Another common stochastic process is an **Ornstein–Uhlenbeck process**.[40] This simulates a spring that can be expanded or contracted by random shocks, but that has an equilibrium point that it "wants" to return to.

$$dx = \lambda(K - x)dt + \sigma d\beta. \tag{3.20}$$

K is the equilibrium position of the spring. When $x = K$, there is no drift term so it doesn't "feel" too tight or too loose. If the spring is stretched beyond equilibrium $(x > K)$, then the term $(K - x)$ is negative so the spring has a tendency to return down to K at the next tick of the clock. Conversely, when the spring is compressed, $(K - x)$ is positive and the next tick of the clock will have a positive drift, giving the spring a tendency to expand.

The positive parameter λ indicates how fast the spring snaps back: λ near zero is a weak spring; while very large λ is a tight spring. So σ is the usual volatility parameter, and $d\beta$ is the usual i.i.d. white noise process – mean 0, standard deviation $\sqrt{t}$, often assumed normal.

A **Markov process** is a stochastic process with no memory: the conditional probability distribution given all previous observations is the same as the conditional probability distribution given only the most recent observation.

$$Pr(X_t = v_t \mid X_{t-1} = v_{t-1}, \ldots, X_0 = v_0] = Pr(X_t = v_t \mid X_{t-1} = v_{t-1}]. \tag{3.21}$$

A **martingale** is a process where knowing the past doesn't help you win. More precisely, a martingale is a stochastic process $\{X_t\}$ (discrete time is OK for our purposes) where the expected value of the absolute value of each X_t is finite, and

$$\mathbb{E}[X_t \mid X_0, \ldots, X_{t-1}] = X_{t-1}. \tag{3.22}$$

While they are similar in concept, neither Markov nor martingale implies the other. Cumulative tosses of a biased coin (X_t = number of heads observed $-$number of tails observed after t^{th} toss) is Markov but not a martingale. On the other hand, suppose X_t is generated from cumulative tosses of a fair coin where

---

40 [Protter 2005], p. 98 (exercise 27).

the payoff is $+1/-1$ for heads/tails if the previous outcome was a tail; and $+2/-2$ for heads/tails if the previous outcome was a head. Then X_t is a martingale but is not a Markov process.

3.8 Term Structure Models

Yield curve models – also called models of the term structure of interest rates – are stochastic processes intended to produce realistic evolutions of an entire yield curve into the future.

A key desire in fixed income is that the term structure be sensible and consistent. We could model each interest rate (1 day, 1 month, 1 year, 5 year, 10 year...) separately and link them together. There is a class of models that do that, but in this chapter we will look at another class of models that use the "short rate" to enforce consistency.

Let $r(t, T)$ denote the current $(t = 0)$ or forward $(t > 0)$ rate of a zero starting at time t and maturing at time $T \geq t$. The **implied short rate** (also called the **implied instantaneous rate**) at time t is $r(t, t)$: the rate of return obtained in the limit on a very short interval of time starting at t:

$$r(t,t) = \lim_{\Delta t \to 0} r(t, t + \Delta t) = \lim_{\Delta t \to 0} r(t - \Delta t, t). \tag{3.23}$$

This assumes that for each t, the two limits in (3.23) are defined, equal, and finite.

Using $s = t$ and $f = t + \Delta t$ (where Δt is a small increment of time) in (3.14) gives (assuming limits and derivatives are well defined):

$$r(t, t + \Delta t) = r(0, t + \Delta t)\frac{t + \Delta t}{\Delta t} - r(0, t)\frac{t}{\Delta t},$$

$$r(t, t + \Delta t) = r(0, t + \Delta t) + t\frac{r(0, t + \Delta t) - r(0, t)}{\Delta t},$$

and

$$r(t,t) = \lim_{\Delta t \to 0} r(t, t + \Delta t) = r(0, t) + t\frac{dr(0, t)}{dt}. \tag{3.24}$$

Thus the implied short rate at some future time t can be expressed as the sum of the currently known rate at maturity t, plus t times the slope of the yield curve at maturity t. Equivalently for well-behaved functions:

$$r(0, t) = \frac{1}{t} \int_0^t r(x, x)dx. \tag{3.25}$$

Figure 3.12 (generated by Code Segment 3.12) shows the latest yearend implied short-rate curve in orange; it's based on the monthly interpolated US Treasury curve in blue. A cubic Hermite spline is applied to the jagged piecewise linear curve that arises from the raw US Treasury data in order to smooth out the derivatives in (3.24).

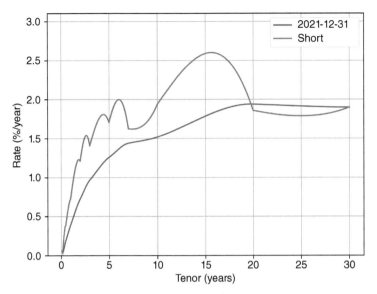

Figure 3.12 Smoothed US Treasury and short-rate curves.

Short-Rate Models: General Framework

A major class of term structure models is based on the assumption that implied short rates are Markovian, that is, the probability distribution of $\{r(\tau,\tau), \tau \geq t\}$ is completely determined by the value of $r(t,t)$ and not the path that was followed to $r(t,t)$. This is not necessarily true: another class of models called forward market models[41] are not Markovian. In this book, we will not study forward market models.

The Markov assumption seems to have first been made by Vasicek (1977), who pointed out that a continuous Markov process is a diffusion process, that is, a process of the form (3.15). Vasicek further assumed that what we have called $Z(s,f)$ (the price $Z(s,f)$ of a zero starting at time s in the future and maturing at 1 at time $f \geq s$) was only dependent on the assessment, at time s, of the set of short rates from time s to time f.

Let R be the random variable giving the short-rate starting at time s, so:

$$dR = \alpha(t,R)dt + \sigma(t,R)d\beta, \tag{3.26}$$

as in (3.16), but with some symbols changed. As we noted above, a stochastic process like (3.26) can be thought of as an algorithm that generates many random paths into the future. The outcome space Ω_s is the set of all paths taken by the short-rate R from starting time s to time f generated by the process (3.26).

---

41 See [Lyashenko and Mercurio 2019].

Let $\omega \in \Omega_s$ be such a path, and define:

$$\overline{R}(\omega) = \frac{1}{f-s} \int_s^f R_\omega(t)dt. \tag{3.27}$$

$\overline{R}$ is a random variable that maps ω into $\mathbb{R}$ by averaging the value of the realized short rate over the path ω. The integral on the right of (3.27) is deterministic given ω. The price of a zero conditional on path ω is $Z_\omega(s,f) = \exp(-(f-s)\overline{R}(\omega))$.

The unconditional expected price $Z(s,f)$ of the zero maturing at 1 at time f is the expected value over all ω of $Z_\omega(s,f)$, together with a risk adjustment. Vasicek shows (his equation 18) that we can write:

$$Z(s,f) = \mathbb{E}_{\Omega_s}\left[\exp\left(-(f-s)\overline{R}(\omega) - Rsk(s,f,\omega)\right)\right]. \tag{3.28}$$

Vasicek's risk adjustment random variable depends on a deterministic function $q(x,y)$ as follows:

$$Rsk(s,f,\omega) = \frac{1}{2}\int_s^f q^2(\tau, R_\omega(\tau))d\tau - \int_s^f q(\tau, R_\omega(\tau))d\beta_\omega. \tag{3.29}$$

While (3.29) covers a wide range of models, it often suffices to assume that the function $q(x,y)$ is a constant, which we will do from now on. That collapses (3.29) into a simpler expression:

$$Rsk(s,f,\omega) = \frac{1}{2}q^2(f-s) - q\int_s^f d\beta_\omega.$$

The first term is nonstochastic and the second term adds q to the σ function in (3.26). So under the assumption that q is a constant, the risk adjustment can be taken into account by making suitable translations of α and σ in (3.26), and we can assume

$$Z(s,f) = \mathbb{E}_{\Omega_s}\left[\exp\left(-(f-s)\overline{R}(\omega)\right)\right]. \tag{3.30}$$

3.8.2 Short-Rate Models: Specific Framework

In an example, Vasicek further assumed that (3.26) was an Ornstein–Uhlenbeck process. This was reasonable, because – like a spring – interest rates and volatilities also have some kind of equilibrium value. If not, then the economy in which they occur is probably broken. A functioning economy can't have interest rates going to infinity: that's hyperinflation,[42] which prevents money from fulfilling the functions listed in Section 1.5. There have been economies with hyperinflation and essentially worthless money, but they quickly stopped functioning altogether.

---

42 Michael K. Salemi, "Hyperinflation," Econlib website. www.econlib.org/library/Enc/
   Hyperinflation.html.

In the past, it was thought that a similar constraint was that nominal interest rates couldn't go negative except in very short technical disruptions. But we've already seen in Figure 3.3 that isn't true; there can be sustained periods of negative nominal (or, as Figure 3.2 shows, real) rates. However, it's generally thought that rates can't be *too* negative for the reasons discussed at the beginning of this chapter. So as we'll see, most modelers tried to put a zero lower bound on rates, or at least discourage them from going significantly below zero.

Vasicek's specific model for the short-rate $R(t)$ was:

$$dR = \lambda(R_\infty - R)dt + \sigma d\beta. \tag{3.31}$$

That's an Ornstein–Uhlenbeck process like (3.20). Here, R_∞ is the equilibrium position of the spring – a target short rate. As with other stochastic processes, (3.31) can be thought of as an algorithm that steps through time increments of dt, starting at $t = 0$ and generating $R(t + dt)$ once $R(t)$ is known.

Before running the algorithm, we need to choose $R(0)$, the current observable short rate. This could be an overnight Fed Funds rate.[43] We also need to choose R_∞, which doesn't have to be a constant. It can vary with time t as long as it's deterministic as we step through time increments. Vasicek actually envisioned a constant R_∞; time-varying R_∞ was introduced by Hull and White (1990). Thus, R_∞ can be the current implied short-rate curve. We choose λ (the spring stiffness) by observing how long it has taken rates to get back to their average historically, and σ, the volatility of shocks to the short rate also by historical observation. Finally, the length of the curve, say, $T = 30$ years, is chosen.

The algorithm runs like this:

1. Set $t = 0$ and decide on a time increment, maybe $dt = 1/12$ for a month.
2. Generate a draw from a white noise (say, standard normal) distribution. Plug it in as $d\beta$ to the RHS of (3.31). Fill in the rest of the RHS of (3.31) using the value of $R(t)$ from the previous iteration, or from observation if $t = 0$. That results in $dR = R(t + dt) - R(t)$, and hence $R(t + dt)$.
3. Increment $t = t + dt$. Repeat Step 2 until T years are generated. That is one path $\omega \in \Omega$, where Ω is the outcome space of all paths from 0 to T.
4. Generate a yield curve from the short curve: $y(t) = \frac{1}{t} \sum_{u=0}^{t} R(u) \cdot dt$. Thus, $y(t)$ is the $\overline{R}(\omega)$ (with $s = 0, f = t$) in (3.27) for this process.

The process can be repeated as many times as desired to generate as many yield curves as desired. These yield curves can then be used in Monte Carlo simulations (see Chapter 8) to price fixed-income instruments.

Let's try it. Using the most recent yearend yield curve and implied short-rate curve shown in Figure 3.12, we set $\lambda = 1$ and $\sigma = .05$ because they generate

---

43 Federal Reserve Bank of New York. "Effective Federal Funds Rate." Website. www.newyorkfed .org/markets/reference-rates/effr.

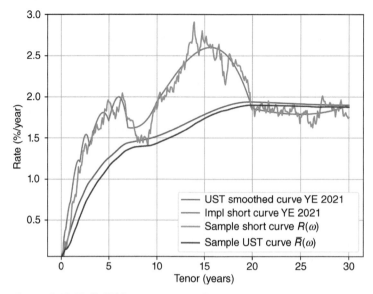

Figure 3.13 Hull–White curve generation.

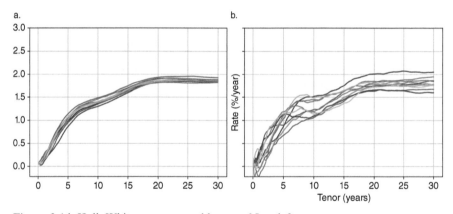

Figure 3.14 Hull–White curves, monthly $\sigma = .05$ and $.2$.

interesting patterns and not because they are particularly realistic. We put σ in monthly units in our example since $dt = 1/12$. Alternatively, we could put σ in annual terms and scale draws from $d\beta$ so they are month-ized, that is, multiply the standard draws by $\sqrt{dt}$.

Figure 3.13 (generated by Code Segment 3.13) shows a random path ω consisting of 360 monthly steps. The orange line is the implied short-rate curve we inferred from the last yearend par curve (which is in blue). We should have used a zero curve, but this suffices for illustrative purposes. The green line is the result of running 360 random draws through the (3.31) process, that is, a sample $R(\omega)$. The red line is the averaged values $\overline{R}(\omega)$ of the green line, giving a randomly drawn yield curve.

Ten randomly generated curves $y(t)$ via the Hull–White model (3.47) with $\lambda = 1$ are shown in Figure 3.14 (generated by Code Segment 3.14). One set has a low σ and one has a higher σ. This is a fairly tight spring. With a lower value of λ, a wider variety of curves would result – but then there would be a larger chance of negative rates.

3.8.3 Expected Value of the Vasicek Model

We can directly integrate the Vasicek process (3.31) after a change of variable $S = e^{\lambda t} R$:

$$d(e^{-\lambda t} S(t)) = \lambda(R_\infty - e^{-\lambda t} S(t) dt + \sigma d\beta \quad \text{and}$$

$$e^{-\lambda t} dS(t) = \lambda R_\infty dt + \sigma d\beta. \tag{3.32}$$

Integrating the differential equation for S and then shifting back to R gives:

$$S(t) = S(0) + R_\infty(e^{\lambda t} - 1) + \sigma \int_0^t e^{\lambda x} d\beta(x) \quad \text{and}$$

$$R(t) = e^{-\lambda t} R(0) + R_\infty(1 - e^{-\lambda t}) + \sigma e^{-\lambda t} \int_0^t e^{\lambda x} d\beta(x). \tag{3.33}$$

We have replicated more formally the process of forming the jagged green line in Figure 3.13. So the short rate can be broken into a nonstochastic part $R_N(t)$ that's just a function of t (with no randomness) and a stochastic part (a random variable $R_S(t)$) that has zero mean but nonzero standard deviation:

$$R(t) = R_N(t) + R_S(t),$$

$$R_N(t) = e^{-\lambda t} R(0) + R_\infty(1 - e^{-\lambda t}), \quad \text{and} \tag{3.34}$$

$$R_S(t) = \sigma e^{-\lambda t} \int_0^t e^{\lambda x} d\beta(x). \tag{3.35}$$

Recall that by definition the rate $r(0,f) = -\frac{1}{f} \ln(Z(0,f))$, so (3.30) can be rewritten as:

$$r(0, T) = \frac{-1}{T} \ln\left(\mathbb{E}\left[\exp\left(-\int_0^T (R_N(s) + R_S(s)) ds\right)\right]\right) = \frac{1}{T} \int_0^T R_N(s) ds$$

$$- \frac{1}{T} \ln\left(\mathbb{E}\left[\exp\left(-\int_0^T R_S(s) ds\right)\right]\right) = r_N(0, T) + r_S(0, T). \tag{3.36}$$

Evaluating the nonstochastic integral after plugging in (3.34) is straightforward:

$$r_N(0, T) = \frac{1}{T} \int_0^T R_N(s) ds = \frac{1}{T} \int_0^T \left(e^{-\lambda s} R(0) + R_\infty(1 - e^{-\lambda s})\right) ds$$

$$= R_\infty + \frac{(R(0) - R_\infty)(1 - e^{-\lambda T})}{\lambda T}. \tag{3.37}$$

The stochastic part of the rate is of the form:

$$r_S(0, T) = -\frac{1}{T}\ln\big(\mathbb{E}[exp(-X)]\big).\tag{3.38}$$

where $X = \int_0^T R_S(s)ds$. With a change of order of integration we have:

$$X = \int_0^T R_S(s)ds = \sigma\int_0^T e^{-\lambda s}\int_0^s e^{\lambda x}d\beta(x)ds = \sigma\int_0^T e^{\lambda x}\left(\int_x^T e^{-\lambda s}ds\right)d\beta(x)$$

$$= \frac{\sigma}{\lambda}\int_0^T \big(1 - e^{-\lambda(T-x)}\big)d\beta(x) = \frac{\sigma}{\lambda}\int_0^T \big(1 - e^{-\lambda x}\big)d\beta(x).\tag{3.39}$$

The last equality replaces $T - x$ with x in the exponent since the order of integration doesn't matter; the $d\beta$ are mean-zero independent random draws.

If the increments $d\beta$ are independent and normally distributed, then by the Central Limit Theorem X is normal. Note that if Y is a normal random variable with mean μ and variance v, $\mathbb{E}[e^{-Y}] = \frac{1}{\sqrt{2\pi v}}\int_{-\infty}^{\infty}e^{-x}e^{-\frac{(x-\mu)^2}{2v}}dx = e^{-\mu+v/2}$. For X, the mean $\mu = 0$ since each $\mathbb{E}[d\beta] = 0$. So we can rewrite (3.38) as:

$$r_S(0, T) = -\frac{1}{T}\ln\big(e^{\mathbb{E}[X^2]/2}\big) = -\frac{1}{2T}\mathbb{E}[X^2].\tag{3.40}$$

The independence of the $d\beta$ means that when squaring X, terms that look like $d\beta(x)d\beta(y)$ where $x \neq y$ have expected value zero. So (by Itô isometry) we can write:

$$\mathbb{E}[X^2] = \frac{\sigma^2}{\lambda^2}\int_0^T \big(1 - e^{-\lambda x}\big)d\beta(x)\int_0^T \big(1 - e^{-\lambda y}\big)d\beta(y)$$

$$= \frac{\sigma^2}{\lambda^2}\int_0^T \big(1 - e^{-\lambda x}\big)^2 d\beta(x)^2 = \frac{\sigma^2}{\lambda^2}\int_0^T \big(1 - e^{-\lambda x}\big)^2 dx$$

$$= \frac{\sigma^2}{2\lambda^3}\big(2\lambda T + 4e^{-\lambda T} - e^{-2\lambda T} - 3\big).\tag{3.41}$$

Combining with (3.40) gives:

$$r_S(0, T) = -\frac{1}{2T}\mathbb{E}[X^2] = -\frac{\sigma^2}{4T\lambda^3}\big(2\lambda T + 4e^{-\lambda T} - e^{-2\lambda T} - 3\big).\tag{3.42}$$

Combining (3.37) and (3.42), the overall expected rate curve is given by:[44]

$$r(0, T) = R_\infty + \frac{(R(0) - R_\infty)(1 - e^{-\lambda T})}{\lambda T} - \frac{\sigma^2}{4T\lambda^3}\big(2\lambda T + 4e^{-\lambda T} - e^{-2\lambda T} - 3\big).\tag{3.43}$$

---

44 With a change of notation, this is the same as Vasicek's (27) and (28) after removing the risk adjustment $\frac{q\sigma}{\lambda^2}(1 - e^{-\lambda T} - \lambda T)$. See also [Wise and Bhansali 2010].

3.8.4 Other Short-Rate Models

Rendleman and Bartter (1980) used a different approach and took what most now believe was a step backward by using a process similar to the lognormal process that Louis Bachelier proposed in 1900 for equity prices:

$$dr = r\mu dt + r\sigma d\beta. \tag{3.44}$$

However, this process can drift to large negative or large positive short rates. This is inconsistent with empirical observation and economic sense.

Cox, Ingersoll, and Ross (1985) combined the mean reversion of an Ohrnstein–Uhlenbeck process with an adjustment for the fact that the volatility of changes in rates is larger as rates get larger. This model can be obtained by assuming that the short-rate $r = s^2$, enforcing positive short rates. Then s, in turn, is assumed to follow the Vasicek process (3.31) with long-term rate $R_\infty = 0$. Applying Itô's Lemma to $r = s^2/2$ and $ds = -as \cdot dt + \sigma d\beta$ gives a process of the form:

$$dr = c(d - r)dt + \sigma\sqrt{r}d\beta. \tag{3.45}$$

The square-root adjustment in the volatility term appears to be supported by empirical patterns.

The Ho and Lee (1986) model allows straightforward fitting to the current curve.

$$dr = \alpha(t)dt + \sigma d\beta. \tag{3.46}$$

So, $\alpha(t)$ is constructed so that r will match the current short-rate curve at the current time and then drift from there.

As we've noted, the Hull and White (1990) model has the same structure as Vasicek's original model, but replaces the constant R_∞ with a time-varying – but nonstochastic – $R_{target}(t)$:

$$dr = \lambda(R_{target}(t) - r)dt + \sigma d\beta. \tag{3.47}$$

This is actually what we used in Figures 3.12 and 3.13.

Black, Derman, and Toy (1990) combine a lognormal process with curve fitting and an Itô volatility adjustment. They further incorporate data from the interest rate derivatives market to fit rate volatilities as well as short-rate levels, so σ is also a function of time:

$$dr = (R_{target}(t) + \sigma^2/2)rdt + \sigma(t)rd\beta. \tag{3.48}$$

Black and Karasinski (1991) is a popular model. They force rates to be nonnegative by substituting the logarithm of short rates for short rates themselves in Vasicek's model, equation (3.31). They further fit both current rates and volatilities into the parameters a, b, and σ. These parameters are nonstochastic but time varying, so they can fit observed market data:

$$d \ln(r) = (b(t) - a(t) \ln(r))dt + \sigma(t)d\beta. \qquad (3.49)$$

This model can be modified to allow rates floored at some value $f < 0$ by replacing $\ln(r)$ with $\ln(r - f)$ in (3.49).

For Code Segments in this chapter, see the Code Appendix starting on p. 440. For executable code, visit www.cambridge.org/9781009209090/ch3

For problem sets for this chapter, visit www.cambridge.org/ 9781009209090/ch3_problems

4 Equity Modeling

While the pricing formula (3.2) is generic enough to cover just about any financial arrangement, it is most useful for fixed-income instruments where the planned cash flows are highly likely. As the times and amounts in (3.2) become less and less certain, the value of enumerating possible but not probable cash flows gets lower and lower.

As a result, equity modelers have taken other approaches that have more dominant random components. In his PhD thesis at the Sorbonne, Louis Bachelier (1900) originated an approach to equity that provides the basis for many current models. His approach was essentially formula (3.17); the key insight was the use of Brownian motion ($d\beta$ in (3.17)) five years before Einstein's paper on the subject. For good measure, Bachelier covered options pricing, anticipating by over 70 years the Black and Scholes (1973) option pricing formula.

Bachelier's work was largely forgotten by financial economists until it was rediscovered and promoted by the statistician Leonard Jimmie Savage[1] in the 1950s. Whether they knew it or not, many economists and financial modelers starting in the 1950s and 1960s were using Bachelier's ideas.

We'll discuss some of the most common equity models, starting with Harry Markowitz's efficient frontier. We'll then briefly review Bayes's Rule, and see how Bayesian adjustments are often used in practical methods to select portfolios with simultaneous risk and reward optimization.

Building on these ideas, we'll show a practical and widely used Bayesian method for equity expected return estimation, the Black–Litterman algorithm.

4.1 Markowitz Efficient Frontier

Harry Markowitz is considered the father of quantitative finance. In Markowitz (1952), he considered the problem of how investors should assemble sets of assets (**portfolios**) from individual assets. He expanded on these ideas in his 1954 PhD thesis at the University of Chicago and in a book (Markowitz 1959).

Prior to Markowitz, investment managers who constructed portfolios had a concept that risk was something you needed to be compensated for bearing. This was compatible with Frank Knight's formulation of risk as lack of information about the future: you needed to be paid to expose your portfolio to an unknown

---

1 [Lindley 1980].

future. However, there was no metric for risk and therefore no precise link between how much risk you took and how much you needed to be compensated for it.

The idea that you could put a number on financial risk – that you could measure your lack of information about the future of an investment – is essentially due to Markowitz, who won the 1990 Sveriges Riksbank Prize in Economic Sciences in Memory of Alfred Nobel[2] for his work. Markowitz continued working and publishing in mathematical finance and was an adjunct professor at the University of California at San Diego[3] until his death at the age of 95 on June 22, 2023.

One way of thinking of a portfolio is as an n-vector w (where n is the number of all the assets in the world) that satisfies the **budget constraint** $w^\mathsf{T}u = 1$ (u is the unit n-vector of all ones). Then w is the vector of weights of assets you own at a certain time, scaled so it represents 100 percent of your wealth. So w can contain negative values.

The **return** or **rate of return** on an asset during a time period is the ending value of the asset divided by the beginning value of the asset, minus one. If there are distributions such as dividends or coupons during the period, they are added (possibly in a time-adjusted way) to the ending value. The returns on the n assets in the world during a period can be characterized by a random variable n-vector r. Thus the scalar random variable giving the return of a portfolio w during the period is $w^\mathsf{T}r$.

Markowitz introduced the idea that investors think of risk as volatility, as measured by the statistic standard deviation (or its square, variance). In our notation, standard deviation σ of a portfolio w is $\sigma = \sqrt{\mathbb{E}[w^\mathsf{T}(r - \mathbb{E}[r])^2]} = \sqrt{w^\mathsf{T}\mathbb{E}[(r - \mathbb{E}[r])(r - \mathbb{E}[r])^\mathsf{T}]w}$. This is sensible and intuitive, as we noted in Chapter 2: there is less information about the future in a high-volatility series than in a low-volatility series.

Based on this intuition, Markowitz's basic formulation was:

Given a choice between two portfolios with the same expected (arithmetic) return, any rational investor will prefer the one with less risk (that is, less variance of returns).

Equivalently:

Given a choice between two portfolios with the same risk (variance of returns), any rational investor will prefer the one with more arithmetic or expected return.

Consider again the Generous Billionaires of Chapter 1. We saw that because of risk aversion, most people would not value a coin toss for $1,000,000,000$ or

2 Nobelprize.org. "Harry M. Markowitz: Facts." Website. www.nobelprize.org/prizes/economic-sciences/1990/markowitz/facts/.
3 UC San Diego Rady School of Management. "Harry Markowitz." Website. https://rady.ucsd.edu/people/faculty/markowitz/.

$0 at the average $500,000,000. Put another way, most people would pay far less than $500,000,000 to purchase a portfolio consisting of one Generous Billionaire tossing a coin for a billion or zero.

But suppose that you were able to form a portfolio of 100 coin-tossing Generous Billionaires, each tossing a different coin and paying $10,000,000 on heads and nothing on tails. Your best and worst cases are still one billion and zero, as they were with the single coin-tossing Generous Billionaire. But the chance of your portfolio being worth nothing is now 2^{-100}, which is effectively zero. The outcomes of your portfolio form a binomial distribution; the chance of you getting less than $310,000,000 is less than 10^{-4}. The average value of the portfolio is still $500,000,000. But by just about any measure, risk has gone down.

So by forming a portfolio, you get the same average reward as a single coin toss, with less risk. In Markowitz's formulation, the portfolio of 100 coin-tossing billionaires is more *efficient* than the portfolio of one coin-tossing billionaire. It has the same expected return, and lower standard deviation ($5 million vs. $500 million).

This is not just financial wizardry; **diversification** is often a better way to allocate human efforts. Pursuing 100 different ventures may be a better technique for progress than everyone working on one venture, just like it was better for the farmer and the hunter in Chapter 1's two-person economy to pool their different food-gathering efforts.

Markowitz's primary risk metric, standard deviation, fails the ADEH monotonicity criterion discussed in Chapter 2, but is otherwise coherent. Actually, the near-coherent risk metric is $\rho(X) = \lambda \sigma(X) - \mu(X)$, where $\lambda > 0$ is a scalar and $\sigma(X)$ and $\mu(X)$ are the standard deviation and mean of X. Suppose R_f and Y are random variables that cost the same at present. Then R_f is the risk-free instrument that will be worth $1 in all future states, while Y will be worth $1 half the time and $3 the other half of the time. $\rho(R_f) = -1$ while $\rho(Y) = \lambda - 2$, so the statewise dominant Y shows more risk than R_f when λ is large enough. Thus standard deviation can say there is risk in taking advantage of riskless arbitrages; that's nonsense. Fortunately, Markowitz's framework had few of the kinds of instruments – like derivatives – that would be the most obvious source of such arbitrage possibilities.

Once you have accepted the idea that a rational investor will choose the less risky portfolio from two with the same arithmetic mean return, you can form an **efficient frontier**: a set of portfolios that have the least possible risk at a given level of return; or the greatest possible return at a given level of risk. An efficient portfolio is one that achieves equipoise between the increase-return and decrease-risk goals.

Let $\boldsymbol{m} = \mathbb{E}[\boldsymbol{r}] = (\mathbb{E}[r_1], \mathbb{E}[r_2], \ldots, \mathbb{E}[r_n])^{\mathsf{T}}$ be the vector of expected returns from now until one period in the future. Here r_i is the scalar random variable giving returns of the ith asset and $\mathbb{E}[]$ is the expected value operator. Then $\mathbb{E}[\boldsymbol{w}^{\mathsf{T}} \boldsymbol{r}] = \boldsymbol{m}^{\mathsf{T}} \boldsymbol{w}$. Let

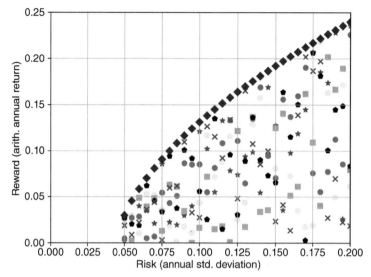

Figure 4.1 Efficient frontier and inefficient portfolios.

$$
C = \begin{bmatrix}
\sigma_1^2 & \sigma_{12} & \cdots & \sigma_{1n} \\
\sigma_{21} & \sigma_2^2 & \cdots & \sigma_{2n} \\
\cdots & & & \\
\sigma_{n1} & \sigma_{n2} & \cdots & \sigma_n^2
\end{bmatrix}
\tag{4.1}
$$

be the covariance matrix of returns, $C = \mathbb{E}[(r - \mathbb{E}[r])(r - \mathbb{E}[r])^{\mathsf{T}}] = \mathbb{E}[rr^{\mathsf{T}}] - \mathbb{E}[r]\mathbb{E}[r]^{\mathsf{T}}$. The (i,j) term looks like $\sigma_{ij} = \mathbb{E}[(r_i - \mathbb{E}[r_i])(r_j - \mathbb{E}[r_j])]$. Note we sometimes write σ_i^2 instead of σ_{ii} for the ith diagonal term.

Then if w is a portfolio n-vector, $Var[w^{\mathsf{T}}r] = w^{\mathsf{T}}Cw$, where Var is the variance (not value-at-risk) operator. If w is a portfolio on the efficient frontier and v is another portfolio with $w^{\mathsf{T}}m = v^{\mathsf{T}}m$ (that is, they have the same expected or arithmetic mean returns), then we must have $Var[v^{\mathsf{T}}r] \geq Var[w^{\mathsf{T}}r]$. Equivalently, if $Var[v^{\mathsf{T}}r] = Var[w^{\mathsf{T}}r]$ then we must have $w^{\mathsf{T}}m \geq v^{\mathsf{T}}m$.

The dark blue curve on top of the dots in Figure 4.1 (generated by Code Segment 4.1) is the efficient frontier – you can't get any higher than that at a given point on the X-axis, nor can you get any further to the left for a given point on the Y-axis. All the other dots represent inefficient portfolios.

4.1.1 Equality-Constrained Frontier

Markowitz did not initially think about multiperiod portfolio construction, as that was too hard to deal with in 1952. Thus, the issue of compounding and the relationship between arithmetic means and geometric (compound) means was avoided. He did not require multivariate normal distributions.

Finding an efficient portfolio n-vector w with a specified mean return μ is a quadratic optimization problem:

$$\text{minimize } w^{\mathsf{T}} C w \qquad (4.2)$$

$$\text{subject to } w^{\mathsf{T}} m = \mu \text{ and } w^{\mathsf{T}} u = 1.$$

Of course, there are many other constraints we might impose, the most obvious being nonnegative holdings. In 1952, there was only one hedge fund[4] that systematically had negative holdings (short sales). Today there are far more such portfolios, but there are also many portfolios that restrict themselves to nonnegative holdings.

Long-only requirements are *inequality constraints*, which don't have a closed-form solution. But to solve just the equality-constrained problem in (4.2), Lagrange multipliers can be used. The derivative with respect to w of the Lagrangian:

$$w^{\mathsf{T}} C w - \lambda_1 (w^{\mathsf{T}} m - \mu) - \lambda_2 (w^{\mathsf{T}} u - 1)$$

is:

$$2 C w - \lambda_1 m - \lambda_2 u = 0.$$

If C is nonsingular, that becomes:

$$w = C^{-1} (\lambda_1 m + \lambda_2 u), \qquad (4.3)$$

where the λ's are rescaled in order to drop a factor of 2.

Left-multiplying (4.3) by m^{T} and u^{T}, respectively, gives:

$$\mu = m^{\mathsf{T}} C^{-1} (\lambda_1 m + \lambda_2 u) \quad \text{and}$$

$$1 = u^{\mathsf{T}} C^{-1} (\lambda_1 m + \lambda_2 u).$$

Solving for the Lagrange multipliers λ_1 and λ_2 gives:

$$\lambda_1 = \frac{(u^{\mathsf{T}} C^{-1} u) \mu - u^{\mathsf{T}} C^{-1} m}{(u^{\mathsf{T}} C^{-1} u)(m^{\mathsf{T}} C^{-1} m) - (u^{\mathsf{T}} C^{-1} m)^2}. \qquad (4.4)$$

We can solve for λ_2 as a function of λ_1:

$$\lambda_2 = \frac{1 - (u^{\mathsf{T}} C^{-1} m) \lambda_1}{u^{\mathsf{T}} C^{-1} u}. \qquad (4.5)$$

Equation (4.4) expresses λ_1 as a function of the desired mean return μ, or μ as a function of λ_1. It will be more convenient to look at it the second way, and retain λ_1 as a varying parameter that moves along the efficient frontier. Together with (4.3), (4.4) and (4.5) give the expression for efficient portfolios w as a function of the varying parameter λ_1:

$$w = \lambda_1 \left(I - \frac{C^{-1} J}{u^{\mathsf{T}} C^{-1} u} \right) C^{-1} m + \frac{C^{-1} u}{u^{\mathsf{T}} C^{-1} u}, \qquad (4.6)$$

---

4 A. W. Jones. "Firm History." Website. https://awjones.com/about-us/firm/.

where $J = uu^\mathsf{T}$ is the n×n matrix of all ones. The variance at the solution is:

$$w^\mathsf{T} Cw = \lambda_1^2 \left(\frac{(u^\mathsf{T} C^{-1} u)(m^\mathsf{T} C^{-1} m) - (u^\mathsf{T} C^{-1} m)^2}{u^\mathsf{T} C^{-1} u} \right) + \frac{1}{u^\mathsf{T} C^{-1} u}. \quad (4.7)$$

Note that the coefficient of the λ_1^2 term is positive.[5] To find the lowest variance portfolio possible, set $\lambda_1 = 0$ to get:

$$w_{minv} = \frac{C^{-1} u}{u^\mathsf{T} C^{-1} u} \quad \text{and} \quad w_{minv}^\mathsf{T} Cw_{minv} = \frac{1}{u^\mathsf{T} C^{-1} u}. \quad (4.8)$$

Equation (4.6) is sometimes called the **Two-Fund Separation Theorem** because of its linear form; efficient portfolios satisfying (4.6) lie along a line in n-space. Let w_1 be the value of (4.6) when $\lambda_1 = 1$; then any w on the (4.6) efficient frontier can be expressed as $w = \lambda w_1 + (1 - \lambda) w_{minv}$ for some $\lambda > 0$. Thus in the simplified world of (4.6), investors don't have to choose between n investments; every investor merely needs to buy some w_{minv} and some w_1, with only the proportion changing from investor to investor.

If we don't care about variance and just want the highest mean portfolio possible, there is no bound. That is because so far we have not prevented leverage, which is measured by the sum of the positive entries in w. Thus, if there are two assets with slightly different expected values, we could weight the higher one with a huge weight approaching infinity, and the lower one with one minus that weight. This two-asset portfolio has an expected return approaching infinity as the weight of the higher returning asset approaches infinity and the weight of the lower returning asset approaches minus infinity.

The hedge fund Long Term Capital Management (LTCM) reportedly used leverage of around 25[6] attempting to get near-infinite returns or at least near-infinite paychecks for its principals. Since $w^\mathsf{T} u = 1$, leverage of 25 means that for every dollar invested in LTCM, the firm borrowed another \$24 through short sales, and put \$25 at risk. It would only take a drop of 4% in the value of its positive holdings (while the negative holdings didn't move) to bankrupt LTCM. LTCM no longer exists and its crash in 1998 nearly destroyed the entire financial system. As a practical matter, limits – on holdings, on leverage – are imposed.

Reversing (4.4) to solve for μ in terms of λ_1, we obtain:

$$\mu = m^\mathsf{T} w = \lambda_1 \left(\frac{(u^\mathsf{T} C^{-1} u)(m^\mathsf{T} C^{-1} m) - (u^\mathsf{T} C^{-1} m)^2}{u^\mathsf{T} C^{-1} u} \right) + \frac{u^\mathsf{T} C^{-1} m}{u^\mathsf{T} C^{-1} u} \quad (4.9)$$

Taking the square root of (4.7) gives the associated standard deviation as a function of λ_1:

$$\sqrt{w^\mathsf{T} Cw} = \sqrt{\lambda_1^2 \left(\frac{(u^\mathsf{T} C^{-1} u)(m^\mathsf{T} C^{-1} m) - (u^\mathsf{T} C^{-1} m)^2}{u^\mathsf{T} C^{-1} u} \right) + \frac{1}{u^\mathsf{T} C^{-1} u}} \quad (4.10)$$

---

5 Covariance matrices are positive semidefinite by construction, and since we're assuming that C is nonsingular, it's positive definite. So C^{-1} is positive definite, forcing $u^\mathsf{T} C^{-1} u$ to be positive. Further, there is a Cholesky factorization $C^{-1} = LL^\mathsf{T}$, so the Cauchy–Schwarz inequality applies to the numerator of the λ_1^2 term, making it positive too.

6 [Lee 2018].

(4.9) and (4.10) allow us to draw an efficient frontier on a graph like Figure 4.1, where the x coordinate is given by (4.10) and the y coordinate is given by (4.9) as λ_1 varies from 0 to infinity.

4.1.2 Equality-Constrained Frontier: Example

We'll work an example using a portfolio of $n = 3$ assets: Swiss francs (CHF), pounds sterling (£ or GBP), and Japanese yen (¥ or JPY). The portfolio is denominated in US dollars.

Code Segment 4.2 retrieves the dollar per currency for these three currencies, and reports the following statistics:

```
From 1971-01-05 to 2021-12-30 ( 12784 observations):

Means: [ 1.1994 -0.4635  0.8866] bps/day
(CHF, GBP, JPY)


    [0.4984 0.2403 0.2132]
C=  [0.2403 0.3542 0.1132]        (4.11)
    [0.2132 0.1132 0.4009]
(%/day)² units
```

The Swiss franc and the Japanese yen have appreciated versus the dollar since 1971, giving positive daily mean returns. The pound sterling has depreciated.

We're going to use the means shown above as the m vector in our calculations. This is a classic, and fatal, error: *we are estimating future characteristics by naively using past characteristics.*

We want to form a portfolio today that will carry us into the future. So we want to know the **expected values**, not the past sample values, of the mean vector and covariance matrix. Past sample values might be good estimators of expected values if the processes in question were **stationary**; that is, if they had unchanging parameters (see Section 9.4 in Chapter 9). But the evidence is overwhelming that financial processes are not stationary over time.

Predicting the future from the past without understanding the generating process is doomed to failure. The comic Stephen Wright said, "I intend to live forever. So far, so good." His projection is so hilarious because it's so myopic: his mortality model doesn't take into account data about humans other than himself.

In fact, using past performance to predict the future is legally discouraged in the USA and other jurisdictions. In the USA, the Code of Federal Regulations (17 CFR 230.156)[7] says

---

7 U.S. Code of Federal Regulations. 2003. Title 17, Volume 2, Section 230-156. Website. www.gpo.gov/fdsys/pkg/CFR-2003-title17-vol2/pdf/CFR-2003-title17-vol2-sec230-156.pdf.

Representations about past or future investment performance could be misleading because of statements ... including:
- (A) Representations, as to security of capital, possible future gains or income,
or expenses associated with an investment;
- (B) Representations implying that future gain or income may be inferred from
or predicted based on past investment performance; or
- (C) Portrayals of past performance, made in a manner which would imply that
gains or income realized in the past would be repeated in the future.

To this point in human experience, the past has been the only time period
on offer for learning purposes: our lives would be very different if we could
learn from the future. But often (as with Stephen Wright's hope for immortality),
it's better to bring in some kind of model (senescence affects all humans;
functionality decreases with age; a Gompertz–Makeham law of mortality applies)
to try to predict the future. The quantitative analyst really wants the most accurate
estimates of future means and covariances; past means and covariances can be as
misleading as Stephen Wright's personal lack of mortality so far.

We're using past sample statistics in this example just because it's a
convenient way to generate numbers of the right order of magnitude to illustrate
the calculations. We'll say more about better estimation methods later in the
chapter.

For now, Code Segment 4.3 computes the inverse of C in (days/pct)^2 units:

$$C\text{-inverse=} \begin{bmatrix} 3.5165 & -1.965 & -1.3152 \\ -1.965 & 4.201 & -0.1411 \\ -1.3152 & -0.1411 & 3.2336 \end{bmatrix} \quad (4.12)$$

(days/%)² units

From this, the key quantities $u^\mathsf{T}C^{-1}u$, $u^\mathsf{T}C^{-1}m$, and $m^\mathsf{T}C^{-1}m$ are computed
in Code Segment 4.4:

```
u'(C-inverse)u = 4.108410547790689 (days/%)²
u'(C-inverse)m = 0.8881677324581263 days
m'(C-inverse)m = 8.006301710547898 bps
```

Filling in these data in equations (4.6), (4.9), and (4.10) gives the numbers
for our three-currency example portfolio computed in Code Segment 4.5. Here
$\sigma = \sqrt{w^\mathsf{T}Cw}$ is the standard deviation of the efficient portfolio w:

```
w'=lambda [ 3.9114 -4.8819  0.9705] + [0.0575 0.5099 0.
      4326]     (4.6)#
mu=(lambda * 7.814295115344305 )+  0.21618280892977973
      bps/day    (4.9)#
sigma=sqrt(lambda² * 7.814295115344305 +
      0.2434031332476627 ) (%/day)   (4.10)#
```

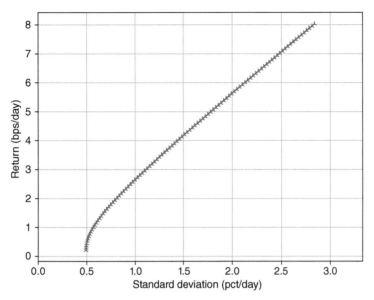

Figure 4.2 Franc, pound, yen efficient frontier.

Note the vector coefficient of λ_1 in (4.6)# has total weight zero (w/roundoff), and the constant vector in (4.6)# has total weight one; it is the global minimum variance solution.

In that solution, pounds sterling (the middle coefficient) have the highest weight. From (4.11) we can see that pounds had the lowest variance, but that alone does not explain why they have the highest weight. There are also second-order effects from correlations with the other currencies. The minimum variance portfolio has a variance that is even lower than the pound's variance.

This shows that *diversification* is a key aspect of portfolio construction – if everything were linear as it is with returns we would have only pounds in the minimum variance solution. We don't because of the quadratic balancing act. Figure 4.2 (generated by Code Segment 4.6) is the classic efficient frontier graph.

The global minimum variance portfolio in this example has positive weights as shown in (4.6)#. From the negative middle entry in the vector multiplying λ_1 in (4.6)#, it follows that the weight of the pound will go negative as λ_1 gets larger, as shown in these results of calculations in Code Segment 4.7:

```
Pound weight goes negative at lambda= 0.1044455026542342
At that point mu= 1.0323507901404427  bps/day
and sigma= 57.327847360205496  bps/day
```

4.1.3 Inequality Constraints

Then as $\lambda_1 \to \infty$, efficient portfolios borrow more and more pounds to fund investments in francs and yen, heading off to an infinite expected return. Figure 4.2 stops at $\lambda_1 = 1$, but it could keep going.

Letting λ_1 get arbitrarily large isn't a sensible thing to do. If an investor starts with a dollar, borrows a billion dollars worth of pounds, and buys a billion and one dollars of francs and yen, then the slightest disturbance in the relationships between francs, yen, and pounds will lead to bankruptcy. Estimated means and covariances can't be treated as certainties, where infinite reliance can be placed on their accuracy.

Even if they were certain, there would be an absorbing barrier problem in the interim. That is, a portfolio can't have a net worth below zero: that's the definition of bankruptcy. **Positive assets** like portfolios, companies, stocks, and bonds will stop operating with a value of zero and will not be allowed to take on negative value. It's possible to draw a line on a graph that starts at $1, meanders down to −$0.10, and ends up at (positive) $3. But that line does not represent a real portfolio. That's similar to an absorbing barrier in physics, where a particle can meander only up to the point where it hits the sides of a container.

One way to avoid unrealistic negative portfolio values is to constrain all the weights in portfolios on the mean-variance efficient frontier to be nonnegative. This changes the problem from one that can be solved in closed form to one that can be solved using a quadratic programming algorithm:

$$\text{minimize} \ -\lambda m^\mathsf{T} w + \frac{1}{2} w^\mathsf{T} C w$$

$$\text{subject to } w^\mathsf{T} u = 1, \text{ each element of } w \geq 0. \tag{4.13}$$

In addition to the nonnegative constraint, we have restated the problem slightly by building in a parameter λ instead of a target mean μ. This is the same idea as flipping (4.4) to (4.9). When $\lambda = 0$, we solve for the global minimum variance portfolio. As λ increases, we care more and more about return maximization and less and less about variance minimization. Thus, λ is a risk tolerance parameter – something like the coefficient of absolute risk tolerance.

Equation (4.13) has a quadratic objective function and linear constraints. It's a special case of a more general group of optimizations with convex objective functions and convex constraints. In the next chapter, we'll delve into convex optimization techniques that can be used for efficient solutions of the great majority of problems likely to arise in portfolio construction.

The solution to the long-only optimization (4.13) is a piecewise series of solutions to the equality-constrained frontier (4.9) and (4.10). In the franc/pound/yen frontier, for example, the equality-constrained minimum variance portfolio has all positive weights so it is also a solution to (4.13). The frontiers continue to coincide until the weight on the pound sterling goes to zero. Then the solution to (4.13) is the efficient frontier consisting only of the Swiss franc and the Japanese yen, shown in orange in Figure 4.3 (generated by Code Segment 4.8). Eventually, the Swiss franc (the highest-returning single asset) becomes the whole portfolio and the (4.13) long-only frontier stops.

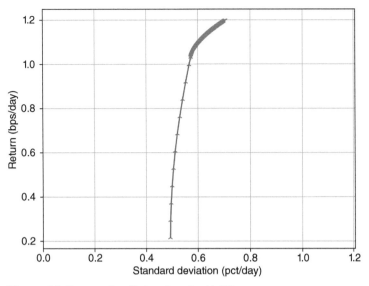

Figure 4.3 Long-only efficient frontier (4.13).

4.1.4 Efficient Frontier and Utility Functions

The connection between portfolios that maximize utility functions and portfolios on the Markowitz efficient frontier is close but not perfect. For example, Pulley (1983, p. 695) concludes:

> ...investors maximizing expected logarithmic utility would hold virtually the same portfolios as investors maximizing certain mean-variance functions.

Similarly, Kroll, Levy, and Markowitz (1984, p. 59) concluded:

> for various utility functions and the historical returns on 3 different sets of securities, when a portfolio may be chosen from any of the infinite number of portfolios of the standard constraint set, the best mean-variance efficient portfolio has almost maximum obtainable expected utility.

One way of making the connection between utility functions and the Markowitz efficient frontier objective function is to consider a quadratic one-period risk-averse utility function on returns, that is, one that looks like $u(z) = -z^2 + az$, $a > 0$. The coefficient of absolute risk aversion is $2/(a - 2z)$ so this is risk-averse when $z < a/2$. That is, $u(z)$ "likes" more return for a while, but if the shock is too big (negative or positive), it gets unhappy.

The investor wants to maximize the expected utility of returns:

$$\mathbb{E}[u(r^\mathsf{T} w)] = \mathbb{E}[-(r^\mathsf{T} w)^2 + a \cdot r^\mathsf{T} w] = -w^\mathsf{T} \mathbb{E}[rr^\mathsf{T}]w + a w^\mathsf{T} \mathbb{E}[r],$$

where r is the random vector of one-period returns. We have already defined the mean vector $m = \mathbb{E}[r]$ and the covariance matrix $C = \mathbb{E}[(r - m)(r - m)^\mathsf{T}]$. Thus,

$$C = \mathbb{E}[rr^\mathsf{T} - 2rm^\mathsf{T} + mm^\mathsf{T}] = E[rr^\mathsf{T}] - mm^\mathsf{T}.$$

So we have:

$$\mathbb{E}[u(r^\mathsf{T}w)] = -w^\mathsf{T}Cw - (w^\mathsf{T}m)^2 + aw^\mathsf{T}m.$$

This is similar to the Markowitz objective function (4.13) (with $a = 2\lambda$ and a change of sign) – although the covariance matrix is not de-meaned.

4.1.5 The Capital Market Line

The *capital market line* is derived from the efficient frontier by the addition of a risk-free asset, that is, a US Treasury or other instrument paying the risk-free rate that we discussed in Chapter 3. We assume the risk-free asset is nonstochastic, so it has no variance and no correlation with anything, including itself.

We can look for an efficient frontier in the usual way and just add the risk-free asset to our universe. However this will make our covariance matrix singular. The usual convention is to separate out the risk-free asset, which has a return r_f. For example, consider the franc, yen, pound efficient frontier. Figure 4.4 (generated by Code Segment 4.9) zooms in to the beginning of the frontier and adds a risk-free asset at $(0,.1)$, that is, $r_f = .1\text{bps/day}$.

We can now be more efficient than the (old) efficient frontier. A straight line that runs between the risk-free asset at $(0, r_f)$ and some point (x, y) that is on the efficient frontier where $y \geq r_f$ will lie above the efficient frontier until (x, y). That line just represents linear combinations of the efficient portfolio at (x, y) and a portfolio consisting only of the risk-free asset.

In fact if the tangency point is chosen to be where the line from $(0, r_f)$ to the efficient frontier just touches the top of the frontier, the line will always be

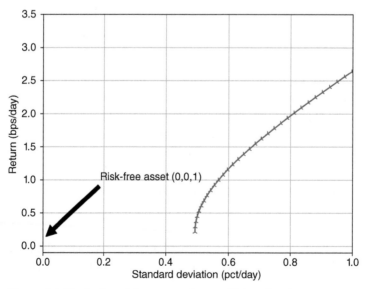

Figure 4.4 Beginning of franc, pound, yen efficient frontier.

above the frontier. That optimal line is the new (including risk-free) efficient frontier and is called the **capital market line**. The two-fund separation theorem in formula (4.6) now becomes even simpler: the new efficient portfolios are linear combinations of the risk-free asset and the tangency portfolio.

To compute the capital market line, note that equations (4.9) and (4.10) specify the old efficient frontier; (4.9) is the y coordinate and (4.10) is the x coordinate. Taking the slope with the chain rule, we see that $\frac{dy}{dx} = \frac{x}{\lambda_1}$. For tangency, this slope must equal $\frac{y-r_f}{x}$, which is the slope of the line between (x,y) and the risk-free asset's representation.

Solving for λ_1 gives $\lambda_1 = \frac{1}{u^\mathsf{T} C^{-1} m - r_f(u^\mathsf{T} C^{-1} u)}$. Putting this λ_1 into (4.3) gives the tangency portfolio w_{tp}:

$$w_{tp} = \frac{C^{-1}(m - r_f u)}{u^\mathsf{T} C^{-1} m - r_f(u^\mathsf{T} C^{-1} u)} = \frac{C^{-1} m_e}{u^\mathsf{T} C^{-1} m_e}, \tag{4.14}$$

where m_e is the excess (over risk-free) return vector $m_e = m - r_f u$.

A portfolio w's *Sharpe Ratio*[8] is $\frac{w^\mathsf{T} m_e}{\sqrt{w^\mathsf{T} C_e w}}$, that is, its excess expected mean return divided by its excess standard deviation.[9] Note that in the mean/standard deviation graphs we have been drawing, the slope of a line that goes through the point $(0, r_f)$ is the Sharpe Ratio of portfolios on that line. Thus the maximum Sharpe Ratio efficient portfolio is the tangency portfolio; to see this, visualize the set of lines from $(0, r_f)$ to points on the efficient frontier.

The tangency (best efficient Sharpe Ratio) portfolio has an excess expected return equal to:

$$w_{tp}^\mathsf{T} m_e = \frac{m_e^\mathsf{T} C^{-1} m_e}{u^\mathsf{T} C^{-1} m_e} \tag{4.15}$$

and a standard deviation:

$$\sqrt{w_{tp}^\mathsf{T} C w_{tp}} = \frac{\sqrt{m_e^\mathsf{T} C^{-1} m_e}}{u^\mathsf{T} C^{-1} m_e}. \tag{4.16}$$

Thus, the Sharpe Ratio of the tangency portfolio is:

$$Sharpe(w_{tp}) = \sqrt{m_e^\mathsf{T} C^{-1} m_e}. \tag{4.17}$$

Code Segment 4.10 adds a risk-free asset with $r_f = .1\text{bp/day}$ to the currency example, giving a tangency portfolio with the following characteristics:

---

8 [Sharpe 1994].

9 C_e is the covariance matrix of excess returns over the risk-free rate. If the risk-free rate really is risk-free – i.e. it never varies – then $C_e = C$. But when we are using sample data over time, the risk-free rate does vary. Practitioners often ignore this and use C in the denominator of the Sharpe ratio. Since the risk-free rate is often far less variable than the assets forming the frontier, leaving it out of the denominator is usually not much of an omission. However, during periods where the risk-free rate is highly variable, the omission can be significant. We used C in the Capital Market Line calculations (4.14) to (4.17), but technically C_e should be used.

```
Tangency portfolio: [ 8.2519 -9.7176  2.4658]
TP mu= 16.58714106615597  bps/day
TP sigma= 5.877123583217739  pct/day
lambda at tangency: 2.095001278500456
```

Drawing the line between the risk-free rate on the Y-axis and the tangency portfolio gives the orange capital market line in Figure 4.5 (generated by Code Segment 4.11).

The efficient frontier in Figure 4.5 is near-linear by the time the capital market line touches it, so there is little difference between the capital market line and the original efficient frontier in this example. When the efficient frontier has more nonlinear shape – for example as a result of multiple constraints – there can be more separation between the capital market line and the efficient frontier.

4.1.6 Benchmark-Relative

As a practical matter, many investment vehicles are constrained to invest in certain segments of the capital markets. For example, a mutual fund may advertise that it is a "large-cap US equity fund." Investors who favor big US companies can give a sum of money to the mutual fund manager, and the manager will decide which big US companies to buy with that money. The manager would be amiss – and legally culpable – if it didn't mostly[10] place its investors' money

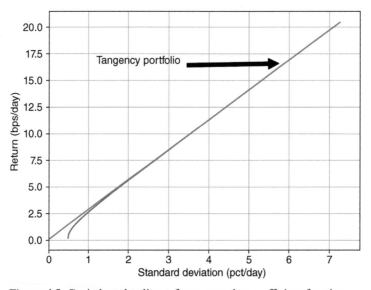

Figure 4.5 Capital market line + franc, pound, yen efficient frontier.

10 In the USA, "mostly" means 80% or more. Securities and Exchange Commission. "Final Rule: Investment Company Names." Release No. IC-24824. Website. www.sec.gov/rules/final/ic-24828.htm.

in big US companies; to do otherwise would be false advertising. By the same token, investors can hardly blame the manager if big US stocks generally do poorly; they knew what they were getting into.

This situation is usually handled with a *benchmark portfolio*. Benchmark portfolios are often constructed by institutions that publish transparent benchmark composition rules intended to select certain market segments mechanically. For example, the FTSE/Russell company publishes the Russell 1000®[11] index of the one thousand largest stocks in Russell's universe; this is widely used as a large-cap US equity benchmark.

Most benchmark indices are **capitalization-weighted**; that is, the holding weights are proportional to the total market values (market price per share time shares outstanding) of the companies in the index. Sometimes caps are put on percentage holdings to attenuate the influence of one dominant player in a market. **Float-weighting** is sometimes used when portions of a company are unavailable to the public, for example due to founding family holdings: the "float" is the portion of the company that trades freely.

Equal-weighting (or the 1/N rule) weighs each of the N securities in an index the same. One argument for this approach notes that if P_M is the market price of a security and P_T is its theoretically correct price if all future information about the company and the economy were known today, then: (a) if $P_M > P_T$, the company is overweighted in capitalization-weighted indices; while (b) if $P_M < P_T$, then the company is underweighted in capitalization-weighted indices. Thus, capitalization-weighted indices overweight overpriced securities and underweight underpriced securities. On the other hand, equal-weighting is random compared to a company's future prospects and so tends to get about half the weights right and half wrong; 50 percent right is better than 0 percent right. However, equal-weighted indices can be impractical if the smaller companies in the index are illiquid.

However a benchmark is constructed, risk is then redefined to be relative to the benchmark b. In our example b = Russell 1000®, which itself would be considered to have no risk, while cash would have quite a lot of risk. Rather than $\sqrt{w^\mathsf{T} C w}$, the relevant volatility would be $\sqrt{(w-b)^\mathsf{T} C(w-b)}$; this benchmark-relative volatility is called *tracking error*. The objective function in an optimization like (4.13) would change to $-\lambda m^\mathsf{T}(w-b) + \frac{1}{2}(w-b)^\mathsf{T} C(w-b)$.

The equivalent of a Sharpe Ratio in a benchmark-relative context is an *information ratio*; it is defined as $\frac{(w-b)^\mathsf{T} m}{\sqrt{(w-b)^\mathsf{T} C(w-b)}}$. The information ratio equals the Sharpe Ratio when the benchmark is the risk-free asset.

---

11 FTSE Russell. "Russell US Indices." Website. www.ftserussell.com/products/indices/russell-us.

4.1.7 Efficient Frontiers: Theory and Practice

While Markowitz started the field of quantitative finance and his work was revolutionary, investors quickly found that it often didn't work as well as the qualitative methods they were using before 1952. One problem is that the quadratic optimization process doesn't know that the numbers (means, covariances) it is given can be wrong. While a human would be skeptical about large, too-good-to-be-true returns, the optimization process is likely to put a heavy weight on a security with a too-good-to-be-true return.

Even realistic returns can lead to unrealistic results. A human would think that the difference between two securities, both with very similar covariances to the rest of the universe, and one with a mean of 1.12345 and the other 1.12346, was random. It wouldn't make much difference if you were buying one or the other. But as we noted when discussing frontier leverage, if you're buying one and selling the other, then any small difference between securities can be exploited with enough leverage. An unconstrained optimizer would go massively long the higher return one and massively short the lower, thereby multiplying random estimation errors.

In fact, most of our currency example efficient frontier was highly leveraged and would be unattainable with the long-only constraint; most of the "results" could be suspect. Thus, as we've already noted, in many cases holdings are constrained to be long only; this stops solutions from having any leverage.

Despite the problems with naively using past statistics to predict the future, past (sample) covariance matrices are often used to estimate expected covariances. In fact, a great deal of effort has been spent on understanding how covariances change over time; we'll discuss these efforts in Chapters 9 and 10. But covariances are less variable than sample mean returns. So there are a number of estimation methods that start with sample covariance matrices and then try to modify them so they are better predictors.

Sample covariance matrices are, by construction, at least positive semidefinite and possibly positive definite. We need n time periods of observation to make an $n \times n$ covariance matrix nonsingular, but even if we have that many periods we still might not have a rich set of data for each entry. There are $\binom{n+1}{2}$ different numbers in a covariance matrix. In every time period we observe n rates of return. So if we have t periods of observations, the number of observables per covariance is $\frac{2t}{n+1}$. For example, for the Russell 1000®index, we would need 5,005 time periods if we wanted to have a not very impressive ten observations per covariance.

Having 5,005 observations is about twenty years at a daily periodicity, which limits the number of companies that can be considered, as many do not have public trading data for that long. Also, daily observations are only valid for the most heavily traded stocks; a lightly traded stock may not have any meaningful trading activity after (say) 2 p.m., while more heavily traded stocks continue trading (and reacting to news) until the close of the market at 4 p.m. The day's return on the lightly traded stock is then asynchronous with the day's returns on more heavily traded stocks. That in turn can lead to misleadingly low correlations. Longer periodicities, like monthly, are often used to address this problem. A few hours of missing price movements out of a month is less noticeable than a few hours missing from a day. But at a monthly periodicity, any sample covariance matrix of the Russell 1000® will be singular. That in turn causes problems with solving optimizations like (4.2), which will no longer have a unique solution.

Even when covariance matrices aren't singular, they can have problems. The *condition number* of a matrix is the ratio of its largest eigenvalue to its smallest eigenvalue. The larger the condition number, the more likely it is that a very small change in input variables (means and covariances) can make a very large change in output variables (weights of the optimal solution).

Because of the generally poor quality of covariance matrices, most users of optimizers put bounds on many quantities in addition to long-only (or not-too-short) constraints. Individual holdings usually have concentration limits – for example, no single stock can occupy more than 5 percent of the portfolio. If the optimization is benchmark-relative, then constraints like "every security must be within plus or minus 2 percent of the benchmark's weight in that security" can be set. Constraints are often placed on other relevant characteristics like industries, countries, property types (in real estate portfolios), and duration/credit quality (in fixed-income portfolios).

Setting limits produces sensible portfolios, since the limits are set sensibly. But in effect it gives the answer to the optimizer – if the user is not careful, an optimizer can become a smokescreen for the judgments of the human who put in very restrictive limits.[12]

4.2 Parameter Estimation Methods

We'll now turn our attention to some of the practical approaches to estimating the parameters m and C used in the construction of efficient portfolios. Many of them rely on Bayes's Rule. We'll begin by reviewing that.

4.2.1 Review of Bayes's Rule

Bayes's Rule is simple to state:

$$Pr(E \mid F) = \frac{Pr(F \mid E)Pr(E)}{Pr(F)}.$$

12 [Michaud 1989].

It is essentially a restatement of the definition of conditional probability in (1.4). Despite this uncomplicated derivation, Bayes's Rule is profound. We'll walk through an example to get an intuitive feel for Bayes's Rule.

Suppose you are worried that you may have a rare disease that makes you forget your personal utility function. Fortunately, there's a very accurate test for this condition. You go to the doctor and take the test, which comes back positive. You are now terrified that if you should run into some Generous Billionaires, you won't know what to do. You contemplate entering an intensive (and expensive) treatment program for the condition. Should you?

We need to be more precise: by "rare," we mean that only 1 in 10,000 people has the disease. And by "very accurate," we mean that the test is right 99 percent of the time.

The relevant outcome space Ω in this case is the set of roughly 8 billion people in the world. Thus, Ω can be divided into four disjoint events:

- People with positive test results who have the disease;
- People with positive test results who don't have the disease;
- People with negative test results who have the disease; and
- People with negative test results who don't have the disease.

From the 10^{-4} probability of having the disease, we know that 800,000 people in the world have the disease. This allows us to start filling in a table:

Outcomes	Have Disease	Don't Have	Total
Test+			
Test−			
Total	800,000	7,999,200,000	8Bn

Of the 800,000 who have the disease, 99% are properly diagnosed and 1% (8,000) are misdiagnosed as not having the disease. Similarly for the 7.999Bn who don't have the disease. So we can completely fill in the table:

Outcomes	Have Disease	Don't Have	Total
Test+	792,000	79,992,000	80,784,000
Test−	8,000	7,919,208,000	7,919,216,000
Total	800,000	7,999,200,000	8Bn

With a positive test result, you are in the Test+ row. But the vast majority of people with a positive test score are test mistakes in the "don't have" column. In fact even with a positive test result, your chance of having the disease is only 1 percent.

If $n = |\Omega|$ is the size of the outcome space, then we know:

- Event E (have disease) has size $10^{-4}n = 800,000$.
- Event W (wrong test result) has size $10^{-2}n = 80,000,000$
- Event F (positive test result) has size $(10^{-2} + 10^{-4} - 2 \cdot 10^{-6})n = 80,784,000$
  Event F's size is not directly given but is computed from the first row of the 2×2 matrix.

Outcomes	Have Disease	Don't Have	Total
Test+	$E \cap F$	$(\Omega \setminus E) \cap F$	F
Test−	$E \cap (\Omega \setminus F)$	$(\Omega \setminus E) \cap (\Omega \setminus F)$	$\Omega \setminus F$
Total	E	$\Omega \setminus E$	Ω

In terms of probabilities, $p_E = 10^{-4}$ is the probability of having the disease, and $p_W = 10^{-2}$ is the probability of a wrong test result. Then the table looks like:

Outcomes	Have Disease	Don't Have	Total
Test+	$p_E(1 - p_W)$	$(1 - p_E)p_W$	$p_F = p_E + p_W - 2p_E p_W$
Test−	$p_E p_W$	$(1 - p_E)(1 - p_W)$	$1 - p_E - p_W + 2p_E p_W$
Total	p_E	$1 - p_E$	1

In our example, we wanted to know the probability of having the utility-forgetting disease (event E) given that we had observed a positive test result (event F). Event E is called the *prior* – what you believed to be true before new information came in. So you believed that the chance of having utility-forgetting disease was very small (.01%) before taking the test.

Event F is the *update*: a positive test result. As we saw, from the fact that the test is wrong $p_W = .01$ of the time and the fact that $p_E = 10^{-4}$, we could compute $p_F = p_E + p_W - 2p_E p_W = .010098$. The conditional probability $Pr(F \mid E)$ = probability positive test result given you have the disease is 99% because the test is 99% accurate independently of whether or not you have the disease. Putting it together, we get $Pr(E \mid F)$ = probability of disease given positive test result = $.99 * .0001 / .010098 = .009804$, or a little less than 1% as we saw.

Bayes's Rule is due to Thomas Bayes, who lived from 1701 to 1761. It is far ahead of its time in its clever use of existing information (e.g. utility-forgetting-disease is rare), new information (test results), and probability theory. This is especially clever because probability theory, at least as we know it today, didn't exist in the early 1700s. Of course the general concept of odds, such as in the

Bernoullis' discussion of St. Petersburg Paradox, existed then. But the formal framework, including sample spaces, σ-algebras, and probability measures, was a few hundred years in the future.

4.2.2 Shrinkage Estimators

Practitioners often use methods intended to improve parameter estimates, sometimes in conjunction with proprietary views on the future direction of markets. Many such methods take the form of *shrinkage estimators*. The general idea is similar to Bayes's Rule: we have some kind of prior belief about a quantity we are trying to estimate, and we "shrink" the deviations from the prior in some way. Often the prior is *centralized*, meaning it is based on some kind of marketwide average value.

An example of a centralized prior for an efficient portfolio is the vector $w = \frac{1}{n}u$; which indicates that everything in the universe is of equal importance without knowing anything about means and covariances. Bouchaud, Potters, and Aguilar (1997)[13] had this prior in mind when they suggested maximizing a nonparametric portfolio diversification measure like Shannon entropy:[14]

$$\exp\left(-\sum |w_i| \cdot \ln(|w_i|)\right)$$

or an inverse Herfindahl–Hirschman[15] index:

$$\frac{1}{\sum w_i^2} = \frac{1}{w^\mathsf{T} w}.$$

Here, w_i are the scalar components of the portfolio vector w, where as usual $w^\mathsf{T}u = 1$. For both metrics, the worst case is the intuitively most concentrated: one $w_i = 1$ and the others equal to zero. Both measures equal one in that case. If $w \geq 0$, then for both measures the best case (where the measures equal n) is $w_i = 1/n$ (in vectors, $w = \frac{1}{n}u$).

The Bouchaud, Potters, and Aguilar (1997) suggestion was to add one of the diversification measures to the portfolio optimization problem, so for example the objective in (4.13) would be changed to:

$$\text{minimize} \; -\lambda m^\mathsf{T} w + \frac{1}{2} w^\mathsf{T}(C + \gamma I) w. \tag{4.18}$$

13 Jean-Philippe Bouchaud, Marc Potters, and Jean-Pierre Aguilar are physicists who now run a quantitative hedge fund in Paris ("CFM: Who We Are." Website. www.cfm.fr/who-we-are/).
14 Shannon defined his entropy function as a measure of the uncertainty of a probability distribution. A set of portfolio weights satisfying the budget contraint can be thought of as a probability mass function when the weights are constrained to be positive, so Shannon entropy can be applied to positive portfolio weights. For portfolios where negative weights are allowed, modifications of Shannon entropy are required to make the measure sensible. One modification is $\exp\left(\sum_{w_i>0} -w_i \ln(w_i)\right)$ which is maximized when there are no short positions and all $w_i = \frac{1}{n}$. However this introduces inequality constraints when used in an optimization [Shannon 1948].
15 [Hirschman 1964].

With a sufficiently large γ parameter, the optimization will focus more on minimizing the nonparametric Herfindahl–Hirschman Index, and less on the quantities m and C that need estimating. This can produce a solution that mitigates the problem of too-heavy reliance on random noise in inputs, pushing solutions toward $w = \frac{1}{n}u$.

The problem of parameter estimation is so large that some have suggested giving up on it altogether. DeMiguel, Garlappi, and Uppal (2009) considered the "1/N rule," which in our notation means giving infinite weight to the γ parameter in (4.18), forcing $w = \frac{1}{n}u$. DeMiguel et al. (p. 1915) evaluated out-of-sample performance of a number of variations on parameter estimation for Markowitz-type mean-variance optimization. They:

> find that none is consistently better than the 1/N rule in terms of Sharpe ratio, certainty-equivalent return, or turnover. This finding indicates that, out of sample, the gain from optimal diversification is more than offset by estimation error. ... This suggests that there are still many "miles to go" before the gains promised by optimal portfolio choice can actually be realized out of sample.

The DeMiguel et al. "1/N rule" is a Bayesian approach with infinite weight on the centralized prior. Other methods also have centralized priors but are less than 100 percent dubious about update information. For example, the *James–Stein shrinkage estimator*[16] for the vector of multivariate normal means can be applied to the prior belief that all means are equal to some common scalar value μ_0. The observed mean vector m is then pushed some way back to this prior. A scalar s is used to calibrate how far to push back:

$$s = \min\left(1, \frac{n-2}{T(m - \mu_0 u)^\mathsf{T} C^{-1}(m - \mu_0 u)}\right), \qquad (4.19)$$

where n is the number of variables in the vectors and T is the number of observations (often time periods). The denominator in (4.19) is a scaled squared **Mahalanobis Distance**.[17]

The revised mean vector estimate is then:

$$m_{new} = (1 - s)m + s\mu_0 u. \qquad (4.20)$$

The default mean μ_0 can for example be the average of all the means in m ($\mu_0 = \frac{m^\mathsf{T} u}{n}$).

This seems like a sensible, quasi-Bayesian, heuristic for not relying too much on possibly erroneous sample data. But James and Stein showed something remarkable about this estimator: if there is a true (but unknown) population mean vector m_{true}, then:

$$(m_{true} - m)^\mathsf{T} C^{-1}(m_{true} - m) \geq (m_{true} - m_{new})^\mathsf{T} C^{-1}(m_{true} - m_{new}). \qquad (4.21)$$

---

16 [James and Stein 1961].
17 [Mahalanobis 1936].

That means that the new estimator is guaranteed to be closer (in Mahalanobis distance) to the unknown true mean vector than the original. That's *for any value of* μ_0! So you can just pick a μ_0 randomly and you'll get closer to the true mean vector than your sample mean vector m. Of course, an outrageous μ_0 will cause the s in (4.19) to be very small, so there won't be much adjustment. But it will be in the right direction!

A similar idea is seen in the *Jorion shrinkage estimator*,[18] formed by taking:

$$s = \frac{n+2}{n+2 + T(m - \mu_{min}u)^\mathsf{T} C^{-1}(m - \mu_{min}u)},$$

where

$$\mu_{min} = m^\mathsf{T} w_{minv} \tag{4.22}$$

and then applying the shrinkage combination in (4.20) with $\mu_0 = \mu_{min}$. Here w_{minv} is the minimum variance portfolio shown in (4.8).

Code Segment 4.12 computes the James–Stein and Jorion estimates of the mean vector for our three-currency example. The last year of sample data is held out so we can later compare the estimates with the last year's out-of-sample mean vector.

```
James-Stein shrinkage factor: 0.09072800398771942 ;
        common mean:
5.929673476567321e-05
James-Stein estimate of mean as of 2020-12-31 :
        [ 1.1906e-04 -3.6734e-05 9.5560e-05]


Jorion shrinkage factor: 0.3232968231767555 ; minimum
        variance mean:
2.622748946290537e-05
Jorion estimate of mean as of 2020-12-31 :
        [ 9.3086e-05 -2.2863e-05  7.5594e-05]
```

Similarly, shrinkage estimators can be applied to the covariance matrix. Elton, Gruber, and Padberg (1978, p. 300) pointed out that there appeared to be little information in covariance matrices off the diagonal. They reluctantly concluded that just setting all off-diagonal correlations to the average value gave better estimates of future correlation matrices:

> In this section, we will assume that all pairwise correlation coefficients are equal. While this probably does not represent the true pattern one finds in the economy, it is very difficult to obtain a better estimate. Elsewhere we have shown that this assumption produces better estimates of future correlation coefficients than do historical correlation coefficients. . . .

---

18 [Jorion 1986].

Thus – just as in the $1/N$ rule or the James–Stein and Jorion shrinkage estimators – Elton, Gruber, and Padberg (1978) came to the idea of a centralized prior. Ledoit and Wolf (2003) used this idea. Let $R = S^{-1}CS^{-1}$, where C is a sample covariance matrix and $S = \sqrt{\text{diag}(C)}$ is the matrix with sample standard deviations on the diagonal and zeroes elsewhere. R is the sample correlation matrix. Let $\rho_{average} = \frac{u^{\mathsf{T}}Ru - n}{n(n-1)}$ be the average off-diagonal correlation. Then the constant correlation covariance matrix is:

$$C_\rho = S(I + \rho_{average}(J - I))S, \tag{4.23}$$

where as usual $J = uu^{\mathsf{T}}$ is the matrix of all ones.

The Ledoit–Wolf constant-correlation covariance shrinkage estimator is:

$$C_{cc} = sC_\rho + (1 - s)C, \tag{4.24}$$

where s is a scalar shrinkage parameter – the larger s is, the less trust you have in your correlations. Note that C_{cc} has the same diagonal as the original C; variances are not changed in this shrinkage method.

Ledoit and Wolf give the following rather elaborate estimate of s:

- First, define y_{it} as the de-meaned observation of the ith security's return in time period t, so that $\sum_t y_{it} = 0$. Then if Y is the sample de-meaned return matrix $(n \times T)$, then $C = \frac{1}{T}YY^{\mathsf{T}}$ is the sample covariance matrix.
- Second, define f_{ij} as the (i,j) element of C_ρ and s_{ij} as the (i,j) element of C.
- Third, compute $\hat{\pi} = \sum_i \sum_k \pi_{ij}$ where $\pi_{ij} = \frac{1}{T}\sum_{t=1}^{T}\left(y_{it}y_{jt} - s_{ij}\right)^2$.
- Fourth, compute $\hat{v}_{ii,ij} = \frac{1}{T}\sum_{t=1}^{T}\left(y_{it}^2 - s_{ii}\right)\left(y_{it}y_{jt} - s_{ij}\right)$. Then compute $\hat{x} = \sum_{i=1}^{n} \pi_{ii} + \frac{\rho_{average}}{2}\sum_{i=1}^{n}\sum_{j=1,j\neq i}^{n}\left(\sqrt{\frac{s_{jj}}{s_{ii}}}\hat{v}_{ii,ij} + \sqrt{\frac{s_{ii}}{s_{jj}}}\hat{v}_{jj,ij}\right)$.
- Fifth, compute $\hat{\gamma} = \sum_{i=1}^{n}\left(f_{ij} - s_{ij}\right)^2$.
- Sixth, set $s = \frac{\hat{\pi} - \hat{x}}{\hat{\gamma}}$. Ledoit and Wolf suggest bounding this between 0 and 1 if necessary.

While this estimate of the optimal shrinkage intensity s is quite complicated to write down, it is not hard to program. An easier heuristic is to set s equal to the fraction of the trace contained in the correlation matrix's first $\sqrt{n}$ eigenvalues.

In a later paper, Ledoit and Wolf (2004) suggest a different prior: rather than keeping variances the same, they shrink them back to the average variance. They also shrink correlations to zero. This second Ledoit–Wolf shrinkage method has been implemented in packages like Scikit–learn.[19]

The second Ledoit–Wolf shrinkage method starts with X, the $T \times n$ matrix of data such as returns or log-returns of n variables observed over T time periods. The sample covariance matrix is $C = \frac{1}{T-1}X'(I - J/T)X$, where I is the $T \times T$

---

19 Scikit-learn. "Sklearn.covariance.ShrunkCovariance." Website. https://scikit-learn.org/ stable/modules/generated/sklearn.covariance.ShrunkCovariance.html.

identity matrix and J is the $T \times T$ matrix of all ones; the $I - J/T$ term de-means the observations. This is shrunk to:

$$C^* = s^*(\bar{v}I) + (1 - s^*)C, \tag{4.25}$$

where $\bar{v}$ is the average variance, that is, the trace of the sample covariance matrix C divided by n, the dimension of C.

The shrinkage intensity s^* is formed as follows: define $d = \|S - \bar{v}I\|$, where $\|x\| = \sqrt{tr(xx^\mathsf{T})/n} = \sqrt{\frac{1}{n}\sum_{i=1}^{n}\sum_{j=1}^{n}x_{i,j}^2}$. Here $tr(z)$ means the trace of the matrix z, so $\|x\|$ is the scaled Frobenius norm of the $n \times n$ matrix x. Define

$$\bar{b}^2 = \frac{1}{T^2}\sum_{i=1}^{T}\|x_i^\mathsf{T}x_i - C\|^2, \tag{4.26}$$

where x_i is the ith row of the de-meaned observation matrix $(I - J/T)X$. Then the shrinkage intensity is $s^* = \min\left(1, \frac{\bar{b}^2}{d^2}\right)$.

A heuristic method combining the two Ledoit–Wolf shrinkage estimators with both variance and correlation priors centralized looks like this:

$$C_{cc}^* = s_{cc}^*\bar{v}(I + \rho_{average}(J - I)) + (1 - s_{cc}^*)C. \tag{4.27}$$

Code Segment 4.13 applies the heuristic Ledoit–Wolf shrinkage method (4.27) to our three-currency example covariance matrix. As above, we hold out the last year of our sample data so we can later compare the estimates with the last year's out-of-sample covariance matrix. For comparison, we show the Scikit–learn version of the (4.25) estimator. Both methods have small shrinkage intensities due to the large number of observations, which increases confidence in the sample covariance matrix C:

```
As of 2020-12-31:
Ledoit-Wolf heuristic shrinkage factor:
      0.028561131922019173
Average correlation: 0.4498706659045772 ; average
      variance:
4.2319336365584934e-05
Ledoit-Wolf heuristic covariance estimate:
 [[5.0287e-05 2.4193e-05 2.1510e-05]
 [2.4193e-05 3.5972e-05 1.1690e-05]
 [2.1510e-05 1.1690e-05 4.0699e-05]]
Scikit-Learn Ledoit-Wolf shrinkage factor:
      0.003352114013335964
Scikit-Learn Ledoit-Wolf covariance estimate:
 [[4.9806e-05 2.3945e-05 2.1246e-05]
 [2.3945e-05 3.5442e-05 1.1280e-05]
 [2.1246e-05 1.1280e-05 4.0093e-05]]
```

4.2.3 Statistical Tests

The shrinkage estimators of the previous section seem plausible. Some of them have theoretical backing based on assumptions about underlying distributions – generally multivariate normal – or about asymptotic behavior. But since any theoretical assumptions about underlying distributions or asymptotic behavior are likely to be violated in practice, it's desirable to have a metric that tests the quality of an estimator.

The ultimate metric is the degree to which using the estimator in a portfolio selection process improves out-of-sample results. But there are common statistical tests for equality of means, variances, and covariance matrices that can be used to check directly whether a method is delivering better out-of-sample prediction.

Typically, such tests are based on a function of observed data that produces a scalar metric whose distribution is known under assumptions about the distribution of the underlying data. It's also common that the test statistic will have a minimum (and best) value of zero. For example, suppose $f(x_1, x_2)$ is the statistic that we test to see whether the means of x_1 and x_2 could be the same, where x_1 and x_2 are sets of observed n-vectors. We will probably have $f(x_1, x_2) = 0$ when $\bar{x}_1 = \bar{x}_2$. $f(x_1, x_2)$ will then increase as $\bar{x}_1$ gets further and further away from $\bar{x}_2$.

Once a test metric like $f(x_1, x_2)$ is computed, a *p*-**value** can be found. The *p*-value is the cdf of the test metric under the test distribution. For example, we'll show a test statistic in (4.28) below that does what we described in the previous paragraph; it tests for equality of means. This statistic follows an F distribution (see below) if the underlying data are multivariate normal. Thus, the larger the cdf of the test statistic, the less likely it is that the two samples were generated by processes with the same mean vector. If the cdf is large enough (typically .95 or .99 for 5% or 1% significance), we might say that we reject the null hypothesis. (In our example the null hypothesis is the equality of means of the generating processes for the two samples.) Otherwise, we **fail to reject the null hypothesis.**

Unfortunately, *p*-values depend on what are usually overly strong assumptions about the underlying generating distributions of the observed data. We agree with the American Statistical Association's statement[20] on *p*-values, which among other things states:

> Scientific conclusions and business or policy decisions should not be based only on whether a p-value passes a specific threshold.

But while the *p*-values might not be realistic, the test metrics might still help to distinguish relative distances. For example, there might be two different

---

20 [Wasserstein and Lazar 2016].

methods of predicting out-of-sample behavior. We can look at the test metric that gives how distant each predictive vector is from out-of-sample data that were generated after the predictions were made. This can help assess predictive quality on a relative basis, but not necessarily on an absolute basis.

4.2.3.1 Equality of Mean Vectors: Hotelling's Test The James–Stein estimator satisfied the property (4.21), which said that in some sense the James–Stein estimator m_{new} was closer to the true (but unknown) population mean vector m_{true} than the sample mean m. The distance metric was based on the inverse of the population covariance matrix C.

A more general form of this metric is Hotelling's T statistic,[21] which in turn is a generalization of the Student's T statistic we will see in Section 7.2 in Chapter 7. Hotelling supposes that we have two groups of data drawn independently from multivariate normal distributions, and we want to test the hypothesis that the mean vectors are the same.

So suppose that group i ($i = 1, 2$) has observations $x_{i,1}, \ldots, x_{i,T_i}$ where each $x_{i,t}$ is a p-vector. Let $m_i = \frac{1}{T_i} \sum_{j=1}^{T_i} x_{i,j}$ and $S_i = \frac{1}{T_i-1} \sum_{j=1}^{T_i} (x_{i,j} - m_i)(x_{i,j} - m_i)^\mathsf{T}$ be the sample mean vector and the sample covariance matrix, respectively, for the ith group. Form the combined covariance matrix $S_{comb} = \frac{(T_1-1)S_1+(T_2-1)S_2}{T_1+T_2-2}$. Then Hotelling's T statistic is:

$$H(1,2) = \left(\frac{T_1 + T_2 - p - 1}{(T_1 + T_2 - 2)p} \right) \left(\frac{T_1 T_2}{T_1 + T_2} \right) (m_1 - m_2)^\mathsf{T} S_{comb}^{-1} (m_1 - m_2). \quad (4.28)$$

Then $H(1,2)$ is distributed as an F distribution[22] with parameters p and $T_1 + T_2 - 1 - p$. Thus if $F(H(1,2), p, T_1 + T_2 - 1 - p) > c$, we reject the null hypothesis that x_1 and x_2 were drawn from distributions with the same mean vectors with confidence c. However, this test is very sensitive to the assumption that the generating distributions were normal.

Code Segment 4.14 applies Hotelling's test to the James–Stein and Jorion estimates of the three-currency mean vector, comparing them to the holdout year's mean vector:

```
Comparing mean vector estimates as of 2020-12-31
    with mean vector for year ending 2021-12-31:

Hotelling statistics for James-Stein, Jorion:
      0.6410467792416411
0.58019978427698
P-values for James-Stein, Jorion: 0.5885261233701685
      0.627956786337834
    Jorion has higher p- value
```

21 [Hotelling 1931].
22 [Shumway and Stoffer 2017], p. 48.

```
James-Stein: Cannot reject null hypothesis of equal means
      at 99% significance
Jorion: Cannot reject null hypothesis of equal means at
      99% significance
```

4.2.3.2 Equality of Variances: Levene's Test

Levene's Test[23] for equality of variances across two samples is less dependent on the assumption of normality than an older test by Bartlett.

Extending the notation used in (4.28), let $x_{i,j,k}$ be the kth element of the p-vector $x_{i,j}$. For each k, Levene's Test tests the hypothesis that the T_1 observations $x_{1,j,k}$ were drawn from a distribution with the same variance as the T_2 observations $x_{2,j,k}$.

To do this, define $z_{i,j,k} = |x_{i,j,k} - m_{i,k}|$, where $m_{i,k}$ is the kth element of the p-vector m_i defined above. Let $z_{i,k} = \frac{1}{T_i} \sum_{j=1}^{T_i} z_{i,j,k}$ be the mean of these absolute values for group i, element k, and let $z_k = \frac{1}{T_1+T_2} \sum_{i=1}^{2} \sum_{j=1}^{T_i} z_{i,j,k}$ be the overall average absolute difference. Then the Levene statistic for the kth element is:

$$L_k = (T_1 + T_2 - 2) \frac{T_1(z_{1,k} - z_k)^2 + T_2(z_{2,k} - z_k)^2}{\sum_{i=1}^{2} \sum_{j=1}^{T_i} (z_{i,j,k} - z_{i,k})^2}. \tag{4.29}$$

Then L_k is distributed as an F distribution with parameters 1 and $T_1 + T_2 - 2$. Thus if $F(L_k; 1, T_1 + T_2 - 1) > c$, we reject the null hypothesis that $x_{1,j,k}$ and $x_{2,j,k}$ were drawn from distributions with the same variances with confidence c.

Code Segment 4.15 applies Levene's Test to the three sample variances from the three-currency example for previous years compared to the latest year:

```
Comparing variances up to 2020-12-31 with year ending
      2021-12-31:
Levene statistic for DEXSZUS:  40.01670112746961 ,
      p-value:
2.601971971216699e-10
Cross-check: results of scipy.stats.levene:
      40.01670112746961
2.6019715443618535e-10
DEXSZUS: Reject null hypothesis of equal variances at 99%
      significance
Levene statistic for DEXUSUK:  13.535888739663358 ,
      p-value:
0.0002350056470314943
Cross-check: results of scipy.stats.levene:
      13.535888739663358
```

---

23 [Gastwirth, Gel, and Miao 2009].

```
0.00023500564703147385
DEXUSUK: Reject null hypothesis of equal variances at 99%
        significance
Levene statistic for DEXJPUS:   34.26963095558968 ,
        p-value:
4.915895357449074e-09
Cross-check: results of scipy.stats.levene:
        34.26963095558968
4.9158953785410015e-09
DEXJPUS: Reject null hypothesis of equal variances at 99%
        significance
```

4.2.3.3 Equality of Covariance Matrices: Box's M Test

Box's M Test[24] can be used to test the equality of covariance matrices. If S_1, S_2, and S_{comb} are as defined in Section 4.2.3.1, then Box's M statistic is:

$$M(1,2) = \big((T_1 + T_2 - 2)\ln\left(\det(S_{comb})\right) - (T_1 - 1)\ln\left(\det(S_1)\right)$$
$$- (T_2 - 1)\ln\left(\det(S_2)\right)\big). \tag{4.30}$$

The statistic is modified by a multiplier that takes into account finite sample size. Box defines (equation (49)):

$$A_1 = \frac{2p^2 + 3p - 1}{6(p+1)}\left(\frac{1}{T_1 - 1} + \frac{1}{T_2 - 1} - \frac{1}{T_1 + T_2 - 2}\right) \tag{4.31}$$

and

$$A_2 = \frac{(p-1)(p+2)}{6}\left(\frac{1}{(T_1 - 1)^2} + \frac{1}{(T_2 - 1)^2} - \frac{1}{(T_1 + T_2 - 2)^2}\right). \tag{4.32}$$

If $A_2 - A_1^2 \leq 0$, $M(1,2)(1 - A_1)$ is distributed as a χ^2 distribution with df_1 degrees of freedom, where $df_1 = \frac{p(p+1)}{2}$. So in this case, the p-value is $\chi^2(M(1,2)(1 - A_1), df_1)$.

Otherwise, define $df_2 = \frac{df_1 + 2}{A_2 - A_1^2}$ and $b = \frac{df_1}{1 - A_1 - (df_1/df_2)}$; then $M(1,2)/b$ is distributed as an F distribution with df_1 and df_2 degrees of freedom. In this case the p-value is $F(M(1,2)/b, df_1, df_2)$.

The null hypothesis is that S_1 and S_2 were formed from samples drawn from multivariate normal distributions with a common covariance matrix. We reject the null hypothesis with confidence c when the p-value is greater than or equal to c.

This test is very sensitive to the assumption of multivariate normality. A useful heuristic is to first use Levene's Test on the diagonals of the covariance matrices. This provides more precise information as to the particular variables

---

24 [Box 1949].

causing hetereoskedasticity, and is less sensitive to non-normality. Once the variances have been checked, the correlation matrices can be extracted from the covariance matrices and Box's M Test can be applied to the correlation matrices.

Code Segment 4.16 segment applies Box's M Test in two parts: first to variances only, and then to correlation matrices. The latest year is compared to previous years' sample data as well as to the Ledoit–Wolf heuristic estimates:

```
Comparing variances up to 2020-12-31 with year ending
        2021-12-31:
Box M-stat and p-value for sample variances only:
        50.32418275579166
1.1102230246251565e-16
Reject null hypothesis of equal sample variances only at
        99% significance


Box M-stat and p-value for sample correlation matrices:
        2.4087684034423615
0.024969986917740106
Cannot reject null hypothesis of equal sample correlation
        matrices at 99%
significance


Box M-stat and p-value for Ledoit-Wolf heuristic vs.
        latest sample correlations:
2.447021893729138 0.02287913453211954
Cannot reject null hypothesis of equal correlation
        matrices at 99% significance
```

4.2.4 Resampled Efficient Frontier

Shrinkage techniques deal with estimation error in means and covariances, but not directly with finding the portfolios on the efficient frontier. Jorion (1992) addressed the problem of finding efficient frontiers directly with the following procedure:

1. Compute the means and covariance matrix from the actual sample of historical returns. Define T as the sample size (number of months, say) and N as the number of assets. Perform the optimization, given the stated objective function and investor constraints.

2. Assume that the estimates from Step 1 are true values. From a multivariate normal distribution with these parameters, draw one random sample of N joint returns. This represents one month of simulated returns. Sample again until T months are generated.

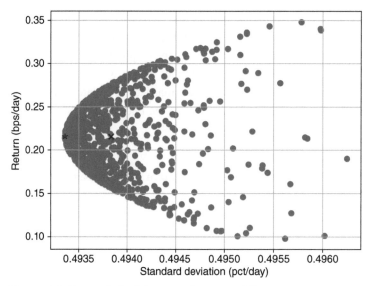

Figure 4.6 Resampled minimum variance portfolios.

3. Estimate from these simulated returns a new set of means and a new variance-covariance matrix; perform an optimization using these inputs. The simulated optimal portfolio provides one observation in the distribution of the original optimal portfolio.

4. Repeat Steps 2 and 3 until the distribution of the optimal portfolio is approximated with enough precision.

We can follow Jorion's procedure to see how much ambiguity there is in the minimum-variance portfolio $w_{minv} = \frac{C^{-1}u}{u^{\intercal}C^{-1}u}$ from our three-currency example.

There's a very large range of mean returns of the resampled minimum variance portfolio shown in Figure 4.6 (generated by Code Segment 4.17). The standard deviations (X-axis) are less variable, but even they show not only a range, but also an inevitable upward bias. The red marker is the original minimum variance portfolio, which is the only efficient portfolio on the graph according to the original parameters. The blue marker is the average of the sample characteristics, which is riskier than the original minimum variance portfolio. The difference between the blue marker and the red marker is an indication of how overly optimistic we were about our ability to get a low-variance portfolio.

There's also uncertainty about the weights. Code Segment 4.18 computes a 95% confidence interval for them from the sample:

```
95% confidence for MV portfolio:
                        (CHF      GBP      JPY)
Bottom of interval:   [0.0113 0.4631 0.3938]
Middle of interval:   [0.0574 0.5105 0.4325]
Original MV port:     [0.0575 0.5099 0.4326]
Top of interval:      [0.106  0.5535 0.4715]
```

Typically, we see that zero is in (or close to) the confidence interval for the first (Swiss franc) weight, so we're not even sure we should have any in the minimum variance portfolio. The pound sterling (second) and Japanese yen (third) confidence intervals are typically about 8 percent wide. And the minimum variance portfolio is generally the most stable since it doesn't use the mean vector as an input!

A *resampled efficient frontier* takes this resampling process and averages it to get a collection of optimal mean-variance portfolios that, it is hoped, will have less dependence on sampling noise. One way of averaging was proposed by Michaud and Michaud (1998); Richard Michaud has a US patent[25] on this method, which is offered commercially through the firm New Frontier Advisors.[26]

Michaud aggregates the minimum variance portfolios from each sample as we did above. He then chops the remainder of the efficient frontier from the minimum variance to the maximum return – assuming there is a maximum return – into an equal number of steps. For example, suppose the original frontier had a minimum return of .2 and a maximum of 2 and there were 10 steps desired along the frontier; then 10 efficient portfolios $P_{1,0}$ with return .2; $P_{2,0}$ with return .4; ...; and $P_{10,0}$ with return 2 would be recorded. Then a resampled frontier would be generated for simulation 1; say, its minimum and maximum returns were .15 and 2.88. The compositions of the 10 portfolios $P_{1,1}$ with return .15; $P_{2,1}$ with return .47; ...; and $P_{10,1}$ with return 2.88 would be recorded. This would be done for S simulations. Then the resampled frontier would consist of the 10 portfolios $\frac{1}{S+1}\sum_{s=0}^{S} P_{i,s}$.

The Michaud method essentially aggregates resampled portfolios by target mean. A method that was used by Ibbotson Associates was described in Idzorek (2006, p. 12). This method essentially aggregates by target standard deviation:

Ibbotson uses a proprietary "bin approach," in which asset allocations from the *simulated* portfolios are grouped together based on narrowly defined standard deviation ranges that cover the risk spectrum. The average asset allocations are then linked back to the original inputs to plot the resampled efficient frontier.

Whichever method is used, the general idea is to (a) lower and (b) estimate sampling noise through a process of resampling. Scherer (2002) points out that resampling methods will average out to the original efficient frontier when there are no constraints in the optimization process, but when there are constraints – for example, long-only holdings – the resampled frontier will generally improve on the original frontier. That is, empirical tests have generally shown that

25 Google Patents. "Portfolio Optimization by Means of Resampled Efficient Frontiers." Website. https://patents.google.com/patent/US6003018A/en.
26 New Frontier. Website. www.newfrontieradvisors.com/.

resampled frontiers do better at predicting out-of-sample (future) behavior than the original efficient frontier. But resampling is a heuristic rather than a proof, and practitioners continue to search for even better heuristics to predict out-of-sample behavior.

4.3 Black–Litterman

Black and Litterman (1991) is another attempt to deal with poor estimation of the Markowitz parameters, in this case through a Bayesian framework. Fischer Black's contributions to mathematical finance include (among many others) the Black–Scholes option pricing formula and two of the short-rate models we discussed. Robert Litterman headed quantitative management at Goldman Sachs Asset Management; in Chapter 3 we discussed Litterman and Scheinkman (1991) about key rates.

In the Black–Litterman framework, we assume there is a true but unobservable expected mean n-vector μ that is associated with the process generating asset returns. Before updating our information to estimate μ, we have a prior belief: namely, that it is consistent with the Capital Asset Pricing Model ("CAPM"), which we will cover in Section 6.1. The prior that comes from that model is:

$$\mu_{CAPM} = r_f u + (\mathbb{E}[r_M] - r_f)\beta, \qquad (4.33)$$

where $\mathbb{E}[r_M]$ is the expected return on the market. $\beta = \frac{w_M^\mathsf{T} C}{w_M^\mathsf{T} C w_M}$, where C is as in (4.1).

Our error of estimate is given by a multivariate normal distribution with mean 0 and covariance matrix sC, where s is a confidence scalar. If s = 0, we are perfectly confident that μ_{CAPM} is the right answer. As s gets larger, we get less confident. C might be estimated from historical returns or from an equity model. Note, however, that a full covariance matrix C is not consistent with the CAPM, which assumes $C = \sigma_M \beta^\mathsf{T} \beta$.

In the Black–Litterman framework, we can express views (opinions) about the actual mean return n-vector μ. A view is a value of some linear combination of returns. The simplest view is that a return on a particular asset will take on a particular value, but we can also (for example) express a view on an industry (a weighted combination of the assets in that industry), or on one group of assets versus another (a hedge or relative value trade). In general, we write:

$$p = V\mu + \epsilon, \qquad (4.34)$$

where V is a $v \times n$ matrix whose rows are the linear combinations expressing the form of our views, of which we have v. The p is a v-vector giving the outcomes of the views. So ϵ is an error v-vector with mean 0.

For example, if we believe pharmaceutical stocks will outperform energy stocks by 12%, a row of V would have positive weights (perhaps capitalization-weighted) on all the pharmaceutical stocks and negative weights on energy stocks, and the corresponding row of the v-column-vector p would be 12%.

We are trying to minimize the error term ϵ on the right-hand side. To do this, we could solve a standard ordinary least squares (OLS) regression using least squares, obtaining $\mu = (V^\mathsf{T}V)^{-1}V^\mathsf{T}p$. However, in accordance with our theme of keeping track of how much we don't trust our parameters, we assume that the error vector ϵ is multivariate normally distributed with mean 0 and $v \times v$ covariance matrix Γ. The smaller the entries of Γ, the more confident we are in our views. Usually we assume off-diagonal elements are 0, and that really is just to make things easier.

When we have an error matrix like Γ, we can use an extension of ordinary least squares regression called generalized least squares (GLS). The idea is to modify OLS regression by weighting the variables we are more sure about more heavily, and the variables we are less sure about less heavily. The GLS solution is:

$$\mu_{views} = (V^\mathsf{T}\Gamma^{-1}V)^{-1}V^\mathsf{T}\Gamma^{-1}p. \tag{4.35}$$

We have two equations involving our estimate of μ – one from the CAPM (4.33) and one from views (4.35). We can put them together and minimize the errors using GLS again. We put everything together into these vectors:

$$y = \begin{pmatrix} \mu_{CAPM} \\ p \end{pmatrix} ; M = \begin{pmatrix} I \\ V \end{pmatrix} ; E = \begin{pmatrix} sC & 0 \\ 0 & \Gamma \end{pmatrix}. \tag{4.36}$$

Plugging the quantities in (4.36) into a GLS like (4.35) gives

$$\mu = \left(\frac{1}{s}C^{-1} + V^\mathsf{T}\Gamma^{-1}V\right)^{-1}\left(\frac{1}{s}C^{-1}\mu_{CAPM} + V^\mathsf{T}\Gamma^{-1}V\mu_{views}\right). \tag{4.37}$$

Recall that s is the scalar that shows how much we disbelieve the prior – the CAPM view. As $s \to 0$, the views become less and less important and the estimate of μ approaches μ_{CAPM}. On the other hand, as $s \to \infty$, the CAPM prior becomes less and less important and the views dominate, giving μ_{views} when the expressions make sense.

In this case – when the matrices are well-behaved enough – we can write:

$$\mu = M_{CAPM}\mu_{CAPM} + (I - M_{CAPM})\mu_{views}, \text{ where}$$

$$M_{CAPM} = \left(\frac{1}{s}C^{-1} + V^\mathsf{T}\Gamma^{-1}V\right)^{-1}\frac{1}{s}C^{-1} \text{ and} \tag{4.38}$$

$$M_{views} = \left(\frac{1}{s}C^{-1} + V^\mathsf{T}\Gamma^{-1}V\right)^{-1}V^\mathsf{T}\Gamma^{-1}V, \text{ so}$$

$$M_{CAPM} + M_{views} = I.$$

However, note that M_{CAPM} is affected by the views, and M_{views} is affected by the CAPM. In fact, views do not only affect the securities for which they are expressed – they are spread out over the entire vector. This reflects the fact that a view on a security passes through the covariance structure and affects other securities.

4.3.1 Black–Litterman Example

We'll work an example of Black–Litterman, using the currency data from earlier in the chapter. For currencies, the concept of "the market" is not as clear as it is for stocks. It's relatively easy to compute the total value of investable shares of Apple Computer or Walmart; it's less easy to compute the total value of investment we could make in Swiss francs. We'll just arbitrarily assign a market portfolio for our three currencies:

$$w_M = \begin{pmatrix} .05 \\ .15 \\ .80 \end{pmatrix}. \tag{4.39}$$

From the three-currency data used above, Code Segment 4.19 computes the expected mean return $m^\mathsf{T} w_M$ of the market, and the market's standard deviation $\sigma_M = \sqrt{w_M^\mathsf{T} C w_M}$:

```
Mkt mu= 0.6996911437388623  bps/day
Mkt sigma²= 0.3136192847913145 (%/day)²
```

Code Segment 4.20 computes the vector of betas of the three individual assets with the market, and from that the μ_{CAPM} vector given by (4.33). The small adjustment of the covariance matrix to an excess covariance matrix is not made here:

```
beta = [0.7382 0.4965 1.1108]
mu-CAPM= [0.5427 0.3977 0.7661]  bps/day
```

Let us now put in a single opinion, which is that pounds will outperform yen by .2bps/day. The CAPM prior says pounds will underperform yen, so we are going in a different direction. In the notation of (4.34) (and assuming the unknown μ vector is in bps/day units), this says:

$$p = .2,$$

$$V = \begin{pmatrix} 0 & 1 & -1 \end{pmatrix}.$$

Let us assume the error of estimate matrix of our views is (in $1/\text{days}^2$ units) $\Gamma = .0001 \cdot I$, where I is the identity matrix (actually a scalar here since $v = 1$). We'll weight our market beliefs with $s = 1$.

We can then compute the term:

$$\left(\frac{1}{s}C^{-1} + V^{\mathsf{T}}\Gamma^{-1}V\right)^{-1}$$

used in (4.37) and (4.38). Code Segment 4.21 computes the term inside the parentheses in days² units. After inverting, Code Segment 4.21 multiplies by 10,000 for display purposes, which converts to (pct/days)² units:

```
C-inverse/s= [[ 35165.3773 -19650.3851 -13151.8981]
 [-19650.3851  42009.9265  -1411.1725]
 [-13151.8981  -1411.1725  32335.7129]]
V'(Gamma-inverse)V= [[     0.        0.        0.]
 [     0.    10000.  -10000.]
 [     0.   -10000.   10000.]]
Sum= [[ 35165.3773 -19650.3851 -13151.8981]
 [-19650.3851  52009.9265 -11411.1725]
 [-13151.8981 -11411.1725  42335.7129]]
Sum inverse (pct/day)**2= [[0.4979 0.236   0.2183]
 [0.236  0.3162 0.1586]
 [0.2183 0.1586 0.3468]]
```

The other terms are $\frac{1}{s}C^{-1}\mu_{CAPM}$ and $V^{\mathsf{T}}\Gamma^{-1}V\mu_{views}$. Note from (4.35) we have $V^{\mathsf{T}}\Gamma^{-1}V\mu_{views} = V^{\mathsf{T}}\Gamma^{-1}p$. Code Segment 4.22 computes these quantities:

```
C-inverse*muCAPM/s= [0.1192 0.4963 1.7075]
V'(Gamma-Inverse)p= [[ 0. ]
 [ 0.2]
 [-0.2]]
Sum= [[0.1192 0.6963 1.5075]]
(All in units of days)
```

Finally, Code Segment 4.23 multiplies the matrix times the vector to produce the Black–Litterman estimate μ as in (4.37):

```
Black-Litterman mu (bps/day): [[0.5528]
 [0.4873]
 [0.6591]]
```

After a great deal of calculation, we have modified the μ_{CAPM} vector a little: the expected mean pound return has increased and the expected mean yen return has decreased, although not enough to fully implement our opinion that pounds would outperform yen by .2bps. The expected return on Swiss francs has changed a little too, even though we didn't have an opinion about it: this is because the covariance structure causes our views to propagate through to the entire market.

Recall that there were some uncertainty parameters – the scalar s and the matrix Γ – that have no obvious calibration process. A Black–Litterman user can adjust them until they give an answer that seems intuitively appealing. The danger is similar to that of overconstraining an optimization – adjusting a quantitative process until it confirms our qualitative biases. Michaud, Esch, and Michaud (2013) captured this concern in the title of their paper: "Deconstructing Black-Litterman: How to Get the Portfolio You Already Knew You Wanted."

Still, such quantitative methods are not without value. It is more important to listen to what the algorithm is saying than to tell it what to do. For example, understanding what relationships caused the change in the Swiss franc's expected return in our Black–Litterman example might lead to some insight: What is it about the pound's and the yen's relationships with the franc that caused that movement? Is there some relationship between the Swiss, British, and Japanese economies that is being revealed, or is it just a statistical artifact? Pursuing these kinds of questions can lead to better results.

Black–Litterman is used by robo-advisers like Betterment,[27] who determine client risk preferences with questionnaires in order to find the appropriate point along an efficient frontier for that client. The expected values of the portfolio components (which for robo-advisers are index funds or exchange-traded funds) are obtained with a Black–Litterman approach.

For Code Segments in this chapter, see the Code Appendix starting on p. 440. For executable code, visit www.cambridge.org/9781009209090/ch4

For problem sets for this chapter, visit www.cambridge.org/ 9781009209090/ch4_problems

27 Betterment. "The Betterment Portfolio Strategy." Website. www.betterment.com/resources/ betterment-portfolio-strategy/.

5 Convex Optimization

In the previous chapter, we saw that finding a Markowitz efficient frontier in an equality-constrained setting was simple: just use Lagrange multipliers and specify a closed-form solution. But finding an efficient frontier got more complicated in Section 4.1.3 when the constraints were inequalities. The example we used there with only three assets was simple enough to think through explicitly. More generally with possibly thousands of assets and thousands of constraints, an algorithm is needed.

In this chapter, we'll discuss **optimization**: the process of finding inputs that maximize or minimize a function (called the **objective function**) subject to constraints on the inputs. In quantitative finance, optimizations are used to find the best fits of parameters to data and to form optimal investment portfolios, among other uses.

Most quantitative finance practitioners and academics will not write their own optimization algorithms since most widely used computer languages already have extensive prepackaged optimization capabilities. However, most users of optimization packages can attest to the fact that "plug and chug" almost never works: the packages require sophisticated users who can understand (a) the best ways to present their problems, and (b) how to fix whatever (inevitably) goes wrong the first several times an optimization is attempted.

The aim of this chapter is to give the reader enough facility so that he or she can wrangle optimization packages into giving fast and accurate answers to the reader's problems. Readers wishing to gain enough facility so they can write their own optimization packages will need further development. Boyd and Vandenberghe (2004) and Bertsekas (1996) provide excellent further foundation in this area.

5.1 Basic Optimization Terminology

The **gradient** of a well-behaved (continuous, differentiable) function $f : \mathbb{R}^n \to \mathbb{R}$ is the column n-vector of partial derivatives:

$$grad(f) = \nabla f = \left(\frac{\partial f}{\partial x_1}, \dots, \frac{\partial f}{\partial x_n} \right)^\mathsf{T}.$$

The **Hessian matrix** of this function is (if it's twice differentiable):

$$\nabla^2 f \equiv \nabla \nabla^\mathsf{T} f = \begin{bmatrix} \frac{\partial^2 f}{\partial x_1^2} & \ddots & \frac{\partial^2 f}{\partial x_1 \partial x_n} \\ \vdots & \cdots & \vdots \\ \frac{\partial^2 f}{\partial x_n \partial x_1} & \ddots & \frac{\partial^2 f}{\partial x_n^2} \end{bmatrix}.$$

Note the ∇ operator produces an $n \times 1$ vector, so to produce the $n \times n$ Hessian matrix the notation should be $\nabla \nabla^\mathsf{T} f$. However, the usual notation is $\nabla^2 f$, or $\nabla^2 f(x)$ to indicate that the Hessian is evaluated at the specific point x.

A point x_m is a **local minimum** of a function f if and only if for all small positive scalars d,

$$f(x_m + e) \geq f(x_m) \quad \forall e | e^\mathsf{T} e < d. \tag{5.1}$$

A **local maximum** is defined analogously. A point is an **extremum** (or just **extreme**) if it is a minimum or a maximum.

If x_m is a local minimum of the function f, then it's a local maximum of the function $-f$, so we'll assume without loss of generality that we're looking for minima. If the idea is to get more of a good thing, then a procedure that gets less of the opposite of the good thing will get to the same place.

Suppose a point x_m is a local minimum of f. Let d_k be the vector of all 0's except for a one in the kth place. By definition,

$$\frac{\partial f}{\partial x_k}(x_m) = \lim_{\delta \to 0} \frac{f(x_m + \delta d_k) - f(x_m)}{\delta}. \tag{5.2}$$

Since x_m is a local minimum, the numerator of the limit in (5.2) is always nonnegative for small enough δ. Approaching x_m from positive δ decreasing to zero gives a positive denominator in (5.2) so $\frac{\partial f}{\partial x_k}(x_m) \geq 0$. Approaching x_m from negative δ increasing to zero gives a negative denominator in (5.2) so $\frac{\partial f}{\partial x_k}(x_m) \leq 0$. Since f is differentiable, the direction of approach to x_m doesn't matter. The only way the gradient can be both ≥ 0 and ≤ 0 is for it to equal zero.

The previous paragraph therefore shows that any local minimum (and analogously any local maximum) of a differentiable function f must be a **critical point** of f, that is, a point where the gradient of f is the zero vector.

Differentiability is theoretically important here: for example, $f(x) = |x|$ has a local (and global) minimum at $x = 0$, but $x = 0$ isn't a critical point because there isn't a critical point. In practice, differentiability might not be so important as bumpy functions can usually be approximated by smooth functions to arbitrary accuracy. For example $f_a(x) = x \cdot \tanh(ax)$ gets closer and closer to $|x|$ as $a \to \infty$, but it is differentiable and has a critical point at $x = 0$.

The other direction isn't generally true: a critical point of a differentiable function might not be a local extremum. A critical point might be a **saddle point** where it's a minimum along one direction of travel and a maximum along another direction.

Generally, it will be desirable to find a global minimum point x_M such that

$$f(x_M) \leq f(x) \quad \forall x.$$

Clearly, global extrema are local extrema but not necessarily vice versa.

A generic optimization problem looks like:

$$\text{minimize}_x f(x)$$

$$\text{subject to } g(x) = 0 \tag{5.3}$$

$$\text{and } h(x) \geq 0.$$

$f(x)$ (a scalar function of $x \in \mathbb{R}^n$) is called the **objective function**. The "subject to" lines are called **constraints**. $g(x)$ is a vector-valued function, so $g(x) = 0$ can comprise multiple scalar equalities; the $g(x) = 0$ requirements are called **equality constraints**. Similarly, $h(x)$ is a vector-valued function and $h(x) \geq 0$ are called **inequality constraints**. A point x that satisfies all the constraints is said to be **feasibile**.

The formulation (5.3) is mildly redundant; the equality constraints are not really needed because they could be encoded in components of h. If $g_1(x)$ is a scalar function and the constraint $g_1(x) = 0$ is desired, then one component of the vector-valued function h could be g_1 and another component could be $-g_1$. It will be algorithmically convenient, however, to separate out the equality constraints from the inequality constraints.

5.2 Convex Properties

A major problem in the optimization of complicated functions is getting stuck at a local extremum that is not a global extremum. An algorithm might check that a small step in any direction away from the point goes up, indicating that the point is a local minimum. But without an exhaustive search, an algorithm can't know that there isn't an even deeper well beyond the next hill.

However, this problem disappears when the objective function of an optimization is convex, that is, where:

$$f(\theta x + (1 - \theta)y) \leq \theta f(x) + (1 - \theta)f(y) \text{ for } 0 \leq \theta \leq 1.$$

Property 5.1: Local minima are global minima for convex functions. |

Proof: Suppose not: Let x_m be a local minimum and x_M a global minimum with $f(x_M) < f(x_m)$. Take a combination $\theta x_m + (1 - \theta)x_M$ where θ is close enough to 1 so that the combination is still within the area around x_m where x_m is a minimum.

By convexity, $f(\theta x_m + (1 - \theta)x_M) \leq \theta f(x_m) + (1 - \theta)f(x_M) < \theta f(x_m) + (1 - \theta)f(x_m) = f(x_m)$. This violates x_m's local minimality, which is a contradiction. That forces $f(x_M) = f(x_m)$ so the local minimum is a global minimum. ∎

Property 5.1 is enormously helpful, as it means that checking locally suffices to find a global minimum when f is convex. Convex functions have other powerful and useful properties:

Property 5.2: If function f is differentiable then it is convex if and only if

$$f(y) \geq f(x) + \nabla f(x)^\mathsf{T}(y - x). \qquad (5.4)$$

Proof: Note that by the definition of convexity,

$$f(x + \epsilon(y - x)) = f(\epsilon y + (1 - \epsilon)x) \leq \epsilon f(y) + (1 - \epsilon)f(x).$$

So:

$$f(x + \epsilon(y - x)) - f(x) \leq \epsilon(f(y) - f(x)).$$

Dividing by $\epsilon > 0$ and taking the limit as $\epsilon \to 0$ proves convexity implies (5.4).

To prove (5.4) implies convexity; let z be some point on the line segment between x and y. That is, $z = \theta x + (1 - \theta)y$, where $0 \leq \theta \leq 1$. Then by (5.4), $f(y) \geq f(z) + (\nabla f(z))^\mathsf{T}(y - z)$ and $f(x) \geq f(z) + (\nabla f(z))^\mathsf{T}(x - z)$. Multiply these two inequalities by $1 - \theta$ and θ, respectively, and add them together. The gradient term drops out and leaves the desired convexity property. ∎

The previous section noted the implication (local minimum) $\implies$ (critical point) for differentiable functions. Property 5.2 establishes the even better reverse implication (critical point) $\implies$ (global minimum) for convex differentiable functions. Together with Property 5.1, that establishes:

Property 5.3: For convex differentiable functions, points are critical if and only if they are global minima.

Convex functions also have a second derivative property when they are twice differentiable:

Property 5.4: A twice differentiable function f is convex if and only if its Hessian matrix is positive semidefinite.

Proof: Let x and y be arbitrary n-vectors, and let:

$$g(x, y, \theta) = \theta f(x) + (1 - \theta)f(y) - f(\theta x + (1 - \theta)y) \qquad (5.5)$$

for $0 \leq \theta \leq 1$. A Taylor expansion of a scalar function h about a point x_0 looks like:

$$h(x) = h(x_0) + (\nabla h(x_0))^\mathsf{T}(x - x_0) + \frac{1}{2}(x - x_0)^\mathsf{T}\nabla^2 h(x_0)(x - x_0) + \cdots + .$$

Let $h(y) = g(x,y,\theta)$ and apply a Taylor expansion of $h(y)$ about $y = x$:

$$h(y) = g(x,y,\theta) = g(x,x,\theta) + \nabla_2 g(x,x,\theta)^\mathsf{T}(y-x)$$
$$+ \frac{1}{2}(y-x)^\mathsf{T}\nabla_2^2 g(x,x,\theta)(y-x) + \cdots +,$$

where ∇_2 means the derivative is taken with respect to the second argument. It follows from the definition of g that $g(x,x,\theta) = 0$ and:

$$\nabla_2 g(x,x,\theta) = (1-\theta)(\nabla f(y))_{y=x} - (1-\theta)\nabla f(\theta x + (1-\theta)y)_{y=x} = 0.$$

That leaves only the Hessian and higher terms. Note:

$$\nabla_2^2 g(x,x,\theta) = (1-\theta)(\nabla^2 f(y))_{y=x} - (1-\theta)^2 \nabla^2 f(\theta x + (1-\theta)y)_{y=x}$$
$$= \theta(1-\theta)\nabla^2 f(x).$$

Thus,

$$g(x,y,\theta) = \frac{\theta(1-\theta)}{2}(y-x)^\mathsf{T}\nabla^2 f(x)(y-x) + \cdots +, \tag{5.6}$$

where the dots represent third-order and higher terms. Suppose f is convex. Then $g(x,y,\theta) \geq 0$ for θ in the unit interval. Set $y = x + \delta z$ where z is an arbitrary n-vector and $\delta > 0$ is a positive scalar. (5.6) becomes:

$$g(x,x+\delta z,\theta) = \frac{\theta(1-\theta)}{2}\delta^2 z^\mathsf{T}\nabla^2 f(x)z + O(\delta^3). \tag{5.7}$$

Both sides of (5.7) are nonnegative by the assumed convexity of f. As $\delta \to 0$, the $O(\delta^3)$ terms become negligible, so the other term must be nonnegative. So if θ is not 0 or 1, we must have $z^\mathsf{T}\nabla^2 f(x)z \geq 0$ for any x and z, proving that the Hessian is positive semidefinite.

For the other direction of Property 5.4, suppose the Hessian is positive semidefinite. Then note that the Mean Value Theorem says there is a z between x and y such that:

$$f(y) = f(x) + (\nabla f(x))^\mathsf{T}(y-x) + \frac{1}{2}(y-x)^\mathsf{T}\nabla^2 f(z)(y-x). \tag{5.8}$$

Rearranging,

$$f(y) - f(x) - (\nabla f(x))^\mathsf{T}(y-x) = \frac{1}{2}(y-x)^\mathsf{T}\nabla^2 f(z)(y-x) \geq 0, \tag{5.9}$$

where the latter inequality holds because of positive semidefiniteness. Applying Property 5.2 proves that f is convex. ∎

If $f(x)$ is concave, then $g(x) = -f(x)$ is convex. So all the properties of convex functions work with obvious substitutions for concave functions: "maximize" replaces "minimize" and "negative semidefinite" replaces "positive semidefinite." The inequality in (5.4) is reversed for concave functions.

Consider the following cautionary example: Idee Adynr is a billionaire whose utility function is $U(w, b) = (5w - w^2)(10b - b^2)$; w is her wealth in billions of dollars and b is the number of best friends she has. Idee wants to maximize her utility.

To stay with our convention of minimizing, let $f(w, b) = -U(w, b)$, that is, the objective will be to minimize Idee's disutility. The gradient is:

$$\nabla f(w, b) = \begin{bmatrix} \frac{\partial f}{\partial w} \\ \frac{\partial f}{\partial b} \end{bmatrix} = \begin{bmatrix} -(5 - 2w)(10b - b^2) \\ -(5w - w^2)(10 - 2b) \end{bmatrix}.$$

Thus the critical point $\nabla f = 0$ when she has $w = \$2.5$ billion wealth and $b = 5$ best friends. Code Segment 5.1 shows how to use a standard scipy.optimize function to find the critical point using a numerical (conjugate gradient) method. The solution is:

```
Critical point wealth = 2.5, friends = 5.0
Objective function at critical point: -156.25
```

The Hessian of Idee's disutility function is:

$$\nabla^2 f = \begin{bmatrix} \frac{\partial^2 f}{\partial w^2} & \frac{\partial^2 f}{\partial w \partial b} \\ \frac{\partial^2 f}{\partial b \partial w} & \frac{\partial^2 f}{\partial b^2} \end{bmatrix} = \begin{bmatrix} 2(10b - b^2) & -2(5 - 2w)(5 - b) \\ -2(5 - 2w)(5 - b) & 2(5w - w^2) \end{bmatrix}.$$

At the critical point $w = 2.5$, $b = 5$, the Hessian evaluates to:

$$\nabla^2 f = \begin{bmatrix} 50 & 0 \\ 0 & 12.5 \end{bmatrix},$$

which is positive definite. So Idee's disutility function is convex at the critical point, and \$2.5 billion and 5 best friends is a local disutility minimum, that is, a local utility maximum. At the critical point, the disutility function is -156.25.

But the objective function is not globally convex. When both wealth w and best friends b are large, the curvature reverses. In fact, Idee can have arbitrarily large utility (arbitrarily large negative disutility) by having huge amounts of money and huge numbers of friends. For example, at $w = 7, b = 12$, the disutility is -336, that is, this is preferable to the critical point $w = 2.5, b = 5$. At $(7, 12)$ the Hessian has one positive and one negative eigenvalue. This can be seen in Figure 5.1 (generated by Code Segment 5.2).

The light blue well centered at wealth = 2.5, friends = 5 has the minimum value -156.25 as noted above. However, the front left corner of the graph at wealth = 7, friends = 12 has a value of -336. If we extended the graph far enough in either direction, we would get arbitrarily large negative values. Because the function is not everywhere convex, the local minimum is not a global minimum.

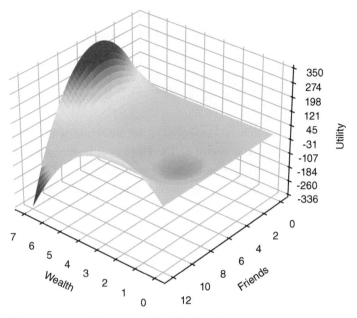

Figure 5.1 Locally convex disutility function.

5.3 | Unconstrained Convex Optimization

The Idee Adymr example shows that functions that are not globally convex can have messy behavior. But even if the function to be minimized is known to be convex, the unconstrained minimization problem might not have a closed-form solution. (Unconstrained means that there are no g or h functions in the generic form (5.3).)

The necessary and sufficient condition for x_M to be a global minimum of a convex function f is that the gradient $\nabla f(x_M) = 0$. But the gradient could be highly nonlinear and difficult to solve in closed form.

A simple example of a convex function is the portfolio mean-variance optimization problem from Chapter 4, or more generally a quadratic objective function:

$$f(x) = -m^\mathsf{T}x + \frac{1}{2}x^\mathsf{T}Cx. \tag{5.10}$$

Here the unknown x is a portfolio vector, that is, an n-vector of amounts of holdings in n possible assets. C is the $n \times n$ covariance matrix (which is symmetric by construction), and m is the n-vector of mean (expected) returns. Property 5.4 indicates that the function f is convex if and only if C is positive semidefinite, which it must be by construction.

If C is strictly positive definite – that is, the function is strictly convex – then C is nonsingular and the critical point is simply $x_{min} = C^{-1}m$.

However if C is singular – positive semidefinite but not positive definite – then there may or may not be a solution to the matrix equation $Cx_{min} = m$. For example, if:

$$C = \begin{bmatrix} 1 & 0 \\ 0 & 0 \end{bmatrix} \quad \text{and} \quad m = \begin{bmatrix} 1 \\ 1 \end{bmatrix},$$

then the objective function is $\frac{1}{2}v^2 - v - w$, where v and w are the two scalar components of the argument vector x. The Hessian is positive semidefinite, but there is no solution to $Cx_{min} = m$ because every multiple of C has a zero in the second component. In this case, the second scalar component w is unbounded and can go to ∞, giving an arbitrarily small objective function.

The Spectral Decomposition Theorem says that a positive semidefinite matrix can be written as $C = E_k D_k E_k^{\mathsf{T}}$, where $k \leq n$ and E_k is the $n \times k$ matrix of eigenvectors of C associated with nonzero eigenvalues; the $k < n$ nonzero eigenvalues are contained in the $k \times k$ diagonal matrix D_k. E_k is standardized so that $E_k^{\mathsf{T}} E_k = I_k$ where I_k is the $k \times k$ identity matrix.

> Property 5.5: For positive semidefinite C, there is a solution to $Cx_{min} = m$ if and only if m is in the nullity of $I - E_k E_k^{\mathsf{T}}$ where the columns of E_k are the standardized eigenvectors of C.

Proof: Recall that the nullity of a matrix M is the set of vectors x such that $Mx = 0$.

Suppose first that there is a solution x_{min} to $Cx_{min} = m$. Set $\lambda = D_k E_k^{\mathsf{T}} x_{min}$ where D_k is the diagonal matrix of associated eigenvalues as above. λ is a k-vector with the property $E_k \lambda = m$, so $E_k^{\mathsf{T}} E_k \lambda = E_k^{\mathsf{T}} m$, that is, $\lambda = E_k^{\mathsf{T}} m$ since E_k was standardized. Thus, $E_k \lambda = E_k(E_k^{\mathsf{T}} m)$, that is, $m = E_k(E_k^{\mathsf{T}} m)$ so $(I - E_k E_k^{\mathsf{T}})m = 0$ proving the desired nullity holds.

In the other direction suppose that $(I - E_k E_k^{\mathsf{T}})m = 0$, that is, $m = E_k E_k^{\mathsf{T}} m$. Set $x_{min} = E_k D_k^{-1} E_k^{\mathsf{T}} m$. Then $Cx_{min} = E_k D_k E_k^{\mathsf{T}} E_k D_k^{-1} E_k^{\mathsf{T}} m = E_k E_k^{\mathsf{T}} m = m$ where the last equality follows by supposition. ∎

In the example above where:

$$C = \begin{bmatrix} 1 & 0 \\ 0 & 0 \end{bmatrix} \quad \text{and} \quad m = \begin{bmatrix} 1 \\ 1 \end{bmatrix}$$

$$k = 1 \quad \text{and} \quad E_1 = E_k = \begin{bmatrix} 1 \\ 0 \end{bmatrix},$$

$$\text{so } I - E_k E_k^{\mathsf{T}} = \begin{bmatrix} 0 & 0 \\ 0 & 1 \end{bmatrix}.$$

Multiplying $\begin{bmatrix} 0 & 0 \\ 0 & 1 \end{bmatrix}\begin{bmatrix} 1 \\ 1 \end{bmatrix} = \begin{bmatrix} 0 \\ 1 \end{bmatrix}$ which is not zero, so m is not in the nullity and Property 5.5 says there is no solution.

For the case where m is in the nullity of $I - E_k E_k^\mathsf{T}$, a solution looks like:

$$x_{min} = E_k D_k^{-1} E_k^\mathsf{T} m + Z_{n-k}\nu, \tag{5.11}$$

where ν is any $(n-k)$-vector. Here Z_{n-k} is the $n \times (n-k)$ matrix of eigenvectors associated with the zero eigenvalue of C. $E_k D_k^{-1} E_k^\mathsf{T}$ is the **pseudo-inverse** of C.

For example, if:

$$C = \begin{bmatrix} 1 & 1 \\ 1 & 1 \end{bmatrix} \quad \text{and} \quad m = \begin{bmatrix} 1 \\ 1 \end{bmatrix},$$

then $k = 1$ and $E_k = \begin{bmatrix} 1/\sqrt{2} \\ 1/\sqrt{2} \end{bmatrix}$. The matrix $I - E_k E_k^\mathsf{T} = \frac{1}{2}\begin{bmatrix} 1 & -1 \\ -1 & 1 \end{bmatrix}$ and m is in its nullity, so there is a solution to $Cx_{min} = m$. In this example, $Z_1 = \begin{bmatrix} 1/\sqrt{2} \\ -1/\sqrt{2} \end{bmatrix}$. The nonzero eigenvalue is $D_1 = 2$. Thus the form of solutions in this case is:

$$x_{min} = \frac{1}{2}\begin{bmatrix} 1 \\ 1 \end{bmatrix} + \nu\begin{bmatrix} 1 \\ -1 \end{bmatrix},$$

where ν is an arbitrary scalar.

5.3.1 Gradient Descent

When the convex objective function f is more complicated, an iterative technique can be applied. The nonoptimality of a point x is $f(x) - f(x_{min})$; this must be nonnegative. Under a condition called **strong convexity**, nonoptimality can be bounded both below and above:

$$\frac{1}{2e_{max}}\nabla f(x)^\mathsf{T}\nabla f(x) \le f(x) - f(x_{min}) \le \frac{1}{2e_{min}}\nabla f(x)^\mathsf{T}\nabla f(x). \tag{5.12}$$

Here x_{min} is the global minimum point, and x is any other point. e_{min} and e_{max} are the minimum and maximum eigenvalues of the Hessian matrix over the domain of f.

Even when (5.12) doesn't hold, it's reasonable to look at $\nabla f(x)^\mathsf{T}\nabla f(x)$ as an indicator of how close x is to x_{min}: after all, when $x = x_{min}$ the gradient $\nabla f(x)$ equals zero. So a small dot product $\nabla f(x)^\mathsf{T}\nabla f(x)$ is a clue that x is close to x_{min}. This idea is used in the **Gradient Descent Method**,[1] which proceeds as follows:

---

1 [Boyd and Vandenberghe 2004], pp. 466ff.

Gradient Descent Method

1. Choose an initial point x_0 and a convergence parameter ϵ. Set $i = 0$.
2. Evaluate $\nabla f(x_i)$, the gradient at x_i.
3. Check convergence $\nabla f(x_i)^\mathsf{T} \nabla f(x_i) < \epsilon$ for some target ϵ. If converged, stop with $x_{min} = x_i$. Otherwise continue.
4. Choose a scalar step size δ_i.
5. Set $x_{i+1} = x_i - \delta_i \nabla f(x_i)$ and $i = i + 1$. Go back to Step 2.

Then ϵ should be chosen so that the gradient is reasonably close to zero before convergence is declared.

The complexity of the objective function f needs to be taken into account when choosing the scalar distance δ_i in Step 4. If it's computationally easy to find the δ_i that minimizes $f(x_i - \delta_i \nabla f(x_i))$, then that's what should be done. For example, if the objective function is the quadratic one (5.10), then a closed-form expression for δ_i can be computed.

For more difficult objective functions, **backtracking** might need to be used. The idea is to take a big step, and then reduce the step size iteratively until it appears to be approximately optimal.

To visualize this, suppose you are walking through hilly countryside and want to find the lowest point of the terrain. You are completely fogged in so you can't see anything around you, but once you step on a point you can check your altimeter and see how high or low you are.

One strategy would be to take very tiny steps, exhaustively covering all the terrain. That would increase the chance that you find your way to the lowest point, but it might take a very long time. On the other hand, you could adopt a strategy of taking giant leaps for each step. That might speed things up, but it would increase the chance that you jump right over the minimum and never find it.

The backtracking method tries to combine the best of both worlds: take a big jump in some direction, and then cut back judiciously until you seem to be converging on the best you can do in that direction. To control the backtracking process, there are two search parameters: $0 < \alpha < \frac{1}{2}$ and $0 < \beta < 1$. β will be a fineness parameter: the closer it is to one, the finer the search. α controls the accuracy of the search in a different way: the closer α is to $\frac{1}{2}$, the more optimal the searched-for distance will be.

The backtracking algorithm chooses δ_i in Step 4 of the Gradient Descent Method, assuming that the current point is x_i. To be more general, we'll just call these items δ and x within the discussion of backtracking.

Given a proposed step direction s – for Gradient Descent, $s = \nabla f(x)$ – and a gradient g – in this case, also $g = \nabla f(x)$ – the Backtracking Algorithm proceeds as follows:

Backtracking Algorithm

1. Set $\delta = 1$.
2. Look at the proposed new objective function $f(x - \delta s)$. Is this larger than $f(x) - \alpha\delta g^\mathsf{T}s$? If not, stop and return the current δ. If so, go to Step 3.
3. Set $\delta = \beta\delta$ and go to Step 2.

Why does the stopping test in Step 2 work when $s = g = \nabla f(x)$? Assuming there is a maximum Hessian eigenvalue e_{max} as above, we can alter (5.8) to say:

$$f(y) \leq f(x) + (\nabla f(x))^\mathsf{T}(y - x) + \frac{e_{max}}{2}(y - x)^\mathsf{T}(y - x). \tag{5.13}$$

So if $y = x - \delta\nabla f(x)$, we can write:

$$f(x - \delta\nabla f(x)) \leq f(x) + \delta\left(\frac{\delta e_{max}}{2} - 1\right)(\nabla f(x))^\mathsf{T}\nabla f(x). \tag{5.14}$$

Note that $\frac{\delta e_{max}}{2} - 1 < -\frac{1}{2}$ when $0 \leq \delta < \frac{1}{e_{max}}$, so for small positive δ, we have:

$$f(x - \delta\nabla f(x)) \leq f(x) - \frac{\delta}{2}(\nabla f(x))^\mathsf{T}\nabla f(x) \leq f(x) - \alpha\delta(\nabla f(x))^\mathsf{T}\nabla f(x), \tag{5.15}$$

where the second inequality holds because $\alpha < \frac{1}{2}$.

Equation (5.15) shows that the condition for the backtracking algorithm will be satisfied for small enough δ. The efficiency of the algorithm depends on how many steps it takes to find a good descent size δ.

As an example, consider the objective function:

$$f(x) = \ln\left(\sum_{i=1}^{3}\exp(a_i^\mathsf{T}x + b_i)\right),$$

where x is a 2-vector and:

$$a_1 = \begin{bmatrix} 1 \\ 3 \end{bmatrix}, a_2 = \begin{bmatrix} 1 \\ -3 \end{bmatrix}, a_3 = \begin{bmatrix} -1 \\ 0 \end{bmatrix}, b_1 = b_2 = b_3 = -.1.$$

We'll start with the initial point $x_0 = \begin{bmatrix} 1 \\ 1 \end{bmatrix}$. We used $\alpha = .25$ and $\beta = .75$. Code Segment 5.3 performs gradient descent, with the following results:

```
Initial point: [1, 1]
Objective function at initial point: 3.9091744845917344
Gradient at initial point: [0.98664717 2.96523407]
0   obj: 3.9091744845917344   grad^2: 9.766085755759542
Delta from backtracking: 0.5625
1   obj: 2.4198033815320383   grad^2: 8.332277507974275
Delta from backtracking: 0.31640625
2   obj: 1.191342005793633   grad^2: 1.8085316901136013
```

```
Delta from backtracking: 0.2373046875
3  obj: 1.0371266525499625  grad^2: 0.4614786912439451
Delta from backtracking: 0.31640625
4  obj: 0.993811097175349  grad^2: 0.3000411969185905
Delta from backtracking: 0.31640625
5  obj: 0.9663931514449048  grad^2: 0.15240881861624558
Delta from backtracking: 0.31640625
6  obj: 0.9513765394485699  grad^2: 0.06234346749137597
Delta from backtracking: 0.31640625
7  obj: 0.9444446348940022  grad^2: 0.021872767145336654
Delta from backtracking: 0.31640625
8  obj: 0.9416102287070496  grad^2: 0.0071421499562395055
Delta from backtracking: 0.421875
9  obj: 0.9406337475243942  grad^2: 0.005013547563411552
Delta from backtracking: 0.31640625
10  obj: 0.9400357387441528  grad^2: 0.0013103159291693281
Delta from backtracking: 0.421875
11  obj: 0.9398762683963624  grad^2: 0.0008968302419736885
Delta from backtracking: 0.31640625
12  obj: 0.9397707581273169  grad^2:
       0.00021282361268819977
Delta from backtracking: 0.421875
13  obj: 0.9397453799577112  grad^2: 0.0001426802968551179
Delta from backtracking: 0.31640625
14  obj: 0.9397285178216892  grad^2:
        3.2757240214948984e-05
Delta from backtracking: 0.421875
15  obj: 0.9397245432286266  grad^2:
        2.1622169910912445e-05
Delta from backtracking: 0.31640625
16  obj: 0.9397219603939353  grad^2: 4.935959607312414e-06
Delta from backtracking: 0.421875
17  obj: 0.9397213421564151  grad^2: 3.214831086458704e-06
Delta from backtracking: 0.31640625
18  obj: 0.9397209529623713  grad^2: 7.381076729893752e-07
Delta from backtracking: 0.421875
19  obj: 0.9397208570272877  grad^2:
        4.7463418119893896e-07
Delta from backtracking: 0.31640625
20  obj: 0.9397207987112907  grad^2:
        1.1013177723974826e-07
```

```
Delta from backtracking: 0.421875
21  obj: 0.9397207838334166  grad^2: 6.991693307399583e-08
Delta from backtracking: 0.31640625
22  obj: 0.9397207751074605  grad^2: 1.643163423666225e-08
Delta from backtracking: 0.421875
23  obj: 0.9397207727999762  grad^2:
       1.0295718246691514e-08
Delta from backtracking: 0.31640625
24  obj: 0.9397207714939018  grad^2: 2.453528614906475e-09
optimal x [-3.46542274e-01  8.52808141e-06]
optimal objective 0.9397207714939018
gradient [3.13159844e-05 3.83775681e-05]
```

The output shows that $f(x_0) = 3.909$ and:

$$\nabla f(x_0) = \begin{bmatrix} .987 \\ 2.965 \end{bmatrix}.$$

The algorithm converged in 24 iterations to a solution $x_{min} = [-.3465, 0]^\mathsf{T}$ and an objective function $f(x_{min}) = .9397$. The backtracking algorithm generally chose δ between .3 and .43.

5.3.2 Newton's Method

Newton's Method is an iterative technique like the gradient descent method, but one that often has faster convergence properties.

Consider a step from x to y as follows:

$$y = x - \delta \left(\nabla^2 f(x)\right)^{-1} \nabla f(x).$$

The gradient step used in the gradient descent method has been modified by left-multiplying by the inverse of the Hessian matrix, which must be strictly positive definite for this approach to work. The idea is to take advantage of the Taylor expansion:

$$f(y) = f(x) + (\nabla f(x))^\mathsf{T}(y - x) + \frac{1}{2}(y - x)^\mathsf{T}\nabla^2 f(x)(y - x) + \cdots +.$$

Substituting $y = x - \delta\left(\nabla^2 f(x)\right)^{-1}\nabla f(x)$ into the Taylor expansion gives:

$$f\!\left(x - \delta\left(\nabla^2 f(x)\right)^{-1}\nabla f(x)\right) = f(x) - \left(\delta - \frac{\delta^2}{2}\right)(\nabla f(x))^\mathsf{T}\left(\nabla^2 f(x)\right)^{-1}\nabla f(x) + O(\delta^3).$$

This shows that for small enough δ and a strictly positive definite Hessian, the step from x to y is guaranteed to be a descent.

The algorithm is straightforward:

Newton's Method Algorithm

1. Pick an initial x_0 and set $i = 1$. Choose a tolerance parameter ϵ and backtracking algorithm parameters α and β.
2. Evaluate the quadratic form $(\nabla f(x_{i-1}))^{\mathsf{T}} (\nabla^2 f(x_{i-1}))^{-1} (\nabla f(x_{i-1}))$. If this is less than the tolerance parameter ϵ, quit and return the result x_{i-1}.
3. Choose a step size δ_i using the backtracking algorithm with step $s = (\nabla^2 f(x_{i-1}))^{-1} \nabla f(x_{i-1})$ and gradient $g = \nabla f(x_{i-1})$.
4. Move to $x_i = x_{i-1} - \delta s$, increment i, and go back to Step 2.

Code Segment 5.4 re-solves the example problem that was used above for the gradient descent method, this time with Newton's Method. The output looks like this:

```
[1, 1]
Objective function at initial point: 3.9091744845917344
Gradient at initial point: [0.98664717 2.96523407]
Hessian at initial point: [[0.02652737 0.03959433]
 [0.03959425 0.14729915]]
Inverse Hessian initial: [[ 62.95504778 -16.92245195]
 [-16.92241874  11.33768788]]
0  obj: 3.9091744845917344  grad_hessinv_grad:
       61.9550186818811
0.1001129150390625 [-0.19488658 -0.69415497]
1  obj: 1.9695284290060509  grad_hessinv_grad:
       5.531911655234065
0.2373046875 [0.58173321 0.05768105]
2  obj: 1.332917842911155  grad_hessinv_grad:
       1.1717248760683536
0.75 [-0.60126449  0.03222069]
3  obj: 0.9735631248857185  grad_hessinv_grad:
       0.07127301938153104
1 [-0.33182959 -0.01084381]
4  obj: 0.9400979212470573  grad_hessinv_grad:
       0.0007467797214999371
1 [-3.46318864e-01 -1.52792099e-04]
5  obj: 0.9397208558231811  grad_hessinv_grad:
       1.6993978123362368e-07
1 [-3.46573538e-01 -3.88955953e-08]
6  obj: 0.9397207708399228  grad_hessinv_grad:
       9.563096791675888e-15
```

```
optimal x: [-3.46573538e-01 -3.88955953e-08]
iterations: 6
optimal objective: 0.9397207708399228
gradient: [ 5.24899427e-08 -1.75030188e-07]
Hessian [[ 9.99999996e-01 -1.64845942e-07]
 [-1.56169838e-07  4.50000025e+00]]
```

Newton's Method arrives at the same answer as gradient descent, but after only six iterations. Each iteration is more computationally costly than gradient descent as a matrix inversion and matrix multiplications are performed. However, overall efficiency is probably better.

There are many variants of descent algorithms, and a number of tuning techniques that can speed unconstrained optimization considerably when there are large numbers of variables. Most scientific computation packages have large numbers of sophisticated methods to solve minimization problems. For example, Code Segment 5.5 solves the example problem yet again using scipy.optimize's Conjugate Gradient (CG) method. The result vector, its objective function, and its gradient are as follows:

```
[-3.46579585e-01 -1.16131017e-07]
0.9397207708579167 [-5.99472090e-06 -5.22586444e-07]
```

5.4 Constrained Optimization

In most practical applications, the objective function $f \colon \mathbb{R}^n \to \mathbb{R}$ is not allowed to operate on the entirety of n-space.

For example, when we considered the simple portfolio optimization example (5.10), we didn't take into account the tautology that 100 percent of a portfolio is all we have to invest, that is, the budget constraint $x^\mathsf{T} u = 1$ where u is the vector of all ones.

More generally, an equality-constrained convex optimization problem looks like:

$$\text{minimize}_x f(x)$$

$$\text{subject to } Ax = b. \tag{5.16}$$

Here A is a $k \times n$ matrix with $k \leq n$ and b is a k-vector. Recall that the generic optimization problem's equality constraints in (5.3) were expressed as components of the vector identity $g(x) = 0$. Here the function $g(x) = Ax - b$ is linear because of the convexity requirement. An equality constraint is the same as two inequality constraints, $g_i(x) \geq 0$ and $-g_i(x) \geq 0$; the only way both can be true and $g_i(x)$ can be convex is for $g_i(x)$ to be linear.

The feasible set for problem (5.16) is the set $F = \{x | Ax = b\}$. Recall from standard calculus that problems like (5.16) can be solved with **Lagrange**

Multipliers. Joseph-Louis Lagrange noticed that if $x_{min} \in F$ and minimizes f among all members of F, then there exists a k-vector λ so that:

$$\nabla f(x_{min}) = A^\mathsf{T}\lambda. \tag{5.17}$$

In effect the Lagrange multipliers – the components of the λ vector – extend the function f on n variables to a function h on $n + k$ variables:

$$h(x_1, \ldots, x_n, \lambda_1, \ldots, \lambda_k) = f(x_1, \ldots, x_n) - \lambda^\mathsf{T}(Ax - b)$$

$$= f(x_1, \ldots, x_n) - \sum_{j=1}^{k} \lambda_j(a_j x - b_j), \tag{5.18}$$

where a_j is the $1 \times k$ vector giving the jth row of A. The function h is called the **Lagrangian** of the problem (5.16). The partial derivative of h with respect to λ_j encodes the jth equality constraint.

Thus unconstrained optimization techniques can be used on the function $h(x_1, \ldots, x_n, \lambda_1, \ldots, \lambda_k)$. The resulting $x^* = (x_1, \ldots, x_n)$ will be the optimal vector that satisfies the equality constraints.

For example, suppose there are linear equality constraints with a portfolio optimization problem like (5.10):

$$\text{minimize}_x - m^\mathsf{T}x + \frac{1}{2}x^\mathsf{T}Cx$$

$$\text{subject to } Ax = b, \tag{5.19}$$

where A is a $k \times n$ matrix and b is a k-vector.

The Lagrangian is:

$$-m^\mathsf{T}x + \frac{1}{2}x^\mathsf{T}Cx + \lambda^\mathsf{T}(Ax - b),$$

where λ is a k-vector. Taking the gradient with respect to the extended (x, λ) vector gives:

$$Cx + A^\mathsf{T}\lambda = m,$$

$$Ax = b.$$

Define an $(n + k) \times (n + k)$ matrix:

$$B = \begin{bmatrix} C & A^\mathsf{T} \\ A & 0 \end{bmatrix}.$$

Then the optimization is just the solution to the linear system:

$$B \begin{bmatrix} x \\ \lambda \end{bmatrix} = \begin{bmatrix} m \\ b \end{bmatrix}.$$

If B is nonsingular then the solution is simply $\begin{bmatrix} x \\ \lambda \end{bmatrix} = B^{-1} \begin{bmatrix} m \\ b \end{bmatrix}$. Otherwise (if B is singular), then the linear dependencies might need to be separated out using a pseudo-inverse as in (5.11).

For more complex problems than (5.19) where the objective function is not amenable to closed-form solution, an iterative method can be used to find the zero gradient of the Lagrangian (5.18).

An explicit way to require feasibility $Ax = b$ is to find the nullity of A, that is, the $n \times (n - k)$ matrix N such that $AN = 0$. (We're assuming that $rank(A) = rowdim(A) = k$. If not, N has more columns.)

The nullity N of A can be found from an eigendecomposition of $A^\mathsf{T}A$, which is an $n \times n$ matrix of rank k assuming full row rank of A. The nullity of $A^\mathsf{T}A$ is made up of the $n - k$ eigenvectors of $A^\mathsf{T}A$ corresponding to zero eigenvalues. These are also in the null space of A since $A^\mathsf{T}Ax = 0$ must mean $Ax = 0$ or else A is not of full row rank. So A's nullity N is the $n \times (n - k)$ matrix whose columns are the zero-eigenvalue eigenvectors of $A^\mathsf{T}A$.

Set $x_0 = A^\mathsf{T}(AA^\mathsf{T})^{-1}b$; x_0 is a solution to $Ax_0 = b$. Thus all solutions to $Ax = b$ can be written as $x = x_0 + Nz$, where z is any (i.e. unconstrained) $(n - k)$-vector.

Because of this, we can rewrite (5.16) as the unconstrained problem:

$$\text{minimize}_z \text{ff}(z), \tag{5.20}$$

where $\text{ff}(z) = f(x_0 + Nz)$. (5.20) can be solved with an unconstrained technique like Newton's Method on a lower-dimensional (i.e. the size of z) problem.

A simple example of constraint mapping is a way to enforce a budget constraint $x^\mathsf{T}u = 1$; simply define the last component x_n of the n-vector x as $x_n = 1 - x_1 - \cdots - x_{n-1}$. Plug this equality into the objective function and the other constraints, reducing the problem to one on $n - 1$ variables where the budget constraint is built in.

5.4.1 Lagrange Duality

Even more generally than (5.16), an optimization problem can be written like this to include inequality constraints:

$$\text{minimize}_x f(x)$$

$$\text{subject to } g_i(x) \le 0, \quad i = 1, \dots, k. \tag{5.21}$$

We won't require that $f(x)$ or $g_i(x)$ are convex for the remainder of this Subsection 5.4.1.

A common technique in optimization is to look for a dual problem: that is, a problem that ends up being equivalent to the original under certain conditions. To this end, define the **Lagrange dual function** of the optimization (5.21) as:

$$L(\lambda) = \inf_{x \in F} \left\{ f(x) + \sum_{i=1}^{k} \lambda_i g_i(x) \right\}. \tag{5.22}$$

Here F is the feasible set, $F = \{x | g_i(x) \le 0, \quad i = 1, \dots, k\}$.

Let M be the global minimum feasible point, that is, $M \in F$ and $f(M) \le f(x)$ for all $x \in F$. In other words, M is a solution to the optimization problem (5.21).

If x is feasible, $\sum_{i=1}^{k} \lambda_i g_i \le 0$ when each $\lambda_i \ge 0$, since feasibility means $g_i(x) \le 0$. Since M is one of the feasible points over which the *inf* in (5.22) is taken, $L(\lambda) \le f(M)$ must hold as long as each element of λ is nonnegative.

The best lower bound that the Lagrange dual function can give can be found by constructing another optimization:

$$\text{minimize}_\lambda - L(\lambda)$$

$$\text{subject to} - \lambda_i \le 0, \quad i = 1, \dots, k. \tag{5.23}$$

Note that:

$$-L(a\lambda_1 + (1-a)\lambda_2)$$

$$= -\inf_{x \in F} \left\{ f(x) + \sum_{i=1}^{k} (a\lambda_{1i} + (1-a)\lambda_{2i}) g_i(x) \right\}$$

$$= -\inf_{x \in F} \left\{ a\left(f(x) + \sum_{i=1}^{k} \lambda_{1i} g_i(x) \right) + (1-a)\left(f(x) + \sum_{i=1}^{k} \lambda_{2i} g_i(x) \right) \right\}$$

$$\le -a \cdot \inf_{x \in F} \left\{ \left(f(x) + \sum_{i=1}^{k} \lambda_{1i} g_i(x) \right) \right\} - (1-a) \inf_{x \in F} \left\{ \left(f(x) + \sum_{i=1}^{k} \lambda_{2i} g_i(x) \right) \right\}$$

$$= -aL(\lambda_1) - (1-a)L(\lambda_2).$$

The inequality follows because allowing inf to work separately on each term allows it to (possibly) find a smaller value, which becomes larger when negated. This proves that the negative of the Lagrange dual function $-L(\lambda)$ is convex no matter what properties the original optimization (5.21) had.

Thus, (5.23) is a convex optimization. Let λ_M be a vector that minimizes $-L(\lambda_M)$ while satisfying the constraint of having all nonnegative entries. Recall that $L(\lambda_M) \le f(M)$. When $L(\lambda_M) = f(M)$, the optimizations (5.21) and (5.23) are said to have **strong duality**.

If strong duality holds, then:

$$f(M) = L(\lambda_M) = \inf_{x \in F}\left\{f(x) + \sum_{i=1}^{k}\lambda_{M_i}g_i(x)\right\}$$

$$\leq f(M) + \sum_{i=1}^{k}\lambda_{M_i}g_i(M) \leq f(M). \tag{5.24}$$

The first inequality in this series holds because the infimum of an expression over all feasible x has to be less than or equal to the value of the expression at a particular feasible x, namely $x = M$. The second inequality holds because M is feasible (so $g_i(M) \leq 0$ as required in (5.21)), and the λ_{M_i} are nonnegative as required in (5.23).

Thus $\lambda_{M_i}g_i(M) \leq 0$ for all i, so $\sum_{i=1}^{k}\lambda_{M_i}g_i(M) \leq 0$. In that case the inequalities in (5.24) are actually equalities, so when strong duality holds then:

$$\sum_{i=1}^{k}\lambda_{M_i}g_i(M) = 0. \tag{5.25}$$

If every summand of the sum in (5.25) is non-positive and the sum is zero, then (under strong duality) every summand must be zero: $\lambda_{M_i}g_i(M) = 0 \ \forall i$. Thus under strong duality, a non-zero Lagrange multiplier $\lambda_{M_i} > 0$ forces $g_i(M) = 0$.

Define a Lagrangian function similar to (5.18):

$$h(x,\lambda) = f(x) + \sum_{i=1}^{k}\lambda_i g_i(x). \tag{5.26}$$

Then under strong duality:

$$\inf_{x \in F}\{h(x,\lambda_M)\} = h(M,\lambda_M).$$

In other words, under strong duality a (5.21) global minimum point M also minimizes the Lagrangian. Minima are critical points as we noted in the paragraph containing (5.2), so:

$$\nabla_x h(M,\lambda_M) = \nabla f(M) + \sum_{i=1}^{k}\lambda_{M_i}\nabla g_i(M) = 0. \tag{5.27}$$

Then (5.27) is a stronger version of Lagrange's (5.17).

Thus under strong duality between (5.21) and (5.23), the following conditions hold on a global minimum point M and the dual optimal Lagrange vector λ_M. These are called the **Karush–Kuhn–Tucker ("KKT")** conditions:[2]

Karush–Kuhn–Tucker Conditions   (5.28)

$$g_i(M) \leq 0,$$

$$\lambda_{M_i} \geq 0, \text{ for all } i,$$

$$\lambda_{M_i} g_i(M) = 0, \text{ for all } i, \text{ and}$$

$$\nabla f(M) + \sum_{i=1}^{k} \lambda_{M_i} \nabla g_i(M) = 0.$$

Strong duality implies KKT (5.28).

5.4.2 KKT Conditions with Convexity

It is not generally true that KKT implies strong duality. Some conclusions can be made in the other direction if the original optimization problem (5.21) is convex. While the previous subsection 5.4.1 was general and didn't require convexity, for the remainder of this subsection 5.4.2 we'll assume that both the objective function $f(x)$ and all the constraint functions $g_i(x)$ are convex.

In that case, note that any equality constraints (where both $g_i(x) \geq 0$ and $-g_i(x) \geq 0$) must be affine (linear), since the only way a function and its opposite can both be convex is if the function is affine.

Assume that there is a y and a λ such that the KKT conditions hold:

KKT Conditions with inputs   (5.29)

$$g_i(y) \leq 0,$$

$$\lambda_i \geq 0, \text{ for all } i,$$

$$\lambda_i g_i(y) = 0, \text{ for all } i, \text{ and}$$

$$\nabla f(y) + \sum_{i=1}^{k} \lambda_i \nabla g_i(y) = 0.$$

---

2 Until about the year 2000, Karush's name was not included in what were just called the "Kuhn–Tucker" conditions based on [Kuhn and Tucker 1951]. For example, [Bertsekas 1996] does not mention Karush. However, some mathematical history detective work by [Kjeldsen 2000] found that William Karush had predated Kuhn and Tucker in [Karush 1939], his master's thesis at the University of Chicago. [Boyd and Vandenberghe 2004] refers to Karush–Kuhn–Tucker.

The first two lines of (5.29) mean that y is feasible for (5.21) and that λ is feasible for the dual problem (5.23).

If the primary optimization (5.21) is convex, then the Lagrangian function $h(y, \lambda)$ defined in (5.26) is a linear combination of convex functions, so it is convex. The last line of (5.29) says that the gradient with respect to y of the Lagrangian is zero. With the assumption of convexity, Property 5.3 can be applied, implying that y minimizes the Lagrangian.

Together with definition (5.22), this shows that:

$$L(\lambda) = \inf_{x \in F} \left\{ f(x) + \sum_{i=1}^{k} \lambda_i g_i(x) \right\} = h(y, \lambda) = f(y) + \sum_{i=1}^{k} \lambda_i g_i(y). \qquad (5.30)$$

The third line of (5.29) implies $\sum_{i=1}^{k} \lambda_i g_i(x) = 0$, so (5.30) says that $L(\lambda) = f(y)$ and strong duality holds.

Another technical condition (that there is at least one feasible point of (5.21) where the inequality constraints hold strictly) is needed to establish that y is a global minimum.

A convex optimization problem like (5.21) can be approached by finding points that satisfy the KKT conditions (5.29). That's often easier than trying to do the optimization with an iterative method.

The third KKT condition $\lambda_i g_i(y) = 0$ for all i separates the conditions of (5.21) into two parts: strict inequality conditions where $g_i(y) < 0$; and equality conditions where $g_i(y) = 0$. For the former, $\lambda_i = 0$ must hold. For the latter, the only information from the third KKT condition is that $\lambda_i \geq 0$ so more work is needed to determine these equality-constraint λ_i.

When the problem and its constraints are convex, the only way to require equality (rather than having it possible but not required) is to have the single affine requirement $a_i^\top y - b_i = 0$. Thus for convex problems, (5.21) can be rewritten as:

$$\text{minimize}_x f(x)$$

$$\text{subject to } g_i(x) \leq 0, \quad i = 1, \ldots, k_{ineq}$$

$$\text{and } Ax = b, \text{ rowdim}(A) = \text{rowdim}(b) = k_{eq},$$

$$f, g \text{ convex.} \qquad (5.31)$$

The KKT conditions for this form of the convex optimization problem are:

$$\text{KKT Conditions for (5.31)} \qquad (5.32)$$

$$g_i(M) \leq 0 \quad i = 1, \ldots, k_{ineq},$$

$$\lambda_{M_i} = 0, \text{ when } g_i(M) < 0,$$

$$\lambda_{M_i} \geq 0, \text{ when } g_i(M) = 0,$$

$$Ax = b, \text{ and}$$

$$\nabla f(M) + \sum_{\lambda_{M_i} \neq 0} \lambda_{M_i} \nabla g_i(M) + A^{\mathsf{T}} \gamma = 0.$$

Here γ is an unconstrained k_{eq}-vector. Note that even though inequality constraints don't require equality, equality may happen to hold at a solution. Thus it can't be assumed that the λ_M associated with the ith inequality constraint is zero.

5.5 Barrier Methods

Equation (5.20) showed that an equality-constrained optimization could be reduced to an unconstrained optimization by using the Lagrangian (5.18). That then allowed iterative methods to be used to solve difficult problems.

Similarly, an inequality-constrained optimization can be reduced to a series of equality-constrained optimizations, since an inequality that is not binding at a point can be ignored in a neighborhood of that point. So previous techniques can be used at least until the algorithm bumps into another constraint, at which point the problem morphs into a new equality-constrained problem.

One way to accomplish a reduction of inequality constraints to equality constraints is with a **barrier method**. With a barrier method, the inequality constraints are put in the objective function with a high penalty if they are not satisfied. The purest form of a barrier is the indicator function:

$$\delta(x) = \begin{cases} 0, & \text{for } x \leq 0, \\ \infty, & \text{for } x > 0. \end{cases}$$

Equation (5.31) can then be reformulated as:

$$\text{minimize}_x f(x) + \sum_{i=1}^{k_{ineq}} \delta(g_i(x))$$

$$\text{subject to } Ax = b, \text{rowdim}(A) = \text{rowdim}(b) = k_{eq}. \tag{5.33}$$

This removes explicit inequality constraints and makes (5.31) equivalent to (5.16). However, the indicator functions are ill behaved: no matter how cautious an algorithm is, at some point its next step will explode as the delta function switches on.

Fortunately, this problem can be mitigated by smoothing the delta functions, that is, replacing δ with a smoother version δ_{sm} that has a parameter that can be

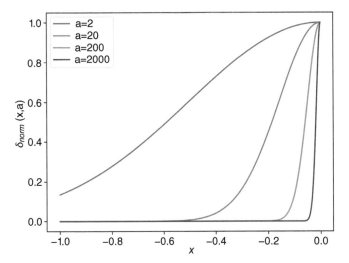

Figure 5.2 Normal pdf-based approximation to delta function.

set to gradually approach the abrupt δ. One smoothing approach is based on the normal pdf:

$$\delta_{norm}(x, a) = \exp\left(ax|x|\right).$$

As $a \to \infty$, the function becomes sharper and more like the indicator function. At $x = 0$ $\delta_{norm}(x, a) = 1$. But for large a, δ_{norm} quickly becomes very large for any positive argument x.

Figure 5.2 (generated by Code Segment 5.6) shows the "bend" in the δ_{norm} function as the a parameter gets larger:

In practice, another parameter ω is used to balance the effect of the indicator function against the rest of the objective function. We'll use δ_{norm} as the smoothed indicator function in what follows, but we'll shift to the more general notation δ_{sm} to indicate that other smoothed indicator functions can be used.

Equation (5.33) is, therefore, changed to:

$$\text{minimize}_x \quad \omega f(x) + \sum_{i=1}^{k_{ineq}} \delta_{sm}(g_i(x))$$

$$\text{subject to } Ax = b, \text{rowdim}(A) = \text{rowdim}(b) = k_{eq}. \tag{5.34}$$

If $g_i(x) < 0$ as desired, $\delta_{sm}(g_i(x))$ is comparatively small. Once $g_i(x)$ goes positive, $\delta_{sm}(g_i(x))$ goes to an increasingly unpleasant large positive number, which the optimizer will seek to avoid. Solving (5.34) with small ω is really just finding a feasible point.

After a solution is obtained for a given level of ω, it can be used as the starting point for a tougher optimization with a bigger ω that gives more emphasis on minimizing $f(x)$. Eventually this process will converge on a solution that satisfies the constraints and minimizes $f(x)$.

The **Barrier Algorithm**[3] to solve (5.33) looks like this:

Barrier Algorithm

1. Set parameters $\omega_0 > 0$, $\alpha > 1$, $\epsilon > 0$. Find an initial feasible point x of the problem (5.33). Set $\omega = \omega_0$.
2. Perform the optimization (5.34) using an iterative technique on its Lagrangian, starting at initial point x. Call the result $x(\omega)$.
3. Set $x = x(\omega)$.
4. If $k_{eq}/\omega < \epsilon$, stop with solution x. Otherwise, set $\omega = \alpha\omega$ and go back to Step 2.

We'll illustrate this method by solving a simple problem based on the efficient frontier optimizations in Chapter 4. We'll just look for a minimum variance portfolio subject to a budget constraint and subject to a convex constraint that the sum of the squares of the weights is less than .4.

$$\text{minimize}_x \frac{1}{2} w^\mathsf{T} C w$$

$$\text{subject to } w^\mathsf{T} u = 1, \quad w^\mathsf{T} w \leq .4.$$

As usual, the dimension of the vectors is n and u is an n-vector of all ones. Using the encoding process for the budget constraint, let w_0 be an n-vector of all zeroes except for a one in the nth place. Let N be an $n \times (n-1)$ matrix with the $(n-1) \times (n-1)$ identity matrix in the first $n-1$ rows, and a row of all -1s in the last row.

$$w_0 = \begin{bmatrix} 0 \\ \vdots \\ 0 \\ 1 \end{bmatrix}, \qquad N = \begin{bmatrix} I_{n-1} \\ -u_{n-1}^\mathsf{T} \end{bmatrix}.$$

Then for any $(n-1)$-vector x, the n-vector $w_0 + Nx$ satisfies the budget constraint since:

$$u_n^\mathsf{T}(w_0 + Nx) = 1 + u_{n-1}^\mathsf{T} I_{n-1} x - u_{n-1}^\mathsf{T} x = 1.$$

The objective function becomes:

$$\frac{1}{2} w^\mathsf{T} C w = \frac{1}{2}(w_0 + Nx)^\mathsf{T} C(w_0 + Nx) = \frac{1}{2} x^\mathsf{T} F x + w_0^\mathsf{T} C N x + const,$$

---

3 [Fiacco and McCormick 1968].

where $F = N^\mathsf{T}CN$. Dropping the constant, the unconstrained objective (as in (5.34)) is to:

$$\text{minimize}_x \quad \omega\left(\frac{1}{2}x^\mathsf{T}Fx + w_0^\mathsf{T}CNx\right) + \delta_{sm}((w_0 + Nx)^\mathsf{T}(w_0 + Nx) - .4).$$

Further simplification:

$$w_0^\mathsf{T}w_0 = 1; \quad w_0^\mathsf{T}Nx = -u_{n-1}^\mathsf{T}x; \quad x^\mathsf{T}N^\mathsf{T}Nx = x^\mathsf{T}x + (u_{n-1}^\mathsf{T}x)^2.$$

The unconstrained problem simplifies to:

$$\text{minimize}_x \quad \omega\left(\frac{1}{2}x^\mathsf{T}Fx + w_0^\mathsf{T}CNx\right) + \delta_{sm}((u_{n-1}^\mathsf{T}x - 1)^2 + x^\mathsf{T}x - .4).$$

We'll use the same Swiss franc/pound/yen data as was used in Chapter 4 to create the C matrix. Code Segment 5.7 brings in that data.

The initial point will be $x_{init} = \left(\frac{1}{2}, \frac{1}{4}\right)$, so that $w_{init} = \left(\frac{1}{2}, \frac{1}{4}, \frac{1}{4}\right)$.

For accuracy and speed of convergence, the non-barrier part of the objective function will be scaled to be on the order of 1. Initial parameters are $\omega_0 = 1$, $\epsilon = 10^{-8}$.

Code Segment 5.8 runs the first pass of the barrier algorithm and produces the following output:

```
Initial point: [0.5, 0.25]
Objective function at initial point: 572.0095937203789
Gradient at initial point: [2.86529901e+04 3.81987775e-02]
0  obj: 572.0095937203789  grad^2: 820993843.7308449
Delta from backtracking: 2.3864747990995235e-06
1  obj: 12.768453271095378  grad^2: 541530.1485572453
Delta from backtracking: 7.533931929047496e-05
2  obj: -0.09288542514530174  grad^2: 1893.775482237069
Delta from backtracking: 0.0017838067156503712
3  obj: -1.054800646845617  grad^2: 8.426110061631583
Delta from backtracking: 0.0031712119389339932
4  obj: -1.062673480054419  grad^2: 1.9414162883166184
Delta from backtracking: 0.0031712119389339932
5  obj: -1.0644352062234936  grad^2: 0.47073322317722044
Delta from backtracking: 0.0031712119389339932
6  obj: -1.0648886764972436  grad^2: 0.10756901910054678
Delta from backtracking: 0.0031712119389339932
7  obj: -1.0649917864283562  grad^2: 0.02536190642741909
Delta from backtracking: 0.0031712119389339932
```

```
8  obj: -1.06501658682627  grad^2: 0.005925357838139831
Delta from backtracking: 0.0031712119389339932
9  obj: -1.0650224237765085  grad^2: 0.0013963038695945257
Delta from backtracking: 0.0031712119389339932
10  obj: -1.065023817199954  grad^2: 0.0003285531874043325
Delta from backtracking: 0.0031712119389339932
11  obj: -1.0650241488395522  grad^2:
      7.747928562280249e-05
Delta from backtracking: 0.0031712119389339932
12  obj: -1.0650242279678375  grad^2:
      1.827064320470491e-05
Delta from backtracking: 0.0031712119389339932
13  obj: -1.0650242468946232  grad^2:
      4.312318261448227e-06
Delta from backtracking: 0.0031712119389339932
14  obj: -1.0650242514078938  grad^2:
      1.0187675766236276e-06
Delta from backtracking: 0.0031712119389339932
15  obj: -1.0650242524934188  grad^2:
      2.406151288415629e-07
Delta from backtracking: 0.0031712119389339932
16  obj: -1.0650242527508393  grad^2:
      5.661118291355651e-08
Delta from backtracking: 0.0031712119389339932
17  obj: -1.0650242528138665  grad^2:
      1.2971437079775402e-08
Delta from backtracking: 0.0031712119389339932
18  obj: -1.065024252828625  grad^2: 3.039836055223908e-09
optimal x: [0.3266502  0.33711115] 0.3362386468404185
iterations: 18
optimal objective: -1.065024252828625
gradient: [-1.76747506e-05 -5.22248911e-05]
```

The gradient descent method got an answer that is roughly equal weighted.

Code Segment 5.9 uses Code Segment 5.8's solution as the initial point for the next optimization with a bigger ω. The algorithm says to iterate until $\frac{k_{eq}}{\omega} < \epsilon$, but we don't have any explicit equality constraints left. Code Segment 5.9 just does five iterations, increasing ω by a factor of 10 each time, to produce the following output:

```
barrier iteration   1
optimal x: [0.30180644 0.35144947] 0.34674408650332245
iterations: 15
optimal objective: -9.855995919080867
gradient: [-1.17239551e-05 -2.80664381e-05]
barrier iteration   2
optimal x: [0.26444077 0.37380701] 0.3617522207132179
iterations: 19
optimal objective: -101.73689269123221
gradient: [-5.11590770e-05 -3.41060513e-05]
barrier iteration   3
optimal x: [0.23193106 0.39393848] 0.3741304563642358
iterations: 23
optimal objective: -1013.539521323303
gradient: [ 4.54747351e-05 -4.54747351e-05]
barrier iteration   4
optimal x: [0.20030194 0.41405373] 0.3856443351111212
iterations: 501
optimal objective: -10108.31594256287
gradient: [0.00145519 0.0007276 ]
barrier iteration   5
optimal x: [0.15873136 0.44118304] 0.4000855930590287
iterations: 501
optimal objective: -101033.80926308232
gradient: [0.00582077 0.00582077]
```

Because of the binding constraint $w^\mathsf{T}w \leq .4$, the solution has a more even distribution of weights than the unconstrained solution in (4.6).

Of course, the reason to do the barrier algorithm is not on such straightforward problems with $n = 3$. In commercial use, there may be thousands or tens of thousands of assets being considered, and a host of portfolio construction constraints, including perhaps regulatory and tax considerations. In that case, a convex optimization might find satisfactory optimal portfolios that no amount of human intuition could find.

Fortunately, many elegant and powerful packages exist to do convex optimization. That's the good news. The bad news was given at the beginning of this chapter: if the user is not aware of how optimization works, algorithm failure or nonsensical results will quickly arise. But in the hands of a skilled user – perhaps you after finishing this chapter? – convex optimization packages can solve tough problems.

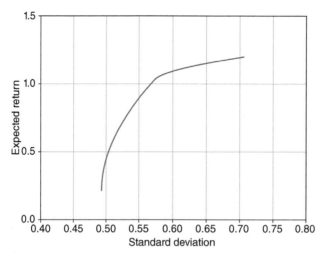

Figure 5.3 Long-only efficient frontier (like Fig. 4.3).

One such package for Python is based on Boyd and Vandenberghe (2004). To close this chapter, we've repeated the long-only optimization (4.13) using the Boyd, Vandenberghe, et al. cvxopt package (Figure 5.3, generated by Code Segment 5.10).

For Code Segments in this chapter, see the Code Appendix starting on p. 440. For executable code, visit www.cambridge.org/9781009209090/ch5

For problem sets for this chapter, visit www.cambridge.org/ 9781009209090/ch5_problems

6 Factor Models

A fundamental premise of security markets is that securities do not move independently of each other. If they did, then buying n equally weighted securities would create a portfolio with variance equal to $\frac{1}{n}$ times the average variance, so any sufficiently large portfolio would effectively be risk free. On the other hand, the portfolio return would still contain the average risk premium, which is most likely positive, leading to a riskless arbitrage: borrow money to buy the large portfolio and risklessly pocket the average risk premium.

We did see in Chapter 4 that well-thought-out diversification led to lower risk than undiversified securities or portfolios. But at some point we reap all the benefits of diversification that we can, and beyond that point adding more securities doesn't help lower risk.

There must therefore be common factors that affect all security returns and that don't diversify away. The Capital Asset Pricing Model (CAPM), which we'll cover below, is an extreme version of this idea: it states that there is a single source of risk that affects all securities, and all other variation in a security's price is specific to that security and is independent of anything else. For a time, most academic work used the CAPM as the five-finger assumption against which departures, called "anomalies," could be investigated. Since the 1990s, the baseline academic assumption has been a four-factor model ("Fama–French–Carhart") that we'll also describe.

These models can be thought of as extensions of the **Efficient Market Hypothesis (EMH)**. An efficient market is one whose prices are at a level that correctly takes into account all the information that is known about the security. If there are factors – like those in the four-factor model – that have positive expected returns in excess of the risk-free rate, then under EMH the excess returns must be compensation for risk. Otherwise, there would be information that allowed an investor to make excess returns with no risk, meaning that prices had not correctly impounded that information. So under EMH, the factors that explain excess returns are the same as the factors that explain systematic risk.

In this chapter, we'll also discuss the Arbitrage Pricing Theory (APT), which is a more general and a more powerful model for the commonalities in security returns than CAPM. Its assumptions are much less restrictive than those required to obtain the CAPM, and much less arbitrary than those in the four-factor model. On the other hand, the APT is so general that it doesn't even specify which common factors affect security returns; it just says they exist.

Practitioners have developed a large number of tools that capture the basic insights of the academic models, while specifying factors and software that allow equity risks to be understood in practice. We will describe some of those models in this chapter.

6.1   The Efficient Market Hypothesis

The **Efficient Market Hypothesis (EMH)** postulates that prices for assets traded in markets are continually updated with all known information about those assets. Eugene Fama,[1] winner of the 2013 Sveriges Riksbank Prize in Economic Sciences in Memory of Alfred Nobel, is perhaps the best-known proponent of EMH: in Fama (1970, p. 383) he defined efficiency:

> In general terms, the ideal is a market in which prices provide accurate signals for resource allocation; that is, a market in which firms can make production-investment decisions, and investors can choose among the securities that represent ownership of firms' activities under the assumption that security prices at any time "fully reflect" all available information. A market in which prices always "fully reflect" available information is called "efficient."

Fama's use of the word "efficient" differs from Markowitz's. Although both applications of the word convey a sense of optimality, one is applied to markets and the other to portfolios.

Fama set out three possible forms of market efficiency:

1. Weak form, in which the information contained in historical prices is fully reflected in current prices. Essentially this says that prices follow a submartingale;
2. Semi-strong form, in which all publicly available information (historical prices, earnings, corporate announcements ...) is fully reflected in current prices; and
3. Strong form, in which all information including, for example, private information only known to corporate insiders is fully reflected in current prices.

Weak-form efficiency is the easiest to test for historically. Fama (citing Niederhoffer and Osborne 1966) noted that there is evidence of tick-by-tick reversals in stock prices, but that two positive (negative) moves are more likely to be followed by a positive (negative) move than to reverse. These phenomena were suspected to be artifacts of market microstructure.

This would contradict weak-form efficiency, but Fama concluded in 1970 that it would not be possible to make trading profits based on these phenomena; they are within the limits of arbitrage and the costs of trading would erase

---

1 NobelPrize.org. "Eugene F. Fama: Facts." Website. `www.nobelprize.org/prizes/economic-sciences/2013/fama/facts/`.

any profits. After citing other evidence, Fama (in 1970, p. 416) optimistically concluded that:

> ...the evidence in support of the efficient markets model is extensive, and (somewhat uniquely in economics) contradictory evidence is sparse.

In the ensuing decades, even Professor Fama backed away from this Panglossian[2] claim. Momentum, for example, has been shown by Jegadeesh and Titman (1993) to be a very real phenomenon that does not disappear after trading costs are taken into account. That is, buying positive momentum stocks and selling negative momentum stocks for no net investment has on average a significant positive return even after transactions costs.

In Chapter 2, we discussed how risk preference finds its way into prices. Current theoretical models admit that there are phenomena – like momentum – that provide predictability to returns that is incompatible with simple weak-form efficiency. However, following a momentum strategy is risky: while it has an overall attractive return like Chapter 2's risky Beyond Vegetables example, sometimes there are violent reversals where momentum doesn't work. Investors quite plausibly would demand to be compensated for this risk. Thus, the existence of a positive long-term return by following a no-investment momentum strategy simply means that momentum is risky, not that there is a riskless arbitrage.

Current models – both academic and practitioner – attempt to identify a spanning set of risk factors that account for known compensated risks in markets. From an academic point of view, a phenomenon that produces excess returns over those accounted for by known risk factors may be a candidate for a new risk factor, or at the very least a published paper.

The practitioner world is broadly split into two camps. One camp, called **passive investors,** generally agrees with the (risk-adjusted) EMH. Passive investors don't try to outperform the market: they simply identify sections of the market that clients might want exposure to, and provide that exposure. The largest passive investors provide low-cost vehicles to invest in broad market indices like the Standard & Poor's 500. Other passive investors take a "smart beta" approach, where they identify a risk factor (like momentum) and invest algorithmically in that factor.

The other practitioner camp, **active investors,** thinks that there is little chance that markets are efficient even after accounting for risk. We've already seen obvious violations of market efficiency, ranging from engineered short squeezes over 100 years ago, to procyclical herd behavior on October 19, 1987, to more recent short squeezes in stocks like Gamestop. We've also seen that people

---

2 Voltaire's satirical novel *Candide* featured a pathologically optimistic character, Dr. Pangloss, who subscribed to Gottfried Leibniz's philosophy that we live in an optimal world. Dr. Pangloss maintained this unrealistic view even as he underwent a violently suboptimal set of disasters. Most active practitioners find the pure EMH to be as out of touch as Dr. Pangloss.

do not behave in the strictly rational ways that utility theory would predict, and that behavioral economics shows that these departures from rationality do not cancel out but rather are systematic.

Active investors believe that there are sufficiently large and predictable market inefficiencies so that they can make a profit over and above compensation for known risks. One type of active investment is factor timing: for example, a momentum-timing investor might attempt to use a momentum strategy when she thinks it will be profitable, and exit or reverse the strategy just before she thinks it will turn unprofitable. Another type of active investing looks for profitable strategies that are orthogonal to known risk factors. In both cases, the active investor is likely to use a risk model that tries to identify known risks in the market: the first to take the risk; the second to avoid it.

6.2 The Capital Asset Pricing Model and the Four-Factor Model

The **Capital Asset Pricing Model ("CAPM")** competes with the Black–Scholes option pricing formula for the title of the most widely known model from the field of quantitative finance. Despite the fact that empirical tests of the CAPM generally fail to show that it holds in practice,[3] it remains wildly popular. The model is variously attributed to Jack Treynor,[4] William Sharpe, John Lintner, and Jan Mossin, who all independently published versions of it in the early 1960s. Sharpe, who was cited in Chapter 2 for his Sharpe Ratio, had been a PhD student of Harry Markowitz at UCLA. Sharpe's 1990 Sveriges Riksbank Prize in Economic Sciences in Memory of Alfred Nobel was awarded largely for his CAPM work.

The Sharpe (1964) version of the CAPM is essentially something we've already seen: Figure 4.5. Sharpe assumed that investors want to choose mean-variance efficient portfolios; that they can borrow and lend at a risk-free rate r_f; and that they all agree on the joint probability distribution of asset returns. The last assumption is particularly counterfactual – investors have wildly different expectations of future returns, volatilities, and correlations. Sharpe acknowledges this is "undoubtedly unrealistic." The hope is that while individual investors may disagree, in aggregate they will act as if they agree.

---

3 There is a vast academic literature, mostly from the early 1970s, attempting to test the CAPM. [Roll 1977] eviscerated most of this work (including his own), saying of CAPM that "(a) No correct and unambiguous test of the theory has appeared in the literature; and (b) there is practically no possibility that such a test can be accomplished in the future." More recent work focuses on exploiting the failings of CAPM; for example, a popular approach is called "Betting against Beta" [Frazzini and Pedersen 2014].

4 Jack Treynor (see www.q-group.org/jack-treynor-prize/) appears to have been the first to develop something like CAPM. William Sharpe says that after writing his own paper on the subject, he "... learned that Mr. Jack L. Treynor, of Arthur D. Little Inc., had independently developed a model similar in many respects to the one described here. Unfortunately Mr. Treynor's excellent work on this subject is, at present, unpublished."

Under Sharpe's assumptions, everyone will want to be somewhere on the orange line in Figure 4.5. In that case, in equilibrium the tangency portfolio will simply be the market portfolio of all available assets, capitalization weighted – that is, weighted by how much of each asset is available in the market. Since all investors will hold linear combinations of the risk-free asset and the market portfolios, individual assets will be forced in equilibrium to fall on that line as well. Thus, each security s's expected return r_s can be expressed as:

$$\mathbb{E}[r_s] - r_f = \beta_s(\mathbb{E}[r_m] - r_f). \tag{6.1}$$

If $\beta_s = 0$, then the security is the risk-free asset; if $\beta_s = 1$, then the security's expected return is the same as the expected return of the market (tangency) portfolio.

Removing expectations, the CAPM says we must have:

$$r_s - r_f = \beta_s(r_m - r_f) + \epsilon_s, \tag{6.2}$$

where $Cov(\epsilon_s, r_m) = Cov(\epsilon_s, \epsilon_t) = 0$ (for $s \neq t$), and $\mathbb{E}[\epsilon_s] = 0$. Then ϵ_s is the *idiosyncratic* or *non-systematic* behavior of the security, while $r_f + \beta_s(r_m - r_f)$ is the *systematic* behavior. Each security has an idiosyncratic variance $\sigma^2_{epsilon_s} = \mathbb{E}[\epsilon_s^2]$. It follows from (6.2) and the assumptions after it that we must have $\beta_s = \frac{Cov(r_s - r_f, r_m - r_f)}{Var(r_m - r_f)} = \frac{Cov(r_s, r_m)}{Var(r_m)}$. The second equality follows from the assumption that the risk-free rate is a constant.

Because of the central role of the beta coefficient, users of the CAPM might simply say they are using betas to describe security behavior.

In the decades since its origin, the CAPM has been massively tested, discussed, modified, and retested. By 1980, Anise Wallace published a cleverly titled article in *Institutional Investor*: "Is Beta Dead?"[5] In corporate finance, betas were (and still are) very much alive for cost-of-capital calculations. In business schools, CAPM is very much alive as it is taught to MBA students as possibly the only market model they need to know.

For portfolio managers composing investment portfolios, beta was never really alive. By assumption the CAPM precludes any systematic ability to beat the market, so active (nonindex) investors will find little to help them find superior investments. They can and do use CAPM as a benchmark, but even that use has only weak empirical support.

In academia, debate about CAPM raged on. If the CAPM is correct and the market is the only systematic factor in security returns, we should not be able to observe systematic correlations between ϵ_s and ϵ_t for $s \neq t$. A large "anomaly" literature developed, showing that certain systematic characteristics could predict security behavior better than the market, so the ϵ_s were not really independent. For example, Banz (1981) and Reinganum (1981) independently showed the

5 [Wallace 1980].

"size anomaly": small companies behave systematically differently than large companies, in a way that can't be explained by differing betas.

Fama and French (1992) considered some previously documented anomalies like company size and "value" (high book-to-price ratios), and defined a three-factor risk model. Later work by Carhart (1997) extended this to what became the standard academic four-factor equity risk model:

$$r_s - r_f = \beta_{m,s}(r_m - r_f) + \beta_{sz,s}SMB + \beta_{val,s}HML + \beta_{mom,s}UMD + \epsilon_s. \quad (6.3)$$

In addition to the familiar market beta (which has been recaptioned $\beta_{m,s}$), three new betas to three new factors are added:

- $\beta_{sz,s}$ is the beta of security s to the size factor SMB ("small minus big"), which captures the difference in returns between a cohort of small stocks and a cohort of big stocks. That is, $\beta_{sz,s} = \frac{Cov(r_s, SMB)}{Var(SMB)}$.
- $\beta_{val,s}$ is the beta of security s to the size factor HML ("high minus low"), which captures the difference in returns between a cohort of high book-to-market ratio stocks and a cohort of low book-to-market ratio stocks.
- $\beta_{mom,s}$ is the factor added due to Carhart's work; it is the beta of security s to the momentum factor UMD ("up minus down"), which captures the difference in returns between a cohort of stocks that have had high momentum over the previous year (i.e. relatively good returns) and a cohort of low momentum stocks.

The Fama–French–Carhart model was dominant in academic work from the 1990s to the late 2010s. Most academic investigations into equity phenomena used the model as a benchmark to make sure that a supposedly new phenomenon was not just a repackaging of the four Fama–French–Carhart factors. Fama and French (2015) introduced a five-factor model that added a profitability factor (RMW, robust minus weak profitability) and an investment factor (CMA, conservative minus aggressive investment, where "investment" means expected growth in book value) to their three 1992 factors (market, HML, and SMB). Subsequently, many academic papers began using the five-factor model to test phenomena.

However, neither model made serious inroads into practical work. Practitioners continue to use commercial models with larger numbers of factors for portfolio construction. These commercial models are described in Section 6.4.

6.3 Arbitrage Pricing Theory

The Arbitrage Pricing Theory (APT) was published in Ross (1976). We've already seen the Ross Recovery Theorem and the Cox-Ingersoll-Ross short-rate model. Ross made these and numerous other contributions to mathematical finance, but when he died on March 3, 2017, his many laudatory obituaries identified him as the "inventor of arbitrage pricing theory."

As the name indicates, APT relies on the principle of arbitrage, or more accurately no-arbitrage. In particular APT relies on the Law of One Price that we saw in Chapter 2; if the same item has two prices then (within the limits of arbitrage such as transactions costs), arbitrageurs will buy the cheaper and sell the dearer until the prices are equalized. Traders speak lovingly of such arbitrage trades and say they will do them "until their fingers bleed," contemplating a lot of furious keyboarding to collect the free money.

6.3.1 APT: Exact Form

To understand the basic idea of the APT, we start with the following exact equation:

$$r = a + Bf. \tag{6.4}$$

Here, r is an n-vector containing the n random variables giving returns over a single period for each of the n assets in the universe. Then a is a non-stochastic n-vector, B is a nonstochastic $n \times k$ matrix, and f is a k-vector containing the k random variables giving returns of factors. We can assume that $\mathbb{E}[f] = 0$ by shifting $a \to a + \mathbb{E}[Bf]$ if necessary. So assume $a = \mathbb{E}[r]$.

We called (6.4) an exact equation because all of the variation of individual securities on the LHS is exactly explained by the variation of the factors f on the RHS. We'll relax that condition in the next section, but for now note that (6.4) is an underdetermined equation. We can "prove" (6.4) simply by setting $a = \mathbb{E}[r], f = r - \mathbb{E}[r]$, and $B = I$ where I is the identity matrix. Clearly there is nothing profound about this. The real insight of the APT is that something like the pricing equation above can work when $k << n$. The APT therefore contemplates a very small number of systematic, market-wide factors that determine the prices of a very large number of assets. In the CAPM, $k = 1$ – the market itself is the only systematic factor. The APT extends that to allow more and different factors.

For example, as we pointed out in Chapter 3, the general level of interest rates is an important factor in an economy. It's plausible that such an important factor would affect most securities in the economy. In that case, one of the elements of f might be a random variable giving the general level of interest rates.

So the f vector contains systematic, market-wide factors, while the B matrix contains the sensitivities of individual securities to these factors. The ith row of the B matrix is the set of sensitivities for the ith security. In the CAPM, B was a single vector of betas; in the APT, there are "betas" or sensitivities to multiple factors in the columns of B. Sometimes these are called "factor loadings."

Note the APT does not say what the factors are or how many there are. It is completely general in that sense. Ross left it to others (including himself in later papers[6]) to try to determine plausible sets of factors.

The APT also contemplates a nonstochastic expected return a_i for each security. Ross showed that, under certain conditions, these expected returns are explained (as specified in (6.7) below) by the factor loadings B plus a constant that is essentially a risk-free rate. This anticipated Ross's Recovery Theorem work by almost 40 years, but it has a similar strategy: eliminate unknowns with some clever math.

To prove (6.7), define a **hedge portfolio** as an n-vector of weights h with $h^\mathsf{T}u = 0$, where as usual u is the unit n-vector of all ones. Arbitrage would exist if there were a hedge portfolio h with:

$$\mathbb{E}[h^\mathsf{T}r] \neq 0 \quad \text{and} \quad Var[h^\mathsf{T}r] = 0. \tag{6.5}$$

This says that we could make money with no investment and no risk by investing in h (or $-h$ if the expected value $\mathbb{E}[h^\mathsf{T}r]$ is negative). Since there is no variance, the expected value is the value in all future states of the world. So under no-arbitrage, there must be no portfolio satisfying these conditions.

The argument to prove (6.7) proceeds as follows: We suppose that n is very large compared to k. (In other words, we have found a comparatively small number k of systematic factors that explain everything going on in the market.)

Let A be the matrix $(u \ B)$; that is, the $n \times (k + 1)$ matrix with all ones in the first column and the coefficient matrix B in the remaining k columns. Consider a vector h where $h^\mathsf{T}A = 0$.

So h is a *factor neutral hedge portfolio*: the zero dot product with the first column of A makes it a hedge portfolio: and the condition $h^\mathsf{T}B = 0$ means there are no systematic risks ("factors") in h. Whatever long exposure h has to any of the systematic factors (i.e. the sum of the positive entries in h) is offset by an exactly equal short exposure (i.e. the sum of the negative entries in h). Since our model has no non-systematic behavior, there is nothing left over. If we left-multiply (6.4) by h^T, we get:

$$h^\mathsf{T}r = h^\mathsf{T}a + (h^\mathsf{T}B)f = h^\mathsf{T}a. \tag{6.6}$$

Therefore, h requires no investment ($h^\mathsf{T}u = 0$) and has no risk because taking *Var* of both sides of (6.6) shows that $Var[h^\mathsf{T}r] = Var[h^\mathsf{T}a] = 0$ because $h^\mathsf{T}a$ is a constant. So the no-arbitrage condition (6.5) tells us its expected value (that is, $h^\mathsf{T}a = \mathbb{E}[h^\mathsf{T}r]$) is zero. Another way of saying this is that if h is a factor-neutral hedge portfolio, then $\mathbb{E}[r]$ is in the null space of h, $\mathbb{E}[r] \in N(h)$.

---

6 [Chen, Roll, and Ross 1986].

More generally, the columns of A form a vector space $c(A)$, and the (left) null space of A forms another vector space $N(c(A))$. That is, $h \in N(c(A)) \iff h^\mathsf{T}w = 0 \quad \forall w \in c(A)$. Consider the null space of the null space, $N(N(c(A)))$. This is the collection of vectors z with $z^\mathsf{T}h = 0$ whenever $h \in N(c(A))$. It can be shown that $N(N(c(A))) = c(A)$.

From the line of reasoning above, and the fact that $h^\mathsf{T}\mathbb{E}[r] = 0$, we see that $\mathbb{E}[r] \in N(N(c(A))) = c(A)$, so $\mathbb{E}[r]$ is a linear combination of the columns of A:

$$a = \mathbb{E}[r] = r_f u + B\lambda. \tag{6.7}$$

Equation (6.7) is what is usually called the *Arbitrage Pricing Theory*; it is the generalization of CAPM's (6.1). Here λ is a k-vector of scalars and r_f is a scalar. If there is a risk-free asset, then r_f is the risk-free rate since the factor loadings for the risk-free asset are zeroes. In other words, the row of B corresponding to the risk-free asset is a row of zeroes. Otherwise r_f is an arbitrary scalar. The λ's are called the **prices of risk** for each of the k factors.

The linear form of the APT, together with the dimensions ($n \gg k$), indicates that we can price excess expected returns solely by reference to their loadings on systematic factors.

6.3.2 APT: Inclusion of Specific Behavior

The exact equation (6.4) was oversimplified; it didn't allow for idiosyncratic behavior, that is, behavior that is independent of systematic factors. For example, if the head of an electric car company tweets about a possible stock buyout and the company's price jumps, that may have nothing to do with the overall economy, with the rest of the automobile industry, or with any other identifiable systematic factor.

We can take into account such **idiosyncratic** or **specific** behavior by introducing a new term to (6.4):

$$r = a + Bf + \epsilon. \tag{6.8}$$

Here ϵ takes into account CEO tweeting and other independent behavior; it is a random n-vector where $\mathbb{E}[\epsilon_i \epsilon_j] = \mathbb{E}[\epsilon_i f_m] = \mathbb{E}[\epsilon_i] = 0 \ \forall i, m, j \neq i$. We can assume as in the exact APT development that $\mathbb{E}[f] = 0$ and $a = \mathbb{E}[r]$. Equation (6.8) is the generalization of the Capital Asset Pricing Model's (6.2).

As we noted after (6.4), (6.8) is trivially true. While (6.7) contains some clever reasoning, (6.4) and (6.8) are just statements about how we intend to think about things and are not theorems.

For the exact equation (6.4), the result was that $a = A\lambda$ for some $(k+1)$-vector λ, where A was the B matrix prepended by the u-vector. For the APT with nonsystematic behavior included, the result is less exact and is stated in the limit as the number n of securities in the market goes to infinity.

The generalization of (6.7) that we seek to prove under model (6.8) (and no-arbitrage) says that with no-arbitrage, there is a constant c such that no matter how big the number of assets n gets, we can find a $(k+1)$-vector λ so that:

$$(a - A\lambda)^{\mathsf{T}}(a - A\lambda) \leq c. \tag{6.9}$$

The n-vector $(a - A\lambda)$ is called the **pricing error** and is the "miss" in the factor model; it is the deviations in expected returns that can't be explained by the factors (and a constant). In the exact form, we were able to eliminate pricing error ($c = 0$). Equation (6.9) doesn't eliminate pricing error, but it does say that the factor model pricing error is bounded in some sense even for a very large number of securities.

To prove (6.9), note first that as a result of (6.8) and the assumptions after it, we can write:

$$
\begin{aligned}
Var[w^{\mathsf{T}}r] &= \mathbb{E}\left[\left(w^{\mathsf{T}}r - w^{\mathsf{T}}\mathbb{E}[r]\right)^2\right] = \mathbb{E}\left[w^{\mathsf{T}}\left(r - \mathbb{E}[r]\right)\left(r^{\mathsf{T}} - \mathbb{E}[r]^{\mathsf{T}}\right)w\right] \\
&= w^{\mathsf{T}}Var[r]w = w^{\mathsf{T}}Var[Bf]w + w^{\mathsf{T}}Var[\epsilon]w \\
&= w^{\mathsf{T}}BVar[f]B^{\mathsf{T}}w + w^{\mathsf{T}}Var[\epsilon]w, \tag{6.10}
\end{aligned}
$$

for any portfolio w.

Thus, if we estimate the $k \times k$ factor covariance matrix $Var(f)$ – a much easier proposition than directly estimating the $n \times n$ full covariance matrix $Var(r)$ – we have under APT obtained the full covariance matrix except possibly for a diagonal matrix of specific (or residual, or idiosyncratic) risks.

If the model (6.8) has any value, the residual risks in the vector ϵ shouldn't be too big. Contrapositively, if the residuals dominate the risks explained by the factors, then (6.8) has no content. This is similar to the idea that (6.4) has no content if n isn't much bigger than k, the number of factors.

Thus, we further assume that the variances of the residuals are bounded above, so that for all i,

$$Var(\epsilon_i) < S^2$$

for some constant S.

The bounded nature of residual variance is perhaps the key requirement. Intuitively, it says that whatever is left over after the factor behavior is removed can't be too important. While the pricing equation (6.8) is completely arbitrary, once we:

1. restrict the number k of systematic factors to be very small; and
2. restrict the residual variances,

we are imposing a view of the world on asset pricing – namely, that the small number of factors essentially controls pricing.

Huberman (1982) strengthened the no-arbitrage condition (6.5) slightly to say that there can be no sequence of hedge portfolios $h_1, \ldots, h_j, \ldots$, such that:

$$\lim_{j \to \infty} \mathbb{E}[h_j^\mathsf{T} r] = \infty \text{ and } \lim_{j \to \infty} Var[h_j^\mathsf{T} r] = 0. \qquad (6.11)$$

If there is a portfolio h satisfying (6.5), then the sequence $h_j = j \cdot h$ (or $-h_j$) satisfies (6.11). The contrapositive of that implication is that the nonexistence of (6.11) sequences implies the nonexistence of (6.5) hedge portfolios, so the (6.11) nonexistence is the stronger condition.

The LHS of the desired inequality (6.9) is the square of the $\mathscr{L}^2$-norm of the pricing miss. We can minimize that by finding λ_{min}:

$$\lambda_{min} = \operatorname{argmin}(a - A\lambda)^\mathsf{T}(a - A\lambda). \qquad (6.12)$$

To find λ_{min}, we take the derivative of the RHS of (6.12) with respect to λ and set it to zero:

$$A^\mathsf{T}(a - A\lambda_{min}) = 0. \qquad (6.13)$$

Let $h_{min} = a - A\lambda_{min}$ be the optimal pricing miss. Then (6.13) tells us that $A^\mathsf{T} h_{min} = 0$, so h_{min} is a factor neutral hedge portfolio. The expected return on h_{min} is:

$$\mathbb{E}[h_{min}^\mathsf{T} r] = h_{min}^\mathsf{T} a, \qquad (6.14)$$

since $a = \mathbb{E}[r]$. Since A is in the null space of h_{min}, we can change the rightmost a to $a - A\lambda_{min}$:

$$\mathbb{E}[h_{min}^\mathsf{T} r] = h_{min}^\mathsf{T} h_{min}. \qquad (6.15)$$

The variance of h_{min}'s return is:

$$Var[h_{min}^\mathsf{T} r] = h_{min}^\mathsf{T} Var[\epsilon] h_{min}. \qquad (6.16)$$

Here we have used (6.10) and the fact that $A^\mathsf{T} h_{min} = 0$ so $B^\mathsf{T} h_{min} = 0$. Our assumptions indicate that the $Var[\epsilon]$ matrix is diagonal and that each term is bounded above by S^2, so:

$$Var[h_{min}^\mathsf{T} r] \le S^2 h_{min}^\mathsf{T} h_{min}. \qquad (6.17)$$

The desired inequality (6.9) contemplates an ever-growing number of assets, so the optimal pricing miss h_{min} is actually $h_{min}(j)$, where j is the number of assets in the iteration. Set:

$$s(j) = \left(h_{min}(j)^\mathsf{T} h_{min}(j)\right)^{-3/4} \qquad (6.18)$$

and define $h_j = s(j) h_{min}(j)$. The $h_{min}(j)^\mathsf{T} h_{min}(j)$ expression on the RHS of (6.18) was already present (with implicit j) in the mean and variance expressions (6.15) and (6.17), so we can write:

$$\mathbb{E}[h_j^\mathsf{T} r] = s(j)\mathbb{E}[h_{min}(j)^\mathsf{T} r] = \left(h_{min}(j)^\mathsf{T} h_{min}(j)\right)^{1/4}, \qquad (6.19)$$

$$Var[h_j^\mathsf{T} r] = s(j)^2 Var[h_{min}(j)^\mathsf{T} r] \leq S^2 \left(h_{min}(j)^\mathsf{T} h_{min}(j)\right)^{-1/2}. \qquad (6.20)$$

Consider the sequence of h_j's in the context of the no-arbitrage conditions (6.11). The expression $h_{min}(j)^\mathsf{T} h_{min}(j)$ is the LHS of (6.11); if it gets bigger and bigger as the number of assets grows, then (6.19) and (6.20) show that (6.11) will be violated. That can't happen, so $h_{min}(j)^\mathsf{T} h_{min}(j)$ is bounded as desired and the APT is proved.

The APT is in some sense far more powerful than the CAPM. It rests almost entirely on the assumption that the market is driven by a small number of factors – from that basic assumption (and no-arbitrage) the rest is logical reasoning. Of course the precise form of that basic assumption (a stationary linear relationship) is also important, but it is less restrictive than the CAPM's assumption that market participants are mean-variance optimizers.

On the other hand, the APT is silent on what the factors are. Subsequent to its publication, many investigators attempted to determine plausible sets of factors. One line of investigation is exemplified by Chen, Roll, and Ross (1986), who concluded that macroeconomic factors – inflation surprise, industrial production, interest rates, credit spreads, and the level of the equity market – were the appropriate factors. The last factor is in effect the CAPM factor. While such macroeconomic factors seem to give a broad historical view of asset relationships – they seem to get things right over decades – few practitioners use them in day-to-day portfolio management.

6.4 Factor Models in Practice

A line of investigation that is more popular with market participants is exemplified by Rosenberg and Marathe (1976), who used microeconomic factors to drive the equity market. Rosenberg went on to form a company called BARRA ("Barr Rosenberg Associates") that offered equity risk models. Over the years, these kinds of factors included:

- Industry or industrial sector
- Country or region (for multinational portfolios)
- Price/ratio factors: book/price, earnings/price, dividend/price, free cash flow/price, sales/price . . .
- Company size (market capitalization)
- Price momentum, earnings momentum – as well as price reversals and earnings reversals over different periods
- Financial leverage (debt/equity ratio); capital expenditures.

BARRA was acquired in 2004 by another company, MSCI,[7] which sells the current versions of these factor-based risk models. Competitors like Axioma[8] and Northfield[9] also offer equity factor models.

Testing the APT is difficult: the main problem is that it only works as $n \to \infty$. We can try to gather a large number of assets on which to test APT, but we can't be sure we have enough since we'll never get to infinity. What we leave out might be crucial.

Informal tests can be made simply by doing regressions. If we are able to identify a set of factors – whether macroeconomic, company specific, or based on principal components analysis – then we can look at the residuals after the systematic portion based on the factors is removed from returns. If these residuals are small, then we have anecdotal but not conclusive evidence of a good model. More importantly, if the out-of-sample residuals are small, then we have informal evidence of having captured a market dynamic.

While it is often possible to obtain reduction in the sizes of the residuals that remain after moving factors from returns, it appears that factors and their loadings are unstable over time, making it impossible to estimate static long-term parameters. However, over shorter periods of time, residual reduction can be found.

The main practical implementation of the APT is (6.9) – that is, the model for the covariance matrix. Stripping out the portfolio vector, we can just write:

$$C = BFB^{\mathsf{T}} + D. \tag{6.21}$$

Here C is the $n \times n$ covariance matrix, where the (i,j) entry is the covariance between asset i and asset j. B is an $n \times k$ matrix, where $k \ll n$. F is the $k \times k$ factor covariance matrix, which is assumed to be much easier to estimate and predict than C directly. D is a diagonal matrix of individual asset residual variances.

In the Rosenberg and Marathe 1976 approach, B is determined by looking at the characteristics of the asset. For example, the columns of B might be of size $k = 100$ with the first 50 columns being mostly zeroes. These 50 columns indicate what industries the company does business in, with a complicated company like Amazon having as many as 5 nonzero entries (such as cloud services, online retail, etc.). The other entries might be things like company size (the logarithm of the company's stock market capitalization), its earnings momentum, and other factors from the list above. The nonindustry items might be standardized across the universe so that they average zero in every cross-section

7 MSCI. "About Us." Website. www.msci.com/who-we-are/about-us.
8 Qontigo.com. "Axioma Equity Factor Risk Models™." Website. https://qontigo.com/products/axioma-equity-factor-risk-models/.
9 Northfield. "About Us." Website. www.northinfo.com/aboutus.php.

and have a cross-sectional standard deviation of one. They might also be Winsorized[10] at around ± 4.5.

The general idea is that the relationships between the $k = 100$ factors are more stable than the relationships between the (say) $n = 8,000$ assets. For example, the relationship between the energy industry and the aircraft manufacturing industry is probably more stable than the relationship between Boeing and Exxon-Mobil. The relationship between "value" companies with high book/market ratios and "small" companies with low market capitalizations is (the theory goes) more stable than the relationship between any two such companies.

The residual (the diagonal entries of D) is used to account for company-specific or idiosyncratic behavior. For example, there is very little difference between Royal Dutch Shell and Exxon-Mobil in terms of systematic exposures: they are both large, multinational – the fact that one is headquartered in the USA and the other in Europe is not particularly important given their global reach – integrated energy companies. Any differences in their returns behavior is most likely due to some specific factors – say, Exxon-Mobil is drilling a particular well that Shell is not.

The residual variance in D can be computed by looking at the variance of the difference between the asset's actual time series of returns (often over the last five years monthly) minus the returns that would have been produced by multiplying the factor loadings times the returns on the underlying factors (energy industry, large-cap companies, etc.). Or residual variance can itself be modeled.

6.5 Principal Components Analysis

Another approach to modeling covariance matrices is **Principal Components Analysis ("PCA")**, which can be described intuitively as a process that reweights the data in a matrix X in order of importance. This intuitive idea of importance turns out to be related to eigenvalues and eigenvectors, which we'll briefly review before returning to the financial application.

Suppose M is a matrix (for simplicity we'll assume herein that M is $n \times n$ square and symmetric), and suppose further that there is a scalar λ and a nonzero vector e with:

$$Me = \lambda e. \tag{6.22}$$

---

10 Winsorization (after biostatistician Charles Winsor) is a truncation process by which outlying data are moderated. A parametric version of the process caps observations at some maximum or minimum numerical amount, so for example any observation over 4.5 would be deemed to equal 4.5. A nonparametric version sorts observations from lowest to highest and then sets (say) the lowest and second-lowest observations equal to the third-lowest observation.

λ is called an *eigenvalue* (or *characteristic value*) of M, and the n-vector e is λ's associated *eigenvector*. Multiplying both sides of (6.22) by a scalar preserves the identity, so any scalar multiple of an eigenvector remains an eigenvector associated with the same eigenvalue. Because of this, we usually require that $e^{\mathsf{T}}e = 1$ to standardize the eigenvector. That doesn't quite specify e uniquely: both $+e$ and $-e$ are standardized in this sense.

The defining equation (6.22) can be rewritten:

$$(M - \lambda I)e = 0. \qquad (6.23)$$

From basic matrix theory, we know this means $M - \lambda I$ is singular, which means:

$$\det(M - \lambda I) = 0. \qquad (6.24)$$

Equation (6.24) becomes a polynomial in λ of order up to n; it is called the *characteristic equation* of M. Every solution to the characteristic equation is an eigenvalue, and vice versa.

The reader should be able to show that:

> The product of all eigenvalues of a matrix equals the matrix's determinant.　　|

Thus a matrix is nonsingular if and only if none of its eigenvalues is zero. A matrix is positive (semi)definite if for any vector $x \neq 0$, we have $x^{\mathsf{T}}Mx \geq 0$, with strict inequality removing the "(semi)." If the matrix is positive definite (semidefinite), then all the eigenvalues are positive (nonnegative).

The reader should also be able to show that:

> The sum of all eigenvalues of a matrix equals the matrix's trace.　　|

If M is a real symmetric $n \times n$ matrix of rank r, then the spectral theorem[11] says that we can write:

$$M = EGE^{\mathsf{T}} \text{ where } E^{\mathsf{T}}E = I \text{ and G is diagonal.} \qquad (6.25)$$

E is $n \times r$ and G is $r \times r$. If M is of full rank (nonsingular), then E is a square matrix and $E^{\mathsf{T}} = E^{-1}$. The decomposition (6.25) is called an **eigendecomposition** or **spectral decomposition**.

The eigenvectors in the columns of a symmetric eigendecomposition (6.25) can be reordered as desired. Let Q be an $r \times r$ permutation matrix (a matrix of 0s and 1s with exactly one 1 in every row and column) reordering the integers from 1 to r, r the rank of the matrix M being decomposed. Note $QQ^{\mathsf{T}} = Q^{\mathsf{T}}Q = I, I$ the identity matrix. Then:

$$M = EGE^{\mathsf{T}} = (EQ)(Q^{\mathsf{T}}GQ)(EQ)^{\mathsf{T}}.$$

Thus, EQ is a rearrangement of the eigenvectors in the columns of E into a new order and $Q^{\mathsf{T}}GQ$ reorders the eigenvalues on the diagonal of G accordingly.

11 [Halmos 1963].

Therefore without loss of generality the eigenvalues along the diagonal of G can be arranged in decreasing order, with the eigenvectors in the columns of E arranged accordingly.

Suppose M is a symmetric positive semidefinite matrix of dimension n and rank r with ordered eigendecomposition $M = EGE^\mathsf{T}$. A series of approximations $M_0 = 0, M_1, M_2, \ldots, M_r = M$ can be created by defining (for $i = 1, \ldots, r$) $M_i = E_i G_i E_i^\mathsf{T}$, where E_i is the $n \times i$ matrix consisting of the first i columns of the eigenvector matrix E and G_i is the $i \times i$ matrix consisting of the upper left corner of the diagonal matrix of eigenvalues G. The eigenvectors have the property that:

$$e_{i+1} = \arg \max_{z^\mathsf{T} z = 1} z^\mathsf{T}(M - M_i)z. \tag{6.26}$$

(Note e_{i+1} is only specified up to a flip of sign here.) In some sense (6.26) says that e_1 is the best single vector fit to M, and that subsequent eigenvectors are the best fits to what's left over after taking out the previous eigenvectors.

We can now make precise the intuition at the beginning of this section that PCA "reweights the data in a matrix X in order of importance." Let E be the column matrix of eigenvectors as shown in (6.25), where $M = X^\mathsf{T} X$. A matrix M of this form is positive semi-definite, so it has non-negative eigenvalues. Then the principal components of X are the columns of XE, where the eigenvectors in the columns of E are in decreasing order of associated eigenvalues. These principal components rotate the original data along orthogonal axes that maximize remaining variance, since e_{i+1} maximizes the expression in (6.26) with a value g_{i+1}.

Since a sample covariance matrix is already of the form $C = X^\mathsf{T} X$ (where X is the periodized, de-meaned matrix of historical data), the relevant information is in the eigenvectors of C. Thus when we refer to the principal components of a covariance matrix, we will just mean the eigenvectors of that matrix in descending order of associated eigenvalues. Similarly we'll refer to the eigenvectors of a correlation matrix as its principal components since a sample correlation matrix R is of the form $R = Y^\mathsf{T} Y$ where $Y = S^{-1} X$ and S is the diagonal matrix of square roots of the diagonal of $X^\mathsf{T} X$.[12]

So to do PCA (in this broader sense) for a covariance matrix C or a correlation matrix R, we use an eigensystem calculator like numpy.linalg.eig rather than feeding C or R into a PCA calculator like sklearn.decomposition.PCA.

If there's an APT-type (or Rosenberg–Marathe-type) factor model with k factors for n assets like (6.8), the $n \times k$ factor loading matrix B uses features of the assets being modeled. For example, if the assets are stocks, many popular models use log-market-capitalization as a factor. Such features are **exogenous** to

12 If M is a correlation matrix, then an approximation M_i using fewer eigenvectors will not itself be a correlation matrix: the diagonal will not consist of ones. This can be repaired by treating M_i as if it was a covariance matrix and setting $R_i = \sqrt{\operatorname{diag}(M_i)^{-1}} M_i \sqrt{\operatorname{diag}(M_i)^{-1}}$, but then R_i will have a different eigensystem than M_i. Analysts using this method should take care that the result is sensible.

the $T \times n$ data matrix X (typically containing de-meaned and scaled log-returns over T periods) that would be used in PCA.

On the other hand, PCA contemplates using **endogenous** data to form the factor model, that is, information that is computed from the data matrix X. If E is the eigenvector matrix of $M = X^\mathsf{T}X$, then the PCA factor model sets $B = E$. The factors are the principal components XE. The factor covariance matrix $F = (XE)^\mathsf{T}XE = E^\mathsf{T}(X^\mathsf{T}X)E = E^\mathsf{T}(EGE^\mathsf{T})E = G$. So (leaving aside specific risk) the full PCA covariance matrix is $C = BFB^\mathsf{T} = EGE^\mathsf{T} = X^\mathsf{T}X$.

But while it's intuitively clear what size or log-market-cap means, what does an eigenvector mean? Sometimes there may be a noticeable pattern that is intuitively meaningful. For example, if an eigenvector looks like $e = u/\sqrt{n}$ where u is the vector of all ones, then it's clear that the factor the eigenvector is specifying is the equal-weighted market. Or, if the eigenvector had positive values in the entries corresponding to large companies and negative values in the entries corresponding to small companies, intuition would say this is a size-related factor. We saw similarly intuitively clear eigenvectors in Chapter 3 when analyzing covariance matrices of interest rate changes. We find intuitive comfort in the idea that comprehensible phenomena like size and market have persisted as explanatory factors over decades, so we expect them to work out-of-sample after the data X are collected.

Unfortunately, much of the time there is no intuitive explanation that springs to mind, and the PCA-derived factor is simply a jumble of numbers specifying a linear combination of the n assets. While we know that the higher-eigenvalue eigenvectors were the best explanatory factors for the in-sample $X^\mathsf{T}X$, how do we know that they will work out-of-sample? We don't really have any guarantee, but the premise of PCA is that these higher-eigenvalue eigenvectors will persist while lower-eigenvalue eigenvectors will not.

The eigenvectors associated with the smaller eigenvalues are called **scree**, a word from geology that means "debris." A **scree plot** shows the percentage of the trace represented by the eigenvalues of a matrix, in descending order. For example, Code Segment 6.1 outputs the eigenvalues of the [CHF,GBP,JPY,EUR] currency correlation matrix and displays their percentages in Figure 6.1:

```
n=4.000000, T=5769.000000
Eigenvalues: [2.44359783 0.89440863 0.47726874 0.1847248 ]
```

Figure 6.1 shows a typical pattern where the eigenvalues drop in size: it is rare that they are close to equal. Usually, as the size of the matrix increases, we see that a small number of eigenvalues account for most of the trace, after which there is an inflection point and the sizes of the eigenvalues drop sharply. This seems to be true of both covariance and correlation matrices: the correlation matrix $R = S^{-1}CS^{-1}$ will have different eigenvalues than the covariance

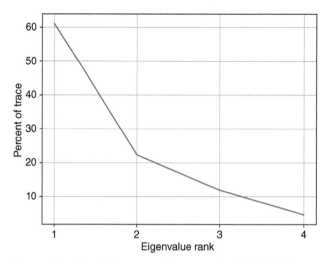

Figure 6.1 Correlation scree plot, currencies 1999–2021.

matrix C, but if the standard deviations on the diagonal of S don't cover too wide a range, R will look like a scalar multiple of C and will have similar eigenvalue patterns.

Financial econometricians have taken the dropoff in eigenvalues as evidence that the Arbitrage Pricing Theory is true. Trzcinka (1986, p. 347) summarized his results as follows:

> We compute sample [stock market] covariance matrices of returns in sequentially larger portfolios of securities. Analyzing their eigenvalues, we find evidence that one eigenvalue dominates the covariance matrix indicating that a one-factor model may describe security pricing .... We find that while only the first eigenvalue dominates the matrix, the first five eigenvalues are growing more distinct.

The dominance of the first eigenvalue seems to be replicable; other markets and other time periods than the ones used by Trzcinka – including our Figure 6.1 and yield curve data in Figure 3.10 – show a similar pattern. Trzcinka concluded that there wasn't strong evidence of another obvious inflection point after the first eigenvalue, but thought that there was weak evidence of an inflection point after the fifth eigenvalue.

Unfortunately, a concentration in larger eigenvalues is not necessarily evidence of underlying factor structure: it may just be random. Suppose a $T \times n$ data matrix X is populated randomly; each of the nT entries is generated by an independent draw from a standard normal distribution. Marchenko and Pastur (1967) found the distribution of the sizes of eigenvalues of $C = \frac{1}{T}X^{\mathsf{T}}X$ as $n, T \to \infty$ with a constant ratio of $1 < \frac{T}{n} < \infty$; it is heavily front loaded.

If G is the diagonal matrix of eigenvalues of a random standard covariance matrix, then in the limit the Marchenko–Pastur pdf of eigenvalues $g \in G$ is:

$$f(g) = \frac{T}{n} \frac{\sqrt{(g_+ - g)(g - g_-)}}{2\pi g},$$

where:

$$g_\pm = \left(1 \pm \sqrt{\frac{n}{T}}\right)^2. \tag{6.27}$$

For g outside of the range $[g_-, g_+]$, the Marchenko–Pastur limit pdf is zero.

A standard random covariance matrix (i.e. one created from mean-0, variance-1 normal draws) is not exactly a correlation matrix since sampling noise may result in non-one diagonals. But the Marchenko–Pastur pdf of a standard random covariance matrix gives an idea of what pattern might be expected of a correlation matrix.

Code Segment 6.2 outputs the $g_\pm$ range for the [CHF,GBP,JPY,EUR] data and produces Figure 6.2 showing the shape of the Marchenko-Pastur limit distribution:

```
Ratio = 0.000693
     Expected range from 0.95 to 1.05
Ratio = 0.500000
     Expected range from 0.09 to 2.91
```

Figure 6.2 shows two limiting pdfs: one for the (very small) ratio of ($n = 4$) to (the number of data points used to create Figure 6.1); and another for a ratio

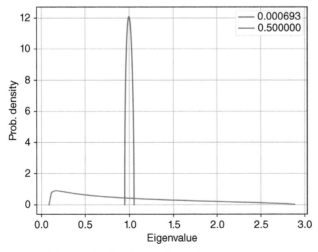

Figure 6.2 Marchenko–Pastur limit pdf.

of .5. Given that there are many years of data for only four points in Figure 6.1, Marchenko–Pastur says that there's a lot of conviction about the eigenvalues all being close to 1 if the matrix is random. (Recall that the eigenvalues of a correlation matrix must average to one because they must sum to the trace.)

On the other hand, with relatively sparser data implied by a .5 ratio of assets to time periods, Marchenko–Pastur expects a more diffuse distribution of eigenvalues.

While Marchenko–Pastur is a limit distribution, one heuristic is to deem any eigenvalues below g_+ (which is about 1.5 given the shape of the data used in Figure 6.1) as scree, that is, noise. With that rule of thumb, only the largest of the four eigenvalues from the Figure 6.1 data is (highly!) significantly nonrandom. The others would be considered noise, so we would use the approximation $M_1 = E_1 G_1 E_1^\mathsf{T}$ to estimate the out-of-sample matrix.

However, this heuristic doesn't preserve the trace of the original matrix M. One simple fix for this is to scale up the entire approximation matrix. If eigenvectors are cut off at $k < r$ by using the approximation $M_k = E_k G_k E_k^\mathsf{T}$, then the modified approximation sM_k will have the right trace, where the scalar $s = \frac{trace(M)}{\sum_{i=1}^{k} g_i}$.

Another heuristic called the **constant residual eigenvalue method** (López de Prado 2020) is similar in spirit to Winsorization. This method averages the eigenvalues below a cutoff point: set $h_i = g_i$ for $i \le k$ where k is the cutoff point, and set $h_i = \frac{1}{r-k} \sum_{j=k+1}^{r} g_j$ for all $i > k$. Then the modfied approximation is $L_k = EH_k E^\mathsf{T}$, where H_k is the diagonal matrix of hs.

The strength of PCA (as well as its weakness) is that it requires no judgment about the data. The Rosenberg–Marathe approach used in most commercial models requires judgment about which characteristics of a security are the important, lasting ones. If these judgments are right, then the model will do a good job predicting future covariance matrices. But as markets change, these models might not keep up. For example, most commercial models didn't have an Internet factor in the late 1990s, although the technology bubble (and its bursting) made Internet companies behave distinctly differently from other companies in that period.

Because PCA infers factors from the data, it is able to discover patterns that human analysts may not see. However, there are some disadvantages to this approach:

- Principal components analysis is backward looking. It cannot "see" a pattern until it is in the data. Similarly, it cannot drop a pattern that is no longer relevant until it drops out of the data. For example, in the runup to the US invasion of Iraq in 2003, virtually the only factor that mattered in the US stock market was a security's relationship to the impending war. After the invasion of Iraq on March 20, 2003, this factor quickly became irrelevant. However a model with (say) a trailing 3-year data window would not know this for 3 years.

- The backward-looking problem would not be a problem if principal components were stable through time. However, usually they are not – a principal component that was present in the data in the last 3 years may disappear completely in the next 3 years. For this reason, some practitioners use PCA as a forensic tool (helping to alert humans to patterns that may be emerging in the data) as opposed to a model.
- Principal components analysis factors are hard or impossible for humans to understand.

To see the time variation in eigenvalues and eigenvectors, Code Segment 6.3 compares the 4×4 covariance matrix using the data behind Figure 6.1 (taken over the period 1999 [when the euro began] to the most recent yearend) with the same currencies from the turbulent year 2008:

```
1999-2021 covariance matrix (Cfull): (5769 days)
      CHF      GBP      JPY      EUR
[ 0.4334   0.1908   0.1594   0.3080]
[ 0.1908   0.3449   0.0526   0.2173]
[ 0.1594   0.0526   0.3877   0.1069]
[ 0.3080   0.2173   0.1069   0.3498]
2008 covariance matrix (C2008):
[ 0.9045   0.3453   0.3816   0.6867]
[ 0.3453   0.9142  -0.2797   0.5875]
[ 0.3816  -0.2797   0.9572   0.0110]
[ 0.6867   0.5875   0.0110   0.8044]
```

The effects of the financial crisis in 2008 are clear: the diagonals of C2008 are larger than the diagonals of Cfull by about a factor of two – that is, volatility was much higher in 2008.

Code Segment 6.4 shows that the eigenvalues and eigenvectors for Cfull were:

```
Full period eigenvalues times 10**6:
[ 92.9893   33.8204   17.7947    6.9809]
Eigenvector (column) matrix:
CHF [-0.6212 -0.0044  0.5418 -0.5662]
GBP [-0.4392 -0.4192 -0.7575 -0.2398]
JPY [-0.3348  0.8861 -0.3150  0.0590]
EUR [-0.5560 -0.1975  0.1828  0.7864]
```

The first column of the eigenvector matrix is the one associated with the largest eigenvalue. All the entries are of the same sign and are roughly the same order of magnitude. There's no guarantee that an eigenvector will have any intuitive meaning, but in this case it's pretty clear what the largest factor is: it's the US dollar, since all these exchange rates were versus the US dollar.

The second column of the eigenvector matrix might be Europe versus Japan, but we're just guessing. We only have 4 items in our universe here. Imagine if there were 4,000 items: it would be very tough to find an intuitive explanation of 4,000 numbers.

Code Segment 6.5 outputs the eigensystem of the 2008 covariance matrix:

```
2008 eigenvalues times 10**6:
[ 196.6205   125.9944    27.9513    7.4675]
2008 eigenvector (column) matrix:
CHF [-0.5949  0.3290  0.3950 -0.6178]
GBP [-0.5133 -0.4496 -0.7044 -0.1956]
JPY [-0.0894  0.8280 -0.5177  0.1960]
EUR [-0.6120 -0.0638  0.2824  0.7359]
```

The overall volatility has gone up a lot as previously noted. The first principal component now seems to be mostly European currencies versus the dollar, whose role as a safe haven currency was even more important in 2008. The second principal component has become more important than in the full matrix (i.e. eigenvalue is larger both on an absolute basis and as a percentage of the total). The second principal component now appears to be currencies that were considered safe havens (Swiss franc and yen) versus less safe-haven currencies (pound and euro).

Often PCA is used for noise reduction. The sequence of approximations $M_1, \ldots, M_r$ to a matrix M noted in (6.26) uses successively more eigenvalues and eigenvectors. For example, we might have concluded after looking at the eigendecomposition of the 4×4 currency covariance matrices that only the first two components were significant, so $M_2 = E_2 G_2 E_2^{\mathsf{T}}$ would be a good compromise to avoid overfitting past data. The premise is that the biggest eigenvectors, or at least some linear combination of them, are the lasting explanations that will continue to predict out-of-sample behavior.

Code Segment 6.6 computes covariance matrices based on fewer eigenvalues. The printed version shows 2 eigenvalues, while the online version allows the user to select a number. Various heuristics for noise reduction are used.

```
Input #eigenvectors to use (1-4), 0 to stop

2

Original matrix:
      CHF      GBP      JPY      EUR
[ 0.4334   0.1908   0.1594   0.3080]
[ 0.1908   0.3449   0.0526   0.2173]
[ 0.1594   0.0526   0.3877   0.1069]
[ 0.3080   0.2173   0.1069   0.3498]
```

```
Truncated matrix:
[ 0.3588   0.2543   0.1921   0.3215]
[ 0.2543   0.2388   0.0111   0.2551]
[ 0.1921   0.0111   0.3698   0.1139]
[ 0.3215   0.2551   0.1139   0.3007]
Scaled truncated matrix:
[ 0.4289   0.3040   0.2296   0.3843]
[ 0.3040   0.2855   0.0133   0.3049]
[ 0.2296   0.0133   0.4421   0.1362]
[ 0.3843   0.3049   0.1362   0.3594]
Constant residual matrix:
[ 0.4349   0.2203   0.1668   0.2786]
[ 0.2203   0.3170   0.0389   0.2146]
[ 0.1668   0.0389   0.3825   0.1125]
[ 0.2786   0.2146   0.1125   0.3814]
Input #eigenvectors to use (1-4), 0 to stop

   0
```

The matrices don't look very different by the time two PCs are used, confirming at least intuitively that the significant movements are in the earlier principal components.

Current commercial risk models may use a hybrid approach, where a specified factor model like (6.3) – or the richer 100-factor models used in practice – is applied first. The residuals ϵ_s from (6.3) (or its commercial big brother) are computed for each security in each time period, typically for 60 months. The residuals are then used to form a residual covariance matrix, and PCA is applied to that matrix. If it looks like there is a large common factor in the residual covariance, the model (6.3) must be misspecified. This process can be used as a forensic tool to guide intuition to find missing factors, or it can be used to add residual PCA factors to the risk model.

For Code Segments in this chapter, see the Code Appendix starting on p. 440. For executable code, visit www.cambridge.org/9781009209090/ch6

For problem sets for this chapter, visit www.cambridge.org/ 9781009209090/ch6_problems

7 Distributions

We noted at the beginning of Chapter 4 that Louis Bachelier's 1900 PhD thesis was far ahead of its time in its use of Brownian motion to model changes in financial markets. The basic assumption of Gaussian/normal (or lognormal) changes in financial values seems plausible, and many subsequent modelers simply assumed normality.

There's a reason why normality seems, well, normal: the Central Limit Theorem, which says that averages of reasonably well-behaved distributions eventually start to look Gaussian. So if (say) one-second changes in logarithms of prices are generated by reasonably well-behaved distributions that satisfy the conditions of the Central Limit Theorem, then one-day log-price changes might start to look normal. Indeed, a histogram of log-price changes usually will have the roughly unimodal, symmetric, bell-shaped look of a Gaussian.

But empiricists[1] soon began to notice that price changes were too "peaked" to be samples of a normal distribution. Here "peaked" means that very small and very large changes happen far more frequently than a normal distribution would predict, while middling changes happen less frequently. Distributions in which large changes happen more often than in a Gaussian are called **fat-tailed**. If the Central Limit Theorem fails empirically, then the component distributions must not be well-behaved in the way the Central Limit Theorem requires.

Mandelbrot (1963) analyzed changes in prices of cotton and concluded that stable distributions with infinite variances gave better explanations of sample behavior than normal distributions. The Central Limit Theorem requires the component distributions to have finite variances, but Mandelbrot thought that this condition was violated. Most current financial economists think Mandelbrot was right about non-normality, but was wrong about the reason for it. The condition that is currently thought to be the culprit is independence: every second's log-price increment must be independent of every other second's log-price increment for the Central Limit Theorem to apply. If increments aren't independent, then behavior very much like observed behavior can occur.

We'll discuss two fat-tailed distributions that are often used to generate more realistic patterns than a normal distribution: Student's T and a mixture of normals.

We will also discuss extreme value distributions, which are fat-tailed and which are particularly helpful for modeling peril-type risks.

---

1 [Mandelbrot 1963] gives credit to a variety of earlier writers for noticing departures from normality, going as far back as Wesley C. Mitchell in 1915.

7.1 Central Limit Theorem

There are many versions of the **Central Limit Theorem ("CLT")**. What they have in common is the idea that in the limit, the average of ever-larger numbers of random variables is distributed normally. The random variables being averaged must be independent, and some of their moments must be finite.

For example, if a fair coin is tossed once, the distribution is binary: 50% heads and 50% tails. But if the coin is tossed twice, the distribution is 25% for two heads, 50% for one head and one tail, and 25% for two tails. After only two tosses, there is a rise in the central probabilities and a falling off in probability at the tails.

By the time the coin is tossed 1,000 times, the distribution of the number of heads looks very much like a normal distribution. Further, the more times the coin is tossed, the more probability mass squeezes toward the center: the standard deviation of n uncorrelated fair coin tosses is $\sqrt{n}/2$. Let P be a \$1 billion portfolio made up of n uncorrelated risky ventures each like Chapter 2's Beyond Vegetables. Then P's dollar standard deviation will be $10^9/(2\sqrt{n})$, which will tend to zero as n tends to infinity. (But as we noted in Chapter 6, putting together larger and larger numbers of assets into a portfolio does not actually result in standard deviation tending to zero. That in turn means there must be the types of common factors we studied in Chapter 6, so as a practical matter it is impossible to find a large number of uncorrelated assets.)

Figure 7.1 (generated by Code Segment 7.1) draws the 1,000-toss binomial distribution's probability mass function together with a normal probability

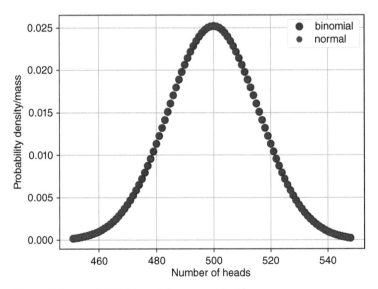

Figure 7.1 $n = 1,000$ binomial vs. normal pdf.

density function with the same mean (500 heads) and variance (250). It's very hard to see any difference.

More formally, we have the following version[2] of the CLT:

Central Limit Theorem (Lyapunov–Lindeberg) *Let $\{X_i\}$ be a discrete scalar stochastic process where each pair $\{X_i, X_j\}$ is independent. Suppose each mean $\mu_i = \mathbb{E}[X_i]$ and each variance $\sigma_i^2 = \mathbb{E}[(X_i - \mu_i)^2]$ is defined and finite. Define $s_n^2 = \sum_{i=1}^{n} \sigma_i^2$, and suppose that:*

$$\lim_{n \to \infty} \frac{1}{s_n^2} \sum_{i=1}^{n} \mathbb{E}[(X_i - \mu_i)^2 \delta(|X_i - \mu_i| > \epsilon s_n)] = 0 \quad \forall \epsilon > 0 \qquad (7.1)$$

where $\delta(b) = 1$ if b is true and $\delta(b) = 0$ otherwise. Then if we define the standardized average:

$$Z_n = \frac{\sum_{i=1}^{n} (X_i - \mu_i)}{s_n}, \qquad (7.2)$$

and if $F_{Z_n}(x)$ is the cumulative distribution function of Z_n, we have:

$$\lim_{n \to \infty} F_{Z_n}(x) = \frac{1}{\sqrt{2\pi}} \int_{-\infty}^{x} \exp\left(-\frac{t^2}{2}\right) dt = F_{Norm}(x) \quad \forall x \in \mathbb{R}. \qquad (7.3)$$

The often-cited Lindeberg–Levy form of the CLT requires **independent and identically distributed (i.i.d.)** X_i. The Lyapunov–Lindeberg form only requires independence, finite first and second moments, and the technical "Lindeberg Condition" (7.1), which essentially says that the contributions to overall variance coming from the tails of the distributions have to become negligible as $n \to \infty$.

For example, we could take second-by-second observations of the percentage price changes of the Swiss franc ("Swissie") versus the dollar. We don't even need to know what distributions are generating these observations: we could be in a state of Knightian Uncertainty. Each second's distribution could be different from the next second's distribution. All we need to know is that each second is independent of each other second; that whatever distributions are generating these price changes don't "go crazy" with infinite moments; and that each second's variance is a small component of the overall variance, as required by (7.1). Currencies trade in New York, London, Tokyo, Hong Kong, and other venues – say, roughly 16 active hours during a day, or 57,600 seconds. If the conditions of the CLT are satisfied, then it's plausible that daily price changes of the Swissie should look normal.

In fact, under conditions similar to those of the CLT, the Berry–Esseen Theorem[3] specifies a rate of convergence:

2 [Durrett 2013], p. 113.
3 [Durrett 2013], p. 118. We have modified Durrett's version to allow for non-identical distributions.

Berry–Esseen Theorem *Let $\{X_i\}$ be a discrete scalar stochastic process where each pair $\{X_i, X_j\}$ is independent. Suppose each mean $\mu_i = \mathbb{E}[X_i]$ and each variance $\sigma_i^2 = \mathbb{E}[(X_i - \mu_i)^2]$ is defined and finite. Let s_n^2, Z_n, $F_{Z_n}(x)$, and $F_{Norm}(x)$ be as defined in the CLT. Then there is a constant C_0 so that:*

$$\sup_{x\in\mathbb{R}} |F_{Z_n}(x) - F_{Norm}(x)| \le \frac{C_0}{\sqrt{n}} \frac{\bar{\rho}_n}{\bar{s}_n^3}, \tag{7.4}$$

where:

$$\bar{s}_n^2 = \frac{1}{n} s_n^2 \quad and \quad \bar{\rho}_n = \frac{1}{n} \sum_{i=1}^n \mathbb{E}[|X_i - \mu_i|^3].$$

Upper bounds on the constant C_0 have been improved gradually since the original publication of the theorem in 1942. Shevtsova (2010) proved that $C_0 < .5600$ for all n, with smaller upper bounds on C_0 for $n \le 10$.

Note that $\bar{\rho}_n$ is the average absolute third moment and $\bar{s}_n^2$ is the average second moment. If the component distributions are i.i.d. normal with common mean μ and common standard deviation σ, then the common absolute third moment is:

$$\rho = \frac{2}{\sqrt{2\pi}\sigma} \int_\mu^\infty (x - \mu)^3 \exp\left(-\frac{(x-\mu)^2}{2\sigma^2}\right) dx$$

$$= \frac{2}{\sqrt{2\pi}\sigma} \int_0^\infty 2^{3/2}\sigma^3 y^{3/2} \exp(-y) \frac{\sigma^2 dy}{\sqrt{2y}\sigma} = \frac{4\sigma^3}{\sqrt{2\pi}}$$

using the change of variable $y = \frac{(x-\mu)^2}{2\sigma^2}$. If we take the ratio $Ratio_{\{X_i\}} = \sup_n \frac{\bar{\rho}_n}{\bar{s}_n^3}$ as a tail thickness measure of the stochastic processes $\{X_i\}$, the i.i.d. normal baseline value is $Ratio_{Norm} = \frac{4}{\sqrt{2\pi}} \approx 1.596$. If we can find an upper bound of the form $Ratio_{\{X_i\}} \le Ratio_{Norm} * k$, then Berry–Esseen will give us a rate of convergence for the composite distributions $F_{Z_n}(x)$.

For example, if we have a log-price process $\{X_i\}$ where $Ratio_{\{X_i\}} \le Ratio_{Norm} * 2$, then we know from (7.4) that by the time there are $n = 10,000$ observations, the composite distribution $F_{Z_n}(x)$ will be everywhere less than $2 \cdot .5600 \cdot \frac{4}{100\sqrt{2\pi}} \approx 1.8\%$ away from the normal cdf $F_{Norm}(x)$.

7.1.1 Checking Normality: Q-Q and P-P Plots

There is a way to demonstrate visually whether or not a sample has been drawn from a particular distribution: a **Q-Q (quantile-quantile) plot**. The idea is to sort the sample observations so that $x_1 \le \cdots \le x_n$. We form standardized observations $z_i = \frac{x_i - m}{s}$, where $m = \frac{1}{n} \sum_{i=1}^n x_i$ is the sample mean and $s^2 = \frac{1}{n} \sum_{i=1}^n (x_i - m)^2$ is the sample variance. If these were distributed according to the cdf $F(x)$, then we could approximate z_i with the inverse distribution function

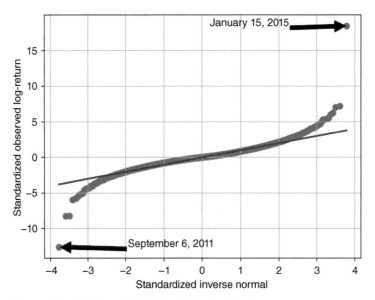

Figure 7.2 Q-Q plot, CHF 1971–2021, 12,784 observations.

$$z_i \approx F^{-1}\left(\frac{i}{n+1}\right). \qquad (7.5)$$

That is, $F(z_i) \approx \frac{i}{n+1}$. A Q-Q plot is a scatter of n points whose (x,y) coordinates are $\left(F^{-1}\left(\frac{i}{n+1}\right), z_i\right)$. If the sample is close to the desired distribution, then the Q-Q plot should be close to a straight line.

Code Segment 7.2 tries this for the Swissie; the desired distribution is normal, $F_{Norm}(x) = \frac{1}{\sqrt{2\pi}} \int_{-\infty}^{x} \exp\left(-\frac{t^2}{2}\right) dt$ as in (7.3). Code Segment 7.2 gathers daily log-changes of the Swissie from 1971 to the end of last year and produces Figure 7.2.

The red straight line shows what Figure 7.2 would look like if Swissie observations were sampled from a normal distribution. They clearly weren't: the green line formed from actual Swissie data is fairly straight in the middle, but begins to curve noticeably away from the red line at about ±2.5 standard deviations. This is a typical fat-tailed (leptokurtic) pattern seen in financial data.

Note, for example, the more than 12 standard deviation fall of the Swissie (versus the US dollar) in the lower left of the graph. That was on September 6, 2011, when the Swiss National Bank (SNB, the central bank of Switzerland) announced that it would do whatever it took[4] to devalue the Swissie, effectively pegging it to the cheaper euro. The bank felt this was necessary because it was getting less and less competitive, losing out to goods and services denominated in euros on world markets.

4 [Wearden 2011].

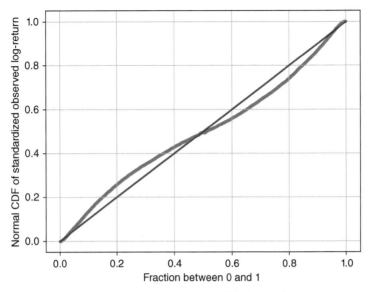

Figure 7.3 P-P plot, CHF 1971–2021, 12,784 observations.

As we will see below, the chance of a 12+ standard deviation move under the assumption of a normal distribution is essentially nil.

On January 15, 2015, the SNB announced that it was abandoning the ceiling[5] on the Swissie's value, and it shot up by 18 standard deviations, an even more improbable chance than before.

When the inverse F^{-1} of the target cdf F is not easily computed, a **P-P (probability-probability) plot** can be used. The scatter points have (x, y) coordinates equal to $\left(\left(\frac{i}{n+1} \right), F(z_i) \right)$. For the Swissie data, Code Segment 7.3 produces the P-P plot in Figure 7.3.

The scatter plot's departure from the target normal distribution is less visually striking in Figure 7.3 than it was in Figure 7.2, but the departure is still present. The fact that the green scatter goes above the red diagonal line in the left half of Figure 7.3 shows that the empirical distribution initially accumulates probability in the below-median region faster than the normal distribution. That's another way of saying that the normal distribution stochastically dominates the empirical distribution below the median. Above the median, the empirical distribution dominates. In both cases, that's because of fatter tails in the empirical distribution.

7.1.2 Jarque–Bera

A more metrical approach to characterizing normality or non-normality was given by Jarque and Bera (1980). They started from the observation that a normal

5 [Petroff 2015].

distribution has zero skewness (third moment) and excess kurtosis ($\equiv$kurtosis minus 3):

$$\frac{1}{\sqrt{2\pi}} \int_{-\infty}^{\infty} t^3 \exp\left(-\frac{t^2}{2}\right) dt = 0; \quad \frac{1}{\sqrt{2\pi}} \int_{-\infty}^{\infty} t^4 \exp\left(-\frac{t^2}{2}\right) dt = 3. \quad (7.6)$$

The Jarque–Bera test forms a statistic that gets larger as S=skewness and K=(excess kurtosis) depart from zero. This statistic is distributed as chi-squared with two degrees of freedom (scipy.stats.chi2.cdf(x,2)), and gives the probability that the observed distribution is non-normal:

$$JB(S,K) = \frac{n}{6}\left(S^2 + K^2/4\right). \quad (7.7)$$

For the Swissie series from 1971 through the previous yearend, visual inspection of Figure 7.2 indicates the data are significantly non-normal. This is confirmed by the Jarque–Bera calculation in Code Segment 7.4, which produces the following output:

```
Skewness 0.396194
Excess Kurtosis 14.499288
Jarque-Bera Statistic 112316.617856
Chi-squared probability non-normal 1.000000
```

The null hypothesis is that the data are normal; we reject that hypothesis when the chi-squared statistic is above a desired confidence level. For the Swissie data, there is almost perfect confidence in rejecting normality.

7.1.3 Causes of Non-Normality

There are at least two phenomena causing the departures from normality reflected in Figure 7.2 and the Jarque–Bera statistic. One is the presence of a large price-maker in the market. The dynamic behind Brownian motion is a series of random collisions of molecules (the equivalent of comparatively small price-takers) moving the location of a particle (the price of the Swissie). If the scientist looking at the particle under the microscope picks up the slide it's on and moves it across the laboratory, that's an intervention on a massively greater scale than random molecule collisions. That's what the Swiss National Bank did on the two highlighted extreme dates.

But even leaving aside the SNB's interventions, there are a good number of observations of regular market days that curve away from the straight (normal) line in Figure 7.2. This empirical failure of the Central Limit Theorem – significant leptokurtosis – appears in virtually every financial time series. Mandelbrot's explanation was essentially that any second could have an arbitrarily large price move, but that doesn't seem consistent with the data. A more reasonable failure point for the Central Limit Theorem's assumptions is independence: there can be periods of systematic trending, so the second-by-second observations don't cancel each other out but rather reinforce each other.

There is a limit to how much weight can be in the tails of a distribution. **Markov's Inequality**[6] says that if Z is a nonnegative random variable and $k > 0$, then:

$$Pr(Z > k\mathbb{E}[Z]) \leq \frac{1}{k}. \tag{7.8}$$

If X is any random variable with finite first and second moments, then letting $Z = (X - \mathbb{E}[X])^2$ and applying (7.8) with $\sigma^2 = \mathbb{E}[Z] = \mathbb{E}\left[(X - \mathbb{E}[X])^2\right]$ proves **Chebyshev's Inequality**:

$$Pr(|X - \mathbb{E}[X]| \geq k\sigma) \leq \frac{1}{k^2} \tag{7.9}$$

when $k > 0$. This says that the probability of being k standard deviations σ away from the mean can be no more than $\frac{1}{k^2}$. Thus a 10 standard deviation event can happen no more than 1/100th of the time. That's about 2.5 times a year assuming daily periodicity. For a normal distribution, 10 standard deviation events are a lot rarer, as shown in Table 7.1 (produced by Code Segment 7.5).

Table 7.1 shows 10 standard deviation events expected to occur in one per 10^{-23} periods. The age of the universe[7] is less than 10^{13} business days, so anything over about 8 standard deviations is effectively never, assuming normality. The fact of the 18 standard deviation event (10^{-72} frequency) in Swissie prices on January 15, 2015, is by itself excellent evidence for non-normality. On the other hand, Chebyshev's Inequality says such events could happen every 324 days – once per 1.3 years of business days. Observed data seem to be well within Chebyshev's bound but well outside normal.

The apparent violation of the Central Limit Theorem's independence condition is due to the fact that financial markets are populated with humans who react to patterns they perceive in history. We've seen that general idea expressed in many different ways. Reactions can be **procyclical** (positively correlated with the past) or **anticyclical** (negatively correlated with the past); neither reaction is independent of the past.

7.1.4 Market Ages

The oldest continuously operating bond market appears to be for British government debt starting around the formation of the Bank of England in 1694.[8] The Bank of England has kept track of rates on consols (perpetual bonds) and other

---

6 [Durrett 2013], p. 25.
7 The age of the universe is about 13.75 billion years, which is about 10^{13} business days. ([Jarosik, Bennett, Dunkley, et al. 2011], Table 8).
8 Bank of England. "Our History." Website. www.bankofengland.co.uk/about/history.

Table 7.1 Normal distribution probabilities (log10)

Std. devs	log10(prob)
0	−0.30103
1	−0.799546
2	−1.64302
3	−2.8697
4	−4.49933
5	−6.54265
6	−9.00586
7	−11.8929
8	−15.2061
9	−18.9475
10	−23.1181
11	−27.7188
12	−32.7504
13	−38.2134
14	−44.1083
15	−50.4352
16	−57.1946
17	−64.3866
18	−72.0114
19	−80.0692
20	−88.5601

long-term borrowings since 1703, as shown in Figure 7.4 (produced by Code Segment 7.6).

Borrowing and lending have been recorded for almost as long as humans have produced records (about 5,000 years[9]), but Figure 7.4 documents the world record of over 300 years of uninterrupted payments from the same non-defaulting entity.

The oldest continuously operating stock exchange in the world is the Amsterdam Stock Exchange, started in 1602.[10]

9 [Homer and Sylla 2005] indicate that Sumerian agricultural loans from about 4 millennia ago are the oldest recorded. They document interest rates century by century to the present, but there does not appear to be another entity that has as long an unbroken record of non-defaulting borrowing as the UK government.
10 [Petram 2014]. [Braudel 1992] found securities being exchanged in Italian city-states in the early 1300s, but these markets have not operated continuously.

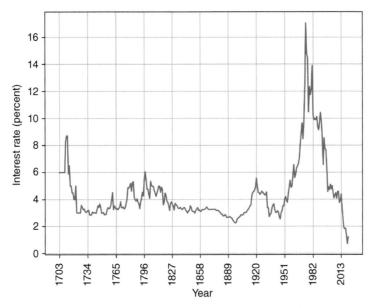

Figure 7.4 UK government bond long-term rates, yearend 1703–2021.

Otherwise, most markets have had lives of less than 200 years.[11] Sometimes market failures have been accompanied by a violent break in the political system as well, with loss of life focusing the mind more than loss of investment. The Russian Revolution repudiated all government debt and abolished private property in a series of steps from 1917 to 1920, so once-thriving stock exchanges in Moscow, Kiev, and St. Petersburg had total losses of value. The Chinese government took similar steps from 1949 to 1953,[12] the Cuban government in 1959.

Thus, in modeling empirical finance, it is usually not reasonable to apply a theorem that has $t \rightarrow \infty$ somewhere in its proof; $t \rightarrow 300$ (years) is more realistic. Arguments that depend on long-term equlibrium taking hold are prone to be emphatically disproven by rebels storming the seat of government.

The oldest operating markets have been in existence for about 10^5 days, so if financial data were normally distributed, we might expect to see a few 4 or 5 standard deviation events during their entire existence. In fact, such events are relatively common. Even in the relatively staid and short 300-plus annual observations of UK rate changes shown in Figure 7.4, the output of Code Segment 7.7 shows that there was a 7 standard deviation event and more than 11 observations greater than expected if the data were normal:

---

11 [Reinhart and Rogoff 2009].
12 Visit www.americanbondholdersfoundation.com/ to see a group of people (or their descendants) who bought Chinese government bonds pre-1938 and are still trying to get their money back. The Shanghai stock exchange also closed in 1949. It reopened in 1990 with completely new listings.

```
Normal standard deviations for one in 318 years:
        2.732303990659007
Observations larger than that:
Date
1977-12-31    -5.902363
1982-12-31    -5.416020
1713-12-31    -4.104369
1975-12-31    -3.323273
1722-12-31    -2.925356
1993-12-31    -2.910619
1978-12-31     2.778117
1994-12-31     2.940231
1710-12-31     3.411836
1973-12-31     3.573950
1974-12-31     7.081513
Name: Rate, dtype: float64
```

On the other hand, overly violent moves are not compatible with ongoing markets: a primary market with regular 90% swings in value will simply scare away participants. So some kind of intermediate distribution – more violent than normal, but less violent than an infinite-variance distribution – is in order.

7.2 Student's T Distribution

There are many natural distributions that are fatter-tailed than normal. One popular choice to fatten tails is the **Student's T-distribution**. The sample means of finite numbers of observations drawn from a normal process are not distributed normally, but rather as a Student's T.

The distribution is generally credited to William Gosset,[13] who wrote under the pen-name "Student." In Student (1908), he reported on the distribution of the error in estimating the mean from small samples of draws from a normal process. While Student (Gosset) gets the credit, the distribution was actually discovered by Jacob Lüroth in 1876.[14] Lüroth's work was in German and was not well known to English statisticians when Student (Gosset) did his work.

The idea is that there are n independent observations $X_1, X_2, \ldots, X_n$ of a random variable that is normally distributed with known mean μ, but whose variance is unknown. The observed mean is $m_n = \frac{X_1 + X_2 + \cdots + X_n}{n}$.

---

13 MacTutor. "William Sealy Gosset." Website. www-history.mcs.st-andrews.ac.uk/Biographies/Gosset.html.

14 MacTutor. "Jacob Lüroth." Website. www-history.mcs.st-andrews.ac.uk/Biographies/Lueroth.html.

An estimate of the unknown variance can be computed from the data in the usual way:

$$s_n^2 = \frac{1}{n-1} \sum_{i=1}^{n} (X_i - m_n)^2. \tag{7.10}$$

The **Student T statistic** is:

$$T_n = \sqrt{n} \left(\frac{m_n - \mu}{s_n} \right), \tag{7.11}$$

where n is the number of observations. Student (Gosset) computed the pdf of this distribution. The usual presentation defines $d = n - 1$ and defines:

$$student_d(t) = \frac{\Gamma\left(\frac{d+1}{2}\right)}{\sqrt{d\pi}\,\Gamma\left(\frac{d}{2}\right)} \left(1 + \frac{t^2}{d}\right)^{-\frac{d+1}{2}}. \tag{7.12}$$

This uses the Gamma function $\Gamma(x) = \int_0^\infty e^{-t} t^{x-1} dt$. For integer i, $\Gamma(i) = (i-1)!$. From Stirling's formula $\Gamma(x) \approx \sqrt{\frac{2\pi}{x}} \left(\frac{x}{e}\right)^x$, it follows that the ratio of the Gamma functions in (7.12) approaches $\sqrt{\frac{d}{2}}$ as $d \to \infty$. Thus, we have:

$$\lim_{d \to \infty} student_d(t) = \frac{1}{\sqrt{2\pi}} \exp\left(-\frac{t^2}{2}\right).$$

That is, for large numbers of observations, the Student's T pdf approaches the normal pdf as the Central Limit Theorem dictates.

The standardized Student's T distribution in (7.12) has odd moments (including mean and skew) equal to zero; variance equal to $d/(d-2)$; and excess kurtosis equal to $6/(d-4)$ when $d > 4$. We can move the mean to a desired quantity a and scale the standard deviation by a desired quantity b by translating and scaling the argument:

$$student_{d,a,b}(t) = student_d \left(\frac{t-a}{b}\right) = \frac{\Gamma\left(\frac{d+1}{2}\right)}{\sqrt{d\pi}\,\Gamma\left(\frac{d}{2}\right)} \left(1 + \frac{\left(\frac{t-a}{b}\right)^2}{d}\right)^{-\frac{d+1}{2}}. \tag{7.13}$$

Code Segment 7.8 produces Figure 7.5, which shows Student's T pdfs for various low d compared to a near-normal ($d = 1,000$) pdf.

The first-order visual impression from the Figure 7.5a is that there is only a slight difference between the distributions. However, it becomes apparent when we zoom in on the left tails in Figure 7.5b that there's a huge difference: for example, a four or worse standard deviation event occurs quite rarely (about once in 117 years with daily periodicity) with d=1000. With d=5, the four or worse standard deviation event occurs about once in 9 months.

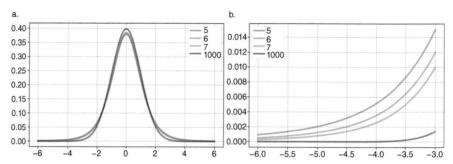

Figure 7.5 a. Overall view of Student's T densities. b. Left cumulative tails of Student's T distributions.

7.3 Mixtures of Normals

A second simple way of fattening tails is to take a **mixture of normals**. This is not to be confused with a sum of (independent) normals $S_m = X_1 + \cdots + X_m$; the random variable S_m is itself normal.

A mixture distribution adds the component probability density functions (or equivalently the cdfs), not the random variables. Suppose there is a finite number m of distributions to be mixed, and that there are weights $w_1, \ldots, w_m$ with $w_i > 0$ and $w_1 + \cdots + w_m = 1$. Let $\mathrm{pdf}_i()$ be the probability density function of the ith distribution. Then the mixture distribution's probability density function is:

$$\mathrm{pdf}_{mix}(t) = \sum_{i=1}^{m} w_i \mathrm{pdf}_i(t). \tag{7.14}$$

Intuitively, the different mixture components represent different states of the world, with weight w_i representing the probability of being in state i. Some states of the world are relatively calm; others are relatively turbulent. Some states of the world have low expected values; others have high expected values.

It's hard to come up with an intuition as to why a Student's T distribution should model a real economic object. The many thousands of Swiss franc observations that gave rise to Figure 7.2 were not small samples of normal distributions. On the other hand, it's plausible that a mixture of distributions reflects the fact that sometimes markets are calm and sometimes they are volatile.

Sampling from a mixture distribution is a two-part process. First a sample u is taken from a uniform distribution on the interval $[0, 1]$. If u is between $\sum_{j=1}^{i-1} w_j$ and $\sum_{j=1}^{i} w_j$, then the mixture sample is taken from the distribution given by pdf_i. Intuitively, the surprise of not knowing which distribution gives rise to any given sample causes fatter tails.

While a sufficiently large number of normal mixture components can approximate any distribution to an arbitrary degree of precision,[15] using large

---

15 [Willkens 2005], p. 214.

numbers of mixture components means a large number of parameters, possibly resulting in overfitting. The power of mixture distributions comes in their ability to model realistic behavior with a small number of components. We'll focus on using mixtures that produce distributions with desired levels of the first four moments: mean, variance, skewness, and kurtosis.

Notation: Let μ_i be the mean of the ith distribution, $\mu_i = \int x \, \text{pdf}_i(x) dx$. The jth central moment of the ith distribution is:

$$c_{i,j} = \int (x - \mu_i)^j \text{pdf}_i(x) dx.$$

Note $c_{i,0} = 1$ and $c_{i,1} = 0$ for all i.

It follows from (7.14) that the mean of the mixture distribution equals the weighted average of the component means:

$$\mu_{mix} = \int x \left(\sum_{i=1}^{m} w_i \text{pdf}_i(x) \right) dx = \sum_{i=1}^{m} w_i \left(\int x \, \text{pdf}_i(x) dx \right) = \sum_{i=1}^{m} w_i \mu_i. \quad (7.15)$$

In general, the kth central moment of the mixture $c_{mix,k}$ can be computed by binomial expansion of the terms.

$$\begin{aligned}
c_{mix,k} &= \int (x - \mu_{mix})^k \left(\sum_{i=1}^{m} w_i \text{pdf}_i(x) \right) dx \\
&= \sum_{i=1}^{m} w_i \left(\int \left((x - \mu_i) + (\mu_i - \mu_{mix}) \right)^k \text{pdf}_i(x) dx \right) \\
&= \sum_{i=1}^{m} w_i \int \left[\sum_{j=0}^{k} \binom{k}{j} (x - \mu_i)^j (\mu_i - \mu_{mix})^{k-j} \right] \text{pdf}_i(x) dx \\
&= \sum_{i=1}^{m} w_i \left[\sum_{j=0}^{k} \binom{k}{j} c_{i,j} (\mu_i - \mu_{mix})^{k-j} \right]. \quad (7.16)
\end{aligned}$$

Applying (7.16) to the second central moment – the variance – shows that:

$$\sigma_{mix}^2 = \sum_{i=1}^{m} w_i [(\mu_i - \mu_{mix})^2 + \sigma_i^2] = \sum_{i=1}^{m} w_i \sigma_i^2 + \left(\left[\sum_{i=1}^{m} w_i \mu_i^2 \right] - \mu_{mix}^2 \right). \quad (7.17)$$

Jensen's Inequality says that the term $\left(\left[\sum_{i=1}^{m} w_i \mu_i^2 \right] - \mu_{mix}^2 \right)$ is non-negative, so the mixture variance σ_{mix}^2 is no less than the weighted average variance of the components.

The mixture's central third moment and its scaled version (skewness) look like this:

$$c_{mix,3} = \sigma_{mix}^3 skew_{mix} = \sum_{i=1}^{m} w_i [(\mu_i - \mu_{mix})^3 + 3\sigma_i^2(\mu_i - \mu_{mix})]. \qquad (7.18)$$

The mixture components are normal so the component skews $c_{i,3} = 0$. Still, there can be nonzero mixture skew unless all the component means are the same.

The fourth central moment is the unscaled absolute (nonexcess) kurtosis:

$$c_{mix,4} = \sigma_{mix}^4 kurt_{mix}$$

$$= \sum_{i=1}^{m} w_i [(\mu_i - \mu_{mix})^4 + 6\sigma_i^2(\mu_i - \mu_{mix})^2 + 4c_{i,3}(\mu_i - \mu_{mix}) + 3\sigma_i^4)]$$

$$(7.19)$$

Recall from (7.6) that the absolute kurtosis of a normal distribution equals 3, that is, $c_{i,4} = 3\sigma_i^4$ for each component. When all of the component means are the same, (7.19) simplifies to $kurt_{mix} = 3\frac{\sum_{i=1}^{m} w_i \sigma_i^4}{\sigma_{mix}^4}$. The ratio on the RHS is greater than one by Jensen's Inequality, meaning that a mixture of same-mean normals is always leptokurtic.

Financial distributions are mostly unimodal. Mixing normals with different means can lead to multimodal distributions, which only occur under special circumstances.[16] However, usually different component means are not needed or wanted: (7.17)–(7.19) show that a distribution with a desired mean, standard deviation, and kurtosis can be generated by mixing normals with the same means and different standard deviations. Such a mixture will have zero skew, but log-return empirical distributions often don't have significant skews. Realistic skew can usually be modeled simply by taking an *exp*, that is, $Y = \exp(X) - 1$ where X is a zero-skew distribution.

A mixture of two normal distributions with the same means has four parameters: the common mean μ; the higher standard deviation σ_1; the lower standard deviation σ_2; and the weight $0 \le w_1 \le 1$ of the more volatile distribution in the mixture. These four parameters can be set to generate a mixture distribution with a desired mean μ_{mix}; standard deviation σ_{mix}; zero skew; and excess kurtosis κ_{mix}.

The mean μ of each distribution is set to the target mean μ_{mix}. Let $r = \frac{\sigma_1^2}{\sigma_2^2} \ge 1$ be the ratio of the larger component variance to the smaller component variance.

---

16 Multimodal distributions can occur, usually temporarily, around events like a possible merger: there may be one mass of probability around prices reflecting success of the merger and another mass around failure prices. Even so, most of the time outcomes are diffuse enough so that distributions are unimodal.

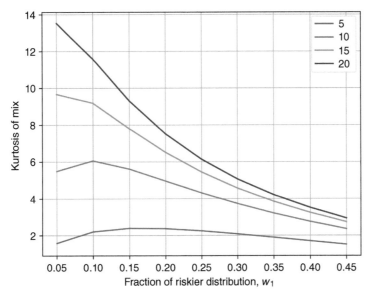

Figure 7.6 Kurtosis of mixtures of normals.

Substituting into (7.17) and (7.19) gives two equations in the three unknowns r, w_1, and σ_2:

$$\sigma_{mix}^2 = \sigma_2^2(w_1 r + 1 - w_1),$$

$$\kappa_{mix} = \frac{c_{mix,4}}{\sigma_{mix}^4} - 3 = 3\frac{\left(w_1 r^2 + 1 - w_1\right)}{\left(w_1 r + 1 - w_1\right)^2} - 3. \tag{7.20}$$

Code Segment 7.9 produces Figure 7.6, which displays excess kurtosis for $r = 5, 10, 15$, and 20 at different values of w_1.

While the curves in Figure 7.6 aren't always monotone, they do show that small exposures to the more volatile component can produce higher kurtosis. For example, a market that has relatively low variance 95% of the time, but that has $20\times$ the usual variance 5% of the time, produces an excess kurtosis of about 14 at the left end of the red curve. More frequent high-volatility regimes lead to lower kurtosis: the shock of more turbulent log-returns wears off.

Mixtures of normals are closely related to regime-switching models, such as those in Ang and Timmerman (2011). They note (p. 2) that:

> Regime-switching models can match the tendency of financial markets to often change their behavior abruptly and the phenomenon that the new behavior of financial variables often persists for several periods after such a change.

Mixtures of normals get the first part of this – the abrupt changes of behavior – but not the second, that is, not the persistence of the new behavior.

To take that into account, we need time series models such as the ones we will study in Chapter 9.

A more powerful way of fitting large mixtures of normals – often called Gaussian Mixture Models – is via a machine learning expectation maximization technique.[17] This is a form of unsupervised learning that determines an optimal clustering of a dataset to a best-fit mixture of normals.

7.4 Stable Distributions

We noted above that sums of normal distributions are normal. **Stable Distributions**[18] generalize the closed-under-sum property. If X_1 and X_2 are independent and identically distributed, then their common distribution is **stable** if any positive linear combination of X_1 and X_2 is distributed the same way (up to positive scaling and translation). This class of distributions was characterized by Paul Lévy in the 1920s;[19] it's also called Lévy α-stable distributions.

More precisely, a cumulative distribution function $F(x)$ is stable if and only if when there are two independent random variables X_1 and X_2, both with cdf's $F(x)$, then for any positive a and b there exists a positive c and a d such that $\frac{aX_1+bX_2}{c} - d$ has cdf equal to $F(x)$.

Stable distributions – other than the normal distribution, which is in some sense the tamest member of the stable distribution family – are used sparingly in mathematical finance for two main reasons. One reason is that, other than the normal, stable distributions have undefined variances, making them less likely to describe observed data than fat-tailed but finite-variance distributions. The second reason is more practical: only a few stable distributions have closed-form density functions. Most require an algorithm to compute even the most basic distributional characteristics, like Value at Risk. As we've noted, mathematical modeling in finance is less about finding physical law and more about guiding intuition; that's more difficult to do when the relationship between inputs and outputs is highly nonlinear.

We will briefly cover stable distributions because, as we noted above, Benoit Mandelbrot proposed them as a way to model the observed leptokurtosis in financial data. Current approaches use more tractable and arguably more realistic techniques, but stable distributions are still good to have in a quantitative analyst's toolkit.

---

17 Scikit-learn.org. "Gaussian Mixture Models." Website. `https://scikit-learn.org/stable/modules/mixture.html`.

18 In this section we have relied on [Nolan 2020] and a prepublication version of [Nair, Wierman, and Zwart 2020].

19 [Nolan 2020], vii.

The closed-under-addition property of stable distributions leads to the:

Generalized Central Limit Theorem[20] *If* $X_1, X_2, \ldots$ *is an infinite sequence of independent and identically distributed variables, and if there are scalar nonstochastic quantities* $a_1 > 0, a_2 > 0, \ldots$ *and* $b_1, b_2, \ldots$ *such that the cdfs of* $a_n(X_1 + X_2 + \cdots + X_n) - b_n$ *converge pointwise to the cdf of a random variable* Z, *then* Z *is stable.*

The finiteness conditions in the Central Limit Theorem are removed. But the same general conclusion can be drawn: there is a distribution – or more generally, a family of distribution – that is the limiting value of some kind of distribution averaging. This is an intuitively reasonable property for financial time series, as it seems desirable to be able to aggregate movements over short time periods into a recognizable distribution over longer periods.

Stable distributions can be specified[21] with closed-form characteristic functions using four parameters:

Letter	Parameter name	Range
α	Stability	$0 < \alpha \leq 2$
β	Symmetry	$-1 \leq \beta \leq 1$
γ	Scale	$0 < \gamma$
δ	Location	$-\infty < \delta < \infty$

Standardized stable distributions can be specified with only the first two parameters (α and β):

$$\varphi(t) = \exp\left(-|t|^\alpha \left[1 - i\beta \tan\left(\frac{\pi\alpha}{2}\right)\mathrm{sgn}(t)\right]\right), \quad \alpha \neq 1, \qquad (7.21)$$

$$\varphi(t) = \exp\left(-|t| \left[1 - i\beta\frac{2}{\pi}\ln(|t|)\mathrm{sgn}(t)\right]\right), \quad \alpha = 1. \qquad (7.22)$$

$\mathrm{sgn}(x)$ is the sign of x (+1 if positive, 0 if 0, -1 if negative). If the distribution is symmetric ($\beta = 0$), then the expression for the characteristic function simplifies considerably to $\varphi(t) = \exp(-|t|^\alpha)$.

The scale parameter (similar to standard deviation) and the location parameter (similar to mean) can be introduced through linear transforms. If Z is a stable random variable whose distribution is given by (7.22), we can define $X = \gamma Z + \delta$ which by definition is also stable. For the $\alpha \neq 1$ case in (7.21), a

---

20 [Nair, Wierman, and Zwart 2020], pp. 123–124.
21 There are so many parameterizations of stable distributions that some authors include a fifth parameter indicating which parameterization scheme is being used. We have adopted the main scheme used by [Nolan 2020], pp. 6–7.

different transform is used to make the resulting characteristic function a little more tractable:

$$X = \gamma \left(Z - \beta \tan \left(\frac{\pi \alpha}{2} \right) \right) + \delta, \quad \alpha \neq 1, \tag{7.23}$$

$$X = \gamma Z + \delta, \quad \alpha = 1. \tag{7.24}$$

The characteristic functions of the resulting four-parameter distributions look like this:

$$\varphi(t) = \exp \left(-|\gamma t|^\alpha \left[1 - i\beta \tan \left(\frac{\pi \alpha}{2} \right) \mathrm{sgn}(t)(|\gamma t|^{1-\alpha} - 1) \right] + i\delta t \right), \quad \alpha \neq 1, \tag{7.25}$$

$$\varphi(t) = \exp \left(-|\gamma t| \left[1 - i\beta \frac{2}{\pi} \ln(|\gamma t|) \mathrm{sgn}(t) \right] + i\delta t \right), \quad \alpha = 1. \tag{7.26}$$

As in the standardized cases (7.21) and (7.22), symmetry considerably simplifies the expression: $\varphi(x) = \exp(-|\gamma t|^\alpha + i\delta t)$.

Code Segment 7.10 generates Figures 7.7a and 7.7b, which are similar to 7.5a and 7.5b, except these use stable distributions with different αs. We have included $\alpha = 1.7$, which was the value that Mandelbrot suggested formed a good fit for the cotton price data he analyzed. The differences in tail probabilities are dramatic.

The range of the $\alpha = 1.7$ distribution is typically 10–20 times the range of the normal distribution. While financial time series are clearly fat-tailed, they are usually not *that* fat-tailed. Even the highly unusual events seen in Figure 7.2 as a result of intervention by the Swiss National Bank were only about 3–4 times the range of normal.

There are three standard closed-form pdfs in the stable distribution family. One is when $\alpha = 2$; in that case $\tan \left(\frac{\pi \alpha}{2} \right) = 0$, removing the asymmetry terms from (7.21). The characteristic function of the standard stable distribution then

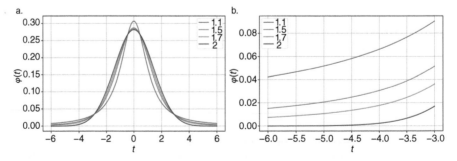

Figure 7.7 a. Overall view of stable distributions. b. Left cumulative tails of stable distributions.

inverse-Fourier-transforms to the normal distribution pdf, although with double the variance of the standard normal:

$$f_{\alpha=2}(t) = \frac{1}{2\sqrt{\pi}} \exp\left(-\frac{t^2}{4}\right). \tag{7.27}$$

The standard symmetric ($\beta = 0$) stable distribution with $\alpha = 1$ is called a **Cauchy distribution**. In this case, (7.22) is simply $\exp(-|t|)$; its inverse Fourier transform is:

$$f_{\alpha=1}(t) = \frac{1}{\pi} \frac{1}{1+t^2}. \tag{7.28}$$

The stable distribution with $\alpha = \frac{1}{2}$ and $\beta = 1$ is called a **Lévy distribution**. Its pdf looks like:

$$f_{\alpha=\frac{1}{2}, \beta=1}(t) = \frac{1}{\sqrt{2\pi t^3}} \exp\left(-\frac{1}{2t}\right). \tag{7.29}$$

This can be a little confusing; the entire stable family is sometimes called the "Lévy α-stable" family, but the "Lévy distribution" is the particular family member given in (7.29). The support of this asymmetric pdf consists of the positive real numbers.

Code Segment 7.11 produces Figure 7.8, which compares these three pdfs, although we have removed the factor of 2 in the normal variance in (7.27). Code Segment 7.11 also computes observation sizes – essentially numbers of standard deviations – for events with probability 10^{-4}:

```
Observation sizes for p=.0001:
Normal: 3.7190164854556804
Cauchy: 3183.098757116829
Levy: 63661976.90343881
```

Consider the point 10^{-4} on the X-axis of Figure 7.8; this represents a frequency that's about once per the number of Swiss franc observations we used for Figure 7.2. The blue line, the normal distribution, shows that observations of size about ± 4 would be expected to be seen that frequently; in fact the straight line in Figure 7.2 is in that vertical range. The red line in Figure 7.8 shows that a Cauchy distribution would produce observations of size ± 3183 once in 10^4 times. The green line shows that a Lévy distribution would produce observations of size $63,661,977$ once in 10^4 times. We noted after Figure 7.7 that $\alpha = 1.7$ gave unrealistically fat tails; the Cauchy and Lévy distributions are even more unrealistic.

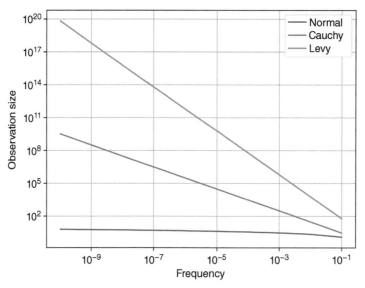

Figure 7.8 Inverse standard Normal, Cauchy, and Levy.

It is natural to ask if we can characterize the behavior of tails of distributions, $Pr(X > z)$ or $Pr(X < -z)$ for a random variable X and a large positive scalar z. For a standard normal random variable X and $z > 0$,

$$Pr(X > z) = \int_z^\infty f(x)dx < \int_z^\infty \frac{x}{z}f(x)dx = \frac{f(z)}{z},$$

where $f(z) = F'(z) = \frac{1}{\sqrt{2\pi}}\exp\left(-\frac{z^2}{2}\right)$ is the standard normal pdf. Thus the tail probability for a normal distribution approaches zero rapidly.

For a random variable X with a general four-parameter stable distribution, the tail dropoff rate is approximated by:[22]

For $0 < \alpha < 2$,

$$Pr(X > z) \approx K_{high}z^{-\alpha}, \tag{7.30}$$

$$Pr(X < -z) \approx K_{low}z^{-\alpha}, \tag{7.31}$$

where the limit as $z \to \infty$ of the ratio of the LHS and the RHS of the $\approx$ signs is one.

Here $K_{high} = \gamma^\alpha \sin\left(\frac{\pi\alpha}{2}\right)\frac{\Gamma(\alpha)}{\pi}(1 + \beta)$ and $K_{low} = \gamma^\alpha \sin\left(\frac{\pi\alpha}{2}\right)\frac{\Gamma(\alpha)}{\pi}(1 - \beta)$. Notice the location parameter δ does not appear in either expression, since a finite shift in location will eventually be overcome as $z \to \infty$.

Thus for standardized symmetric stable distributions ((7.21) and (7.22) with $\beta = 0$), the tail probabilities begin to look like Figure 7.9 (generated by Code Segment 7.12).

22 [Nolan 2020], p. 22.

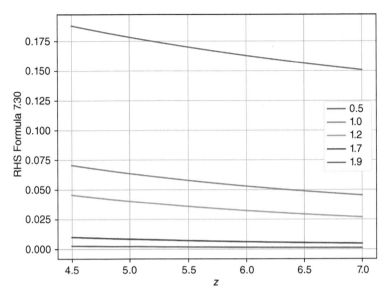

Figure 7.9 Tail cdf approximations, Formula (7.30).

7.5 Extreme Value Distributions

The Central Limit Theorem and the Generalized Central Limit Theorem addressed average values of random variables. In a financial context, averaging makes sense for quantities like log-returns: the annualized log-return over n periods is the average of the n per-period annualized log-returns.

However, there are other contexts where the "worst of" is of more concern than the "average of." A financial entity cannot continue operating for long if it can't pay its bills, so it has to assess the worst case for its assets versus its liabilities. Insurance companies can't just plan for average claims; they need an understanding of worst cases.

Thus, instead of thinking about $Average(X_1, X_2, \ldots, X_n)$, at times we want to think about $\max(X_1, X_2, \ldots, X_n)$, where the X_i might be loss amounts or (minus) capital levels. If $X_1, X_2, \ldots, X_n$ are i.i.d. with common cdf $F(x)$, then the maximum has a convenient distribution function: $Pr(\max(X_1, X_2, \ldots, X_n) \leq x) = F^n(x)$.

For example, consider the uniform distribution $F(x) = x$ on $[0, 1]$. Intuitively, it's clear that the more points we sample from the uniform distribution, the higher the probability that the maximum is close to one. In fact, we have $\mathbb{E}[\max(X_1, X_2, \ldots, X_n)] = \int_0^1 x dF(x)^n = \frac{n}{n+1}$ where the X_i are i.i.d. uniformly distributed. Code Segment 7.13 generates Figure 7.10, which is a histogram of maxima from uniform samples. Figure 7.10 shows that as expected the density function is proportional to x^{n-1}.

There is an analog to the Central Limit Theorem that says that if suitably normalized maxima converge, they converge to a particular type of distribution

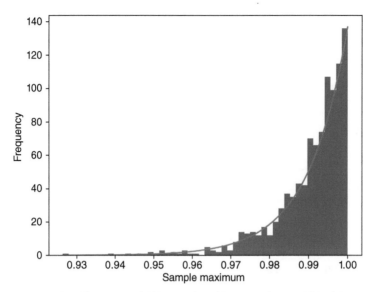

Figure 7.10 Histogram of 100-sample uniform maxima, 1,000 trials.

called a **generalized extreme value (GEV) distribution**. Standard (location 0, scale 1) GEV distributions can be parameterized with a scalar γ:

$$GEV_\gamma(x) = \exp\big(-(1+\gamma x)^{-1/\gamma}\big), \quad 1+\gamma x > 0, \tag{7.32}$$

When $\gamma > 0$, the GEV is also called a *Fréchet distribution*; when $\gamma < 0$, the GEV is also called a *Weibull distribution*. The limiting case $\gamma = 0$ is called a *Gumbel distribution*:

$$GEV_0(x) = \exp\big(-\exp(-x)\big). \tag{7.33}$$

The associated pdfs are:

$$gev_\gamma(x) = (1+\gamma x)^{-1/\gamma - 1} GEV_\gamma(x), \quad \gamma \neq 0, \tag{7.34}$$

$$gev_0(x) = \exp(-x)GEV_0(x). \tag{7.35}$$

The Central Limit Theorem analog is due to Fisher, Tippet, and Gnedenko,[23] and says:

Extreme Value Theorem *Suppose that $X_1, X_2, \ldots$ are i.i.d. and that there exist sequences m_n and $s_n > 0$ of constants and a nondegenerate cdf $G(x)$ so that*

$$\lim_{n \to \infty} Pr\Big(\frac{\max(X_1, X_2, \ldots, X_n) - m_n}{s_n} \leq x\Big) = G(x). \tag{7.36}$$

Then $G(x)$ is a generalized extreme value (GEV) function as defined in (7.32).

---

23 [Nair, Wierman, and Zwart 2020], p. 160.

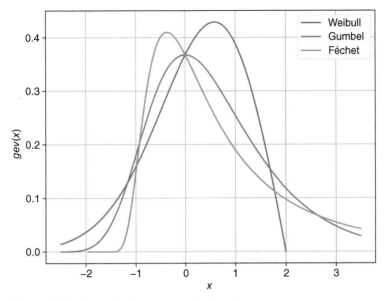

Figure 7.11 Generalized extreme value densities.

Here the degenerate cdfs being ruled out are those with 100% probability of a single outcome.

The condition in (7.32) shows that the support of Fréchet distributions is bounded below by $-\frac{1}{\gamma} < 0$, while the support of Weibull distributions is bounded above by $-\frac{1}{\gamma} > 0$. Gumbel distributions have support across the entire real line.

Code Segment 7.14 generates a graph of the standard GEV pdf's with $\gamma = \pm.5$ shown in Figure 7.11.

Just as we did with stable distributions, we can introduce location and scale parameters to the standard GEV distributions. The general cdf is:

$$GEV_{\mu,\sigma,\gamma}(x) = GEV_\gamma\left(\frac{x-\mu}{\sigma}\right). \tag{7.37}$$

The general pdf is:

$$gev_{\mu,\sigma,\gamma}(x) = \frac{1}{\sigma}gev_\gamma\left(\frac{x-\mu}{\sigma}\right). \tag{7.38}$$

The additive location parameter μ and the multiplicative scale parameter σ are not the mean and standard deviation of the distribution; in fact, GEV's have no mean when $\gamma \geq 1$. For a Gumbel distribution ($\gamma = 0$), the mean is $\mu + \sigma K$ where $K \approx .577$ is Euler's constant $-\int_0^\infty \exp(-x)\ln(x)dx$.

Otherwise, when $\gamma < 1$, the mean of the GEV given by (7.38) is $\mu + \sigma(\Gamma(1-\gamma)-1)/\gamma$, where Γ is the standard Gamma function.

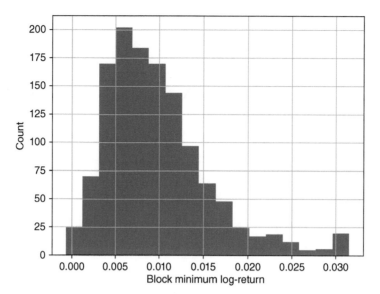

Figure 7.12 Block minima, CHF/USD 1971–2021, 1,278 blocks.

7.5.1 Block Maxima

Estimating the parameters of a GEV is sometimes a difficult process. The **method of block maxima** is a simple approach; it's not the most efficient but it can give a quick start to understanding empirical data.

If we have T observations, we can group the observations in m blocks of t, where $mt \approx T$.

We'll compute block maxima for the 1971-present Swiss franc data that were analyzed in Figure 7.2. We could group the 12,000+ days of data into 10-day periods and form a histogram of the biggest loss in each 10-day period (changing signs so a loss is a positive number). Code Segment 7.15 does that and computes the histogram of outcomes shown in Figure 7.12. Code Segment 7.15 also displays the following extremes:

```
Worst observation: 0.08890689133141738
Best block: -0.0006642311768628944
```

There was one 10-day period where all the log-returns were gains, so the maximum loss was negative. The worst 1% was forced into the bin starting at the 99th percentile because the positive tail is very long. It seems probable from the shape of the histogram in Figure 7.12 that the distribution is Fréchet.

To determine best fit parameters, we can use a maximum likelihood method – that is, we maximize (over distribution parameters μ, σ, γ) the product of the probability densities of the observations. As is often the case, it's more convenient to take the logarithm and maximize the sum, which we'll call "LML" (Log-Maximum-Likelihood). Define $z_i = \frac{M_{t,i}-\mu}{\sigma}$. Then we have (using (7.38)):

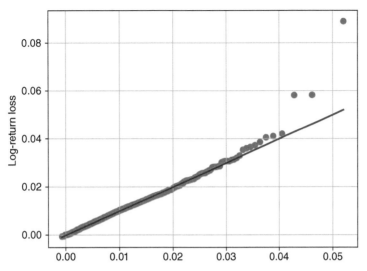

Figure 7.13 Q-Q plot, CHF 10-day max loss vs. Fréchet, 1971–2021.

$$LML_{(\mu,\sigma,\gamma)}\big(M_{t,1}, \ldots, M_{t,m}\big) = \ln\left(\prod_{i=1}^{m} gev_{\mu,\sigma,\gamma}(M_{t,i})\right)$$

$$= -m\ln(\sigma) + \sum_{i=1}^{m} \ln\big(gev_\gamma(z_i)\big). \qquad (7.39)$$

We can further define $y_i = 1 + \gamma z_i$ and state:

$$LML_{(\mu,\sigma,\gamma)}\big(M_{t,1}, \ldots, M_{t,m}\big)$$

$$= -m\ln(\sigma) - (1 + 1/\gamma)\sum_{i=1}^{n} \ln(y_i) - \sum_{i=1}^{m} y_i^{-1/\gamma}, \quad \gamma \neq 0,$$

$$LML_{(\mu,\sigma,\gamma)}\big(M_{t,1}, \ldots, M_{t,m}\big) = -m\ln(\sigma) - \sum_{i=1}^{m} z_i - \sum_{i=1}^{m} \exp(-z_i), \quad \gamma = 0.$$

$$(7.40)$$

A nonlinear optimizer can be used to find the parameters, although the optimization can be unstable.

A simple heuristic is to find the parameters that minimize the Q-Q plot distance. That is, assume our maxima observations are sorted so that $M_{t,1} \leq M_{t,2} \leq \cdots \leq M_{t,m}$. Then find the parameters μ, σ, γ that minimize:

$$\sum_{i=1}^{m} \left(\frac{i}{m+1} - GEV_{(\mu,\sigma,\gamma)}\big(M_{t,i}\big)\right)^2. \qquad (7.41)$$

Code Segment 7.16 produces Figure 7.13, which is the Q-Q plot that results from using the scipy.stats best fit function for the Swiss franc block maxima data. Code Segment 7.16 also outputs the following parameter values:

```
Gamma= 0.1010694768360614
Mu= 0.00692267514422739
Sigma= 0.004302550116011067
```

Except for three outlying values, the Q-Q plot in Figure 7.13 is reasonably straight as desired.

If the Extreme Value Theorem holds, then the γ we obtain from block maxima is expected to be the same (except for sampling error) across all block sizes t. μ and σ will vary as the block size changes.

7.5.2 Domains of Attraction

We could restate the conclusion of the Extreme Value Theorem (7.36) as:

$$\lim_{n \to \infty} \left[F^n(s_n x + m_n) \right] = GEV_\gamma(x). \tag{7.42}$$

Consider, for example, the exponential distribution whose cdf is $F(x) = 1 - \exp(-\lambda x)$ for $x \geq 0$ and a parameter $\lambda > 0$. The pdf is $\lambda \exp(-\lambda x)$, so the mean μ equals the standard deviation σ; both are $1/\lambda$. If in (7.42) we set $s_n = \sigma = 1/\lambda$ and $m_n = (\ln n)\mu$, then we have:

$$
\begin{aligned}
\lim_{n \to \infty} \left[F^n(s_n x + m_n) \right] &= \lim_{n \to \infty} \left[\left(1 - \exp(-\lambda(s_n x + m_n)) \right)^n \right] \\
&= \lim_{n \to \infty} \left[\left(1 - \exp(-(x + \ln n)) \right)^n \right] \\
&= \lim_{n \to \infty} \left[\left(1 - \frac{e^{-x}}{n} \right)^n \right] = GEV_0(x). \tag{7.43}
\end{aligned}
$$

So maxima of exponential distributions are Gumbel distributed.

Generally we say that a cdf F is in the **maximum domain of attraction**[24] of a GEV distribution with parameter γ if, when we apply the Extreme Value Theorem (7.36) to maxima of F, the result is GEV_γ. In that case we write $F \in MDA(GEV_\gamma)$. Thus we've just shown that the exponential distribution is in $MDA(GEV_0)$.

For the uniform distribution $F(x) = x$ on $[0, 1]$, we saw above that $m_n = \frac{n}{n+1}$ was probably a good choice. Set $s_n = \frac{1}{n+1}$. Then:

$$
\lim_{n \to \infty} \left[F^n(s_n x + m_n) \right] = \lim_{n \to \infty} \left[\left(\frac{x+n}{n+1} \right)^n \right] = \lim_{n \to \infty} \left[\left(1 + \frac{x-1}{n+1} \right)^n \right]
$$
$$
= \exp(-(1-x)) = GEV_{-1}(x).
$$

The uniform distribution is in $MDA(GEV_{-1})$, that is, the Weibull family.

---

24 [Nolan 2020], p. 21.

If $F(x)$ is normal as in (7.3), it is in $MDA(GEV_0)$, that is, the Gumbel family. One standardizing sequence – there are others – is given in Gasull, Jolis, and Utzet (2015): $m_n = F^{-1}\left(1 - \frac{1}{n}\right)$ and $s_n = \frac{m_n}{1+m_n^2}$. Thus,

$$F^n(y) = \exp\left(-\exp\left(\frac{y-m_n}{s_n}\right)\right) = \exp\left(-\exp\left(-(m_n + \frac{1}{m_n})y - (m_n^2 + 1)\right)\right).$$

Recall that the mean of a translated Gumbel distribution is $m_n + s_n K$, where $K \approx .577$ is Euler's constant. This shows that normal maxima increase very slowly: $m_n = 10$ when n is about 10^{23}. Thus, in order to get an expected maximum of a little more than 10, the sample size has to be about 10^{23}.

Necessary and sufficient conditions are known for the parameter of the MDA family if one exists:

If F is a cdf where $F(x) < 1$ for all finite x, then $F \in MDA(GEV_\gamma)$ for $\gamma > 0$ (i.e. a Fréchet distribution) if and only if:

$$\lim_{t \to \infty} \frac{1 - F(tx)}{1 - F(t)} = x^{-1/\gamma}.$$

The $\gamma < 0$ (Weibull) case is similar. Define $x_{sup} = \sup\{x : F(x) < 1\}$. If $x_{sup} < \infty$, then $F(x) \in MDA(GEV_\gamma)$ for $\gamma < 0$ if and only if:

$$\lim_{t \to \infty} \frac{1 - F\left(x_{sup} - \frac{1}{tx}\right)}{1 - F\left(x_{sup} - \frac{1}{t}\right)} = x^{1/\gamma}.$$

The conditions for Gumbel ($\gamma = 0$) distributions are more technical.

7.6 Tail Distributions

The methods we have just discussed for estimating generalized extreme value distributions may be helpful in thinking about protecting something: a bank's capital, an insurance company's ability to cover a disaster, a hedge fund's ability to operate, a long-only asset manager's relationship with its clients. With an estimate of the distribution of maximum losses, a risk manager can take steps – setting aside a buffer, buying put options, reinsuring, changing positions – so the enterprise can continue to operate.

While the distribution of maximum losses is one important characteristic of the tails of a distribution, estimating the behavior of the tail distribution itself can also be of interest. That is, contingent on being beyond some point u in the support of a distribution, what does the rest of the distribution look like? This can be of interest to a reinsurer, who covers losses over a certain amount.

If $F(x)$ is a cdf, the **excess or tail distribution** $F_u(x)$ is:

$$F_u(x) = Pr(X - u \le x \mid X > u) = \frac{F(x+u) - F(u)}{1 - F(u)}. \tag{7.44}$$

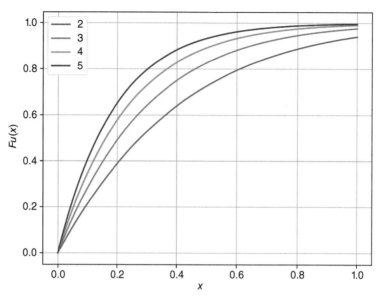

Figure 7.14 Standard normal tails.

The denominator is necessary to normalize $F_u(x)$, so it ranges from 0 to 1 as x ranges from 0 to ∞. Figure 7.14 plotted by Code Segment 7.17 shows the tail distributions based on a standard normal distribution for u=2,3,4,5.

We can see that F_u stochastically dominates F_v if $u < v$; the further out in the tail we are, the faster the cdf rises at the beginning.

There is a third natural class of distributions called **Generalized Pareto Distributions (GPDs)** that, like stable and GEV distributions, are the limiting values of certain behaviors. Stable distributions are the limiting values of sums (or averages after normalization); GEVs are the limiting values of maxima; and GPDs are the limiting values of tail distributions $\lim_{u \to m_F} F_u(x)$ where $m_F = \max\{x \in domain(F)\}$. They have this form:

$$GPD_{\gamma, \beta}(x) = 1 - \left(1 + \frac{\gamma x}{\beta}\right)^{-1/\gamma}, \quad \gamma \neq 0,$$

$$GPD_{0, \beta}(x) = 1 - \exp\left(-\frac{x}{\beta}\right). \tag{7.45}$$

Here $\beta > 0$. The support $supp(GPD_{\gamma, \beta}) = [0, m_F)$ where $m_F = \infty$ if $\gamma \geq 0$, and $m_F = -\frac{\beta}{\gamma}$ otherwise.

Using the exponential distribution $F(x) = 1 - \exp(-\lambda x)$ as an example, we see that:

$$F_u(x) = \frac{1 - \exp(-\lambda(x+u)) - (1 - \exp(-\lambda u))}{1 - (1 - \exp(-\lambda u))}$$
$$= \frac{\exp(-\lambda(x+u)) - \exp(-\lambda u)}{\exp(-\lambda u)} = F(x).$$

So (unlike the normal distribution) the exponential distribution doesn't care where in the tail it is – the tail distribution equals the distribution. Also note that $F(x) = GPD_{\gamma, \beta}(x)$ where $\gamma = 0$ and $\beta = 1/\lambda$.

Thus the tail distribution of a GPD with $\gamma = 0$ is also a GPD with $\gamma = 0$. This property holds as well for $\gamma \neq 0$. If $F(x) = GPD_{\gamma, \beta}(x)$, then:

$$F_u(x) = \frac{-\left(1 + \frac{\gamma(x+u)}{\beta}\right)^{-\frac{1}{\gamma}} + \left(1 + \frac{\gamma u}{\beta}\right)^{-\frac{1}{\gamma}}}{\left(1 + \frac{\gamma u}{\beta}\right)^{-\frac{1}{\gamma}}} = 1 - \left(1 + \frac{\gamma x}{\beta + \gamma u}\right)^{-1/\gamma}$$

$$= GPD_{\gamma, \beta + \gamma u}(x).$$

The tail GPD has the same parameter γ, but shifts the scale parameter from β to $\beta + \gamma u$.

We saw in (7.43) that the exponential distribution was in $MDA(GEV_0)$. We saw above that the tail behavior of the exponential was GPD_0. That's not a coincidence:

> **Theorem (Pickands)**[25] *If (and only if) $F(x) \in MDA(GEV_\gamma)$, then there exists a function $\beta(u)$ such that:*
>
> $$\lim_{u \to m_F} \sup_{x < m_F - u} \left| F_u(x) - GPD_{\gamma, \beta(u)}(x) \right| = 0 \qquad (7.46)$$
>
> *where* $\max\{x \in domain(F)\} = m_F$.

Pickands Theorem ties together maximum behavior and tail behavior through the parameter γ – if a distribution F has maxima that approach GEV_γ, then its tail distribution approaches (in the way shown in (7.46), as the threshold u is raised in the limit as far as it can go) the GPD_γ family. And vice versa.

7.6.1 Fitting Parameters to Tail Distributions

Unfortunately, in practice it is often difficult to collect enough data to estimate the relevant parameters. By definition, tail phenomena occur rarely. Imposing a model or borrowing data from other markets can help, but ultimately judgment needs to be used.

Despite the difficulty of this problem, we'll try to apply the framework we've just seen in practice. Let $F(x)$ be a cdf with support on the real line up to m_F. We'll make these heroic assumptions:

- The Extreme Value Theorem applies so that $F \in MDA(GEV_\gamma)$ for some γ.
- Pickands Theorem then applies, and we are far enough along into the tail that the limit (7.46) is a reasonable description of tail behavior.

---

25 [Charras-Garrido and Lezaud 2013].

To implement these assumptions, samples are taken from the distribution F, say $X_1, \ldots, X_T$. Then the **exceedance set** $EX_u(X_1, \ldots, X_T) = \{Y_i = X_i - u \mid X_i \geq u\}$ is formed. These are the overages of the set of observations that are beyond the threshold u. For an insurance company u might be the deductible on an insurance policy, or the amount it has reinsured with other insurance companies – in that case the exceedance set contains the amounts the insurance company will actually have to pay. Similarly tranches of structured financial products may only be affected by exceedances of their subordination.

The **exceedance count** EC_u is the number of items in the exceedance set EX_u. We will leave out the arguments $X_1, \ldots, X_T$ when it is clear what they are. They are sometimes used as risk metrics, but exceedance counts suffer from lack of coherence in a way that is similar to Value at Risk – they don't provide much information on how bad things can get in the tail.

The **peaks over thresholds ("POT")** method is the application of Pickands Theorem in this situation. The POT method entails choosing a cutoff point u and then finding the parameters of a Generalized Pareto Distribution (GPD) that best fit the exceedance set. A large body of literature addresses methods to find good cutoff points u and good parameter estimates; Goldberg and Giesecke (2004) give a good overview.

We'll use a standard log-maximum-likelihood method for our parameter estimation. This involves multiplying together the probability densities of observing the exceedances and taking the logarithm. Taking the derivative of (7.45) gives:

$$gpd_{\gamma,\beta}(x) = \frac{1}{\beta}\left(1 + \frac{\gamma x}{\beta}\right)^{-1/\gamma-1}, \quad \gamma \neq 0,$$

$$gpd_{0,\beta}(x) = \frac{1}{\beta}\exp\left(-\frac{x}{\beta}\right). \tag{7.47}$$

As Figure 7.15 (generated by Code Segment 7.18) shows, there is ugly behavior when $\gamma < -1$: the pdf blows up as x approaches the upper limit $m_F = -\beta/\gamma$ of the support. Maximum likelihood becomes problematic. Fortunately most real data seems to have $\gamma > -1$.

To find γ and β from observed data $X_1, \ldots, X_n$, the log-likelihood function is maximized:

$$LML_{\gamma,\beta}(EX_u(X_1, \ldots, X_n)) = -EC_u \ln(\beta) + \sum_{Y_i \in EX_u(X_1, \ldots, X_n)} \ln(gpd_{\gamma,\beta}(Y_i))$$

$$= -EC_u \ln(\beta) - \left(1 + \frac{1}{\gamma}\right)\sum_{Y_i \in EX_u(X_1, \ldots, X_n)} \ln\left(1 + \gamma\frac{Y_i}{\beta}\right),$$

$$\gamma \neq 0,$$

$$= -EC_u\left(\ln(\beta) + \frac{\bar{Y}}{\beta}\right), \gamma = 0, \tag{7.48}$$

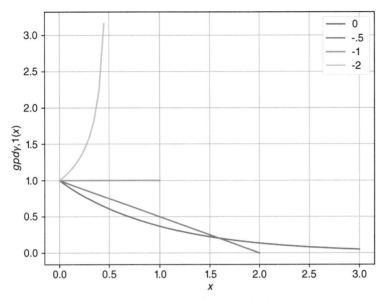

Figure 7.15 Generalized Pareto densities using (7.47).

where $\bar{Y}$ is the average value of the nonzero exceedances Y_i. For the Gumbel family ($\gamma = 0$), this shows that the maximum value of the log-likelihood function occurs when $\beta = \bar{Y}$.

For an example, we'll use draws from a standard normal distribution. We know from above that the normal is in $MDA(GEV_0)$, that is, the Gumbel family. So from Pickands Theorem we know that the tails should approach an exponential distribution (GPD_0 as in (7.45)). Thus we should find that the maximum likelihood occurs when $\gamma = 0$ and $\beta = \bar{Y}$, the average exceedance. Code Segment 7.19 generates 10,000 standard normal draws and takes exceedances over a threshold of 2. It finds as follows:

```
Sample number of exceedances over 2: 236
Theoretical number of exceedances: 228

Sample average exceedance: 0.35425370003744094
Theoretical average exceedance: 0.37321553282284103

Sample maximum likelihood function at beta:
    8.907101559107904
Theoretical maximum likelihood function at beta:
    -3.2833846264013493
```

There were more exceedances than the $10,000 \cdot F_{norm}(-2) = 228$ than were expected simply due to sampling error. Sampling error has a comparatively small

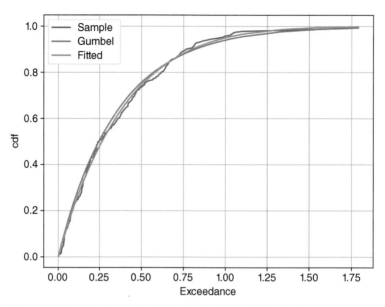

Figure 7.16 cdfs of empirical, Gumbel, and fitted distributions.

effect on the number of exceedances and on the average exceedance, but has a large effect on the (unfortunately) sensitive maximum likelihood function.

Code Segment 7.20 performs the LML optimization without forcing $\gamma = 0$:

```
Optimal gamma: -0.12229649326542354
Optimal beta: 0.39723275375440636
Support cap mF: 3.2481123795780547
Optimal LML: 10.744930456472616
```

The optimization process returns a Weibull ($\gamma < 0$) distribution, even though the data were generated by sampling a normal distribution that we know to be in the Gumbel MDA family. This gives an idea of the confidence interval around parameter estimates.

Figure 7.16 (generated by Code Segment 7.21) shows that both the theoretically appropriate Gumbel distribution and the LML-optimal Weibull distribution do a good job of fitting the empiricals.

A similar result is obtained by Code Segment 7.22, which uses the scipy.stats Generalized Pareto application:

```
scipy.stats optimal gamma, (7.48) gamma:
     -0.11828514339286177  -0.12229649326542354
```

```
scipy.stats optima mu, (7.48) mu:
      0.0018525166876476764 0.0
scipy.stats optimal beta, (7.48) beta: 0.393752301002408
      0.39723275375440636
```

The genpareto.fit algorithm solves for a location parameter μ that we didn't include; the value is close to zero, and the γ and β parameters are close to the ones from our maximum likelihood method.

For Code Segments in this chapter, see the Code Appendix starting on p. 440. For executable code, visit www.cambridge.org/9781009209090/ch7

For problem sets for this chapter, visit www.cambridge.org/ 9781009209090/ch7_problems

8 Simulation, Scenarios, and Stress Testing

In the previous chapter, we saw a variety of distributions that can be used for situations that fall into Knight's a priori risk category. If we are confident that a known distribution describes all the outcomes and all the associated probabilities for a set of variables, then we might even be able to get a closed-form description of relevant risk metrics for these variables.

But even if that situation obtains, our work isn't done. For financial applications, we'll probably want to know the rate of return of a portfolio. The portfolio could be a mutual fund, hedge fund, or institutional portfolio managed by an asset manager; it could be the positions on a trading desk; or it could be aggregate holdings of a sovereign wealth, pension, or endowment fund belonging to an asset owner.

The behavior of a portfolio of securities will be determined by a set of k factors describing the financial and economic state of the world. These factors might come from a factor model like (6.8); they might be key rates; or they might just be individual securities. Whatever the inputs are, the sample space of interest will consist of k-vectors sv ("state variable(s)") giving possible future states of the world. Often the convention is that such a state-of-the-world vector is expressed as a change from the current state.

Once we have the relevant state-of-the-world variables, we will also need deterministic pricing functions $R_i(\text{sv})$ that give the rate of return of the ith security in a portfolio one period forward, conditional on state-of-the-world sv being realized. Another function is then applied to the individual pricing functions to form a desired statistic at the portfolio level; for example, $\text{Port}(R_1(\text{sv}), \ldots, R_n(\text{sv})) = \ln\left(1 + \sum w_i R_i(\text{sv})\right)$ would give the portfolio's log-returns where w is the portfolio weight vector.

For example, there are four parameters (β_0, β_1, β_2, and τ) that describe a Nelson–Siegel curve in (3.10). If we are interested in modeling possible returns on a portfolio of bonds, then we might think that the relevant state-of-the-world sample space consists of 4-vectors giving the possible future values of the four Nelson–Siegel parameters. We might even think we have a state of Knightian Risk with respect to the Nelson–Siegel parameters: we have a good description of their probability distribution. But to value a portfolio of bonds being discounted by such a curve, we'll need to pass the four parameters through the formula

Table 8.1 Simulation functions and datasets

Item	Description	Type
sv	Environmental (state-of-the-world) variables	k-vector
$R_i(\text{sv})$	Pricing (rate-of-return) function for i^{th} security	Function
$\text{Port}(R_1(\text{sv}),\dots,R_n(\text{sv}))$	Composition function forming portfolio-level datum (return/log-return/price)	Function

(3.10), and then apply the pricing equation (3.2) in order to get a pricing function $R_i(\text{sv})$ for an individual bond. The portfolio return's response to changes in the four Nelson–Siegel parameters will therefore be highly nonlinear.

Simulation is used in cases where the responses to the state-of-the-world variables are complex. A process is developed to describe the sample space: this can be a closed-form approach, or a random-number generator producing a large number of samples of the state-of-the-world vector. Then, conditional on the future evolving according to the sample draw, the object of interest – such as a portfolio of bonds discounted by the Nelson–Siegel curve based on the sample parameters – is valued. The distribution of portfolio results is then analyzed for relevant statistics.

We've already described the basic inputs for simulation. They're collected in Table 8.1.

We have seen this technique already. The short-rate models in Sections 3.8.2 through 3.8.4 are examples of simulations; they generate a distribution of yield curves that can be used to value fixed-income instruments. The resampled efficient frontier in Section 4.2.4 is another example. An efficient portfolio is a highly nonlinear function of inputs such as a mean vector, a covariance matrix, and constraints. The resampling process is designed to produce an informative distribution of portfolios from which either a range or a center can be chosen.

We can consider these techniques *guided looks into the future*. If the technique is good, then the future that actually does unfold (and futures reasonably like the true one) will be among the outcomes, and their associated probabilities will cause us to plan appropriately.

8.1 Historical Simulation

Perhaps the simplest way to generate outcomes and probabilities is **historical simulation**. In its purest form, this method requires no model other than the empirical history of the securities in a portfolio. The sample space is simply what happened in the past, and the associated probabilities can be totally agnostic –

each historical observation has the same weight – or weighted according to a model such as: more recent observations are more important than older observations.

As we noted in Chapter 4, the most naive forms of historical simulation – where an analyst simply expects the past to repeat itself – can be misleading guides to the future. Good judgment is required to find the frontier between the advantages of being model free and the prediction failures of being too literal.

One commonly used version of historical simulation attempts to get the best of both worlds by using factor models for securities. As we saw in Chapter 6, not only do factor models help give better predictions of future behavior; they also help with missing data. For example, a portfolio may contain Snap (SNAP), the company behind the Snapchat application. Snap common stock started trading in 2017, so an analyst in the year 2022 may determine that there isn't enough SNAP history to infer patterns reliably. But SNAP might be modeled as some combination of factors like technology and growth; these factors have long histories and more reliable relationships than do individual securities.

We'll analyze a historical simulation involving the Swissie, pound, yen example from Section 4.1.2, using data going back to 1971. The sample space will simply be all T 3-vectors of (CHF,GBP,JPY) log-returns that were observed in the past, and individual pricing functions will be $R_i(\text{sv}) = \exp(\text{sv}_i) - 1$, where sv is one of the 3-vectors in the sample space.

Suppose that the portfolio of interest is an equal-weighted portfolio of the three currencies, $w = (1/3, 1/3, 1/3)^{\mathsf{T}}$. Let X be the $T \times 3$ matrix whose (t, i) entry is the {(dollars per currency i on day t) divided by (dollars per currency i on day $t-1$)} minus one. X is the priced sample space. The T-vector of log-returns at the portfolio level would be $\text{Port}(X) = \ln(1 + Xw)$.

The ith observation of the T observations in $\text{Port}(X)$ is assumed to have a probability p_t of being observed. In this context, the time index runs backward so $\text{Port}(X_1)$ is the most recent observation and $\text{Port}(X_T)$ is the oldest observation. In the agnostic version where there is no information to prioritize observations, $p_t = \frac{1}{T} \ \forall t$.

It would be reasonable to assume that going forward, the world will look more like it did last year than it did in 1971. In that case, an observation distribution p_t (where $p_i \geq p_j$ when $i \leq j$) would be appropriate. A common technique is an **exponentially weighted moving average ("EWMA")**: the observation probabilities are given by:

$$p_t = \frac{2^{-h(t-1)}}{\sum_{s=0}^{T-1} 2^{-hs}} = \frac{2^{-h(t-1)}(1 - 2^{-h})}{1 - 2^{-hT}} \approx 2^{-h(t-1)}(1 - 2^{-h}) \approx 2^{-h(t-1)} \frac{h \cdot \ln(2)}{1 + \frac{h \cdot \ln(2)}{2}}.$$

$$(8.1)$$

So, $h = 1/252$ in (8.1) would be a one year half-life if the observation periodicity was business-daily, since there are about 252 business days in a year.

In that case, the observations from a year ago would be half as probable as the most recent observation; three years ago would be one-eighth as probable.

More generally, the idea of **importance ranking** resonates intuitively: distinguishing which past data are more or less relevant to the future is a sensible approach. In EWMA, a simple distance metric (time) was used for ranking. Other kinds of importance ranking look at richer feature sets describing time periods. For example, a set of economic features including a stock market earnings/price ratio, interest rates, GDP changes, and unemployment rates might be used to describe conditions at each time period. Then a distance metric between current features and past features can be used to rank or filter other past period data for use in a predictive model.

Czasonis, Kritzman, and Turkington (2022) define "relevance" as a Mahalanobis distance between past features and present features, and use this relevance metric to filter out past data whose features are far from current features. The Mahalanobis distance is $(f_0 - f_t)^\mathsf{T} C^{-1} (f_0 - f_t)$, where f_0 (f_t) is the current (past) feature vector, and C is the feature covariance matrix. Since the covariance matrix may have poor condition, inverting it might have a stability problem. A metric that avoids inverting the matrix is $\frac{1-\rho}{1+\rho}$ where ρ is the correlation between feature vectors: this can be used to downgrade or eliminate low- or negative-correlation past periods.

Returning to the simple equally weighted (in time) data, Code Segment 8.1 produces statistics and a histogram of the outcomes for the three-currency portfolio (equally weighted by currency) in Figure 8.1. The pattern looks familiar:

Statistic	Value
Count	12784
Min	−0.041114
Max	0.0516067
Mean	7.5e-05
Median	1.73e-05
Standard Deviation	0.0051541
Skewness	0.241948
Excess Kurtosis	4.79666
Jarque–Bera	12380.3
Chi-Squared p	0
Serial Correlation	0.0255342
99% VaR	0.0131703
99% cVaR	0.0170842

```
Portfolio cumulative return: 1.2012038506475355
Portfolio annual return: 0.015905251399260356
```

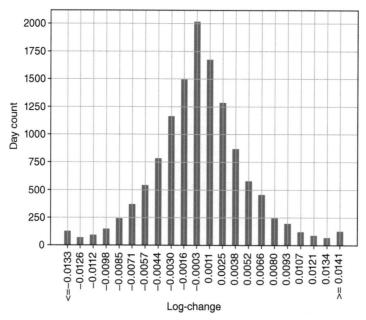

Figure 8.1 Histogram of equal-weighted CHF+GBP+ JPY daily log-changes, 1971–2021.

The statistics table is based on daily portfolio returns. So a very simple look into the future of an equally weighted portfolio of Swissies, pounds, and yen tells us that IF we expect the future to be like the historical record since 1971, we will be drawing log-returns from the distribution shown in Figure 8.1 that looks normal at first glance, but is actually fat-tailed.

As it turns out, the daily-rebalanced equally weighted portfolio would have made a profit – more than doubling since 1971. If an analyst has no model of expected returns and is just looking to estimate higher (second and above) moments, then quite often the historical mean is ignored or set to zero.

This example's mean is typical of short-term financial data in that it is negligible compared to the volatility. Over longer periods such as a year, the mean may not be negligible. That's because when there isn't too much serial correlation, the mean scales linearly with time, while standard deviation scales as the square root of time.

8.2 Delta-Normal

A second common method for generating future distributions is **delta-normal**. This method assumes that input variables – rates of return[1] of the three

---

1 As we've previously noted, it's more likely that log-returns follow a multivariate normal distribution than simple returns. To compute portfolio log-returns, security log-returns need to be converted to simple returns, combined, and then converted back to log-returns: that's what was done in the historical simulation. In the delta-normal illustration, we've just modeled returns themselves as normal for simplicity.

currencies in our example – will follow a multivariate normal distribution. Often the mean of the multivariate normal is assumed to be zero; as noted above, for short periodicities the mean is usually negligible compared to the higher moments.

The delta-normal method starts by mapping portfolio holdings into the appropriate exposure vector w. As with the historical example, this vector may simply be a vector of weights of the securities in the portfolio, with an associated covariance matrix C. A (6.21)-type model $C = BFB^\mathsf{T} + D$ is often assumed.

For large institutional portfolios, the security-specific variance matrix D in (6.21) might be ignored. This is because only the squares of security weights appear in the quadratic form $w^\mathsf{T}Dw$. In a large portfolio, it is unlikely that any one security occupies more than a few percent. Squaring a few percent gets down to basis points. Further, if the factor model is well specified, the entries of D are small. This is basically the argument that was made in the development of the Arbitrage Pricing Theory in Chapter 6.

Thus, a vector of security weights w can be mapped into factor loadings $b = B^\mathsf{T}w$, where B is the factor loading matrix in (6.21). In that case, the associated covariance matrix is the F in (6.21).

Generally, if x is an asset and f is a factor that might affect x, $\delta_f(x) = \frac{\partial x}{\partial f}$. That is, the Greek letter δ (delta) is generally used to denote the first-order sensitivity of an asset to a factor. In the delta-normal method, the deltas of more complex securities like options are added in to the exposure vector.

Thus in the delta-normal method, the appropriate statistics can be formed directly without simulation. Say e is the exposure n-vector (either a security weight vector w or a factor exposure vector b), and M is the associated covariance matrix. Then the variance of the distribution of portfolio outcomes is $e^\mathsf{T}Me$ and the standard deviation is $\sigma = \sqrt{e^\mathsf{T}Me}$.

The Value at Risk at probability p is $v = -(\mu + \sigma * Norm^{-1}(1 - p))$ as in (2.9). At $p = 99$, that's 2.326σ. The cVaR (= Expected Shortfall since Norm is continuous) (expressed as a loss amount) is:

$$-\mu + \frac{\sigma}{(1-p)\sqrt{2\pi}} \exp\left(\frac{-v^2}{2\sigma^2}\right)$$

as in (2.10).

Code Segment 8.2 draws the histogram in Figure 8.2 directly from the multivariate normal distribution, and generates the statistics table under the delta-normal assumption. The mean from the historical data has been used in order to make the statistics more directly comparable; in practice as noted above, a zero mean might be assumed.

Statistic	Value
Count	12784
Min	−0.0194116
Max	0.0195616
Mean	7.5e-05
Median	7.5e-05
Standard Deviation	0.00515432
Skewness	0
Excess Kurtosis	0
Jarque–Bera	0
Chi-Squared p	1
Serial Correlation	0
99% VaR	0.0119158
99% cVaR	0.0141338

Figure 8.2 looks generally similar to Figure 8.1, but Figure 8.2 falls off at the tails while Figure 8.1 has extra probability at the two extremes as a result of its leptokurtosis.

Note that the standard deviations of the historical simulation and the delta-normal method agree to four decimal places. That's not a coincidence: if X is the $T \times 3$ matrix of daily returns of the three currencies, then the covariance matrix of

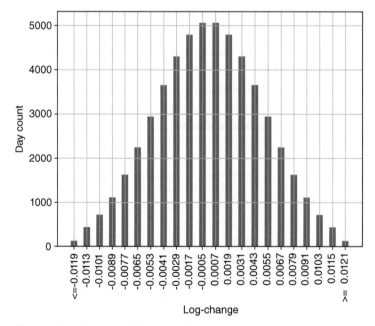

Figure 8.2 Histogram, delta-normal.

returns is $C_{returns} = (X - JX/T)^{\mathsf{T}}(X - JX/T)/T$, where J is the $T \times T$ matrix of all ones. The delta-normal calculation of standard deviation was $\sigma_{delta-normal} = \sqrt{w^{\mathsf{T}} C_{returns} w}$.

The historical simulation's standard deviation was obtained by forming the T-vector $r = (X - JX/T)^{\mathsf{T}} w$, and then taking component-wise logs, $r_{log} = log(1 + r)$. The standard deviation of log-returns is $\sigma_{log-historical} = r_{log}^{\mathsf{T}} r_{log}/T$. Since daily returns are on the order of 10^{-4}, $log(1 + r) \approx r$ is a good approximation. So $\sigma_{delta-normal} \approx \sigma_{log-historical}$ to several decimal places.

While the delta-normal method doesn't give a realistic picture of tail risk, it has a great advantage: the **Euler Rule**[2] can be applied. This decomposes overall standard deviation into its component parts.

It works like this: let $f(x)$ be a positive homogeneous and continuously differentiable scalar function of an n-vector $x = (x_1, \ldots, x_n)$. Positive homogeneity of scalar degree k means that $f(zx) = z^k f(x)$ for all real scalar $z > 0$. If $f(x)$ is such a function, the Euler Rule states that:

$$k \cdot f(x) = \sum_{i=1}^{n} x_i \frac{\partial f}{\partial x_i}(x) = x^{\mathsf{T}}(\nabla f(x)). \tag{8.2}$$

So $\nabla f(x) = (\frac{\partial f}{\partial x_1}(x), \ldots, \frac{\partial f}{\partial x_n}(x))^{\mathsf{T}}$ is the gradient vector of x.

We know from the discussion of coherent risk measures that standard deviation $\sigma(w) = \sqrt{w^{\mathsf{T}} C w}$ is positive homogenous with $k = 1$. The gradient of standard deviation is $g = \nabla \sigma = \frac{1}{\sigma(w)} C w$. Applying (8.2) decomposes standard deviation into the influences of each component:

$$\sigma(w) = w^{\mathsf{T}} g. \tag{8.3}$$

The right-hand side of (8.3) is a vector dot product – the vector version of the Euler decomposition in (8.2). The ith summand ($i = 1$ to n) in the dot product is $w_i g_i$, the contribution of the ith element to the overall delta-normal standard deviation.

Code Segment 8.3 computes these quantities for the three-currency example, giving the following:

```
Gradient (bps/day): [0.00616951 0.00457384 0.00471963]
Contributions to Std Dev: [0.0020565  0.00152461
        0.00157321]
```

The Swissie is the biggest contributer to standard deviation. If an analyst expects one of the other currencies to outperform Swissies, some weight could

---

2 More precisely, this is Euler's Homogeneous Function Theorem. It follows directly from the definition of homogeneity $f(zx) = z^k f(x)$ by differentiating both sides with respect to z, applying the chain rule, and setting $z = 1$. Eric W. Weisstein, "Euler's Homogeneous Function Theorem." Wolfram MathWorld. https://mathworld.wolfram.com/EulersHomogeneousFunctionTheorem.html.

be shifted from Swissies to that other currency, giving a win-win. Such a move would increase expected return while lowering expected risk. This works on the margin, but large changes in weights require a reassessment of overall risk.

This framework helps with risk/reward decisions. In more complex covariance matrices, there might be some items with a negative contribution $w_i g_i$ to overall standard deviation; those are diversifiers. If an analyst expects that a diversifier is going to generate more return than items with positive contributions, increasing the exposure to the diversifier will produce more expected return while reducing risk.

8.2.1 The Cornish–Fisher Expansion

One way of correcting the delta-normal approach's underestimation of tail risk is to adjust statistics like Value at Risk with a **Cornish–Fisher expansion**. In the delta-normal approach, VaR is simply $z\sigma$, where σ is standard deviation and $z = Norm^{-1}(p)$; for example, $z = 2.326$ when $p = .99$. We saw, however, that Historical Simulation VaR was higher than delta-normal VaR, meaning the empirical z multiple was bigger than the Gaussian z.

The Cornish–Fisher expansion (from Cornish and Fisher 1938) is essentially a Taylor series that takes into account moments of the distribution beyond the second moment to get a better estimate of the multiplier z. Taking into account the skewness and kurtosis terms gives:

$$z_{new} = z - \frac{1}{6}(z^2 - 1)m_3 + \frac{z}{24}(z^2 - 3)m_4 - \frac{z}{36}(2z^2 - 6)m_3^2. \qquad (8.4)$$

Here m_3 is skewness and m_4 is (excess) kurtosis. For a normal distribution, skewness and excess kurtosis are zero, so the Cornish–Fisher adjustment makes no change in that case.

Maillard (2012) pointed out that the expansion only works in a certain range of skewness and kurtosis parameters. The absolute value of skewness must be outside a middle range, as shown:

$$6(\sqrt{2} - 1) \geq |m_3|, \quad 6(\sqrt{2} + 1) \leq |m_3|. \qquad (8.5)$$

So $|m_3|$ must be less than about 2.485, or greater than about 14.485. The top range – where skewness is greater than 14.485 – is generally beyond repair by a simple adjustment. So the main applicability of Cornish–Fisher is in the lower range of skewness.

Kurtosis must be between the two roots of a quadratic:

$$4(1 + 11s^2 - \sqrt{s^4 - 6s^2 + 1}) \leq m_4 \leq 4(1 + 11s^2 + \sqrt{s^4 - 6s^2 + 1}), \qquad (8.6)$$

where $s = m_3/6$. Thus, when $s = 0$, kurtosis must be between 0 and 8.

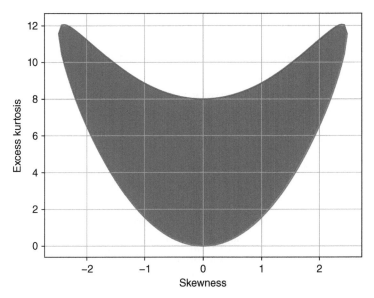

Figure 8.3 Allowed parameter combinations for Cornish–Fisher.

Figure 8.3 (generated by Code Segment 8.4) shows the valid parameter area for Cornish–Fisher in the lower range of skewness. Excess kurtosis is on the vertical axis; skewness is on the horizontal axis.

Code Segment 8.5 applies (8.4) to the Historical Simulation data above, producing the following:

```
Normal 99 pct z:  2.32635
Cornish-Fisher:  3.27137
Historical:  2.58673


Normal 99 pct VaR:  0.01192
Cornish-Fisher VaR:  0.01679
Historical VaR:  0.01326
```

So in this case, the Cornish–Fisher expansion overcorrects, giving a more conservative Value at Risk than the one that arose from historical experience.

8.3 Monte Carlo Simulation

A third technique for generating distributions of portfolio outcomes is the **Monte Carlo** method. Monte Carlo is a reference to the casinos in Monaco, and indicates that a large number of random trials are generated to form a sample distribution. This idea was first conceived by Stanislaw Ulam in 1946 as a way of harnessing the nascent power of computers to find the probability of winning at solitaire.

It was so named by Nicholas Metropolis based on the gambling habits of Ulam's uncle.[3]

To illustrate this, we'll start with a delta-normal model but then will add complexity.

Suppose then that we have an $n \times n$ covariance matrix M and an exposure n-vector e for a portfolio. We want to draw an n-vector of factor (or security returns) from the multivariate normal distribution with covariance matrix M. To do this, we must **Cholesky factor**[4] M:

$$M = LL^\mathsf{T}, \text{ where } L \text{ is lower triangular.} \qquad (8.7)$$

If M is positive semidefinite, then such a factorization is possible.

The algorithm for Cholesky factorization is straightforward. The lower triangular Cholesky factor of the three-currency log-return covariance matrix (4.11) is computed by Code Segment 8.6:

```
(8.8) Cholesky decomposition of 3-currency sample
      covariance matrix:
  [[0.70595279 0.          0.         ]
   [0.34035761 0.4882504  0.         ]
   [0.30198568 0.02130788 0.55610753]]
```

To generate vectors drawn from a multivariate normal distribution with covariance M, the Monte Carlo process starts by generating n-vectors s_j ($j = 1$ to T, where T the number of Monte Carlo trials desired) of independent draws from a standard (mean 0, standard deviation 1) normal distribution. Each s_j consists of n scalars, each drawn independently from a standard normal distribution.

The vector $r_j = Ls_j$ is a draw from a multivariate normal with the desired covariance structure. This is because:

$$\mathbb{E}[r_j r_j^\mathsf{T}] = \mathbb{E}[Ls_j s_j^\mathsf{T} L^\mathsf{T}] = L\mathbb{E}[s_j s_j^\mathsf{T}]L^\mathsf{T} = LL^\mathsf{T} = M. \qquad (8.9)$$

Code Segment 8.7 runs T trials (where T is the number of days in the currency dataset), generating 3-vectors $s_1, \ldots, s_T$. It then forms draws $r_i = Ls_i$. These return-vector draws are then dotted with the weight vector $w = (1/3, 1/3, 1/3)$ to generate T rates of return. The statistics for this simulated portfolio look like this:

3 [Metropolis 1987].
4 [Gentle 1998], p. 93.

Monte Carlo with simple normal draws

Statistic	Value
Count	12784
Min	−0.0204272
Max	0.0185333
Mean	−4.3e-06
Median	1.08e-05
Standard Deviation	0.0051776
Skewness	0.0277483
Excess Kurtosis	−0.0306785
Jarque–Bera	2.14188
Chi-Squared p	0.342687
Serial Correlation	0.0068568
99% VaR	0.01189
99% cVaR	0.0135764

These statistics are close to the statistics from the delta-normal method. There are some subtleties of the sampling distributions – even though we generated future outcomes by using draws from a normal distribution, there is some variation in what we will observe. For example, the skewness and kurtosis were not exactly zero in our sample, although they are zero in a true normal distribution. The standard deviation was slightly different.

The artificial future generated using simple Monte Carlo looked a lot like the artificial future generated using delta-normal, and the reasons for the differences are well understood. Sampling error is limited and can be made smaller simply by running more trials. We're not going to learn anything very interesting this way, except perhaps to get a feel of the impact of sampling error.

However, there's no reason why the Monte Carlo process has to draw from a normal distribution. A wide variety of more realistic distributions could be used to give more realistic tail behavior. For example, Code Segment 8.8 fits a mixture of normals to each currency separately. The mixture targets the currency's mean, standard deviation, and excess kurtosis along with zero skewness. Correlation structure is introduced by multiplying by the Cholesky factor of the correlation matrix.

The result of the Monte Carlo simulation in Code Segment 8.8 is much more realistic than the Monte Carlo with simple normal draws:

Monte Carlo with leptokurtic mixtures of normals

Statistic	Value
Count	12784
Min	−0.05194
Max	0.0419218
Mean	7.12e-05
Median	0.0001153
Standard Deviation	0.0054495
Skewness	−0.277349
Excess Kurtosis	8.62665
Jarque–Bera	39804.5
Chi-Squared p	0
Serial Correlation	0.0113249
99% VaR	0.015351
99% cVaR	0.0232959

The true power of the Monte Carlo approach comes in applying a full valuation to every instrument in the portfolio. Suppose a portfolio contains derivatives or other complex instruments. Monte Carlo-ing – even when imitating realistic leptokurtic behavior – will not help if the pricing functions are simply based on delta (i.e. linear). The portfolio manager needs to know when derivatives might provide protection and when they might blow up. Using the full valuation formula, not an approximation, provides this information.

In full generality – as described at the beginning of this chapter – a k-vector sv of state variables describes the relevant financial and economic state of the world, or at least the parts of the world that are relevant to the portfolio under analysis. A full Monte Carlo approach first generates T draws of the state variable vector sv from an appropriate distribution, which may be empirical, normal, Student's T, a mixture of normals, stable, or others.

A series of transformations and back-transformations might be applied to the state variables. For example, suppose we think there is significant serial correlation so that $sv_{i,t} = a_i sv_{i,t-1} + \epsilon_{i,t}$, where $\epsilon_{i,t}$ is a draw from a normal distribution that is independent of any previous $\epsilon_{i,s}$, $s < t$. In that case, we would form the time series $sv_{i,t} - a_i sv_{i,t-1} = \epsilon_{i,t}$ and estimate $\epsilon_{i,t}$'s volatility and relationships with other transformed state variables. We would then Cholesky factor the state variable covariance matrix as in (8.7), and draw T values of $\epsilon_{i,t+1}$ from a multivariate normal distribution that included the other transformed state variables. Of course, other multivariate distributions could be used, and relationships could be captured by a copula function rather than a covariance matrix as described in Chapter 10.

When a vector of transformed state variables has been produced, a back-transformation (in the example, $sv_{i,t+1} = a_i sv_{i,t} + \epsilon_{i,t+1}$) is applied to get the right inputs for the pricing functions $R_i(sv)$ ($i = 1, \ldots, n$) shown in Table 8.1.

As noted above, these pricing functions give the rates of return of each instrument given the state variable changes in sv. The pricing functions may have nonlinear or other complex aspects. They may even use their own Monte Carlo simulations based on variables that are different from the portfolio-wide state variables in sv.

The final step in Monte Carlo simulation is aggregation of individual prices (or rates of return) to an overall portfolio price, rate of return, or other statistic such as a log-return. The resulting distribution of portfolio prices, returns, or log-returns can be used to judge risk and reward. Sample statistics like mean, standard deviation, and Expected Shortfall can be computed, or we can just map the distribution and see if it has an acceptable shape.

8.3.1 Delta-Gamma, Delta-Gamma-Theta Simulations

The detailed Monte Carlo process we just described can be difficult to implement fully. Even when the resources are available to gather all the requisite data and to code all the requisite algorithms, the time required to run all the simulations can be prohibitive. An institution requiring daily risk assessments may have difficulty completing all the calculations between the close of yesterday's markets and the open of today's markets, and an institution requiring continuously updated risk assessment may find the task hopeless.

We've seen that delta-normal simulations, which are usually computationally tractable, can oversimplify. We've noted that detailed Monte Carlo simulations can take too many resources and too much time. Compromises between these extremes use more terms of a Taylor series in an attempt to tune the trade-off between speed and power.

A **delta-gamma** simulation includes both first- and second-order terms in the pricing functions. For a multivariate simulation, that means that a **Hessian matrix** of mixed partial derivatives must be estimated for every instrument. The (i,j) entry of the Hessian Γ_i is $\frac{\partial R_i}{\partial sv_i \partial sv_j}$, where R_i is the ith pricing function and sv is the vector of state variables as in Table 8.1.

The rate of change with respect to time is often included along with the first- and second-order dependencies on the state variables. Let $\theta_i = \frac{\partial R_i}{\partial t}$ be the rate of change of the ith instrument's pricing function with respect to time. If the ith instrument is cash, for example, then θ_i is the risk-free rate.

The addition of time dependence to a delta-gamma approximation makes it a **delta-gamma-theta** approximation. The approximate pricing delta-gamma-theta pricing function is:

$$\tilde{R}_i(\Delta sv) = \Delta sv^\mathsf{T} \Gamma_i \Delta sv + \delta_i^\mathsf{T} \Delta sv + \theta_i \Delta t. \qquad (8.10)$$

Here we have made the pricing function explicitly dependent on changes rather than on levels; Δt is the length of time in a simulation step. Of course, without the last term on the RHS, (8.10) is just a delta-gamma approximation.

The goal of replacing full valuation functions R_i with approximations $\tilde{R}_i$ is, as noted above, to save simulation time and complexity. However, each Hessian matrix Γ_i requires f^2 parameters, where f is the number of state variables. Reliable estimation of this many parameters can be unrealistic, so lower-dimensional models can be used. In some cases, the off-diagonal elements of the Hessian matrix are assumed to be zero and only the diagonal elements are estimated.

8.4 Markov Chain Monte Carlo

The **Markov Chain Monte Carlo ("MCMC")** method, like the other Monte Carlo methods explored in this chapter, uses random sampling from a distribution to explore a sample space. But unlike simple Monte Carlo methods, MCMC guides itself through the sample space in a way that is intended to enrich the predictive validity of the sample.

As we noted in Section 3.7, a Markov Chain only depends on the previous state. So the first "MC" in "MCMC" means that sampling can be done sequentially through an algorithm that only needs to remember the previous iteration. A Markov Chain on a finite sample space with n states $[1, \ldots, n]$ can be embodied in a transition matrix T (similar to the ones used in Ross Recovery in Section 2.9) where the (i,j) entry is the probability of moving from state i to state j. In that case, T is row-stochastic (its row sums equal one), because when leaving state i the next state has to be in the sample space.

In the continuous case, there is a transition probability density function $Tr(y \mid x)$ that gives the probability of moving from state x to state y. For example a normal transition function $Tr_{norm}(y \mid x) = \frac{1}{\sqrt{2\pi}\sigma} exp\left(\frac{-(y-x)^2}{2\sigma^2}\right)$ for some standard deviation parameter σ.

Under reasonable conditions a unique **stationary distribution** $\pi(x)$ of a Markov Chain can be computed: $\pi(x)$ is the long-run probability that the chain is in state x, that is, the probability that an infinite-length chain with transition probability Tr is in state x. If the state space is finite, taking the dot product of the ith column of the transition matrix T with the stationary probability vector π gives π_i. This happens because we can enumerate all the states j that could have transitioned into state i: the probability of being in state j over the long run is π_j and the probability of transitioning from j to i is the (j,i) entry of T. So running through all n states that could have transitioned to i gives the aforementioned dot product, which must result in the probability of being in state i which is π_i.

As a matrix equation, $T^\mathsf{T}\pi = \pi$. That is, the stationary distribution vector π is a left eigenvector of the transition matrix T with eigenvalue 1. For the continuous case, $\pi(y) = \int \pi(x) Tr(y \mid x)dx$.

The **Metropolis–Hastings Algorithm**[5] takes advantage of the Markov Chain properties noted above to randomly sample a chain of values $x_0, x_1, \ldots, x_n$ that are drawn from the stationary distribution, even if that distribution is not directly known. The algorithm assumes $Tr(x \mid y)$ is known. We'll assume a strong property that describes the relationship between the stationary distribution and the transition probability:

$$\frac{\pi(x)}{\pi(y)} = \frac{Tr(x \mid y)}{Tr(y \mid x)}. \tag{8.11}$$

Some of the initial values (called **burn-in**) in the chain $x_0, x_1, \ldots, x_n$ may be discarded as the algorithm finds the proper range; often the first 20% of the n values are treated as burn-in. At each step of the algorithm, a random sample is taken from a **proposal distribution** $p(s \mid x_t)$; often the proposal distribution is a normal $N(x_t, \sigma)$, where σ is an algorithm parameter that represents a trade-off between speed and accuracy. More generally, the proposal distribution may be asymmetric.

Here's the Metropolis–Hastings algorithm:

1. Pick a starting value x_0. Set $t = 0$.
2. Generate a random sample s_t from the proposal distribution $p(s \mid x_t)$.
3. Compute an acceptance ratio:

$$r(s_t, x_t) = \frac{Tr(s_t \mid x_t) \, p(x_t \mid s_t)}{Tr(x_t \mid s_t) \, p(s_t \mid x_t)}. \tag{8.12}$$

4. Generate a random sample u_t from the uniform distribution over $[0, 1]$. If $r(s_t, x_t) \geq u_t$, set $x_{t+1} = s_t$. Otherwise set $x_{t+1} = x_t$.
5. Increment t and go back to Step 2 unless stopping. Stopping may occur after a predetermined number of steps, or when it appears that the sample distribution is not changing much.

Because of the assumption (8.11), the acceptance ratio (8.12) is the same as $\frac{\pi(s_t)}{\pi(x_t)} \frac{p(x_t \mid s_t)}{p(s_t \mid x_t)}$; this produces the desired sample distribution from the algorithm.

We'll show a toy example of Metropolis–Hastings based on a symmetric 3×3 transition matrix:

$$T = \begin{bmatrix} .6 & .3 & .1 \\ .3 & .5 & .2 \\ .1 & .2 & .7 \end{bmatrix}.$$

For a symmetric stochastic matrix T, $Tu = u$ where u is the vector of all ones, so the stationary distribution is uniform.

We'll use a tent proposal distribution, that is, $p(i \mid i) = \frac{2}{3}$ and $p(i \mid \neq i) = \frac{1}{6}$ where i is one of the three states. Code Segment 8.9 runs the algorithm and

---

5 [Metropolis et al. 1953] described the symmetric case, while [Hastings 1970] (https://doi.org/10.1093/biomet/57.1.97) added asymmetry.

compares the sample frequencies of being in each of the three states with the uniform distribution:

```
State: 0 MCMC: 0.315 Theoretical: 0.333
State: 1 MCMC: 0.321 Theoretical: 0.333
State: 2 MCMC: 0.364 Theoretical: 0.333
```

Metropolis–Hastings can be used to generate samples when there are transition matrices or transition probability distributions.

Another MCMC method used in finance is a **Gibbs Sampler**,[6] which among other things is useful for implying missing data. The Gibbs Sampler is a bootstrap process that constructs samples from an unknown joint distribution when only conditional distributions are known.

More specifically, suppose there is an unknown joint density function $f(x,y)$ of two variables (which could each be a vector). While $f(x,y)$ is not known, the conditional density $f(x \mid y) = \frac{f(x,y)}{f_Y(y)}$ is known. Here $f_Y(y)$ is the marginal density for the second variable, that is, $f_Y(y) = \int f(x,y)dx$ where the (possibly multiple) integral is over the domain of x. Similarly assume $f(y \mid x)$ is known.

The Gibbs Sampler works like this:

1. Pick a starting value for the x variable, x_1. Set $t = 1$.
2. Generate a random sample y_t of the y variable from the conditional distribution $f(y \mid x_t)$.
3. Generate a random sample x_{t+1} from the conditional distribution $f(x \mid y_t)$.
4. Increment t and go back to Step 2 unless stopping.

The stopping rule can be a fixed number of iterations, or a method that looks for stable statistical properties.

To illustrate this method, we'll modify an application from O'Cinneade (2012). Suppose D_m is an $n_m \times T_m$ data matrix containing monthly log-returns of n_m market assets, and D_e is an $n_e \times T_e$ data matrix containing quarterly economic data over the same time span. We'll work an example that uses the 10 years ending at the end of the most recent year, so $T_m = 120$ months for the monthly data and $T_e = 40$ quarters for the quarterly data.

Market data often anticipate economic data. For example, the US stock market dropped about 20% in first quarter of 2020 due to COVID-19 pandemic fears. But the US GDP was roughly unchanged in first quarter 2020. US GDP was down about 10% in *second* quarter 2020 while the stock market recovered. Thus, we'll put a one quarter lag in the market data.

With the lag, the first three months of market data in D_m will be from October/November/December, while the corresponding first quarter of economic data in D_e will be from the first quarter of the next year. The last three months of market data in D_m will be from July/August/September, while the corresponding

---

6 [O'Cinneade 2012].

last quarter of economic data in D_e will be from the fourth quarter. This means there will be a predictive component to this application: the most recent market data will anticipate not-yet-seen economic data. We'll expand on this below.

We'd like to understand the relationships between market data and economic data. The most obvious thing to do is to dumb down the monthly market data by combining the months into quarters, and then looking at the relationships in the quarterly data. However, this seems wasteful: it coarsens the precision of the monthly data.

A different approach is to smarten up the quarterly data: use the existing information to guess what the missing monthly returns of the quarterly data should look like. The resulting pseudo-monthly economic series can then be compared to other monthly series. We will:

1. Infer relationships between n_m monthly series and n_e quarterly series by coarsening the monthly series to quarterly and seeing how the quarterly series relate; and
2. Use those relationships (via a Gibbs Sampler) to generate likely values for the missing monthly data points of the quarterly series.

We can then use the pseudo-monthly economic series along with other monthly data in simulations and other historical studies.

We first estimate the following quantities from the data D_m and D_e. Then u_s is the $s \times 1$-vector of all ones.

- $\mu_m = \frac{1}{T_m} D_m u_{T_m}$, the n_m-vector of monthly mean log-returns of the market series estimated from all T_m monthly market log-returns;
- $C_m = \frac{1}{T_m}(D_m - \mu_m u_{T_m})(D_m - \mu_m u_{T_m})^\mathsf{T}$, the $n_m \times n_m$ covariance matrix of the market data;
- $\mu_e = \frac{1}{3T_e} D_e u_{T_e}$, the n_e-vector of month-ized quarterly mean returns of the n_e economic series estimated from all T_e quarterly economic returns;
- $C_e = \frac{1}{3T_e}(D_e - \mu_e u_{T_e})(D_e - \mu_e u_{T_e})^\mathsf{T}$, the $n_e \times n_e$ month-ized covariance matrix of the economic data;
- $C_{me} = \frac{1}{3T_e}(D_m - \mu_m u_{T_m}^\mathsf{T})MQ(D_e - 3\mu_e u_{T_e})^\mathsf{T}$, the $n_m \times n_e$ month-ized matrix of covariances between quarterly market data and quarterly economic data. MQ is a $T_m \times T_e$ matrix with three consecutive ones in each column and zeroes elsewhere. The ones start in row $3(j-1)+1$ of the jth column.

From these quantities we can compute the conditional mean $\mu_{e|m}(t)$ and the conditional covariance matrix $C_{e|m}$ of the missing monthly observations of the quarterly data in month t. Actually, the conditional mean is dependent on the month but the conditional covariance matrix isn't:[7]

---

7 [O'Cinneade 2012], p. 105. There is an error in O'Cinneade's formula at the bottom of p. 105. In his notation, $\Sigma_{J|I}$ in the formula for $\mu_{t,J|I}$ should actually be Σ_{JI}.

$$\mu_{e|m}(t) = \mu_e + C_{me}C_m^{-1}(D_m(t) - \mu_m), \qquad (8.13)$$

$$C_{e|m} = C_e - C_{me}^{\mathsf{T}}C_m^{-1}C_{me}. \qquad (8.14)$$

Here, $D_m(t)$ is the tth column of the data matrix, that is, the log-returns of the monthly data in month t.

With these quantities defined, we can apply Gibbs sampling by letting:

- $x_t = \mu_{e|m}(t)$ be the conditional mean of the missing monthly economic data in month t; and
- y_t be the n_e-vector of missing monthly economic series returns in month t.

Following O'Cinneade (2012), the steps of the Gibbs Sampler in this case look like the following:

1. Let x_1 be μ_e. Set t=1.
2. Randomly sample an n_e-vector from $N(x_t, C_{e|m})$. Call this sample vector z_t.
3. (a) If t is not a quarter-end month, go to Step 4. (b) If t is a quarter-end month, let $Z_t = z_t + z_{t-1} + z_{t-2}$ be the most recent quarterly log-return vector produced by this process. Let $D_e(t/3)$ be the column of D_e containing the actual quarterly log-return for this quarter. Set $y_{t-j} = z_{t-j} + (D_e(t/3) - Z_t)/3$ for $j = 0, 1, 2$.
4. Increment t. Stop when $t > T_m$. Otherwise, set $x_t = \mu_{e|m}(t)$ as defined in (8.13).

Step 3b ensures that the quarterly log-returns of filled-in monthly series y_t match the original data. Step 2 in this algorithm looks like Step 2 in the generic Gibbs Sampler, but Step 3 here doesn't actually generate a random sample from $f(x \mid y_t)$ as in the generic case.

Code Segment 8.10 implements this algorithm using stock market indices for the USA, Europe, and Japan as the market data, and Gross Domestic Product information as the economic data. Both are converted to log-changes (log-returns). The market data are aligned so that it is three months earlier than the economic data, that is, the first quarter market returns are aligned with the second quarter GDP data. Figures 8.4, 8.5, and 8.6 (generated by Code Segment 8.10) show the original GDP levels and the pseudo-monthly GDP levels that are computed from the output of the Gibbs Sampler.

The more jagged blue lines are the pseudo-monthly GDP series. Each quarter the blue line coincides with the orange line: the orange line is the original quarterly GDP data.

The pseudo-monthly series can be mixed with other monthly data for historical studies. There is also a prediction at the tail end of the data: the market data in D_m ended in September, while the GDP data ended in December. We didn't use the fourth quarter market data, which aligns with first quarter economic

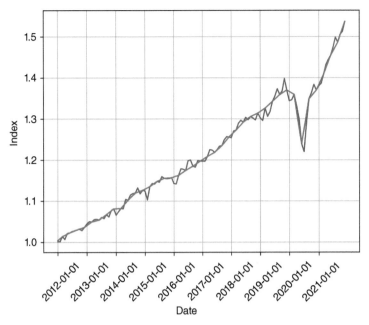

Figure 8.4 SPASTT01USM661N (US).

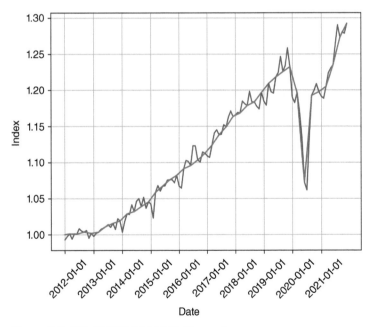

Figure 8.5 SPASTT01EZM661N (Europe).

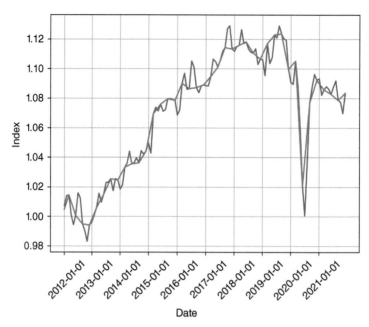

Figure 8.6 SPASTT01JPM661N (Japan).

data. The prediction is simply that first quarter economic data will be drawn from $N(x_t, C_{e|m})$. Code Segment 8.11 displays these numbers:

```
Final quarterly mean vector for GDP log-changes, quarter
        ending 2021-12-31
US        : 0.022253
Europe    : 0.017542
Japan     : 0.0047175


Conditional covariance matrix:
7.26966e-05 8.94213e-05 4.51411e-05
8.94213e-05 0.000136545 6.16223e-05
4.51411e-05 6.16223e-05 5.83646e-05


Actual log-changes of GDPs, first quarter 2022
US        : 0.015868
Europe    : 0.014866
Japan     : 0.0015012
```

There is nothing new about the prediction contained in $\mu_{e|m}$: it's just a lagged regression. Market participants are able to react quickly to news such as the onset of a pandemic, while large economies are like massive container ships at sea: it takes a long time for them to turn around. So it isn't surprising when market data precede economic data, and $\mu_{e|m}$ is sometimes close to the actual subsequent

GDP change. At other times, $\mu_{e|m}$ is so far off that Paul Samuelson's quip about the market predicting nine of the last five recessions comes to mind.

While the predictive component of this process has varying results, the real contribution of this application of MCMC is the ability to fill in missing data in a Bayesian framework. As we noted above, this makes the resulting pseudo-monthly series useful in simulations and other historical studies.

8.5 Stress Testing and Scenario Analysis

We have noted that financial markets are subject to Knightian Uncertainty. Efforts to generate a realistic returns distribution for a portfolio assume counterfactually that we are in a world of Knightian Risk, that is, that we can know all the outcomes and all their associated probabilities.

While we clearly aren't always in a world of Knightian Risk, much of the time we are, especially in developed financial markets. For example, if we discard the leftmost and rightmost bars of the histogram in Figure 8.1, the remaining observations of an equally weighted portfolio of currencies do look remarkably normal. But the tail events destroy any hope of normality.

We would still have work to do even if we reacquired a state of Knightian Risk at the portfolio level. Suppose that we find a fat-tailed cdf $F(x)$ that is the true generating distribution for portfolio log-returns, so that $F(x)$ describes (to within negligible sampling error) the probability that future empirical log-returns at the portfolio level will be less than or equal to x.

Knowing $F(x)$ would be helpful, but we still wouldn't know which combination of state variables led to which outcome. Maybe the lower part of the distribution is caused by a cluster of state variables associated with hyperinflation, or maybe it's caused by a cluster of state variables associated with deflation. Or maybe some of the lower tail is caused by each of these, that is, by completely opposite effects. The cdf $F(x)$, even if it's spot on, might say "how much" but it doesn't say "why."

But if we're going to prepare our portfolios for the future, we need to have an idea of why they might get into the tails. Because there is typically not enough data to estimate "why" – that is, which highly unusual combination of state variables might be the one that will lead to the next tail event – we need to use a more intuitive approach.

Stress testing takes one or a small number of key factors in our state variable vector sv and **shocks** it (them) by a very large move. For example, interest rates generally move by 10 or fewer basis points a day. An interest rate stress test might move rates up or down by 200 basis points. Suppose that the US Treasury 10-year rate is the factor in sv representing interest rates; then we would form $\text{sv}_\pm = \text{sv} \pm \delta_{UST10YR}.02$, where $\delta_{UST10YR}$ is a k-vector of zeroes except for a one in the US Treasury 10-year element. We would then reprice the portfolio

Port($R_1(\mathrm{sv}_+), \ldots, R_n(\mathrm{sv}_+)$) (and similarly for Port($R_1(\mathrm{sv}_-), \ldots, R_n(\mathrm{sv}_-)$)) to get an idea of the portfolio's response to extreme changes in interest rates.

Scenario analysis envisions a full economic situation affecting many if not all of the factors. **Historical** scenario analysis attempts to reproduce the changes in factors during unusual historical periods, such as the Great Depression starting in 1929, or the technology bust of 2000, or the Global Financial Crisis of 2008–2009.

Hypothetical scenario analysis envisions a possible future stressful scenario, such as hyperinflation following a policy error by central banks. Hypothetical scenario analysis starts with a qualitative narrative, but must finish with a k-vector $\mathrm{sv}_{hypothetical}$ that specifies levels or changes in the state variables so that Port($R_1(\mathrm{sv}_{hypothetical}), \ldots, R_n(\mathrm{sv}_{hypothetical})$) can be formed.

This can be difficult: for example, in a US dollar hyperinflation scenario, analysts might focus carefully on financial variables in the USA. But what would happen to the USD/JPY (Japanese yen) exchange rate? Maybe the yen would have even worse hyperinflation, or maybe it would be a haven of stability.

If analysts don't have the expertise to form opinions on certain state variables like the Japanese yen, they might seek to fill in the missing variables. Suppose sv_0 is the vector containing changes in the variables where expert opinions are available and sv_1 is the vector containing the unknown variables. Then either historical information or a model could be used to obtain conditional distributions $f(\mathrm{sv}_0 \mid \mathrm{sv}_1)$ and $f(\mathrm{sv}_1 \mid \mathrm{sv}_0)$, which would allow a Gibbs sampler to be run to fill in the agnostic variables, as shown in the previous section.

Both historical analysis and hypothetical scenario analysis require as much art as science. As Mark Twain is supposed to have said, "History never repeats itself. But it does rhyme." There may be a global pandemic in the year 2050, but it will certainly not be precisely like the COVID-19 pandemic starting in the year 2020. Still, subjecting a portfolio in the year 2050 to the pandemic state variable changes from 2020 might rhyme – maybe the 30-year-old financial variable changes will be helpful in alerting human analysts to possibilities. But there are an infinite number of possible extremely unusual versions of the future: human judgment needs to be used to determine which ones deserve our attention.

For Code Segments in this chapter, see the Code Appendix starting on p. 440. For executable code, visit www.cambridge.org/9781009209090/ch8

For problem sets for this chapter, visit www.cambridge.org/9781009209090/ch8_problems

9 Time-Varying Volatility

Benjamin Graham[1] famously anthropomorphized the US stock market, attributing wild emotional swings to "Mr. Market."[2] Sometimes Mr. Market was fearful, usually after a sufficiently traumatic negative event. At those times Mr. Market would sell valuable assets cheaply. Other times Mr. Market was greedy, and was willing to pay unrealistically high prices. The essence of "value investing" espoused by Graham – and later by his most successful student, Warren Buffett[3] – was to take advantage of Mr. Market's changing moods.

Mr. Market's moods affect both valuation and volatility. We noted when discussing mixtures of normals in Section 7.3 that authors such as Ang and Timmerman (2011) found that markets:

> often change their behavior abruptly and … the new behavior of financial variables often persists for several periods after such a change. (p. 2)

In Section 7.3, we explored a model that does a good job of embodying the observation that markets "often change their behavior abruptly": mixtures of normals. But mixtures of normals don't address the persistence that Ang and Timmerman (2011) and others have observed. In this chapter, we'll study volatility models that are aimed at *both* realistic behavior change and realistic persistence.

9.1 Historical Volatility

We know that even draws taken from a well understood distribution will have considerable sampling variation. So is it possible that abrupt changes and regime persistence in volatility are just due to ordinary sampling variation?

Let's examine the volatility of the US stock market starting in July 1926. To start, Code Segment 9.1 computes the annualized standard deviation of monthly log-returns from July 1926 to the end of last year:

```
Annualized standard deviation of US stock market,
192607-202112(95.5 years): 18.42%
```

---

1 Columbia250. "Benjamin Graham." Website. http://c250.columbia.edu/c250_cele brates/your_columbians/benjamin_graham.html.
2 [Graham 1949].
3 Biography.com. "Warren Buffett." Website. www.biography.com/business-figure/ warren-buffett.

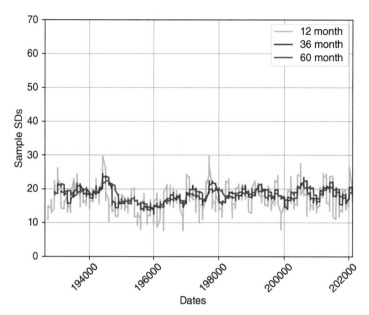

Figure 9.1 Virtual US stocks 1926-07–2021-12, annual sigma = 18.42.

To show what sampling variation looks like, Code Segment 9.2 generates Figure 9.1, which shows draws from a normal distribution with mean 0 and standard deviation equaling the historical standard deviation we just obtained.

We've labeled Figure 9.1 with dates. But these are not real dates – they are *merely corroborative detail intended to give artistic verisimilitude*[4] to the figure. Figure 9.1 is composed of the same number of observations that we used above to find the long-term volatility of the US stock market, which is the target volatility in Figure 9.1. Otherwise, Figure 9.1 is virtual.

The yellow line shows sample standard deviations computed over rolling 12-month periods; blue shows annualized 36-month sample standard deviations; and red shows 60-month. The red line is the smoothest, as it has the most opportunity to average out individual sampling quirks.

By comparison, Figure 9.2 (generated by Code Segment 9.3) shows reality: sample annualized standard deviations taken from real US stock market data over 12-, 36-, and 60-month trailing periods.

The differences between Figure 9.1 and Figure 9.2 are dramatic. The most obvious difference is the long high-volatility regime in Figure 9.2 consisting of the Great Depression of the 1920s and 1930s. This was far beyond the kind of sampling variation shown in Figure 9.1. Actual reality is more complicated than virtual reality. It would be nice to ignore that, but acting on the mistaken belief that we live in the world of Figure 9.1 will inevitably lead to a painful adjustment.

---

4 [Gilbert and Sullivan 1885].

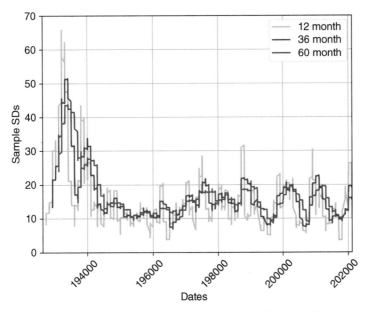

Figure 9.2 Actual US stocks sample std dev 1926-07–2021-12.

The standout features of Figure 9.2 are the spikes – especially evident in the yellow line – that occur because of large negative shocks: the Great Depression; the stock market crash of October 1987; and in 2008–2009. None of these would have been observed if we had just sampled from a lognormal.

In addition to protruding periods of very high volatility in the real data, a close look reveals regimes of persistent low volatility. For example, the two decades of the 1950s and the 1960s showed volatility mainly in the low teens, as did the period 2003–2006.

It certainly seems plausible that major economic events cause the financial markets to have volatility memory. In the Great Depression, it was not clear for quite a while whether the USA would survive without major changes, if at all.

Fortunately there was not a complete break in the rule of law in the USA. Complete breaks occur frequently, almost inevitably, in history, as we pointed out in Section 7.1.4 with examples in Russia, China, and Cuba. On the other hand, it could be argued that the New Deal legislation passed in the USA in the wake of the Great Depression reshaped the social and economic contract, so there was a partial break.

The calm period of the 1950s and 1960s corresponded to a number of soothing factors – the end of a world war, stable demographics, household formation, and so on.

The reasoning applied to these large macroeconomic regimes can be extended to lesser events such as the 1986 Tax Reform Act[5] in the USA.

5 [Bolster, Lindsey, and Mitrusi 1988].

Anticipation and eventual passage of this law created short-term market volatility: the yellow line in Figure 9.2 spiked to over 30 percent for three months at the end of 1986. But eventually markets adjusted to the new rules and volatility subsided.

9.2 Options and Volatility

We have noted that Harry Markowitz was apparently the first (in 1952) to suggest that volatility (standard deviation) was a good metric for how much information we lack about the future, that is, Frank Knight's concept of risk.

We have also noted that we live in a world of Knightian Uncertainty, where we don't know the probability distribution of outcomes. If we did, we would know future volatilities. But we don't even know how much we don't know about the future.

This lack of knowledge about our lack of knowledge is good news for market participants called **volatility traders**: they would not have jobs if everyone knew future volatility. But in fact there are lively markets where participants are able to express views about future volatility.

Many of the strategies to bet on future volatility involve options, so the next section briefly reviews options terminology.

9.2.1 Review of Options Terminology

The owner of a **European call option** has the right (but not the obligation) to purchase an **underlying** entity (such as a share of a particular stock; a unit of an index such as the Standard & Poor's 500; or an ounce of gold) at an agreed-on price (called the **strike price**) on a certain date in the future. This date is called **maturity** or **expiration** of the option; after that date, the option no longer confers any power on its owner. If the call option owner chooses to use its right to purchase, it is said to have **exercised** the option. An **American call option**[6] has the same properties, except it can be exercised on or before (not just on) a certain date in the future.

A **call writer** is the entity on the other side of the transaction from the call owner: the call writer agrees, at the call owner's discretion, to sell the underlying entity at the agreed-on price on (or before, if American) a certain date. The call writer has no discretion; it merely awaits a command from the call owner that the call owner may or may not choose to exercise. Because the call writer is

---

6 Most individual equity options are American-style whether they are traded in the USA or in Europe: option style is not a geographical descriptor. Witty options traders have riffed on the American and European style names to come up with other styles, like Bermudian. Bermudian-style options have features of both American-style options and European-style options, and Bermuda is somewhere between the USA and Europe. But Bermudian-style options are not native to Bermuda.

submitting to the call owner's self-interest, the call owner must pay the call writer an inducement to cede power. The consideration paid by the call owner to the call writer is the **call premium**.

Many options are **cash settled**, meaning the purchase of the underlying entity does not actually occur. For example, if a call owner exercises the right to buy an underlying entity at a strike price of $100 at a time when its market price is $120, under cash settlement the call writer would simply pay $20 to the call owner. However, if the option has **physical settlement**, upon exercise the call owner pays the strike price to the call writer, who simultaneously delivers a unit of the underlying to the call owner.

Whether through cash or physical settlement, a European call option is worth $\max(X_T - K, 0)$ at maturity time T, where X_t is the market price of the underlying at time t and K is the option's strike price. Then $\max(X_T - K, 0)$ is called the **payoff** of the call option.

In practice in many cases, calls are not bilateral contracts. Instead, an exchange (such as the Cboe, formerly the Chicago Board Options Exchange[7]) stands between all call owners and all call writers. Call owners pay the premium to the exchange and call writers receive the premium from the exchange, but the exchange collects collateral (called **margin**) from call writers to minimize the chance that they collectively fail to fulfill their obligations in the event of exercise. Upon exercise, physical or cash settlement also takes place through the exchange.

The owner of a **put option** has the right (but not the obligation) to sell an underlying entity to a **put writer** (or to an exchange standing between owners and writers) with conditions similar to a call option. A European put option has payoff equal to $\max(K - X_T, 0)$ at maturity time T.

Consider an investor who establishes a three-position portfolio UPC consisting of:

- a unit of the underlying;
- a put on that underlying; and
- a written (short) call on that underlying.

The put and the call have the same maturity and the same strike price. If, at maturity, the underlying is worth less than the common strike price, then the call will be worthless but the put will be worth the difference between the strike price and the underlying, so the portfolio UPC will be worth the strike price. Similar logic shows that if the underlying is worth more than the strike price at maturity, then UPC will also be worth the strike price. Thus, by no-arbitrage, the portfolio UPC is the same as a risk-free zero-coupon bond that will be worth the strike price at maturity time T.

---

7 Cboe.com. Website. www.cboe.com.

This relationship for same-parameter European options on the same non-dividend-paying underlying is called **put-call conversion** or **put-call parity**:

$$X_t + P_t - C_t = \exp(-r(T - t))K. \qquad (9.1)$$

Here, as above, T is the maturity time; X_t is the price of the underlying at time $0 \leq t \leq T$; and K is the common strike price of the options. Then P_t and C_t are the put and call premia, respectively, at time t, of options on the underlying struck at K with maturity time T. The RHS of (9.1) is the current price of a riskless zero-coupon bond that pays the common strike price K at the common maturity T; r is the riskless discount rate over the horizon T.

Options are a type of **derivative security**. Such securities derive their prices from other more fundamental observables, including stock prices, bond prices, commodity prices, and interest rates.

The prices (premia) of many options derive from the following five inputs. We've seen the first four already; the fifth input is new but not surprising:

- X, the current price of the underlying asset (such as the S&P 500);
- K, the strike price of the option;
- T, the time to maturity of the option;
- r, the risk-free rate of interest; and
- $f(x)$, the probability density function of the underlying asset's price at time T.

More complex options may have other inputs; for example, if the underlying pays dividends, then the dividend rate or even a calendar of scheduled dividend payments may be input. In narrative form, a generic formula for the price of a simple option looks like this:

$$Price(\text{option}) = f(\text{underlying price, strike price, time,}$$
$$\text{rf rate, underlying density function}). \qquad (9.2)$$

In order to move from the generic formula (9.2) to a specific formula, assumptions about the behavior of the underlying asset need to be made. We noted at the beginning of Chapter 4 that the Black–Scholes option formula (Black and Scholes 1973) is based on the assumption that underlying assets follow lognormal random walks as in (3.17).

Using the lognormal assumption and an arbitrage argument, Black and Scholes showed that the price of a call option could be approximated by a continuously updated combination of the underlying and cash. That led them to a differential equation for the price of a call option. The mean of the underlying distribution did not appear in this differential equation and thus didn't appear in the Black–Scholes formula: the only distribution parameter needed is the underlying's standard deviation of log-returns.

Black and Scholes solved the differential equation to obtain their well-known formula for the price of a call option $C(X, K, T, r, \sigma)$:

$$C(X, K, T, r, \sigma) = X \cdot N(d_1) - K \cdot \exp(-rT)N(d_2), \qquad (9.3)$$

where:

$$d_1 = \frac{\ln\left(\frac{X}{K}\right) + \left(r + \frac{\sigma^2}{2}\right)T}{\sigma\sqrt{T}} \quad \text{and} \quad d_2 = d_1 - \sigma\sqrt{T}.$$

9.2.2 Market Volatilities and Volatility Markets

We already know from Chapter 7 that Black–Scholes's basic assumption of underlying lognormal random walks isn't true. We'll explore the implications of non-normality further below.

For now, note that the first four Black–Scholes inputs are easily observable. The fifth (volatility) can be observed in the past, but as we've pointed out above, volatility is not constant and we don't know what it will be over the future life of option.

While we can't observe future volatility, we might be able to observe current options prices. So when the options of interest are traded in a market like the Cboe or the Eurex,[8] we can rearrange (9.3) so that observables are on the right-hand side:

$$ImpVol(\text{option}) = g(\text{underlying price, strike price, time,}$$

$$\text{rf rate, option price}). \qquad (9.4)$$

The standard deviation that was an input to (9.3) is rebranded as **implied volatility** in (9.4): its value is implied under the assumption that (9.3) holds. Often, an iterative procedure rather than a closed-form formula is applied to (9.3) to determine the g function in (9.4).

Higher underlying standard deviation means that more probability mass is pushed away from the center of the underlying's distribution, out to the tails. More probability in the tails means a higher probability of high values for an option. Thus, Black–Scholes (9.3) will have a positive derivative with respect to its fifth argument, that is, $\frac{\partial C}{\partial \sigma} > 0$.

This indicates that the expectation of an underlying's volatility over the life of an option is closely linked to the price of that option. More expected volatility means a higher option price when all other arguments are held constant, and a higher option price reflects more expected volatility through (9.4). Because of this tight connection, sometimes options prices are quoted in volatility units rather than in monetary units.

8 Eurex.com. "About Us." Website. www.eurex.com/ex-en/find/about-us.

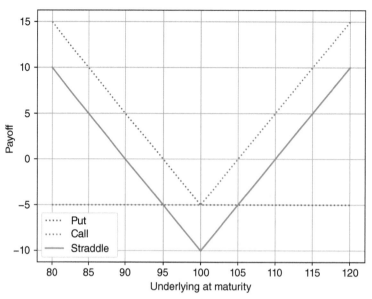

Figure 9.3 Put, call, straddle payoffs.

So options markets can be seen as markets where underlying volatility is traded. A simple strategy that can express a view of future volatility is to buy or write a **straddle**, which is a put option and a call option struck at-the-money and expiring at the same time in the future. (**The money** means the current price of the underlying.)

If we pay p for the put and c for the call, then if the underlying moves more than $p + c$ in either direction away from its current price, we will profit. If we knew future volatility, we would be able to tell if $p + c$ was too low (buy the straddle) or too high (write the straddle). Figure 9.3 (generated by Code Segment 9.4) shows the payoff patterns of the put, the call, and the straddle at time of maturity, where the strike is 100 and both the put and the call are assumed to cost 5.

The most widely observed implied volatilities are those of the Standard & Poor's 500®,[9] who created the Cboe Volatility Index®, more widely known as the VIX® Index,[10] to "measure the market's expectation of future volatility … based on options of the S&P 500® Index." VIX® actually uses a more sophisticated methodology that we'll explore below, but for now it suffices to understand that VIX® extracts levels of underlying S&P 500 volatility from options prices.

The VIX® has been published daily by the Cboe[11] since the early 1990s, and data have been backfilled to the beginning of 1986. An older series called

9 S & P Dow Jones Indices. "S&P 500®." Website.
10 Cboe. "Cboe VIX/textregistered Index." Website. www.cboe.com/vix.
11 See www.cboe.com/micro/vix/historical.aspx.

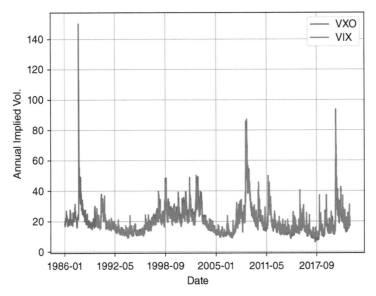

Figure 9.4 Implied volatilities, 1986–2021.

VXO is based on a different methodology, but basically tells the same story as VIX. Figure 9.4 (generated by Code Segment 9.5) shows the historical values of VXO and VIX retrieved from the FRED database. Code Segment 9.5 also outputs the dates of the 10 largest VIX moves, as well as the recent yearend VIX level:

```
Dates of 10 largest
['1987-10-19', '1987-10-20', '1987-10-26', '1987-10-22',
        '1987-10-23',
'1987-10-27', '2020-03-16', '2020-03-12', '2020-03-18',
        '2008-11-20']
Yearend VIX 17.22
```

The very large spike on the left of Figure 9.4 is the all-time high annualized implied volatility of 150, observed as a result of the stock market crash on and around October 19, 1987. The second-highest spike activity was on March 16, 2020, as the markets were shocked by the COVID-19 pandemic. And a spike of about 80 was observed on November 20, 2008, as markets considered the possible breakdown of the global financial system. For context, we've seen above that the annualized volatility of the US stock market since July 1926 is between 18 and 19 (percentage points).

Given the variation that is apparent in Figure 9.4, it is not surprising that markets for volatility are quite active. There are vehicles like volatility and variance swaps[12] and VIX® futures[13] that allow positions to be taken on the

---

12 [Demeterfi, Derman, Kamal, and Zou 1999b].
13 Cboe. "Volatility Index VIX®Futures." Website. www.cboe.com/tradable_products/vix/vix_futures/.

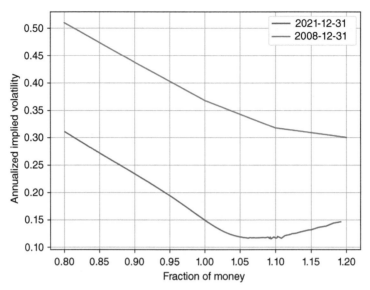

Figure 9.5 Moneyness skew SPX options: expiry 2022-03-18, quoted 2021-12-31, compared with 2008-12-31 quotes.

future level of certain asset volatilities. This activity is called **vega trading** since "vega" is the term often used to denote an instrument's sensitivity to changes in underlying volatility.[14]

9.2.3 Volatility Skews

Figure 9.4 showed a single time-varying option-implied volatility for the Standard & Poor's 500. But at any given time, for the same underlying there are many traded options with varying strike prices and varying maturities. Each of these options has an implied volatility obtained from (9.4). Since the underlying asset can have only one actual volatility, we might hope that all options on the same underlying have the same implied volatility.

They don't. Figure 9.5 (generated by Code Segment 9.6) shows implied volatilities for options on the same underlying (S&P 500) with the same maturity, but with moneyness varying along the X-axis. (Moneyness is the ratio of the strike price of the option to the current price of the underlying.)

The blue line in Figure 9.5 shows implied volatilities of S&P 500 options as of the end of last year, with expiration about three months after that. The value

14 "Option Greeks" are terms that denote the derivatives of an instrument's price with respect to various factors such as interest Rates (rho) or the passage of Time (theta). These two examples are Greek letters and have the first-letter mnemonic T-theta-time and R-rho-rates. There is no Greek letter that starts with "v," so some use Vega (actually a star in the Lyra constellation) as a pseudo-Greek to maintain the V-vega-volatility mnemonic. Purists who insist on actual Greek letters use "kappa" for volatility sensitivity, losing the first-letter mnemonic. We will look at option Greeks in more detail in Chapter 12.

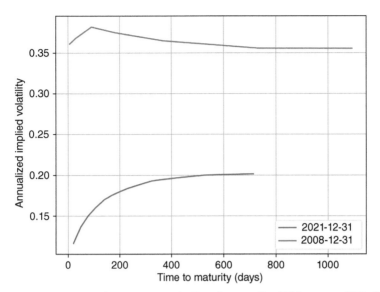

Figure 9.6 Maturity skew ATM SPX options: strike 4775, money 4782.4502, quoted 2021-12-31, compared with 2008-12-31 quotes.

of the blue line on Figure 9.5 at "Fraction of money" equal to 1.00 is very close to the rightmost value of Figure 9.4.

As moneyness varies, the blue line decreases monotonically except for slight perturbations at the high end where options are more thinly traded and the data are less reliable.

The red line in Figure 9.5 is the set of implieds on December 31, 2008, in the thick of the Global Financial Crisis. It's similar in shape to the blue line, but it's translated up on the Y-axis.

This kind of monotone pattern, typical of equity options, is called a **volatility skew**. In some cases – currency options, often – the moneyness curve dips in the middle but comes up at both ends; this is called a **volatility smile**.

In Figure 9.5 maturity was held constant while moneyness varied. If we hold moneyness constant (at 100%, referred to as at-the-money, or ATM) while maturity varies, we get the patterns shown in Figure 9.6 (generated by Code Segment 9.7).

The blue line in Figure 9.6 is a skew, although its range is not as wide as the moneyness skew in Figure 9.5.

The red line in Figure 9.6 is an upside-down smile, so of course it's called a **volatility frown**. In addition to the obvious highly elevated overall level, the red line shows the market's expectation that volatility would increase for about three months before subsiding slightly.

The downward slope – implied volatility decreases as moneyness increases – in Figure 9.5 is reliable, although the magnitude varies. Figure 9.7b (generated by Code Segment 9.8) is 120%–80% moneyness skew in six-month options; it's

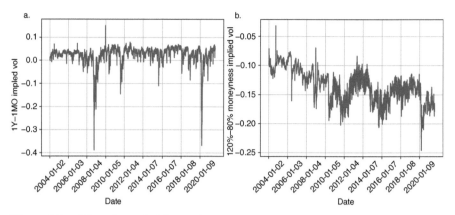

Figure 9.7 a. Time skews. b. Money skews.

always negative, usually more than 10%. That is, 120% moneyness annualized implied volatilities have been less than 80% moneyness implied volatilities of six-month options since at least 2004. There is some tendency for moneyness skew to increase during periods of market distress, like the terrorist attacks of September 11, 2001, or the Global Financial Crisis.

Code Segment 9.8 also generates Figure 9.7a, which extends the anecdotal evidence of Figures 9.5 and 9.6: time skew is not as pronounced as moneyness skew. Figure 9.7a shows one year implied volatility minus one month implied volatility, both of at-the-money (100% moneyness) Standard & Poor's 500 options. We used one year–one month because they are both heavily traded. This difference is usually (over 80% of the time) positive – during normal markets, investors tend to demand a volatility time premium so that future implied volatility is higher than present implied volatility. But in market shocks, investors tend to buy short-term options rapidly and drive up near-term implied volatility. Thus time skew is a reasonably reliable market stress indicator. The percentage of time that the time skew was positive computed by Code Segment 9.8 is:

```
Percent time skew positive: 86.19%
Source: Cboe Exchange, Inc. (Cboe)
```

9.3 Volatility Models

The nonconstant implied volatilities in Figures 9.5 and 9.6 are further evidence – not that any was needed – that the simple lognormal random walk model of underlying prices (3.17) is wrong. There is no way to reconcile the different implied volatilities with the idea of a lognormal underlying distribution with a single, time-invariant volatility parameter.

The Black–Scholes formula (and other option pricing formulas like Cox, Ross, and Rubenstein (1979)) are essentially theorems that follow from certain axioms. If a theorem doesn't work empirically, then one of the axioms must be an incorrect description of reality. Mandelbrot used this line of reasoning as he examined the empirical failure of the Central Limit Theorem.

So we now turn our attention to what could be wrong with the assumptions behind the classical option pricing formulas, with the hope that we can get further insight, if not a perfect model. While the existence of active volatility markets means that future volatility is unknown, that doesn't mean that we can't find patterns in volatility that can be used to generate descriptive models of the future.

These models are not prescriptive – they don't predict volatility. But they do generate patterns of volatility that are very much like the patterns we see in the markets. Thus, the versions of the future that they generate are more likely to encompass the possible outcomes and their associated probabilities than are constant volatility models.

9.3.1 Risk-Neutral Density Recovery

Breeden and Litzenberger (1978) decided to let the options market tell them what the underlying's distribution is, rather than try to tell the options market what it should be. Their approach is one of the ways to recover a risk-neutral cdf or pdf; from there, the Ross Recovery Theorem can be applied as in Chapter 2.

A general way to write the price of a European call option is:

$$C(X, K, T, r, f_{X,T}) = \exp(-rT) \int_K^\infty (y - K) f_{X,T}(y) dy. \qquad (9.5)$$

This is a more explicit version of (9.2), using the notation of Section 9.2.1. But this is less explicit than Black–Scholes (9.3) because Black–Scholes's assumption of underlying lognormality has not been made. Instead, the underlying X's probability density function at time T, $f_{X,T}$ has been included as an argument to the pricing function.

Breeden and Litzenberger's (1978) technique recovers $f_{X,T}$ from options price data. This technique does not disentangle risk preferences from probabilities, so the density function recovered using their method will be risk neutral like $q(x)$ in Chapter 2, not real world like $p(x)$.

Manipulating (9.5) gives:

$$\exp(rT) C(X, K, T, r) = \left(\mu - \int_{-\infty}^K y f_{X,T}(y) dy \right) - K(1 - F_{X,T}(K)). \qquad (9.6)$$

Here, μ is the average value of the underlying over the pdf $f_{X,T}$, and $F_{X,T}(x)$ is the cumulative distribution function arising from the density function $f_{X,T}$.

Taking the derivative of both sides of (9.6) with respect to the exercise price K gives:

$$\exp(rT) \frac{\partial C(X, K, T, r)}{\partial K} = -K f_{X,T}(K) - 1 + F_{X,T}(K) + K f_{X,T}(K).$$

The $Kf_{X,T}(K)$ terms cancel, giving:

$$F_{X,T}(K) = \exp(rT)\frac{\partial C(X,K,T,r)}{\partial K} + 1. \tag{9.7}$$

This gives an expression for the previously unknown cumulative density function in terms of the rate of change in the prices of options as strike prices change. We can approximate the derivative on the RHS of (9.7) by taking successive differences of observable options prices with incrementally higher strike prices, that is, by using finite differences $\Delta C/\Delta K$. For example, if we have a 3-month option struck at 90 and another 3-month option struck at 90.5, then two times the difference between their market prices will approximate the 3-month forward cdf around 90.25.

Taking the derivative of (9.7) produces the pdf:

$$f_{X,T}(K) = \exp(rT)\frac{\partial^2 C(X,K,T,r)}{\partial K^2}. \tag{9.8}$$

So if C_1, C_2, and C_3 are the market prices of options struck at 90, 90.5, and 91, respectively, then:

$$\exp(rT)\frac{C_3 - 2C_2 + C_1}{.5^2}$$

is an approximation to the risk-neutral pdf of the underlying around 90.5.

In practice, applying (9.8) (or its finite difference approximation) produces bumpy distributions. Some options may be thinly traded, producing asynchronous quotes that lead to noisy pdfs. Often some kind of smoothing method, like a cubic spline, is applied to fill and smooth the recovered pdf. Another approach is to fit a smooth function to the observed moneyness volatility curve like those in Figure 9.5. Then the smoothed volatilities can be used as inputs to (9.3) to get prices that are input to (9.8).

The risk-neutral distribution that results from this recovery and smoothing process can be used by traders to suggest arbitrage ideas in places where the trader feels the options market is being particularly unreasonable, too risk averse, or not risk averse enough.

9.3.2 Real-World Density Recovery

The recovered risk-neutral density function can be used together with the Ross Recovery Theorem (Section 2.10 in Chapter 2) to find real-world densities implied by observable options prices under Ross's assumptions.

We noted in Section 2.10 that observable options prices could be used to produce a square $n \times n$ matrix Q whose (i,j) entry is the probability of transitioning from state i to state j over a given time period. To form Q we need to observe options prices at many different strikes and maturities.

For example, suppose we can observe prices of options expiring in one month with strikes of $90, 90.5, \ldots, 110$. That would allow us to form $n = 39$ second differences, corresponding to 39 states to which the Ross Recovery Theorem can be applied. State 1 is a price of 90.5; state 2 is a price of 91, ..., state 39 is a price of 109.5.

Let's say the current state's index is $c = 20$, that is, a price of \$100. Then the prices of one-month options that are currently trading will let us fill in the cth row of the desired Q matrix, where Q's given time period is one month. But what do we do to fill in other rows of Q? For example suppose i indexes the state where the underlying's price is 105 and j indexes the state where the underlying's price is 98.5. How do we find $q(i,j)$, the probability of transitioning from \$105 to \$98.5 over one month?

To fill in the rest of Q, we'd need to look at prices of options that expire in 2 months; in three months; ...; in 39 months. In practice, it would be unlikely that we'd have all the necessary observations, but we might be able to fill in all the requisite data by interpolating between observed prices.

Once we have all n second differences of prices (39 in our example, derived from 41 strike prices) over all the maturities (each of the next 39 months in our example), we can form an $n \times n$ matrix Q_c whose (i,t) entry is $q(c,i,t)$: the probability of transitioning from the current state c to state i between now and time $t, t = 1, \ldots, 39$.

The c row of the desired matrix Q is the first column of the matrix Q_c, that is, the vectors marked in red below are the same:

$$Q = \begin{bmatrix} \vdots & \ddots & \vdots \\ q(c,1) & \cdots & q(c,m) \\ \vdots & \ddots & \vdots \end{bmatrix},$$

$$Q_c = \begin{bmatrix} q(c,1,\Delta t = 1) & \ddots & q(c,1,\Delta t = m) \\ \vdots & \cdots & \vdots \\ q(c,m,\Delta t = 1) & \ddots & q(c,m,\Delta t = m) \end{bmatrix}.$$

From this observation, we can bootstrap the rest of Q by noting that going from now (time 0) to state i at time t means we went from now to state j at time $t - 1$, and then did a one-month transition from state j to state i. Summing, we get:

$$q(c,i,\Delta t = t) = \sum_{j=1}^{n} q(c,j,\Delta t = t-1)q(j,i).$$

In other words, the (i,t) entry of the known matrix Q_c is the dot product of:

- column i of the as-yet-unknown $n \times n$ matrix Q; and
- column $t - 1$ of Q_c.

We also know – since things have to transition from somewhere or to somewhere – that $Qu = Q^\mathsf{T}u = u$ where u is the vector of all ones.

Putting the observations of the previous two paragraphs together in a matrix equation gives:

$$\left(Q_c(2,n)|u\right) = Q^\mathsf{T} \times \left(Q_c(1, n-1)|u\right),$$

where $Q_c(a,b)$ consists of columns a through b of Q_c and "$|u$" means a column of all ones is appended after the last column of the matrix.

Solving for Q^T gives:

$$Q^\mathsf{T} = \left(Q_c(2,n)|u\right)\left(Q_c(1, n-1)|u\right)^{-1}. \tag{9.9}$$

This retrieves the entire risk-neutral one-period state transition matrix from the Breeden–Litzenberger risk-neutral probabilities extracted from multiple time periods.

Getting this process to work in practice requires a lot of assumptions and a lot of data. We won't really have the $n(n+2)$ independent observations needed, and the way we fill in missing observations can affect the spectral analysis described in Section 2.10. But when used with caution, this process can deliver a partial description of a possible real-world density function of an underlying implied by market prices of its options.

9.3.3 Stochastic Volatility Modeling

The Black–Scholes model for option pricing started with the assumption that the underlying variable x_t – for example, the price of a stock at time t – followed a lognormal stochastic process like the ones we introduced in Chapter 3:

$$\frac{dx}{x} = \alpha dt + \sigma d\beta. \tag{3.17}$$

Of course, our point in this chapter is that it's unrealistic to assume that σ is a constant. We see σ varies in every way possible – over time; as x_t varies; even when none of the variables in (3.17) vary, that is, across option strike prices or expiration times.

So starting in the 1980s, a number of models were created that attempted to improve (3.17) by removing the requirement that volatility is constant:

$$\frac{dx_t}{x_t} = \alpha dt + \sigma(t,x_t)d\beta. \tag{9.10}$$

But (9.10) is just notation. The difficulty is in finding a realistic model for $\sigma(t,x_t)$. For one thing, realistic models will need to reflect the fact that volatilities are range bound: they can't be negative and they can't increase forever. In fact, volatilities of risky assets can't even stay near zero for very long periods because then the asset would be risk free.

If volatilities could increase forever, then swings would get more and more violent, and the stability necessary for market participants to have enough confidence to trade would be lost. William Butler Yeats (1919) poetically expressed conditions of unbounded volatility:

> *Turning and turning in the widening gyre / The falcon cannot hear the falconer / Things fall apart; the centre cannot hold / Mere anarchy is loosed upon the world*

Yeats was commenting on the chaos leading to World War I. As we've previously seen, the complete demises of markets in Russia, China, and Cuba were consequences of wider societal restructurings where "things fell apart." Wild market swings accompany wars and revolutions; they both reflect the widening gyre and add to it. Anecdotally, it appears that the centre cannot hold above a sustained 50% annualized standard deviation of log-returns, although short-lived spikes above this level are often seen.

So modelers used Ornstein–Uhlenbeck processes to capture the range-bound nature of variance (and volatility, its square root). The Heston (1993) model, for example, is:

$$dv(t) = \kappa[\theta - v(t)]dt + \varphi\sqrt{v(t)}dz(t). \tag{9.11}$$

Here, $v(t) = \sigma^2(t,x)$ is variance, but Heston's model does not make use of the x argument. Thus, dz is a Wiener process with correlation ρ with the underlying's process $d\beta$, and κ, θ, and φ ("volvol," the volatility of volatility) (e constant parameters. Heston notes that (9.11) is the same equation as Cox, Ingersoll, and Ross's short-rate model (3.45).

Models like (9.11) are called **Stochastic Volatility Models**. If $2\kappa\theta > \varphi^2$ (the "Feller Condition"), then the variance will almost surely stay above zero.[15]

Heston (1993) derives a closed-form formula for stock, bond, and currency options based on (9.10) and (9.11). The formulas are messy and involve some numerical integration. A large literature accompanied and followed Heston's results with variants and generalizations.

We noted in Chapter 3 that the original Vasicek model for short interest rates contemplated constant parameters. This was later generalized by Hull and White (and others) to allow nonstochastic but time-varying parameters to better capture interest rate curves. Similarly, parameters in (9.11) can be made to vary in a way that models the various types of skew that we saw in Section 9.2.

9.3.4 Local Volatility Modeling

Dupire (1994) and others took a different approach to the varying nature of $\sigma(t,x_t)$. Dupire's approach relied on the Breeden–Litzenberger process to extract

---

15 [Gikhman 2011] has a nice one-page proof of this.

from options price an implied time-varying probability density function $f(t,x)$ for the underlying asset x.

The **local volatility model** ("LVM") gathers data for as many option expiration times $tex_1, tex_2, \ldots, tex_n$ as possible, that is, for which robust data at many strike prices are available. For each tex_i, LVM computes the density function $f(tex_i, x)$ using (9.8) and some kind of interpolation/smoothing algorithm to treat the market's inconsistency. Another interpolation/smoothing algorithm is applied between expiration times to produce a single smooth density function $f(t,x)$.

Dupire's insight was that the density function could be mapped into a volatility surface $\sigma(t,x)$. That is, it is possible to find a volatility function $\sigma(t,x)$ that:

- when used with (9.10) and an option pricing method like Black–Scholes produces the observed option prices in the market; and
- is consistent with the market-derived density function $f(t,x)$.

Dupire used the Fokker–Planck equation that ties together volatilities and density functions. Dupire shows that when applied to (9.10), it says:

$$\frac{\partial f(t,x)}{\partial t} = \frac{\partial}{\partial x}\left(\alpha x f(t,x)\right) + \frac{\partial^2}{\partial x^2}\left(\frac{\sigma^2(t,x)}{2}f(t,x)\right). \qquad (9.12)$$

We've dropped the subscript "t" on x here, but it's the same x as in (9.10). Equation (9.12) can be solved for $\sigma(t,x)$ so that the two conditions above are satisfied.

Black–Scholes and the related Black model for forward contracts have become familiar quoting conventions. Market participants essentially pretend that the innovations in (9.10) are normal and put the non-normality in the variable $\sigma(t,x)$. The local volatility model ties together time-varying volatility and the underlying distribution, so that the shapes (skews, smiles, smirks, frowns...) that are empirically evident can be mapped into a distribution. This allows options traders to think in terms of volatility surfaces (graphical representations of $\sigma(t,x)$) rather than in terms of pdfs.

9.3.5 SABR Modeling

Unfortunately, there is a flaw in the LVM. It does not actually reflect reality as current prices change. We'll show how the problem arises and give a brief description of the widely used SABR model that solves the problem. A full investigation of SABR is beyond our scope.

Massimo Morini[16] notes the following: Let the current price (the "money") of the underlying be x_0. Extend our notation so that $\sigma(x_0; t, x)$ means the volatility

16 [Morini 2011], pp. 230–231.

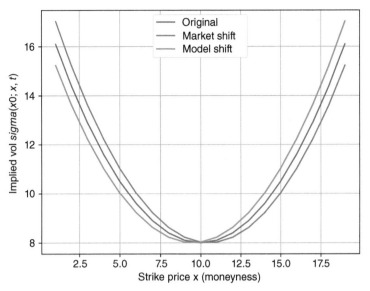

Figure 9.8 LVM does not shift the way the market shifts.

surface estimated through the LVM process when the current ($t = 0$) price is x_0, the time to expiration is t, and the strike price is x.

Then instantaneously shock the current price up a little bit, $x_0 \rightarrow x_0 + $ *epsilon*. The volatility surface will change. It's reliably observed in practice that the surface shifts up, $\sigma(x_0 + \epsilon, t, x) \approx \sigma(x_0; t, x - \epsilon)$. This is shown in Figure 9.8 (generated by Code Segment 9.9), where the red curve is the original blue curve shifted right by 0.5.

It can be shown that the LVM does the exact opposite: it shifts the perturbed curve to the left (green curve). I have shown a perfect smile in the graph, but the right shift seems to occur with imperfect smiles and with skews. I don't have a lot of intuition about why this occurs, but when a model contradicts a reliable market phenomenon, the model is wrong.

Hagan et al. (2002) helpfully pointed out the shortcomings of the LVM model and put forward a new model that is still widely used. We'll just state the basic components of the **SABR (Stochastic Alpha, Beta, Rho)**, but won't pursue it further:

$$dx(t) = \sigma(t)x(t)^{\beta} dZ_x(t),$$

$$d\sigma(t) = \varphi\sigma(t)dZ_{\sigma}(t); \quad \sigma(0) = \alpha, \tag{9.13}$$

$$\mathbb{E}[dZ_x dZ_{\sigma}] = \rho dt.$$

Like the Heston model (9.11), SABR has a volvol ϕ and a correlation ρ between volatility and the underlying. However, the dynamics are different and seem to fit market behaviors better.

9.3.6 VIX® Calculations

The fact of volatility skew means that no single option's implied volatility gives the whole picture. That's because the underlying distribution isn't really lognormal. We saw that Breeden–Litzenberger allows the risk-neutral distribution to be recovered from options prices. Wouldn't it make more sense to compute the standard deviation of that distribution than to use the varying implied volatility from a single option?

Rhetorical question: of course it would make more sense, assuming there's a deep enough options market to get sufficient reliable data. In a Goldman, Sachs March 1999 white paper, Demeterfi, Derman, Kamal, and Zou (1999a) provided an elegant methodology to recover a risk-neutral standard deviation. Their approach was adopted by the Cboe in its official calculations to produce the VIX® index.[17]

Demeterfi, Derman, Kamal, and Zou (1999a) note that Itô's Lemma applied to (3.17) results in the stochastic process identity:

$$\frac{dX}{X} - d(\ln(X)) = \frac{\sigma^2}{2} dt. \tag{9.14}$$

This relationship does not depend on strong assumptions about the nature of the underlying's distribution: the $d\beta$ term that contains those assumptions has canceled out. All that is required is that σ, which is possibly time varying, be reasonably well behaved without large discontinuous jumps.

Integrating over time and taking the risk-neutral expectation of (9.14) gives:

$$\sigma_{RN}^2 = \frac{2}{T}\mathbb{E}\left[\int_0^T \frac{dX}{X} - \ln\left(\frac{X_T}{X_0}\right)\right] = \frac{2}{T}\left[rT - \mathbb{E}\left[\ln\left(\frac{X_T}{X_0}\right)\right]\right]. \tag{9.15}$$

The latter equality is the result of the fact that in the risk-neutral measure, $\frac{dX}{X} = rdt + \cdots +$. Intuitively, the $\frac{dX}{X}$ term represents a continuously rebalanced portfolio of $\frac{1}{X}$ units of the underlying X, which is always worth 1 and therefore has no risk; it must then match the risk-free return.

The log term in (9.15) can be replicated by a portfolio of options, as follows: First, because in-the-money options are less liquid, we choose a strike price K_0 so that in the replicating portfolio put options are used for strikes below K_0 and call options for strikes above K_0. Then K_0 will actually be close to the forward value $\exp(rT)X_0$ of the underlying. Using a cutoff like K_0 is intended to improve data quality but doesn't change the theoretical argument.

---

17 Cboe. "Cboe VIX FAQ." Website. www.cboe.com/tradable_products/vix/faqs/.

Demeterfi, Derman, Kamal, and Zou (1999a) note the following identity that works for any K_0:

$$\frac{X_T - K_0}{K_0} - \ln\left(\frac{X_T}{K_0}\right) \tag{9.16}$$
$$= \int_0^{K_0} \frac{1}{K^2} \max(K - X_T, 0)dK + \int_{K_0}^{\infty} \frac{1}{K^2} \max(X_T - K, 0)dK.$$

The two integrals on the RHS calculate the payoff at maturity time T (with underlying price X_T at that time) of a portfolio Π. So Π consists of (a) in the first integral, put options struck at every strike price K from 0 to some cutoff strike K_0, where the option struck at K is given a weight $\frac{1}{K^2}$; and (b) in the second integral, call options struck at every strike price from K_0 to ∞, with the same weighting scheme. All the options are on the same underlying X. One integral or the other will have no value depending on whether X_T is above or below K_0; it is not hard to verify that the nonzero integral will equal the quantity on the LHS.

The logarithm $\ln\left(\frac{X_T}{X_0}\right)$ appearing in (9.15) didn't have a K_0 term, and the logarithm $\ln\left(\frac{X_T}{K_0}\right)$ appearing in (9.16) didn't have an X_0 term. That's easily addressed by the decomposition:

$$\ln\left(\frac{X_T}{X_0}\right) = \ln\left(\frac{X_T}{K_0}\right) + \ln\left(\frac{K_0}{X_0}\right).$$

So $\ln\left(\frac{K_0}{X_0}\right)$ is known at time $t = 0$ and thus can be safely extracted from the expectation operator. Thus (9.15) becomes:

$$\sigma_{RN}^2 = \frac{2}{T}\left[rT - \ln\left(\frac{K_0}{X_0}\right) - \mathbb{E}\left[\ln\left(\frac{X_T}{K_0}\right)\right]\right]. \tag{9.17}$$

The risk-neutral expectation at time $t = 0$ of the value at time T of the replicating portfolio Π whose payoff in (9.16) is:

$$\mathbb{E}\left[\ln\left(\frac{X_T}{K_0}\right)\right] = \exp(rT)\frac{X_0}{K_0} - 1 +$$
$$\exp(rT)\left(\int_0^{K_0} \frac{1}{K^2}P(K)dK + \int_{K_0}^{\infty} \frac{1}{K^2}C(K)dK\right) \tag{9.18}$$

Here, $P(K)$ and $C(K)$ are prices of the replicating portfolio's put and call options on the underlying X maturing at time T and struck at K. Market-observed prices can be used here; of course, there aren't continuously available options at every possible strike, but a finite approximation to (9.18) can be made.

Combining (9.18) with (9.17) gives the estimate of variance from a replicating portfolio of options:

$$\sigma_{RN}^2 = \frac{2}{T}\left[rT - \ln\left(\frac{K_0}{X_0}\right) - \exp(rT)\frac{X_0}{K_0} + 1 \right. \tag{9.19}$$
$$\left. - \exp(rT)\left(\int_0^{K_0}\frac{1}{K^2}P(K)dK + \int_{K_0}^\infty \frac{1}{K^2}C(K)dK\right)\right].$$

If K_0 is set to equal the forward price $\exp(rT)X_0$, the terms on the first line of (9.19) add to zero, leaving only the adjusted value of the portfolio of options.

The actual formula for VIX® is the square root of a finite approximation to (9.19):

$$\sigma^2 = \frac{2\exp(rT)}{T}\sum_i \frac{\Delta K_i}{K_i^2}O(K_i) - \frac{1}{T}\left(\frac{F}{K_0}-1\right)^2, \tag{9.20}$$

where:

- the index i runs over the set of strike prices for which options with reasonable liquidity are available;
- K_i is the strike price of the ith option used in the calculation where $K_i < K_j$ if $i < j$;
- ΔK_i is half the distance between adjacent strike prices, $\Delta K_i = \frac{K_{i+1}-K_{i-1}}{2}$;
- T is the time to expiration (30 days is targeted by taking an average of the calculation at the longest expiration less than 30 days and the shortest expiration greater than 30 days);
- r is the risk-free (US Treasury bill) rate for maturity T;
- $O(K_i)$ is the observable bid-asked average price of the option used at strike K_i;
- F is the forward price of the underlying, roughly $\exp(rT)X_0$ (more below); and
- K_0 is the dividing strike price where puts are used at strikes below K_0 and calls are used above K_0. Both a put and a call are used at K_0.

Put-call parity (9.1) shows that the price of a call equals the price of the put with the same parameters when their common strike price equals $\exp(rT)X_0$, that is, the forward price of the underlying. The VIX® methodology looks for the strike price K_{min} where the absolute difference between the put P and the call C struck at K_{min} is the smallest. The F in formula (9.20) is defined as $F = K_{min} + \exp(rT)(C - P)$. F should be very close to the forward price $\exp(rT)X_0$. The dividing line K_0 between puts and calls used in (9.20) is the highest available strike price less than or equal to K_{min}. This makes the term $\frac{1}{T}(\frac{F}{K_0} - 1)^2$ small, similar to the terms on the first line of (9.19).

Code Segment 9.10 uses a replicating portfolio of Black–Scholes puts and calls to calculate the value of (9.20) at different values of X_T. The options all have $\sigma = .2$, so we expect the variance-replicating calculation to return .04. Figure 9.9 (generated by Code Segment 9.10) shows the results.

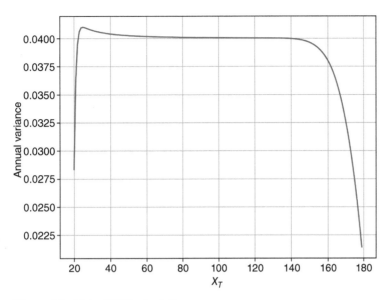

Figure 9.9 Virtual VIX calculations.

Figure 9.9 shows that the calculation works well in a wide neighborhood around the center (100) of available options. Actual S&P 500 strikes are about 20bps apart as a fraction of S&P price, which is even closer than the 1 percent strike spacing used here.

9.4 Time Series Terminology

We will finish our study of time-varying volatility with the work of Robert Engle, Tim Bollerslev, and others who used time series techniques. For that, we'll need the terminology that we'll use for basic time series analysis. This section sets out our terminology and is not intended as a course in time series. There are many excellent texts on time series analysis, such as Shumway and Stoffer (2017).

A **time series** is a set of data X_t indexed by time. Typically, values of X_t where t is in the past are simply data, while future values of X_t are assumed to follow a stochastic process. For our purposes, the stochastic process will be discrete and will contain data at a certain **periodicity**. The period can be a microsecond, a minute, a decade, or any other fixed amount of time.

We can define conditional distributions based on previous observations of the time series. When $t_1 > t_2$, the notation $F[X_{t_1}|\{X_s, s \leq t_2\}]$ indicates the cdf for a future value X_{t_1} of the time series given the information in previous values $\{X_s, s \leq t_2\}$. If we have a closed form for the conditional distribution $F[X_{t_1}|\{X_s, s \leq t_2\}]$, then the time series is **autopredictive**.

The conditional distribution framework reasonably contemplates us updating our beliefs. As the clock ticks (as t increases), we build up more and more history.

We get closer to the present, and eventually as the future becomes the present, variables become fixed and not stochastic. Suppose, for example, that $t_1 =$ the year 2050 and we form our belief as to the distribution of stock prices in 2050 based only on information about the stock market up to the year $t_2 = 2010$. That distribution will be different from the one we form if we have information about the stock market up to $t_2 = 2049$.

A time series is **strongly stationary** if $F(X_i, \ldots, X_m) = F(X_{i+j}, \ldots, X_{m+j})$ for all $i \leq m$ and $j \geq 0$. It is **nonstationary** if not. A weaker form of stationarity is **covariance stationarity**, meaning $\mathbb{E}[X_t]$ is a constant independent of t, and $Cov(X_t, X_s)$ is only a function of $t - s$. Thus, Variance(X_t) is only a function of $t - t = 0$, that is, like the mean, variance is a constant independent of t for a covariance stationary time series. A strongly stationary time series is covariance stationary if it has finite variance; it is, however, possible to find infinite variance strongly stationary time series that are not covariance stationary.

Many time series are not stationary, but often techniques are used to transform them into stationary series, which are easier to deal with.

The (possibly time-varying) mean $\mu(t)$ of a time series is straightforward: $\mu(t) = \mathbb{E}[X_t]$. The **autocovariance function** of a time series is $\sigma(s,t) = \mathbb{E}[(X_s - \mu(s))(X_t - \mu(t))]$. The **autocorrelation function** is $\rho(s,t) = \frac{\sigma(s,t)}{\sqrt{\sigma(s,s)\sigma(t,t)}}$.

If the time series is covariance stationary, then we can define the autocovariance function as $v(s - t) \equiv \sigma(s,t)$, that is, all that matters is the difference in times. Similarly, the autocorrelation function can be written $r(s - t) \equiv \rho(s,t) = v(s - t)/v(0)$ for a covariance stationary time series.

A time series is **autoregressive of order p** (written $AR(p)$) if the following holds for all t:

$$X_t = c + \sum_{i=1}^{p} a_i X_{t-i} + \epsilon_t. \tag{9.21}$$

Here $c, a_1, \ldots, a_p$ are constants and the ϵ_t are i.i.d. with mean 0 and variance σ^2. Often we start with initial conditions, where $X_0, \ldots, X_{p-1}$ are known with certainty. We then begin introducing randomness through **shocks** (or **innovations**) embodied in the ϵ_t.

Consider for simplicity an AR(1) process:

$$X_t = c + a X_{t-1} + \epsilon_t. \tag{9.22}$$

The first step from the initial condition brings us to:

$$X_1 = c + a X_0 + \epsilon_1.$$

Iterating the AR(1) relationship up to time t, we obtain:

$$X_t = \left(c \sum_{i=0}^{t-1} a^i + a^t X_0 \right) + \sum_{i=1}^{t} a^{t-i} \epsilon_i = \left(c \frac{1 - a^t}{1 - a} + a^t X_0 \right) + \sum_{i=1}^{t} a^{t-i} \epsilon_i. \tag{9.23}$$

Note that if $|a| < 1$, the term in large parentheses in (9.23) converges to $c/(1-a)$ as $t \to \infty$, and if $|a| \geq 1$, the term is either unbounded or does not converge. For the AR(1) process to be stationary, we must have $|a| < 1$.

More generally for an AR(p) process, we can define the **characteristic equation**

$$z^p - a_1 z^{p-1} - \cdots - a_p = 0. \tag{9.24}$$

The AR(p) process will be stationary iff the roots of this characteristic equation are all less than one in absolute value; that is, they lie inside the unit circle on the complex plane. If any roots are outside the unit circle, the process is ill behaved: it rapidly heads off to infinite values. If there are roots on the unit circle and none outside the unit circle, then the process is a nonstationary **unit root** process that meanders.

Recall from Chapter 3 that a Markov process is one where the current distribution's dependence on the past is limited to its dependence on the immediate previous distribution, not the entire history of how it got there.

$$Pr[X_n = v_n | X_{n-1} = v_{n-1}, \ldots, X_0 = v_0] = Pr[X_n = v_n | X_{n-1} = v_{n-1}]. \tag{3.21}$$

Thus, an AR(1) process is essentially a Markov process, since (using (9.22)):

$$
\begin{aligned}
Pr[X_n = v_n | X_{n-1} = v_{n-1}, \ldots, X_0 = v_0] &= Pr[\epsilon_n = v_n - c - a v_{n-1}] \\
&= Pr[X_n = v_n | X_{n-1} = v_{n-1}].
\end{aligned}
$$

A generalized definition of a Markov process is one where the current distribution depends only on a fixed finite number p of previous observations, not the entire history. Thus, an AR(p) process fits this more general definition of a Markov process.

Assume for simplicity that the parameter c in an AR(p) process (9.21) is zero and therefore all means are zero. Multiply the defining equation by $X_{t-k}(k > 0)$ and take expectations to get:

$$\mathbb{E}[X_t X_{t-k}] = \sum_{i=1}^{p} a_i \mathbb{E}[X_{t-i} X_{t-k}]. \tag{9.25}$$

If the process is stationary, only the difference in times matters in defining autocovariances, so we have:

$$v(k) = \sum_{i=1}^{p} a_i v(k-i) \quad \text{and} \quad v(0) = \sum_{i=1}^{p} a_i v(-i) + \text{ff}^2 = \sum_{i=1}^{p} a_i v(i) + \text{ff}^2. \tag{9.26}$$

Dividing both sides of the left-hand equation by $v(0)$ converts the v's (autocovariances) to r's (autocorrelations) and gives rise to a series of linear equations called the **Yule–Walker equations** (noting $r(-i)=r(i)$):

$$
\begin{bmatrix} r(1) \\ r(2) \\ \vdots \\ r(p) \end{bmatrix} = \begin{bmatrix} 1 & r(1) & \dots & r(p-1) \\ r(1) & 1 & \dots & r(p-2) \\ \vdots & & \dots & \dots \\ r(p-1) & r(p-2) & \dots & 1 \end{bmatrix} \begin{bmatrix} a_1 \\ a_2 \\ \vdots \\ a_p \end{bmatrix}. \tag{9.27}
$$

A **moving average process MA(q)** is one where:

$$
X_t = c + \epsilon_t - b_1 \epsilon_{t-1} - \cdots - b_q \epsilon_{t-q}. \tag{9.28}
$$

The ϵ's are i.i.d. with mean 0 and variance σ^2. We showed above in (9.23) that a stationary AR(1) process can be transformed into something that looks like an infinitely expanding MA process going back to the first shock ϵ_1. An actual MA process (9.28) only goes back a fixed number q of terms. Similarly, iterating an MA(1) process back to inception gives:

$$
X_t = c \left(\frac{1 - b_1^{t+1}}{1 - b_1} \right) + \epsilon_t - \sum_{i=1}^{t} b_1^i X_{t-i}. \tag{9.29}
$$

This looks something like an AR process, but it is infinitely expanding.

Similar to (9.24), define the characteristic polynomial for an MA(q) process:

$$
z^q - b_1 z^{q-1} - \cdots - b_q = 0. \tag{9.30}
$$

Then if the roots of (9.30) are inside the unit circle (absolute value less than one), we can invert the MA(q) process into a stationary AR process. That is, for each X_t in the MA(q) process, there will be a way to write X_t as a stationary AR(t) process similar to (9.29).

Combining AR and MA processes, we can define an **ARMA(p,q) process** as one where

$$
X_t = c + a_1 X_{t-1} + \cdots + a_p X_{t-p} + \epsilon_t - b_1 \epsilon_{t-1} - \cdots - b_q \epsilon_{t-q}. \tag{9.31}
$$

It is convenient to introduce the **backward and forward operators** B and F. For any time series Y_t, $BY_t = Y_{t-1}$, and $FY_t = Y_{t+1}$. B is sometimes called the **lag operator**.

These operators make it easier to define and manipulate time series equations. We can rewrite an ARMA(p,q) process as:

$$
X_t = c + \left(\sum_{i=1}^{p} a_i B^i \right) X_t + \left(1 - \sum_{i=1}^{q} b_i B^i \right) \epsilon_t. \tag{9.32}
$$

Assuming no unit roots of the AR characteristic equation, we can move the X_t terms to the LHS and solve for X_t:

$$X_t = \frac{c}{1 - \left(\sum_{i=1}^{p} a_i\right)} + \frac{1 - \sum_{i=1}^{q} b_i B^i}{1 - \sum_{i=1}^{p} a_i B^i}\epsilon_t. \tag{9.33}$$

We can also solve for the innovations ϵ_t:

$$\epsilon_t = \frac{-c}{1 - \left(\sum_{i=1}^{q} b_i\right)} + \frac{1 - \sum_{i=1}^{p} a_i B^i}{1 - \sum_{i=1}^{q} b_i B^i}X_t. \tag{9.34}$$

9.5 ARCH and GARCH Modeling

The **ARCH (Auto–Regressive Conditional Heteroskedasticity)** model was introduced by Robert Engle (1982). Engle started a decades-long series of investigations into related time-series-based models, and won the 2003 Sveriges Riksbank Prize in Economic Sciences in Memory of Alfred Nobel[18] for his work.

The 1982 ARCH model started with the standard Itô process for log-prices like (3.16):

$$dx = \alpha(t,x)dt + \sigma(t,x)d\beta. \tag{3.16}$$

The $\alpha(t,x)$ term is not important for volatility purposes, so Engle assumed $\alpha(t,x) = 0$. He also assumed that $\sigma(t,x) = \sigma_t$, that is, volatility is time varying but not a function of the (log) price level x. Let $y = dx$ be the time series of changes in x. Then the ARCH model is:

$$y_t = \sigma_t d\beta(t). \tag{9.35}$$

As before, each $d\beta(t)$ is an independent draw from a standard normal (or more generally mean 0, variance 1) distribution. However now σ_t – actually its square, the variance – is similar to an AR(p) process as in (9.21):

$$\sigma_t^2 = c + \sum_{i=1}^{p} a_i y_{t-i}^2 = c + \left(\sum_{i=1}^{p} a_i B^i\right) y_t^2. \tag{9.36}$$

Equations (9.35) and (9.36) together (along with the condition that y is a strongly stationary time series) constitute the ARCH(p) model.

The relationship (9.36) is not exactly autoregressive in σ_t^2, as σ_t^2 does not directly depend on earlier values of the σ^2 series. Nor is it exactly a moving average, as the y's are not i.i.d. like the ϵ's of (9.28). But it has aspects of both kinds of standard time series. Also, the time is offset so that $\sigma(t)$ is not influenced by the latest shock $d\beta(t)$; otherwise, (9.35) and (9.36) would be circular.

---

18 Nobelprize.org. "Robert Engle: Facts." Website. www.nobelprize.org/prizes/economic-sciences/2003/engle/facts/.

Heteroskedasticity (as opposed to the more tractable **homoskedasticity** that the usual condition of i.i.d. shocks imposes) refers to differing variances in the random draws taken to produce the shocks $y(t)$ in (9.35). The heteroskedasticity is conditional because it depends on previous observations of the shocks.

The ARCH model captures some aspects of the kinds of volatility regimes that we saw in the US stock market graphs. The simple relationship (9.35) indicates that when volatility is high, the shocks to our series (S&P 500 log-prices, for example) will be higher. That in turn feeds into (9.36), which averages recent shocks to get today's volatility, which will tend to be higher, which feeds on itself...

The c term in (9.36), which can be thought of as an anchor to the long-term average volatility, will dampen runaway tendencies. If the current volatility is high, then having c in the expression will pull it down; if the current volatility is low, then having c in the expression will pull it up. This is the same general idea as the long-term variance θ in the Heston model (9.11).

In practice, p is usually small; in fact, often $p = 1$. If we square (9.35) (using (9.36) with $p = 1$), the equation simplifies to:

$$y_t^2 = (c + a_1 y_{t-1}^2)d\beta(t)^2. \tag{9.37}$$

Taking expectations of both sides of (9.37) shows that in order to avoid volatility becoming unbounded over time, $|a_1| < 1$ and the long-term expected variance (as $t \to \infty$) $\mathbb{E}[\sigma_t^2] \to c/(1 - a_1)$.

Squaring both sides of (9.37) and taking expectations gives:

$$\frac{\mathbb{E}[y_t^4]}{\mathbb{E}[d\beta(t)^4]} = c^2 + 2ca_1\mathbb{E}[y_{t-1}^2] + a_1^2\mathbb{E}[y_{t-1}^4]. \tag{9.38}$$

The denominator of the left-hand side of (9.38) is the kurtosis κ_β of the innovation process; if the innovations are normal, then $\kappa_\beta = 3$. If the series is covariance stationary, then further manipulation (including the observation above that the limit as $t \to \infty$ of $\mathbb{E}[y_t^2]$ is $c/(1 - a_1)$) allows us to find the long-term equilibrium kurtosis κ_y:

$$\kappa_y = \frac{(1 - a_1^2)\kappa_\beta}{1 - a_1^2\kappa_\beta}. \tag{9.39}$$

Under reasonable conditions ($\kappa_\beta > 1$, the denominator of (9.39) is positive), we will have $\kappa_y > \kappa_\beta$. In other words, the ARCH(1) process fattens the tails and creates more unusual events than would be found in a similar homoskedastic process.

Tim Bollerslev (1986) extended the ARCH model into the **GARCH(p,q) (Generalized Auto-Regressive Conditional Heteroskedasticity)** model that is now widely used:

$$\sigma_t^2 = c + \sum_{i=1}^{p}\left(b_i\sigma_{t-i}^2\right) + \sum_{j=1}^{q}\left(a_jy_{t-j}^2\right) = c + \sum_{i=1}^{p}\left(b_iB^i\right)\sigma_t^2 + \sum_{j=1}^{q}\left(a_jB^j\right)y_t^2. \quad (9.40)$$

The GARCH model of course includes (9.35), only with the more complex variance updates shown in (9.40) replacing (9.36).

The new term is directly autoregressive in σ^2 and is similar the ARMA(p,q) model in (9.31). The autoregressive terms give persistence to volatilities, so if past volatilities were high (low) then future volatilities will tend to be high (or low). Shocks (y's) get bigger too as volatilities increase, but if there happens to be some smaller shocks then the process will go the other way and there will tend to be a prolonged period of lower variance. The constant c serves as an anchor, pulling the variance to some long-term average over time.

To make the process reasonable and stationary, we must have:

$$c > 0; \quad a_i \geq 0; \quad b_j \geq 0; \quad \sum_{i=1}^{p}b_i + \sum_{j=1}^{q}a_j < 1. \quad (9.41)$$

As with ARCH, the most commonly used form of GARCH(p,q) is the simplest: GARCH(1,1). The variance equation becomes:

$$\sigma_t^2 = c + b_1\sigma_{t-1}^2 + a_1y_{t-1}^2. \quad (9.42)$$

It can be shown that a GARCH(1,1) process has bounded volatility if and only if $a_1 + b_1 < 1$. Further, the long-term expected variance (as $t \to \infty$) is $\mathbb{E}[\sigma_t^2] = c/(1 - a_1 - b_1)$. As with ARCH(1), it can be shown that a nontrivial GARCH(1,1) process increases the kurtosis of the innovation process.

We can estimate parameters of a GARCH model by maximum likelihood. Here we assume the innovations $d\beta$ are normal. In that case, the usual log-likelihood function on normal density can be used:

$$LML(c,a_1,b_1|y_1,\ldots,y_t) = -\sum_{i=1}^{t}\ln(\sigma_i) - \sum_{i=1}^{t}\frac{y_i^2}{2\sigma_i^2}. \quad (9.43)$$

As with all log-maximum-likelihood functions, this is obtained by looking at the product $f_1(y_1)f_2(y_2),\ldots,f_t(y_t)$ where $f_i(x)$ is the appropriate pdf and y_i are the observed data. In this case, the pdfs are normal with mean 0 and standard deviations σ_i. Maximizing this product is the same as maximizing the logarithm of the product, which is the sum of the logs of the pdfs. That's what is shown in (9.43).

This is used in conjunction with the recursion for variance, (9.42). The variance series must be seeded with an initial value, which is often just taken to be the sample variance of the observations $y_1,\ldots,y_t$. That's a kind of cheating, since at time 0 we couldn't know what the future y_i's were going to be. A purer initial guess would use only information known at time 0. However, the initial guess usually doesn't make that big a difference in a sufficiently long time series.

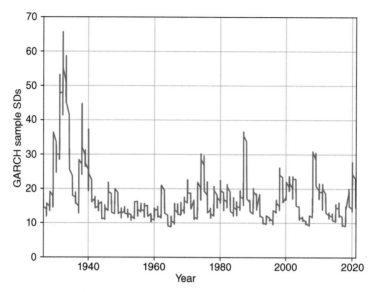

Figure 9.10 GARCH(1,1) fit to US stock market data.

Let's try this with the monthly US stock market data we showed above. We will use the cheat described in the previous paragraph and seed the process with the long-term volatility from mid-1926 to the end of last year. We found that initial value in the first code segment of this chapter. The resulting LML fit to the data is shown in Figure 9.10 (generated by Code Segment 9.11, which also outputs GARCH characteristics):

```
a=0.135
b=0.847
c=0.692

Annual sample std dev 18.4174528766247 = monthly variance
     of 28.266880871890958 bps
Stationary check (a+b less than one):  0.9819816664200475
Monthly target variance 38.422024062429585 bps
Target annualized standard deviation:  21.47240761417208
```

The parameters show that the LML solution was stationary. The long-term annualized standard deviation projected at the end of last year was a little higher than the sample standard deviation over the entire period back to mid-1926, but is of the same order of magnitude.

The "de-GARCHed" series is y_i/σ_i. Code Segment 9.12 shows that its excess kurtosis drops to about one-third of the original. It's not quite zero which would make the distribution pretty close to normal. But it's much closer:

```
Excess kurtois before and after deGarching:
     6.728574706975481 2.314680942506488
```

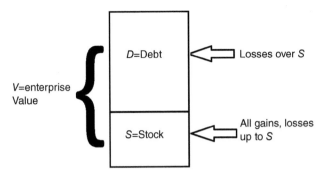

Figure 9.11 Merton model.

9.5.1 ARCH and GARCH variants

Over the years, an enormous set of variations on GARCH have been proposed and used. We will mention a few of them.

A recurring empirical regularity is an asymmetric response to returns: positive returns tend to be followed by less of an increase in volatility than do negative returns. But all the y terms in (9.40) are squared, so the GARCH(p,q) model does not differentiate between volatility responses to positive and negative returns.

For theoretical background on why this asymmetry might exist, we turn to the **Merton model**, named after Robert Merton. Merton received the Sveriges Riksbank Prize in Economic Sciences in Memory of Alfred Nobel[19] in 1997. We will talk more about this model in Chapter 11, but for now we'll see why it might suggest asymmetry.

At its simplest, the Merton (1974) model (Figure 9.11) assumes that companies (also called "enterprises") have two kinds of obligations: they have borrowed a certain amount of money, called D (for "debt"), which they need to pay back; and they have stockholders who own whatever is left over after the enterprise pays off its debt. Thus, if the enterprise's entire value is V, we have $S = V - D$ where S is the stock (also called "equity") portion of the enterprise.

But if $D > V$, that's not true: there's nothing left over for the stockholders. So more precisely, $S = \max(0, V - D)$. If $D > V$, then the debtholders don't get fully repaid; they just get V/D dollars back per dollar that they loaned. On the other hand, D is fixed – the debt holders don't participate if the company grows.

19 Nobelprize.org. "Robert C. Merton: Biographical." Website. www.nobelprize.org/prizes/economic-sciences/1997/merton/biographical/.

Merton (1974) noted that the payoff pattern to debtholders – linearly increasing in V for $0 < V < D$, and capped at D when $V > D$ – is the same as the payoff pattern to someone who owns the corporation (i.e. owns V) but who has also sold a call option on the corporation struck at price D. The stockholders own the call option on the enterprise value, struck at D.

When the call option is far in the money – that is, the value of the enterprise is much higher than D – then changes in the value of the enterprise cause comparatively small percentage changes in the value of the stock (i.e. the option on the enterprise that the stockholders own).

However, as the value of the enterprise gets smaller and closer to the value of the debt D, the percentage swings in the stock get larger and larger as the company approaches bankruptcy and the shareholders approach zero value.

This argues in favor of asymmetric impact of returns. If there is a downward shock, that gets the value of the enterprise closer to the debt barrier and should increase volatility. If there is an upward shock, that gets the value of the enterprise further away from the debt barrier and should decrease volatility. This argument – essentially that leverage increases with negative shocks – has some practical problems as it has been shown to not fully explain asymmetries, but the empirical fact of asymmetry is unassailable.

One way of dealing with asymmetry is to have a threshold on the shocks y_t. This gives rise to a variety of models with names like TARCH, TGARCH, and QTARCH. The Glosten, Jagannathan, and Runkle (1993) GJR TARCH model added a term that gave an extra boost to variance when there were negative returns:

$$\sigma_t^2 = a_1 y_{t-1}^2 + \delta(y_{t-1} < 0) a_1^- y_{t-1}^2. \tag{9.44}$$

The δ function equals one when its Boolean argument is true, and equals zero otherwise. This is like (9.36) with $p = 1$, but the extra term adds the desired asymmetry. An obvious extension can be made for $p > 1$.

Another straightforward implementation is a TGARCH (also called GJR-GARCH[20]) model, where another term for down-shocks is added to the GARCH(1,1) model in (9.42):

$$\sigma_t^2 = c + b_1 \sigma_{t-1}^2 + a_1 y_{t-1}^2 + \delta(y_{t-1} < 0) a_1^- y_{t-1}^2. \tag{9.45}$$

---

20 VLAB. "Documentation: GJR-GARCH." Website. vlab.stern.nyu.edu/docs/volatility/GJR-GARCH.

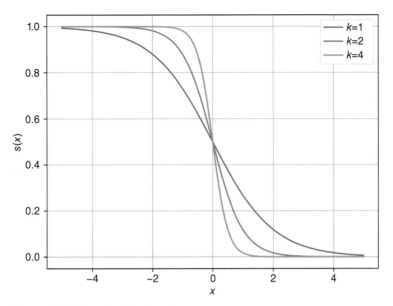

Figure 9.12 Pseudo-delta functions.

GJR-GARCH is the main market volatiity model used by the Volatility Laboratory at New York University ("V-Lab."). The V-Lab notes that if all parameters are positive and $b_1 + a_1 + \frac{a_1^-}{2} < 1$, then σ_t^2 is mean-reverting to $\frac{c}{1-b_1-a_1-\frac{a_1^-}{2}}$.

The QTARCH model generalizes the delta function from positive/negative to pick out segments of the shock distribution – for example, we could have different responses if the shock was between -1% and -5% than if it was between -5% and -12%. Of course, the more parameters that are added to a model, the more chance there is of overfitting past data and degrading out-of-sample performance.

An approach that may not suffer as much from overfitting is to change the abrupt transition caused by the delta functions in (9.44) and (9.45) to a smoother transition. Let $s(x) = 1/(1 + \exp(kx))$. Note that as $k \to \infty$, $s(x)$ becomes the delta function $\delta(x < 0)$. As we lower k, $s(x)$ still looks like the delta function but transitions more smoothly. We can use $(x - m)$ instead of x to shift the transition point. Figure 9.12 (generated by Code Segment 9.13) illustrates this pseudo-delta function for some different values of k.

Another GARCH variant is EGARCH, or Exponential GARCH. The idea is that there are various contortions of the GARCH parameters that are required to make sure that the variance comes out positive. Those contortions can be avoided by taking the log of the variance, which can range over the positive and negative real numbers while still preserving positive variance.

The EGARCH model was specified in Nelson (1991). Nelson didn't mimic the original GARCH specification directly. He had a term that took into account asymmetric responses to positive and negative shocks. Translating into terms we have used, the EGARCH(1,1) model is:

$$\ln(\sigma_t^2) = c + b_1 \ln(\sigma_{t-1}^2) + a_1 y_{t-1}^2 + \delta(y_{t-1} < 0) a_1^- y_{t-1}^2. \tag{9.46}$$

While this seems plausible, empirical tests done by Engle and Ng (1993) show that EGARCH overweights the effects of big shocks and ends up fitting actual data more poorly than the GARCH model.

For Code Segments in this chapter, see the Code Appendix starting on p. 440. For executable code, visit www.cambridge.org/9781009209090/ch9

For problem sets for this chapter, visit www.cambridge.org/ 9781009209090/ch9_problems

10 Modeling Relationships

In the previous chapter, we saw that markets in effect have moods – at times nervous, at times overconfident – that persist for a while but eventually revert to some long-term middle-of-the-road mood. We don't find it unusual when our high-strung friend has a meltdown because his socks don't match, but the same behavior in someone who is normally unflappable makes us sit up and take notice. It's the sudden change from a calm mood to panic, and the eventual relaxation back to calm, that produces fat-tailed distributions.

Fat tails would not be so concerning if they were idiosyncratic. A 10-standard-deviation event that affected only a small percentage of a portfolio would be attenuated if all the other assets in the portfolio were conducting business as usual. Fortunately, that does sometimes happen, strengthening further the case for diversification.

But relationships between securities are themselves not stable, so what may be uncorrelated behavior in one period can become correlated in another period. In this chapter, we'll analyze relationships between securities and their time-varying properties.

10.1 Pearson Correlation

The standard measure of a relationship between two random variables X and Y is due to Karl Pearson[1] and is accordingly called the **Pearson correlation**:

$$\rho(X,Y) = \frac{\mathbb{E}[(X - \mathbb{E}[X])(Y - \mathbb{E}[Y])]}{\sigma_X \sigma_Y}. \tag{10.1}$$

The standard deviations in the denominator follow from the usual definition of variance:

$$\sigma_X^2 = \mathbb{E}[(X - \mathbb{E}[X])^2]$$

and similarly for σ_Y.

Some obvious facts about the Pearson correlation follow directly from (10.1):

$$\rho(X, aX) = \begin{cases} 1, & \text{for } a > 0, \\ 0, & \text{for } a = 0, \\ -1, & \text{for } a < 0, \end{cases} \tag{10.2}$$

---

1 Encyclopedia of Mathematics. "Pearson, Karl." Website. https://encyclopediaofmath.org/wiki/Pearson,_Karl.

$$F_{X,Y}(x,y) = F_X(x)F_Y(y) \implies \rho(X,Y) = 0. \qquad (10.3)$$

In words, (10.3) says that if X and Y are independent then they are uncorrelated.

However, it is not necessarily true that if X and Y are uncorrelated, then they are independent. For example, let X be a standard normal random variable and let $Y = X^2$. Then $\mathbb{E}[X] = 0$, so $\mathbb{E}[(X - \mathbb{E}[X])(Y - \mathbb{E}[Y])] = \mathbb{E}[XY] = \mathbb{E}[X^3] = 0$ with the last equality coming about because the skewness of a normal distribution is zero. Thus, X and Y are uncorrelated. But it's intuitively clear they aren't independent; formally we could, for example, look at $F_{X,Y}(1,1)$ and note that it's the same as $F_{X,Y}(\infty, 1)$ since $Y \le 1$ means $X \le 1$. But it's not true that $F_X(1)F_Y(1) = F_X(\infty)F_Y(1)$, so they aren't independent.

Pearson correlations are very widely used and even non-statisticians have a general sense of what correlation means. News media frequently report social science studies whose main results are correlations between socially desirable or undesirable outcomes. For example, a correlation between early childhood education programs and later reduction in poverty rates might be reported. While the general public might not be able to write down (10.1) if given a spot quiz, most people understand that the reported study implies that more early childhood education helps lower poverty.

But that may not be true. Virtually every statistics class repeats the warning that **correlation is not causation**. A standard example is the supposed correlation between ice cream sales and the homicide rate. Ice cream does not cause homicides; warmer weather does. That's because more people are outside interacting, sometimes murderously. By coincidence, ice cream sales also go up in warmer weather. Clearly, banning ice cream sales would not lower the homicide rate. Would increasing early childhood education cause poverty rates to go down? Correlation neither proves nor disproves that link; it's a necessary but not sufficient condition for the link to exist.

Correlation is a unitless quantity ranging from minus one to one. Even without the complications of causation, the existence of a nonzero correlation might not even be significant. The **Fisher z-test** allows us to estimate the statistical significance of an observed correlation. The test uses the **Fisher z-transform**:

$$z(\rho) = \frac{1}{2} \ln\left(\frac{1+\rho}{1-\rho}\right) = \operatorname{arctanh}(\rho) \qquad (10.4)$$

Figure 10.1 (generated by Code Segment 10.1) shows that the z-transform is near-linear when the correlation is small in absolute value. The straight line on the graph goes through the points where the z-transform equals ± 1.

Often we are interested in whether there is any correlation between two items; in other words, we want to see if we can reject the hypothesis that the correlation is zero. The standard error (standard deviation of the sampling

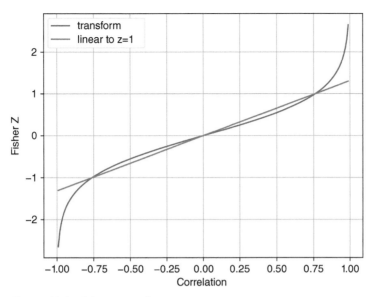

Figure 10.1 Fisher z-transform.

distribution) of the Fisher z-transform is $\frac{1}{\sqrt{n-3}}$, where n is the number of points in the sample from which we compute the sample correlation. This depends on the assumption that the two variables being correlated are bivariate normal.

So, for example, if there are 15 subjects in a sample, we need arctanh(r) > $\frac{1}{\sqrt{12}}$, or r > tanh($\frac{1}{\sqrt{12}}$) = 28.1% (or r < −28.1%) for the sample correlation r to have less than a 16% chance $(1 - F^{-1}(1)$ where F is the normal cdf) of being zero. Under the assumption of normality, an observed correlation outside the range ±56.2% has less than a 2.5% chance of occurring when the true correlation is zero.

The Fisher z-transform significance test is most useful when dealing with small samples – if n is very large, the standard error is extremely small.

10.2 Spearman Correlation

The Pearson correlation is widely used, but it has some problems. If we have observations $(x_1, y_1), \ldots, (x_n, y_n)$, then the finite version of the Pearson correlation in (10.1) is:

$$\rho(x, y) = \frac{\sum_{i=1}^{n}(x_i - \bar{x})(y_i - \bar{y})}{(n-1)s_X s_Y} \tag{10.5}$$

and $\bar{x}$, $\bar{y}$, s_x, and s_y are the sample means and standard deviations.

Large unusual observations – or just plain data errors – can affect the number disproportionately. For example, suppose we have the following observations of two quantities at six different times:

Time period	x observation	y observation
1	1	1
2	−0.1	−0.1
3	1.5	1.5
4	1.7	1.7
5	−1	−1
6	5	−2

The first five observations are the same and therefore have 100% correlation. However, the last large observation makes the overall correlation (10.5) negative (−28%). Depending on one's intuition about the importance of the dissonant observation, this may seem dissatisfying.

A variation on Pearson correlation that addresses this problem is due to Charles Spearman.[2] The **Spearman correlation** works from ranks rather than from direct data.

Looking down the "x observation" column of the data table above, we see that in the first time period, the x observation is the number 1 which is the fourth biggest x: 5, 1.7, and 1.5 are bigger and −0.1 and −1 are smaller. For y observations, the 1 in the first time period is the third biggest. To compute a Spearman correlation, we would replace the first time period's observations with their ranks 4 and 3. Transforming the whole data table into a table of ranks gives:

Time period	x rank	y rank
1	4	3
2	5	4
3	3	2
4	2	1
5	6	5
6	1	6

The Spearman correlation is just the Pearson correlation of the rank table. The Pearson correlation between the two rank columns (i.e. the Spearman correlation of the original data) is 14.3 percent. The fact that the components

2 The Royal Society Publishing. "Biographical Memoirs of Fellows of The Royal Society: Charles Spearman." Website. https://doi.org/10.1098/rsbm.1947.0006.

of the last pair of observations are at complete opposite ends of the spectrum does bring down the correlation, but it doesn't make it negative since the other five observations are more aligned.

More generally, if we have a rank function r_x so that $x(r_x(1)) \geq x(r_x(2)) \geq \cdots \geq x(r_x(n))$, and similarly for y, then we look at the pairs $(r_x^{-1}(1), r_y^{-1}(1)), (r_x^{-1}(2), r_y^{-1}(2)), \ldots, (r_x^{-1}(n), r_y^{-1}(n))$. Ties are treated by taking the average of the ranks that are tied, that is, if the fourth and fifth biggest observations are the same then they are both given rank 4.5. The average of the numbers from 1 to n is $(n+1)/2$. So for the Spearman correlation, (10.5) becomes:

$$\rho_{Spearman}(x,y) = \frac{\sum_{i=1}^{n}\left(r_x^{-1}(i)r_y^{-1}(i)\right) - n\frac{(n+1)^2}{4}}{(n-1)s_{r_x^{-1}}s_{r_y^{-1}}}. \tag{10.6}$$

Here $s_{r_x^{-1}}$ is the standard deviation of the ranks of the x's, which will be roughly $\sqrt{\frac{n^2-1}{2}}$, with variation depending on how many ranks are tied. Similarly for $s_{r_y^{-1}}$.

Code Segment 10.2 performs calculations for the Pearson/Spearman example, producing the following output:

```
X data: [1, -0.1, 1.5, 1.7, -1, 5]
X ranks: [4. 5. 3. 2. 6. 1.]
Y data: [1, -0.1, 1.5, 1.7, -1, -2]
Y ranks: [3. 4. 2. 1. 5. 6.]
Pearson correlation: -0.2844419046262927
Spearman correlation from Pearson ranks:
       0.14285714285714285
Spearman from scipy: 0.14285714285714288
```

10.3 Conditional Correlation

Often in financial applications there are time series of prices or returns or log-returns, and we're interested in estimating future correlations between them. The correlations we've seen so far are static. They assume that there is a stationary underlying process being analyzed. But what if that's not true?

Conditional correlation is defined in a time series context. Assume we are observing stochastic processes X_u and Y_u. We want to know what we expect the correlation to be at some later time t based on what we knew at some earlier time s. That is, if $s < t$, we compute:

$$\rho_s(X_t, Y_t) = \frac{\mathbb{E}_s[(X_t - \mathbb{E}_s[X_t])(Y_t - \mathbb{E}_s[Y_t])]}{\sigma_s(X_t)\sigma_s(Y_t)}. \tag{10.7}$$

Is this necessary? Maybe correlations are constant over time and we just need to compute a single unconditional correlation. It should be pretty clear that things will not be this easy, but let's check the data.

Code Segment 10.3 imports daily log-returns of three regional stock indices – North America, Europe, and Japan – going back to mid-1990. However, daily returns will give us misleading correlations due to **asynchronous trading**. The time zones of the three regions are quite different: during overlapping daylight savings regimes, London markets are open from 3 a.m. to 11:30 a.m. New York time. Tokyo markets are open from 8 p.m. to 2 a.m. New York time; Hong Kong from 9:30 p.m. to 4 a.m. New York time, both one day ahead across the International Date Line. Thus a given date's closing price reflects different sets of information across geographically disparate markets, lowering correlation artificially.

Over longer time periods this effect is less noticeable – a matter of hours out of a month or even a week is not as significant. So we'll mitigate the asynchronous trading effect by changing the daily log-returns to weekly (Wednesday-Wednesday) returns. Wednesdays are usually preferred for weekly data as they tend to be least subject to holidays and end-of-week economic data announcements. We use a weekly periodicity rather than a monthly periodicity because it removes most of the asynchronicity while still having a robust number of observations. Code Segment 10.3's output looks like this:

```
Inputting   Europe
Inputting   North_America
Inputting   Japan
1644   weekly observations starting 1990-07-04 ending
       2021-12-29
```

With the data acquired, Code Segment 10.4 computes the 3×3 correlation matrix and the standard deviations of these securities:

```
Correlation matrix and standard deviations (10.8):
                 Europe  North_America      Japan
Europe         1.000000       0.759062   0.500087
North_America  0.759062       1.000000   0.400097
Japan          0.500087       0.400097   1.000000
Annualized standard deviations:
 [0.1841786644194622, 0.16588764601126615,
    0.20247265313094603]
Correlation significance: 0.02468070178833984
```

Comparing these correlations with $\tanh\left(\frac{1}{\sqrt{n-3}}\right)$ (see text after (10.4)) shows that all are significantly nonzero, as we would expect with so much data.

Using these correlations (and variances), Code Segment 10.5 computes the global minimum variance portfolio of the three regional indices:

```
Minimum variance portfolio:
Europe          0.085593
North_America   0.595845
Japan           0.318562
Minimum variance portfolio annualized std deviation: 0.
      15054193150005715
Lowest component annualized std deviation
      0.16588764601126615 ( North_America )
```

Recall from Chapter 4 that the variance of the global minimum variance portfolio is $\frac{1}{u^\intercal C^{-1} u}$ where C is the covariance matrix. Expanding the data in (10.8) into a covariance matrix and performing the calculation gives an annualized standard deviation that is lower than that of the lowest individual component standard deviation. Once again, portfolio construction taking advantage of diversification mitigated the risk while still participating in the linear combination of returns of the components.

But that was in the past. What about the future?

We'll first test the stability of an artificially generated series as we did in Chapter 9. Code Segment 10.6 takes weekly draws from an artificial reality generated by a multivariate normal distribution with zero means and covariance matrix equal to the correlation matrix in (10.8). It then shows the three trailing 52-week correlation pairs in Figure 10.2.

```
Cholesky:
  [[1.          0.          0.         ]
   [0.75906193 0.65101843 0.         ]
   [0.50008736 0.03148857 0.86540228]]

Standard Error =   0.14189319376693255
```

There's a lot of sampling variation. The standard error of a 52-week sample is 14.2%, which is larger than the difference between the two smaller correlation pairs. Figure 10.2 shows at most times that Europe/North America is the highest correlation, but the other two correlation pairs are often reversed.

Taking longer samples – three years (156 weeks) with standard error $\tanh\left(\frac{1}{\sqrt{156-3}}\right) \approx 8.1\%$ – produces a clearer picture (Figure 10.3, generated by Code Segment 10.7).

```
Standard Error =   0.08066953425829816
```

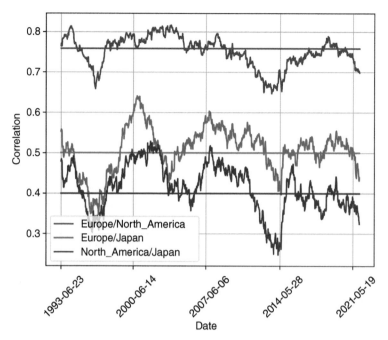

Figure 10.2 Simulated 52-week sample correlations.

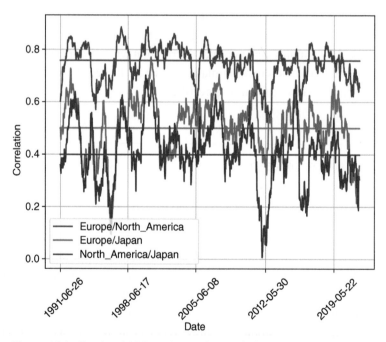

Figure 10.3 Simulated 156-week sample correlations.

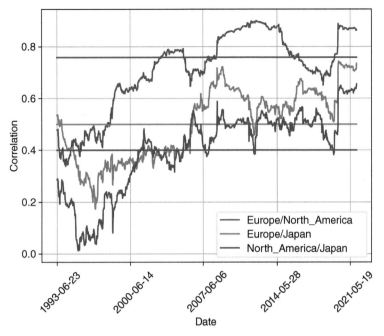

Figure 10.4 Historical 156-week sample correlations.

Figure 10.4 (generated by Code Segment 10.8) shows the historical 156-week correlations. It's clear that something more than sampling variation is going on. For example, over the first three years of the dataset, the Europe/North America sample correlation was lower than the Europe/Japan sample correlation.

10.4 Correlations and the Economy

It's important to try to anticipate what correlations will be.[3] This matters not just to investment portfolios, but also to the economy as a whole. A portfolio or economy that is diversified can better withstand the inevitable shocks that come as the unknown future unfolds.

Countries whose economies are driven by a single commodity are vulnerable to price and demand shocks in that commodity. These countries often seek to diversify their economies by encouraging the development of businesses that have low correlation with the primary commodity. For example, Saudi Arabia has been trying for decades to lower its dependence on oil revenues. The current plan, Saudi Vision 2030,[4] boasts that:

---

3 *Anticipating Correlations* is the title of a book by Robert Engle, stressing the importance of this kind of forecasting activity [Engle 2009]. The implementations reported in Section 10.8 are based on [Engle 2009].

4 Kingdom of Saudi Arabia. "Vision 2030." Website. https://vision2030.gov.sa/en.

> We are determined to reinforce and diversify the capabilities of our economy, turning our key strengths into enabling tools for a fully diversified future. As such, we will transform Aramco from an oil producing company into a global industrial conglomerate. ...

A polite word to use about the Saudis' success with these plans so far is "mixed."

But in broadly diversified economies like those of the USA and the EU, regions and industries that have low (or at least not perfect) correlation provide opportunities to keep most workers engaged in productive activity. If the construction industry in Nevada is doing badly, then maybe the meat packing plant in Nevada is thriving and hiring workers. Or maybe the construction industry in Iowa is booming.

If the vast majority of a nation's workforce is productively employed, then they have a better chance of collectively producing enough goods and services to make the nation prosper. But in an economy where all business activity is highly correlated, a downturn will lead directly to unemployment: there's nowhere else to work. The idling of significant portions of the workforce lowers the chance that net output is enough to have general prosperity.

Even good times in a highly correlated economy or market can lead to problems. Economies and markets need creative destruction – there have to be losers such as obsolete industries or technologies that go into decline when new industries or technologies come along. If everything is going up, people lose their motivation to distinguish between the good and the less good and to seek a reasonable price level. This creates bubbles. For example, average house prices in the USA went up every quarter for almost 15 years, from third quarter 1992 through first quarter 2007. Figure 10.5 (generated by Code Segment 10.9) shows that runup in prices, and what happened after that.

House prices fell every quarter from second quarter 2007 through second quarter 2011 before finally starting to recover. It took nine years for house prices to get back to their level at the end of first quarter 2007.

A key component of the overheated market leading to this crash was a mistaken belief that house prices in the USA were geographically well diversified. It was thought that house prices in Florida had little relationship to house prices in (say) Nevada. This in turn led to banks and investors believing that they would be protected against large downturns if they had a geographically diversified portfolio of mortgages. Investors badly misestimated the correlation matrix between segments of the housing market.

As a result of this misestimation, what in retrospect were too many dollars then flowed into the housing market, misdirecting productive activity into building houses that were not needed. In the second quarter of 2007 the bubble began to burst as house prices declined in a highly correlated way virtually everywhere in the USA.

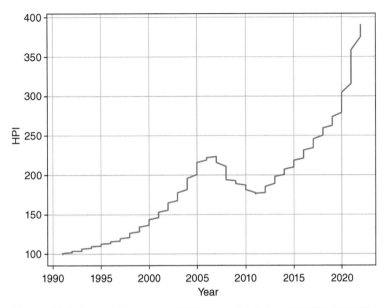

Figure 10.5 Seasonally adjusted US house price index 1991Q1–2022Q2.

If we could simply predict precisely which activities were going to be useful and therefore profitable, we wouldn't need to worry about predicting correlations. But if we had such predictive powers, there would be neither Knightian Risk nor Knightian Uncertainty in the world. That's not the world we live in.

Thus, to form a good investment portfolio – which in turn helps to direct the economy in the appropriate directions – we want to avoid gross errors in estimating correlations like those made in the housing market. A well-diversified portfolio is a portfolio that is resilient to the future unfolding in ways we couldn't anticipate.

Unfortunately, there is a tendency for correlations to go up in bad markets as investors and business owners become more concerned with the overall economy than with the health of a particular venture. This can lead to "risk-on/risk-off" (sometimes called "RORO") regimes where most risky assets rise together when there is overall good economic news ("risk-on") and most risky assets fall together when there is overall bad economic news ("risk-off").

However, even in risk-off regimes, not everything does poorly. Some assets are considered safe havens against economic storms. They may be deemed too unexciting in a risk-on regime, but when things are going badly the cliché is that "return of capital becomes more important than return on capital." In that case, boring but safe is exactly what investors want.

Safety assets can include US Treasurys, Japanese Government Bonds ("JGBs"), gold, and sometimes cryptocurrencies. The correlations between these safety assets become extremely high in risk off regimes, while their correlations

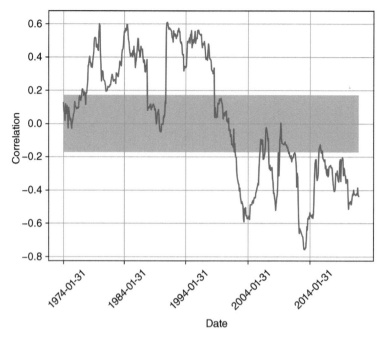

Figure 10.6 US stock/bond 36-month correlations 1974-01-31 to 2021-12-31 (gray=insignificant).

with risky assets become quite negative. This is another example of the type of regime shifting we have discussed.

But there are no guarantees. For example while US Treasurys have provided good diversification from US stocks since the late 1990s, before that they tended to correlate positively with US stocks, as shown in Figure 10.6 (generated by Code Segment 10.10).

The positive correlations seen in the USA before the 2000s were more like stock/bond correlations in emerging markets, where both government bonds and the stock market are strongly influenced by the health of the overall economy and thus have generally positive correlations. It is anyone's guess how long US Treasurys or JGBs will continue to provide safety in market downturns.

10.5 Implied Correlations

In Chapter 9, we looked both at volatilities obtained from historical log-returns, and at volatilities implied by option prices. The attraction of option-implied volatilities is that since the prices of options move every time the option trades, we get an instant update on the implied volatility. We don't have to smooth over many months or years.

Are there option-implied correlations? Not exactly. There are correlations implied from models of tranched credit; we'll discuss those later in this chapter.

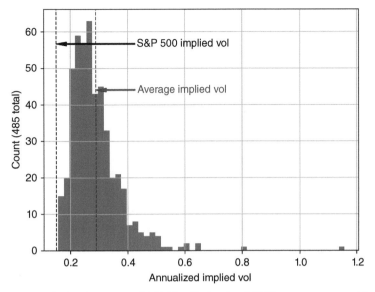

Figure 10.7 Histogram of ATM implied vols of SPY components expiring 2022-03-18, quoted 2021-12-31.

However, these correlations are narrowly applicable to the default times of particular assets such as specific pools of loans and are not broadly applicable.

There is a method that uses option-implied volatilities to infer a single marketwide average correlation between a typical pair of stocks. For this method to work, there must exist traded options on a portfolio (such as the Standard & Poor's 500® Index) and on all the components of the portfolio (such as the 500 stocks in the S&P 500). The general idea is that the implied volatility of the portfolio is a function of the covariance matrix, which contains variances and correlations. The method extracts an average correlation from the difference between the portfolio's variance and its component variances.

Specifically, if Var_{port} is the variance of the portfolio, then:

$$Var_{port} = w^{\mathsf{T}} C w = \sum_{i=1}^{n} \sum_{j=1}^{n} w_i w_j \sigma_i \sigma_j \rho_{ij}. \tag{10.9}$$

The volatilities (σ_i's) of component securities have a wide range. Figure 10.7 (generated by Code Segment 10.11) shows the distribution of annualized volatilities of 500 stocks that make up the exchange-traded-fund (ETF) SPY,[5] which is close to the S&P 500. Code Segment 10.11 also produces the following statistics regarding the SPY and its components:

---

5 State Street Global Advisors. "SPDR®S&P 500®ETF Trust." Website. www.ssga.com/us/en/ individual/etfs/funds/spdr-sp-500-etf-trust-spy.

```
506 SPY tickers input,    0.790 seconds
48618 SPY options input,   45.119 seconds
496 SPY tickers matched with options,   6.770 seconds
7612 SPX options input,    7.024 seconds

SPX implied: 0.15005000000000002
Number greater: 495
Average implied: 0.2893586525537634
Implied correlation per formula (10.10):
        0.29993803783291334
```

Figure 10.7, which is based on cross-sectional rather than time series data, looks roughly lognormal. Note the "Number greater" output by the previous code cell shows that almost all of the individual stocks in the S&P 500 have greater implied volatilities than does the index itself, as expected. This means the portfolio is benefiting from diversification, that is, comparatively low average correlations.

Note that the weighted average correlation between a pair of different stocks in a portfolio of n stocks looks like $\sum_{i=1}^{n} \sum_{j\neq i} x_{i,j} \rho_{i,j}$, where $x_{i,j} > 0$ is the weight given to the (i,j) correlation. The weights must sum to one: $1 = \sum_{i=1}^{n} \sum_{j\neq i} x_{i,j}$.

A natural weighting scheme is $x_{i,j} = \dfrac{v_i v_j}{\sum_{k=1}^{n} \sum_{m\neq i} v_k v_m}$, where $v_i = w_i \sigma_i$. This gives:

$$\rho_{average} = \sum_{i=1}^{n} \sum_{j\neq i} x_{i,j} \rho_{i,j} = \frac{\sum_{i=1}^{n} \sum_{j\neq i} v_i v_j \rho_{ij}}{\sum_{i=1}^{n} \sum_{j\neq i} v_i v_j} = \frac{Var_{port} - \sum_{i=1}^{n} v_i^2}{\overline{\sigma}_{port}^2 - \sum_{i=1}^{n} v_i^2}, \quad (10.10)$$

where Var_{port} is from (10.9) and the average portfolio standard deviation is $\overline{\sigma}_{port} = \sum_{i=1}^{n} v_i$.

The rightmost equality in (10.10) is computed from market observables:

- Var_{port} is the square of volatility implied by the prices of S&P 500 (portfolio) options; and
- $v_i = w_i \sigma_i$ is the product of the known weight w_i of the ith portfolio component times σ_i, the volatility implied by prices of options on component i.

Inputting these observables into (10.10) as of the end of last year gave the "Implied correlation" number reported by Code Segment 10.11.

Note that if $\sqrt{Var_{port}} = \overline{\sigma}_{port} = \sum_{i=1}^{n} v_i$, there has been no diversification benefit in the portfolio. That provides an intuitive checkpoint for the rightmost expression in (10.10): in that case, the numerator and denominator are the same and the average correlation is 1 as expected.

Another intuitive checkpoint can be seen when all the correlations are zero: in that case, the variance of the portfolio results only from the diagonal terms

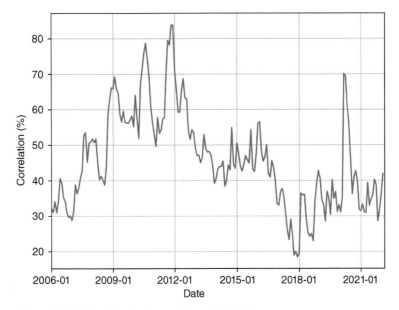

Figure 10.8 Cboe implied correlations COR3M.

of the covariance matrix: $Var_{port} = \sum_{i=1}^{n} w_i^2 \sigma_i^2 = \sum_{i=1}^{n} v_i^2$. In that case, the numerator of the rightmost expression in (10.10) is indeed zero.

Cboe, the largest US options exchange, maintains an index that continually carries out the calculation in (10.10).[6] Figure 10.8 (generated by Code Segment 10.12) shows how average US stock correlations have moved since 2007.

Before the GFC ("Global Financial Crisis") of 2008–2009, average pair correlations in the USA were around 40%. During and after the GFC, correlations shot up in the RORO markets that ensued. It took about 10 years for average pair correlations to drop back down to the vicinity of 40%. Correlations shot up again in March 2020 in response to the COVID-19 pandemic and were unstable for more than a year after that.

While Figure 10.8 appears to show that implied correlation is a trailing indicator of market conditions, Buss, Schönleber, and Vilkov (2019) show empirical evidence that implied correlation is a robust predictor of long-term market returns.

Buss et al. note that the individual variances σ_i^2 seen in (10.10) can be decomposed into a β_i component (i.e. a Capital Asset Pricing Model beta to the market portfolio *port*) and an idiosyncratic (non-market) component. They consider the interplay between implied market variance Var_{port}, implied idiosyncratic variance, and the implied dispersion of market betas across the members of the portfolio. By looking at the interplay between these components

---

6 Cboe actually uses a sampling technique; only the 3-month implied volatilities of the 50 largest components of the 500-security index are taken into account. https://go.cboe.com/l/77532/2021-10-14/bwm39g.

of the implied correlation calculation, Buss et al. find evidence that implied correlation is a leading procyclical state variable for macroeconomic conditions up to 18 months ahead. This work was done before the COVID-19 pandemic.

10.6 Copula Functions

To understand fully the relationships between a number of different items – say, scalar random variables $X_1, \ldots, X_n$ – we need to know the full joint distribution:

$$F_{\mathbf{X}}(x_1, \ldots, x_n) = Pr(X_1 \leq x_1, \ldots, X_n \leq x_n). \tag{10.11}$$

Here $\mathbf{X} = (X_1, \ldots, X_n)$ is the vector containing all the scalar random variables. This joint distribution function contains much more information than a covariance matrix, which averages over the entire distribution in some way.

We saw, for example, that the Europe/North America correlation was high over the many hundreds of weekly observations that we used. So there was a strong tendency for Europe to do well when North America did well. But it's possible that there were nonlinear complications to this relationship. Suppose as a thought experiment that when returns were less than 5 percent in absolute value, there was no relationship between Europe and North America, and only extreme returns were highly correlated. We might have been planning to incorporate an options strategy that limited large moves, so in this case we would be able to use Europe and North America to diversify each other if we thought the past relationships would continue.

We've been using covariance matrices to describe relationships (which are contained in a correlation matrix) and volatility levels (which can be specified in a vector or in a diagonal matrix). In Chapter 9, we saw how constant scalar volatilities were unrealistic descriptions of empirical reality, and how models like GARCH could better describe and anticipate real-world financial distributions.

The process of decomposing a covariance matrix into a correlation matrix and a set of volatilities has an analogy in the context of joint distributions: Define scalar **marginal distributions** F_i:

$$F_i(x) = Pr(X_1 \leq \infty, \ldots, X_i \leq x, \ldots, X_n \leq \infty). \tag{10.12}$$

By setting all the arguments (except the ith) of the joint distribution function to infinity, we remove any variation due to those other items. F_i is a univariate cumulative distribution function for each i.

The marginal distributions contain information on each variable's volatility, but they contain much more than that. What's left over after the marginal distributions are removed is a copula function, which is analogous to the correlation matrix that is left over after volatilities are removed from the covariance matrix.

To develop this intuitive idea formally, we start by noting that if a scalar real random variable Y has a cdf F, we can define another random variable U with range equal to the unit interval $[0,1]$ as $U = F(Y)$. U is called the **quantiles** of Y. If the original cdf F is invertible, then the cdf of U is:

$$F_U(u) = Pr(U \le u) = Pr(F(Y) \le u) = Pr(Y \le F^{-1}(u)) = F(F^{-1}(u)) = u. \quad (10.13)$$

Equation (10.13) says that U is a uniform random variable. The process of moving from the original random variable X to its quantiles U is essentially the same as finding quantiles for a P-P plot (Section 7.1.1). This process was also used to move from the Pearson correlation to the Spearman correlation in Section 10.2. While that section used a discrete approach, more generally we can define:

$$Corr_{Spearman}(W,Y) = Corr_{Pearson}(F_W(W),F_Y(Y)) = Corr_{Pearson}(U_W, U_Y),$$

where $F_W(w)$ and $F_Y(y)$ are the cdfs for W and Y, respectively. U_W and U_Y are their respective quantiles. $Corr_{Pearson}$ is the ρ defined in (10.1).

For each one of the random variables $X_1, X_2, \ldots, X_n$ whose joint distribution was given in (10.11), we can define its quantiles $U_i = F_i(X_i)$ from its marginal distribution F_i. If the marginal distributions are invertible, then the random variables $U_1, \ldots, U_n$ are all uniformly distributed and thus don't contain much information by themselves. But the relationships between them can be quite complex, as dictated by the original joint distribution function (10.11).

Formally, a **copula function** is the joint distribution of the U_i:

$$C(u_1, \ldots, u_n) = Pr(U_1 \le u_1, \ldots, U_n \le u_n). \quad (10.14)$$

The domain of a copula function on n variables is the unit n-cube $[0,1]^n$, while its range is the unit interval $[0,1]$. It's a joint distribution function like (10.11), but its marginal distributions are all uniform. We can remind ourselves explicitly of the connection between the original joint distribution function (10.11) and the uniform-ized copula (10.14) by writing it like this:

$$C(u_1, \ldots, u_n) = Pr(X_1 \le F_1^{-1}(u_1), \ldots, X_n \le F_n^{-1}(u_n)). \quad (10.15)$$

The decomposition of (10.11) into marginals (10.12) and a copula function (10.14) is summed up in:

Sklar's Theorem[7] *Any joint distribution $F_X(x_1, \ldots, x_n)$ can be represented as a copula function $C(\cdot)$ of its univariate marginal distributions:*

$$F_X(x_1, \ldots, x_n) = C(F_1(x_1), \ldots, F_n(x_n)). \quad (10.16)$$

When the marginals are continuous, $C(\cdot)$ is uniquely defined. Conversely, any copula function taking any univariate distributions $\{F_i(x_i)\}$ as its arguments defines a valid joint distribution with marginals $\{F_i(x_i)\}$.

7 Sklar's Theorem is due to Abe Sklar in 1959. This version is from [Eidan 2012], p. 41.

Moving from the joint cdf to the joint pdf is straightforward as long as $C(\cdot)$ has nth partial derivatives. Taking the partial derivative of (10.16) with respect to every variable gives the pdf, which we denote by lowercase letters to distinguish it from the cdf:

$$\frac{\partial^n F_{\mathbf{X}}(x_1,\ldots,x_n)}{\partial x_1,\ldots,\partial x_n} = c(F_1(x_1),\ldots,F_n(x_n))f_1(x_1)\cdot f_2(x_2),\ldots,f_n(x_n). \quad (10.17)$$

Here, $f_i(x_i) = \frac{dF_i(x_i)}{dx_i}$ is the ith marginal density and $c(u_1,\ldots,u_n) = \frac{\partial^n C(u_1,\ldots,u_n)}{\partial u_1,\ldots,\partial u_n}$. (10.17) is analogous to saying that the covariance between two items equals their correlation times their standard deviations.

10.6.1 Copula Example: Gaussian Copulas

The **Gaussian (normal) copula** is widely used in practice. Let $F_S(x)$ be the standard mean-zero variance-one normal cdf. Let R be an $n \times n$ correlation matrix. Let $F_{Norm,R}(x_1,\ldots,x_n)$ be the joint cdf of a multivariate normal distribution with mean vector all zeroes and covariance matrix R. (Among other things, that means that the marginal variances of this distribution are all one.) The Gaussian (normal) copula is:

$$C_{Norm,R}(u_1,\ldots,u_n) = F_{Norm,R}(F_S^{-1}(u_1),\ldots,F_S^{-1}(u_n)). \quad (10.18)$$

It may seem disappointing that, after developing the powerful and fully general copula mechanism in the previous section, a model just slips back into using a familiar (and unrealistically low-kurtosis) multivariate normal distribution. But there is a benefit even in this familiar setup. When the full joint distribution is written using Sklar's Theorem:

$$F_{\mathbf{X}}(x_1,\ldots,x_n) = C_{Norm,R}(F_1(x_1),\ldots,F_n(x_n)),$$

any univariate distributions can be used as the marginals $F_i(x_i)$. These marginals could be Student's T distributions, mixtures of normals, or even empirical distributions gathered from observed historical data without imposing a model. A Gaussian copula model can therefore aim for more realistic fat-tailed behavior while preserving simple relationships.

We'll show how Gaussian copulas are applied to financial structures called **collateralized debt obligations ("CDOs")**.[8] CDOs are financially engineered products that aim to tailor risk levels to investors' requirements. We will assume away many of the complications that are found in practice since we just want to give the general idea of the application of copulas to these products.

---

8 There are many collateralized products with initials "CxO," where in addition to x = D for debt, there can be x = B for bond, x = L for loan; x = M for mortgage; and other kinds of **structured finance** arrangements. There are even CxOs consisting of CxOs, called CxO-squareds. We will use CDO as a generic term for these kinds of structures.

The assets of a CDO consist of a portfolio of bonds. For simplicity, let's suppose that there are 100 bonds each priced at par at the outset of the CDO. Further suppose that the CDO invests $1 million in each bond, so that the CDO's total assets are worth $100 million at its inception. The bonds in a CDO are not default free.

Ownership of these assets is sliced up into several pieces. The French word for "slice" is *tranche*; the process of dividing up ownership of one of these structures is called "tranching" in Franglais. For simplicity we'll assume that three tranches are used, although in practice the number of tranches is often much higher.

The three parts in our simplified example are:

- A **senior tranche** that has a claim on the first $60 million of assets;
- A **mezzanine tranche** that has a claim on the middle $25 million of assets; and
- An **equity tranche** that has a claim on the bottom $15 million of assets.

At maturity of the CDO, if its total assets are worth more than $60 million, the senior tranche is fully repaid. If the CDO's total assets are worth more than $85 million, both the senior and mezzanine tranches are fully repaid. Any value over $85 million is paid to the equity tranche. The delimiters of each tranche are called its **attachment point** (bottom) and its **detachment point** (top). In the example, the mezzanine tranche's attachment point is at $15 million and its detachment point is at $40 million.

Thus, the senior tranche is the safest and is appropriate for investors with low risk tolerance. These tranches are often rated AAA – highest credit quality – by credit rating agencies. Even when bonds, loans, and mortgages default, there is some recovery of principal. Typical recovery rates are around 40%. So virtually every asset in our example structure would have to default before 40% of the value was destroyed and the senior tranche was impaired. That level of defaults has never been experienced, not even in the Global Financial Crisis of 2008. Of course, a particular structure could consist of particularly unlucky assets, but it would be fantastically unlikely that the senior tranche would be impaired. Accordingly, a comparatively small percentage of the coupon payments being collected on the entire CDO is allocated to the senior tranche.

While a senior tranche is engineered to be especially safe, an equity tranche is engineered for investors with high risk tolerances. Any default in the pool of 100 CDO assets will hurt the equity tranche, up to 15% of value. After that, it doesn't matter because the equity tranche has lost all its value. Dour wits in the financial markets have nicknamed equity tranches "toxic waste" because the bad debts in the CDO pool will collect there. Why would anyone buy toxic waste? Because the compensation is high: a comparatively large percentage of the coupon payments being collected on the entire CDO is allocated to the equity tranche.

To value these tranches, investors focus on a key variable for defaultable bonds: the time between now and when the bond's issuer will run out of money and not be able to repay its debts. That time is not knowable in the present, so time to default is modeled as a random variable. If the average of the time to default variable is centuries from now and the bond matures in 10 years, then default is not a concern. But if the average time to default is earlier than the maturity, the investor will probably not be repaid.

For a CDO and its tranches, the relationships between the asset times to default (100 of them in our example) are crucial. If times to default are independent, then there may be a few defaults affecting the equity tranche, but it's unlikely that so many defaults will pile up that the senior tranche is affected. But if there is a strong relationship between times to default, it's possible that in a bad market there could be a lot of defaults at the same time and the higher tranches could be affected.

Li (2000) introduced the use of Gaussian copulas to model relationships between times to default. For about seven years thereafter, trillions of dollars worth of collateralized obligations were modeled using Gaussian copulas.

This model – or more precisely the assumptions people used when applying this model – proved to disastrously overvalue many tranches of collateralized obligations. A typical post-crash comment on the Li copula function model is an article by Felix Salmon with the sensational title "Recipe for Disaster: The Formula That Killed Wall Street."[9]

Li assumed that the default time of the ith asset in a CDO is modeled as an exponential, that is, the ith asset has a hazard rate λ_i so that $F_i(t) = 1 - \exp(-\lambda_i t)$ is the cdf of the asset's default time. So if τ_i is the random variable giving the default time of the ith asset, then the probability that the asset defaults before time t is $F_i(t)$.

In this framework, there is a common market factor M that affects all assets, so we can define:

$$Norm^{-1}(F_i(\tau_i)) = X_i = \sqrt{\rho_i}M + \sqrt{1 - \rho_i}\epsilon_i. \qquad (10.19)$$

Li transformed $\tau_i = F_i^{-1}(Norm(X_i))$ since it will turn out to be more convenient to let X_i give the correlation structure of defaults. $Norm()$ is the standard normal cdf. M and ϵ_i are standard normals, and correlations between M and ϵ_i and between ϵ_i and $\epsilon_j, j \neq i$ are zero.

ϵ_i is the idiosyncratic default behavior of the ith asset in the CDO. The correlation matrix R therefore has $Corr(X_i, X_j) = \sqrt{\rho_i \rho_j}$, while the correlation (and covariance) of X_i with itself is one.

---

9 [Salmon 2009].

The connection between τ_i and X_i can be rewritten:

$$F_i(t) = Pr(\tau_i \le t) = Pr(F_i(\tau_i) \le F_i(t)) = Pr(Norm(X_i) \le F_i(t)). \quad (10.20)$$

This shows that $Norm(X_i)$ is the uniformly distributed marginal that appears in a copula function. Further, at a given level m of the market variable M, we have:

$$Pr(Norm(X_i) \le F_i(T)|M = m) = Pr(\epsilon_i \le \frac{Norm^{-1}(F_i(t)) - \sqrt{\rho_i M}}{\sqrt{1 - \rho_i}}|M = m). \quad (10.21)$$

Putting all the variables together as in Sklar's Theorem, we have:

$$Pr(\tau_1 \le t_1, \ldots, \tau_n \le t_n) = C_{Gauss, R}(F_1(t_1), \ldots, F_n(t_n)). \quad (10.22)$$

The residuals ϵ_i are independent by construction. So we can put (10.21) and (10.22) together and integrate over all realizations of the market factor M to get:

$$Pr(\tau_1 \le t_1, \ldots, \tau_n \le t_n)$$
$$= \frac{1}{\sqrt{2\pi}} \int_{-\infty}^{\infty} \left[\left(\prod_{i=1}^{n} Norm \left(\frac{Norm^{-1}(F_i(t_i)) - \sqrt{\rho_i}m}{\sqrt{1 - \rho_i}} \right) \right) \exp(-m^2/2) \right] dm$$
$$\quad (10.23)$$

This is a messy integral, but it can be done numerically. The marginal hazard rates λ_i can be obtained from market observables like credit default swap spreads. We can then compute the probability that enough assets default to impair a tranche of interest. For example the mezzanine tranche in our three-tranche example would not be impaired until 15% of the asset value was destroyed. After 40% of the asset value was destroyed, the mezzanine tranche would be worthless.

For convenience, market participants make the heroic leap that $\rho_i = \rho$ for all i. That is, there is only one average correlation that matters. This is thought of something like an implied volatility in an option pricing context: we can solve for the ρ that makes the observed price of a tranche of a structure equal to the market price.

There isn't the slightest chance that this assumption actually reflects reality; it's simply a computational convenience. The general idea was that the differing correlations would average out in some way so that a single correlation would be good enough. After all, as we saw in a different context in Chapter 4, Elton, Gruber, and Padberg (1978) claimed that the only information off the diagonal in an equity correlation matrix was the average correlation. So why not default times?

Two things went badly wrong with this assumption. One, which should have been a clue that something was wrong, was that in many cases in order to fit observed market prices, a tranche correlation of $\rho > 100\%$ needed to be assumed. This was assumed to be a quirk of the market and a method (called **base correlation**) was contrived to avoid seeing correlations over 100%.

A second related problem was that in projecting forward what tranche prices should be based on this model, the assumed physical (as opposed to risk-neutral) correlations were far too low. In fact it turned out that the correlation of subprime mortgages and many other kinds of collateral was far greater than assumed, so that when defaults started, the AAA-rated senior tranches that expected to benefit from a low-correlation subordination buffer below them in fact found that everything went bad at once. Some of the senior tranches were compromised, and even more of them were feared to be compromised whether or not they actually were compromised.

The insurance company AIG got into trouble insuring senior tranches of structured products. Normally, insurance companies need to set aside large buffers to make sure that if something bad happens, they can pay off insurance claims. But structured product insurance was exempt from normal insurance rules. AIG was allowed to rely on the assumption that correlations would be low enough between the assets in the structures they insured that they would never have to pay off. When they insured subprime mortgage structures, for example, they assumed that cheap houses in Las Vegas would be uncorrelated with cheap houses in Florida. They were wrong, and ended up needing a large government bailout.[10]

10.7 Historical Estimation of Correlation Matrices

The two most widely used models for future correlation matrices are simple historical samples and exponentially weighted moving averages.

Assume we have observations of log-returns $x(i,t)$ of $i = 1, \ldots, n$ items over $t = 1, \ldots, T$ time periods, where time period 1 is the most recent. Let X be the $n \times T$ matrix containing these observations, and let the centered observation matrix be $X_C = X(I_T - J_T/T)$, where I_T is the $T \times T$ identity matrix and J_T is the $T \times T$ matrix of all ones. Then the maximum likelihood historical sample covariance matrix is $C = (X_C X_C^\mathsf{T})/T$. For an unbiased estimate we would use $T - 1$ instead of T in the denominator, but for most practical implementations T is big enough so it doesn't make a difference.

The **sample correlation matrix** is:

$$R = S^{-1} C S^{-1},$$

where S is the $n \times n$ diagonal matrix whose diagonal is the square root of the diagonal of C.

10 [Amadeo 2020].

Exponentially weighted moving averages ("EWMA"), which we saw in Section 8.1, are based on the premise that older observations are less important than newer ones. They are a special case of GARCH(1,1), which in Chapter 9 we saw was:

$$\sigma_t^2 = c + b_1\sigma_{t-1}^2 + a_1 y_{t-1}^2. \tag{9.42}$$

EWMA simply sets $c = 0$ and $a_1 = 1 - b_1$.

With GARCH, the time index increases as time goes into the future. When taking samples, the time index increases as time goes into the past. We'll use the past-increasing convention here, so period 1 is the most recent past period and period T is the longest-ago period in our sample. So we associate these weights with the log-return observations:

$$p_\lambda(t) = \frac{(1-\lambda)\lambda^{t-1}}{1-\lambda^T}. \tag{10.24}$$

This is the same as (7.1) with $\lambda = 2^{-h}$.

The recentered EWMA observation matrix is $X_\lambda = XP_\lambda(I_T - J_T/T)$, where P_λ is the $T \times T$ matrix with $p_\lambda(t), t = 1, \ldots, T$ on its diagonal and zeroes elsewhere. The EWMA covariance matrix is $C_\lambda = X_\lambda X_\lambda^\mathsf{T}$. When $\lambda = 1$, $p_\lambda(t) = \frac{1}{T}$ and this is the same as the maximum likelihood historical sample covariance matrix.

EWMA (and therefore historical) covariance and correlation matrices are by construction positive semidefinite, and possibly strictly positive definite. This is because for any n-vector z, we can define $y = X_\lambda^\mathsf{T} z$. Since $y^\mathsf{T}y$ is a sum of squares, it must be nonnegative. But $y^\mathsf{T}y = z^\mathsf{T}C_\lambda z$, proving that the quadratic form is always nonnegative, which is the definition of positive definite.

Most commercial systems in use today (Qontigo/Axioma or Northfield for equities, the Yield Book for fixed income, MSCI for multiple asset classes) have exponential weighting as an option, often the default option.[11]

There is widespread skepticism among practitioners over the use of historical and exponentially weighted models, however. These models project either the recent past (exponentially weighted) or a longer view of the past (historical unweighted) forward. As we saw in Figure 9.4, leading up to the Global Financial Crisis of 2008 there was a period of unusually low volatility caused in part by the relatively low correlations shown on the left of Figure 10.8.

These benign conditions began to change in 2007, and then changed massively in the fall of 2008. Many practitioners feel that projecting the past forward works only when you don't really need it to work, that is, when times are calm. When times are turbulent, projecting the past forward is dangerous.

---

11 Qontigo/Axioma, Northfield, Yield Book, MSCI. Websites. https://qontigo.com/products/axioma-equity-factor-risk-models/; www.northinfo.com/; www.yieldbook.com/m/home/index.shtml; https://www.msci.com/analytics.

On the other side of the 2008 GFC, most backward-looking models continued to have a large influence from the high volatilities and correlations for years afterward. That led to very large estimates of variance and very poor expectations of diversification – except between safety assets and risk assets – in a period where volatility was on the way down and diversification was improving.

Effects like these are called **procyclical**. When conditions were recently good, procyclical risk models say it's OK to take more risk, which is a bad feedback loop leading to a bubble. When conditions were recently bad, procyclical risk models say that just about anything you do except diversifying into safety assets will be very risky, which is a bad feedback loop that drives already-low economic activity even lower.

One way to aim for **countercyclicality**, the beneficial opposite of procyclicality, is to use very long-run estimates of relationships and volatilities. But John Maynard Keynes[12] nicely captures the problems of long-run estimates in one of his most famous quotes:

> [The] long run is a misleading guide to current affairs. In the long run we are all dead. Economists set themselves too easy, too useless a task if in tempestuous seasons they can only tell us that when the storm is past the ocean is flat again.

The USA in the 1920s was a manufacturing economy, while today it is a service and knowledge-based economy. Mixing in data from the 1920s with more current data doesn't necessarily lead to the discovery of a universal long-run truth: there may not be a universal long-run truth to discover. Further, even if there is some long-run equilibrium, the sojourns away from that equilibrium can be painfully long. A witty summation of this phenomenon, sometimes attributed to Keynes,[13] is:

> The markets can remain irrational longer than you can remain solvent.

A technique that is sometimes used to mediate between the long term and the short term is to scale historical estimates of volatilities by option-implied volatilities and to scale historical correlations by option-implied correlations from (10.10). This assumes that the options market quickly impounds information that seeps more slowly into historical data.

Unfortunately, the options market tends to overreact: implied volatilities are almost always higher than subsequent realized volatilities. Implied volatilities spike up briefly on just about any piece of news, and usually quickly subside.

---

12 [Keynes 1929], p. 80.
13 The financial analyst A. Gary Shilling seems to be the actual source of this saying, although it's often attributed to Keynes. Quote Investigator. "The Market Can Remain Irrational Longer Than You Can Remain Solvent." Website. https://quoteinvestigator.com/2011/08/09/remain-solvent/.

Even so, a thoughtful approach to finding the right mix of quick-reaction data and slow-reaction data is necessary to avoid procyclicality without underreaction.

10.8 Time Series Estimates of Covariances and Correlations

The success of GARCH models in lowering kurtosis of de-GARCHed financial time series leads to an obvious suggestion: why not construct analogous models for covariances? We might try a variant of (9.42):

$$\sigma_{i,j,t}^2 = c_{i,j} + b_{i,j}\sigma_{i,j,t-1}^2 + a_{i,j}y_{i,t-1}y_{j,t-1}. \tag{10.25}$$

As in Chapter 9, the y's are mean 0 shocks. But the problem is apparent: if there are n securities in the universe, then there will be about $n^2/2$ correlation pairs to estimate. Equation (10.25) needs to estimate three parameters ($c_{i,j}$, $b_{i,j}$, and $a_{i,j}$) per covariance pair. Unless the number of time periods is substantially larger than the square of the number of securities, each covariance will have little statistical validity.

For this reason, individual correlation GARCH models like (10.25) just don't work very well empirically. To have any hope of producing statistically robust estimates, we will need to make some decisions about how to restrict the number of parameters.

10.8.1 Constant and Dynamic Conditional Correlation

Tim Bollerslev, who was a PhD student of Robert Engle and who extended Engle's ARCH model to the more widely used GARCH model, described **constant conditional correlation** ("CCC") in Bollerslev (1990). The model simply postulates a constant correlation matrix with time-varying volatilities:

$$\sigma_{i,j,t}^2 = \rho_{i,j}\sigma_{i,i,t}\sigma_{j,j,t}. \tag{10.26}$$

But we've seen above that constant correlations seem unlikely to fit empirical data. The Engle (2002) **dynamic conditional correlations** ("DCC") seem to be more realistic. In this model, shocks are first standardized:

$$\epsilon_{i,t} = \frac{y_{i,t}}{\mathbb{E}_{t-1}[y_{i,t}^2]}. \tag{10.27}$$

Then time-varying correlations between standardized shocks are computed:

$$\rho_{i,j,t} = \frac{\mathbb{E}_{t-1}[\epsilon_{i,t}\epsilon_{j,t}]}{\sqrt{\mathbb{E}_{t-1}[\epsilon_{i,t}^2]\mathbb{E}_{t-1}[\epsilon_{j,t}^2]}} = \mathbb{E}_{t-1}[\epsilon_{i,t}\epsilon_{j,t}]. \tag{10.28}$$

Substituting the dynamic correlation $\rho_{i,j,t}$ for the constant correlation $\rho_{i,j}$ in (10.26) produces DCC covariances.

Both CCC and DCC separate the problem of estimating covariances into a problem of estimating variances, followed by a problem of estimating correlations. As we've noted, this is not a perfect model since in times of stress it's often the case that both volatilities and correlations go up. Thus, the two estimation problems are not as independent as this method indicates. Still, we might be able to get better estimates than we have previously.

An obvious way of approaching DCC is to use GARCH for the volatilities, as we noted for CCC. The denominator terms $\mathbb{E}_{t-1}[y_{i,t}^2]$ in (10.27) could be computed with a GARCH model. We could also use EGARCH or TARCH or any of the other ARCH-like models that we thought were appropriate.

Let's return to the regional stock market index data to see how this works. First we need to estimate GARCH volatilities of each of the region indices separately. Using the log-maximum-likelihood function (9.43), Code Segment 10.13 computes the following parameters and shows the evolution of the GARCH processes in Figure 10.9:

```
Europe a=0.1909 b=0.7515 c=0.00003922 AnnEquilibStd=0.1882
North_America a=0.1775 b=0.7617 c=0.00003450
       AnnEquilibStd=0.1719
Japan a=0.1169 b=0.8332 c=0.00004122 AnnEquilibStd= 0.2072
```

The separation of relationships and marginal distributions embodied in Sklar's Theorem, or in the two-part de-GARCHing and correlation estimation, seems to fit the patterns we see here.

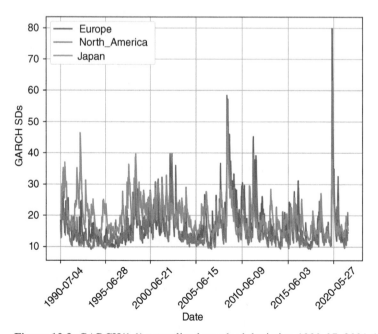

Figure 10.9 GARCH(1,1) annualized standard deviation 1990-07–2021-12.

The next step is to use these volatilities to de-GARCH the three time series of Europe, North America, and Japan shocks. We divide y_t by σ_t because σ_t is a function of the previous y's and doesn't "know" y_t. We did actually cheat a little bit when forming Figure 10.9: we used the long-term average volatility over the entire sample to start the process. But we couldn't have known the end-of-sample information back in 1990. This doesn't make a huge difference, though: we could have just held out a year at the beginning of the sample to form an initial volatility that would have been of the same order of magnitude as the overall volatility. Similarly, we used an overall mean to center the series but could have used a trailing mean, or even ignored the mean, without too much impact.

We noted in Chapter 9 that de-GARCHing often improves the properties of the time series. Code Segment 10.14 checks that and produces the following output:

```
Europe
    DeGARCHed Mean: -0.005893477107448027
    Raw annualized Std Dev: 0.18412264048982568
    DeGARCHed Std Dev: 1.0009208480512117
    Raw excess kurtosis: 6.220045614600393
    DeGARCHed Excess Kurtosis: 1.609790869370185
North_America
    DeGARCHed Mean: -0.016313959090731925
    Raw annualized Std Dev: 0.16583718588963886
    DeGARCHed Std Dev: 1.0001415608212971
    Raw excess kurtosis: 6.05442111241195
    DeGARCHed Excess Kurtosis: 2.5632192573140795
Japan
    DeGARCHed Mean: -0.011105611175006004
    Raw annualized Std Dev: 0.2024110644897854
    DeGARCHed Std Dev: 1.0011888821834636
    Raw excess kurtosis: 2.214332485567999
    DeGARCHed Excess Kurtosis: 1.8649442768900748
```

The de-GARCHed means are no longer zero because the scaling changes them, but they aren't very large. The de-GARCHed time series is scaled so that the weekly standard deviation is close to one, so the means are small fractions of a weekly standard deviation.

The scaling worked well: all three regions have standard deviations close to one. Since σ_t didn't "know" what y_t was going to be, this is a good test of persistence of standard deviation estimates.

The de-GARCHing process also took a dent out of excess kurtosis, lowering it in all three regions. The world is still not multivariate normal even after de-GARCHing, but it's not as bad as it was before. Intuitively, this means that

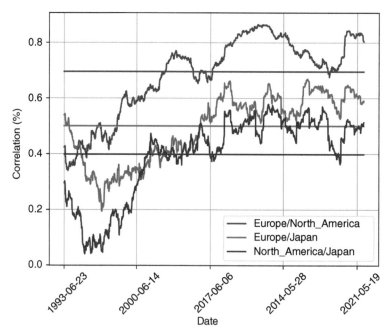

Figure 10.10 Historical de-GARCHed 156-week sample correlations.

big shocks (the ones that cause positive kurtosis) don't come out of the blue as much as we might think. The March 2011 earthquake and tsunami in Japan were shocks out of the blue. But in fact such shocks do not seem to move the financial markets as much as self-caused shocks, like the bankruptcy of Lehman Brothers in September 2008. And the latter seems to come only after a buildup that the GARCH model can (partially) catch.

Figure 10.10 (generated by Code Segment 10.15) shows the historical correlations of the de-GARCHed time series. Comparing this to Figure 10.4 (raw historical correlations) shows that de-GARCHing doesn't seem to make the time series of correlations any steadier.

10.8.2 Implementation of Dynamic Conditional Correlations

Equations (10.27) and (10.28) give a theoretical model for dynamic conditional correlations. But there's more work to be done to get to a practical implementation, since these equations call for taking expected values. We'd have to know the relevant distributions in order to be able to take expected values.

Practical implementations of dynamic conditional correlations focus on the time evolution of the **quasi-correlation matrix**. The quasi-correlation matrix is the covariance matrix of the de-GARCHed series; it's called quasi-correlation because the variances are (we hope) close to, but not exactly equal to, one.

There are three common specifications of how the quasi-correlations evolve: integrated, mean-reverting, and asymmetric.

Integration refers to the time series property that differences are stationary. The **integrated model** is similar to the exponentially weighted estimation method, except that it's applied to standardized shocks. The matrix specification is:

$$Q_t = \lambda \epsilon_{t-1} \epsilon_{t-1}^{\mathsf{T}} + (1 - \lambda)Q_{t-1}. \tag{10.29}$$

Here the Q's are $n \times n$ matrices and ϵ's are n-vectors.

Integrated models have no tendency to return to any sort of long-term average, so if we believe that the economic environment is constantly changing so that correlations are never stable, this is the appropriate model. Note that as long as the process is originally seeded with a positive semidefinite Q_0, the Q_t will stay positive semidefinite as long as λ is in the unit interval.

If we believe that there is a long-term mean correlation matrix that is similar to the equilibrium value in an Ornstein–Uhlenbeck process, then the **mean-reverting model** is appropriate:

$$Q_t = \Omega + a \epsilon_{t-1} \epsilon_{t-1}^{\mathsf{T}} + \beta Q_{t-1}. \tag{10.30}$$

If R is the long-term mean correlation matrix we want to target in (10.30), then we set $\Omega = (1 - \alpha - \beta)R$. We must also have positive α, β, and $1 - \alpha - \beta$. The initial quasi-correlation matrix Q_0 must be positive semidefinite.

The Ω parameter matrix doesn't change with time, but it does introduce approximately $n^2/2$ values to be estimated. Usually, we simply assume that the long-term mean correlation matrix $R = \Omega/(1 - \alpha - \beta)$ will be the past sample correlation matrix; this is called **correlation targeting**.

The **asymmetric model** uses the insight behind TARCH that we saw in Chapter 9: downward movements tend to cause higher correlations than upward ones. We modify (10.30) by adding a term that increases correlations when there are joint down-moves:

$$Q_t = \Omega + a \epsilon_{t-1} \epsilon_{t-1}^{\mathsf{T}} + \gamma \eta_{t-1} \eta_{t-1}^{\mathsf{T}} + \beta Q_{t-1}, \quad \eta_{t-1} = \min(\epsilon_{t-1}, 0). \tag{10.31}$$

The minimization in the definition of η_{t-1} is component-by-component, so η_{t-1} is the same as ϵ_{t-1} where ϵ_{t-1} has a negative entry, and zero otherwise. Thus, the added term $\gamma \eta_{t-1} \eta_{t-1}^{\mathsf{T}}$ will have a zero in cell (i,j) if either $\epsilon_{t-1}(i)$ or $\epsilon_{t-1}(j)$ is positive. Otherwise, this new term will have a positive entry (since we assume $\gamma > 0$), boosting correlation when both elements of the correlation pair have negative returns.

The anchor matrix Ω can be targeted to equal $(1 - \alpha - \beta)R - \gamma N$, where N is the sample correlation matrix of the (negative-only) η's. If $(1 - \alpha - \beta - \gamma)$ is positive, α, β, and γ are also all positive, and the initial Q_0 is positive semidefinite, then the Q_t will remain positive semidefinite. The positivity of $(1 - \alpha - \beta - \gamma)$ is an overly strong condition that can be relaxed a bit, but it doesn't hurt much to insist on it.

In all three models – integrated, mean-reverting, and asymmetric – there is no guarantee that the diagonals of the quasi-correlation matrices Q_t will be all ones. As we saw above when comparing before and after statistics of our three regional indices, de-GARCHing does a good but not perfect job of predicting next-period variance. That's why the Q_t are quasi-correlation matrices but not correlation matrices.

This is easily cured by scaling. We treat the quasi-correlation matrix like it is a covariance matrix to get the actual estimates of correlation:

$$\rho_{i,j,t} = \frac{q_{i,j,t}}{\sqrt{q_{i,i,t} q_{j,j,t}}}. \tag{10.32}$$

In matrix form, that is:

$$R_t = \left(\mathrm{diag}(Q_t)\right)^{-1/2} \cdot Q_t \cdot \left(\mathrm{diag}(Q_t)\right)^{-1/2}. \tag{10.33}$$

We now have a process for estimating dynamic conditional correlations. It remains only to find the familiar maximum likelihood estimator of the parameters in our models. This is a three-step process:

- First, estimate each GARCH series separately using (8.42).
- Second, if necessary (mean-reverting or asymmetric), compute the average R (sample correlation) and N (asymmetric correlation) matrices from the de-GARCHed series. These can be done with simple historical estimates, or using exponential weighting.
- Third, minimize the (opposite of) the log-likelihood function:

$$LML_{corr} = \sum_{t=1}^{T} \left[\ln(\det(R_t)) + \epsilon_t^\mathsf{T} R_t^{-1} \epsilon_t\right]. \tag{10.34}$$

The likelihood function doesn't look intimidating when written in matrix form, but the variables to be estimated are contained in highly nonlinear ways in the function. For example, if we're using the integrated model, there's only one variable (λ) to be estimated in the third step. However, when we apply (10.33) to rescale the quasi-correlation matrix Q_t to the actual correlation matrix R_t, we get a complex expression in λ. The determinant of R_t and the quadratic form in the inverse of R_t shown in (10.34) make things even more complicated.

It is still possible to find a minimum of (10.34) (and hence a maximum of the log-likelihood function), but there is a chance that an optimizer will get stuck. The statistical properties such as confidence intervals around the statistics are also hard to compute.

We soldiered through these potential problems and computed the λ for the integrated model of correlations for our three regional stock market indices in Code Segment 10.16, which also produces Figure 10.11.

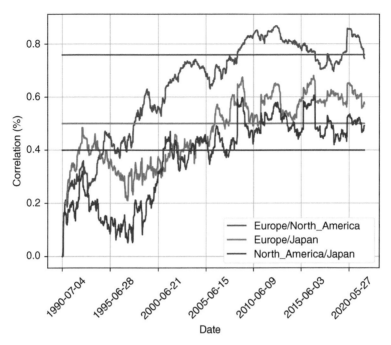

Figure 10.11 Integrated correlations $\lambda = 0.01118$, 1990-07-04:2021-12-29.

```
Optimal lambda: 0.011184559944661282
Optimal objective function: 3305.2122319031564
Half-life (years): 1.1851221760570019
```

Comparing Figure 10.11 with Figure 10.4 doesn't reveal much difference. Figure 10.4 abruptly forgets data beyond 156 weeks, while Figure 10.11 remembers data longer but de-emphasizes it faster.

The objective function (10.34) is very smoothly sloped in λ. The vertical range of Figure 10.12 (produced by Code Segment 10.17) is less than 1% while half-life varies about half a year in either away from the optimal value:

This makes it hard to trust the λ value resulting from this process.

Let's try the mean-reverting model (10.30). It has two parameters, α and β, along with the anchor matrix Ω. Perhaps this formula will lead to a better objective function. Code Segment 10.18 performs the mean-reverting calculations and produces Figure 10.13.

```
Optimal alpha, beta: 0.014473612560970664
        0.9766134450628321
Optimal objective function: 3279.846605143996
Half-life (years): 0.5632839147429579
```

The improvement in the objective function from the integrated model is marginal. The optimal α and β sum to less than one, so the correlation matrices retain positive definiteness as they evolve.

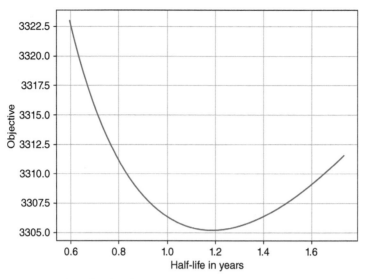

Figure 10.12 Objective function as half-life changes.

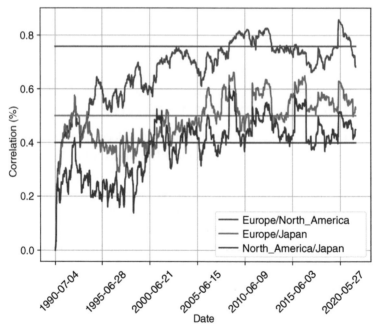

Figure 10.13 Mean reverting correlations $\alpha = 0.01447, \beta = 0.97661$, 1990-07-04:2021-12-29.

The half-life for the mean-reverting model is determined by β since iterating (10.30) backward gives increasing powers of β next to the shocks $\epsilon\epsilon^\mathsf{T}$. Even though the solution β is not far from the $1 - \lambda$ from the integrated method, the half-life is noticeably smaller than the one resulting from the integrated model. This is consistent with the shape of Figure 10.12.

10.8.3 MacGyver Method

The sad fact of estimating parameters by maximum likelihood methods is that the assumptions behind maximum likelihood are likely to be violated. The idea is to find the parameters that produce a pattern that is most likely to match the empirical data, but the assumptions about the underlying distribution necessary to compute the likelihood are often unrealistic.

There is a variety of quasi-maximum-likelihood methods that may not be as statistically pure as maximum likelihood but that seem to make sense. Robert Engle suggests the **MacGyver method** to estimate parameters in correlation modeling. This is named after a television series[14] where the protagonist, MacGyver, used clever scientific tricks to solve problems. The MacGyver (really Engle) method is to estimate the parameters (λ for the integrated model, α and β for the mean-reverting model, etc.) for each pair of assets separately.

This is exactly what we said not to do at the beginning of Section 10.8! However, the MacGyver method doesn't stop at the individual parameters: it combines them by taking the mean or the median, thus producing the necessary parameter restriction. This method also gives an idea of a confidence interval around the parameter by looking at the range of individual parameters.

Since the MacGyver method calls for looking at one quasi-correlation at a time, the integrated method would become a series of scalar equations:

$$q_{i,j,t} = \lambda_{i,j}\epsilon_{i,t-1}\epsilon_{j,t-1} + (1 - \lambda_{i,j}q_{i,j,t-1}). \tag{10.35}$$

The (opposite of) the log-likelihood function, that is, what we want to minimize, is:

$$LML_{q_{i,j,t}} = \sum_{t=1}^{T}\left[\ln\left(1 - q_{i,j,t}^2\right) + \frac{\epsilon_{i,t}^2 + \epsilon_{j,t}^2 - 2q_{i,j,t}\epsilon_{i,t}\epsilon_{j,t}}{1 - q_{i,j,t}^2}\right]. \tag{10.36}$$

A trick similar to pseudo-delta functions (Figure 9.12) can be used to force parameters (λ in the integrated model, α and β in the mean-reverting model) to lie in the interval $(0, 1)$. Set the parameter equal to an expression of the form $\frac{\exp(s)}{1+\exp(s)}$, where s is an unconstrained real number. Then solve for s instead of the original parameter.

Code Segment 10.19 tries the MacGyver technique for the three correlation pairs in our regional stock index example.

```
Europe North_America
    Optimal lambda: 0.030286039199903934
    Optimal objective function: 2118.933741568306
    Half-life (years): 0.43342960925094237
```

14 CBS. *MacGyver*. Website. www.cbs.com/shows/macgyver/.

```
Europe Japan
    Optimal lambda: 0.009509218717723778
    Optimal objective function: 2818.8779337054375
    Half-life (years): 1.3950961871326746
North_America Japan
    Optimal lambda: 0.006421768799189656
    Optimal objective function: 2986.3935339666
    Half-life (years): 2.0690416665085523

Median MacGyver lambda: 0.009509218717723778
```

The median MacGyver λ is not too far from the λ we got from the integrated method as shown in Figure 10.11. The range of half-lives doesn't give us much confidence in the central value.

In addition to giving an idea of the confidence interval around the parameter, the MacGyver method is useful for incomplete data. For example, when we brought the euro into our currency data to form Figure 5.1, we needed to restrict the time period to start in 1999. The Swissie, pound sterling, and the yen have data going back decades before that, but the euro didn't start trading until the beginning of 1999. Before that, each eurozone country had its own currency. The MacGyver method would allow us to use the extra decades of data for parameter estimation between pairs that existed before the euro, while restricting the time period for pairs that include the euro.

However, if after examining parameter ranges we find that we don't have confidence in one of the DCC models, we can simply take rolling historical or EWMA correlations as a low-tech way of predicting future correlations.

For Code Segments in this chapter, see the Code Appendix starting on p. 440. For executable code, visit www.cambridge.org/9781009209090/ch10

For problem sets for this chapter, visit www.cambridge.org/ 9781009209090/ch10_problems

11 Credit Modeling

Chapter 3 investigated the seeming impossibility of uncertainty arising from certainty: even when we know exactly when and how much money we will get in the future, the value we assign today to that future money can be highly variable.

The uncertainty doesn't stop there. "Fixed-income" (US usage) or "fixed-interest" (UK usage) securities are those for which the parties agree in advance on the schedule of future cash flows. But the "fixed" cash flows may be anything but certain. For example, there may be an arrangement where the amount of money to be exchanged is contingent on an interest rate that is unknown today, like the level of the Secured Overnight Financing Rate ("SOFR")[1] at the time of the payment. Securities that make payments contingent on future benchmark interest rates are called **floating rate** instruments.

It's also possible that the uncertainty is unwanted. A borrower and a lender may agree on specific dollar amounts to be paid by the borrower in the future, but the borrower may be unable or unwilling to pay the agreed amounts. **Credit risk** is the uncertainty about whether a borrower will make agreed cash flows in the agreed amounts and/or at the agreed times.

In this chapter, we'll discuss credit risk arising from corporate and sovereign borrowers. Lenders typically perform credit risk assessments themselves as they assemble credit portfolios, but they may also rely on information providers (**credit rating agencies**) that provide scores to potential lenders. We'll discuss some of the qualitative and quantitative methods that lenders and credit rating agencies use.

11.1 Basic Credit Risk Concepts

Chapter 3 noted that a generic financial instrument contemplates a series of cash flows $c_1, \ldots, c_n$ at times $0 \leq t_1, \ldots, t_n$. Perhaps the simplest example of this is a default-free zero-coupon bond where there are two cash flows: one amount $c_1 < 0$ from the lender to the borrower at time $t_1 = 0$, and another one for a predetermined amount $c_2 > 0$ from the borrower to the lender at a predetermined time t_2 in the future.

To reflect the value now (time t) of cash flows c_i at times t_i in the future, Chapter 3 contemplated discount rates r_i that would reflect current market views

---

1 Federal Reserve Bank of New York. "Secured Overnight Financing Rate Data." Website. https://apps.newyorkfed.org/markets/autorates/sofr.

of what those future cash flows are worth today. We saw that those discount rates could be used to "bring back" the expected future cash flows to the present time t:

$$P_t = \sum_{i=1}^{n} \frac{\mathbb{E}[c_i]}{(1 + r_{i,t})^{t_i - t}}, \tag{11.1}$$

$$P_t = \sum_{i=1}^{n} \mathbb{E}[c_i] \exp(-r_{i,t}(t_i - t)). \tag{11.2}$$

The two formulas represent different discounting conventions. Equation (11.1) (which is the same as (3.2)) represents a discrete period discounting method, which is often close to what is used in practice. Equation (11.2) represents continuous compounding, which often is easier than (11.1) to manipulate in formulas. Recall from Section 3.2 that setting $r_{i,t}(b) = \ln(1 + r_{i,t}(a))$, often a very slight change, makes the two equal.

In Chapter 3, $\mathbb{E}[c_i] = c_i$, that is, the planned cash flows were constants. But credit risk contemplates a stochastic **time to default** $t_d > 0$: that is, a time, not currently known, at which the borrower becomes unable to fully pay scheduled cash flows $c_j, c_{j+1}, \ldots, c_n,$[2] where j indexes the first $t_j \geq t_d$.

Post-default, the lender may receive nothing ($c_j = \cdots = c_n = 0$), although this is rare and usually occurs only in situations where the entire economic system has broken down.

More likely, there is a **recovery amount** that is greater than zero but less than the scheduled amounts. **Loss given default ("LGD")** is the complement of recovery: it is the difference between the amount scheduled to be received and the amount actually received. **Severity** is another term for LGD, although severity is often expressed in percentage terms while LGD is often expressed in monetary terms. **Expected loss** is the probability of default times the expected loss given default.

Credit-risky bonds understandably command lower prices than otherwise identical default free bonds. A common way to account for this is to introduce a **spread** (denoted here by "s") into the discounting formula:

$$P_t^{CR} = \sum_{i=1}^{n} \frac{\mathbb{E}[c_i]}{(1 + r_i + s)^{t_i - t}}, \tag{11.3}$$

$$P_t^{CR} = \sum_{i=1}^{n} \mathbb{E}[c_i] \exp(-(r_{i,t} + s)(t_i - t)). \tag{11.4}$$

As in Chapter 3, the $r_{i,t}$ are based on some default-free curve, such as the US Treasury curve, the UK gilt curve, and so on. Thus, these $r_{i,t}$ are the same as those used in (11.1) and (11.2) for default-free bonds.

2 Many credit instruments involve a single initial loan payment by the lender to the borrower, with all subsequent coupon and principal payments made by the borrower to the lender. So after the initial loan, future obligations are usually all on the part of the borrower. In our notation, that means an initial $c_0 < 0$ and then all planned $c_i > 0$ for $i > 0$.

But if the bond in question has credit risk (denoted by the superscript CR on the price), then $P_t^{CR} < P_t$, where P_t is the price of an identical default-free bond. The default-free discount rates $r_{i,t}$ will not be big enough; the future cash flows of the credit-risky bond need to be discounted even more to bring the price down from P_t to P_t^{CR}.

The additional discount amount s is simply a plug number: it's the amount that makes the pricing equation ((11.3) or (11.4) depending on the discounting convention we want to use) come out right. Every other term is known: the price P_t^{CR} is observed in the market, the default-free discount rates $r_{i,t}$ are observed from the market prices of default-free bonds; and the planned cash flows and times are specified in advance.

How big does s have to be? That depends on (a) the market's assessment of the expected loss; (b) the market's risk appetite; and (c) other factors like taxes and liquidity. The expectation $\mathbb{E}[c_i]$ does not itself take into account default; it is the same time-t expectation as if the bond were default-free. So item (a) is an adjustment for the lender's possible injury from default. But that possibility of default also makes the bond riskier, so s will also contain item (b), compensation for that risk.

In theory, if the market thinks the bond is truly default-free, then we should see $s = 0$. But in practice, the (c) "other" category can be quite significant. For example, corporate bonds are generally less liquid than major government bonds, so corporate spreads include some compensation for the perceived difficulty in buying or selling the instrument. Figure 11.4 will show that historically a typical spread for very high credit quality corporate bond was more than $s = 50$bps per year. Very little of this was compensation for loss given default.

As with many other pricing equations, (11.3) and (11.4) can be used as quoting conventions, where price can be found as a function of spread. Thus, a credit-risky issuer's bond might be quoted as "200 over," meaning that a spread s of 200 basis points over default-free discounting will give the market price when plugged into the appropriate pricing equation (11.3) or (11.4).

11.2 Credit Ratings

For centuries, lenders have tried to find out as much as possible about potential borrowers so that they (the lenders) can assess their chances of being repaid. Borrowers need to demonstrate to lenders that they (the borrowers) have a reasonable chance of repaying the money loaned to them, or they simply won't be able to borrow. Insisting that the borrower have a tenable fiscal position is the first line of defense against default for any lender.

Some lenders rely on personal knowledge. In the classic 1946 film *It's a Wonderful Life*,[3] George Bailey runs the Bailey Building and Loan company

---

3 IMDb. "*It's a Wonderful Life* (1946): Plot." Website. www.imdb.com/title/tt0038650/plotsummary.

in the tiny town of Bedford Falls, where he personally knows every actual and potential borrower. While George has near-perfect information about his cohort of borrowers, he has no ability to expand and diversify his business by making loans outside his immediate community.

Making loans to strangers involves less information – which by definition means more risk – than making loans to family, friends, and neighbors. On the other hand, making loans to strangers allows lenders to diversify and expand. Thus, a key focus of economic history is the rise of information networks that supplied financial data and assessments of creditworthiness of businesses and individuals to potential lenders.

For example, Hoffman, Postel-Vinay, and Rosenthal (2019) found that starting in the seventeenth century a robust network of notaries public arranged transactions between French borrowers and lenders who didn't know each other. Hoffman et al. (2019) highlight (p. 72) transactions between parties in the French province of Burgundy with parties in Lyon and Paris:

> For transactions to take place over such distances, lenders in large and distant cities such as Lyon or Paris had to believe that collateral pledges of Burgundian lands were valuable and plausible. That required information, and if intermediaries had not provided it, then the nobles in Burgundy could only have borrowed from other Burgundians. ... The implication is that our intermediaries – the notaries – furnished information services over a broad geographical area.

In this network, the borrower and the lender didn't need to know each other directly, but personal knowledge was still important: a Burgundian borrower knew a Burgundian notary who knew a Parisian notary who knew a Parisian lender.

Eventually, such personal knowledge chains were dispensed with in favor of data, as computers and communications expanded to where vast amounts of information about individuals could be collected and analyzed. In 1958, engineer Bill Fair and mathematician Earl Isaac formed the Fair, Isaac Company. Currently called FICO, the company provides FICO®Scores[4] rating millions of potential individual borrowers looking for credit cards, mortgages, automobile loans, student loans, and the like. The consumers of these scores are generally financial institutions. More recently, fintech companies gather variables from borrowers' digital footprints. Berg et al. (2018) find that the footprints "equal or exceed the information content of credit bureau scores."

In addition to services providing credit information and credit scores of individuals, services exist to supply this information about companies. One of the earliest such services in the USA was the Mercantile Agency of the mid-1800s. This was a forerunner of Dun & Bradstreet, which continues to offer

---

4 FICO®. "About Us." Website. www.fico.com/en/about-us#history; myFICO. "What Is a Credit Score?" Website. www.myfico.com/credit-education/credit-scores.

corporate credit information to this day. The history section of the company's website says:[5]

> To help American merchants in their decision-making, an enterprising busi-
> nessman named Lewis Tappan began, in 1841, to establish a network of
> correspondents that would function as a source of reliable, consistent and
> objective credit information. His Mercantile Agency, located in New York City,
> was one of the first organizations formed for the sole purpose of providing
> business information to customers.

The "network of correspondents" established by the Mercantile Agency in the mid-1800s was similar to the network of notaries public that Hoffman et al. documented in 1600–1800s France. Over time, personal reporting gave way to the corporate information databases now in use.

Mercantile Agency (subsequently Dun & Bradstreet) ratings were applied to companies and were generally used by suppliers wanting to know their chances of getting paid. In the early 1900s, John Moody adapted the application of credit rating systems to a new subject: corporate bonds. Moody eventually assigned letter grades to most corporate bonds in the USA, from Aaa (meaning the highest credit quality with virtual certainty of repayment) down to D (meaning defaulted). Today, Moody's Corp.[6] is one of the largest bond rating services, rating a large portion of all bonds issued worldwide. These include the original corporate bonds as well as sovereign (government) bonds and structured credit, which we'll discuss below.

White (2009) summarized the establishment of corporate bond credit rating agencies in the early twentieth century:

> Moody's firm was followed by Poor's Publishing Company in 1916, the Standard
> Statistics Company in 1922, and the Fitch Publishing Company in 1924. These
> firms sold their bond ratings to bond investors in thick rating manuals.

Poor's and Standard Statistics eventually merged into Standard & Poor's, which continues to provide credit ratings today as part of S&P Global Corp. The "Big Three" credit rating agencies today consist of Moody's, Standard & Poor's, and Fitch.[7] In 2011, they collectively comprised a market share of roughly 95% according to Rönsberg (2011).

The provision of accurate credit rating opinions is considered as important to the smooth functioning of the economy as the provision of accurate accounting audits. Just as accountants need to be certified by their local or national government, so too do credit rating agencies. In the USA, the Securities and

---

5 Dun & Bradstreet. "Our History." Website. www.dnb.com/about-us/company/history
  .html. See www.dnb.com.lv/en/D&B-Sample.html for a sample report.
6 Moodys.com. "About Moody's: Moody's History." Website. https://web.archive.org/
  web/20051103055906/www.moodys.com/moodys/cust/AboutMoodys/AboutMoodys
  .aspx?topic=history.
7 S&P Global Ratings. "About S&P Global Ratings." Website. www.spglobal.com/ratings/
  en/about/index.aspx; Fitch Ratings. "About Us." Website. www.fitchratings.com/
  about-us.

Exchange Commission maintains a list of Nationally Recognized Statistical Ratings Organizations, or "NRSROs."[8] The list currently includes the Big Three and seven others.

In Europe, the European Securities and Markets Authority has a registration and certification program for credit rating agencies. The ESMA approved list, like the US list, includes the Big Three and others.[9]

The Big Three have similar but not identical rating scales for long-term debt. Moody's scale has notches that look like Aaa, Aa1, Aa2, Aa3, A1, ..., Caa3, Ca, and C in descending order (Table 11.1). Standard & Poor's scale is very similar, but (along with Fitch) uses all capital letters and plusses and minuses.[10] Hence, Moody's rating Aa3 is similar to Standard & Poor's rating AA-. Moody's definitions of its major notches are quite qualitative (Table 11.1).

We'll examine historical data below that give some specificity to terms like "highest quality."

Despite generally using the same financial data inputs and having similar ratings scales, credit rating agencies don't always agree with each other. Most famously, at this writing there is disagreement about the world's biggest borrower: Standard & Poor's rates the US government a notch below the highest rating at AA+. Moody's and Fitch rate it Aaa (highest).[11]

11.2.1 Investment Grade and Speculative Grade

Most credit rating agencies divide the bond market broadly into two quality levels:

- **Investment-Grade Bonds** that are expected to have a very high chance of avoiding default; and
- **Speculative-Grade Bonds** (also called **High Yield Bonds**) that have higher chances of default than investment-grade bonds.

---

8 U.S. Securities and Exchange Commission. "Learn More About NRSROs." Website. www.sec.gov/ocr/ocr-learn-nrsros.html.

9 ESMA: European Securities and Markets Agency. "What Is the CRA Regulation and What Does It Cover?" Website. www.esma.europa.eu/supervision/credit-rating-agencies/supervision; https://www.esma.europa.eu/supervision/credit-rating-agencies/risk.

10 Moody's Investors Service. "Rating Symbols and Definitions." October 3, 2022. www.moodys.com/sites/products/AboutMoodysRatingsAttachments/MoodysRatingSymbolsandDefinitions.pdf; S&P Global Ratings. "S&P Global Ratings Definitions." November 10, 2021. www.standardandpoors.com/en_US/web/guest/article/-/view/sourceId/504352.

11 S&P Global Ratings. "Research Update: United States of America Long-Term Rating Lowered to 'AA+' on Political Risks and Rising Debt Burden; Outlook Negative." August 5, 2011. www.standardandpoors.com/en_US/web/guest/article/-/view/sourceId/6802837; Moody's Investors Service. "Moody's Affirms United States' Aaa Rating; Maintains Stable Outlook." April 25, 2018. www.moodys.com/research/Moodys-affirms-United-States-Aaa-rating-maintains-stable-outlook--PR_382024; Fitch Ratings. "2020 North American Sovereign Outlook Stable Despite Fiscal Pressures." November 26, 2019. www.fitchratings.com/site/pr/10103089.

Table 11.1 Moody's qualitative rating descriptions	
Moody's rating classification	Explanation
Aaa	Obligations rated Aaa are judged to be of the highest quality, subject to the lowest level of credit risk
Aa	Obligations rated Aa are judged to be of high quality and are subject to very low credit risk
A	Obligations rated A are judged to be upper-medium grade and are subject to low credit risk
Baa	Obligations rated Baa are judged to be medium-grade and subject to moderate credit risk and as such may possess certain speculative characteristics
Ba	Obligations rated Ba are judged to be speculative and are subject to substantial credit risk
B	Obligations rated B are considered speculative and are subject to high credit risk
Caa	Obligations rated Caa are judged to be speculative of poor standing and are subject to very high credit risk
Ca	Obligations rated Ca are highly speculative and are likely in, or very near, default, with some prospect of recovery of principal and interest
C	Obligations rated C are the lowest rated and are typically in default, with little prospect of recovery of principal and interest

This bifurcation was a result of the New Deal legislation and regulations in the USA that followed the Great Depression of the 1930s. According to White (2009), in 1936:

> ...the Office of the Comptroller of the Currency prohibited banks from investing in "speculative investment securities," as determined by "recognized rating manuals" (i.e., Moody's, Poor's, Standard, and Fitch). "Speculative" securities were bonds that were below "investment grade," thereby forcing banks that invested in bonds to hold only those bonds that were rated highly (e.g., BBB or better on the S&P scale) by these four agencies. In effect, regulators had endowed third-party safety judgments with the force of law.
>
> In the following decades, insurance regulators and then pension fund regulators followed with similar regulatory actions that forced their regulated financial institutions to heed the judgments of a handful of credit rating agencies.

Bond ratings are typically assigned when a bond is first issued and then are updated as warranted when new financial information becomes available.

Often, good or bad news is reflected in stock and bond prices before rating agencies update their ratings. But ratings do change: many bonds undergo **ratings migration** over their lives as the financial position of the issuer changes. An investment grade company that gets into financial trouble might see its bonds become **fallen angels**, that is, bonds that are downgraded to speculative grade although they haven't (yet) defaulted. Sometimes these bonds recover and become **rising stars**, bonds that were speculative grade but that have been upgraded to investment grade. However, if instead the financial deterioration continues, the bonds may default.

The ratings migration process may take years, so it may be that a bond that is currently rated at the high end of investment grade will default 10 years from now after migrating down to the low end of speculative grade. In fact, this is a typical path to default: bonds do default while they are rated investment grade, but more often defaulters migrate down to speculative grade before defaulting.

Until the 1980s, virtually all high yield bonds were fallen angels: there was very little original issuance of speculative-grade bonds. Standard & Poor's[12] notes that:

> The first real boom in the [high yield] market was in the 1980s, however, when leveraged buyouts and other mergers appropriated high-yield bonds as a financing mechanism. Probably the most famous example is the $31 billion LBO [Leveraged Buyout] of RJR Nabisco by private equity sponsor Kohlberg Kravis & Roberts in 1989 (the financing was detailed in the best-selling book *Barbarians at the Gate*).

Much of the growth of the original issuance high yield market in the 1980s was due to Michael Milken,[13] who was known as the "junk bond king." ("Junk" is a mildly pejorative way of saying "high yield" or "speculative grade.") Milken pointed out to investors that a diversified portfolio of speculative-grade bonds would yield more than enough to pay for the expected 3% or less default rate. Nicholas and Preble (2016) note that Milken himself served two years in jail for securities and tax felonies, but the "junk bond" market he created continues to thrive.

11.2.2 Historical Default Frequencies

Qualitative phrases like a "very high chance of avoiding default" are used to describe investment-grade bonds. But what do these terms mean in precise numbers?

12 Standard & Poor's. "High Yield Bond Market Primer." 2007. www.spglobal.com/marketintelligence/en/documents/hybprimer.pdf.
13 Forbes. "Profile: Michael Milken." Website. www.forbes.com/profile/michael-milken.

Traditional rating agencies do not directly target a particular percentage chance of avoiding default. Instead, they look at various factors comprising the legal and business environment and the company's fiscal health, such as these listed (among others) by Standard & Poor's:[14]

- Creditworthiness before external support
- Future income and cash flows
  - Sources (ongoing operations or investments)
  - Potential variability
- Economic conditions
- Regulatory environment
- Economic projections and forecasts
- Liquid assets
- Accounting principles and practices
- Key financial indicators
  - Profitability
  - Leverage
  - Cash flow adequacy
  - Liquidity
  - Financial flexibility
- Trends over time
- Peer comparisons
- External influence
- Likelihood and potential amount of external support
- Existence of guarantee by higher-rated guarantor
- Affiliated business entities
- Negative influences, for example, weaker parent draining cash flows or assets.

These factors are then considered by analysts and discussed by a committee that issues a rating opinion.[15]

While the rating agencies don't want to be pinned down to exact metrics, there are fairly reliable feature sets that separate ratings. Moody's periodically publishes key ratios by rating, such as the ones in Table 11.2 (generated by Code Segment 11.1).

---

14 S&P Global Ratings. "General Criteria: Principles of Credit Ratings." February 16, 2011. Updated December 14, 2020. www.standardandpoors.com/en_US/web/guest/article/-/view/sourceId/6485398.

15 [White 2009] notes that "The rating agencies favor that term ['opinion'] because it allows them to claim that they are 'publishers' and thus enjoy the protections of the First Amendment of the U.S. Constitution (e.g., when the agencies are sued by investors and issuers who claim that they have been injured by the actions of the agencies)."

Table 11.2 Moody's financial metrics Key ratios by rating for global non-financial companies, 2021 update

Item	Aaa	Aa	A	Baa	Ba	B	Caa-C
Debt/EBITDA	1.400	1.700	2.800	3.300	4.000	6.300	9.700
EBITDA/Interest Expense	48.400	25.400	10.200	5.800	3.600	1.700	0.600
Revenue	125.300	89.900	19.600	7.800	2.900	0.900	0.600
EBITDA Margin	0.374	0.180	0.127	0.131	0.128	0.120	0.063
Operating Margin	0.327	0.153	0.101	0.109	0.103	0.072	0.017
FFO/Debt	0.651	0.508	0.296	0.248	0.191	0.094	0.033
(FFO + IntExp) / IntExp	46.000	26.000	13.700	8.100	5.000	2.600	1.400
EBITA / Average Assets	0.193	0.117	0.068	0.068	0.072	0.059	0.033
CAPEX / Depreciation	1.700	1.200	1.200	1.200	1.100	1.000	0.900
Revenue Volatility	13.800	11.400	10.400	11.900	14.400	18.300	17.600

Accounting expertise isn't needed to see which metrics are desirable and which aren't: they are mostly monotone increasing or decreasing. The first item is the ratio of the company's debt to its earnings: EBITDA is "earnings before interest, taxes, depreciation, and amortization." It's intuitively clear that the lower the ratio of debt to earnings, the better chance a company will pay back its debt. This is borne out by the numbers.

These ratios, with minor adjustments, were as relevant one hundred years ago as they are today. From a data science perspective, a simple support-vector machine could be used to assign credit ratings based on features like those in Table 11.2, or to predict directly the chance of default. We'll talk about methods based on that idea in Section 11.8.

The rating agency process produces ratings that tend to be reliably ordinal but not reliably cardinal. With a few small exceptions, the default rates of classifications higher up in Table 11.1 are lower than the default rates of inferior classifications in every year.

But the actual level of defaults varies year by year depending on economic conditions. Code Segment 11.2 uses data from *Moody's Annual Default Study: Corporate Default and Recovery Rates* to generate Figure 11.1. This figure shows the year-by-year default rates for investment-grade bonds (left axis, blue) and speculative-grade bonds (right axis, red) since 1920. Code Segment 11.2 also generates the following summary statistics:

```
Investment grade:
    Min:  0.0
    Avg: 0.140. Since 1983: 0.080
    Max:  1.5503839897212  Year:  1938
    Percentage of years with no defaults:
      56.86274509803921
```

```
Speculative grade:
    Min:   0.0
    Avg: 2.850. Since 1983: 4.303
    Max:   15.7695717129538   Year:   1933
    Percentage of years with no defaults:
        11.764705882352942
```

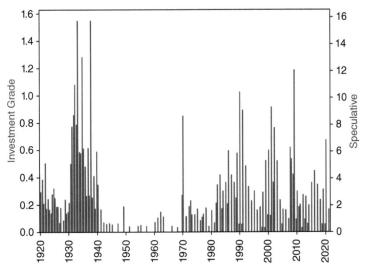

Figure 11.1 Moody's corporate default rates, 1920–2021. Source: *Moody's Annual Default Study: Corporate Default and Recovery Rates*.

The average default rate of investment-grade ("IG") bonds was a fraction of a percentage point per year, while the average default rate of speculative-grade bonds was less than 3% per year. For IG bonds the worst default rate in the last century was 1.55% in 1938. Thus, IG defaults, even in the Great Depression, were relatively rare. It is apparent from Figure 11.1 that the IG median and mode default rates are both zero. That's why there had to be a different scale for IG (left) as opposed to speculative (right); the IG defaults would barely have been visible otherwise.

As we saw above, the rating agencies look largely to time-invariant quantities such as leverage (the ratio of enterprise value to equity) to set the ratings. An enterprise that is largely funded through debt is probably going to have a higher chance of default on that debt than an enterprise that is largely funded through equity. That leads to the ordinal reliability that we noted above.

But it's clear from the historical record that the chance of default varies widely over time. 15.77% of speculative bonds defaulted in 1933; none in 1946. Thus the cardinal meaning of credit ratings needs to be understood in context. In a low-volatility market, the chance of a move in asset value down to the point of default is lower than the chance of a move to default in a high-volatility market.

While Figure 11.1 shows that investment-grade defaults are rare, it doesn't take into account ratings migration. The large credit rating agencies track historical cumulative probabilities of default by year after a bond has a particular rating. Table 11.3 (generated by Code Segment 11.3) shows Moody's cumulative default rates taking into account migration.

Table 11.3 Moody's average corporate cumulative default rates (percents, 1.0=1%) by letter rating, 1983-2021

Rating/horizon	Aaa	Aa	A	Baa	Ba	B	Caa-C	IG	SG	All
1	0.00	0.02	0.05	0.15	0.81	3.14	9.34	0.08	4.11	1.65
2	0.01	0.06	0.16	0.38	2.29	7.58	16.74	0.22	8.33	3.29
3	0.01	0.11	0.33	0.66	4.03	12.19	23.06	0.40	12.33	4.80
4	0.04	0.19	0.51	1.00	5.88	16.38	28.59	0.61	15.91	6.11
5	0.06	0.30	0.73	1.34	7.54	20.16	33.43	0.84	19.03	7.21
6	0.09	0.39	0.97	1.72	9.08	23.50	37.45	1.09	21.70	8.15
7	0.12	0.48	1.23	2.06	10.50	26.45	40.83	1.33	24.00	8.93
8	0.13	0.55	1.49	2.42	11.84	29.04	43.85	1.57	26.03	9.61
9	0.13	0.63	1.74	2.79	13.13	31.36	46.65	1.81	27.86	10.23
10	0.13	0.71	1.98	3.18	14.44	33.36	48.98	2.05	29.50	10.78
11	0.13	0.80	2.23	3.60	15.63	35.10	50.92	2.30	30.92	11.28
12	0.13	0.92	2.46	4.05	16.82	36.74	52.10	2.56	32.23	11.74
13	0.13	1.03	2.70	4.53	17.92	38.37	53.17	2.83	33.47	12.19
14	0.13	1.11	2.98	5.02	18.96	40.04	53.88	3.10	34.69	12.64
15	0.13	1.18	3.29	5.48	20.08	41.51	54.59	3.38	35.84	13.07
16	0.13	1.26	3.60	5.97	21.14	42.89	55.39	3.66	36.94	13.49
17	0.13	1.35	3.93	6.44	22.07	44.13	56.06	3.95	37.91	13.89
18	0.13	1.49	4.29	6.85	22.96	45.36	56.73	4.24	38.85	14.28
19	0.13	1.67	4.59	7.21	23.89	46.52	57.50	4.50	39.78	14.64
20	0.13	1.83	4.90	7.52	24.47	47.77	58.19	4.75	40.55	14.96

For example, Table 11.3 shows that a very small fraction of Aaa bonds defaulted two years after being rated Aaa. Since no bonds defaulted within one year of being rated Aaa, there must have been down-migrations in ratings for the tiny fraction that did default after two years.

Table 11.3 also confirms that the ordinal property always holds for credit ratings: as one reads across the rows of the table, default frequencies go up as the notches go down in quality. In some historical time periods there have been slight disruptions in monotonicity, but generally the order holds.

Table 11.4 (generated by Code Segment 11.4) shows Standard & Poor's version of Table 11.3.

Table 11.4 Standard & Poor's average global corporate cumulative default rates (percents, 1.0=1%) by letter rating, 1981-2021

Rating/Years	AAA	AA	A	BBB	BB	B	CCC/C	IG	SG	All
1	0.00	0.02	0.05	0.15	0.60	3.18	26.55	0.08	3.60	1.50
2	0.03	0.06	0.13	0.41	1.88	7.46	36.74	0.23	6.97	2.93
3	0.13	0.11	0.21	0.72	3.35	11.26	41.80	0.40	9.86	4.17
4	0.24	0.20	0.32	1.09	4.81	14.30	44.74	0.61	12.23	5.22
5	0.34	0.30	0.44	1.48	6.19	16.67	46.91	0.83	14.16	6.10
6	0.45	0.40	0.57	1.85	7.47	18.59	47.95	1.05	15.75	6.83
7	0.50	0.48	0.73	2.18	8.57	20.10	49.08	1.26	17.06	7.45
8	0.58	0.55	0.87	2.50	9.56	21.34	49.82	1.45	18.16	7.97
9	0.64	0.62	1.01	2.80	10.45	22.45	50.48	1.63	19.14	8.43
10	0.69	0.68	1.15	3.10	11.24	23.50	51.05	1.81	20.04	8.86
11	0.72	0.74	1.28	3.40	11.90	24.40	51.49	1.98	20.80	9.23
12	0.75	0.80	1.40	3.64	12.52	25.10	51.92	2.13	21.44	9.54
13	0.78	0.86	1.52	3.86	13.09	25.75	52.45	2.27	22.05	9.84
14	0.83	0.91	1.63	4.09	13.57	26.35	52.91	2.40	22.58	10.10
15	0.89	0.96	1.76	4.34	14.08	26.92	52.97	2.55	23.09	10.36

The two tables are similar. S&P has more AAA defaults than Moody's, but otherwise Moody's default rates tend to be larger than S&P. There are methods that directly target default levels using algorithms intended to find a firm's **expected default frequency (EDF)** given its financial condition and other inputs. These methods are usually based on the Merton structural model that we first saw in Chapter 9. For example, Barclays Bank developed a Corporate Default Probability Model that directly estimated default probabilities. Figure 11.2 (generated by Code Segment 11.5) shows the Barclays model estimated probabilities compared to Moody's historical frequencies on a log-scale.

The Barclays estimates were made in 2009 at the height of the Global Financial Crisis, so they are understandably higher than the long-term Moody's frequencies. But the orders and shapes are similar. Both methods produce something that looks like a straight line on a log-scale, which means that default probabilities/frequencies increase exponentially as ratings go down. For the Barclays estimates, the ratings were not an input but rather were used to group the bonds after the estimates were made.

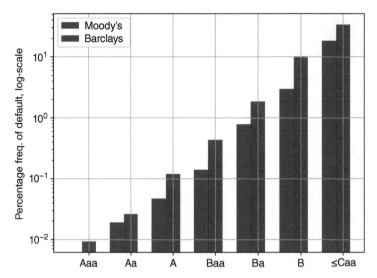

Figure 11.2 Default rates, Moody's historical 1920–2021 and Barclays' model 2009, log-scale.

11.2.3 Sovereign Debt Ratings

Credit ratings are also applied to sovereign (government) bonds, including national governments and local authorities like states, provinces, cities, and government agencies like the Port Authority of New York and New Jersey or Eksportfinans ASA.[16]

There is a saying that "corporations default because they have to; sovereigns default because they want to." This is an exaggeration, but sovereigns may have options that corporations don't:

- Sovereigns can raise taxes or tolls on their subjects;
- Sovereigns can nationalize private property by law or by force – an extreme form of taxation;
- Conversely, sovereigns can privatize or franchise public property (e.g. airports, bridges, roads), realizing revenues and fees;
- If a sovereign controls the central bank that regulates the supply of the currency in which the debt is to be repaid, it can create more money and pay back its debt in devalued currency;
- Sovereigns can choose to abrogate other obligations like payments to retired workers.

16 Port Authority New York New Jersey. "Consolidated Bonds & Notes: Investor Information." Website. www.panynj.gov/corporate/en/financial-information/consolidated-bonds-and-notes.html. Eksportfinans Norway. "Eksportfinans ASA." Website. www.eksportfinans.com/.

Table 11.5 Argentina's debt history	
Year	**Event**
1816	Argentina declares independence from Spain
1827	Defaults on debt because Bank of England hiked interest rates
1890	Default; contributed to Bank of England need to rescue House of Baring
1951	Default
1956	Restructuring; military coup
1982	Default
1989	Default; general emerging market debt crisis
2001	Default; unsustainable heavy borrowing during 1990s
2014	Default
2017	Sells 100-year bond that is 4x oversubscribed
2019	Begins restructuring "massive" debt in August. Defaults again in December. Gets IMF bailout
2020	Misses interest payment of $500 million; negotiates writedown in debt of $66 billion

For a corporation, default is an existential choice: after default, a corporation may cease to exist altogether. At the very least, it will be significantly restructured. So corporations generally default only as a last resort when they just can't pay their debts.

But sovereigns may have a choice as to how much pain they want to inflict on their citizens using the options listed above. Sovereigns also don't face the existential threat from default that corporations do: the sovereign will continue to exist after default. It may find some of its assets seized in partial payment of the debt, and it may very well find that it can't borrow again for quite a while after default. But a sovereign won't perish simply due to default.

In fact, even financial punishments for sovereign default – like inability to borrow further – are uncertain. Consider Argentina's debt history in Table 11.5.[17]

After becoming a nation in 1816 and fighting a war of independence, Argentina was able to borrow from international banks largely based in London.

---

17 Through 2001: [Reinhart and Rogoff 2009]. 2014 default: BBC News. "Argentina Defaults for Second Time." July 31, 2014. www.bbc.com/news/business-28578179. 2017 100-year bond: Financial Times. "How did Argentina pull off a 100-year bond sale?" www.ft.com/content/5ac33abc-551b-11e7-9fed-c19e2700005f. 2019 Restructuring: Congressional Research Service. "Argentina's Economic Crisis and Default." June 15, 2020. https://crsreports.congress.gov/product/pdf/IF/IF10991. 2020: Congressional Research Service. "Argentina: An Overview." July 29, 2022. https://crsreports.congress.gov/product/pdf/IF/IF10932.

By 1827, however, as part of a general crisis in Latin American debt, Argentina defaulted. Understandably, international lenders would not loan money to Argentina for decades after that.

But 50 years after the 1827 default, Argentina had a completely different government and a completely different economy. So it's also understandable that foreign lenders would feel that they could return. In particular, the British House of Baring was heavily involved in loans to Argentina when Argentina defaulted again in 1890. Argentina's default would have led to Barings' default but for a rescue operation by the Bank of England.[18]

Again, it's understandable that Argentina was not able to borrow for quite a while after the 1890 default. But by the mid-1900s it built up debt as, once again, lenders could reason that there was a completely different government and a completely different economy than the one that defaulted so long ago in 1890.

The next default was in 1951. Using the reasoning outlined above, Argentina should have been unable to borrow for a number of decades as international lenders penalized the country and waited for a complete change in people, government and economy.

But Table 11.5 shows a pattern of rapid-fire defaults, in some cases only a few years apart, after the 1951 default. Argentina was even able to sell a "century bond" – a bond not requiring repayment of principal for 100 years – three years after its 2014 default. Two years after that, Argentina restructured its debt again.

Why would any lender trust a country with a long history of defaulting on debt, and with a fresh default in the recent past? Part of the answer to that question is in the satirical title of Reinhart and Rogoff (2009): *This Time Is Different: A Panoramic View of Eight Centuries of Financial Crises*. Financial actors convince themselves that *this time is different* even though it isn't. Noting that investors were rushing to buy Argentina's 100-year bond, Mander and Wigglesworth (2017) observed:

> [The Argentines] "cured" the latest default in 2016, and times have changed, said Joe Harper, a partner at Explorador Capital Management, an investment fund focused on Latin America. "The policy pendulum in Argentina has shifted to the centre, and the country's next 100 years will be very different than the last century."

Two years into the "very different" century after 2017, there was a new government and a new debt restructuring in Argentina.

---

18 [Mitchener and Weidenmier 2008].

Witty credit market participants have characterized restructuring as "amend, extend and pretend." This means that when a debtor cannot pay, the lenders amend the debt agreements, extend the time allowed to repay, and pretend that these measures will somehow allow them eventually to recover their principal and interest.

Another, more hard-headed, rationale for lending to a serial defaulter is that a bond's default does not necessarily mean that investing in that bond was a bad idea. Argentina's 100-year bonds paid almost 8% a year. At the time, that was about 5.1% a year higher than the US Treasury long-term rate. An investor might have no illusions about Argentina's ability to last 100 years without defaulting. But an investor might more realistically think that the next default would be at least 20 years in the future. By that time, given the high coupon on the bonds, the investor would have recovered principal and made some profit. Further, a keen-eyed investor might note that there is often some partial recovery of principal in default or restructuring. So with a high coupon, some recovery, and a sufficiently long time to default, an investor might expect to turn a nice profit even with a default.

And that was just the downside scenario. There was also an upside scenario where, at least for a while, Argentina's fiscal picture improved and the 5.1% spread over US Treasurys tightened by (say) 2%, leading to a rapid double-digit percentage increase in the price of the bonds.

With the benefit of hindsight, we can see that the upside didn't happen, nor did the default scenario take a comfortably long time to play out. But it was not completely daft in 2017 to expect that it might be longer than two years until Argentina's next default.

Empirically, there is an offset between the many options that sovereigns have that corporations don't – which would tend to lower sovereign defaults – and the relatively mild punishment for sovereign default compared to corporate default – which would tend to increase sovereign defaults. Sovereigns rated AAA and AA have used the tools available to them to prioritize maintaining their high ratings and relatively low borrowing costs: Table 11.6 (generated by Code Segment 11.6) shows they had no defaults at all over the subsequent 15 years.

But as ratings got lower, the frequency of sovereign default in Table 11.6 compared to corporate default in Table 11.4 got higher. After two years, a CCC or below sovereign was more likely than not to default. However the overall IG and SG default frequencies for sovereigns were quite similar to the overall IG and SG default frequencies for corporates. This was due to different mixes of ratings within those categories.

Table 11.6 Standard & Poor's average sovereign foreign currency cumulative default rates (percents, 1.0=1%) by letter rating, 1975-2021

Rating/Years	AAA	AA	A	BBB	BB	B	CCC/C	IG	SG	All
1	0	0	0.00	0.00	0.38	2.42	37.50	0.00	3.14	1.18
2	0	0	0.00	0.41	1.37	6.12	44.20	0.10	5.77	2.23
3	0	0	0.23	1.07	1.98	9.54	51.48	0.31	8.09	3.22
4	0	0	0.72	1.53	2.61	12.65	54.03	0.53	10.07	4.09
5	0	0	1.23	2.02	3.94	15.38	57.09	0.76	12.17	5.00
6	0	0	1.76	2.55	5.34	17.70	63.22	1.00	14.18	5.88
7	0	0	2.33	3.11	6.82	20.21	66.57	1.25	16.23	6.76
8	0	0	2.92	3.41	8.63	22.69	66.57	1.45	18.28	7.61
9	0	0	3.53	3.74	10.01	24.58	66.57	1.65	19.84	8.28
10	0	0	4.18	4.10	10.89	26.34	66.57	1.87	21.11	8.85
11	0	0	4.85	4.50	11.53	28.28	69.91	2.10	22.47	9.46
12	0	0	5.58	4.92	12.21	30.09	69.91	2.34	23.64	10.00
13	0	0	6.37	5.39	12.96	31.32	69.91	2.60	24.56	10.47
14	0	0	6.80	6.39	13.77	32.72	69.91	2.87	25.58	10.96
15	0	0	7.74	6.94	14.22	34.33	69.91	3.17	26.50	11.44

11.2.4 Sovereign Spreads in the Eurozone

The eurozone or euro area consists of the member states of the European Union[19] that have adopted the euro as their currency. At this writing, there are 19 countries that use the common currency.

There is a single monetary policy for the entire eurozone, run by the European Central Bank.[20] Thus, a Greek citizen can spend her euros in Germany, or France, or Greece without any conversion needed. But there are 19 different fiscal policies: each country decides how much to tax and spend. Each country also borrows money separately. Naturally, relatively higher-spending countries are considered less likely to repay their debt.

Germany is considered to have the strongest fiscal position in the European Union. (Norway is in Europe and is considered by some to have an even stronger fiscal position than Germany, but Norway is not a member of the European Union.) Bonds issued by the German government are considered to be the default-free references from which discount rates are formed for euro-denominated cash flows.

---

19 European Commission. "What Is the Euro Area?" Website. https://ec.europa.eu/info/business-economy-euro/euro-area/what-euro-area_en. European Union. "Aims and Values." Website. https://europa.eu/european-union/about-eu/eu-in-brief_en.

20 European Central Bank. "Eurosystem." Website. www.ecb.europa.eu/home/html/index.en.html.

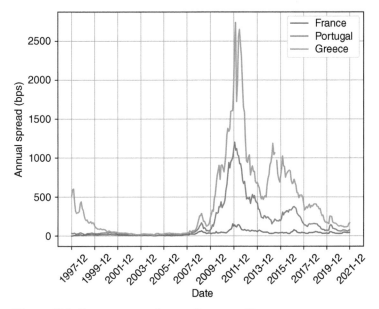

Figure 11.3 European spreads over Germany, 10-year rates.

Other eurozone countries' bonds have higher yields than Germany, reflecting less confidence in their ability to repay their debts. The **sovereign spreads** over Germany range from a little (France) to a lot (Greece). In general, sovereign spreads are like the credit spreads in (11.3) and (11.4) and arise when a sovereign issues debt in a currency that its government does not control.

Figure 11.3 (generated by Code Segment 11.7) shows historical sovereign spreads of three eurozone countries over Germany and also outputs recent values of those spreads:

```
Ending values (2021-12-31) of spreads over Germany in bps/
    year
France  43.4
Portugal  74.4
Greece  167.4
```

The European debt crisis starting in 2009 is apparent in the alpine prominences on the graph. Alessi and McBride (2015) observe that Greece, Ireland, and Portugal all took bailouts from the "Troika" of international institutions composed of the European Commission, the European Central Bank, and the International Monetary Fund.[21] While Portuguese and Irish debts were fully repaid with the help of the bailout, private Greek bondholders were forced to take

---

21 European Commission. Website. https://ec.europa.eu/info/index_en. International Monetary Foundation. Website. www.imf.org/en/home.

a "voluntary" 50% reduction in their principal amount. The difference between a voluntary reduction and a default is measured in lawsuits rather than in euros.

More recently, European sovereign spreads have abated to non-crisis levels. France and Portugal have spreads over Germany that are tighter than AAA corporate bonds (see Figure 11.3). Greece's spread over Germany is similar to a BBB corporate bond.

11.3 The Credit Spread Premium Puzzle

When corporate bonds did default in the years since 1983, Moody's recovery rates given default ("RGDs") were a little higher for investment grade than for speculative grade, as computed by Code Segment 11.8:

```
1983-2021 Investment-Grade Average 5-Year Recovery: 44.64
    percent
1983-2021 Speculative-Grade Average 5-Year Recovery: 38.
    70 percent
```

We've used cumulative five-year recoveries here as an indicator of ultimate recovery, since it may take some time for resolution in a default situation. A rough calculation of the average annual loss rate for investment-grade bonds can therefore be made by Code Segment 11.9 by multiplying loss rates (the complements of recovery rates) times the average annual default rates computed just after Figure 11.1:

```
1983-2021 Investment-Grade Rough Annual Loss Rate: 4.43
    basis points per year
1983-2021 Speculative-Grade Rough Annual Loss Rate: 263.
    76 basis points per year
```

This isn't quite right, as we've multiplied an average times an average. Moody's calculated loss rates directly each year since 1983; the average annual loss rates retrieved by Code Segment 11.10 were:

```
1983-2021 Investment-Grade Average Annual Loss Rate: 4.97
    basis points per year
1983-2021 Speculative-Grade Average Annual Loss Rate:
    253.43 basis points per year
```

These were close to the rough calculations, and show that there has been very little average credit loss from investment-grade bonds, and less than 3% per year average credit loss from speculative-grade bonds. Most losses occur in fallen angels, the bonds that started out as investment grade but were downgraded to speculative grade.

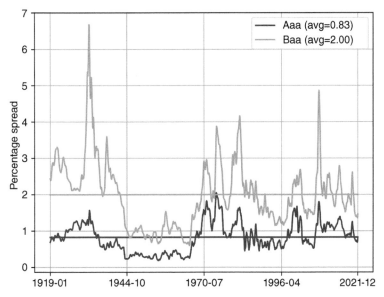

Figure 11.4 Moody's smoothed yield spreads over Treasurys.

Investment-grade bonds would therefore only need to yield a single-digit number of basis points more than US Treasurys to make up for credit losses over average credit cycles. In fact, investors receive far more than single-digit basis points extra yield over Treasurys on investment-grade bonds.

Figure 11.4 (generated by Code Segment 11.11) shows the extra yield (over comparable Treasurys) received by investment-grade corporate bonds: the lower line is for the highest-rated investment-grade bonds (Aaa Moody's=AAA S&P), while the higher line shows the extra yield received for the lowest-rated investment-grade corporate bonds (Baa Moody's=BBB S&P). Code Segment 11.11 also computes the following statistics:

```
Spread and Treasury data starts 1919-01
Aaa/Baa level correlation: 0.73862
Aaa/Tsy difference correlation: -0.36996
Baa/Tsy difference correlation: -0.24246
Aaa/Baa difference correlation: 0.67662

Aaa mean since 1983: 0.9115362211858987
Baa mean since 1983: 1.911852460502137
```

The cumulative 20-year default rate for Aaa bonds in Table 11.3 is a small fraction of the one-year mean Aaa spread since 1983! The Baa cumulative 20-year default in Table 11.3 is not quite so spectacularly low, but it only represents less than 4 years of the mean Baa spread since 1983. Taking into account recovery would make the mismatch even larger.

So it appears that the spreads were too big compared to the loss rates they compensated for. Of course, risk-neutral prices include a component of risk preference, and it seems reasonable that bondholders would be highly risk-averse. So spreads should be bigger than loss rates. But these numbers are different by an order of magnitude, which is impossible to explain by appealing to the different data sources or time periods.

There is a more salient possible explanation for the difference: there is a methodological problem with using the average yield spreads shown in Figure 11.4. Aaa spreads are formed by taking the average of spreads of bonds that are rated Aaa at the time the average is computed. When a bond is downgraded below Aaa, its spread increases and the bondholder suffers a negative return, but it is no longer included in the Aaa spread calculation. Hence the real-world negative effect of downgrades is not taken into account in the Figure 11.4 calculations. Downgraded bonds simply disappear without any consequences.

It is more realistic to track the rates of return of investable portfolios of bonds. That's done by Code Segment 11.12:

```
Annualized rates of return from 1986-08-31 to 2021-12-31
      (35.3 years)
US Treasury 10-year: 0.0568, Vol: 0.0740
US Corp Master (IG): 0.0686, Vol: 0.0527
  (spread over Tsy): 0.0118
US HY Master 2     : 0.0812, Vol: 0.0813
  (spread over Tsy): 0.0244
```

Since September 1986, investing in an index of investment-grade bonds had a higher return than US Treasurys *while experiencing lower volatility*. The lower volatility results from negative rate/spread correlations; we'll explore that in Section 11.5. Speculative-grade (high yield) bonds beat US Treasurys by more, although with slightly higher volatility. These are (except for comparatively small transactions costs) realistic numbers that include price drops due to downgrades and defaults, as well as price increases due to upgrades and other positive news.

Thus, the puzzle of (apparently) too-high credit spreads is real: corporate bonds, both investment grade and speculative grade, return quite a bit more than US Treasurys after paying for defaults. The higher returns could be risk compensation, except that corporate bond index risk is comparable to, or lower than, US Treasury risk when risk is defined as volatility. It may be that bond investors are concerned with tail risk: corporate bonds might not provide safety during extreme financial disruptions. Even so, the numbers intuitively seem too big for the risks involved, especially with investment-grade corporates.

Krainer (2004) reviewed some explanations for the credit spread: tax treatment, bond market illiquidity, and generally changing levels of systemic risk aversion that can't be diversified away. Krainer (p. 3) concludes that:

> High-yield spreads are clearly tied to fundamentals such as future expected default rates. But spreads are also related to market liquidity in ways that are not yet well understood.

Feldhütter and Schaefer (2018) left little doubt as to their point of view in the title of their paper: "The Myth of the Credit Spread Puzzle." In it, they argued that empirical tests of structural models have not been calibrated on sufficiently long historical datasets. When they included data going back to the 1920s, they found that a structural model fits observed credit spreads quite well for investment-grade corporate bonds, although there is still some unexplained spread in speculative-grade corporate bonds.

The debate continued, though, as Bai, Goldstein, and Yang (2018, p. 7) examined Feldhütter and Schaefer's (2018) methodology and found that:

> ... their results are reversed when their model is calibrated to *market* values of debt as required by theory rather than *book* values.

Below, we'll explore what is meant by market value and book (par) value. While the credit spread premium changes depending on model and calibration, we do believe that the puzzle continues to exist: compensation for credit risk is enigmatically large.

11.4 The Merton Model

The Merton (1974) model was briefly described in Section 9.5.1. Now we'll return to that model in greater detail.

Merton assumed that a corporate enterprise had borrowed a principal amount D_{par} in the form of a single zero-coupon bond due at time T from now. In order for a company to be a going concern[22] and not enter bankruptcy, its enterprise value at time T, $V(T)$, will need to be at least D_{par}. Anything left over will go to the stockholders, so at time T a going concern will have $V(T) = D_{par} + S(T)$, where $S(T) \geq 0$ is the value of the company's stock (equity) at time T.

---

22 AICPA®: Statement on Auditing Standards. "The Auditor's Consideration of an Entity's Ability to Continue as a Going Concern." February 2017. www.aicpa.org/research/standards/auditattest/downloadabledocuments/sas_132.pdf.

Merton further assumed that the enterprise value V follows a lognormal process like (3.17):[23]

$$dV = \mu_V V dt + \sigma_V V d\beta,\qquad(11.5)$$

where μ_V is the enterprise value's mean return. An application of Itô's Lemma gives:

$$d\ln(V) = \left(\mu_V - \sigma_V^2/2\right)dt + \sigma_V d\beta.$$

Thus, the logarithm of enterprise value follows a diffusion process that starts at the current point $\ln(V(0))$. At time T from now, log of enterprise value is normally distributed with mean $\mathbb{E}[\ln(V(T))] = \ln(V(0)) + \left(\mu_V - \sigma_V^2/2\right)T$ and standard deviation $\sigma_V\sqrt{T}$.

The part of the time-T distribution of enterprise values in which the company is in default is the part where $\ln(V(T)) < \ln(D_{par})$. We can compute the **distance to default**, which is the number of standard deviations between the mean and the default threshold:

$$d_{Def} = \frac{\mathbb{E}[\ln(V(T))] - \ln(D_{par})}{\sigma_V\sqrt{T}} = \frac{\ln(V(0)/D_{par}) + \left(\mu_V - \frac{\sigma_V^2}{2}\right)T}{\sigma_V\sqrt{T}}.\qquad(11.6)$$

Under Merton's assumption that the diffusion process is normal, this means that the real-world (as opposed to risk-neutral) probability of default in the Merton model is $N(-d_{Def})$, where $N()$ is the standard normal cumulative distribution function.

Option pricing formulas can be used to obtain the risk-neutral (market-observed) prices of stock and debt. This follows from the observation that in addition to the going-concern case, we know the behavior of the non-going-concern (bankruptcy) case at time T. In that case, $V(T) < D_{par}$ and $S(T) = 0$; the lenders only get back a recovery fraction $V(T)/D_{par} < 1$ of the amount they loaned. (As we've seen above that recovery fraction averages around $40\% - 44\%$ of D_{par}.)

Both Merton (1974) and Black and Scholes (1973) pointed out that under these assumptions, the company's stock value S has the same payoff pattern as a European call option.

In our notation, the Black–Scholes–Merton call option pricing formula says:

$$Call = S(0) = V \cdot N(d_1) - \exp(-rT)D_{par}N(d_2),$$

$$d_1 = \frac{\ln(V(0)/D_{par}) + \left(r + \frac{\sigma_V^2}{2}\right)T}{\sigma_V\sqrt{T}},\qquad(11.7)$$

$$d_2 = d_1 - \sigma_V\sqrt{T}.$$

[23] Merton assumed a process that included a constant dividend or interest payment, but that doesn't change the substance of the conclusions.

Put-call parity, also called the **conversion equation**, can be applied to this model to price debt. Put-call parity says that for European options on non-dividend-paying underlying assets X, we have:

$$V(0) + Put - S(0) = \exp(-rT)D_{par}. \tag{11.8}$$

Here, the put and the call (which is the stock $S(0)$) have the same underlyings, same maturities T, and same strike prices D_{par}. Put-call parity follows from the fact that the left-hand side of (11.8) will always be worth D_{par} at time T; either the put or the call will be in the money exactly enough to make up the difference between the underlying value $V(T)$ and the strike price D_{par}. The put's value is therefore:

$$Put = -V \cdot N(-d_1) + \exp(-rT)D_{par}N(-d_2). \tag{11.9}$$

Rearranging (11.8) and using the accounting identity $V(t) = S(t) + D(t)$,

$$V(0) - S(0) = D(0) = \exp(-rT)D_{par} - Put. \tag{11.10}$$

The term $\exp(-rT)D_{par}$ is the current price of a default-free zero-coupon bond maturing at time T from now at the par value of the debt. The possibility of default is reflected by subtracting the value of a put on V struck at D_{par} at time T from now.

Equation (11.10) gives the current market value of the enterprise's debt $D(0)$. Debt par value can be decomposed into three components:

$$D_{par} = D(0) + D_{par}(1 - \exp(-rT)) + Put. \tag{11.11}$$

The $D_{par}(1 - \exp(-rT))$ term is the time value of the debt, while the put value gives the credit risk.

This additive credit risk value is related to the multiplicative spread value s in the pricing equation (11.4):

$$D(0) = \exp(-(r+s)T)D_{par} = \exp(-rT)D_{par} - Put$$

so:

$$s = -\frac{1}{T}\ln\left(1 - \exp(rT)\frac{Put}{D_{par}}\right). \tag{11.12}$$

11.4.1 Merton's Term Structure of Credit Spreads

Merton (1974) uses his debt value (11.10) to compute a theoretical term structure of credit spreads. Define:

$$Spr(T) = -\frac{1}{T}\ln\left(\frac{D(0)}{D_{par}}\right) - r = -\frac{1}{T}\ln\left(\frac{\exp(-rT)D_{par} - Put}{D_{par}}\right) - r$$

$$= -\frac{1}{T}\ln\left(\frac{\exp(-rT)D_{par} + V\cdot N(-d_1) - \exp(-rT)D_{par}N(-d_2)}{D_{par}}\right) - r$$

$$= -\frac{1}{T}\ln\left(1 + \frac{1}{d}\cdot N(-d_1) - N(-d_2)\right) = -\frac{1}{T}\ln\left(\frac{1}{d}N(-d_1) + N(d_2)\right)$$

$$(11.13)$$

to be the spread over the risk-free rate r due to credit risk, where d is:

$$d = \frac{D_{par}\exp(-rT)}{V}.$$

Merton calls d the **"quasi" debt-to-firm value ratio**: it is a kind of leverage ratio.

Note from (11.7) that:

$$d_1 = \frac{-\ln(d) + \frac{s^2}{2}}{s}, \qquad (11.14)$$

where $s = \sigma_V\sqrt{T}$, and $d_2 = d_1 - s$. Thus, $Spr(T)$ is actually a function of three variables: σ_V, T, and d.

Figure 11.5 (generated by Code Segment 11.13) is similar to Figure 1 in Pitts and Selby (1983), which corrects Merton's partially incorrect Figure 3.

The parameters for Figure 11.5 describe highly indebted or near-insolvent companies with high enterprise volatility ($\sigma_V \approx .45$), so the credit spreads are dramatically high.

In the next section, we'll look at some actual values of these parameters.

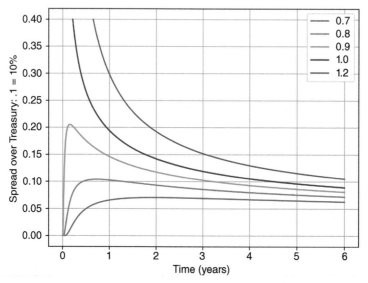

Figure 11.5 Term structure of Merton credit spreads, $\sigma_v^2 - 0.20$.

Image 11.1 Bloomberg enterprise value screen. Source: Used with permission of Bloomberg Finance L.P.

Enterprise Value Example

Image 11.1 is a Bloomberg enterprise value screen for the pharmaceutical giant Johnson & Johnson.[24] Moody's and Standard & Poor's both rate Johnson & Johnson ("JNJ") at the highest possible rating, that is, in aggregate better than the US Treasury. Figure 11.6 (generated by Code Segment 11.14) shows a simplified capital stack for JNJ.

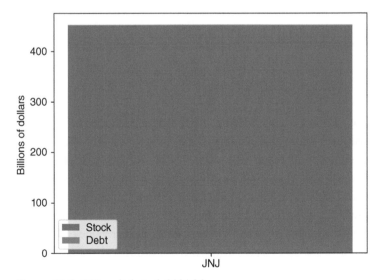

Figure 11.6 JNJ capital stack 2021Q3.

24 Bloomberg. "The Company and Its Products." Website. www.bloomberg.com/company; Johnson & Johnson. "About Johnson & Johnson." Website. www.jnj.com/about-jnj.

We'll discuss some complications in estimating enterprise value below. For now we'll assume that enterprise value number is the sum of S and D_{par}.

Code Segment 11.15 plugs in JNJ's numbers, or first-pass estimates of them from observable numbers, in the formulas above. We've assumed – counterfactually, but in the spirit of the Merton model – that JNJ has a single zero-coupon debt issue maturing in $T = 10$ years. For context, Code Segment 11.15 shows the Aaa default rate from Table 11.3 above times one minus the investment grade recovery rate:

```
Ratios for JNJ:
    D/V: 0.006940028263557669
    D/S: 0.006988528851306424
    S/V: 0.9930599717364423
 ln(V/D): 4.970449431912975


Computations for JNJ:
    S/V-scaled enterprise vol: 0.17135249812312314
Risk-neutral growth rate r-sig^2/2: 0.0005191606934825399
Risk-neutral distance to default: 9.18245060591977
    Default probability N(-d_def): 2.1069519756909534e-20


Debt components for JNJ:
            Par value of debt: 3.142999999999997
        Time value of par debt: 0.44319983363064863
            Value of default put: 0.0
    Current market value of debt: 2.699800166369357


Table 11.3 10-year Aaa default  * (1-IG-recovery) * D_par:
        0.002206987186031947
```

Over 120 years the Merton model gives virtually no chance of default, and assigns a value of close to zero to the default put. There is no noticeable correction to the default-free debt model needed for Johnson & Johnson. Nonetheless, Johnson & Johnson bonds have a spread over US Treasurys on the order of 62bps a year,[25] consistent with the credit spread premium puzzle. Historically, multiplying the cumulative 10-year default rate for Aaa bonds times the investment grade loss rate, and then times the par value of JNJ debt, gives the

25 Option-Adjusted Spread (OAS) from Bloomberg YAS screen for JNJ 4.95 of 05/15/33 as of December 31, 2021. Retrieved February 24, 2022.

final number shown above: it is small but a little bigger than the essentially zero value of the default put under the Merton model.

11.4.3 Model Improvement: Iterative Enterprise Value

While Image 11.1 shows an enterprise value that we took to equal $V(0)$ above, enterprise value can't be directly observed. So D_{par}, how much the company owes, can be observed. If there is publicly traded stock, then $S(0)$, the company's market value, can be observed. But $D(0)$ and $V(0)$ are derived from those observations.[26] For good measure, the unobservability of $V(0)$ means that enterprise volatility σ_V is also unobservable.

Fortunately, there are iterative approaches that can be used to estimate current enterprise value $V(0)$ and enterprise volatility σ_V.

One approach[27] applies Itô's Lemma to (11.5) with $f(V) = Call(V)$. That gives the following expression as the coefficient of the random term $d\beta$:

$$\frac{\partial Call}{\partial V}\sigma_V V = N(d_1)\sigma_V V. \qquad (11.15)$$

For a publicly traded company we can observe σ_S, the volatility of stock prices, through option-implied volatilities or directly from historical price data. Stock prices themselves are often modeled as lognormal processes, at least in the random diffusion term $d\beta$. In that case, the coefficients of the random terms are approximately equal:

$$S\sigma_S \approx N(d_1)\sigma_V V,$$

which gives:

$$\sigma_V \approx \frac{S\sigma_S}{N(d_1)V}. \qquad (11.16)$$

Equations (11.7) and (11.16) give two equations in the two unknowns V and σ_V. The quantities r, T, S, and D_{par} are observable. Stock volatility σ_S is observable in the past and can be estimated in the future via options or using the techniques of Chapter 9.

Code Segment 11.16 applies this approach to JNJ:

```
JNJ enterprise value at par:       452.880
JNJ enterprise value at market:    452.437
JNJ enterprise volatility:         0.172
```

---

26 The company might have publicly traded debt, making the market value observable. But we want to derive the Merton model's value of $D(0)$.

27 [Jones, Mason, and Rosenfeld 1984].

```
                         D_par: 3.142999999999997
Market value of debt (D_par-Put=V-S): 2.6998001632180717
             Time value of par debt: 0.44319983363064863
             Implied default put value: 3.1512854548054747e-09
Default put value as a fraction of par: 1.0026334207324794e-09
                     d_1 at solution: 9.658807077790133
(34 iterations for accuracy 1.000000e-08)
```

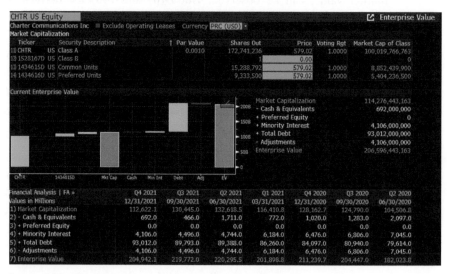

Image 11.2 Bloomberg enterprise value page for Charter. Source: Used with permission of Bloomberg Finance L.P.

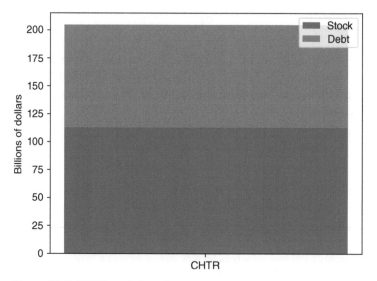

Figure 11.7 CHTR capital stack.

With a more realistic enterprise value and volatility, there is now slightly more value to the default put over the next ten years. But it's still effectively zero, far less than the annual credit spreads that Johnson&Johnson bonds display in the market.

For a lower-rated company, consider Charter Communications, Inc.[28] It is rated BB+/Ba1, that is, speculative grade.

Image 11.2 is the Bloomberg enterprise value page for Charter.

Charter's capital stack display in Figure 11.7 (generated by Code Segment 11.17) is an immediate tipoff that it will have different behavior than Johnson & Johnson.

Plugging in Charter's parameters to the iterative method and assuming for illustrative purposes 10-year debt, Code Segment 11.18 obtains the following:

```
CHTR enterprise value at par:      204.942
CHTR enterprise value at market:   189.526
CHTR enterprise volatility:        0.191


                            D_par: 92.32000000000001
  Market value of debt (D_par-Put=V-S): 76.90437553599988
             Time value of par debt: 13.018201921979486
         Implied default put value: 2.3974225420206494
Default put value as a fraction of par:
    0.02596861505654946

                   d_1 at solution: 1.3994357073170307
(31 iterations for accuracy 1.000000e-08)
Table 11.3 10-year Ba default  * (1-SG-recovery) * D_par:
    8.17512764245547
```

The final number based on Table 11.3's cumulative 10-year Ba default rate, times the speculative-grade loss rate, times the par value of Charter debt, is about four times as large as the default put value from the pure structural model. Actual credit spreads for long-term Charter debt are 351bps *per year*. While the order of magnitude of the default put is not quite as far off as with investment-grade debt, the pure structural model still underestimates actual spreads.

11.4.4 Model Improvement: KMV model

Merton's pure structural model is too elegant to survive in the wild. For example, large companies have many different debt issues maturing at different times and usually paying coupons. This drives a wedge between the Merton model's mathematically tractable assumption of a single zero-coupon debt issue and the multi-date credit obligations of a real company. The simple European put option

---

28 Charter Communications. "About Charter." Website. https://corporate.charter.com/about-charter.

that contains the value of default is, in reality, more like a complicated barrier option: it might forcibly be exercised at a number of different times. This can radically change the value of the default option.

Another deep flaw: Chapter 7 pointed out that empirical financial distributions are almost always leptokurtic. The convenient assumption of lognormality is especially weak at the tails of distributions. Since defaults are neither common nor impossible, they generally live in the tails of distributions.

For example, Table 7.1 shows that a four standard deviation event would mean virtually no (.3bps) chance of default assuming lognormal returns. But Kealhofer (2003a) notes that empirically, a four standard deviation distance to default is associated with approximately a 50bps chance of default, that is, such defaults are over 150 times more common than lognormality implies.

Even with these flaws, the structural model can be useful for assessing ordinal if not cardinal default risks. Distance to default (11.6) seems intuitively to be associated with its eponymous quality even if it is not exactly what it purports to be. So, for example, distance to default calculations might (with some adjustment) help a bank decide how much capital to set aside to protect against losses in its loan portfolio.

With this in mind, Stephen Kealhofer, John McQuown, and Oldrich Vasicek[29] put their initials together to form **KMV** in 1989. KMV computed **expected default frequencies (EDFs)** based on a modified version of the structural model. KMV was very successful and was acquired in 2002 by Moody's Corp, where it is now part of Moody's Analytics.

Crosbie and Bohn (2003, p. 3) describe the KMV model. They point out a number of unrealistic assumptions by the pure Merton model.

> In our study of defaults, we have found that generally firms do not default when their asset value reaches the book value of their total liabilities. While some firms certainly default at this point, many continue to trade and service their debts. The long-term nature of some of their liabilities provides these firms with some breathing room. We have found that the default point, the asset value at which the firm will default, generally lies somewhere between total liabilities and current, or short-term, liabilities.

Kealhofer (2003a), describing the KMV method, therefore makes the distance to default more practical than the pure Merton version (11.6):

$$d_{Def}^{KMV}(h) = \frac{\ln(V) - \ln(DefaultPoint) + \left(\mu_V - \frac{\sigma_V^2}{2}\right)h}{\sigma_V\sqrt{h}}. \tag{11.17}$$

29 Moody's Analytics. "History of KMV." Website. www.moodysanalytics.com/about-us/history/kmv-history.

Here V is the market value of the enterprise's assets and μ_v and σ_V are the expected value and standard deviation of V as in the Merton model (11.6). The parameter h is the horizon (in years) over which the distance to default is to be computed. The default point takes into account the issues noted by Crosbie and Bohn.

Further, KMV takes fat tails into account by using an empirical dataset rather than a lognormal assumption. For corporate bonds, the models build a dataset of past characteristics and default indicators in order to associate distance to default (11.17) with observed default frequencies. That's where Kealhofer got the 50bps estimate of default frequency for a four distance to default cited above.

To estimate the unobservable V and σ_V, KMV-type models use an iterative method like the one we saw above. By using historical information as well as current information, these models can converge on reasonable estimates for the unknowns.

The KMV method starts by making a guess as to the current enterprise value of the company in question, denoted by V_0^0. The market value of the company's stock at the present time, denoted by S_0, can be observed if it's publicly listed. If not, a factor model as in Chapter 6 can be used so that company characteristics like book-to-price, market capitalization, and industry can be projected into an estimated market value. The equity (stock) volatility σ_S can also be observed either from implied volatilities of the company's options, or from historical log-prices, or from historical factors projected into log-prices. An initial guess as to enterprise volatility $\sigma_{V,0}$ can be made with a simple proportional estimate $\sigma_{V,0} = \frac{\sigma_S S_0}{V_0^0}$.

So far, the method is the same as the simple Merton model, with extended notation. But then KMV begins to diverge. Instead of a European option valuation formula, KMV uses a custom option pricing formula developed by Vasicek and Kealhofer (the "VK" formula). The VK formula prices a perpetual option where the strike price (the default point) is an absorbing barrier – whenever the enterprise value hits the default point, the firm is forced to default. The firm can't wait until some future expiration date to recover. The default point takes into account points at which similar firms have defaulted in the past and looks at multiple classes of the firm's liabilities.

KMV then uses the VK option formula to compute an implied time series of past enterprise values $V_0^t, t = 0, \ldots, T$ where a higher t means further in the past; $t = 0$ is the present.

$$[Market - Value - of - Stock]_t = VK(V_0^t, \sigma_{V,0}, DP, r). \qquad (11.18)$$

In (11.18), all but one variable is either observable (historical market values of stock; default point DP computed from capital structure of the firm and analysis of comparable firms; risk-free rate r) or previously assumed (enterprise value

Table 11.7 First four steps of KMV iterative method

Step 1: Get time series V_0^t	Step 2: Compute $\sigma_{V,1}$ from time series	Step 3: Get time series V_1^t	Step 4: Compute $\sigma_{V,2}$ from time series...
$[MVS]_0 = V_0^0$		$[MVS]_0 = V_1^0$	
$VK(V_0^0, \sigma_{V,0}, DP, r)$		$VK(V_1^0, \sigma_{V,1}, DP, r)$	
$[MVS]_1 = V_0^1$		$[MVS]_1 = V_1^1$	
$VK(V_0^1, \sigma_{V,0}, DP, r)$		$VK(V_1^1, \sigma_{V,1}, DP, r)$	
...	...	...	...
$[MVS]_T = V_0^T$		$[MVS]_0 = V_1^T$	
$VK(V_0^T, \sigma_{V,0}, DP, r)$		$VK(V_1^T, \sigma_{V,1}, DP, r)$	

volatility $\sigma_{V,0}$). The variable left to be computed at each time period is the implied enterprise value V_0^t.

Equation (11.18) is used to form a time series of enterprise values V_0^t. The sample volatility $\sigma_{V,1}$ of this time series can then be computed and the process repeated again and again for $i = 1, \ldots$ until it converges:

$$[Market - Value - of - Stock]_t = VK(V_i^t, \sigma_{V,i}, DP, r). \tag{11.19}$$

The ith iteration inputs $\sigma_{V,i}$ and outputs $\sigma_{V,i+1}$. When these are sufficiently close to each other, say at iteration n, the process stops. At that point the values V_n^0 and $\sigma_{V,n}$ can be used as current enterprise value and current enterprise volatility, respectively. Table 11.7 summarizes the first four steps of the process.

Much of this effect is due to the use of stock market information in the KMV method: for most companies, the stock market very quickly impounds new information in prices while ratings agencies are deliberate in re-rating bonds. Thus much of the power of methods like KMV consists of using new but widely known information quickly. Bond traders and portfolio managers would already be well aware of this information before seeing KMV estimates. Still, having the information in a convenient expected default frequency number is quite useful.

11.4.5 Predictive Power of Default Estimates

It's clear from Figure 11.1 that the bifurcation of bonds into investment and speculative grades is meaningful: there has never been a year in which investment-grade defaults were greater than speculative-grade defaults, for example. On the other hand, there's plenty of room for improvement: two broad categories are not very informative. The average man is significantly taller than the average woman, but the average Women's National Basketball Association player[30] is even more significantly taller than the average man.

In fact, it's easy to predict defaults better than agency ratings: just predict that everything will default. Of course, that extreme level of caution will be maximally bad in terms of **Type II error** (the prediction of events that do not occur). Similarly, being extremely reckless and predicting that nothing will default will never mistakenly sound the alarm (no Type II error), but will be maximally bad in terms of **Type I error** (the underprediction of events that do occur).

What is needed is a balancing act between Type I error and Type II error. Suppose there is a sliding scale like distance to default (11.17) or agency rating level (AAA down to D, translated to a numerical scale), and an analyst is trying to decide where to set the cutoff between predicting default and not predicting default. There are about 20 agency rating levels (including $+$ and $-$ notches), and distance to default is continuous, so there are ample opportunities to decide where to set a cutoff to get the best Type I/Type II trade-off.

An extremely cautious analyst would say that a bond is not safe until distance to default is infinite, or until its rating is (impossibly) better than AAA. At these levels of hypercaution, the proportion x of bonds predicted to default would be $x = 1$ (all of them). At the other end of the scale, an extremely reckless analyst would deem bonds safe at any distance to default or at any credit rating: for this analyst, $x = 0$ (no bonds predicted to default).

For such a scale of caution/recklessness that maps a parameter onto the interval $x \in [0, 1]$ of fraction of bonds predicted to default, define $t_1(x)$ ($t_2(x)$) as the standardized fraction of bonds experiencing Type I (Type II) error. By "standardized," we mean adjusted for the fraction of the population q that actually does default.

For example, at maximum caution $x = 1$, $t_1(1) = 0$ and the fraction of bonds experiencing Type II error will be $1 - q$, so we define $t_2(x)$ as the fraction of bonds experiencing Type II error, divided by $1 - q$. Similarly at maximum recklessness $x = 0$, $t_2(0) = 0$ and Type I error is q, so we define $t_1(x)$ as the fraction of bonds experiencing Type I error, divided by q. Thus, t_1 and t_2 both have domain and range equal to $[0, 1]$; $t_1(x)$ is decreasing in x and $t_2(x)$ is increasing in x.

What happens in between the extremes can differ. A parameter like distance to default or credit rating would be good if it minimized Type I error for a given level of Type II error. Thus Kealhofer (2003a) proposes a power measure:

$$p(x) = 1 - t_1\left(t_2^{-1}(x)\right) \tag{11.20}$$

to balance Type I and Type II error. At the cautious end of the domain $x = 1$, Type II error is $1 - q$ so $t_2(1) = 1$, giving $t_2^{-1}(1) = 1$. Hypercaution means no

Type I error, so $t_1(1) = 0$: hence $p(1) = 1 - t_1(1) = 1$. At the reckless end of the domain $x = 0$, Type II error is 0 so $t_2(0) = 0$, giving $t_2^{-1}(0) = 0$. Recklessness maximizes Type I error, so $t_1(0) = 1$: hence $p(0) = 1 - t_1(0) = 0$.

So p is something like a cumulative distribution function with domain $[0, 1]$. A more desirable p is stochastically dominated by a less desirable p, as it is preferable for p to head to 1 (no Type I error) as quickly as possible.

While Kealhofer (2003a) is not a disinterested observer, he shows evidence that the p-curves for the KMV method are stochastically dominated by the p-curves for credit ratings, that is, the KMV method has a better power curve.

A predictive method with a good power curve can help lenders make money, as they want to minimize Type I error in the loans they do make and they want to minimize Type II error in the loans they don't make. However, the time-varying nature of overall default levels can be damaging: just getting things right on average over a long period of time can be of little comfort during a severe economic meltdown. So power consistency over time is also important.

There is little evidence that ratings or default frequency estimates help bond market investors make money by revealing previously unknown default information. Bond ratings are essentially public information,[31] so rating changes are quickly reflected in bond prices and confer no competitive advantage on any particular investor.

Default frequency estimators like KMV rely heavily on stock market levels as inputs, so the majority of information has already been reflected in market prices. Kealhofer (2003b, p. 88) summarizing an earlier study by Vasicek that showed KMV EDFs predicting over- and under-pricing of bonds, disclaims a profitable arbitrage strategy and attributes the reveal over- and under-pricing to bad market making:

> This result is consistent with findings that reported bond pricing does not necessarily reflect actual trades, but, rather, dealer indications or model prices.

Ironically, one popular money-making strategy based on credit ratings is to buy fallen angels, the bonds that were downgraded from investment to speculative grade. Proponents of this strategy point out that many investors have

---

31 The "issuer-pay" business model maintained by the largest credit rating agencies means that the borrower pays the rater to rate the borrower's bonds. The rating is then freely publicized to potential and actual bond buyers. The issuer-pay model has caused discomfort among many who point out an apparent conflict of interest in which issuers might pressure raters to give better scores, thus lowering the issuers' borrowing costs. While there is little evidence of ratings being raised in response to issuer pressure, there is the possibility of rating-shopping where a bond issuer finds the rater whose methodology will give the highest rating.

statutory or regulatory requirements to hold only investment-grade bonds, so they become forced sellers after a downgrade. The fallen angel buyers hope that this leads to an overreaction (too big a price drop) that unconstrained investors can benefit from. The success of this strategy depends on (a) how many other investors are following the same strategy and (b) timing, as buying fallen angels just before a market crash will probably be unprofitable.

11.5 Credit Spread Correlates

While structural models continue to have puzzling faults, their prediction that volatility is an important factor in explaining credit spreads is certainly borne out empirically. Code Segment 11.19 computes correlations between the time series of the VIX® Index of option-implied volatilities on the US stock market and the time series of credit spreads that was shown in Figure 11.4:

```
VIX data starts 1986-01 ends 2021-12; 432 periods
Aaa/VIX level correlation: 0.49461
Baa/VIX level correlation: 0.65096
Aaa/VIX difference correlation: 0.43444
Baa/VIX difference correlation: 0.47541
Reject null hypothesis of zero correlation with
    probability at least one minus:
    2.870537133566415e-21
```

Both level-based and difference-based correlations are high and significantly different from zero. Thus, over long time spans, a large portion of credit spread movement is due to changes in market volatility. The connection is most pronounced during market shocks when both volatilities and credit spreads suddenly expand; during other times, the connection can be more tenuous.

Credit spreads also often have a relationship to interest rates. Generally, when the economy is doing well, interest rates rise as (1) people and companies are more eager to borrow to finance current consumption and investment; and (2) the central bank raises rates to cool things off. During such good economic times, corporate health also improves and credit spreads tighten as the compensation for the risk of default seems less necessary. This reverses during bad times: falling interest rates, widening credit spreads.

This dynamic is similar to the one shown in Figure 10.5, where stock/bond correlations were shown to be negative since the 1990s. However credit spread/interest rate correlations in the USA have been reliably negative for all but one of the last 10 decades, as Figure 11.8 (generated by Code

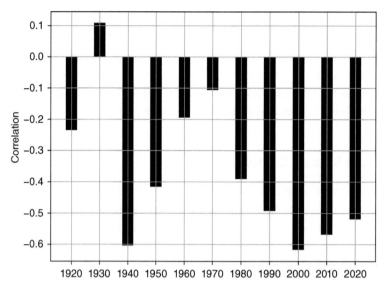

Figure 11.8 Correlations by decade: AAA/BBB average spd chgs versus Treasury rate chgs.

Segment 11.20) shows. Code Segment 11.20 also computes the following correlations and *p*-values:

```
Spread and Treasury data starts 1919-01 ends 2021-12;
     periods: 1236
AAA/Tsy difference correlation: -0.36996 p-value:
     2.3834590494321165e-41
BBB/Tsy difference correlation: -0.24246 p-value:
     5.5525122618123324e-18
```

While most decades have a clearly negative correlation, the 1930s show that unusual economic stress, together with fiscal and monetary response, can cause a regime shift. There was a slightly positive correlation between rates and spreads in the 1930s: as in Argentina and other credit-risky countries, the survival of the country's overall economy became the single paramount factor linking rates and spreads. In other words, there was doubt that the default-free rate really was default-free.

11.6 Credit Spread Metrics

In Chapter 3, we found that Macaulay duration and modified duration were eminently reasonable first-order measures of bond return sensitivity to changes in interest rates. For default-free instruments with simple cash flows, these definitions of duration suffice. But as the instruments get more complex, the cash flows c_i (and possibly their times t_i) contemplated in the generic pricing equation (3.2) also become more complex.

A common feature in a corporate bond, for example, is a **call schedule**: the borrower can pay off the principal early if it wants to retire the debt. Usually, this will only happen if prevailing rates have dropped, leaving the lender with an unwanted return of principal in a low-interest environment. We noted earlier that this can lead to lower, or even negative, convexity.

Of course, credit risk can cause the cash flows to drop due to the borrower's inability to repay. If a credit-risky bond defaults before maturity, repayment of any recovery amount will be accelerated, decreasing duration. Or the cash flows can be based on a formula that floats with the current rate of interest. Thus, there can be a breakdown in the equivalence between (1) Macaulay's original concept of duration as the average time at which cash flows are received; and (2) a multiple of the first derivative of the price with regard to a parallel shift in the discount curve.

Equation (3.6) – in which the relationship between cash flows and first and second derivatives was shown explicitly – can become difficult to evaluate if the cash flows are contingent on future events. Here $y = 1/(1 + r)$, r being the discount rate:

$$P'_t = -y \sum_{i=m}^{n} (t_i - t) c_i y^{t_i - t} \qquad P''_t = y^2 \left(\sum_{i=m}^{n} (t_i - t)^2 c_i y^{t_i - t} \right) - y P'_t. \quad (3.6, \text{again})$$

Instruments may even be path-dependent. For example, **knockout options** automatically exercise themselves as soon as the underlying asset goes above or below certain prices. If we knew that a bond was at 100 at inception of a knockout option and was again at 100 at maturity of the knockout option, we wouldn't have enough information to know how the option would have behaved. If the knockout strike was at 90, then if the bond's price looked like $100(1 + \sin(\pi t)/2)$ as t went from 0 at inception to 1 at maturity, the knockout would not have been triggered. But with a price path looking like $100(1 - \sin(\pi t)/2)$, the option would have exercised.

To take into account these complexities, we assume there is a pricing function $P(r, s)$ that takes a number of arguments, only two of which we list explicitly: r, the vector (or continuous function) of default-free discount rates, and s, the scalar spread that we need to add to the default-free discount rates to make the price of the bond equal the market observed price.

In (11.3) and (11.4) we showed a simple version of the pricing formula as a function of a credit spread. However, when there are complex features to the bond, we may need to use a Monte Carlo simulation run over many possible paths of interest rates or credit events to see what the price should be. The spread s that makes the more complex pricing function equal the market price is called the **option-adjusted spread (OAS)**.

Effective duration is a generalization of the durations we've previously seen. To compute effective duration, the r vector in the complex pricing function $P(r, s)$ is perturbed by a small scalar amount Δr, so r becomes $r \pm u \Delta r$, where

u is the vector of all ones. This gives a finite difference approximation to the (negative of) the derivative of the price with respect to a parallel shift in the discount curve:

$$D_E(r,s,\Delta r) = \frac{P(r - u\Delta r,s) - P(r + u\Delta r,s)}{2\Delta r P(r,s)}. \tag{11.21}$$

Similarly, we can define **effective convexity** as a finite difference approximation to the second derivative divided by price:

$$\begin{aligned} C_E(r,s,\Delta r) &= \frac{P(r - u\Delta r,s) - 2P(r,s) + P(r + u\Delta r,s)}{(\Delta r)^2 P(r,s)} \\ &\approx \frac{D_E(r - u(\Delta r/2),s,\Delta r/2) - D_E(r + u(\Delta r/2),s,\Delta r/2)}{\Delta r P(r,s)}. \end{aligned} \tag{11.22}$$

The second line of (11.22) is an approximation, not an equality, because the denominators of the D_E's are not quite the same as the denominator in the definitional first line. The difference is a higher-order effect, so it's usually not noticeable.

The effective duration D_E will approximate a suitably scaled version of our previous definitions of duration when the cash flows are simple enough, but in the presence of optionality, floating rates, and possible default, D_E may differ. Similarly for effective convexity.

We can also define **option-adjusted spread duration (OASD)**. Not surprisingly, this is:

$$OASD(r,s,\Delta s) = \frac{P(r,s - u\Delta s) - P(r,s + u\Delta s)}{2\Delta s P(r,s)}. \tag{11.23}$$

The definition (11.21) of effective duration contemplates adding (and subtracting) a scalar perturbation Δr to every point on the discount curve. The definition (11.23) of spread duration contemplates adding (or subtracting) a scalar perturbation Δs to the scalar s that is already being added to the discount curve. In both cases, the discount factor is changed from r_i to $r_i + \Delta something$. So shouldn't spread duration be the same as effective duration?

In many cases, the two are equal. However, when optionality or the coupon in a bond depends on rates but not on spread, then effective duration (sometimes called rate duration) and spread duration can differ. For example, when the discount curve is flat a default-free floating-rate security maturing in 30 years will have effective duration close to zero, but very long spread duration.

Risk in credit portfolios is often assessed by spread duration exposure. A manager might say, "I'm 2 years long telecoms spread duration." As we noted with overall duration, spread duration only makes sense as a measure when it is applied to similar things. For example a year's spread duration of the African mobile telecom operator MTN Limited is not really comparable to a year's spread duration of China Mobile Limited.

11.7 Credit Factor Models

Fixed-income portfolios often use factor models like the ones we saw in Chapter 6:

$$C = BFB' + D. \tag{6.21, again}$$

Recall that B is an $n \times k$ factor loading matrix giving the exposures of the $n >> k$ securities in the universe to the comparatively small number of systematic factors explaining the market's behavior. Term D is a (sometimes omitted) diagonal matrix of systematic risks uncorrelated with anything else.

For fixed-income factor risk models, the k factors usually consist mainly of the following: 1. Key rate durations on a number of default-free curves, or more precisely the moves of rates at certain points of the curve; and 2. Spread movements for key sectors like UK investment-grade financials.

For a given security x, its first-order Taylor series approximation may look like:

$$\frac{\Delta P_x}{P_x} = \theta \Delta t - \sum_i (KRD_{x,i} \Delta r_i) - SD_x \Delta s_x. \tag{11.24}$$

Here $KRD_{x,i}$ is the security's key rate duration to the ith point on the security's discount curve – for example, the US Treasury curve for US corporate bonds or the Japanese government curve for Japanese corporate bonds. Then Δr_i is the movement of the yield curve at that point; SD_x is the bond's spread duration (usually zero if this is a default-free government bond. although there can be small spreads on government bonds since yield curves are not perfect). Then, Δs_x is the move in the bond's own spread and θ is the sensitivity to the passage of time, including carry (which captures regular payments like coupons) and rolldown (Section 3.5.5). While carry and rolldown influence rates of return, they are known in advance so they're not considered risk factors.

When modelers want to capture systematic risk, Δs_x might be replaced by Δs_j, where j is a group that the instrument belongs to and that (it is hoped) has homogeneous within-group spread movements. For example, the sector might be UK investment-grade financials. The risk factors going into the factor covariance matrix F in (6.21) would then be (1) changes in rates Δr_i and (2) changes in group spreads Δs_j.

However, substituting a cohort spread change Δs_j for a security spread change Δs_x might not be realistic: the cohort spread level s_j might be significantly different from the security spread level s_x, so changes, while perhaps highly correlated, might be of different sizes. One popular substitution is called **duration times spread (DTS)** and is based on the tautological identity:

$$SD_x \Delta s_x = (SD_x s_x) \frac{\Delta s_x}{s_x}. \tag{11.25}$$

The $SD_x s_x$ term multiplies x's duration times its spread, hence the name DTS. DTS is considered the exposure metric, and $\frac{\Delta s_x}{s_x}$, which is a percentage change in x's spread, is the variable to which x is exposed. So $\frac{\Delta s_x}{s_x}$ is likely to be more statistically well behaved than Δs_x and thus is likely to be more predictable.

In a factor model, individual variables like $\frac{\Delta s_x}{s_x}$ are modeled by systematic factors. It is not unreasonable to assume that x's spread percentage changes would be similar to spread percentage changes in its cohort j:

$$\frac{\Delta s_x}{s_x} \approx \frac{\Delta s_j}{s_j}. \tag{11.26}$$

This is likely to be a much better substitution than Δs_j for Δs_x. Thus, in the DTS model the contribution to x's security return coming from x's spread changes is assumed to be:

$$SD_x \Delta s_x \approx \left(SD_x s_x \right) \frac{\Delta s_j}{s_j}. \tag{11.27}$$

DTS ($SD_x s_x$) is the exposure metric and $\frac{\Delta s_j}{s_j}$ is the risk factor to which the asset's returns are exposed.

The DTS approach has the drawback that the exposure metric can change rapidly. Spread duration SD_x changes as discount curves and spreads change, but typically changes slowly over time. But spread s_x can change quite rapidly. This makes a portfolio manager's task difficult: the manager might decide today on a certain exposure to a risk factor $\frac{\Delta s_j}{s_j}$, but tomorrow changing market conditions can radically change the exposure. This might give the manager the choice of staying with an exposure that was not desired, or of excessive trading just to maintain the desired exposure. In a nutshell: DTS is a moving target.

Another approach that has less of a moving-target problem is **adjusted spread duration**. It starts with a tautology like (11.25):

$$SD_x \Delta s_x = \left(SD_x \frac{s_x}{s_j} \right) \frac{s_j}{s_x} \Delta s_x. \tag{11.28}$$

An approximation similar to (11.26) is then made:

$$\frac{s_j}{s_x} \Delta s_x \approx \Delta s_j. \tag{11.29}$$

This approximation takes into account the possibly different sizes of security spreads s_x and cohort spreads s_j. Putting these together, the adjusted spread duration model is:

$$SD_x \Delta s_x \approx \left(SD_x \frac{s_x}{s_j} \right) \Delta s_j. \tag{11.30}$$

Adjusted spread duration $SD_x \frac{s_x}{s_j}$ is the exposure metric, which is likely to move far more slowly than DTS. The risk factor Δs_j contains changes in cohort credit spreads. This risk factor is likely to be more badly behaved (leptokurtic, for example) than percentage changes $\frac{\Delta s_j}{s_j}$, but the bad behavior can be addressed with GARCH-type models. De-GARCHed spread changes are at least as good risk model citizens as are percentage spread changes.

11.8 Z-Scores, Reduced-Form, and Hybrid Models

Because of the disproportionate importance of default, many methods have been used to try to predict defaults. In addition to the Merton model discussed in Section 11.4, quantitative methods based on accounting and economic data have had success.

Credit ratings use accounting and economic data, but they aren't purely quantitative. While criteria like debt-to-equity ratios are used by credit rating company analysts, there isn't an exact formula associating ratings with criteria. Tables like Table 11.3 and Table 11.5 show historical default frequencies for cohorts of issuers and ratings, but we know these averages belie considerable variability over different economic conditions.

Edward Altman (1968) originated a quantitative method to tie default probabilities to observable accounting criteria. Rating agencies had been doing this qualitatively when assigning ratings; eventually they began compiling data such as Table 11.2 to show the relationships between accounting features and ratings assigned by analysts. Altman dispensed with the analysts and went directly from the features to default probabilities.

Altman (1968) analyzed a sample of sixty-six US corporations. Thirty-three of them had filed for bankruptcy in the period 1946–1965. Thirty-three other firms were found that had similar characteristics but that had not filed for bankruptcy. It was, in 1968, onerous to compile this much data, but Altman did so and applied multiple discriminant analysis (MDA) to see what differentiated the two cohorts. MDA is a statistical technique apparently invented in the 1930s by the ubiquitous R. A. Fisher; it's similar in spirit to what are now called support vector machines.

Altman called the result a **Z-score**. His original Z-score formula was:

$$Z = .012X_1 + .014X_2 + .033X_3 + .006X_4 + .999X_5, \tag{11.31}$$

where:

- X_1 = (Working Capital)/(Total Assets);
- X_2 = (Retained Earnings)/(Total Assets);
- X_3 = EBIT/(Total Assets);
- X_4 = (Market Value of Equity)/(Book Value of Debt);
- X_5 = Sales/(Total Assets).

Total Assets is what we called V above. Working capital is the difference between current assets and current liabilities, Retained earnings is the cumulative net income of the company not paid out in dividends; Altman notes that this measure discriminates against younger firms but that is realistic since younger firms default more. EBIT is Earnings Before Interest and Taxes; more modern accounting treatments would use EBITDA as we saw in Table 11.2. Altman's X_4 is a ratio of quantities we've already seen: S/D_{par} using our notation above. The last ratio, involving annual sales per total assets, is one that Altman notes has little discriminatory power on its own, but that improves the model significantly in the context of the other variables.

The Z-score in (11.31) was calibrated so that a value over 3 meant that the company was relatively safe from bankruptcy; all of the X_i are desirable features of a strong company so the higher the score, the better. A Z-score of under 2 meant that the company was bankrupt or near-bankrupt; and between 2 and 3 was ambiguous.

Prof. Altman and others have updated, recalibrated, and expanded his Z-score many times since its original publication. The method is clearly sensible from a corporate fundamentals point of view, although the exact calibration can vary over time and over cohorts.

One drawback of the method is latency in the publication of accounting data: publicly traded US companies publish accounting data in "K's and Q's" – Form 10-K and Form 10-Q – on an annual and a quarterly basis, respectively. Both are available online,[32] but with a lag. So Z-scores will not be able to keep up with fast-changing events, especially when a company is in trouble. Non-publicly-traded companies and companies in other jurisdictions might publish accounting data on an even less frequent basis.

Also, fitting the coefficients to past data might lead to good in-sample fit, but it isn't necessarily predictive. As is always true in the financial markets, participants adapt. A corporate treasurer who notices that lenders are going to be unfriendly when .012 times the working capital to total assets ratio gets too low might try to improve that ratio artificially with legal (or in some cases illegal[33]) accounting gimmicks.

Still, this is a powerful method and the attempt to predict defaults based on accounting measures remains a rich field today.

Altman's Z-score is an example of a **reduced-form model**, which uses market variables and company information to predict default using regression or other statistical techniques. Altman's Z-score used only company-specific information. Other information that could be used would be general financial distress indicators such as the level of the VIX; time skew in option-implied volatilities; or even macroeconomic variables such as GDP, inflation, and unemployment.

In practice, some market participants use hybrid models that combine the Merton-model distance to default (11.6), company-specific variables like Altman's (11.31), risk-neutral probabilities of default q_d derived from market prices (see next section), and market variables.

---

32 Investor.gov.   "Form   10-K."   www.investor.gov/introduction-investing/
investing-basics/glossary/form-10-k.   "Form   10-Q."   www.investor.gov/
introduction-investing/investing-basics/glossary/form-10-q.   U.S.
Securities and Exchange Commission. "Edgar: Company Filings." Website. www.sec.gov/
edgar/searchedgar/companysearch.html.

33 FBI. "Enron." Website. www.fbi.gov/history/famous-cases/enron.

These can be combined into an overall variable that estimates a probability of default p_{hybrid}:

$$Z_{hybrid} = a_0 + a_1 d_{Def} + a_2 q_d + \sum_{i=1}^{m} a_{i+2} MarketMacroFactor_i$$

$$+ \sum_{j=1}^{cf} a_{j+m+2} CompanyFactor_i, \tag{11.32}$$

$$p_{hybrid} = \frac{1}{1 + \exp(-Z_{hybrid})}.$$

The coefficients are calibrated so that companies with low probabilities of default have a large negative Z_{hybrid}. A term structure can be applied so that probabilities of default are predicted for a number of years forward. For example, a company with a large amount of debt coming due 5 years from now might have a spike in probability of default at that time.

The Li (2000) copula model that was discussed in Section 10.6.1 can be generalized, giving another way to incorporate multiple factors into default predictions.[34] Instead of just one common factor M as in Section 10.6.1, a model can have m common factors $M_1, \ldots, M_m$. For model simplicity, assume the factors are distributed multivariate normal with covariance matrix C.

Suppose there are n debt instruments in a portfolio. Let $Y_i = 0$ if the ith instrument doesn't default in some time frame of interest, and let $Y_i = 1$ if it does default in the time frame. We assume that there is a known probability p_i of the ith instrument defaulting; this may be obtained from another model or inferred from market prices as described in subsequent sections.

In Section 10.6.1, a latent variable X carried the dependency structure of times to default; here a latent variable X will carry the dependency structure of the default indicators Y_i. In particular, we will describe a standard normal latent variable X_i that specifies $Y_i = 1$ when $X_i > N^{-1}(1 - p_i)$ and $Y_i = 0$ otherwise. Here, N is the standard normal cdf. Thus, the unconditional default probability satisfies:

$$Pr(Y_i = 1) = Pr(X_i > N^{-1}(1 - p_i)) = 1 - N(N^{-1}(1 - p_i)) = p_i$$

as desired.

The common factors M_j $(j = 1, \ldots, m)$ are incorporated into the default indicators as follows: Let $C = LL^T$ be the covariance matrix of the factors and its Cholesky factorization. Then as in Section 8.3, we can write $M = LZ$, where M is the m-vector of random variables giving the factors and Z is an m-vector of uncorrelated standard normal random variables. Dependence is transmitted linearly through the relationship $X = AZ + BE$, where:

- X is the n-vector of default propensities X_i described above;
- A is an $n \times m$ matrix of factor loadings; the row a_i of A gives debt instrument i's dependencies on the standardized common factors Z. ($A = FL^{-1}$ where F is

---

34 See for example [Glasserman and Li 2005].

the factor loading matrix on the original nonstandardized factors.) It's assumed that factors are chosen so the elements of A are nonnegative and $a_i a_i^T \leq 1$ for all i;

- Z is an m-vector of the uncorrelated standard normal factors;
- B is a diagonal matrix with $\sqrt{1 - a_i a_i^T}$ in the (i, i) element; and
- E is an n-vector of idiosyncratic risks with standard normal distribution and independent of everything else.

The specification of B ensures that each X_i is standard normal.

Glasserman and Li (2005) note that the default probability conditional on a particular realization of the standardized common factors Z satisfies:

$$Pr(Y_i = 1 \mid Z) = Pr(X_i > N^{-1}(1 - p_i) \mid Z) = Pr(a_i Z + b_i e_i > N^{-1}(1 - p_i))$$

$$= Pr\left(e_i > \frac{-N^{-1}(p_i) - a_i Z}{b_i}\right) = 1 - N\left(\frac{-N^{-1}(p_i) - a_i Z}{b_i}\right)$$

$$= N\left(\frac{N^{-1}(p_i) + a_i Z}{\sqrt{1 - a_i a_i^T}}\right), \tag{11.33}$$

where e_i is the ith standard normal idiosyncratic risk in the E vector. Note that an asset i that has only idiosyncratic risk and no factor dependence ($a_i = 0$) has $Pr(Y_i = 1 \mid Z) = p_i$, that is, the conditional probability is the same as the unconditional probability as expected.

For assets that have no idiosyncratic behavior, the denominator $\sqrt{1 - a_i a_i^T}$ becomes infinite in (11.33). As a consistency check, note that in this case there will be no default if the numerator $N^{-1}(p_i) + a_i Z$ in (11.33) is negative, that is, default probability is zero if $N^{-1}(p_i) = -N^{-1}(1 - p_i) \leq -a_i Z = -X_i$, which means $X_i \leq N^{-1}(1 - p_i)$ which by definition means $Y_i = 0$. Similarly if the numerator $N^{-1}(p_i) + a_i Z$ is positive in the no idiosyncratic case then by definition $Y_i = 1$, that is, there will be a default.

Equation (11.33) provides a structure for correlated portfolio defaults to be estimated conditional on factor realizations. For example, if w_i is the weight of the ith debt instrument in a portfolio and LGD is the loss given default in dollars expected for debt instruments like the ones in the portfolio (perhaps in the .55–.62 range, as in Section 11.3), then the expected portfolio loss due to defaults is:

$$LGD \sum_{i=1}^{n} w_i Pr(Y_i = 1 \mid Z) = LGD \sum_{i=1}^{n} w_i N\left(\frac{N^{-1}(p_i) + a_i Z}{b_i}\right), \tag{11.34}$$

where (11.33) was used in the second equality.

11.9 Implied Default Rates

Financial markets produce myriad implied variables: implied discount rates (internal rates of return); implied volatilities; implied probability densities (Breeden–Litzenberger). In credit markets, it would be helpful to try to recover implied default rates from probabilities. We know that risk-neutral default rates will tend to be high compared to real-world default rates because of risk preference. But it's still informative to try to recover them.

To start, suppose there is a zero-coupon credit-risky bond that matures in T years, and suppose that it either defaults at maturity or it doesn't. In practice, there could be interim default caused by other events in the issuer's corporate structure, but we'll ignore that possibility for now.

This situation is amenable to a binomial tree approach. If the bond defaults, which it will do with a risk-neutral probability we'll call q_d, the lender will get a recovery amount R. If it doesn't default (probability $1 - q_d$), the lender will get full repayment of 100 principal. If the current market-observed price is P, and the observable T-year default-free discount rate is r_T, then we must have:

$$P = \frac{q_d R + (1 - q_d)100}{(1 + r_T)^T},$$

$$q_D = \frac{100 - P(1 + r_T)^T}{100 - R}. \tag{11.35}$$

The numerator $100 - P(1 + r_T)^T$ has to be positive because the current credit-risky price P has to be less than the price $100(1 + r_T)^{-T}$ of a default-free zero-coupon bond.

For illustration, suppose T is 5 years and the default-free 5-year discount rate from the zero curve is $r_T = .04$. Then the price of a default-free zero is 82.19. If the price of a credit-risky 5-year zero is 80, then from (11.35) we see that $q_d = .053$, that is, there is a 5.3% risk-neutral probability of default.

Kealhofer (2003b) gives a simple framework for comparing the risk-neutral q_d with a real-world probability of default p_d. Assuming the zero-coupon credit-risky bond is the only liability of a corporation with enterprise value mean and standard deviation μ_V and σ_V as in the Merton model (11.6), then under the Merton lognormal assumption,

$$q_d = N\left(N^{-1}(p_d) + \frac{\mu_v - r}{\sigma_V}\sqrt{T}\right).$$

It's unlikely that a single zero-coupon bond comprises the entire debt structure of the issuer. Kealhofer (2003b) (citing a result of Vasicek) suggests an adjustment based on a perpetuity model with an absorbing barrier:

$$q_d = 2N\left(N^{-1}\left(\frac{p_d}{2}\right) + \frac{\mu_v - r}{\sigma_V}\sqrt{T}\right). \tag{11.36}$$

Using the illustration above where $q_d = .053$, suppose the enterprise characteristics are $\mu_V = .05$ and $\sigma_V = .2$. Then $\frac{\mu_V - r}{\sigma_V}\sqrt{T} = .112$ and $N^{-1}\left(\frac{q_d}{2}\right) = -1.935$. Using (11.36) shows that $p_d = 2N(-1.935 - .112) = .041$. This real-world probability p_d depends heavily on the hard-to-estimate enterprise mean return μ_V, so Kealhofer suggests using the Capital Asset Pricing Model to estimate enterprise mean returns. This method of estimating real-world and risk-neutral probabilities can provide a second opinion on values obtained using the recovery methods of Chapter 2.

Returning to the binomial tree approach, we can break the tree into finer and finer periods. For a coupon-paying bond, we could have a node of a binomial tree at each coupon payment. Since coupon payments are generally every 3 or 6 months, the approximation that there is default only at the nodes of the tree is more realistic.

The root of the tree at time 0 branches to default or to no default at time 1. If the bond defaults (with probability q_d), there will be a cash flow of $R = $ recovery value. This is a leaf of the tree: there are no further developments after default.

However, if the bond doesn't default (with probability $1 - q_d$), there will be a coupon cash flow of amount c at time 1, and the tree will continue to time 2. Once again, there are two possibilities: a default leaf with cumulative probability $q_d(1 - q_d)$ and a continuation path with cumulative probability $(1 - q_d)^2$. At time 2, recovery R is received in case of default, while another coupon cash flow of c is received in case of no default.

In general, at time period t, default with recovery R happens with cumulative probability $q_d(1 - q_d)^{t-1}$. A coupon c is received with cumulative probability $(1 - q_d)^t$. If the bond survives to maturity without defaulting, a final repayment of 100 principal is received at period T with probability $(1 - q_d)^T$.

Collecting all the probability-weighted cash flows and discounting them to the present, we have the pricing equation:

$$P = \left(\frac{q_d R}{1 - q_d} + c\right) \sum_{i=1}^{T} \frac{(1 - q_d)^i}{(1 + r_i)^i} + 100 \frac{(1 - q_d)^T}{(1 + r_T)^T}. \qquad (11.37)$$

There is no spread s because we are treating the cash flows as default-free once we have determined the path they will travel. That is, we will definitely get R at (say) time 3 conditional on default occurring between time 2 and time 3.

As we did with (11.35), if we have an observed price P then we can turn around the pricing equation (11.37) and solve for the risk-neutral periodic default probability q_d. This won't generally be possible in closed form, but an iterative method can be used.

11.10 Credit Default Swaps

Credit Default Swaps (CDS) were invented by Blythe Masters at JP Morgan in London in 1994.[35] The market for these instruments, especially those referencing indexes rather than single securities, has become large and vibrant.

CDS are simply insurance policies on bonds or groups of bonds. A **protection buyer** pays a fixed amount each year to a **protection seller**; the item being insured is called the **reference entity**. The protection seller is also called the **CDS writer**. The reference entity can be a corporate bond, a government bond, or (probably the most common) an index of bonds such as SOV-X (a group of government bonds); NA.IG or SNAC (Standard North American Contract) (US investment-grade corporate bonds); CMBX (commercial mortgage-backed securities); ABX (subprime mortgage-backed bonds); and many others.[36]

If the reference entity has a **credit event**, a carefully legally defined concept that is more or less equivalent to default, then the seller of protection has to make sure the buyer of protection receives par. So if recovery $R = 40$, the protection seller is responsible for making up the missing 60 to the protection buyer. Most CDS are **cash settled**, so the protection seller just gives the monetary amount to the buyer. A few CDS are **physically settled**, meaning the protection buyer gives the defaulted reference entity to the protection seller, who gives the protection buyer 100. Then the protection seller tries to recover as much as possible from the reference entity it now owns.

CDS terminology is a little confusing: a protection seller hopes that the reference entity does well, and so is doing something more like buying the reference entity than selling it. Similarly, the protection buyer has a negative view of the reference entity.

Originally, CDS were simply bilateral contracts between the protection buyer and the protection seller. This led to an additional risk, called **counterparty risk**: if the protection seller defaulted at the same time as the reference entity, then the protection buyer's "insurance policy" was worthless. This happened during the GFC with the insurance company AIG. McDonald and Paulson (2015, p. 91) explained that:

> As of December 31, 2007, AIG had written credit default swaps with a notional value of $527 billion. ... The [$78 billion] of credit default swaps written

---

35 Masters became, at age 28, the youngest female managing director in JP Morgan's history. While some (like Warren Buffett) claimed that credit default swaps (CDS) exacerbated the Global Financial Crisis, Masters sniffed, "I do believe CDS have been miscast, much as poor workmen tend to blame their tools." (Email reported in *The Guardian*, September 19, 2008. www.theguardian.com/business/2008/sep/20/wallstreet.banking.) Masters's point of view was largely corroborated in [Tett 2009].

36 S&P Global Offerings, IHS Markit®. "iTraxx SovX Indices." https://ihsmarkit.com/products/markit-itraxx-sovx.html; "CDX: Tradable CDS Indices." https://ihsmarkit.com/products/markit-cdx.html; "CMBX Index: Commercial Mortgage Backed Securities Index." https://ihsmarkit.com/products/markit-cmbx.html; "ABX Index: Subprime Mortgage Backed Securities Index." https://ihsmarkit.com/products/markit-abx.html.

on multisector collateralized debt obligations proved the most troublesome... AIG insured collateralized debt obligations backed by a variety of assets, but including a substantial share backed by mortgages – both residential and commercial as well as prime, subprime, and Alt-A (which fall between prime and subprime on the risk spectrum). It is important to realize that AIG's credit default swap exposure resulted in a "one-way" bet on real estate: that is, a decline in real estate prices and a rise in foreclosures would impose costs on AIG, but AIG had no offsetting hedging position that would show gains if real estate prices fell.

AIG faced bankruptcy as much of the collateral (reference entities) for which it had provided protection began to default. The protection buyers were virtually all other large multinational financial institutions, so AIG's failure could have started a cascade of failures across the global financial system. The US federal government stepped in and bailed out AIG at a cost of $182 billion. According to the U.S. Department of the Treasury, by 2013 the US federal government had entirely exited the Orwellian-named "AIG Investment Program." In retrospect, the bailout really was an investment: the government not only was fully repaid, but also made a $22.7 billion profit.[37]

In 2010, the Dodd-Frank Act[38] required that index-based CDS be **centrally cleared**, meaning that CDS contracts trade through financially secure clearing-houses in a way that makes it less likely that the default of a counterparty like AIG would be so catastrophic. According to Aldasoro and Ehlers (2018), the majority of CDS trading is now centrally cleared.

In practice in the USA, there are only two standard payment spreads: 100bps (for investment-grade reference entities) and 500bps (for speculative-grade reference entities). There is an upfront payment at the outset of a CDS that trues up the expected cash flows to the variable CDS spread s that the parties expect. In Europe, there are different standard spreads.[39]

A portfolio consisting of a bond together with bought credit protection on that bond is (absent counterparty risk) roughly equivalent to a default-free bond, although cash flow timing may be different. So (roughly) $B + C = T$, where B = bond; C = CDS, T = US Treasury or similar default-free instrument. So (roughly) $C = T - B$: buying protection is similar to going long a default-free bond and shorting a credit-risky bond.

This line of reasoning is directionally correct, but it leaves out a number of structural features of credit default swaps. It also omits the fact that markets are not always efficient: during the GFC, capital was scarce so the prices of bonds were depressed, causing their option-adjusted spreads (OASs) to be very large.

37 U.S. Department of the Treasury. "Investment in American International Group (AIG)." Website. https://home.treasury.gov/data/troubled-assets-relief-program/aig.

38 Congress.gov. "H.R. 4173 - Dodd-Frank Wall Street Reform and Consumer Protection Act." Website. www.congress.gov/bill/111th-congress/house-bill/4173/text.

39 International Capital Market Association. "The European Corporate Single Name Credit Default Swap Market." February 2018. Website. www.icmagroup.org/assets/documents/Regulatory/Secondary-markets/The-European-Corporate-Single-Name-Credit-Default-Swap-Market-SMPC-Report-150218.pdf

But entering into a credit default swap took little capital. So swap spreads were not as large as cash bond OASs. An entity that had the capital could buy a cash bond with a very large OAS and simultaneously buy credit protection. The CDS spread, while large, was not as large as the underlying bond OAS. This dual position would have been very profitable during the GFC, but fear of counterparty risk and lack of capital limited its use.

CDS prices are quoted in spread terms. For example, a CDS spread of 60bps means that the protection buyer pays the protection seller at an annual rate of .006 times the notional (par) amount of the reference entity covered by the CDS. Thus, a protection buyer of CDS covering $1,000,000 par value of bonds would pay the protection seller $6,000 a year if the swap spread was $s = 60$bps. In practice, the payments might be periodic on a monthly, quarterly, or semi-annual basis.

In fact, real-world CDS have a number of features intended to alleviate counterparty risk in addition to central clearing. These features make it hard to specify the way CDS work in closed-form formulas; in fact, the definitive way of pricing CDS spreads is through an algorithm[40]

We'll give a stylized version of CDS that omits some features but that conveys some of the basic ideas.

We start with a **hazard rate model**: if t_d is the random variable giving the time to a credit entity's default, then a simple hazard rate model says that its cumulative distribution function looks like:

$$Pr(t_d \leq t) = 1 - \exp(-\lambda t).$$

Then λ is the hazard rate; as it goes up, the entity is more likely to default sooner rather than later. For example, if $\lambda = 1\%$, then the half-life is about 69 years (i.e. $Pr(t_d \leq 69) \approx \frac{1}{2}$). A little more generally, a positive exponent α can be included on the time so that the probability looks like:

$$Pr(t_d \leq t) = 1 - \exp(-\lambda t^{\alpha}).$$

Using the simple hazard rate model, we can form a probability-weighted sum of the amounts that the protection buyer is expected to pay to the protection seller over the life of a CDS:

$$B(s,\lambda) = s \sum_{i=1}^{N} \exp(-ri) \exp(-\lambda i) = s \cdot \exp(-(r+\lambda)) \frac{1 - \exp(-(r+\lambda)N)}{1 - \exp(-(r+\lambda))}.$$

$$(11.38)$$

Here:

- s is the swap spread, that is, the fraction of notional paid per year by the protection buyer;
- λ is the reference entity's hazard rate;

40 ISDA®. "CDS Standard Model." Website. www.cdsmodel.com/cdsmodel/.

- N is the number of annual payments to be made over the life of the CDS, assuming no default; and
- r is the discount rate.

We have assumed continuous discounting, a flat discount curve, and protection payments made on an annual basis. The summands in the calculation (11.38) multiply the discount factor at year i times the risk-neutral probability of surviving to year i.

If R is the expected recovery amount given default, then the seller of protection is expected to pay (and the buyer is expected to receive):

$$S(s, \lambda) = (1 - R)(1 - \exp(-\lambda)) \sum_{i=1}^{N} \exp(-ri) \exp(-\lambda(i - 1))$$

$$= (1 - R)(e^{\lambda} - 1) \exp(-(r + \lambda)) \frac{1 - \exp(-(r + \lambda)N)}{1 - \exp(-(r + \lambda))}. \qquad (11.39)$$

Here, s has been included as an argument of the seller's expected payment amount $S(s, \lambda)$, although it is not directly used in that function. However, it is conventional in financial markets to price swap so that, at inception, the buyer's expected payments equal the seller's expected payments. As time goes on, of course, one or the other gains an advantage. But at inception we have $B(s, \lambda) = S(s, \lambda)$, which gives a CDS swap spread of:

$$s = (1 - R)(e^{\lambda} - 1). \qquad (11.40)$$

Solving for λ gives:

$$\lambda = \ln\left(1 + \frac{s}{1 - R}\right). \qquad (11.41)$$

For example, with recovery $R = 50\%$ and a 200bps CDS spread, the risk-neutral hazard rate is $\lambda = \ln(1.04) = 3.92\%$.

Conceptually, the risk-neutral hazard rate λ recovered in (11.41) from CDS prices is similar to the risk-neutral probability of default q_d recovered from bond prices in (11.37). They aren't exactly comparable since a hazard rate gives a time-varying probability of default while q_d is constant. We also used different discounting conventions. But in the limit as time periods get shorter and shorter, these differences will become less important, so comparing the two figures can be informative.

For Code Segments in this chapter, see the Code Appendix starting on p. 440. For executable code, visit www.cambridge.org/9781009209090/ch11

For problem sets for this chapter, visit www.cambridge.org/ 9781009209090/ch11_problems

12 Hedging

A **hedge** is a strategy intended to remove or lower a source of uncertainty about the future rate of return of a portfolio or company. The ultimate hedge is the creation of a risk-free arbitrage like the ones discussed in Section 2.7, although as we noted there it's unlikely that profitable riskless arbitrages can last long.

But an old joke points out a logical problem: A patient rushes into a doctor's office and says, "Doctor, I broke my arm in five places!" The doctor's prescription: "Stay out of those places."

Similarly, why would a manager need a hedging strategy to remove or lower risk? Why not just stay out of those places and avoid unwanted risks in the first place?

An answer can be found by considering the first hedge fund, established by Alfred Winslow Jones in 1949.[1] It simultaneously bought and sold stocks. The idea was to hedge out the risk that the overall stock market rose or fell, while attempting to benefit from picking outperformers on the long side and underperformers on the short side. (Today this strategy is called **market-neutral**.) By taking positions in individual securities, Jones couldn't avoid also getting exposures to the overall stock market. The Capital Asset Pricing Model lay in the future, but Jones (and others) had a qualitative understanding that all stocks were exposed to market risk. To avoid that unwanted risk, Jones had to hedge it away. That left the selection risks he did want.

This chapter explores five reasons why managers engage in strategies that are more sophisticated than just staying out of those places and the techniques that are used to implement hedging when avoidance alone won't do.

12.1 Risk Unbundling

Sometimes a financial security, a company, or other economic structure will naturally contain a package of risks, only some of which are desired.

Consider the case of Philippe, a French investor with a euro-based portfolio. Philippe wants to invest in Tesla, the American vehicle and energy company. He sees that he can easily buy US-dollar-denominated shares of Tesla under the symbol TSLA on the Nasdaq exchange.[2]

---

1 [Stulz 2007].
2 Most large multinational companies trade in multiple venues in multiple currencies. Tesla, Inc. is traded on the Frankfurt Börse in euros, so Philippe could have easily avoided taking on unwanted

When Philippe buys dollar-denominated shares of Tesla, Inc., he will expose his portfolio to the unknown outcomes of the company's success or failure in electric vehicles, batteries, and solar facilities. But he will also take on currency risk: his portfolio will be exposed to the euro/dollar foreign exchange (f/x) rate since shares of TSLA bought on the Nasdaq are denominated in dollars.

Suppose that Philippe wants the company risk but not the f/x risk. That motivates him to look for an **unbundling hedge** that neutralizes, or at least mitigates, the f/x risk while still allowing his portfolio to participate in the company risk.

It's not hard to find such a hedge: the major world currencies trade heavily both in the **spot market** and the **forward market**. The spot market simply exchanges one currency for another "on the spot," that is, instantaneously. The forward market locks in an exchange of currencies in the future at a rate determined today.

For Philippe's purpose, the currency forward market is ideal. If he invests in dollar-denominated Tesla shares, he'll have future dollars that he doesn't want. He'll want to convert them to euros. That's exactly what a **currency forward** does: it's a contract in which parties agree in advance that one currency will be sold and another bought for a currently specified price at a specified time in the future. A forward is not an option: the parties have no choice but to complete the transaction at the specified time in the future.

The future swap of currencies required by a currency forward is equivalent[3] to buying a default-free zero-coupon bill in one currency (in this case euros, that is, a German government bill) and selling a default-free zero-coupon bill in another currency (in this case dollars, i.e. a US Treasury). Recall from Section 11.2.4 that Germany sets the benchmark default-free rates in the eurozone, so German government debt is used here even though Philippe is a French investor.

Thus a currency forward is itself a bundle consisting of two components that are similar to (but not actually) (1) US Treasury bills and (2) German government bills. Philippe's side of the forward consists of borrowing dollars at the US T-bill rate to buy euros at the German government bill rate. Another party – Philippe's counterparty – borrows euros at the German government bill rate and buys dollars at the US T-bill rate. In T years Philippe will get the matured value of the German bill in euros. Simultaneously he will need to pay back the matured

---

currency exposure. This example is just for illustrative purposes. Nasdaq. "About Nasdaq." Website. www.nasdaq.com/about; Nasdaq. "Tesla, Inc. Common Stock." Website. www.nasdaq.com/market-activity/stocks/tsla; Börse Frankfurt. "Tesla, Inc." Website. www.boerse-frankfurt.de/equity/tesla-inc.

3 "Equivalent" is an overstrong word: there are small differences between currency forwards and an exchange of zero-coupon default-free instruments due to the limits of arbitrage. But the two alternatives are very similar.

value of the US Treasury bill in dollars. Philippe's counterparty will do the mirror transactions.[4]

Let r_f be the default-free rate on US Treasury bills (in dollars); the "f" subscript here means "foreign" (to Philippe). Let r_d ("d" for "domestic") be the default-free rate on German government bills (in euros). Let $(f/d)_0$ be the foreign/domestic spot exchange rate, that is, the current number of dollars required to buy a euro.

Using the continuous discounting convention, a zero-coupon German government bill worth €1 in T years will cost €$\exp(-r_d T)$ now. Thus, the current price in dollars to buy the zero-coupon German government bill is $(f/d)_0 \exp(-r_d T)$.

The current price in dollars to buy a zero-coupon US Treasury bill worth \$1 in T years is \$$\exp(-r_f T)$. This allows us to solve for fwd, the number of US zeroes required to buy a German zero:

$$\text{fwd} \cdot \exp(-r_f T) = (f/d)_0 \exp(-r_d T). \tag{12.1}$$

Here fwd is called the **forward rate**; it is the equalizer that makes future dollars ("f" or foreign currency) equal to future euros ("d" or domestic currency) today. Put another way, the forward rate is the rate that causes the cost of entering into a currency forward to be exactly balanced so that neither the buyer of foreign nor the seller of foreign has an advantage; the time-zero market value of the currency forward is zero. As time goes on and f/x and interest rates change, one party or the other will benefit and the other party will be disadvantaged.

Making the notation more explicit, we have:

$$\text{fwd}(f, d, T) = (f/d)_0 \exp\big((r_f - r_d)T\big). \tag{12.2}$$

Suppose that Philippe wants to invest €10,000 in dollar-denominated TSLA as of the most recent yearend, and that he wants to hedge out $T = 1$ year of currency movements. Code Segment 12.1 retrieves the three inputs to (12.2) and computes $\text{fwd}(f, d, T)$.

```
As of: 2021-12-30
    Spot dollars per euro (f/d) 1.1318
    US 1-year rate rf 0.3800
    German 1-year rate rd -0.7300 as of 2021-12


    1yr forward dollars per euro 1.1444
```

---

4 In practice, there may be departures from the simple bilateral transaction described here. The forward may be cash settled: instead of the parties exchanging the two currencies, the losing party may just pay the winning party in one of the currencies, usually the more heavily traded currency. There may also be a central counterparty as described in Section 12.2.6.

Table 12.1 Hedging EUR 10,000			
Item	Dollars (USD=f)	Euros (EUR=d)	Ratio
Time 0	11,318.0	10,000.0	Spot USD/EUR 1.1318
1yr rfree	0.380	-0.730	
Time 1	11,361.1	9,927.3	Fwd USD/EUR 1.1444

Table 12.2 Hedging plus gain			
Item	Dollars (USD=f)	Euros (EUR=d)	Ratio
Time 0	11,318.0	10,000.0	Spot USD/EUR 1.1318
1yr rfree	0.380	-0.730	
Time 1	11,361.1	9,927.3	Fwd USD/EUR 1.1444
T=1 TSLA	13,581.6		0.2000
T=1 Unhdgd	2,220.5	444.1	Crash USD/EUR 5.0000
Final amt		10,371.4	Final return 0.0371
No hedge	13,581.6	2,716.3	Final no hdg -0.7284

Table 12.1 (generated by Code Segment 12.2) shows Philippe's hedging strategy given these numbers. He takes €10,000 and converts it to dollars at the spot rate. He simultaneously enters into a currency forward that sells that number of dollars forward for one year and buys the equivalent amount of euros forward for one year. Here "buy forward" or "sell forward" means to buy (sell) a one-year zero-coupon government bill that is currently worth the given amount.

Philippe will convert euros to dollars as shown at time zero. He will invest the dollars in dollar-denominated shares of Tesla, Inc. At time one, his currency forward will automatically convert dollars back to euros as shown.

To see how the hedge works, suppose that over the year horizon two things happen: Tesla, Inc.'s business is successful and dollar-denominated TSLA goes up 20%; but, the dollar crashes to $5/€.

Philippe may think that the crash of the dollar is irrelevant to him as a euro-based investor since he hedged dollars versus euros. But Table 12.2 (generated by Code Segment 12.3) extends Table 12.1 to summarize the full accounting.

Had Philippe not hedged at all, his dollar-based TSLA investment would have been mutilated by the crash of the dollar, losing $1 - .24(\$/)_0$, or around 70%, of its value. But he didn't escape without bruises: he did not receive anywhere near the 20% rate of return that dollar-based investors got.

These bruises were the result of underhedging. His currency forward covered the increase in dollars that would have occurred if he had invested in a US

Treasury bill, but he actually invested in TSLA. If Philippe had somehow known at the beginning of his year investment period that TSLA would be up 20%, he could have bought a currency forward that would have exactly covered his dollar gain, giving him:

$$10,000 \frac{(f/d)_0 \cdot 1.2}{\text{fwd}(f,d,T)} = 12,000 exp(r_£ - r_\$)$$

euros at the end of the year. He still wouldn't have gotten a 20% rate of return because euro rates are lower than dollar rates, but he would have been close.

But in fact Philippe had no way of knowing TSLA's risky future: if he had hedged anticipating a 20% rise in TSLA but had actually experienced a 20% drop with a radical strengthening of the dollar to .2 per euro, he would have ended up owing money:

$$10,000 \cdot (f/d)_0 \left(\frac{1.2}{\text{fwd}(f,d,T)} - \frac{1.2 - .8}{.2} \right) < 0.$$

Guessing is not a good hedging strategy.

12.1.1 Quantity-Adjusting Options

Suppose Philippe wants to hedge the risk of the first scenario we described above: TSLA appreciates more than Treasurys in dollars. At time 0, Philippe wants to enter into a contingent trade that, if necessary, sells his excess (over Treasury) dollars at time T in exchange for euros at the forward rate fwd(f,d,T) rather than at the new spot rate $(f/d)_T$. Like the currency forward, this hedge can be advantageous (if dollars weaken) or disadvantageous (if dollars strengthen). Either way, it removes uncertainty about the future.

The sale of the excess dollars can be accomplished with a familiar instrument: a "plain vanilla" dollar-denominated European[5] call option on the underlying TSLA. We discussed these instruments in Section 9.2.1. Let X_t be the dollar value of the underlying risky asset TSLA at time $0 \le t \le T$; in our example $X_0 = 10,000(f/d)_0$. Writing (selling) a call option with time-T payoff:

$$\max(X_T - K_f, 0) \quad \text{where} \quad K_f = X_0 \exp(r_f T) \tag{12.3}$$

will neutralize any dollars over K_f, the amount covered by the currency forward discussed above.

The pricing of such options was also discussed in Section 9.2.1. Under the assumption that the underlying asset follows a lognormal random walk, the price of the option is given by the Black–Scholes formula (8.3). Adapted to the current notation, that is:

---

5 Despite the fact that we are working through an example where the euro currency is involved, the only currency referenced by this option is the dollar. The word "European" here refers to the style of the option and means – as noted in Section 9.2.1 – that the option can only be exercised at maturity.

$$C(X_0, K_f, T, r_f, \sigma_X) = X_0 N(d_1) - K_f \exp(-r_f T) N(d_2), \qquad (12.4)$$

where:

$$d_1 = \frac{\ln\left(\frac{X_0}{K_f}\right) + \left(r_f + \frac{\sigma_X^2}{2}\right) T}{\sigma_X \sqrt{T}} \quad \text{and} \quad d_2 = d_1 - \sigma_X \sqrt{T}.$$

Here r_f is the annual risk-free rate in dollars and σ_X is the annualized volatility of TSLA log-returns. Philippe will receive the amount given by (12.4) in exchange for writing an option that gives away his excess dollars.

What about the other side of the transaction described in the first paragraph of this section: receiving euros at the forward rate rather than at the new spot rate? Philippe would like to purchase (at time 0) a derivative with time-T euro (domestic) payoff:

$$\frac{\max(X_T - K_f, 0)}{\mathrm{fwd}(f, d, T)}. \qquad (12.5)$$

Such a derivative would lock in the time-zero forward rate despite the fact that at the time it's needed – at time T – a new f/x rate will prevail. This derivative is called a **quantity-adjusting**, or **quanto**, call option.

For notational simplicity, we'll price a quanto call with euro payoff equal to (12.3), that is, with a locked-in exchange rate of 1. Philippe will buy $\frac{1}{\mathrm{fwd}(f,d,T)}$ such quantos to get the desired payoff (12.5).

The price of the quanto call option depends on two stochastic variables: X_T, the value of the underlying, and $(f/d)_T$, the future f/x rate. While the future f/x rate is not explicitly referenced in (12.3), it needs to be referenced in order to understand the cost of converting the dollar (foreign) amount to the fixed euro (domestic) amount at time T.

The quanto call price can be derived using the assumption of joint lognormality $(X_T$ and $(f/d)_T)$ and a continuous arbitrage approach similar to Black–Scholes.[6] The pricing formula for the quanto call with euro payoff $\max(X_T - K_f, 0)$ is:

$$QuantoCall = X_0 \exp(-qT) N(d_+) - K_f \exp(-r_d T) N(d_-), \qquad (12.6)$$

where:

$$d_\pm = \frac{\ln\left(\frac{X_0}{K_f}\right) + \left(r_d - q \pm \frac{\sigma_X^2}{2}\right) T}{\sigma_X \sqrt{T}} \quad \text{and} \quad q = r_d - r_f - \rho \sigma_X \sigma_R.$$

Notation summary (example in parentheses):

- f is foreign currency (dollars);
- d is domestic currency (euros);

---

6 [Teng, Ehrhardt, and Günther 2015]. We have adapted their formulas (16) and (17). The authors solve for time-varying correlation but we have simplified the formula so that correlation is fixed.

- X_t is the foreign currency price of the underlying at time t (TSLA);
- T the horizon of the option (1 year);
- $N()$ is the standard normal cdf;
- r_f and r_d are default-free rates in the respective currencies for horizon T;
- K_f is the foreign currency strike price ($X_0 \exp(r_f T)$);
- $R_t = (f/d)_t$ is the exchange rate of foreign per domestic at time t;
- σ_X is the annualized volatility of log-returns of the underlying;
- σ_R is the annualized volatility of log-returns of the exchange rate; and
- ρ is the correlation between $\ln(X)$ and $\ln(R)$.

Note that setting $f = d$ removes the currency adjustment and forces $r_f = r_d$ and $q = 0$. In that case (12.6) becomes the same as Black–Scholes (12.4).

To hedge the second situation described above – TSLA drops in dollar price – Philippe could buy $\frac{1}{\text{fwd}(f,d,T)}$ **quanto puts** with time-T euro payoff:

$$\max(K_f - X_T, 0). \tag{12.7}$$

He would simultaneously sell an ordinary dollar-denominated European put option with the same time-T payoff (12.7) – but in dollars, not in euros.

Equations (12.3) and (12.7) show that buying a quanto put and simultaneously selling a quanto call has a linear time-T payoff pattern in euros:

$$X_T + QuantoPut_T - QuantoCall_T = K_f.$$

Here the quantities X_T and K_f, which are nominally in foreign (dollars), are converted to domestic (euros) at a 1:1 exchange rate. The RHS is non-stochastic; K_f is a known quantity at time 0. The LHS is a portfolio of three items: buy foreign (dollar)-denominated underlying TSLA and convert to euros at 1:1; buy quanto put; sell quanto call. Since the time-T value of that portfolio is a nonstochastic domestic (euro) amount, the portfolio must be equivalent to a domestic (euro) risk-free instrument. This gives a quanto put-call parity relationship that holds at any time $0 \leq t \leq T$:

$$X_t + QuantoPut_t - QuantoCall_t = \exp(-r_d(T - t))K_f. \tag{12.8}$$

Equation (12.8) is the quanto equivalent of (8.1).

Using put-call parity (12.8), the price of a quanto put is:

$$QuantoPut = -X_0\big(1 - \exp(-qT)N(d_+)\big) + K_f\exp(-r_dT)N(-d_-). \tag{12.9}$$

Code Segment 12.4 summarizes the key inputs for Philippe's quanto hedging strategy:

```
Data from 2010-07-31 to 2021-12-31
            Current price of underlying X_0: 11318.00
                            Time horizon T: 1.000000
                  Domestic riskfree rate r_d: -0.7300
```

```
            Foreign riskfree rate r_f: 0.3800
       Foreign currency strike price K_f: 11361.09
Annualized volatility of underlying sigma_X: 0.5562
  Annualized volatility of f/x rate sigma_R: 0.0843
     Correlation between underlying and f/x: 0.1512
```

With these inputs, Code Segment 12.5 can compute the cost of Philippe's hedging strategy in each direction: underlying up and underlying down.

```
          Buy Quanto call: 2234.26
   Write Dollar-only call: 2479.48
Cost of hedging TSLA upside: -245.21


        Write Quanto put: 2344.65
      Buy Dollar-only put: 2479.48
Cost of hedging TSLA downside: 134.83


     Total cost of hedging: -110.39
```

Note that the dollar-only call and the dollar-only put have the same price. This is because of put-call parity and the fact that we have set $K_f = \exp(r_f T)X_0$. For the dollar-only options, we have $r_f = r_d = r_\$$. That means $\exp(-r_d T)K_f = X_0$ in this case, forcing $QuantoPut = QuantoCall$.

Also note that the cost of hedging is negative! That's because the correlation between TSLA and the dollar/euro exchange rate is low, while TSLA's volatility is high. TSLA's high volatility means that the dollar-only options have high premia. The low correlation between TSLA and dollars-per-euro means that there is a comparatively high probability of TSLA up/dollar strengthens or TSLA down/dollar weakens; these are the scenarios where it would have been better not to hedge. That makes the quanto premia relatively less valuable than the dollar-only premia.

Unfortunately for Philippe, there is no regular market for dollar-euro-TSLA quantos. There are only a few quanto instruments that trade regularly. The best known is the Nikkei 225 future trading on the CME (formerly Chicago Mercantile Exchange). Investors can buy futures on Nikkei 225 Index that pay the dollar amount of the Japanese yen-denominated index. For example, if the Nikkei 225 is worth ¥20,000, the Nikkei 225 dollar future will pay $20,000.[7]

---

7 CME Group. "About Us." Website. www.cmegroup.com/company/about-us.html;
  CME Group. "Nikkei 225 Index Futures Spread Opportunities." Website. www.cmegroup
  .com/education/featured-reports/nikkei-225-spread-opportunities.html;
  Nikkei Indexes. "Nikkei 225." Website. https://indexes.nikkei.co.jp/en/nkave/.

Philippe's dollar-euro-TSLA quantos would be bespoke (custom-built) instruments, and a notional size of €10,000 would not be enough to induce a financial institution to create these instruments just for Philippe. So in practice, Philippe would have to use a dynamically adjusted portfolio of dollars and TSLA to try to replicate the behavior of the quantos.

In summary, unbundling hedging requires some thought. The efficacy of a strategy to remove a particular risk from a package of risks depends on understanding the relationships between wanted and unwanted risks.

12.2 Franchise Preservation

A second type of hedging aims at **franchise preservation**, where a company wants to neutralize risks that are outside of its area of expertise or control. For example, aluminum is lighter than steel so automobile companies purchase aluminum to provide lighter car bodies and engines for some models. If the price of aluminum skyrockets, an automobile company may not be able to pass on costs to its customers fast enough and may find itself unprofitable. Thus, the automobile company may buy aluminum futures covering its next year's worth of aluminum purchases so it can stabilize the prices it charges.

For a detailed example to illustrate franchise preservation hedging, we'll return to Philippe, the French (euro-based) investor who wanted to hedge the US dollar exposure he took on when he bought dollar-base Tesla, Inc. Let's suppose that when Philippe is not dabbling in the stock market, he owns a business that imports California wines into France.[8, 9]

Informed by his recent experience with cross-currency investing, Philippe begins to worry about the currency risk to the Philippe Wine Company ("PWC") franchise. The company has an overall budget of €20,000,000 per year. It converts euros to dollars at the current exchange rate and buys California wines with dollars; it then imports them to France and sells them for euros at a 10% markup. But Philippe now realizes that if the dollar strengthens significantly, PWC will be squeezed: he won't be able to raise euro prices because he is competing with French (and other European) wine producers, but he'll be paying more.

Table 12.3 (generated by Code Segment 12.6) summarizes PWC's business.

---

8 France produces about 4.47 billion liters of wine per year. It imports about 6.2 million liters per year from the USA. So Philippe's business is more of a thought experiment than a reality, but it's helpful to illustrate our points. Statista. "Official Wine Production in France." Website. www.statista.com/statistics/747272/official-wine-production-france/; USDA Foreign Agricultural Service. "France: Wine Annual Report and Statistics." July 29, 2015. www.fas.usda.gov/data/france-wine-annual-report-and-statistics.

9 I have borrowed the unlikely but amusing paradigm of a French importer of California wines from Mark Kritzman's excellent explanation of Siegel's Paradox in [Kritzman 2000].

Table 12.3 Philippe Wine Company summary	
Location	France
CEO	Philippe
Import budget	EUR 20,000,000.0
Cost/bottle	USD 11.3180
Sales price	EUR 11.0000
Num imported	2,000,000.0
T=0 USD/EUR	USD 1.1318
Cost/bot, lcl	EUR 10.0000
Profit	EUR 2,000,000.0
Bad USD/EUR	USD 1.0289
Cost/bot, lcl	EUR 11.0000
Profit	EUR 0.0

Philippe considers engaging in a hedging program similar to the one that was outlined for his cross-currency investment in TSLA. But he would rather build a business that is naturally immune to the franchise risk of currency movements.

So he decides to split his company in half. The first half will be the original PWC that imports US wines to France, but with half the original budget. The new second half will be a subsidiary that exports French wines to the USA. This will provide natural diversification; the French subsidiary will do well (poorly) on a strong (weak) euro; while the American subsidiary will do poorly (well) on a strong (weak) euro. Philippe is optimistic that he can mitigate franchise currency risk without elaborate trading strategies.

He calls his friend Ken in the USA. After explaining the situation to Ken, he asks him to be the head of the American subsidiary. He tells Ken that the original €20,000,000 budget will be split in half and converted to dollars so that Ken's subsidiary can purchase and import French wines.

The new company, the Philippe-Ken Wine Company ("PKWC") will thus initially be split evenly between the two countries as shown in Table 12.4 (generated by Code Segment 12.7).

Philippe and Ken now calculate what might happen to PKWC in the situation that Philippe feared: a strong dollar. Naturally, they expect the volume and profit of the French half of the business to suffer, but the American subsidiary should do well. Their intuition tells them that the overall business should end up pretty much unscathed by the change in exchange rate.

In fact, as Table 12.5 (generated by Code Segment 12.8) shows, the PKWC franchise does better than "unscathed." The results after currency movement are actually better than the original results. The volume of bottles handled by the

Table 12.4 Philippe-Ken Wine Company: unchanged f/x

Location	France	USA	Total
CEO	Philippe	Ken	
Import budget	EUR 10,000,000.0	USD 11,318,000.0	
Cost/bottle	USD 11.3180	EUR 10.0000	
Sales price	EUR 11.0000	USD 12.4498	
USD/EUR	1.1318		
Cost/bot lcl	EUR 10.0000	USD 11.3180	
Num imported	1,000,000.0	1,000,000.0	2,000,000.0
Profit	EUR 1,000,000.0	USD 1,131,800.0	EUR 2,000,000.0

Table 12.5 Philippe-Ken Wine Company: strong dollar

Location	France	USA	Total
CEO	Philippe	Ken	
Import budget	EUR 10,000,000.0	USD 11,318,000.0	
Cost/bottle	USD 11.3180	EUR 10.0000	
Sales price	EUR 11.0000	USD 12.4498	
USD/EUR	1.0000		
Cost/bot lcl	EUR 11.3180	USD 10.0000	
Num imported	883,548.3	1,131,800.0	2,015,348.3
Profit	EUR -280,968.4	USD 2,772,683.6	EUR 2,491,715.3

business has gone up to more than the original 2 million shown in Table 12.4, and the profit has increased over the original €2 million.

Philippe and Ken feel that this is too good to be true. They were just hoping to stay even by diversifying, but they're actually improving. Perhaps there was something inadvertently asymmetric about the new PKWC structure; maybe they'll do worse if the dollar weakens. Table 12.6 (generated by Code Segment 12.9) shows that scenario.

Strangely, the business has also done better in this direction: both bottle volume and profits have increased due to the weakening of the dollar.

12.2.1 Siegel's Paradox

It seems paradoxical that both non-monetary (bottle volume) and monetary metrics got better no matter which way the dollar–euro exchange rate moved in our examples. Could this be a coincidence because we just chose fortunate numbers?

Location	France	USA	Total
	Table 12.6 Philippe-Ken Wine Company: weak dollar		
CEO	Philippe	Ken	
Import budget	EUR 10,000,000.0	USD 11,318,000.0	
Cost/bottle	USD 11.3180	EUR 10.0000	
Sales price	EUR 11.0000	USD 12.4498	
USD/EUR	1.5000		
Cost/bot lcl	EUR 7.5453	USD 15.0000	
Num imported	1,325,322.5	754,533.3	2,079,855.8
Profit	EUR 4,578,547.4	USD-1,924,210.9	EUR 3,295,740.2

It's not hard to see that this was no coincidence. Let $z = \frac{(f/d)_T}{(f/d)_0}$ be the ratio of the future (time-T) foreign/domestic exchange rate to the spot (time-zero) rate. In our example, $z > 1$ means the dollar weakened and $z < 1$ means the dollar strengthened.

The French part of the Philippe-Ken Wine Company will import $1,000,000z$ bottles after the f/x change, while the US part of the company will import $1,000,000\frac{1}{z}$ bottles. So total PKWC bottle volume will be:

$$1,000,000 \left(\frac{1}{z} + z \right).$$

Jensen's Inequality[10] gives:

$$\frac{1}{2} \exp(y) + \frac{1}{2} \exp(-y) \geq \exp(0) = 1$$

since exp is convex; multiply both sides by 2 and set $y = \ln(z)$ to get:

$$z + \frac{1}{z} \geq 2.$$

Thus, total PKWC bottle volume will be strictly larger than $2,000,000$ if $z \neq 1$; *any* f/x rate change will increase the company's volume.

Figure 12.1 (generated by Code Segment 12.10) shows the number-of-bottles response curve.

Before changes to f/x rates, PKWC annual profits were €2,000,000, as shown in Table 12.4. Once again letting $z = \frac{(f/d)_T}{(f/d)_0}$ be the ratio of post-change exchange rate to original exchange rate, company profits in euros look like this:

$$\frac{1,000,000}{z} \left(\frac{11}{z} - 10 \right) + 1,000,000z \left(11 - \frac{10}{z} \right). \qquad (12.10)$$

---

10 [Jensen 1906].

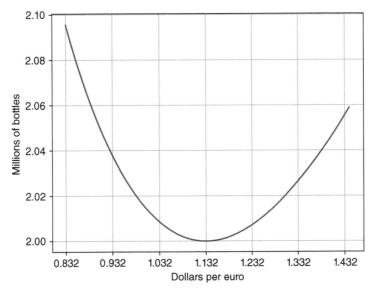

Figure 12.1 Total bottle volume of Philippe–Ken Wine Company.

The first summand is the contribution of the US subsidiary to profits as a product of number of bottles imported times converted-to-euro profit per bottle. The US business's costs are fixed at €10 per bottle. Its proceeds are fixed in dollars at $11 $(f/d)_0$, but the proceeds are variable at €$\frac{11}{z}$ when converted back to euros.

Similarly, the second summand is the contribution of the French part of PKWC to profits. The French proceeds per bottle are fixed at €11, but the cost in euros is variable at €$\frac{10}{z}$ per bottle.

Manipulating (12.10) into a polynomial gives:

$$\frac{1,000,000}{z^2}(z+1)(11z^2 - 21z + 11). \tag{12.11}$$

The roots of the quadratic in (12.11) are imaginary, so profits are positive as long as z is positive, which it must be. Thus, the combined PKWC franchise never loses money, alleviating Philippe's original concern.

While the franchise never loses money, it can make less money than the original €2, 000, 000 profit enjoyed by the undiversified PWC, or by PKWC before f/x rate changes. Subtracting (12.11) from €2, 000, 000, we see that PKWC dips below the original profit level when:

$$(z-1)(11z^2 - z - 11) < 0. \tag{12.12}$$

Code Segment 12.11 finds the roots of the quadratic and translates to actual exchange rates:

```
Roots of (12.12) polynomial: -0.9555779793429654 1
    1.0464870702520563
Profit less than original between (f/d)= 1.1318 and 1.
    1844140661112772
Minimum profit at z= 1.0233800320326436  (f/d)=
    1.1582615202545459
Minimum hedged profit 1988770.9045979201
Percentage profit giveup at minimum: 0.56
Unhedged (PWC) profit at minimum hedged profit: 2514360.
    7047181595
```

When the new/old exchange rate ratio z is between 1 and 1.0465, the hedged franchise PKWC makes a little less than the unhedged enterprise, with a minimum at $z = 1.02338$. The profit at that point is €1, 988, 771, only 56bps below the original franchise profit of €2, 000, 000.

If Philippe had kept the entire €20, 000, 000 in France importing California wine at \$11.227 and selling it for €11, his cost per bottle would be €$\frac{10}{z}$, so he would buy 2, 000, 000z bottles. He sells each one for €11, so his profit would be €20, 000, 000(1.1z − 1).

Figure 12.2 (generated by Code Segment 12.12) compares the France-only franchise PWC's profits with the diversified franchise PKWC's profits. Figure 12.3 (also generated by Code Segment 12.12) zooms in on the profits around the neighborhood of the time-zero exchange rate.

Figure 12.2 shows that the franchise preservation strategy is successful. The original France-only franchise (PWC, blue line) looks more like a currency

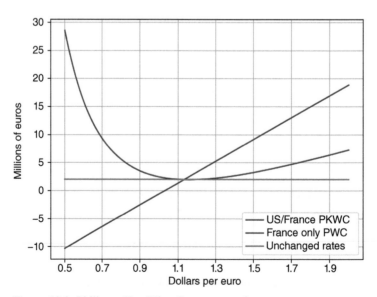

Figure 12.2 Philippe–Ken Wine Company profit.

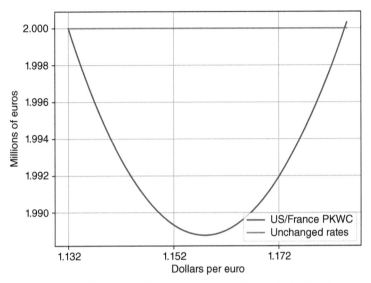

Figure 12.3 Philippe–Ken Wine Company profit – neighborhood.

business than a wine importing business. It is at the mercy of exchange rates. The diversified franchise (PKWC, red line) is positively convex as a result of (12.11) and is almost always above the original €2,000,000 profit line in green.

Figure 12.3 shows that for a small neighborhood around the time-zero f/x rate, the diversified franchise gives up a little profit – at most 56bps, as we saw above. This seems a small price to pay for protection against potentially ruinous large currency moves.

While this exploration provides yet another hearty endorsement of the power of diversification, it doesn't explain the apparent paradox of positive convexity in Figures 12.2 and 12.3. If any change at all in exchange rates increases both non-monetary volume (number of bottles) and monetary profits, then it would appear that we've found the key to unlimited prosperity. World governments need merely work with each other to whip their exchange rates into a volatile frenzy. That will cause more wine, more Tesla Model Ss, and more Airbus 380s to appear effortlessly.[11]

That idea is manifestly absurd. But the number-of-bottle and profit formulas are correct, so what prevents this absurd idea from working? The apparent contradiction has a name, as the title of this subsection indicates: Siegel's Paradox. Jeremy Siegel, currently a Wharton School Emeritus Professor,[12] observed in Siegel (1972) that Jensen's Inequality gives rise to certain counterintuitive phenomena concerning exchange rates.

---

11 Tesla. "Model S." Website. www.tesla.com/models; Airbus. "A380." Website. www.airbus
.com/aircraft/passenger-aircraft/a380.html.
12 University of Pennsylvania, Wharton. "Jeremy Siegel." Website. https://fnce.wharton
.upenn.edu/profile/siegel.

The logical fallacy that gives rise to the "paradox" comes in the assumption that economic participants don't change their behavior. This is the kind of fallacy discussed in Chapter 2, where phenomena like Goodhart's Law and the Lucas Critique were different versions of a similar underlying dynamic: people react.

If the euro strengthens, Philippe buys more California wine. The California wine producers will eventually respond to the increased demand by raising prices – perhaps not for the several thousand extra bottles in our example, but in aggregate to all the increased demand for American goods due to the changed f/x rates. Before they change prices in response to higher demand, the wine producers who produce the extra bottles are economic losers because they have not yet responded to market forces.

But the Law of Demand[13] is as close to an immutable physical law as there is in economics. Eventually prices will adjust. Thus, Siegel's Paradox is a result of myopic vision. If we only look at the Philippe-Ken Wine Company and ignore all the other economic participants, it looks like PKWC wins no matter what. But American or French wine producers lose (gain) because they are working harder (less hard) for less (more) real money. In the aggregate, all we have done by changing f/x rates is shift wealth from one country to another in a way that may be quickly counteracted by adjusting prices.

In fact, in an era of floating exchange rates,[14] the change in f/x rates was probably a response to, and not a cause of, shifting wealth and other factors like interest rates, balance of trade, and national debt.

Thus, the Philippe-Ken Wine Company has not fully eliminated risk, as the assumptions about unchanging same-currency wine prices are unrealistic. Still, the diversified franchise is clearly a more resilient business than the undiversified franchise.

12.2.2 Modigliani–Miller and Franchise Hedging

Modigliani and Miller (1958) developed what is sometimes called the **Modigliani–Miller Indifference Theorem**. Miller received a Sveriges Riksbank Prize in Economic Sciences in Memory of Alfred Nobel in 1990 for his work. Modigliani, who was previously cited in Section 2.3.2, was a 1985 recipient of the same prize.[15] Their 1958 work states that the cost of capital of a firm

13 David Henderson, Econlib. "Demand." Website. www.econlib.org/library/Enc/Demand.html.
14 International Monetary Fund. "Exchange Rate Regimes in an Increasingly Integrated World Economy." June, 2000. Website. www.imf.org/external/np/exr/ib/2000/062600.htm.
15 Nobelprize.org. "Merton H. Miller: Biographical." Website. www.nobelprize.org/prizes/economic-sciences/1990/miller/biographical/; Nobelprize.org. "Franco Modigliania: Biographical." Website. www.nobelprize.org/prizes/economic-sciences/1985/modigliani/biographical/.

(as defined below) is independent of – indifferent to – the proportion of debt in its capital structure.

Modigliani and Miller (1958) define cost of capital as the ratio of two quantities. The denominator is the current market value V_0 of the enterprise (including debt and equity) as first defined in Section 9.5.1. The numerator is $\mathbb{E}[V_T] - V_0$, the expected monetary return on the enterprise over some horizon T. The Modigliani–Miller Indifference Theorem (Proposition I of their cited paper) states that under assumptions of perfect frictionless markets, $\frac{\mathbb{E}[V_T]-V_0}{V_0}$ is invariant to changes in the proportion of debt versus equity in V_0.

With perfect frictionless markets, an investor can create a portfolio by (1) buying equity shares of a company, and (2) borrowing or lending. This portfolio is a synthetic version of the original company with more or less debt than the original company. Modigliani and Miller (1958) show with a no-arbitrage argument that the synthetic company's cost of capital $\frac{\mathbb{E}[V_T]-V_0}{V_0}$ must be the same as the original company's cost of capital. Their use of a no-arbitrage argument allowed them to avoid making assumptions about risk preferences.

Following Modigliani and Miller (1958), many researchers pursued other forms of inside–outside indifference. If an investor outside a company can synthetically create a different debt–equity ratio by making adjustments outside the company, can't the investor make other adjustments outside the company? Hedging is just such a potential adjustment.

At the beginning of this section, we pointed out that automobile companies are exposed to the risk of volatile aluminum prices. But in the spirit of Modigliani–Miller, investors can buy aluminum companies[16] as well as automobile companies. If an investor is worried about aluminum price effects on an automobile company in his or her portfolio, s/he can just add an aluminum company to the portfolio in an appropriate proportion to offset the risk.

If aluminum goes down in price, the investor's aluminum company will do worse but the car company will do better because its materials will be cheaper. If aluminum goes up in price, the car company will suffer but the aluminum company will make up for it. If the automobile company hedges aluminum, that could confuse investors who might become overhedged, thereby re-establishing an unwanted exposure to aluminum. Thus, some argue that it's best to leave hedging to the end investor.

This line of reasoning ignores what academics disapprovingly call "imperfections," that is, the ways in which insubordinate reality departs from assumptions. Transactions costs, taxes, and bankruptcy are real-world considerations that violate the pure Modigliani–Miller axioms and invalidate the irrelevance theorem. If aluminum prices change so dramatically that the automobile company

---

16 Alcoa®. "Aluminum." Website. www.alcoa.com/global/en/what-we-do/aluminum/default.asp.

has to declare bankruptcy, there will be a discontinuous loss of value: the value of a car manufacturer as a going concern is greater than just the auction value of its plant and equipment. As we saw in Chapter 11, recovery given default is only around 40%. Thus, companies rightly attach a high value to self-preservation.

In practice, franchise preservation hedging involves gamesmanship and prediction of future outcomes. If all but one of a group of competitive automobile companies hedge aluminum, then the non-hedger may go bankrupt if aluminum prices skyrocket. But if aluminum prices crash, the non-hedger will have a big competitive advantage over its rivals who have locked in the old higher prices. The non-hedger might drive some of the hedgers into bankruptcy by its ability to lower automobile prices.

This dynamic played out in the gold mining industry starting in the 1980s. Some gold mining companies argued that they were good at mining, but that they couldn't control the price of gold. During the 1980s and 1990s, many (but not all) gold miners hedged the price of gold in order to purify their reliance on their own skill in driving down mining costs while avoiding the external risk of fluctuating gold prices.

By 1999, Ashanti Goldfields (a large Ghanaian gold miner) had sold forward a large portion of its reserves at a locked-in price. Gold prices then spiked up, meaning that Ashanti owed money on its hedges while its gold reserves got more valuable. By definition "reserves" are in the ground; Ashanti could only mine about 15% a year of the gold it had hedged. The bankers demanding cash payment on the hedges were very much above the ground. Ashanti was able to negotiate with its creditors to avoid outright bankruptcy, but shareholder value was decimated.[17]

This and other bad outcomes of gold hedging programs caused the industry fashion to shift. Adam and Fernando (2006) argued that gold hedging was profitable because gold miners were uniquely able to reap the risk premium ("contango") usually found in the gold futures market. But this argument did not stay the course of the gold industry: Foster (2018) indicated that as of 2018, gold miners had virtually no gold hedges.

To preserve their franchises, companies generally hedge the relative risk, not the absolute risk, of price shocks to their inputs. This is similar to benchmark-relative risk discussed in Section 4.1.6: here the benchmark is the industry. If almost everyone in the industry is exposed to aluminum prices because no one hedged, then they might all raise or lower prices together if necessary due to aluminum shocks. Aluminum shocks confer no competitive advantage or disadvantage in that case: in that case a hedger is taking the most risk. Similarly if

---

17 AngloGoldAshanti. Website. www.anglogoldashanti.com/; GhanaWeb. "Ashanti: A Hedge Too Far." February 23, 2002. www.ghanaweb.com/GhanaHomePage/features/ASHANTI-A-Hedge-Too-Far-21933.

almost everyone hedges, then a non-hedger is taking the most risk. There's only a potential problem (or reward) for a company that has a very different risk profile from its competitors. Since the potential reward from being different is probably not due to skill – automobile companies are not aluminum traders – it is usually not one that companies want to embrace.

Empirical evidence of the effect of franchise preservation hedging on actual franchise value is mixed. Allayannis and Weston (2001) concluded that f/x hedging added a statistically significant 5% to the value of firms that hedged.[18] Despite this, a 2013 survey[19] showed that only about half of multinational firms engaged in currency hedging: perhaps some of them felt that, like PKWC, they were naturally hedged.

On the other hand, Jin and Jorion (2006) studied 119 oil and gas producers and analyzed 330 firm-years worth of hedging oil prices; gas prices; neither; or both. They did not find any significant effect of hedging on firm market value, but they did find that hedging lowered the hedging firm's stock price sensitivity to price movements of the hedged commodity.

In addition to investigating the effectiveness of franchise preservation hedging, scholars have investigated hedging rationale. Geyer-Klingeberg et al. (2018) summarized dozens of previous studies that had investigated reasons to hedge. They found four main reasons for franchise preservation hedging:

1. reducing the corporate tax burden;
2. lowering bankruptcy and financial distress costs;
3. mitigating asymmetric information and agency costs of equity;[20] and
4. improving the coordination of financing and investment policy while alleviating agency conflicts of debt.

None of these reasons is directly observable, but there are observable proxy variables: for example, tax-loss carryforwards on the balance sheet proxy for "reducing the corporate tax burden." Geyer-Klingeberg et al. (2018) find weak evidence for reasons 1 and 4 (taxes and financing coordination), and no evidence for reason 3 (mitigating asymmetric information). But they do find strong

18 [Allayannis and Weston 2001] use Tobin's Q as the measure of firm value. This is the ratio of market value (V_0 in our notation) to replacement cost of assets; it can be thought of as an adjusted market-to-book value ratio. Replacement cost of assets is difficult to calculate; [Allayannis and Weston 2001] use an accounting method where they infer the vintages and depreciation pattern of in-place gross fixed assets, and add in the book value of inventories and LIFO reserves.

19 CFO. "Only Half of Companies Hedging Currency and Other Risks." Website. www.cfo.com/risk-management/2013/10/half-companies-hedging-currency-risks/.

20 Asymmetric information can refer to knowledge that a company's managers have that external shareholders don't, so the ability of external shareholders to replicate managers' actions as contemplated by Modigliani and Miller may not exist. Asymmetric information can also mean that a company's managers do not have knowledge that others do have: for example, an automobile manufacturer may not be fully informed about aluminum prices.

evidence for reason 2, lowering bankruptcy and financial distress costs. Thus, franchise preservation hedging does seem to be a key activity in corporations.

12.2.3 Bank Franchise Hedging

For banks, franchise preservation hedging is a matter of urgency.

Deposits in banks are short term: a checking account depositor can remove its money at any time. Such monies are called **demand deposits** and are ultra-short-term liabilities of the bank. Banks do have longer-lasting deposits and do borrow money for longer periods, but demand deposits are usually a key source of funding.

Theoretically, a bank could make money simply by accepting deposits and charging fees for transactions and storage. Banks would then just be electronic warehouses, and would always be able to repay their depositors instantaneously. But in fact banks are not electronic warehouses: they use most of their customers' funds to form a portfolio of risky investments like loans and securities. This portfolio's returns accrue to the bank and its shareholders, not to the bank's customers. A warehouse-only bank would have to charge such high fees that it would not be able to attract customers from banks who don't have to make a profit from warehousing.

Table 12.7 shows a simplified "T-account" statement for JP Morgan Chase & Co. as of December 31, 2021, summarizing its assets and liabilities.[21]

On the right side of the balance sheet, deposits and short-term liabilities are dominant. On the left side, securities and loans – assets that generally have longer maturities and less liquidity – are dominant. This creates a potentially dangerous **asset–liability mismatch**.

Table 12.7 JP Morgan Chase T-account statement December 31, 2021 ($Mn)

Assets		Liabilities	
Cash & equivs	1,002,532	Deposits	2,462,303
Securities	1,311,878	Short-term	675,382
Loans	1,061,328	Long-term	311,755
Other	367,829	Stk equity	294,127
Tot assets	3,743,567	Total liabs	3,743,567

21 JPMorgan Chase & Co. "2021 Annual Report." Website. www.jpmorganchase.com/content/dam/jpmc/jpmorgan-chase-and-co/investor-relations/documents/annualreport-2021.pdf.

Because of this danger, banks are heavily regulated. One requirement is that banks must act as partial, or fractional, warehouses: they are required by national authorities to keep some minimum fraction of their customers' deposits in reserve, ready to repay customers demanding their cash back. This practice is called **fractional reserve banking**. For large banks in the USA, the minimum reserve fraction was 10% until March 26, 2020. At that point, reserve requirements were lowered to zero on an emergency basis as a result of the COVID-19 pandemic.[22]

The unreserved fraction of deposits and other bank liabilities is loaned out or invested at higher rates than depositors are paid. And, as in Table 12.7, bank assets usually have significantly longer maturities than their liabilities. Most of the time – about 89 percent of the time, as we saw in Chapter 3 – this is a naturally profitable position, as yield curves tend to be upward sloping. The rates on the longer-term assets then tend to be higher than the rates on the shorter-term liabilities. But even more than that, banks charge a significant spread: the rate a depositor is paid to loan money to the bank for x years is considerably lower than the rate the bank is paid to loan money to borrowers for the same x years.

There are two problems with the mismatch between long asset maturities and short liability maturities:

1. The possibility of a **run on the bank**: short-term depositors might all show up at the same time and demand their money back. This hasn't happened much recently for reasons we'll discuss below, but there were limited bank runs in the USA at IndyMac Bank in 2008 and in the UK at Northern Rock in 2007.[23]
2. The possibility of yield curve movement that overwhelms the bank's spread, making their liabilities more expensive than their assets.

We first consider bank runs. Before the COVID-19 crisis, US banks were required to keep 10% of the amount of customer deposits in reserve, that is, in unencumbered cash warehoused and ready to repay customers. Normally, far fewer than 10% of depositors show up on any given day wanting to retrieve their money, so this is normally more than enough. But suppose that more than 10% of the deposits were demanded for withdrawal by customers. What would the bank do after it exhausted its reserves?

The bank may have used some of the unreserved money to make mortgage loans lasting 30 years to people buying houses. These mortgagors may be fully creditworthy and may be faithfully making the required payments on their mortgages, but there is no mechanism by which a bank can force accelerated

---

22 Office of the Comptroller of the Currency. Website. www.occ.treas.gov/; Board of Governors of the Federal Reserve System. "Reserve Requirements." Website. www.federalreserve.gov/monetarypolicy/reservereq.htm.
23 FDIC. "Failed Bank Information: Information for IndyMac Bank, F.S.B." Website. www.fdic.gov/bank/individual/failed/indymac.html; [Cunliffe 2017].

Image 12.1 Northern Rock run in 2007. Source: Peter Macdiamid / Getty Images News / Getty Images Europe

repayment. Stretching out payments over time is the very point of long-term borrowing. As we'll see later in this chapter, for residential mortgages the right to accelerate repayment rests with the borrower and not with the lender.

Unable to retrieve the money from the borrower, the bank would have to try to sell the mortgage to a more patient investor who can wait 30 years to receive all the scheduled cash flows. But it might take time to arrange a sale at a fair price. The fact that the bank is desperate to sell the mortgage in order to raise cash immediately (a "fire sale") will depress the price. Similarly, the fire sales of other long-term assets will depress the bank's asset-to-liability ratio, thereby lowering confidence in the bank and incenting more depositors to run to the bank to get their money out before the bank is not able to pay them back. That causes more fire sales of assets until the bank, which might have been perfectly solvent before its depositors panicked, fails. Image 12.1 shows a crush of panicked depositors trying to get their money out of Northern Rock in 2007.

Diamond and Dybvig's[24] classic paper (1983) on bank runs, points out that there are two equilibria with respect to depositor confidence in banks: a calm equilibrium in which depositors expect that withdrawals are random and uncorrelated, and a turbulent equilibrium in which depositors expect that other depositors have lost faith in the bank and are rushing to take their money out. In the calm equilibrium, there is no reason for a depositor to take its money out other than its own liquidity needs; in the turbulent equilibrium, there is every reason for a depositor to take its money out as soon as possible before the bank runs out of money.

24 Diamond and Dybvig (along with former US Federal Reserve chair Ben Bernanke) won the 2022 Sveriges Riksbank Prize in Economic Sciences in Memory of Alfred Nobel. www.nobelprize .org/prizes/economic-sciences/2022/summary/.

Diamond and Dybvig (1983) note that general poor economic conditions, rumors, or actual disturbing bank-specific news can trigger a transition from the calm equilibrium to the panicked, turbulent equilibrium. Once the regime switch is made, the bank is doomed as it becomes rational for each depositor to panic. Legally, the bank has the right to suspend withdrawals, but such a step will be fatal to future confidence in the bank and damaging to trust in the general financial system.

Diamond and Dybvig (1983) showed that there is only one way to prevent a switch into the doomed equilibrium: the Hobbes (1651) Leviathan of government intervention. Only the assurance of inexhaustibly deep pockets can remove the incentive to panic. This idea was recognized in practice 50 years before Diamond and Dybvig (1983): the US Federal Deposit Insurance Corporation ("FDIC") was formed in 1933 to insure bank acounts.[25] So both Diamond and Dybvig theory and practical experience bear out the conclusion that there is no way for a bank to hedge itself against bank runs: it must appeal to the higher power of government backing.

Systems of government intervention to prevent bank runs vary from country to country. The US system collects an insurance payment from each bank based on an assessment of the bank's size and risk level. Depositors are insured up to $250,000 per account. The insurance payments go into a Deposit Insurance Fund that amounted to about 1.27% of the total amount being insured as of September 2021; this percentage is called the reserve ratio. The September 2021 reserve ratio was below the statutory minimum 1.35% due to the COVID-19 pandemic. The insurance provided to depositors is backed by the "full faith and credit" of the US government, so if the Deposit Insurance Fund were to run out, the US Treasury would have to step in.[26]

In practice, bank failure in the USA has become routine: about five banks fail each year, on average. Typically, government regulators like the FDIC will swoop in over a weekend and move deposit accounts of a failed bank to a stronger bank in the area, so that on Monday morning depositors can go about their business at a new address. The shareholders of the failed bank will probably lose all or virtually all their investment, and creditors (landlords, bondholders, e.g.) might get only partial payment. But depositors will suffer no loss up to the insured amount, so they will have no reason to panic.

In the UK, a less formal system of government backing prevailed going into the Global Financial Crisis. Deposits were only guaranteed up to £2,000; beyond that, there was a misguided policy of "constructive ambiguity." British policymakers thought that it would be good to maintain some mystery about

---

25 FDIC. "History of the FDIC." Website. www.fdic.gov/about/history/.
26 FDIC. "Deposit Insurance Assessments: FDIC Assessment Rates." Website. www.fdic.gov/deposit/insurance/assessments/proposed.html; [Ellis 2021].

government backing as (they thought) that would incent depositors to be extra careful about where they deposited their money. But depositors are not bank examiners; they generally assume that a government-licensed bank is solid.

Confusion over exactly what the government was going to do led to the chaotic scene shown in Image 12.1. The Chancellor of the Exchequer – essentially the British taxpayer – did eventually (on September 17, 2007) guarantee Northern Rock deposits. A year later, far larger bank failures of RBS and Lloyds led to even deeper raids on the British taxpayer's pocket.

Subsequently, the UK adopted quite detailed bank stabilization and resolution regimes intended to avoid ambiguity, constructive or otherwise. Among other measures, a Financial Services Compensation Scheme[27] was adopted that insured deposits up to £85,000 per account, or £170,000 for joint accounts.

Both theory and practice have borne out Diamond and Dybvig's two-equilibrium model: it's not possible for banks to stop runs without some kind of government backing. However, some resilience is better than none. In 2014, the Basel III international banking regulatory framework adopted requirements for a Net Stable Funding Ratio requiring banks to hold a stock of high-quality liquid assets in order to lower the chances of a switch into the panicked equilibrium. While fractional reserve banking will never be free of the potential for runs, the requirement to hold more assets that can be easily converted to cash can help ward off some problems.[28]

12.2.4   Asset–Liability Management: Interest Rate Swaps

The second asset–liability mismatch problem is the **possibility of yield curve movement that overwhelms the bank's spread.**

At any point in time a bank will make sure that it lends at higher rates than it borrows. If short-term default-free rates are 1% and long-term default-free rates are 2%, a bank might make a 20-year loan at 3.5%, taking advantage both of the steepness of the yield curve and its ability to add a spread. But once the 3.5% rate has been established, the bank is stuck with it for 20 years. Meanwhile, demand deposit rates are resetting overnight, and other short-term rates are resetting frequently. If short-term default-free rates rise to 4% at any time in the next 20 years, the 3.5% loan becomes unprofitable. At the same time, the rise in short-term rates may be accompanied by a rise in long-term rates, which causes the existing fixed-rate loans and bonds owned by the bank to be discounted more and to drop in value.

---

27 Bank of England. "Financial Services Compensation Scheme." Website. www.bankofengland .co.uk/prudential-regulation/authorisations/financial-services-compe nsation-scheme.

28 BIS. "Basel III: international regulatory framework for banks." Website. https://www.bis.org/ bcbs/basel3.htm; Basel Committee on Banking Supervision. "Basel III: The Net Stable Funding Ratio." October 2014. Website. www.bis.org/bcbs/publ/d295.pdf.

In the early 1980s, hundreds of savings and loans (a type of bank) went bankrupt in the USA, largely due to rapid rises in interest rates and the resulting asset–liability mismatch. Savings and loan banks had their own government insurance entity, the Federal Savings and Loan Insurance Corporation ("FSLIC"). This proved inadequate to backstop the losses, and taxpayer assistance of about $124 billion was used to clean up the mess.[29]

Today banks are required to practice **asset–liability management (ALM)** so that changes in interest rates are not overwhelming. ALM seeks to protect a franchise from unfavorable yield curve reshaping. For banks, the business model consists of short-term (rapidly changing or "floating") interest rates providing funding, while long-term (unchanging or "fixed") interest rates provide revenue. So, banks naturally have negative positions short-term and positive positions long-term. An **interest rate swap** can hedge away that exposure.

A standard ("plain vanilla") interest rate swap is a contract between two parties that lasts for a predetermined time. The parties agree to swap payments at regular intervals, for example, every six months, during the life of the swap. One party is the **fixed payer** who sends the other party (the **fixed receiver**) an unchanging amount, determined at inception of the swap, at every payment period. (The fixed payer owns a **payer swap**.) At the same payment period, the fixed receiver (who owns a **receiver swap**) sends an ever-changing ("floating") amount to the fixed payer. In fact, the two parties just net the amounts and whichever party owes the greater amount sends money to the other. The floating amount is determined by reference to the current value of a benchmark, which for the vast majority of US interest rate swaps is SOFR, the Secured Overnight Financing Rate. SOFR replaced LIBOR, the London Inter-Bank Offered Rate, on January 1, 2022. In Europe, EURIBOR and ESTR, Euro Short-Term Rate, are used as the reference rates.[30]

The fixed and floating sides are specified as interest rates that are translated into monetary amounts by multiplying by the size of the swap, called its **notional amount**. For example, suppose the notional amount is $1 million; the annual fixed swap rate set at the inception of the swap is 5%; and at a particular 6-month payment period the then-current annualized reference rate is 4%. Then the fixed payer would send $1,000,000(.05 - .04)/2 = $5,000$ to the fixed receiver, dividing the annual amount by two because the interval is 6 months in our

---

29 [Robinson 2013].
30 Federal Reserve Bank of New York. "Secured Overnight Financing Rate Data." Website.
   https://apps.newyorkfed.org/markets/autorates/sofr;   ICE   Benchmark
   Administration. "LIBOR®." Website. www.theice.com/iba/libor; European Money Markets
   Institute.   "Euribor®."   Website.   www.emmi-benchmarks.eu/benchmarks/euribor/;
   European Central Bank. "Euro short-term rate." Website. www.ecb.europa.eu/stats/
   financial_markets_and_interest_rates/euro_short-term_rate/html/
   index.en.html.

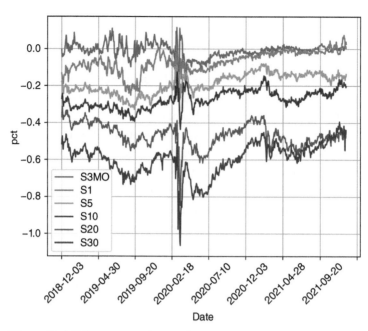

Figure 12.4 US swap spreads over Treasurys (by maturity). Source: IHS Markit.

example. If the reference rate had been 6% instead of 4%, the cash flow would have gone in the other direction, paid by the fixed receiver to the fixed payer.

In the USA, swap rates referencing SOFR have been a little lower than US Treasury rates as shown in Figure 12.4 (generated by Code Segment 12.13).

The lowest (30-year) line shows that swap rates were consistently, and significantly, lower than US Treasury rates. This suggests a strategy for a bank:

1. Set aside $100 million of short-term deposits where the depositors are getting paid a short-term rate like SOFR.
2. Buy $100 million of US Treasurys yielding a fixed rate fix_{30}.
3. Enter into a 30-year payer swap at rate $SW(30)$.
4. Use the floating-rate payments received from the swap to pay the costs of the borrowing in Step 1.
5. Pocket $100 million times $(\text{fix}_{30} - SW(30))$ per year.

Code Segment 12.14 computes recent profits from this strategy:

```
Profit from $100Mn 30-year spread: $439,330.0 as of
    2021-12-31
```

The fact that this apparently profitable strategy continues to be available is a complex function of government issuance, capital availability, regulation, and preferred habitat.[31]

31 Treasury Borrowing Advisory Committee. "Swap Spreads." Website. https://home.treasury .gov/system/files/221/TBACCharge2Q12021.pdf.

Boyarchenko et al. (2018) note that regulatory changes make it less attractive to enter into the strategy described above. Under post–Global Financial Crisis regulations, a bank would have to set aside risk capital to buffer any problems with the trade. There are few foreseeable problems with the trade given the existence of central counterparties (CCPs), but that does not change the fact that regulatory capital would need to be used. The fact that the negative spreads persist is evidence that banks have judged they have more profitable uses of their regulatory capital.

12.2.5 Interest Rate Swaps: Simplified Model

Just as a currency forward is basically an exchange of short-term bonds in different currencies, so an interest rate swap is basically an exchange of bonds: a fixed-rate bond is exchanged for a floating-rate bond. The two bonds have the same maturity and the same principal, so the final repayments of principal cancel out and all that is left are the periodic exchanges of coupons.

As we saw with credit default swaps in Section 11.9 and with currency forwards in Section 12.1, at the outset of an interest rate swap the fixed rate is set so that the expected values of the two bonds being exchanged are equal and the swap has no current value to either the fixed receiver or the fixed payer. Over time as rates change, one side will gain value and the other side will lose value.

In practice, interest rate swaps have collateral–collection features designed to lower the risk that the losing side does not honor its obligations ("counterparty risk"). We'll work through a simplified version of an interest rate swap that ignores some of these features in order to illustrate the main exposures.

Let $SW(T)$ be the to-be-determined annual swap rate paid to the fixed receiver for a swap that starts now (time 0) and ends $T > 0$ years from now with n payments received p times per year (so $n/p = T$). Assume that the notional value of this swap is one monetary unit. If there are p payments per year, then each payment is $SW(T)/p$.

Let $s(x,y)$ be the annual rate from the zero swap curve (essentially SOFR) that discounts a payment received at time $y > x$ back to time x. Using discrete compounding to discount the fixed payments back to the present gives the value of the fixed cash flows now:

$$Value(fixed, T) = \frac{SW(T)}{p} \sum_{i=1}^{n} \frac{1}{\left(1 + s(0, \frac{i}{p})\right)^{\frac{i}{p}}}. \tag{12.13}$$

The floating rate payer will pay the then-current reference rate over a period $\frac{1}{p}$ years. There is a one-period offset, so the amount paid at time $\frac{i}{p}$ ($i = 1, \ldots, p$) will be:

$$\frac{s\left(\frac{i-1}{p}, \frac{i}{p}\right)}{p}.$$

The expected value of the future rate can be obtained from (3.12):

$$\mathbb{E}\left[s\left(\frac{i-1}{p}, \frac{i}{p}\right)\right] = \frac{\left(1 + s\left(0, \frac{i}{p}\right)\right)^i}{\left(1 + s\left(0, \frac{i-1}{p}\right)\right)^{i-1}} - 1.$$

Thus, the expected value of the floating cash flows is:

$$Value(floating, T) = \frac{1}{p}\sum_{i=1}^{n} \frac{\dfrac{\left(1 + s\left(0, \frac{i}{p}\right)\right)^i}{\left(1 + s\left(0, \frac{i-1}{p}\right)\right)^{i-1}} - 1}{\left(1 + s\left(0, \frac{i}{p}\right)\right)^{\frac{i}{p}}} \tag{12.14}$$

$$= \frac{1}{p}\sum_{i=1}^{n} \left(\frac{\left(1 + s\left(0, \frac{i}{p}\right)\right)^{i\left(1 - \frac{1}{p}\right)}}{\left(1 + s\left(0, \frac{i-1}{p}\right)\right)^{i-1}} - \frac{1}{\left(1 + s\left(0, \frac{i}{p}\right)\right)^{\frac{i}{p}}} \right).$$

Solving for the fixed swap payment $SW(T)$ that causes $V(fixed, T) = V(floating, T)$ gives:

$$SW(T) = \frac{\sum_{i=1}^{n}\left(\dfrac{\left(1 + s\left(0, \frac{i}{p}\right)\right)^{i\left(1 - \frac{1}{p}\right)}}{\left(1 + s\left(0, \frac{i-1}{p}\right)\right)^{i-1}} - \dfrac{1}{\left(1 + s\left(0, \frac{i}{p}\right)\right)^{\frac{i}{p}}} \right)}{\sum_{i=1}^{n} \dfrac{1}{\left(1 + s\left(0, \frac{i}{p}\right)\right)^{\frac{i}{p}}}}. \tag{12.15}$$

If the periodicity is annual ($p = 1$), then (12.14) becomes a telescoping sum where all but the first and last terms cancel:

$$Value(floating, T, p = 1) = 1 - \frac{1}{\left(1 + s(0, T)\right)^T}. \tag{12.16}$$

This gives the simplified expression:

$$SW(T, p = 1) = \frac{1 - \dfrac{1}{\left(1 + s(0, T)\right)^T}}{\sum_{i=1}^{T} \dfrac{1}{\left(1 + s(0, i)\right)^i}}. \tag{12.17}$$

Once the swap is established, the swap rate $SW(T)$ is fixed for the next T years. However, the swap curve $s(x, y)$ is in motion. Extending the notation, let $SW(t, T)$ be a swap rate established $t > 0$ years ago. If swap rates have risen ($SW(T) = SW(0, T) > SW(t, T)$), then the fixed receiver of the seasoned swap established at time t in the past loses value. In the other direction the fixed receiver gains value. This is similar to a bondholder losing (gaining) value as discount rates increase (increase).

The value of a **seasoned receiver swap** established $t > 0$ years in the past is:

$$SeasonedRcvr(t,T) = \frac{SW(t,T)+1}{p} \sum_{i=1}^{p(T-t)} \frac{1}{\left(1+s\left(0,\frac{i}{p}\right)\right)^{\frac{i}{p}}} -$$

$$\frac{1}{p} \sum_{i=1}^{p(T-t)} \left(\frac{\left(1+s\left(0,\frac{i}{p}\right)\right)^{i\left(1-\frac{1}{p}\right)}}{\left(1+s\left(0,\frac{i-1}{p}\right)\right)^{i-1}} \right). \qquad (12.18)$$

When $p = 1$ the expression simplifies to:

$$SeasonedRcvr(t,T,p=1) = SW(t,T,p=1) \sum_{i=1}^{T-t} \frac{1}{\left(1+s(0,i)\right)^i}$$

$$- 1 + \frac{1}{\left(1+s(0,T-t)\right)^{T-t}}. \qquad (12.19)$$

A seasoned payer swap's value is the opposite of the seasoned receiver swap's value.

Forward-starting swap rates can also be computed from the current swap curve. The fixed leg of a swap beginning at time $b > 0$ and ending at time $e > b$ is a modification of (12.13):

$$FwdValue(fixed,b,e) = \frac{SF(b,e)}{p} \sum_{i=1}^{p(e-b)} \frac{1}{\left(1+s\left(b,b+\frac{i}{p}\right)\right)^{\frac{i}{p}}}. \qquad (12.20)$$

Here $SF(b,e)$ is the to-be-determined forward-starting swap rate. The floating leg changes from (12.14) to:

$$FwdValue(floating,b,e)$$

$$= \frac{1}{p} \sum_{i=1}^{p(e-b)} \left(\frac{\left(1+s\left(b,b+\frac{i}{p}\right)\right)^{i\left(1-\frac{1}{p}\right)}}{\left(1+s\left(b,b+\frac{i-1}{p}\right)\right)^{i-1}} - \frac{1}{\left(1+s\left(b,b+\frac{i}{p}\right)\right)^{\frac{i}{p}}} \right). \qquad (12.21)$$

Solving for the $SF(b,e)$ that equates fixed and floating gives the forward-starting swap rate analogous to (12.15):

$$SF(b,e) = \frac{\sum_{i=1}^{p(e-b)}\left(\frac{\left(1+s\left(b,b+\frac{i}{p}\right)\right)^{i\left(1-\frac{1}{p}\right)}}{\left(1+s\left(b,b+\frac{i-1}{p}\right)\right)^{i-1}} - \frac{1}{\left(1+s\left(b,b+\frac{i}{p}\right)\right)^{\frac{i}{p}}}\right)}{\sum_{i=1}^{p(e-b)}\frac{1}{\left(1+s\left(b,b+\frac{i}{p}\right)\right)^{\frac{i}{p}}}}. \quad (12.22)$$

When $p = 1$, the numerator telescopes and the expression simplifies to the analog of (12.17):

$$SF(b,e,p=1) = \frac{1 - \frac{1}{\left(1+s(b,e)\right)^{e-b}}}{\sum_{i=1}^{e-b}\frac{1}{\left(1+s(b,b+i)\right)^{i}}} = \frac{\frac{1}{\left(1+s(0,b)\right)^{b}} - \frac{1}{\left(1+s(0,e)\right)^{e}}}{\sum_{i=1}^{e-b}\frac{1}{\left(1+s(0,b+i)\right)^{b+i}}}, \quad (12.23)$$

where the second equality gives the current expectation of $SF(b,e,p=1)$.

12.2.6 Interest Rate Swaps: Market

Since 2013 most interest rate swap transactions have been done through central counterparties (CCPs) that are AAA-rated. So the transaction is:

- fixed payer — CCP — fixed receiver

The CCP steps in if one side or the other fails, as the graphic in Figure 12.5 illustrates. Here the central counterparty is the Japan Securities Clearing Corporation (JSCC).

The largest CCPs are LCH (formerly London ClearingHouse), about 90% of the market in USD; and CME (a combination of the former Chicago Mercantile Exchange and the former Chicago Board of Trade), about 10% in USD. These

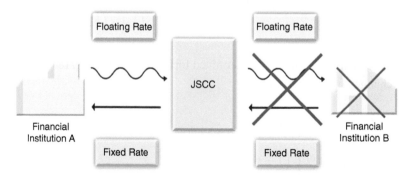

Figure 12.5 Fixed payer failure mitigated by CCP. Source: Japan Securities Clearing Corporation, www.jpx.co.jp/jscc/en/cash/irs/clearing.html

Table 12.8 Market sizes		
Statistic	Size (US$Trillions)	As/of date
Interest rate swaps	$488 Notional, $8.9 Net	June 2021[a]
Interest rate options	$42 Notional, $0.7 Net	June 2021[a]
F/X forwards	$102 Notional, $2.4 Net	June 2021[a]
Credit default swaps	$8.8 Notional, $.205 Net	June 2021[b]
Market value of all listed stocks (world)	$124.6	December 2021[c]
Market value of all bonds (world)	$125	June 2021[d]
Gross domestic product (world)	$102.4	December 2021[e]
Total household wealth (world)	$418.3	December 2020[f]
US residential mortgage-backed securities	$11.905	September 2021[g]
US housing debt	$11.25	December 2021[h]
Value of US housing	$43.4	December 2021[i]

Sources:

a) Bank for International Settlements 1. `https://stats.bis.org/statx/srs/table/d5.1?f=pdf`;
b) Bank for International Settlements 2. `https://stats.bis.org/statx/srs/table/d10.1?f=pdf`;
c) World Federation of Exchanges. `https://focus.world-exchanges.org/issue/february-2022/market-statistics`;
d) SIFMA 1. `www.sifma.org/resources/research/research-quarterly-fixed-income-issuance-and-trading/`;
e) International Monetary Fund. `www.imf.org/external/datamapper/NGDPD@WEO/OEMDC/ADVEC/WEOWORLD`;
f) Credit Suisse global wealth report. `www.credit-suisse.com/corporate/en/research/research-institute/global-wealth-report.html`;
g) SIFMA 2. `www.sifma.org/resources/research/research-quarterly-fixed-income-outstanding`;
h) New York Federal Reserve Bank. `www.newyorkfed.org/microeconomics/hhdc.html`;
i) Zillow. `www.zillow.com/research/us-housing-market-total-value-2021-30615/`

two also dominate other currencies, with Eurex and JSCC having smaller parts of EUR, JPY and other markets.[32]

The size of the interest rate swap market is astonishing. Table 12.8 shows the sizes of major world markets and economies.

32 LCH. "Swapclear." Website. `www.lch.com/services/swapclear`; CME Group. "Cleared OTC Interest Rate Swaps." Website. `www.cmegroup.com/trading/interest-rates/cleared-otc.html`; Eurex. "Eurex Clearing." Website. `www.eurex.com/ec-en/clear/eurex-exchange`; Japan Securities Clearing Corporation. "OTC Derivatives Clearing." Website. `www.jpx.co.jp/jscc/en/otc/index.html`.

The notional amount of outstanding swaps is more than all the wealth in the world. The notional amount is a multiplier that does not actually change hands; it is used to determine the flows back and forth between fixed payer and fixed receiver. So the actual movements of cash are about two orders of magnitude less than the notional even before the fixed-floating offset. The net amount, essentially the sum of the values of seasoned swap as in (12.18), is much less. But it's still a formidable figure.

One of the reasons the interest rate swap market is so large is the previously mentioned use of swaps by banks for asset–liability management. Consider the bank in our example at the beginning of Section 12.2.4: short-term rates were 1% and long-term rates were 2%. The bank made a 20-year loan at 3.5%. If short-term rates rose to 4%, the loan would be unprofitable.

To hedge away this risk, the bank could enter into a 20-year payer swap for the same notional as the loan. The swap rate $SW(20)$ would likely be close to long-term rates of 2%; say $SW(20) = 2.25\%$. The floating payments the bank receives as part of the swap offset the payments it owes to its short-term depositors, while the swap's fixed payments subtract from the fixed payments the bank is receiving from the loan, locking in a 1.25% spread with virtually no risk.

The only thing left unhedged in our simple example is the final repayment of capital on the loan, which can be handled by a zero coupon swap. In fact, the bank will simply look at everything going out or coming in for the next 30 years or so, and make sure it has hedged the asset–liability mismatch.

The other side of this hedge is often taken by pension plans (called superannuation schemes in UK usage). Such plans set aside funds to provide for workers after retirement; they typically have very long horizons as some members of the current workforce will not retire for decades.

Like banks, these plans have a maturity mismatch, but it's the opposite of the bank mismatch. Pension plans have long-term liabilities and short-term assets. They therefore often engage in liability-driven investment ("LDI"),[33] which is just the mirror image of the asset–liability management practiced by banks.

This is fortunate as it creates a natural offset. The individuals borrowing from banks are interested in building businesses, getting educations, and buying houses for family formation. All of these activities need capital now for long-term payoffs. The workers covered by pension plans are setting aside capital now to pay for their retirement in the long term, so they are interested in long-term payoffs. It's a beautiful match, intermediated by banks, pension plans, and other financial institutions. Interest rate swaps – as Table 12.8 shows – are a huge part of this horizon transfer process.

---

33 Dan Tammas-Hastings. "Beyond Modern Portfolio Theory: Liability-Driven Investment Strategies." CFA Institute. November 21, 2017. `https://blogs.cfainstitute.org/investor/2017/11/21/beyond-modern-portfolio-theory-liability-driven-investment-strategies/`.

12.2.7 Longevity Risk

We noted in the previous section that there is a natural offset between banks and pension plans. But the offset relies on the pension plan's knowledge of what its obligations are going to be, and that knowledge requires accurate demographic life span projections. The uncertainty around these projections is called **mortality risk** when life spans are shorter than expected, and **longevity risk** when life spans are longer than expected. Current economic concerns are focused on longevity risk.

If populations simply scale up their productivity as they live longer – say, a population living to be 90 becomes 9/8 as productive as they were when they were living to be 80 – then there won't be a mismatch between resources and demand for resources. Recognizing this, Denmark's pension system[34] has a program of raising retirement age and encouraging pension deferral with a formula based on national longevity. Other countries have not been as explicit but have moved to increase retirement age.

But in many areas, the extra years of a longer life are simply tacked on to retirement years without changing productive years. That causes a concomitant lowering in the ratio of resource production to resource use. The most obvious implication of that lower ratio is to disadvantage public and private pension plans that promise to pay a regular amount for the remaining life of a retiree ("defined benefit" plans). They will need more money if people extend their retirement period. It's no coincidence that Stanford University's Center on Longevity has a number of corporate affiliates (donors) such as the American Association of Retired Persons, which markets medical insurance to older people.[35]

Medical insurance companies may need to pay out more if people live longer. Insurance companies paying annuities[36] (fixed payments for the life of an individual) are another form of pension plan and are also exposed to longevity risk.

Beneficiaries of increased longevity include companies that are paid to provide care to the elderly like nursing home operators, pharmaceutical companies, and medical equipment producers. Life insurance companies will be able to postpone payments if people live longer, which is why insurance companies often diversify by offering both annuities and life insurance with opposite exposures to increasing longevity.

---

34 Social Security Office of Retirement and Disability Policy. "Denmark." Website. www.ssa.gov/policy/docs/progdesc/ssptw/2016-2017/europe/denmark.html.

35 Stanford Center on Longevity. "About the Center." Website. http://longevity.stanford.edu/about/; Stanford Center on Longevity. "Corporate Affiliates Program." Website. http://longevity.stanford.edu/scl-corporate-affiliates-program/; American Association of Retired Persons. Website. www.aarp.org/.

36 Insurance Information Institute. "The Difference between Annuities and Life Insurance." Website. https://www.iii.org/article/the-difference-between-annuities-and-life-insurance.

There have been attempts to create longevity swap markets, where one side might pay a fixed rate and the other side would receive the current average life span in a country. In 2020, life expectancy at birth in the USA was 77.0 years.[37] A longevity swap established now might have the payer receiving a fixed $77 and paying whatever the latest life expectancy figure is each year. So if life expectancy becomes 79 years, the longevity payer loses $2; if life expectancy becomes $76, the longevity payer gains $1.

With such a swap, a defined benefit pension plan could be a longevity receiver, exchanging payments with a nursing home operator who was a longevity payer. The nursing home operator would look at the longevity payments as franchise preservation hedging, while the pension plan would be able to invest less in stocks and bonds because it wouldn't have to anticipate worst case longevity.

While a huge portion of world productive resources is subject to longevity risk, there is no active capital market in longevity swaps. The imbalance between the size of natural longevity receivers (very large) and natural longevity payers (not so large) is more of a societal problem than a problem that can be fixed by a clever capital markets solution.

Some insurance companies offer insurance policies against longevity risk, as explained by the trade group Institutional Longevity Markets Association.[38] These policies, generally called pension risk transfer insurance, offload longevity risk from a pension plan (which pays a fixed fee) to an insurance company (which guarantees lifetime payments to retirees). However the capacity for such policies is not large enough to cure a demographic imbalance across an entire country.

12.3 Illiquidity Hedging

GARP (2017, p. 3) defines **asset and market liquidity** as:

> The degree to which a financial instrument can be converted to cash within a specified time horizon and at a specified cost.

If the act of buying or selling does not have much impact on the asset's price, then it is liquid; if there is a big impact, then the asset is illiquid. Liquidity is dependent on size and urgency. An asset may be liquid if only a small amount is being transacted, but illiquid in larger size. Similarly, an asset may be illiquid if it needs to be transacted over the next minute, but liquid over the next year. Market conditions also play a role in liquidity: in some markets, it may be easier to buy than sell or vice versa.

---

37 [Murphy et al. 2021].

38 Institutional Longevity Markets Association. "Longevity-Mortality Markets: General Background." Website. https://lifemarketsassociation.org/about-ilma/longevity-mortality-markets/.

The third hedging category is **illiquidity hedging**. We've already seen a possible illiquidity problem in banks that can't meet short-term demands even if they have substantial long-term but illiquid investments or loans. Risks arising from yield curve reshaping can be hedged with interest rate swaps, but there is no hedge for the negative feedback loop caused once there are forced sales of illiquid assets.

We've seen that for banks, there is a mechanism of government support to help stop bank runs. But other investors don't enjoy this backing.

If a portfolio manager decides that conditions have changed for Apple Computer stock (AAPL), precipitating a decision to buy or sell, there will be no problem transacting. AAPL daily trading volume is routinely in the tens of billions of dollars, so the portfolio manager's trade is likely to be absorbed virtually instantly. With that much volume, the portfolio manager is likely to be a **price taker**, transacting with virtually no impact on AAPL's price.

But what if the portfolio manager owns (or wants to own) an office building and decides that conditions have changed and a transaction is desired? Commercial real estate typically has a time on market ("TOM") of 10–20 months.[39] During that time, conditions may change radically. If the originator of the transaction wants to speed things up, the price will move in the wrong direction or the transaction just won't happen.

There is no perfect hedge for this kind of illiquidity. Liquid assets are generally fungible: there are large numbers of functionally identical versions of the asset, like a share of Apple Computer. Illiquid assets are generally idiosyncratic: no office building is exactly like any other office building.

However, even illiquid assets have characteristics like location, square feet, amenities, and quality that are more systematic than idiosyncratic. These systematic characteristics can sometimes be mapped onto liquid instruments that might be used to mitigate some of the risk in the illiquid investment. For example, the CMBX index[40] and its many sub-indices are based on a number of commercial mortgage-backed securities. Trading in credit default swaps based on this family of indices is liquid, so a portfolio manager can add or subtract commercial mortgage exposure easily. If commercial buildings are doing well (poorly), then commercial mortgages are probably also doing well (poorly).

---

39 The 10–20 month TOM range for US commercial properties is the result of data kindly supplied by Eugene Page and Martin Nguyen from Centre Urban Real Estate Partners (www.centre-urban.com). The data were compiled in April 2020 from Costar Group (www.costargroup.com) and cover the period 2005 through March 2020.

40 S&P Global Offerings: IHS Markit®. "CMBX Index: Commercial Mortgage Backed Securities Index." Website. https://ihsmarkit.com/products/markit-cmbx.html.

However, the hoped-for relationship between an actual set of commercial buildings and a traded index like CMBX may break down. This is another form of **basis risk**: the risk that the item being hedged is not fully matched with the hedge. The idiosyncratic properties of the commercial real estate being hedged may dominate its systematic properties, or the fact that CMBX credit default swaps are based on mortgages and not property ownership may come into play. It is possible to have a wrong-way hedge – one in which the item being hedged goes down and the item doing the hedging goes up, which (since the hedge is short) is a lose-lose situation. Thus, like longevity risk, illiquidity risk is very hard to hedge successfully.

12.4 Distribution Reshaping

The fourth kind of hedging seeks to reshape an outcome distribution. There are many techniques to reshape distributions, but none of them can produce a distribution that stochastically dominates the original distribution. However, reshaping can be done to produce an outcome distribution that has higher utility to an investor.

Selling (buying) **futures** is a simple way to decrease (increase) market exposure without selling (buying) individual securities and without committing a lot of capital. Properly done, futures transactions scale the volatility of a portfolio's outcome distribution up or down.

A future is similar to a forward purchase: one party agrees to buy and another party agrees to sell an asset S at a price agreed on today, T years from now. If $\mathrm{fut}(S, T)$ is the agreed-on price, then the party who will be buying can borrow $\mathrm{fut}(S, T) \exp(-rT)$ today (at the T-year default-free rate r) in order to have the purchase price T years from now. The selling party can just buy the underlying at the current price S_0 in order to have it for sale. Equating the two sides in the usual way gives:

$$\mathrm{fut}(S, T) = S_0 \exp(rT). \tag{12.24}$$

This is equivalent to (12.2).

In practice, forwards are bilateral contracts, while futures are traded on exchanges and require frequent exchanges of collateral. Exchange-traded instruments have extensive procedures to avoid counterparty default, so futures traders need to maintain cash in a margin account that can and will be seized if the trader defaults on its obligations. Adjustments might need to be made if the underlying asset pays dividends. If the underlying asset is physical – for example, if it's oil, a metal, or an agricultural commodity – adjustments might need to be made to reflect storage costs and spoilage. Thus, a more precise version of (12.24) requires further adjustment to reflect these additional factors.

Very active futures markets exist for most developed countries' stock and government bond indices, including:[41]

- USA: Standard & Poor's 500; US Treasurys
- UK: FTSE; Gilts
- Germany: DAX; Bunds, Bobls, and Schatzes
- Japan: Nikkei 225; JGBs.

Selling appropriate futures against a long-only portfolio can lower variance by lowering exposure to a close substitute for its first principal component, like the overall stock or bond market. Similarly, buying futures can scale up variance. Finer tuning with other futures transactions can add or remove other systematic exposures and their associated volatilities, like style tilts in equity or key rate exposures in fixed income. Basis risk is always a concern, though: care must be taken to see that the original assets really do respond to the systematic factors being hedged.

12.4.1 Distribution Reshaping with Options

Hedging techniques using European put and call options can surgically reshape outcome distributions, since strike prices can be set in a way that cuts and pastes segments of distributions.

Perhaps the simplest example of a static technique is the purchase of a European put option maturing at time T on an underlying asset with a lognormal outcome distribution. That snips out the lower tail of the time-T distribution, but moves the rest of the cdf left, as shown in Figure 12.6b (generated, along with Figure 12.6a, by Code Segment 12.15). Figure 12.6a shows the payoff pattern at time T of the underlying versus the underlying plus the put.

The blue lines show the underlying's time-T payoff pattern (Figure 12.6a) and lognormal distribution (Figure 12.6b), $T = 1$ in these examples. The time-zero price of the underlying ("the money") is 100, and the center of the time-T distribution is $100 \exp(rT)$.

41 CME Group. "S&P Index Futures and Options on Futures." www.cmegroup.com/trading/equity-index/us-index/sp-index-futures-and-options.html; CME Group. "Welcome to U.S. Treasury Futures." www.cmegroup.com/trading/why-futures/welcome-to-us-treasury-futures.html; ICE Futures Europe. "FTSE 100 Index Future." www.theice.com/products/38716764/FTSE-100-Index-Future; ICE Interest Rates. "ICE Gilt Futures & Options." www.theice.com/interest-rates/gilt-futures-and-options; Eurex. "DAX®Futures." www.eurex.com/ex-en/markets/idx/dax/DAX-Futures-139902; Eurex. "Euro-Bund Futures." www.eurex.com/ex-en/markets/int/fix/government-bonds/Euro-Bund-Futures-137298; Japan Exchange Group. "Nikkei 225 Futures (Large Contracts)." www.jpx.co.jp/english/derivatives/products/domestic/225futures/01.html; Japan Exchange Group. "JGB Futures." www.jpx.co.jp/english/derivatives/products/jgb/jgb-futures/01.html.

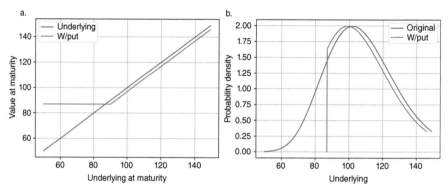

Figure 12.6 a. Payoff of put plus underlying: strike = 90, cost = 3.02. b. Density function with and w/out put.

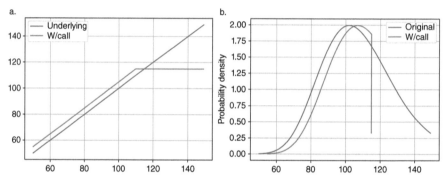

Figure 12.7 a. Payoff of underlying minus call: strike = 110, cost = 4.94. b. Density function with and w/out written call.

The orange line in Figure 12.6a shows the payoff pattern of the underlying plus a put option struck at 90 when the put option matures at time T; the orange line in Figure 12.6b shows the pdf (density function) of the underlying+put at time T.

The underlying-plus-put pdf has no probability of any outcome below 90 minus the cost of the put, that is, disastrous outcomes are avoided. The rest of the distribution is shifted left to pay for the option. Which shape – the blue or the orange – is better is a matter of risk preference.

If an investor thinks that the cost of buying a put option is too low because the market's expectation of the future distribution is just wrong, then the investor might buy a put option to express a directional view rather than, or in addition to, a risk preference.

For the remainder of this section, we'll show a number of other static option techniques that are commonly used to reshape distributions. Traders have given some of them colorful names, and they are only a sample of a vast arsenal.

Figures 12.7a and 12.7b (generated by Code Segment 12.16) show what happens when a call struck at 110 is written (sold).

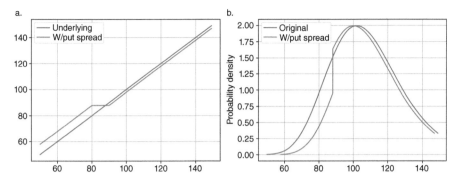

Figure 12.8 a. Payoff of put spread plus underlying: HighStrk = 90, HighCst = 3.02; LowStrk = 80, LowCst = 0.96. b. Density function with and w/out put spread.

Writing a call is in a way the mirror image of buying a put. The written call gives away the upper end of the outcome distribution and redistributes it across the rest of the distribution by profiting from the call premium as shown above.

A **put spread** provides limited downside protection, as shown in Figures 12.8a and 12.8b (generated by Code Segment 12.17).

A put is bought down from the money while another put is written even further down from the money. We used 90 for the bought put strike and 80 for the written put strike. Above the higher strike put, nothing happens except for the loss of the put cost. But the cost is lower than just buying a put because money was gained by writing the lower strike put. The net is still negative, but not as negative as just buying a put.

There will probably be a benefit from volatility skew as the lower-struck put probably has a higher implied volatility than the higher-struck put as shown in Figure 9.5. Between the two strikes, the higher-struck put provides downside protection. Below the lower strike, the downside protection is capped at the difference between the two strikes, minus the cost.

A **call spread** sells off upside participation, as shown in Figures 12.9a and 12.9b (generated by Code Segment 12.18).

Like a put spread, one option is bought and one is sold. In this case, a call option up from the money is sold, and another call even further up from the money is bought. As with the put spread, volatility skew may work in favor of such a trade. (A volatility smile may work against the trade.) The payoff pattern looks like a cheap call until the higher call kicks in, at which point the contribution is capped.

Figures 12.10a and 12.10b (generated by Code Segment 12.19) show a **"straddle,"** which is a way to bet on large moves. We've already seen this trade in Figure 9.3: both a put and a call are purchased at-the-money. If the underlying stays at-the-money, the straddle purchaser loses the put and call premia. But as the underlying moves away from the money, either the put (on a down move) or

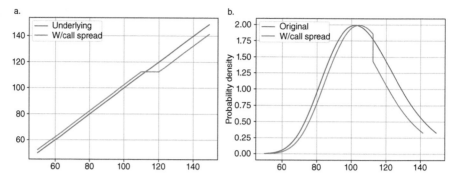

Figure 12.9 a. Payoff of call spread plus underlying: HighStrk = 120, HighCst = 2.55; LowStrk = 110, LowCst = 4.94. b. Density function with and w/out call spread.

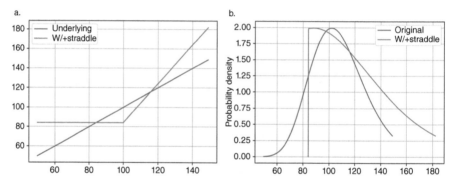

Figure 12.10 a. Payoff of underlying plus straddle: Call Strike = Put Strike = 100, Call Cost = 8.92, Put Cost = 6.94. b. Density function with and w/out +straddle.

the call (on an up move) starts becoming more valuable. If the underlying moves far enough, then the put value (down) or call value (up) will become big enough to pay for the combined premia, plus a profit.

Together with the underlying, a straddle caps the loss on the downside and enhances the win on the upside. Thus, a bought straddle anticipates more probability in the tails of the underlying distribution than was priced into options, while a sold straddle anticipates more probability in the center of the distribution than was priced in.

A straddle is a type of **gamma** trade. Gamma, explained more fully in Section 12.4.2, is the Greek letter that denotes the second derivative of changes in the price of an option with respect to changes in the price of the underlying: it is essentially the same as convexity, which we studied in Chapter 3. Bought options have positive gamma, that is, positive convexity, and they like big moves.

A **short straddle** sells both a put and a call at-the-money; this trade enhances the center of the distribution at the expense of the tails, as shown in Figures 12.11a and 12.11b (generated by Code Segment 12.20).

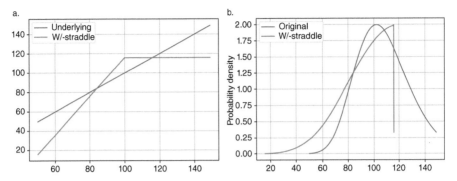

Figure 12.11 a. Payoff of underlying minus straddle: Call Strike = Put strike = 100, Call Cost = 8.92, Put cost = 6.94. b. Density function with and w/out −straddle.

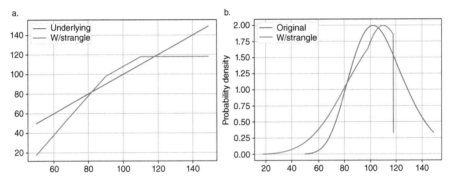

Figure 12.12 a. Payoff of underlying with strangle: Call Strike = 110, Call Cost = 4.94, Put Strike = 90, Put Cost = 3.02. b. Density function with and w/out strangle.

A **strangle** (sometimes called a **short strangle**) is similar to a short straddle, but with a little different payoff pattern.

As shown in Figures 12.12a and 12.12b (generated by Code Segment 12.21), a strangle brackets the money by writing a put struck down from the money and writing a call struck up from the money. The owner of a strangle benefits if the price doesn't move outside the bracket. The further outside the bracket the price moves, the worse things get. A strangle therefore has virtually unlimited liability: it trades the tails of the distribution for the center of the distribution. If the strikes are set reasonably far away from the money, a strangle works most of the time, but on a big move a lot of money can be lost.

Trades like strangles and short straddles are not-so-jokingly called "picking up dimes in front of a steamroller," since most of the time there is a small profit. However, when there is a big move, it's like getting run over by a steamroller. That's especially true when only the options part of the trade is done; if options plus underlying are in place, then the underlying provides some offset.

Options traders can wax lyrical, as evidenced by the **butterfly spread** shown in Figures 12.13a and 12.13b (generated by Code Segment 12.22).

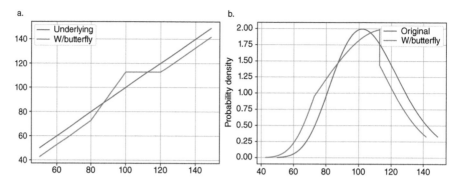

Figure 12.13 a. Payoff of underlying w/butterfly spread: Low = 80, Mid = 100, High = 100; trade cost = 7.26. b. Density function w/and w/out butterfly.

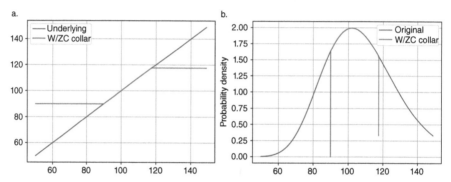

Figure 12.14 a. Payoff of underlying with ZC collar: Put Strike = 90, Call Strike = 118; option costs = 3.02. b. Density function with and w/out ZC collar.

The butterfly spread is a limited loss version of a strangle. A typical butterfly spread consists of call options at three different strikes: a call bought down from the money (say, at strike S_d); two calls written at-the-money (at strike S_0), and another call bought up from the money (at strike S_u). Note that a butterfly spread is essentially a second difference if the strikes are evenly spaced; thus, the Breeden and Litzenberger (1978) method described in Section 9.3.1 was a way to use the prices of butterfly spreads to retrieve underlying risk-neutral distributions.

If the underlying is outside the bracket $[S_d, S_u]$ at maturity, the trade contributes a constant negative amount (the cost of putting on the position) not dependent on the level of the underlying. Inside the bracket, the trade contributes an upside-down "V" peaking in the middle (S_0).

A **zero cost collar** (shown in Figures 12.14a and 12.14b, generated by Code Segment 12.23) consists of buying a put down from the money (say, at 90%) and writing a call up from the money where the strike is chosen so that the written call exactly offsets the cost of the put. The collar sells off the tails – no big drops, no big gains. If there is volatility skew, the strike on the upside is closer to the money than it would be if the underlying were lognormal.

There are infinite combinations of options, so infinite new shapes of distributions can be crafted. If the options are fairly valued, the payoff pattern will always have some losses and some wins, and will have zero expected value in the risk-neutral probability measure. More complicated strategies can be designed by putting together portfolios of options with varying times to maturity, and even more complicated strategies can be designed by dynamically trading options rather than just buying them and waiting for them to expire.

12.4.2 Option Greeks

There are five basic parameters in the Black–Scholes formula (12.4). Partial derivatives of the call and put formulas show how option prices will react to small changes in these parameters. As we noted in Chapter 9 (Footnote 14), these derivatives are called **option Greeks** because they are usually (but not always) denoted by Greek letters. Option Greeks are used to establish hedging positions that are first-order (and sometimes second-order) neutral, or that have desired tilts.

Table 12.9 summarizes the more common derivatives. The notation is from (12.4).

Table 12.9 has one second-order and four first-order derivatives. Since each option has a different set of Greeks, a portfolio with the desired Greeks can be formed with five reasonably different options by solving five equations in the five unknowns (weights of the options in the portfolio). For example, an options portfolio that has vega exposure and nothing else could be formed. That portfolio of options will give pure exposure to changes in volatility.

Table 12.9 Option Greeks

Name	Derivative wrt	Call	Put
Delta δ	Underlying price X_0	$N(d_1)$	$N(d_1) - 1$
Gamma Γ	Delta δ	$\dfrac{1}{X_0 \sigma_X \sqrt{T}} \left(\dfrac{\exp\left(\frac{-d_1^2}{2}\right)}{\sqrt{2\pi}} \right)$	same
Vega/ kappa κ	Volatility σ_X	$X_0 \sqrt{T} \left(\dfrac{\exp\left(\frac{-d_1^2}{2}\right)}{\sqrt{2\pi}} \right) = \left(T X_0^2 \sigma_X \right) \Gamma$	same
Rho ρ	Rate r_f	$K_f T \exp(-r_f T) N(d_2)$	$\rho_{Call} - K_f T \exp(-r_f T)$
Theta θ	Time (T)	$\frac{1}{2} \left(X_0 \sigma_X \right)^2 \Gamma + \frac{r_f}{T} \rho_{Call}$	$\theta_{Call} - K_f r_f \exp(-r_f T)$

Since time and the price of the underlying are two of the key variables, the linear combination of five options that exhibits the desired exposure at a given point in time might not be the linear combination that exhibits the key exposures tomorrow. Thus, some cleverness is required to come up with a set of options that gives the desired exposures but that doesn't require too much adjustment, especially procyclical adjustment. A portfolio manager would rather not be selling calls or buying puts because the market moved down, nor would the manager want to be buying calls or selling puts because the market moved up.

Code Segment 12.24 shows an example where $\sigma_X = .2$, $r_f = 2\%$, $X_0 = K_f = 100$, and $T = .25$:

```
    Original X0:  100.00
 Original Price:  4.2322
          Delta:  0.5398

        New X0:  100.10
     New Price:  4.2863
Difference delta:  0.5418
```

The finite difference delta from a small change in price is close to, but not the same as, the instantaneous delta from Table 12.9.

Options are usually wasting assets, since as time passes the option owner's power wanes until it disappears entirely at expiration. Thus, the derivative of option price with respect to time is usually positive: longer-maturity options have higher prices. There are a few exceptions, but most of the time options lose value as they get closer to maturity. The worst time decay is at the strike price.

Code Segment 12.25 uses the parameters in the previous example, but varies the strike price, to produce Figure 12.15 and the following at-the-money ("ATM") calculations:

```
ATM call theta 8.93406342873292
ATM put theta 10.924088387118283
```

Here the ATM call (strike price 100) is losing value at about 8.93/year; the put is losing value at about 10.92/year. The maximum theta strikes are a little higher than ATM.

The benefit gained from buying options (whether puts or calls) requires constant infusions of money, just like an insurance policy requires that its premiums be paid on an ongoing basis. This is reflected in positive theta, sometimes called "theta bleed" or "theta decay." Negative theta positions are usually similar to selling insurance: as we noted with strangles and short straddles, they are "dimes in front of a steamroller" trades that usually make money but that can result in spectacular losses when they don't.

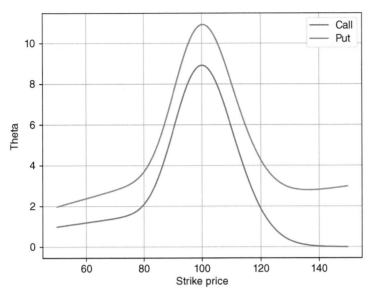

Figure 12.15 Theta as a function of strike price: Price $= 100$, $r = 0.02$, $T = 0.02$, sigma $= 0.20$.

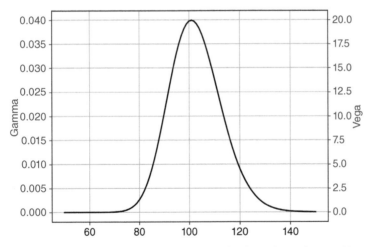

Figure 12.16 Gamma, vega as a function of strike price: Price $= 100$, $r = 0.02$, $T = 0.25$, sigma $= 0.20$.

Gamma is the second derivative with respect to the price of the underlying: it adjusts for responses to large moves. It peaks when the option is at-the-money, as shown in Figure 12.16 (generated by Code Segment 12.26). So does vega, the response to changes in volatility. The ratio of vega to gamma is $X_0^2 \cdot T \cdot \sigma$; since X_0 and σ are common properties of the underlying, the only way to differentiate between vega and gamma is to use options with different expiration times T.

```
ATM delta 0.539827837277029
ATM gamma  0.039695254747701185
ATM vega  19.847627373850596
Vega/gamma ratio  500.0
```

Since time $T = .25$ is constant in Figure 12.16, the vega/gamma ratio is constant at 500. Thus, the shapes of the vega and gamma curves are exactly the same: the only difference is in scale with the gamma scale on the left and the vega scale on the right.

For our example, when price = strike = 100, a one-unit increase in price will increase the delta by about $\Gamma = .0397$, that is, from the .5398 noted above to .5795. This provides the same kind of positive convexity that benefits bond prices. Similarly, a one-unit decrease in price will decrease delta to .5001, thereby cushioning the fall. Taking the derivative of Γ in Table 12.9 with respect to strike price shows that Γ is maximized when the strike price equals the current price times $\exp((r_f + \sigma^2/2)T)$.

The ATM vega of about 19.8 means that if standard deviation were to increase from the 20% used in our example to 21%, the option price would go up by $19.8 \cdot (.21 - .20) = .198$.

Trading desks at broker-dealers make money through a mix of risk taking and risk hedging. The Greeks are used to protect broker-dealer franchises, as follows:

A **broker** is a matchmaker who takes no principal risk. An options broker would find a client who wants to buy an option and a client who wants to sell the exact same option and get them together for a fee. If the transaction is "DvP," or **delivery versus payment**, the dealer just acts as the middleman and has no exposure to movements in the markets or in the creditworthiness of the clients.

Very few broker-dealers actually have such a pure transaction-based business. Most also act as **dealers** who maintain inventory and who take risks with their own capital to facilitate trades and for other reasons. Consider a situation in which a dealer has a client who wants to buy a call option on Google (Alphabet).[42] The particular option wanted by the client may not trade very heavily, so there may be no seller at the moment. However, the dealer knows that the option trades every hour or so. So the dealer may temporarily take the other side of the trade, and an hour later when a seller shows up, the dealer can unwind.

Over the course of a day for a large dealer, there may be thousands of such transactions. At any given time there may be hundreds or thousands of options in the dealer's inventory awaiting disposition. Sometimes the dealer may decide to "sail close to shore" and hedge away most risks in the "book," the collection

42 Nasdaq. "GOOG Option Chain." Website. www.nasdaq.com/market-activity/stocks/goog/option-chain.

of positions. The Greeks – actually many more than we have shown, going into mixed partial second and third derivatives – are computed, and the dealer can enter into offsetting transactions in heavily traded options to neutralize the book. Or the dealer may decide to lean in a certain direction by tilting Greeks.

Delta hedging is comparatively easy, since the underlying has delta exposure but nothing else. So going long or short the underlying, perhaps through a futures transaction, can neutralize delta. In terms of overall dollar exposures, the most likely thing that would bankrupt a dealer would be a large move in the underlying when there is a material delta exposure, so most options dealers hedge away delta for franchise preservation.

12.4.3 Fixed-Income Options

In the fixed-income market, commonly used derivatives are called **caps, floors, and collars**.

Caps are molecules composed of atomic units called **caplets**. A caplet pays the buyer if a benchmark interest rate (typically SOFR) is above a strike price at a given date in the future. The payoff function for a caplet looks like:

$$\text{notional} * \max(0, index - strike) / \text{periodicity}.$$

For example, suppose an investor owns a caplet with 6-month SOFR as the index (periodicity 2 per year), struck at 1%, maturing a year from now, on \$1Mn notional. If the 6-month SOFR rate from 6 months from now to one year from now is an annual 2.5%, the caplet owner will receive \$7,500 from the caplet writer. Note that the 6-month SOFR rate used to determine the payoff on the caplet maturing one year from now was already known 6 months prior to the payoff.

A cap strings together caplets struck at the same level over time. For example, a 5-year cap might have caplets maturing \$.5, 1, 1.5, 2, ..., \$ and 5 years from now and all struck at 1% and all with \$1Mn notional. A cap can be synchronized with an interest rate swap, so that a portfolio consisting of a receiver swap and a cap limits the payments the fixed receiver (floating payer) has to make during the life of the swap/cap to be no more than the cap's strike price. Each of the cap's caplets covers one payment during the life of the swap/cap.

A floor is an analogous collect of **floorlets**; each floorlet pays its owner if interest rates go below its strike price with payoff function:

$$\text{notional} * \max(0, strike - index) / \text{periodicity}.$$

A **fixed-income collar** is the simultaneous purchase of a cap struck at s_c and sale of a floor struck at s_f, with $s_c > s_f$, both with identical maturities, notionals, and periodicities. This protects against higher rates while selling off the benefit of lower rates.

The equivalent of put-call parity (8.1) is established by the following two-position portfolio:

- A payer interest rate swap with fixed rate s;
- A maturity- and notional-matched floor struck at s.

Suppose $index > s$ at some payment time. Then (per unit of notional) the owner of the swap receives $index - s$ from the swap; the floorlet at this time is worthless. In total, the owner of the payer swap/floor combination receives $index - s$.

Suppose $index < s$ at some payment time. Then (per unit of notional) the owner of the swap receives $index - s$ from the swap (which is actually a negative, i.e. a payment to the swap counterparty); the floorlet at this time produces $s - index$. Together, the two cancel so the owner of the combination receives 0.

Thus, the combination of a payer swap and a matched floor has the same payoff pattern as a cap,

$$Cap = PayerSwap + Floor \tag{12.25}$$

as long as everything is matched in strike, maturity, periodicity, and notional. Equivalently,

$$ReceiverSwap = Floor - Cap. \tag{12.26}$$

12.5 Convexity Hedging

The fifth type of hedging is **convexity hedging**.[43] There are some kinds of exposures that can change precipitously as conditions change. In that case, the very act of trading to try to hedge the exposure can exacerbate the situation. Instead, a hedge should be designed that will anticipate and mitigate possible large market moves. Epigrammatically: prepare, not repair. We'll use **mortgage convexity hedging** to illustrate this problem.

As Table 12.8 showed, about one-third of the value of US residential housing stock is mortgaged (borrowed). Table 12.8 further shows that the great majority of mortgages have been securitized: that is, they have been placed in pools that allow the originators (banks and other financial institutions) to diversify and offload their mortgage lending exposures. The US MBS (mortgage-backed security) market is larger than the entire fixed-income market of any other country in the world other than China and Japan.[44]

---

43 A good discussion of mortgage convexity hedging can be found in [Modukuri et al. 2003], a white paper by the MBS Strategies group at Lehman Brothers. Ironically, Lehman Brothers declared bankruptcy in September 2008 largely because of misinvestment in mortgage-backed securities. See [TMPG 2021] for a more recent example of convexity hedging.

44 Bank for International Settlements, "Summary of Debt Securities Outstanding." Website. https://stats.bis.org/statx/srs/table/c1?f=pdf.

Many of these pools have been created through three large government agencies: "Fannie Mae" (the Federal National Mortgage Association); "Freddie Mac" (the Federal Home Loan Mortgage Corporation); and "Ginnie Mae" (the Government National Mortgage Association).[45]

Mortgage loans are secured by a property and typically have long maturity dates: 15 to 30 years. The standard fixed-rate mortgage is attractive to borrowers as it typically entails a fixed monetary payment each month, making housing expenses more predictable and (since they are spread out over a long period) affordable. Each month's payment for a fixed-rate mortgage consists of interest on the remaining principal, plus some repayment of principal. As time passes, the proportion of the fixed monthly payment that is principal increases, and the proportion that is interest decreases.

Let P be the principal amount borrowed in a mortgage, n the number of months (e.g. $n = 360$ for a 30-year mortgage), and r the annual mortgage rate. Then at the end of the first month the interest owed is Pr_m where $r_m = r/12$. There is also some principal repayment p_1 in the first monthly payment. Since each payment is the same, it must be true that the first month's payment equals the second month's payment, so:

$$Pr_m + p_1 = (P - p_1)r_m + p_2,$$

where p_2 is the principal repayment in the second month. Thus, $p_2 = (1 + r_m)p_1$. Repeating this reasoning shows that $p_i = (1 + r_m)^{i-1}p_1$ for any $i = 1, \ldots, n$. The entire principal P must be repaid over n months, so:

$$P = \sum_{i=1}^{n} p_i = p_1 \frac{(1 + r_m)^n - 1}{r_m}.$$

Thus, the ith month's principal payment is:

$$p_i = (1 + r_m)^{i-1} \frac{Pr_m}{(1 + r_m)^n - 1} \tag{12.27}$$

and the cumulative principal paid through month i equals:

$$P \left(\frac{(1 + r_m)^i - 1}{(1 + r_m)^n - 1} \right).$$

The constant monthly payment of both principal and interest equals:

$$Pr_m \left(1 + \frac{1}{(1 + r_m)^n - 1} \right). \tag{12.28}$$

---

45 Fannie Mae®. Website. www.fanniemae.com/; Freddie Mac. Website. www.freddiemac .com/; Ginnie Mae. Website. www.ginniemae.gov/.

For example, a 360-month mortgage on a principal amount of $300,000 at an annual fixed rate of 4% has a monthly payment of $1,432.

If a borrower fails to make payments, eventually a mortgage lender can take possession of the mortgaged house and sell it to recover unpaid principal and interest. That allows lenders to charge lower rates for mortgages than they would for unsecured loans. However, quite often people move house before they have finished repaying their mortgage. The lender would lose security if it continued the loan arrangement all the way to its full term. Instead, lenders allow homeowners to prepay the remaining principal on their loans. This prepayment can occur at any time, not just when the homeowner is moving.

The option to prepay a fixed-rate mortgage is valuable and gives rise to prepayment risk on the part of the lender, as noted in Section 3.4. The fixed-rate mortgage lender has conceded something like an interest rate floor to the mortgage borrower, struck at the current mortgage rate. If interest rates drop, large numbers of mortgage borrowers will get a new loan at the new prevailing lower interest rate. They exercise their right to prepay the old loan with the proceeds of the new loan.

Some mortgages are ARMs (adjustable-rate mortgages); that is, the borrower pays a floating interest rate that changes with a benchmark like a Constant Maturity Treasury Rate.[46] For example, a **5/1 ARM** is a mortgage with a fixed rate for the first five years, followed by an annual reset frequency where the rate for the next year is updated based on the current value of the reference rate, plus a spread. ARMs have much less negative convexity than do fixed-rate mortgages. However, the vast majority of residential mortgages in the USA (94.8% at the end of 2021) were fixed-rate.[47]

A wave of prepayments can wash over the MBS market as MBS holders are suddenly given large amounts of cash that they will need to reinvest at the lower rates that caused them to get the cash in the first place. That buying wave can force rates down still further. Given the vast size of the MBS market, this procyclical behavior can become a systemic problem. For example, on March 4, 2020, Olick (2020) reported that weekly mortgage refinances had spiked 26% as interest rates fell due to coronavirus fears.

On the flip side, when interest rates rise, the durations of MBS extend, as fewer people than normal pay back their existing mortgages. Having duration extending when interest rates are going up is doubly bad for an MBS holder: that is, it's negative convexity.

46 U.S. Department of the Treasury. "Interest Rates – Frequently Asked Questions." Website. https://home.treasury.gov/policy-issues/financing-the-government/interest-rate-statistics/interest-rates-frequently-asked-questions.
47 ICE Mortgage Technology™ Origination Insights Report December 2021, page 5 (All Loans). www.icemortgagetechnology.com/mortgage-data/origination-insight-reports.

How can MBS holders hedge this problem? They could try to delta-hedge by adjusting durations as they change. As interest rates rose, duration would go up, so to adjust delta the MBS holder could enter into payer swaps or could sell US Treasury futures. Similarly, as interest rates fell, duration would be going down, so the MBS holder could enter into receiver swaps or could buy US Treasury futures.

But in a market whose size is over \$10 trillion, the size of the swap or Treasury future trades required to make a dent in rapidly changing MBS durations would be ruinous. Even though swaps and Treasurys are themselves enormous markets, they would be moved procyclically by the volume of trading required to keep MBS durations in check. This effect has been mitigated by the US Federal Reserve's quantitative easing program: as of March 2021, the Fed was buying about 25% of MBS production, which it does not hedge.[48] But the volume of MBS held by banks and investors who are prone to hedging is still enormous.

The savvy hedger would try to be in a position to avoid pouring fuel onto the fire. If you're short-rate gamma (convexity), you can use an options position to buy rate gamma. Then the options position will automatically adjust your duration for you. In effect, you would try to buy back the optionality that was given away to mortgagees.

The preferred market for rate gamma hedging is the **swaptions market**.[49] Table 12.8 shows that the notional and gross amounts of interest rate options (largely swaptions) are about one-tenth of the notional and gross amounts of interest rate swaps. This is enough to handle the sudden flows that occur because of mortgage rate changes.

A European payer swaption gives the holder the right but not the obligation to enter into a payer swap. A swaption has an **optionality period**, the length of time for which the holder can exercise the right to enter into a swap, and a **swap tenor**, which is the length of time the optioned swap is active. Thus, a swaption is described as an "$m \times n$" ("m by n" or "m into n") swaption, where m is the optionality period and n is the swap tenor. The swaption also has a strike price, which is the fixed annual rate K that the fixed payer will owe (while receiving the floating reference rate) if the swaption is exercised and the swap is entered into.

---

48 Tatevossian, Leon, "Can We Still Blame MBS Hedgers?," March 25, 2021, lecture at New York University Tandon School Finance and Risk Engineering Department.

49 Given the vastness of the MBS market, many instruments are available to manage MBS portfolios and their risks. US Treasurys, US Treasury futures, and US Treasury future options can be used to hedge mortgage exposures, but they have basis risk: mortgage rates don't always move in lockstep with Treasury rates. The mortgage TBA (to-be-announced) market (SIFMA) ("TBA Market Fact Sheet." 2015. www.sifma.org/wp-content/uploads/2011/03/SIFMA-TBA-Fact-Sheet.pdf) provides mortgage-related forward instruments that lower basis risk. But while mortgage TBAs are very liquid, they provide only first-order (delta) exposure adjustments. The mortgage TBA option market, which does provide second-order (convexity) exposure adjustments, is not very liquid.

A European receiver swaption has the same parameters, but the optioned swap is a receiver swap.

To price a payer swaption, note that m years from now, the swaption owner will look at the then-prevailing swap rate for n-year swaps; call that rate S. The swaption owner will compare S to the swaption strike price K to determine if $S > K$.

- If so, the swaption holder can exercise the swaption and get a payer swap, while simultaneously entering into a receiver swap. The floating legs of the payer and receiver swaps cancel each other. If p is the periodicity (number of times per year there are payments), then the fixed legs bring in (receiver) S/p and pay out (payer) K/p, so the swaption holder benefits by $(S - K)/p > 0$ in each payment period, per unit of notional.
- If not, the swaption isn't exercised.

Thus, the payment received at time $m + \frac{i}{p}$ ($i = 1, \ldots, pn$) is $\max(0, S - K)/p$. This is the payoff on a forward-starting caplet, that is, one that is exercised at time m based on the level of S at the time, but whose payoff doesn't come until time $m + i/p$.

The value of such an caplet is given by a variant on Black–Scholes, which is simply called the Black model (Black 1976). It's a modification of (8.3) that takes into account forward-starting instruments:

$$CL(F, K, T, r, \sigma) = \exp(-rT)\big(FN(d_1) - KN(d_2)\big), \qquad (12.29)$$

$$d_1 = \frac{\ln\left(\frac{F}{K}\right) + \frac{\sigma^2}{2}T}{\sigma\sqrt{T}}, d_2 = d_1 - \sigma\sqrt{T}.$$

The Black formula for the corresponding floorlet is:

$$FL(F, K, T, r, \sigma) = \exp(-rT)\big(-FN(-d_1) + KN(-d_2)\big). \qquad (12.30)$$

Applied to forward-starting caplets and floorlets, the forward parameter F becomes the forward-starting swap rate $SF(m, m + n)$ given by (12.22). The time parameter T is the optionality period m. Then σ is the volatility of swap rates and r is an appropriate discount rate, which we'll take from the swap curve, although conventions may vary.

The payer swaption is a series of these forward-starting caplets. The decision to exercise is taken at the common expiration of the optionality period m years from now, but the cash flows come at different times during the n-year life of the optioned swap and thus need to be discounted differently. Summing up the discounted values of the caplets gives:

$$PayerSwaption(m,n,K) =$$

$$\frac{(SF(m,m+n)N(d_1) - KN(d_2))}{p} \sum_{i=1}^{pn} exp\left(-s\left(0, m+\frac{i}{p}\right)\left(m+\frac{i}{p}\right)\right),$$

(12.31)

$$d_1 = \frac{\ln\left(\frac{SF(m,m+n)}{K}\right) + \frac{\sigma^2}{2}m}{\sigma\sqrt{m}}, \quad d_2 = d_1 - \sigma\sqrt{m}.$$

A receiver swaption is a series of forward-starting floorlets, so by analogous reasoning together with parity (12.25), we can say:

$$RcvrSwaption(m,n,K) =$$

$$\frac{(-SF(m,m+n)N(-d_1) + KN(-d_2))}{p} \sum_{i=1}^{pn} exp\left(-s\left(0, m+\frac{i}{p}\right)\left(m+\frac{i}{p}\right)\right)$$

(12.32)

Terms d_1 and d_2 are as in (12.31).

A simple form of mortgage convexity hedging can now be seen. Suppose a portfolio manager owns a mortgage-backed security with 11 years of life left. The component mortgages are paying 4% interest. The manager expects based on a mortgage prepayment model[50] that if 10-year rates fall below 2.5%, 30% of the mortgages will suddenly prepay.

To hedge this risk over the next year, the manager could buy a 1×10 receiver swaption struck at 4% on 30% of the principal. Suppose rates hit 2.5% in one year and 30% of the principal is repaid. The manager takes three actions:

- Invests the repaid principal in a fixed rate bond;
- Enters into a payer swap; and
- Exercises the swaption, getting a receiver swap at 4%.

The floating legs of the two swaps cancel, leaving the manager with a stream of $4 - 2.5 = 1.5\%$ incoming payments. The fixed rate bond delivers 2.5% or close to it, so all told the manager maintains a 4% income stream even though mortgage rates dropped and many mortgages prepaid.

For Code Segments in this chapter, see the Code Appendix starting on p. 440. For executable code, visit www.cambridge.org/9781009209090/ch12

For problem sets for this chapter, visit www.cambridge.org/ 9781009209090/ch12_problems

50 [Hall and Maingi 2019].

Appendix: Code Segments

#Code Segment 1.1:

```python
import numpy as np
import matplotlib.pyplot as plt
%matplotlib inline
plt.rcParams['figure.dpi']= 300

starting_wealth=10**5
def util_fn(x):
    #log utility function with starting wealth
    return(np.log(x+starting_wealth))

x=np.arange(-starting_wealth+.01,10**9,10**6)
y=util_fn(x)
plt.title("Figure 1.1: Concave upside utility")
plt.xlabel("Added Wealth")
plt.ylabel("Utility")
plt.grid()
plt.annotate('500Mn', xy=(5*10**8, util_fn(5*10**8)), \
            xytext=(5*10**8, 10),arrowprops= \
            dict(arrowstyle='->',facecolor='black'))
plt.annotate('1Bn', xy=(10**9, util_fn(10**9)), \
            xytext=(.9*10**9, 11),arrowprops= \
            dict(arrowstyle='->',facecolor='black'))
plt.plot(x,y)
#Show linear increase from utility of $500Mn
y2=x*(util_fn(5*10**8)-util_fn(0))/(5*10**8)+util_fn(0)
plt.annotate('2*u(500Mn)-u(0)', xy=(10**9, \
            2*util_fn(5*10**8)-util_fn(0)), \
            xytext=(.5*10**9, 26), arrowprops \
            =dict(arrowstyle='->',facecolor='black'))

plt.plot(x,y2);
```

440

#Code Segment 1.2:

```
def thug_fn(x):
    #log utility function for number of broken fingers
    return(-np.log(x+1))


x=np.arange(0,10,1)
y=thug_fn(x)
plt.title("Figure 1.2: Convex downside utility")
plt.xlabel("Fingers Broken")
plt.ylabel("Utility")
plt.grid()
plt.annotate('1 Finger', xy=(1, thug_fn(1)), \
            xytext=(1, -3),arrowprops \
            =dict(arrowstyle='->',facecolor='black'))
plt.annotate('2 Fingers', xy=(2, thug_fn(2)), \
            xytext=(5, -.25), arrowprops \
            =dict(arrowstyle='->',facecolor='black'))
plt.plot(x,y)
#Show linear decrease from utility of 1 broken finger
y2=x*thug_fn(1)
plt.annotate('2*u(1 Finger)', xy=(2, 2*thug_fn(1)), \
            xytext=(3, -4),arrowprops=dict(arrowstyle \
            ='->',facecolor='black'))

plt.plot(x,y2);
```

#Code Segment 1.3:

```
#Kahneman's decision weights function

x=[0,1,2,5,10,20,50,80,90,95,98,99,100]
y=[0,5.5,8.1,13.2,18.6,26.1,42.1,60.1,71.2,79.3,87.1, \
    91.2,100]
plt.title("Figure 1.3: Kahneman's empirical decision \
    weights d(p)")
plt.xlabel("Probability")
plt.ylabel("Decision Weight")
plt.grid()
plt.plot(x,x,label="linear")
plt.plot(x,y,label="d(p)")
plt.legend();
```

#Code Segment 2.1:

```
#Generate a high volatility and a low volatility price \
    series
import numpy as np
import matplotlib.pyplot as plt
%matplotlib inline

x=np.arange(0,1.01,.01)
rng = np.random.default_rng(27182818)   #Use seed \
    so repeatable
r1=rng.normal(loc=0.,scale=.3,size=100)
r2=rng.normal(loc=0.,scale=.01,size=100)
#Force both series to end up in the same place
r1+=.002-np.average(r1)
r2+=.002-np.average(r2)
#Start both series at a value of 1 and
#switch from log(pnew/pold-1) to pnew/pold-1
y1=np.append(np.array(1),np.exp(np.cumsum(r1)))
y2=np.append(np.array(1),np.exp(np.cumsum(r2)))
plt.title("Figure 2.1 - High vs. low volatility: \
    same returns")
plt.xlabel('Time')
plt.ylabel('Value of a dollar')
plt.grid()
plt.plot(x,y1)
plt.plot(x,y2);
```

#Code Segment 2.2:

```
import matplotlib.pyplot as plt
%matplotlib inline
import numpy as np
import scipy.stats as spst

#Generate some random numbers and show VaR and cVaR

#Generate 90% low vol, 10% high vol random numbers; \
    this creates a fat-tailed distribution
trials=1000
rng = np.random.default_rng(314159)   #Use seed \
    so repeatable
```

```python
y=np.concatenate((rng.normal(0.,1.,int(.9*trials)), \
                  rng.normal(0.,10.,int(.1*trials))))
y.sort()   #Put them in order

p=.99
p100=p*100.
p_string="%0.0f"% p100

# Compute sample p-VaR; n=trials
# We assume there is probability mass = 1/(n+1) at each \
      of the n observations.
# So the smallest observation has cumulative probability \
      mass 1/(n+1) and
# the largest observation has cumulative probability \
      mass n/(n+1)
# From (2.4) we want the smallest k such that
# k/(n+1) >= 1-p, i.e. k>=(n+1)(1-p)

breakpoint=(trials+1)*(1-p)
k=int(breakpoint)
#Python list convention is: first list element is index 0
#So if breakpoint is an integer, decrement k
#Otherwise leave it alone to get the next one up
if k==breakpoint:
    k-=1
VaRp=-y[k]
#Compute cVaR
#Standardization factor is (sum of probabilities \
      <= VaRp). Here that's (k+1)/(n+1).
#As n->infinity that will get closer and closer to 1-p, \
      but for the finite case
#it's a little off.
cVaRp=-np.sum(y[:k+1])/(k+1)

plt.scatter(range(1,21),-y[:20])
plt.annotate(p_string+"% VaR", xy=(10.0, VaRp), \
             xytext=(10.0, VaRp+1), \
             arrowprops=dict(arrowstyle='->', \
                   facecolor='black'))
plt.hlines(VaRp,0,20)
```

```python
plt.annotate(p_string+"% cVaR", xy=(10.0, cVaRp), \
             xytext=(10.0, cVaRp+1),color='red', \
             arrowprops=dict(arrowstyle='->', \
                        facecolor='red'))
plt.hlines(cVaRp,0,20,colors='red')

plt.title('Figure 2.2: Worst 20 losses out \
      of '+str(trials))
plt.xlabel('Observation number')
plt.ylabel('Loss amount')
plt.show();

pv_string=p_string+"% VaR is "
print(pv_string,VaRp)
pcv_string=p_string+"% cVaR is "
print(pcv_string,cVaRp)

#For comparison, generate VaR and cVaR with interpolation
#numpy percentile function does the wrong thing - \
      assumes first observation
#is 0 percentile and last is 100th. Cure that by adding \
      extra observations
#at each end.
z=np.insert(y,0,y[0]-1)
z=np.append(z,z[-1]+1)
VaRp_interp=-np.percentile(z,(1-p)*100)
# Compute sample p-cVaR without interpolation
nexceed=max(np.where(y<=-VaRp_interp)[0])
#-VaRp is (1-p) of the way between y[nexceed] \
      and y[nexceed+1]
cVaRp_interp=-(np.sum([yy for yy in y if
      yy<=-VaRp_interp])-(1-p)*VaRp_interp)/
      (nexceed+2-p)
pv_string=p_string+"% interpolated VaR is "
print(pv_string,VaRp_interp)
pcv_string=p_string+"% interpolated cVaR is "
print(pcv_string,cVaRp_interp)
```

#Code Segment 2.3:

```python
#Get mean and standard deviation of the data
samp_mean=np.mean(y)
samp_std=np.std(y)
```

```
#Show normal VaR vs sample VaR
nVaRp=-(samp_mean+samp_std*spst.norm.ppf(1-p))
pv_string=p_string+"% Sample VaR is "
print(pv_string,VaRp)
pvn_string=p_string+"% Normal VaR is "
print(pvn_string,nVaRp)

# Get normal cVaR
ncVaRp=-samp_mean+samp_std*np.exp(-.5*(nVaRp/
    samp_std)**2)/((1-p)*np.sqrt(2*np.pi))
pcv_string=p_string+"% Sample cVaR is "
print(pcv_string,cVaRp)
pncv_string=p_string+"% Normal cVaR is "
print(pncv_string,ncVaRp)
```

#Code Segment 2.4:

```
def SharePrice(f,p):
    #Price to pay when a fraction f of
    #wealth is invested in a gamble that pays 1 with \
        probability
    #p and 0 otherwise, log-utility
    #See formula 2.17 above
    if (f<0) or (f>=1) or (p<=0) or (p>1): #Can't bet \
        anything
        return(0.0)
    if (f==0.0):                 #Limiting amount to be \
        risk-neutral
        return(p)
    if (p==1.0):
        return(1.0)
    one_minus_f=1-f
    denom=one_minus_f**(1-1/p)-one_minus_f
    return(f/denom)
#Done with SharePrice

#Generate isoprobability graphs

frac_wealth = np.arange(0,1.01,.01) #compute at \
    fractions of wealth
                                    #ranging from 0 to \
    1 by .01's
```

```
prob = np.arange(.1,1.1,.1) #Compute isoprobability \
    curves every 10%
                         #of probability
#y is a list of lists - each contained list is an \
    isoprobability curve
y=[[SharePrice(fw,pr) for fw in frac_wealth] for pr \
    in prob]

#Display the graph
for i in range(len(prob)):     #Do each isoprobability line
    plt.plot(frac_wealth,y[i])

plt.xticks(rotation=45)
plt.grid()
plt.title('Figure 2.3: Isoprobability (constant p) \
    curves')
plt.xlabel('Fraction of wealth')
plt.ylabel('Share price q')
plt.axis([0,1,0,1])
plt.show();
```

```
#Code Segment 2.5:
```

```
#Display GME short squeeze 2020-2021
import yfinance as yf
from datetime import datetime

tix = yf.Ticker("GME")
# get historical market data
hist = tix.history(period="max")

#Drop rows with any NaNs
hist = hist.dropna()

#Plot prices
start_date = datetime.strptime("2020-06-30", "%Y-%m-%d")
x=hist[hist.index>=start_date].index    #dates
y=hist[hist.index>=start_date].Close    #adjusted prices
i=np.arange(len(y))    #index
plt.plot(i,y)

#Display about 10 dates on the x axis
stride=int(len(y)/10)
```

```
plt.xticks(i[::stride],x[::stride].strftime("%Y-%m-%d"), \
    rotation=45)

plt.title("Figure 2.4 - GME short squeeze")
plt.xlabel('Date')
plt.ylabel('Price')
plt.grid()
plt.show();
```

#Code Segment 3.1:

```
import qrpm_funcs as qf
import matplotlib.pyplot as plt
%matplotlib inline
import numpy as np

#FRED code for wholesale price series 1914-1968
seriesnames=['M0448CUSM350NNBR']

dates,prices=qf.GetFREDMatrix(seriesnames)

## Configure the graph
x=np.arange(len(dates))
plt.plot(x,prices)
plt.title('Figure 3.1 - US wholesale prices')
plt.xlabel('Date')
plt.ylabel('Price Level')
plt.xticks(x[::120],dates[::120],rotation=45)
plt.grid(True)
plt.show();
```

#Code Segment 3.2:

```
#FRED code for 5-year TIPS returns
seriesnames=['FII5']

dates,prices=qf.GetFREDMatrix(seriesnames)

#reformatting needed for fill_between
#prices is actually an array of singleton arrays,
#which fill_between doesn't like
p=[prices[i][0] for i in range(len(prices))]
```

```
## Configure the graph
x=np.arange(len(dates))
zeroline=np.zeroes(len(dates))
plt.plot(x,p)
plt.plot(x,zeroline,color='black')
plt.fill_between(x,p,zeroline,where=zeroline >= p, \
    facecolor='red')
str_title='Figure 3.2 - 5-year US real rates '
str_title+=dates[0][:7]+' to '+dates[-1][:7]
plt.title(str_title)
plt.xlabel('Date')
plt.ylabel('Percentage')
plt.xticks(x[::36],dates[::36],rotation=45)
plt.grid(True)
plt.show();
```

#Code Segment 3.3:

```
#FRED code for Swiss 10-year rates
seriesnames=['IRLTLT01CHM156N']

dates,rates=qf.GetFREDMatrix(seriesnames, \
    startdate='2014-01-02')

#reformatting needed for fill_between
#prices is actually an array of singleton arrays,
#which fill_between doesn't like
r=[rates[i][0] for i in range(len(rates))]

## Configure the graph
x=np.arange(len(dates))
plt.plot(x,r)
#Put in a horizontal line at 0 and shade negative rates \
    in red
zeroline=np.zeroes(len(dates))
plt.plot(x,zeroline,color='black')
plt.fill_between(x,r,zeroline,where=zeroline >= r, \
    facecolor='red')
#titles and labels
str_title='Figure 3.3 - Swiss 10-year nominal rates '
str_title+=dates[0][:7]+' to '+dates[-1][:7]
plt.title(str_title)
plt.xlabel('Date')
```

```
plt.ylabel('Rate (%)')
plt.xticks(x[::12],dates[::12],rotation=45)
plt.grid(True)
plt.show();
```

#Code Segment 3.4:

```
# Plot bond prices using Formula 3.3
# Function formula3p3 is in qrpm_funcs
x = np.arange(0, 14.25, .25)
coupon=7
years=29
y=[qf.formula3p3(coupon,rate,years) for rate in x]
plt.plot(x, y)

## Configure the graph
str_title='Figure 3.4 - Seasoned %d'% years
str_title+='-year %d'% coupon
str_title+='% Coupon Bond Price'
plt.title(str_title)
plt.xlabel('Discount Rate (%)')
plt.ylabel('Price')
plt.xlim(0,14)
plt.grid(True)
plt.show();
```

#Code Segment 3.5:

```
#Plot duration of a newly issued bullet bond
#with (coupon=discount rate)
x = np.arange(0, 14.25, .25)
years=30
y=[qf.formula3p7(coupon,coupon,years) for coupon in x]
plt.plot(x, y)

#Show the duration of the 7% coupon bond for reference
coupon_7_dur=[qf.formula3p7(7.,7.,years)]*len(x)
plt.plot(x,coupon_7_dur,color='black')

## Configure the graph
str_title='Figure 3.5 - New %d'% years
str_title+='-year bond duration'
plt.title(str_title)
```

```
plt.xlabel('Coupon Rate')
plt.ylabel('Macaulay Duration (years)')
plt.xlim(0,14)
plt.grid(True)
plt.show()
```

#Code Segment 3.6:

```
#Show a graph of true price of a 7% coupon, 30-year bond
#at different discount rates; compare with duration
#approximation and duration+convexity approximation
x = np.arange(0, 14.25, .25)
years=30
baserate=7
#Get the base price from formula 3.3
baseprice=qf.formula3p3(baserate,baserate,years)
#Get the base duration from formula 3.7
basedur=qf.formula3p7(baserate,baserate,years)
#Get the base convexity formula 3.8
basecvx=qf.formula3p8(baserate,baserate,years)
#y holds prices computed from formula 3.3 at different \
    discount rates
y=[qf.formula3p3(baserate,rate,years) for rate in x]
# Duration-only
y1=[baseprice-basedur*(rate-baserate) for rate in x]
# Duration and convexity
y2=[y1[i]+.5*basecvx*(rate-baserate)**2/100 for i, \
    rate in enumerate(x)]

plt.plot(x, y, label='True price')
plt.plot(x, y1, label='Dur approx')
plt.plot(x, y2, label='Dur+Cvx approx')
## Configure the graph
plt.title('Figure 3.6: First- and second-order \
    approximations')
plt.xlabel('Discount Rate')
plt.ylabel('Price')
plt.legend()
plt.grid(True)
plt.show();
```

#Code Segment 3.7:

```python
import pandas as pd
#Plot the 2010, 2019, and most recent yearend
#US Treasury curves

seriesnames=['DGS1MO','DGS3MO','DGS6MO','DGS1','DGS2', \
             'DGS3','DGS5','DGS7','DGS10','DGS20','DGS30']
cdates,ratematrix=qf.GetFREDMatrix(seriesnames)

#Form the list of curve dates to display
lastday=qf.LastYearEnd()
displaydates=['2010-12-31','2019-12-31',lastday]
tenors=qf.TenorsFromNames(seriesnames)

#Plot the three lines
for i in range(3):
    year=displaydates[i][:4]
    plt.plot(tenors, ratematrix[cdates. \
        index(displaydates[i])], label=year)

## Configure the graph
plt.title('Figure 3.7: US Yearend Treasury curves')
plt.xlabel('Tenor (years)')
plt.ylabel('Rate (%/year)')
plt.legend()
plt.grid(True)
plt.annotate('Upward sloping', \
             xy=((tenors[-2]+tenors[-1])/2., \
           (ratematrix[cdates. \
             index(displaydates[1])][-1]+ \
             ratematrix[cdates.\
             index(displaydates[1])][-2])/2.), \
             xytext=(21.25, 0), \
          arrowprops=dict(arrowstyle='<->', \
             facecolor='black'))
plt.text(.5, 1, 'Short end')
plt.text(10, 2.5, 'Belly')
plt.text(25, 4, 'Long end')
plt.show;
```

```
#Display most recent curve
print("Most recent yearend curve ("+displaydates[-1]+")")
for i in range(len(seriesnames)):
    print(seriesnames[i][-len(seriesnames[i])+3:], \
            ratematrix[cdates.index(displaydates[-1])][i])
```

#Code Segment 3.8:

```
#Show the inverted Treasury curve from 2001-01-02

targetdate='2001-01-02'
#Note no one-month rate on this date
    snames_target=['DGS3MO','DGS6MO','DGS1',
                'DGS2','DGS3','DGS5','DGS7',
                'DGS10','DGS20','DGS30']
dates_target,ratematrix_target=qf.GetFREDMatrix( \
    snames_target,startdate=targetdate,enddate=targetdate)

plt.plot(qf.TenorsFromNames(snames_target), \
        ratematrix_target[0])
## Configure the graph
plt.title('Figure 3.8: US Treasury curve '+targetdate)
plt.ylim(0,max([x for x in ratematrix_target[0] if pd. \
    notna(x)])+.5)
plt.xlabel('Tenor (years)')
plt.ylabel('Rate (%/year)')
plt.grid(True)
plt.show;
```

#Code Segment 3.9:

```
#Code to get data for 10y - 3m US Treasury steepness and
#compare with NBER recessions since 1962

#Get 3 month rates and 10-year rates (monthly first \
    of month)
#USREC is 0,1 indicator of NBER US recession
cdates_steep,ratematrix_steep=qf. \
    GetFREDMatrix(['TB3MS','GS10','USREC'], \
    startdate="1962-01-01",enddate=lastday)

steeps_not_nan = [(not (np.isnan(x) or np.isnan(y) or \
    np.isnan(z))) for [x,y,z] in ratematrix_steep]
```

```python
steeps = [y-x for ([x,y,z],bool) in \
    zip(ratematrix_steep,steeps_not_nan) if bool]
nber = [z for ([x,y,z],bool) in \
    zip(ratematrix_steep,steeps_not_nan) if bool]
steeps_dates = [d[:7] for (d,bool) in \
    zip(cdates_steep,steeps_not_nan) if bool]

#Compute percentage negative
n_steeps=len(steeps)
num_neg=sum(x<0 for x in steeps)
pct_neg_str="%.2f"%float(100*num_neg/n_steeps)

#Make the graph; different colors of positive and \
    negative slopes
x=np.arange(n_steeps)
plt.plot(x,[0 if steep < 0 else steep for steep in \
    steeps],color='b')
plt.plot(x,[0 if steep >=0 else steep for steep in \
    steeps],color='r')

#Mark recessions \
    (http://www.nber.org/cycles/cyclesmain.html) in red
rec_starts=[]
rec_finishes=[]
in_recession = (nber[0] == 1.)
for t in range(1,len(nber)):
    if in_recession:
        if nber[t] == 0.:
            rec_finishes.append(steeps_dates[t-1])
            in_recession = False
    else:
        if nber[t] == 1.:
            rec_starts.append(steeps_dates[t-1]) \
                #t-1 lines up with NBER
            in_recession = True

#Check if still in recession
if len(rec_starts) > len(rec_finishes):
    rec_finishes.append(steeps_dates[-1])

for idx in range(len(rec_starts)):
    rec_start=steeps_dates.index(rec_starts[idx])
    rec_finish=steeps_dates.index(rec_finishes[idx])
```

```
    plt.axvspan(rec_start, rec_finish, alpha=0.5, \
        color='gray')
## Configure the graph
plt.title('Figure 3.9: 10-year, 3-month US \
    Treasury steepness ('+pct_neg_str+'%neg)')
stride=int(len(steeps)/10)
plt.xticks(x[::stride],steeps_dates[::stride],rotation=45)
plt.ylabel('Steepness (%/year)')
plt.grid(True)
plt.show;
```

#Code Segment 3.10:

```
#Plot first 3 principal components from Table 2 in
#https://pdfs.semanticscholar.org/c0ca/
    bab4aebf9d04e58a3084e4f35ea4d57045aa.pdf
tenornames=['3mo','6mo','1yr','2yr','3yr',
    '4yr','5yr','7yr','10yr','30yr']
tenornumbers=range(len(tenornames))
pc1=[0.21,0.26,0.32,0.35,0.36,
    0.36,0.36,0.34,0.31,0.25]
pc2=[-0.57,-0.49,-0.32,-0.1,0.02,
    0.14,0.17,0.27,0.3,0.33]
pc3=[0.5,0.23,-0.37,-0.38,-0.3,
    -0.12,-0.04,0.15,0.23,0.46]
plt.plot(tenornumbers, pc1, label='PC1')
plt.plot(tenornumbers, pc2, label='PC2')
plt.plot(tenornumbers, pc3, label='PC3')

## Configure the graph
plt.title('Figure 3.10: UST curve principal components')
plt.xlabel('Tenor')
plt.ylabel('Level')
plt.legend()
plt.xticks(tenornumbers, tenornames)
plt.grid(True)
plt.show;
```

#Code Segment 3.11:

```
## Nelson-Siegel curve components
## Use tenornames and tenornumbers from previous \
    code segment
```

```
def ns_slope(t):
    #Nelson-Siegel slope component
    return((1-np.exp(-t))/t)


def ns_twist(t):
    #Nelson-Siegel twist component
    return((1-np.exp(-t)*(1+t))/t)


tenors=[.25, .5, 1., 2., 3., 4., 5., 7., 10., 30.]
n=len(tenors)
plt.plot(tenornumbers, [1.]*n, label="Level")
plt.plot(tenornumbers, [ns_slope(t) for t in tenors], \
    label="Slope")
plt.plot(tenornumbers, [ns_twist(t) for t in tenors], \
    label="Twist")


## Configure the graph
plt.title('Figure 3.11: Nelson-Siegel Components')
plt.xlabel('Tenor')
plt.ylabel('Level')
plt.legend()
plt.xticks(tenornumbers, tenornames)
plt.grid(True)
plt.show;
```

#Code Segment 3.12:

```
#Get most recent yearend US Treasury curve
#Interpolate with cubic spline to monthly and compute \
    a short
#rate curve based on that
#Plot both
import scipy.interpolate as spyi


lastday=qf.LastYearEnd()
seriesnames=['DGS1MO','DGS3MO','DGS6MO','DGS1',
            'DGS2','DGS3','DGS5','DGS7',
            'DGS10','DGS20','DGS30']
cdates,ratematrix=qf.GetFREDMatrix(seriesnames, \
            startdate=lastday,enddate=lastday)
tenorsfromtsy=qf.TenorsFromNames(seriesnames)
```

```
#Get monthly piecewise linear interpolated curve and \
    short-rate curve
tenors,curvemonthly,shortrates=qf. \
    InterpolateCurve(tenorsfromtsy,ratematrix[0])


# Replace piecewise linear curve with smoothed cubic \
    Hermite spline cureve
dydx=[(ratematrix[0][i]-ratematrix[0][i-1])/
    (tenorsfromtsy[i]-tenorsfromtsy[i-1]) \
    for i in range(1,len(tenorsfromtsy))]
dydx.append(0.)
z=spyi.CubicHermiteSpline(tenorsfromtsy, \
    ratematrix[0],dydx)
curvemonthly=z.__call__(tenors)
#Formula 3.24
shortrates=curvemonthly+np.multiply(tenors, \
    z.__call__(tenors,nu=1))


plt.plot(tenors, curvemonthly, label=lastday)
plt.plot(tenors, shortrates, label='Short')
## Configure the graph
plt.title('Figure 3.12: Smoothed US Treasury and \
    short-rate curves')
plt.xlabel('Tenor (years)')
plt.ylabel('Rate (%/year)')
plt.ylim(0,max(shortrates)+.5)
plt.legend()
plt.grid(True)
plt.show;
```

#Code Segment 3.13:

```
import random
#Plot an observed year-end Treasury curve;
#a short-rate curve based on that;
#a Hull-White randomly generated short-rate curve;
#and a yield curve integrating the Hull-White short curve

def hull_white_path(xlam,sig,shortrs,tens,fixedseed):
    #Generates one Hull-White path using parameters
    #xlam (lambda) and sig (sigma) in 3.31
    #shortrs is time-varying r-infinity; tens are \
        associated tenors
```

```python
    #returns randomwalk (the path) and curvesample \
        (the averaged cumulative path)
    randomwalk=[]
    curvesample=[]
    #Do we want the same omega every time?
    if fixedseed:
        random.seed(5772157)
    for i,rate in enumerate(shortrs):
        if i==0: # initialize
            randomwalk.append(shortrs[i])
            curvesample.append(randomwalk[i])
        else:
            delta_t=tens[i]-tens[i-1]
            deterministic=(xlambda* \
                (shortrs[i]-randomwalk[i-1]))*delta_t
            stochastic=sigma*np.sqrt(delta_t)* \
                random.gauss(0,1)
            randomwalk.append(randomwalk[i-1]+ \
                deterministic+stochastic)
            #sample curve is average of short rate
            #random walk to this point
            curvesample.append((curvesample[i-1]*i+ \
                randomwalk[i])/(i+1))
    return(randomwalk,curvesample)
#Done with hull_white_path

#Use short-rate curve (tenors, shortrates) obtained in \
    previous code segment

#set parameters for Ornstein-Uhlenbeck process
#xlambda is spring stiffness; sigma is volatility
xlambda=1
sigma=.05*np.sqrt(12)
randomwalk,curvesample=hull_white_path(xlambda,sigma, \
    shortrates,tenors,True)

#Plot the four curves
minrate=min(curvesample)
maxrate=max(curvesample)
plt.ylim(min(.5,minrate),max(3,maxrate))
plt.plot(tenors, curvemonthly, \
    label='UST Smoothed Curve YE '+lastday[:4])
```

```
plt.plot(tenors, shortrates, \
    label='Impl Short Curve YE '+lastday[:4])
plt.plot(tenors, randomwalk, \
    label='Sample Short Curve $R(\omega)$')
plt.plot(tenors, curvesample, \
    label='Sample UST Curve $\overline{R}(\omega)$')
## Configure the graph
plt.title('Figure 3.13: Hull-White Curve Generation')
plt.xlabel('Tenor (years)')
plt.ylabel('Rate (%/year)')
plt.legend()
plt.grid(True)
plt.show;
```

#Code Segment 3.14:

```
#Plot 10 Hull-White paths based on yearend US Treasury \
    curve

#do one graph with sigma=.05 and another with sigma=.2
#keep track of range
minrate,maxrate=1000,-1000
fig, (ax1, ax2) = plt.subplots(1, 2, figsize=(12,4), \
    sharey=True)
fig.suptitle("Figure 3.14: 10 Hull-White curves, monthly \
    $\sigma$=.05 and .2")
plt.ylabel("Rate (%/year)")

#set parameter for Ornstein-Uhlenbeck process
xlambda=1
ax=ax1

for sigma in (.05*np.sqrt(12),.2*np.sqrt(12)):
    #generate and plot 10 sample curves
    for sample_number in range(10):

    randomwalk,curvesample=hull_white_path(xlambda, \
        sigma,shortrates,tenors,False)
        minrate=min(curvesample+[minrate])
        maxrate=max(curvesample+[maxrate])
        ax.plot(tenors,curvesample)
    plt.xlabel('Tenor (years)')
```

```
    ax.grid(True)
    ax=ax2

plt.ylim(min(.5,minrate),max(3,maxrate))
plt.show;
```

#Code Segment 4.1:

```
#Graph an efficient frontier with inefficient
#points below it
import matplotlib.pyplot as plt
%matplotlib inline
import numpy as np

# evenly sampled standard deviation
t = np.arange(0.05, .2, 0.005)

#Plot the frontier
plt.plot(t, .7*(t-.04)**.5-.04, 'D', color='darkblue')
markers=['o','*','8','s','p','x']
colors=['yellow','red','green','orange','black','magenta']
#Six sets of random inefficient portfolios
np.random.seed(602215)
for i in range(6):
    s=np.random.uniform(0,1,len(t))
    plt.scatter(t, s*(.7*(t-.04)**.5-.04), \
        marker=markers[i], color=colors[i])
plt.axis([0,.2,0,.25])
plt.title('Figure 4.1: Efficient frontier and \
    inefficient portfolios')
plt.xlabel('Risk (annual std. deviation)')
plt.ylabel('Reward (arith. annual return)')
plt.grid(True)
plt.show();
```

#Code Segment 4.2:

```
import pandas as pd
import qrpm_funcs as qf
#Get 3 currencies until the end of
#previous year. Form sample covariance matrix
#and do simple efficient frontier calculations
```

```
lastday=qf.LastYearEnd()
#Swiss franc, pound sterling, Japanese Yen
seriesnames=['DEXSZUS','DEXUSUK','DEXJPUS']
cdates,ratematrix=qf.GetFREDMatrix(seriesnames, \
    enddate=lastday)
multipliers=[-1,1,-1]

lgdates,difflgs=qf.levels_to_log_returns(cdates, \
    ratematrix,multipliers)

#Mean vector and covariance matrix are inputs to \
    efficient frontier calculations
d=np.array(difflgs)
m=np.mean(d,axis=0)
c=np.cov(d.T)

#display the output
#vectors and matrices are in fractional units;
#    fraction*100=percent
#    fraction*10000=basis point
#    (fraction^2)*10000=percent^2
np.set_printoptions(precision=4)
print("From",lgdates[0],"to",lgdates[-1], \
    "(",len(lgdates),"observations):")
print("\nMeans:",m*10000,"bps/day")
print("(CHF, GBP, JPY)\n")
print("   ",c[0]*10000)
print("C=",c[1]*10000,"    (4.20)")
print("   ",c[2]*10000)
print(f'(%/day)\N{SUPERSCRIPT TWO} units')
```

#Code Segment 4.3:

```
#invert the c matrix, which is in (fraction/day)^2 units
#so ci (c-inverse) is in (days/fraction)^2 units
ci=np.linalg.inv(c)
print("          ",ci[0]/10000)
print(f'C-inverse=',ci[1]/10000,"    (4.21)")
print("          ",ci[2]/10000)
print(f'(days/%)\N{SUPERSCRIPT TWO} units')
```

#Code Segment 4.4:

```
#sum entries in ci
uciu=np.sum(ci)
print(f'u\'(C-inverse)u =',uciu/10000, \
    f'(days/%)\N{SUPERSCRIPT TWO}')
ucim=np.sum(ci @ m)
print(f'u\'(C-inverse)m =',ucim,'days')
mcim = m @ (ci @ m)
print(f'm\'(C-inverse)m =',mcim*10000,'bps')
```

#Code Segment 4.5:

```
#Vectors for equation 4.6
u=[1]*3
vec2=(ci @ u)/uciu
vec1=np.subtract(ci @ m,vec2*ucim)
print(f"w'=lambda",vec1,"+",vec2,"    (4.6)#")

lambdacoeff=(uciu*mcim-ucim*ucim)/uciu
constmu=ucim/uciu
print(f'mu=(lambda *',lambdacoeff*10000,")+", \
    constmu*10000," bps/day    (4.9)#")

print(f'sigma=sqrt(lambda\N{SUPERSCRIPT TWO} *', \
    lambdacoeff*10000,'+',10000/uciu,') (%/day) \
    (4.10)#')
```

#Code Segment 4.6:

```
#Draw graph of simple efficient frontier
lambda1s=np.arange(0,1.01,.01)
xrisk=100*np.sqrt(lambdacoeff*lambda1s**2+1/uciu) \
        #Multiply * 100 for percent/day units
yreturn=10000*(lambdacoeff*lambda1s+constmu) \
        #Multiply * 10000 for bp units

plt.figure(1)
plt.plot(xrisk,yreturn,marker='2')
plt.title("Figure 4.2: Franc, pound,\
    yen efficient frontier")
plt.xlabel("Standard Deviation (pct/day)")
plt.ylabel("Return (bps/day)")
```

```
plt.xlim(0,max(xrisk)+.5)
plt.grid()
plt.show();
```

#Code Segment 4.7:

```
print(f'Pound weight goes negative at lambda=', \
    -vec2[1]/vec1[1])
print('At that point mu=',-10000*lambdacoeff* \
    vec2[1]/vec1[1]+10000*constmu,' bps/day')
print('and sigma=',10000*np.sqrt(lambdacoeff* \
    (vec2[1]/vec1[1])**2+1/uciu),' bps/day')
```

#Code Segment 4.8:

```
#Draw graph of long-only efficient frontier
#Segment with pounds
lambda_nopound=-vec2[1]/vec1[1]
lambda1s=np.arange(0,lambda_nopound,.01)
lambda1s=np.append(lambda1s,lambda_nopound)
x1=100*np.sqrt(lambdacoeff*lambda1s**2+1/uciu) \
    #Multiply by 100 for percent/day units
y1=10000*(lambdacoeff*lambda1s+constmu) \
    #Multiply by 10000 for bp units

#Get franc/yen portfolio at the point where pounds \
    disappear
vec3=lambda_nopound*vec1+vec2
#rest of frontier decreases yen and increases francs
deltas=np.arange(0,vec3[2]*1.01,vec3[2]/100.)
x2=[100*np.sqrt(((vec3+[delta,0,-delta]) @ c) @ \
    (vec3+[delta,0,-delta]))for delta in deltas]
y2=[10000*((vec3+[delta,0,-delta]) @ m) for delta in \
    deltas]

plt.figure(1)
plt.plot(x1,y1,marker='2')
plt.plot(x2,y2,marker='1')
plt.title("Figure 4.3: Long-only efficient frontier \
    (4.13)")
plt.xlabel("Standard Deviation (pct/day)")
plt.ylabel("Return (bps/day)")
```

```
plt.xlim(0,max(x2)+.5)
plt.grid()
plt.show();
```

#Code Segment 4.9:

```
#Add a risk-free asset at .1 bps/day
rfrate=10**(-5)
plt.figure(2)
plt.plot(xrisk,yreturn,marker='2')
plt.title("Figure 4.4: Beginning of franc, pound, \
    yen efficient frontier")
plt.xlabel("Standard Deviation (pct/day)")
plt.ylabel("Return (bps/day)")
plt.xlim(0,1)
plt.ylim(-.1,3.5)
plt.annotate('Riskfree asset (0,'+str(10000*rfrate)+')', \
            xy=(0, 10000*rfrate),xytext=(.2, 1), \
            arrowprops=dict(facecolor='black', \
            shrink=0.05),)
plt.grid()
plt.show();
```

#Code Segment 4.10:

```
#Print the tangency portfolio
rfvec=[rfrate]*3
tangencyport=(ci @ (m-rfvec))/(ucim-rfrate*uciu)
print('Tangency portfolio:',tangencyport)
#Solve for the lambda1 at tangency
mutp=tangencyport @ (m.T)
sigmatp=np.sqrt((tangencyport @ c) @ (tangencyport.T))
tpl1=(mutp-constmu)/lambdacoeff
print('TP mu=',mutp*10000,' bps/day')
print('TP sigma=',sigmatp*100,' pct/day')
print(f"lambda at tangency:",tpl1)
```

#Code Segment 4.11:

```
#Show capital market line
#Extend frontier
lambda1s=np.arange(0,tpl1+.5,.01)
```

```
xrisk=100*np.sqrt(lambdacoeff*lambda1s**2+1/uciu)
yreturn=10000*(lambdacoeff*lambda1s+constmu)

#Compute line
x=np.arange(0,max(xrisk),.01)
y=100*((mutp-rfrate)/sigmatp)*x+10000*rfrate

plt.figure(3)
plt.plot(xrisk,yreturn)
plt.plot(x,y)
plt.annotate('Tangency portfolio', \
            xy=(sigmatp*100, mutp*10000), \
            xytext=(1,mutp*10000), \
            arrowprops=dict(facecolor='black', \
            shrink=0.05),)
plt.title("Figure 4.5: Capital market line + franc, \
    pound, yen efficient frontier")
plt.xlabel("Standard Deviation (pct/day)")
plt.ylabel("Return (bps/day)")
plt.xlim(0,max(xrisk)+.5)
plt.grid()
plt.show;
```

```
#Code Segment 4.12:
```

```
#Compute James-Stein and Jorion estimates of mean based \
    on previous year
import scipy.spatial as spsp

#Search for end of previous year
for i in range(260,200,-1):
    if lgdates[-i][:4]==lastday[:4]:
        prev_year_n=len(lgdates)-i
        prev_year_date=lgdates[-i-1]
        break

#Form mean vector and covariance matrix up to end of \
    previous year
prev_m=np.average(d[:prev_year_n],axis=0)
prev_c=np.cov(d[:prev_year_n].T)
prev_ci=np.linalg.inv(prev_c)
prev_dim=len(prev_m)
#Set the central prior
central_m=[np.average(prev_m)]*prev_dim
```

```python
#James-Stein estimate of mean
#Compute scale factor s
s_js=min(1.,(prev_dim-2)/(prev_year_n*spsp.distance. \
    mahalanobis(prev_m,central_m,prev_ci)**2))
james_stein_m=np.multiply(1-s_js,prev_m)+np. \
    multiply(s_js,central_m)
print("James-Stein shrinkage factor:",s_js,"; \
    common mean:",np.average(prev_m))
print("James-Stein estimate of mean as of  \
    "+prev_year_date,":",james_stein_m)


#Jorion estimate - get minimum variance portfolio's mean
prev_min_var_mean=(prev_m @ (prev_ci @  \
    ([1]*prev_dim)))/np.sum(prev_ci)
central_m_jorion=[prev_min_var_mean]*prev_dim
s_jorion=spsp.distance. \
    mahalanobis(prev_m,central_m_jorion,prev_ci)**2
s_jorion=min(1.,(prev_dim+2)/ \
    (prev_dim+2+prev_year_n*s_jorion))
jorion_m=np.multiply(1-s_jorion,prev_m)+np. \
    multiply(s_jorion,central_m_jorion)
print("\nJorion shrinkage factor:",s_jorion,"; \
    minimum variance mean:",prev_min_var_mean)
print("Jorion estimate of mean as of "+prev_year_date, \
    ":",jorion_m)
```

#Code Segment 4.13:

```python
# Ledoit-Wolf heuristic covariance estimator 4.27
# Scikit-Learn Ledoit-Wolf covariance estimator

# Form the three-currency correlation matrix as of \
    previous year
prev_sig=np.sqrt(np.diag(np.diag(prev_c)))
prev_sig_inverse=np.linalg.inv(prev_sig)
prev_r_matrix=(prev_sig_inverse @ prev_c) @ \
    prev_sig_inverse

# Get average correlation (off-diagonal)
prev_avg_corr=(np.sum(prev_r_matrix)-prev_dim)/ \
    (prev_dim**2-prev_dim)
```

```python
# Get average variance
prev_avg_variance=np.matrix.trace(prev_c)/prev_dim
# Centralized prior
prev_prior=prev_avg_variance* \
    (np.ones((prev_dim,prev_dim))*prev_avg_corr+ \
    np.identity(prev_dim)*(1-prev_avg_corr))

# Compute shrinkage intensity modified from 4.47
shrink_d=np.linalg.norm(prev_c-prev_prior)/np. \
    sqrt(prev_dim)

# b-squared as in 4.26
shrink_b_sq=0
for i in range(prev_year_n):
    mtrx=d[i].reshape(-1,1)
    shrink_b_sq+=np.linalg.norm(mtrx.dot(mtrx.T) \
        -prev_c)**2
shrink_b_sq/=prev_year_n**2
shrink_b_sq/=prev_dim

s_ledoit_wolf_heuristic = min(1,shrink_b_sq/shrink_d**2)

# Ledoit-Wolf estimate
ledoit_wolf_est = \
    np.multiply(1-s_ledoit_wolf_heuristic,prev_c) + \
    np.multiply(s_ledoit_wolf_heuristic,prev_prior)

print("As of",prev_year_date+":")
print("Ledoit-Wolf heuristic shrinkage factor: \
    ",s_ledoit_wolf_heuristic)
print("Average correlation:",prev_avg_corr,"; \
    average variance:",prev_avg_variance)
print("Ledoit-Wolf heuristic covariance estimate: \
    \n",ledoit_wolf_est)

# Use Scikit-Learn version
from sklearn.covariance import LedoitWolf
cov = LedoitWolf().fit(d)
print("Scikit-Learn Ledoit-Wolf shrinkage factor:", \
    cov.shrinkage_)
print("Scikit-Learn Ledoit-Wolf covariance estimate: \
    \n",cov.covariance_)
```

#Code Segment 4.14:

```python
import scipy.stats as spst
#Hotelling's test for james_stein and jorion

def hotelling(T1,T2,p,m1,m2,s1,s2):
    #Compute Hotelling's statistic and p value

    #Combined covariance matrix
    scomb=((T1-1)*s1+(T2-1)*s2)/(T1+T2-2)

    #Multiplier for statistic
    hmult=(T1+T2-p-1)*T1*T2/((T1+T2-2)*p*(T1+T2))

    #Matrix algebra for statistic
    if p==1:
        h12=hmult*(m1-m2)**2/scomb
    else:
        h12=hmult*((m1-m2) @ np.linalg.inv(scomb)) @ \
            (m1-m2)

    p_value = 1.0 - spst.f.cdf(h12, p, T1+T2-1-p)
    #Note when the dimension p=1, p_value will equal \
        spst.ttest_ind(x1,x2)

    return(h12,p_value)

# Compute mean vector of latest year

latest_m = np.average(d[prev_year_n:],axis=0)

# Compute covariance matrix of latest year
latest_c = np.cov(d[prev_year_n:].T)

# James-Stein
h12_js, p_js = hotelling(prev_year_n,len(d)-prev_year_n, \
    prev_dim,james_stein_m, latest_m, prev_c, latest_c)

# Jorion
h12_jo, p_jo = hotelling(prev_year_n,len(d)-prev_year_n, \
    prev_dim,jorion_m, latest_m, prev_c, latest_c)

print("Comparing mean vector estimates as of", \
    prev_year_date)
```

```
print("    with mean vector for year ending", \
    lastday+":\n")
print("Hotelling statistics for James-Stein,\
    Jorion:",h12_js,h12_jo)
print("P-values for James-Stein, Jorion:",p_js,p_jo)
if p_js > p_jo:
    print("    James-Stein has higher p-value\n")
else:
    print("    Jorion has higher p- value\n")

def signif_print(thresh,str_name,str_type,p_value):
#Print out text explaining significance
    one_minus_thresh=(1-thresh)*100

    if p_value < thresh:
        str_p=str_name+"Reject null hypothesis of \
            equal "+str_type
        str_p+=" at %2.f" % one_minus_thresh
    else:
        str_p=str_name+"Cannot reject null hypothesis \
            of equal "+str_type
        str_p+=" at %2.f" % one_minus_thresh
    str_p+="% significance"
    print(str_p)
#Done with signif_print

thresh=.01
signif_print(thresh,"James-Stein: ","means",p_js)
signif_print(thresh,"Jorion: ","means",p_jo)
```

#Code Segment 4.15:

```
# Apply Levene's Test to three-currency example with \
    previous years
# compared to latest year
#Note the results shown are the same as
#scipy.stats.levene(d[:prev_year_n,k],d[prev_year_n:,k], \
    center='mean')

def levene(x1,x2):

    #Numbers of observations
    T1=len(x1)
```

```python
    T2=len(x2)
    #Could also use median
    m1=np.average(x1)
    m2=np.average(x2)
    #Form absolute difference observations
    z1j=[np.abs(x1[j]-m1) for j in range(T1)]
    z2j=[np.abs(x2[j]-m2) for j in range(T2)]
    #Average absolute difference in each set
    z1=np.average(z1j)
    z2=np.average(z2j)
    #Overall average difference
    z=(T1*z1+T2*z2)/(T1+T2)


    levene_mult=T1+T2-2
    levene_numer=T1*(z1-z)**2+T2*(z2-z)**2
    levene_denom=np.sum((z1j-z1)**2)+np.sum((z2j-z2)**2)


    levene_stat=levene_mult*levene_numer/levene_denom


    p_value = 1 - spst.f.cdf(levene_stat, 1, T1+T2-2)


    return(levene_stat,p_value)
#Done with levene

print("Comparing variances up to",prev_year_date, \
    "with year ending "+lastday+":")
for i in range(prev_dim):

    lstat, p_value = levene(d[:prev_year_n,i], \
        d[prev_year_n:,i])
    print("Levene statistic for "+seriesnames[i]+": \
        ",lstat,", p-value: ",p_value)
    x,y = spst.levene(d[:prev_year_n,i], \
        d[prev_year_n:,i],center='mean')
    print("Cross-check: results of scipy.stats.levene:", \
        x,y)
    signif_print(thresh,seriesnames[i]+": \
        ","variances",p_value)
```

#Code Segment 4.16:

```
# Box M Test for covariance matrices
# From G.E.P. Box, "A General Distribution Theory for \
    a Class of Likelihood Criteria",
# Biometrika 36, December 1949, pp. 317-346.


def BoxM(T1,T2,s1,s2):
    #Tests for equality of two covariance matrices,\
        s1 and s2
    #T1 and T2 are numbers of observations for s1 and s2
    #Returns M statistic and p-value

    #Make sure dimension is common
    if len(s1)!=len(s2):
        print("Error: different dimensions in Box M \
            Test:",len(s1),len(s2))
        return(0,0)
            .

    #Matrices are pxp
    p=len(s1)

    #Form the combined matrix
    scomb=(T1*s1+T2*s2)/(T1+T2)

    #Box M statistic
    Mstat=(T1+T2-2)*np.log(np.linalg.det(scomb))-(T1-1)* \
        np.log(np.linalg.det(s1))-(T2-1)*np. \
        log(np.linalg.det(s2))

    #Multipliers from equation (49) in Box 1949.
    A1=(2*p**2+3*p-1)/(6*(p+1))
    A1*=(1/(T1-1)+1/(T2-1)-1/(T1+T2-2))

    A2=(p-1)*(p+2)/6
    A2*=(1/(T1-1)**2+1/(T2-1)**2-1/(T1+T2-2)**2)

    discrim=A2-A1**2

    #Degrees of freedom
    df1=p*(p+1)/2

    if discrim <= 0:
        #Use chi-square (Box 1949 top p. 329)
```

```
            test_value=Mstat*(1-A1)
            p_value=1-spst.chi2.cdf(test_value,df1)
        else:
            #Use F Test (Box 1949 equation (68))
            df2=(df1+2)/discrim
            b=df1/(1-A1-(df1/df2))
            test_value=Mstat/b
            p_value=1-spst.f.cdf(test_value,df1,df2)


    return(test_value,p_value)
#Done with BoxM

print("Comparing variances up to",prev_year_date, \
    "with year ending "+lastday+":")

#Apply to sample variances
stat, p_value = BoxM(prev_year_n,len(d)-prev_year_n, \
                    np.diag(np.diag(prev_c)), \
                    np.diag(np.diag(latest_c)))
print("Box M-stat and p-value for sample variances \
    only:",stat,p_value)
signif_print(thresh,"","sample variances only",p_value)

#Compute latest correlation matrix
latest_sig=np.sqrt(np.diag(np.diag(latest_c)))
latest_sig_inverse=np.linalg.inv(latest_sig)
latest_r_matrix=(latest_sig_inverse @ latest_c) @ \
    latest_sig_inverse

#Apply to sample correlations
stat, p_value = BoxM(prev_year_n,len(d)-prev_year_n, \
    prev_r_matrix, latest_r_matrix)
print("\nBox M-stat and p-value for sample correlation \
    matrices:",stat,p_value)
signif_print(thresh,"","sample correlation matrices", \
    p_value)

#Apply to Ledoit-Wolf heuristic correlations
lwh_sig=np.sqrt(np.diag(np.diag(ledoit_wolf_est)))
lwh_sig_inverse=np.linalg.inv(lwh_sig)
lwh_r_matrix=(lwh_sig_inverse @ ledoit_wolf_est) @ \
    lwh_sig_inverse
```

```
stat, p_value = BoxM(prev_year_n,len(d)-prev_year_n, \
    lwh_r_matrix, latest_r_matrix)
print("\nBox M-stat and p-value for Ledoit-Wolf \
    heuristic vs. "+"latest sample correlations:", \
    stat,p_value)
signif_print(thresh,"","correlation matrices",p_value)
```

#Code Segment 4.17:

```
#Resample the minimum variance portfolio from 3-currency \
    example
np.random.seed(662607)

samp_size=1000
samp_time_periods=1000
samp_stds=[]
samp_means=[]
samp_portfolios=[]
for trial in range(samp_size):
    #Generate a virtual history of returns in x
    x=np.random.multivariate_normal(m,c,samp_time_periods)
    #Compute the virtual history's mean, covariance, and \
        inverse covariance
    samp_m=np.mean(x,axis=0)
    samp_c=np.cov(x.T)
    samp_ci=np.linalg.inv(samp_c)
    #Compute minimum variance portfolio s_vec2 according \
        to new parameters
    s_uciu=np.sum(samp_ci)
    s_vec2=(samp_ci @ u)/s_uciu
    #Find the mean and standard deviation of
    #this portfolio according to the old parameters
    samp_means.append(10000*(s_vec2 @ m))
    samp_stds.append(100*np.sqrt((s_vec2 @ c) @ s_vec2))
    samp_portfolios.append(s_vec2)

#Plot the minimum variance portfolios
plt.scatter(samp_stds,samp_means,marker='o',color='green')
#Plot the original MV portfolio
plt.scatter(np.sqrt(10000./uciu),10000.*ucim/uciu, \
    marker='*',color='red')
#Plot the average of the resampled MV portfolios
```

```
plt.scatter(np.mean(samp_stds),np.mean(samp_means), \
    marker='x',color='blue')
#Zoom in on the x-range
xdiff=np.max(samp_stds)-np.min(samp_stds)
plt.xlim(np.min(samp_stds)-.05*xdiff, \
    np.max(samp_stds)+.05*xdiff)
plt.title('Figure 4.6: Resampled minimum variance \
    portfolios')
plt.xlabel('Standard Deviation (pct/day)')
plt.ylabel('Return (bps/day)')
plt.grid(True)
plt.show();
```

#Code Segment 4.18:

```
#Show the 95% confidence intervals for the MV portfolio
bottom=np.percentile(samp_portfolios,5,axis=0)
middle=np.percentile(samp_portfolios,50,axis=0)
top=np.percentile(samp_portfolios,95,axis=0)
print("95% confidence for MV portfolio:")
print("                    (CHF     GBP     JPY)")
print("Bottom of interval: ",bottom)
print("Middle of interval: ",middle)
print("Original MV port:   ",vec2)
print("Top of interval:    ",top)
```

#Code Segment 4.19:

```
#Fake "market" for the three currencies
wmkt=np.array([.05,.15,.8])
mumkt=wmkt @ (m.T)
varmkt=(wmkt @ c) @ (wmkt.T)
print('Mkt mu=',mumkt*10000,' bps/day')
print(f'Mkt sigma\N{SUPERSCRIPT TWO}=',varmkt*10000, \
    f'(%/day)\N{SUPERSCRIPT TWO}')
```

#Code Segment 4.20:

```
betavec=(c @ wmkt)/varmkt
print('beta =',betavec)

mucapm=np.multiply(10000,rfvec+(mumkt-rfrate)*betavec)
print('mu-CAPM=',mucapm,' bps/day')
```

\#Code Segment 4.21:

```python
#View that pounds will outperform yen
view=np.array([0,1,-1])
pview=.00002

gamma=np.matrix([.0001])
sweight=1

#First Black-Litterman matrix calculation
print('C-inverse/s=',ci/sweight)
#Second matrix
v1=(np.matrix(view).T) @ np.linalg.inv(gamma)
vgvmtrx=v1 @ np.matrix(view)
print('V\'(Gamma-inverse)V=',vgvmtrx)
#Sum of the two
print('Sum=',ci/sweight+vgvmtrx)

m1inv=np.linalg.inv(ci/sweight+vgvmtrx)
print('Sum inverse (pct/day)**2=',m1inv*10000)
```

\#Code Segment 4.22:

```python
cimcs=(ci @ (mucapm/sweight))*10**(-4)
print('C-inverse*muCAPM/s=',cimcs)

print('V\'(Gamma-Inverse)p=',v1*pview)
m2=cimcs+v1.T*pview
print('Sum=',m2)
print("(All in units of days)")
```

\#Code Segment 4.23:

```python
mufinal=(m1inv @ (m2.T))*10000
print('Black-Litterman mu (bps/day):',mufinal)
```

\#Code Segment 5.1:

```python
#Optimize Idee's utility function
import numpy as np
import scipy.optimize as scpo
```

```python
def util(params):
    w,b=params
#Want to maximize utility, so minimize -disutility
    ufunc=(5*w-w**2)*(10*b-b**2)
    return(-ufunc)


#initial guess for parameters
init_params=[1.,0.]
#Run the minimization.
results = scpo.minimize(util,init_params,method='CG')
wealth, friends = results.x
print("Critical point wealth = %.1f, friends = %.1f" \
    % (wealth, friends))
print("Objective function at critical point: %.2f" \
    % results.fun)
```

#Code Segment 5.2:

```python
#Graph Idee's disutility function

import matplotlib.pyplot as plt
%matplotlib inline
import scipy.stats as spst
from mpl_toolkits.mplot3d import Axes3D
from matplotlib import cm
from matplotlib.ticker import LinearLocator, \
    FormatStrFormatter


#draw surface
fig, ax = plt.subplots(subplot_kw={"projection": "3d"}, \
    dpi=1200)


# Make data.
X = np.arange(0.,7.05,.05)
Y = np.arange(0.,12.05,.05)
X, Y = np.meshgrid(X, Y)
Z = util([X,Y])


# Plot the surface.
surf = ax.plot_surface(X, Y, Z, cmap=cm.rainbow, \
    linewidth=0, antialiased=False)
```

```
# Customize the z axis.
ax.zaxis.set_major_locator(LinearLocator(10))
ax.zaxis.set_major_formatter(FormatStrFormatter('%.0f'))
ax.view_init(ax.elev, ax.azim-170)

#Label axes
ax.set_xlabel('Wealth')
ax.set_ylabel('Friends')
ax.set_zlabel('Utility')

s_title="Figure 5.1: Locally convex disutility function"
plt.title(s_title)

plt.show();
```

#Code Segment 5.3:

```
#Gradient descent method for log(sum(exp(ai'x+bi))) \
    objective function

#Problem parameters
n=2; m=3    #variables, components of sum
a=np.zeroes((m,n))
a[0]=[1,3]
a[1]=[1,-3]
a[2]=[-1,0]
b=[-.1,-.1,-.1]
def objfunc(x):
    #This objective function is reasonably scaled so \
        not using order_magnitude adjustment
    sumexps=sum([np.exp(np.matmul(a[i],x)+b[i]) \
        for iin range(m)])
    return(np.log(sumexps))

#gradient of this objective function
def gradfunc(x):
    gradvec=np.zeros(n)
    sumexps=0.
    for i in range(m):
        this_exp=np.exp(np.matmul(a[i],x)+b[i])
        gradvec+=this_exp*a[i]
        sumexps+=this_exp
    return(gradvec/sumexps)
```

```python
def gradientmethod(xinit,objfunc,gradfunc,talkative):
    global order_magnitude    #variable used to size \
        objective function around 1
#Gradient descent method
    #Starting point
    x=xinit
    iteration=0
    #initialize order of magnitude - objfunc uses this \
        to scale objective
    order_magnitude=0.

    if talkative:
        print("Initial point:",x[0])
        print("Objective function at initial point:", \
            objfunc(x[0]))
        print("Gradient at initial point:",gradfunc(x[0]))

    #Parameters for backtracking
    alpha=.25
    beta=.75
    epsilon=10**(-8)
    maxiter=500

    #Iterate as long as necessary
    while True:
        deltax=-gradfunc(x[iteration])
        delta=1

        #Backtracking
        current_obj=objfunc(x[iteration])
        grad_squared=np.matmul(deltax,deltax)
        if talkative: print(iteration," obj:", \
            current_obj," grad^2:",grad_squared)
        if grad_squared < epsilon:
            break      #Done

        while True:
            y=x[iteration]+delta*deltax
            new_obj=objfunc(y)
            if new_obj > current_obj-delta*alpha* \
                grad_squared:delta*=beta
            else:
                break   #Backtracking done
```

```
        if talkative: print("Delta from backtracking:", \
        delta)
        x.append(y)
        iteration+=1
        if iteration > maxiter:
            break
    return(x)

#Starting point
xinit=[[1]*n]
x=gradientmethod(xinit,objfunc,gradfunc,True)

print("optimal x",x[-1])
print("optimal objective",objfunc(x[-1]))
print("gradient",gradfunc(x[-1]))
```

#Code Segment 5.4:

```
# Use Newton's method to optimize the previous function

def hessfunc(x,epsilon):
    #Hessian function computed by differencing gradient
    hessmatrix=np.zeroes((n,n))
    for i in range(n):
        deltai=np.zeroes(n)
        deltai[i]=epsilon
        xx=np.array(x)
        hessmatrix[i]=(gradfunc(xx+deltai)-gradfunc(xx)) \
            /epsilon
    return(hessmatrix)

def newtonmethod(xinit,objfunc,gradfunc,hessfunc):
    global order_magnitude     #variable used to size \
        objective function around 1

#Run Newton's Method with calls to objfunc, gradfunc,  \
    and hessfunc
    #Starting point
    x=xinit
    print(x[0])
```

```python
iteration=0
#initialize order of magnitude - objfunc uses this \
    to scale objective
order_magnitude=0.

#Parameters for backtracking
alpha=.25
beta=.75
epsilon=10**(-8)
maxiter=500

print("Objective function at initial point:", \
    objfunc(x[0]))
print("Gradient at initial point:",gradfunc(x[0]))
print("Hessian at initial point:",hessfunc(x[0], \
    epsilon))
print("Inverse Hessian initial:",np.linalg. \
 inv(hessfunc(x[0],epsilon)))

#Iterate as long as necessary
while True:
    deltax=-np.matmul(np.linalg. \
        inv(hessfunc(x[iteration],epsilon)), \
        gradfunc(x[iteration]))
    delta=1

    #Backtracking
    current_obj=objfunc(x[iteration])
    grad_hessinv_grad=np. \
        matmul(gradfunc(x[iteration]),deltax)
    print(iteration," obj:",current_obj, \
        " grad_hessinv_grad:",-grad_hessinv_grad)
    if -grad_hessinv_grad < epsilon:
        break        #Done

    while True:
        y=x[iteration]+delta*deltax
        new_obj=objfunc(y)
        if new_obj > current_obj+delta*alpha* \
            grad_hessinv_grad:
            delta*=beta
        else:
            break    #Backtracking done
```

```
        y=x[iteration]+delta*deltax
        print(delta,y)
        x.append(y)
        iteration+=1
        if iteration > maxiter:
            break
    #x has the x vector for each iteration, with the \
        last one
    #being the optimal (or last if ran out of iterations)
    return(x)


xinit=[[1]*n]
x=newtonmethod(xinit,objfunc,gradfunc,hessfunc)

print("optimal x:",x[-1])
print("iterations:",len(x)-1)
print("optimal objective:",objfunc(x[-1]))
print("gradient:",gradfunc(x[-1]))
print("Hessian",hessfunc(x[-1],10**(-8)))
```

#Code Segment 5.5:

```
# Use built-in scipy.optimize function to minimize
# the previous function

#initial guess for parameters
init_params=[1.]*n
#Run the minimization.
results = scpo.minimize(objfunc,
                        init_params, jac=gradfunc,
                        method='CG')
print(results.x)
print(objfunc(results.x),gradfunc(results.x))
```

#Code Segment 5.6:

```
#Illustrate smoothed delta function

def delta_norm(x,a):
    exparg=a*(x**2)
    return(a*np.exp(np.sign(x)*min(exparg,600)))
```

```
x=np.arange(-1.,-.001,.001)
for a in [2,20,200,2000]:
    scale=delta_norm(x[-1],a)
    y=[delta_norm(xx,a)/scale for xx in x]
    plt.plot(x,y,label="a="+str(a))

plt.title("Figure 5.2: Normal pdf-based approximation \
    to delta function")
plt.legend()
plt.show();
```

#Code Segment 5.7:

```
import pandas as pd
import qrpm_funcs as qf
#Get 3 currencies until the end of
#previous year. Form sample covariance matrix

lastday=qf.LastYearEnd()
#Swiss franc, pound sterling, Japanese Yen
seriesnames=['DEXSZUS','DEXUSUK','DEXJPUS']
cdates,ratematrix=qf.GetFREDMatrix(seriesnames, \
    enddate=lastday)
multipliers=[-1,1,-1]

lgdates,difflgs=qf.levels_to_log_returns(cdates, \
    ratematrix,multipliers)

#Mean vector and covariance matrix are inputs to \
    efficient frontier calculations
d=np.array(difflgs)
m=np.mean(d,axis=0)
c=np.cov(d.T)
```

#Code Segment 5.8:

```
#Do the optimization:
#minimize 1/2*w'Cw
#Subject to w'u=1
#           sum(wi^2)<= k
#where w is n-vector, u is unit n-vector
```

```
#Change to unconstrained barrier function where
# w=w0+Nx, x an n-1 vector.
#w0 is vector of all zeroes except for 1 in nth place
#N is nx(n-1) matrix with (n-1)x(n-1) identity matrix \
    I(n-1) in first
#n-1 rows, -u(n-1) in last row (u(n-1) unit vector of \
    size n-1)
#This gives function to be minimized over x:
# f(x)=omega*((1/2)*x'Fx+x'N'Cw0)- \
    delta((u(n-1)'x-1)^2+x'x-k)

#Parameters
omega=1
epsilon=10**(-8)
k_parameter=.4

def delta_smooth(x):
    #Compute smoothed delta function
    a=2000.
    exparg=a*x**2
    return(a*np.exp(np.sign(x)*min(exparg,600.)))

def barrierfunc(x):
    global k_parameter, omega, c, epsilon, order_magnitude
    #Create N matrix
    n=len(x)+1
    nmatrix=np.vstack([np.identity(n-1),[-1]*(n-1)])
    #Create w0 vector
    w0=[0]*(n-1)+[1]
    #Create F matrix = N'CN
    fmatrix=(nmatrix.T @ c) @ nmatrix
    #First part of objective function 1/2*x'Fx
    objfunction=((x @ fmatrix) @ x)/2.
    #Second part of objective function w0'CNx
    objfunction+=(w0 @ (c @ nmatrix)) @ x
    #Make order of magnitude of this part about one - \
        otherwise convergence is slow
    if order_magnitude == 0.:
        order_magnitude=np.abs(objfunction)
    objfunction*=(omega/order_magnitude)
    #Add in barrier
    u_times_x=sum(x)
```

```
        arg_delta = (u_times_x-1)**2 + (np.array(x) @ x) - \
            k_parameter
        objfunction+=delta_smooth(arg_delta)
        return(objfunction)

def barriergrad(x):
    #Take gradient of function by differencing
    n=len(x)
    epsilon=10**(-8)/n
    bf_x=barrierfunc(x)

    gradvec=np.array([-bf_x]*n)
    for i in range(n):     #perturb each argument a little
        little_vec=np.zeroes(n)
        little_vec[i]=epsilon
        gradvec[i]+=barrierfunc(np.add(x,little_vec))
    gradvec/=epsilon
    return(gradvec)

#Run initial step of barrier algorithm
i=0
xinit=[1/2,1/4]

order_magnitude=0.
x=gradientmethod([xinit],barrierfunc,barriergrad,True)

print("optimal x:",x[-1],1-sum(x[-1]))
print("iterations:",len(x)-1)
print("optimal objective:",barrierfunc(x[-1]))
print("gradient:",barriergrad(x[-1]))

#Pass on initial value for Barrier Algorithm iterations
xinit=x[-1]
```

#Code Segment 5.9:

```
#Iterate the barrier method using starting
#value from previous code segment

alpha=10
iter_barrier=1
omega*=alpha
```

```
while True:

    x=gradientmethod([xinit],barrierfunc,barriergrad,False)

    print("barrier iteration ",iter_barrier)
    print("optimal x:",x[-1],1-sum(x[-1]))
    print("iterations:",len(x)-1)
    print("optimal objective:",barrierfunc(x[-1]))
    print("gradient:",barriergrad(x[-1]))

    if iter_barrier == 5:
        break    #Done

    #Keep going with a bigger omega
    #Use solution as initial guess for next pass
    xinit=x[-1]
    iter_barrier+=1
    omega*=alpha
```

#Code Segment 5.10:

```
# Modified from cvxopt - originally for Figure 4.12 \
    in Boyd
# and Vandenberghe book. https://cvxopt.org/install/

from cvxopt import matrix
from cvxopt.blas import dot
from cvxopt.solvers import qp, options

n = 3
S = matrix(c)
pbar = matrix(m)

G = matrix(0.0, (n,n))
G[::n+1] = -1.0
h = matrix(0.0, (n,1))
A = matrix(1.0, (1,n))
b = matrix(1.0)

N = 100
mus = [ 10**(5.0*t/N-1.0) for t in range(N) ]
options['show_progress'] = False
xs = [ qp(mu*S, -pbar, G, h, A, b)['x'] for mu in mus ]
```

```
returns = [ dot(pbar,x) for x in xs ]
risks = [ np.sqrt(dot(x, S*x)) for x in xs ]

plt.plot(np.multiply(100.,risks), \
    np.multiply(10000.,returns))
plt.xlabel('standard deviation')
plt.ylabel('expected return')
plt.axis([0.4, 0.8, 0, 1.5])
plt.grid()
plt.title('Figure 5.3: Long-only efficient frontier \
    (like Fig 4.3)')
plt.yticks([0.0, 0.5, 1.0, 1.5])
plt.show();
```

#Code Segment 6.1:

```
import matplotlib.pyplot as plt
%matplotlib inline
import numpy as np
import pandas as pd
import qrpm_funcs as qf

#get sorted eigenvalues and eigenvectors
def eig_get(M):
    evals,evecs=np.linalg.eigh(M)   #eigh is for \
        symmetric M
    #Put the eigensystem in decreasing order of \
        eigenvalues
    sortorder=evals.argsort()[::-1]
    evals=evals[sortorder]
    evecs=evecs[:,sortorder]
    return(evals,evecs)

#Get 4 currencies until the end of previous year.
firstday='1999-01-04'
lastday=qf.LastYearEnd()
seriesnames=['DEXSZUS','DEXUSUK','DEXJPUS','DEXUSEU']
cdates,ratematrix=qf.GetFREDMatrix(seriesnames,
            startdate=firstday,enddate=lastday)
multipliers=[-1,1,-1,1]
```

```
lgdates,difflgs=qf.levels_to_log_returns(cdates, \
    ratematrix,multipliers)

#compute correlation matrix and covariance matrix \
    for later use
R=np.corrcoef(np.array(difflgs).T)
c=np.cov(np.array(difflgs).T)

#Make the scree plot
evals,evecs=eig_get(R)
plt.plot(range(1,5), list(evals*100/sum(evals)))

## Configure the graph
plt.title('Figure 6.1: Correlation scree plot,\
    currencies 1999-'+lastday[:4])
plt.xlabel('Eigenvalue rank')
plt.ylabel('Percent of trace')
plt.xlabel('Eigenvalue rank')
plt.xticks(range(1,5),range(1,5))
plt.grid(True)
plt.show;

#Display shape for Marchenko-Pastur
T,n = np.shape(difflgs)
print('n=%2f, T=%2f' % (n, T))

#Display eigenvalues
print('Eigenvalues:',evals)
```

#Code Segment 6.2:

```
#Graph Marchenko-Pastur PDF

for ratio in [n/T,.5]:
    g_minus=(1-np.sqrt(ratio))**2
    g_plus=(1+np.sqrt(ratio))**2

    print('Ratio = %2.6f' % ratio)
    print('    Expected range from %4.2f to %4.2f' \
        % (g_minus, g_plus))
```

```python
    x=np.arange(g_minus,g_plus,(g_plus-g_minus)/100)
    y=[(1/ratio)*np.sqrt(np.abs((g_plus-g)*(g-g_minus))) \
        /(2*np.pi*g) for g in x]
    label = '%2.6f' % ratio
    plt.plot(x, y, label=label)

## Configure the graph
plt.title('Figure 6.2: Marchenko-Pastur limit pdf')
plt.xlabel('Eigenvalue')
plt.ylabel('Prob. density')
plt.legend()
plt.grid(True)
plt.show;
```

#Code Segment 6.3:

```python
#Display the 4x4 covariance matrix
np.set_printoptions(precision=4,floatmode='fixed', \
    sign=' ')
print('1999-'+lastday[:4]+' covariance matrix (Cfull): \
    (%d days)' % len(difflgs))
print('      CHF     GBP     JPY     EUR')
for i in range(4):
    print(c[i]*10000)

#Compute 2008 covariance matrix
s2008=lgdates.index('2008-01-02')
e2008=lgdates.index('2008-12-31')
c2008=np.cov(np.array(difflgs[s2008-1:e2008+1]).T)
#Display the 4x4 covariance matrix
print('2008 covariance matrix (C2008):')
for i in range(4):
    print(c2008[i]*10000)
```

#Code Segment 6.4:

```python
#Display the eigenvalues
evals,evecs=eig_get(c)
print('Full period eigenvalues times 10**6:')
print(evals*1000000)

#Display the eigenvectors
print('Eigenvector (column) matrix:')
```

```
labels=['CHF','GBP','JPY','EUR']
for i in range(4):
    print(labels[i],evecs[i])
```

#Code Segment 6.5:

```
#get eigenvalues and eigenvectors of the 2008 matrix
evals2008,evecs2008=eig_get(c2008)

#Display the 2008 eigenvalues
print('2008 eigenvalues times 10**6:')
print(evals2008*1000000)

#Display the 2008 eigenvectors
print('2008 eigenvector (column) matrix:')
for i in range(4):
    print(labels[i],evecs2008[i])
```

#Code Segment 6.6:

```
#Compute and display currency covariance matrix
#based on fewer principal components with various \
    heuristics

def display_trunc(matrix,n_2_use=2):
    #Display matrix with truncated eigensystem

    #Round to integer
    num_2_use=int(n_2_use)

    evals,evecs=eig_get(matrix)

    #Form truncated diagonal matrix G of eigenvalues
    g_trunc=np.diag(evals)[:num_2_use]
    del_cols=np.arange(num_2_use,len(evals))
    g_trunc=np.delete(g_trunc,del_cols,1)

    #Form truncated matrix E_k of eigenvectors
    e_trunc=np.delete(evecs,del_cols,1)

    m_trunc=(e_trunc @ g_trunc) @ e_trunc.T
    m_scale=np.multiply(np.matrix.trace(matrix)/np. \
        matrix.trace(m_trunc),m_trunc)
```

```
    #Constant residual
    h=np.copy(evals)
    if n_2_use >= 4:
        residual=0
    else:
        residual=np.sum(evals[n_2_use:])/(4-n_2_use)
    for i in range(n_2_use,4):
        h[i]=residual
    m_constres=(evecs @ np.diag(h)) @ evecs.T

    print('Original matrix:')
    print('     CHF      GBP      JPY      EUR')
    for i in range(4):
        print(matrix[i]*10000)
    print('Truncated matrix:')
    for i in range(4):
        print(m_trunc[i]*10000)
    print('Scaled truncated matrix:')
    for i in range(4):
        print(m_scale[i]*10000)
    print('Constant residual matrix:')
    for i in range(4):
        print(m_constres[i]*10000)

while True:
    print("Input #eigenvectors to use (1-4), 0 to stop")
    n_to_use=int(input())
    if n_to_use<1:
        break
    display_trunc(c,n_to_use)
```

#Code Segment 7.1:

```
#Compare 1000 coin tosses to a normal distribution
import scipy.stats as spst
import numpy as np
import matplotlib.pyplot as plt
%matplotlib inline

n, p = 1000, 0.5
mean, var, skew, kurt = spst.binom.stats(n, p, \
    moments='mvsk')
```

```
x = np.arange(spst.binom.ppf(0.001, n, p), \
    spst.binom.ppf(0.999, n, p))
plt.plot(x, spst.binom.pmf(x, n, p), 'bo', ms=8, \
    label='binomial')
plt.plot(x, spst.norm.pdf(x, loc=mean, \
    scale=np.sqrt(var)), 'ro', label='normal')
plt.title('Figure 7.1: n=1000 binomial vs. normal pdf')
plt.xlabel('Number of heads')
plt.ylabel('Probability density/mass')
plt.legend(loc='best')
plt.grid(True)
plt.show();
```

#Code Segment 7.2:

```
import matplotlib.pyplot as plt
%matplotlib inline
import numpy as np
import pandas as pd
import qrpm_funcs as qf
#Get 3 currencies until the end of previous year.

lastday=qf.LastYearEnd()
#Swiss franc, pound sterling, Japanese Yen
seriesnames=['DEXSZUS','DEXUSUK','DEXJPUS']
cdates,ratematrix=qf.GetFREDMatrix(seriesnames, \
    enddate=lastday)
multipliers=[-1,1,-1]
lgdates,difflgs=qf.levels_to_log_returns(cdates, \
    ratematrix,multipliers)

#Make the Q-Q plot of Swiss francs
chf=[row[0] for row indifflgs]
mean_chf=np.mean(chf)
stdev_chf=np.std(chf)
nobs_chf=len(chf)

#Plot the diagonal
x=spst.norm.ppf([i/(nobs_chf+1) for i in
        range(1,nobs_chf+1)])
line=plt.plot(x, x)
plt.setp(line, linewidth=2, color='r')
```

```
#Plot the actuals
y=np.sort(np.array((chf-mean_chf)/stdev_chf))
plt.scatter(x, y, s=40, c='g')

#Find positive outlier
bigplus=max(y)
plt.annotate('January 15, 2015', xy=(max(x), bigplus), \
            xytext=(0, bigplus),arrowprops= \
            dict(facecolor='black', shrink=0.02),)

#Find negative outlier
bigminus=min(y)
plt.annotate('September 6, 2011', xy=(min(x), bigminus), \
            xytext=(.5*min(x), bigminus),
            arrowprops=dict(facecolor='black', \
            shrink=0.02),)

# Configure the graph
plt.title('Figure 7.2: Q-Q plot, CHF '+ \
        lgdates[0][:4]+'-'+lastday[:4]+ \
        ', '+str(nobs_chf)+' observations')
plt.xlabel('Standardized Inverse Normal')
plt.ylabel('Standardized Observed Log-return')
plt.grid(True)
plt.show;
```

#Code Segment 7.3:

```
#Make the P-P plot of Swiss francs
x=[i/(nobs_chf+1) for i in range(1,nobs_chf+1)]
#Plot the diagonal
line=plt.plot(x, x)
plt.setp(line, linewidth=2, color='r')
#Plot the actuals
y=np.sort(np.array(spst.norm.cdf((chf-mean_chf)/ \
    stdev_chf)))
plt.scatter(x, y, s=5, c='g')
## Configure the graph
plt.title('Figure 7.3: P-P plot, CHF  \
        '+ lgdates[0][:4]+'-'+lastday[:4]+ \
        ', '+str(nobs_chf)+' observations')
```

```
plt.xlabel('Fraction between 0 and 1')
plt.ylabel('Normal cdf of standardized observed \
    log-return')
plt.grid(True)
plt.show;
```

#Code Segment 7.4:

```
#Jarque-Bera
sk=spst.skew(chf)
ku=spst.kurtosis(chf)      #This gives excess kurtosis
jb=(nobs_chf/6)*(sk**2+(ku**2)/4)
chi2=spst.chi2.cdf(jb,2)
print('Skewness %f' % sk)
print('Excess Kurtosis %f' % ku)
print('Jarque-Bera Statistic %f' % jb)
print('Chi-squared probability non-normal %f' % chi2)
```

#Code Segment 7.5:

```
#Normal distribution probabilities
from tabulate import tabulate

out_table = [['%3.0f' % i,'%15.9f' % np.log10(spst. \
    norm.cdf(-i))] for i in range(21)]
headers=['Std. Devs','log10(prob)']

print('Table 7.1: Normal distribution probabilities \
    (log10)')
print(tabulate(out_table, headers, tablefmt='fancy_grid'))
```

#Code Segment 7.6:

```
#Get long bond/consol rates from 1703 to present
import matplotlib.pyplot as plt
%matplotlib inline
from urllib.request import Request, urlopen
import numpy as np
import pandas as pd
import datetime as datetime
import qrpm_funcs as qf
```

```python
lastday=qf.LastYearEnd()

#Get annual and monthly data from Bank of England \
    millenium study
url="www.bankofengland.co.uk/-/media/boe/files/ \
    statistics/research-datasets"
url+="/a-millennium-of-macroeconomic-data-for-the-uk.xlsx"
sheet1='A31. Interest rates & asset ps '    #Annual data \
    starting 1703
sheet2='M10. Mthly long-term rates'         #Monthly \
    data starting 1753
historical_lt=pd.read_excel(url,engine="openpyxl", \
    sheet_name=[sheet1,sheet2])

#Annual data
dates=[]
rates=[]
for i in range(21,71):
    end_year=str(historical_lt[sheet1]. \
        iloc[i][0])+"-12-31"
    dates.append(datetime.datetime. \
        strptime(end_year, "%Y-%m-%d"))
    rates.append(historical_lt[sheet1].iloc[i][19])

#Monthly data
end_days={'Jan': 31, 'Feb': 28, 'Mar': 31, 'Apr': 30, \
        'May': 31, 'Jun': 30,'Jul': 31, 'Aug': 31, \
        'Sep': 30, 'Oct': 31, 'Nov': 30, 'Dec': 31}
for i in range(12,len(historical_lt[sheet2])-5): \
        #Problems at the end of the sheet
    end_month=str(historical_lt[sheet2].iloc[i][0])+ \
        '-'+historical_lt[sheet2].iloc[i][1]
    end_month+='-'+str(end_days[historical_lt[sheet2]. \
        iloc[i][1]])
    dates.append(datetime.datetime.strptime(end_month, \
        "%Y-%b-%d"))
    rates.append(historical_lt[sheet2].iloc[i][10])

#Get recent long-term rates from Bank of England (up to \
    end of last year)
#Using format indicated in
#https://www.bankofengland.co.uk/boeapps/database/ \
    help.asp? Back=Y&Highlight=CSV#CSV
```

```python
#20-year rates splice the best with consol data
url="www.bankofengland.co.uk/boeapps/database/ \
    _iadb-fromshowcolumns.asp?csv.x=yes"
url+="&Datefrom=01/Jan/2016&Dateto=31/Dec/"+lastday[:4]
url+="&SeriesCodes=IUMLNZC&CSVF=TN&UsingCodes=Y"
myHeaders = {'User-Agent': 'Mozilla/5.0 (X11; Linux \
    x86_64) AppleWebKit/537.36 (KHTML, like Gecko) \
    Chrome/55.0.2883.87 Safari/537.36', \
            'Referer': 'https://www.bankofengland \
    .co.uk', 'Accept': 'text/html,application/xhtml+xml,\
    application/xml;q=0.9,image/webp,*/*;q=0.8'}
url_request = Request(url, headers=myHeaders)
data = urlopen(url_request )
recent_lt=pd.read_csv(data)

last_historic = dates[-1]
for i in range(len(recent_lt)):
    this_date = datetime.datetime. \
        strptime(recent_lt["DATE"].iloc[i], "%d %b %Y")
    if this_date>last_historic:
        dates.append(this_date)
        rates.append(recent_lt["IUMLNZC"].iloc[i])

df_longterm = pd.DataFrame(data={'Date': dates, \
    'Rate': rates})

df_long_annual = df_longterm.resample('A', on='Date'). \
    last()

years = [df_long_annual["Date"].iloc[i].year for i in \
    range(len(df_long_annual))]

#Display plot

n_years = len(df_long_annual)
stride = int(n_years/10)

plt.plot(range(n_years), df_long_annual["Rate"])
plt.xticks(np.arange(0,n_years,stride), \
    years[::stride],rotation='vertical')
str_title='Figure 7.4: UK government bond long-term \
    rates YE '
str_title+=str(df_long_annual["Date"].iloc[0].year)+'-'
```

```
str_title+=str(df_long_annual["Date"].iloc[-1].year)
plt.title(str_title)
plt.xlabel('Year')
plt.ylabel('Interest rate (percent)')
plt.grid(True)
plt.show;
```

#Code Segment 7.7:

```
#Compute lag-1 differences of long-term UK rate levels
df_diffs=df_long_annual.diff(). \
    drop(index=df_long_annual.index[0])

#Standardize
diff_mean=df_diffs["Rate"].mean(axis=0)
diff_std=df_diffs["Rate"].std(axis=0)
df_diffs["Rate"]=(df_diffs["Rate"]-diff_mean)/diff_std

#Find large moves
expected_max=-spst.norm.ppf(1./len(df_diffs))
bigger_count=abs(df_diffs["Rate"])>expected_max
print('Normal standard deviations for one in {} \
    years: {}'.format(len(df_diffs),expected_max))
print('Observations larger than that:')
print(df_diffs[bigger_count].sort_values \
    (by=['Rate'])['Rate'])
```

#Code Segment 7.8:

```
from scipy.stats import t
import matplotlib.pyplot as plt

highend=[6.,-3.]
title_strings=["Figure 7.5a: Overall view of \
    Student\'s T densities",
                "Figure 7.5b: Left cumulative tails of \
    Student\'s T distributions"]
plt.figure(figsize=(12,4))
for sp, top in enumerate(highend):
    plt.subplot(1, 2, sp+1)
    x = np.linspace(-6., top, 100)
    for d in (5,6,7,1000):
        if sp==0:
```

```
            plt.plot(x, t.pdf(x, d), lw=3, alpha=0.6, \
                label=str(d))
        else:
            plt.plot(x, t.cdf(x, d), lw=3, alpha=0.6, \
                label=str(d))
    plt.grid()
    plt.legend()
    plt.title(title_strings[sp])

plt.tight_layout()
plt.show();
```

#Code Segment 7.9:

```
#Generate mixed normal kurtosis graph using formula 7.20

#x contains fractions of the riskier distribution going \
    into the mix
x=np.arange(.05,.5,.05)

#y contains the multiple (how much riskier the riskier \
    distribution is than the less risky)
y=[5,10,15,20]

z=np.zeroes((len(y),len(x)))
for i,multiple in enumerate(y):
    for j,mixamount in enumerate(x):
        #numerator 7.20
        z[i,j] = mixamount*multiple**2
        z[i,j] = mixamount*multiple**2+1-mixamount
        #denominator 7.20
        z[i,j] /= (mixamount*multiple+1-mixamount)**2
        #multiply by 3 and subtract 3
        z[i,j] -= 1
        z[i,j] *= 3
    plt.plot(x,z[i,:],label=str(multiple))

plt.grid()
plt.legend()
plt.xlabel('Fraction of riskier distribution, '+r'$w_1$')
plt.ylabel('Kurtosis of mix')
plt.title('Figure 7.6: Kurtosis of mixtures of normals')
plt.show;
```

#Code Segment 7.10:

```
highend=[6.,-3.]
beta = 0      #symmetric
title_strings=["Figure 7.7a: Overall view of stable \
                distributions",
               "Figure 7.7b: Left cumulative tails of \
                stable distributions"]
plt.figure(figsize=(12,4))

for sp, top in enumerate(highend):
    plt.subplot(1, 2, sp+1)
    x = np.linspace(-6., top, 100)
    for alpha in [1.1,1.5,1.7,2]:
        if sp==0:
            plt.plot(x, spst.levy_stable.pdf(x, alpha, \
                beta),
                label=str(alpha))
        else:
            plt.plot(x, spst.levy_stable.cdf(x, alpha, \
                beta),
                label=str(alpha))
    plt.grid()
    plt.xlabel("t")
    p.t.ylabel("phi (t)"0)
    plt.legend()
    plt.title(title_strings[sp])

plt.tight_layout()
plt.show();
```

#Code Segment 7.11:

```
#Generate graph comparing standard Cauchy, Levy, and \
    normal densities
p10=np.arange(1,11,1)
x=np.exp(-p10*np.log(10))
ynormal=-spst.norm.ppf(x,0,1)
ycauchy=-spst.cauchy.ppf(x,0,1)
ylevy=spst.levy.ppf(1-x,0,1)

plt.plot(x,ynormal,label='Normal')
plt.plot(x,ycauchy,label='Cauchy')
plt.plot(x,ylevy,label='Levy')
```

```
plt.grid()
plt.xscale('log')
plt.xlabel('Frequency')
plt.yscale('log')
plt.ylabel('Observation size')
plt.legend()
plt.title('Figure 7.8: Inverse standard Normal, Cauchy,  \
    and Levy')
plt.show();

print('Observation sizes for p=.0001:')
print('Normal:',ynormal[3])
print('Cauchy:',ycauchy[3])
print('Levy:',ylevy[3])
```

#Code Segment 7.12:

```
import scipy as sp
#Generate tail densities for various alpha's
#using formula 7.30
x=np.arange(4.5,7.1,.1)
beta=0.0
gamma=1.0
alpha=[0.5,1.0,1.2,1.7,1.9]

for i,a in enumerate(alpha):
    tailscale=gamma**a
    tailscale*=np.sin(np.pi*a/2)
    tailscale*=sp.special.gamma(a)/np.pi
    tailscale*=(1+beta)
    row=[tailscale*x**(-a)]
    plt.plot(x,np.array(row[0]),label=str(a))

plt.grid()
plt.xlabel("z")
plt.ylabel("RHS Formula 7.30)
plt.legend()
plt.title("Figure 7.9: Tail cdf approximations,  \
    Formula 7.30")
plt.show;
```

#Code Segment 7.13:

```
#Generate maxima of uniform samples
maxima=[]
n_sample, n_trials=100, 1000

rng = np.random.default_rng(111)    #Use seed so repeatable
maxima=np.amax(np.split(rng.uniform(size=n_sample* \
    n_trials),n_trials),axis=1)

#generate histogram
n_per_bin, bins, patches = plt.hist(maxima, 50)

#generate theoretical density function; scale so area \
    under curve = n_trials
y=bins**(n_sample-1)
y*=n_trials/sum(y)

plt.plot(bins, y)
plt.title("Figure 7.10: Histogram of "+ \
        str(n_sample)+"-sample uniform maxima, " \
        +str(n_trials)+" trials")
plt.xlabel("Sample maximum")
plt.ylabel("Frequency")
plt.show();
```

#Code Segment 7.14:

```
#Generate Weibull, Gumbel and Frechet densities
#using 7.34 and 7.35

def gev(gamma,x):
    #Return pdf of a gev with parameter gamma at point x
    if gamma != 0:
        op_gamma_x = 1 + gamma*x
        if op_gamma_x > 0:     #make sure in the support
            oo_gamma_power=op_gamma_x**(-1/gamma)
            gev_cdf=np.exp(-oo_gamma_power)
            gev_pdf=oo_gamma_power*gev_cdf/op_gamma_x
        else:
            gev_pdf = np.nan
    else:   #gumbel
        gev_cdf = np.exp(-np.exp(-x))
        gev_pdf = np.exp(-x)*gev_cdf
    return(gev_pdf)
```

```
gamma_list=[-0.5,0.0,.5]
name_list=['Weibull','Gumbel','Frechet']
x_list=np.arange(-2.5,3.55,.05)

for i,gamma in enumerate(gamma_list):
    y=[gev(gamma,x) for x in x_list]
    plt.plot(x_list,y,label=name_list[i])

plt.grid()
plt.xlabel("X")
plt.ylabel("gev(x))
plt.legend()
plt.title('Figure 7.11: Generalized extreme value \
    densities')
plt.show();
```

```
#Code Segment 7.15:
```

```
#Get block maxima (actually minima since looking for big \
    losses) by
#grouping into 10-day blocks; using Swiss francs chf
blocksize=10; iblox=int(len(chf)/blocksize)
worstguys=-np.amin(np.split(np.array \
    (chf[:iblox*blocksize]),iblox),axis=1)

#Plot a histogram of block maxima. histogram is
#Long-tailed to the right so have a "more" category
num_bins=int(np.sqrt(len(worstguys))/2)
#Winsorize so long tail doesn't give unrealistic scale \
    of histogram.
#Winsorized values will show up in the highest bin of \
    the histogram.
prettybad=np.percentile(worstguys,99)
sortaworst=[min(x,prettybad) for x in worstguys]

n, bins, patches = plt.hist(sortaworst, num_bins)
plt.title('Figure 7.12: Block minima, CHF/USD 1971-' \
        +lastday[:4]+', '+str(len(worstguys))+' blocks')
plt.ylabel('Count')
```

```
plt.xlabel('Block minimum log-return')
plt.grid()
plt.show;
print('Worst observation:',np.max(worstguys))
print('Best block:',np.min(worstguys))
```

#Code Segment 7.16:

```
#Find the best fit extreme value distribuion to CHF \
    block maxima

xsample=np.sort(worstguys)
m_sample=len(xsample)
ysample=[(i+1)/(m_sample+1) for i in range(m_sample)]

#Use scipy.stats.genextreme to fit - "c" parameter is \
    minus gamma in our notation
fit_params = spst.genextreme.fit(xsample)
dist_name=['Frechet','Gumbel','Weibull'] \
    [int(np.sign(fit_params[0]))+1]

gma=-fit_params[0]; mu=fit_params[1]; sigma=fit_params[2]

print("Gamma=",gma)
print("Mu=",mu)
print("Sigma=",sigma)

#Make the Q-Q plot of extremes versus the best fit \
    distribution
#Inverse cumulative distribution of a probability p is:
#sigma*{((-ln(p))^(-gma)-1)/gma}+mu
#Equally spaced p's are in ysample. Don't have to \
    worry about gma=0 due to sampling noise
xgenex=(-np.log(ysample))**(-gma)-1
xgenex*=sigma/gma
xgenex+=mu
#Plot the diagonal
line=plt.plot(xgenex,xgenex)
plt.setp(line, linewidth=2, color='r')
#Plot the actuals
plt.scatter(xgenex,xsample, s=40, c='g')
tstr='Figure 7.13: Q-Q plot, CHF %d-day max loss vs. ' \
    % blocksize
```

```
tstr+=dist_name+', '+lgdates[0][:4]+'-'+lastday[:4]
plt.title(tstr)
plt.ylabel('Log-return loss')
plt.grid(True)
plt.show;
```

#Code Segment 7.17:

```
#Generate normal tails according to 7.44
xlist=np.arange(0,1.01,.01)
ulist=[2,3,4,5]

for u in ulist:
    fofu=spst.norm.cdf(u)
    y=[(spst.norm.cdf(x+u)-fofu)/(1-fofu) for x in xlist]
    plt.plot(xlist,y,label=str(u))

plt.grid()
plt.xlabel('x')
plt.ylabel('$F_u(x)$')
plt.legend()
plt.title('Figure 7.14: Standard normal tails')
plt.show();
```

#Code Segment 7.18:

```
#Create Generalized Pareto densities using 7.47
xlist=np.arange(0,3.05,.05)

#gamma=0; density is exp(-x)
plt.plot(xlist,[np.exp(-x) for x in xlist],label='0')

#gamma=-.5; upper limit is 2
shortlist=np.arange(0,2.05,.05)
y=[1-x/2 for x in shortlist]
y+=[np.nan]*(len(xlist)-len(shortlist))
plt.plot(xlist,y,label='-.5')

#gamma=-1; constant value of 1 up to 1
shortlist=np.arange(0,1.05,.05)
y=[1]*len(shortlist)
y+=[np.nan]*(len(xlist)-len(shortlist))
plt.plot(xlist,y,label='-1')
```

```
#gamma=-2; blows up at x=.5
#1/sqrt(1-2x)
shortlist=np.arange(0,.5,.05)
y=[1/(1-2*x)**.5 for x in shortlist]
y+=[np.nan]*(len(xlist)-len(shortlist))
plt.plot(xlist,y,label='-2',color='y')

plt.grid()
plt.xlabel("x")
plt.ylabel(gpd_gamma1(x))
plt.legend()
plt.title('Figure 7.15: Generalized Pareto densities \
    using 7.47')
plt.show();
```

#Code Segment 7.19:

```
#Generate 10,000 standard normal draws
#Take exceedances over threshold; show number and \
    average exceedance
threshold=2
n_sample=10000

rng = np.random.default_rng(314159)    #Use seed so \
    repeatable
sample = rng.normal(size=n_sample)

exceeds=[s-threshold for s in sample if s>threshold] \
    #Exceedance set over u=threshold

numex=len(exceeds)     #exceedance count
#Theoretical exceedance count
theo_numex=int(n_sample*spst.norm. \
    cdf(-threshold)+.5)

avex=np.mean(exceeds) #y-bar
#Theoretical average exceedance
theo_avex=np.exp(-threshold)/((1-spst.norm.
        cdf(threshold))*np.sqrt(2*np.pi))-threshold

#Sample maximum likelihood function 7.48
maxlike=-numex*(np.log(avex)+1)
```

```
#Theoretical maximum likelihood function
theo_maxlike=-theo_numex*(np.log(theo_avex)+1)

print('Sample number of exceedances over {0}: {1}'. \
    format(threshold,numex))
print('Theoretical number of exceedances: {0}'. \
    format(theo_numex))
print('\nSample average exceedance:',avex)
print('Theoretical average exceedance:',theo_avex)
print('\nSample maximum likelihood function at beta: \
    {0}'.format(maxlike))
print('Theoretical maximum likelihood function at beta: \
    {0}'.format(theo_maxlike))
```

#Code Segment 7.20:

```
import scipy.optimize as scpo

#Log-max-likelihood for GPD. Sign is reversed since \
    we are using minimize.
def gpd_lml(params):
    gma,beta_log=params
    #enforce positive beta
    beta=np.exp(beta_log)
    #check if gamma=0
    tolerance=10**(-9)
    if abs(gma)<tolerance:
        return(numex*(beta_log+avex/beta))
    #uses "exceeds" vector computed above
    log_sum=0
    #sum ln(1+gamma*yi/beta) when positive
    for i in range(numex):
        arg_log=1+gma*exceeds[i]/beta
        if arg_log<=0:
            log_sum+=1000*np.sign(1+1/gma)  #put a \
                very discouraging amount in the sum
        else:
            log_sum+=np.log(arg_log)
    #scale
    log_sum*=(1+1/gma)
    if beta<=0:
        log_sum+=1000
    else:
```

```
        log_sum+=numex*np.log(beta)
    return(log_sum)

#initial guess for parameters is gumbel
init_params=[0.,np.log(avex)]
#Run the minimization.
results = scpo.minimize(gpd_lml,
                        init_params,
                        method='CG')
gma_res,beta_res=results.x
beta_res=np.exp(beta_res)    #move back from log space

print("Optimal gamma:",gma_res)
print("Optimal beta:",beta_res)
print("Support cap mF:",-beta_res/gma_res)
print("Optimal LML:",-results.fun)
```

#Code Segment 7.21:

```
#Show the CDF plot
#x's are sorted values of the exceedances
xsample=np.sort(exceeds)
ysample=[(i+1)/(numex+1) for i in range(numex)]
ygumbel=[1-np.exp(-x/avex) for x in xsample]
yfitted=[1-(1+gma_res*x/beta_res)**(-1/gma_res) for x \
    in xsample]

plt.plot(xsample,ysample,label='Sample')
plt.plot(xsample,ygumbel,label='Gumbel')
plt.plot(xsample,yfitted,label='Fitted')

plt.grid()
plt.xlabel('Exceedance')
plt.ylabel('cdf')
plt.legend()
plt.title('Figure 7.16: cdfs of empirical, Gumbel,\
    and fitted distributions')
plt.show;
```

#Code Segment 7.22:

```
#Find the best fit generalized pareto distribution \
    to normal extrema

xsample=np.sort(exceeds)
m_sample=len(xsample)
ysample=[(i+1)/(m_sample+1) for i in range(m_sample)]

#Use scipy.stats.genpareto to fit
#The fit also finds a location parameter mu
gma_spst, mu_spst, beta_spst = spst.genpareto. \
    fit(xsample,gma_res)

print("scipy.stats optimal gamma, (7.48) gamma:", \
    gma_spst,gma_res)
print("scipy.stats optima mu, (7.48) mu:",mu_spst,0.)
print("scipy.stats optimal beta, (7.48) beta:", \
    beta_spst,beta_res)
```

#Code Segment 8.1:

```
%matplotlib inline
import pandas as pd
import qrpm_funcs as qf
import numpy as np
import matplotlib.pyplot as plt
from tabulate import tabulate
import scipy.stats as spst
#Get 3 currencies until the end of
#previous year. Form sample covariance matrix
#and do simple efficient frontier calculations

lastday=qf.LastYearEnd()
#Swiss franc, pound sterling, Japanese Yen
seriesnames=['DEXSZUS','DEXUSUK','DEXJPUS']
cdates,ratematrix=qf.GetFREDMatrix(seriesnames, \
    enddate=lastday)
multipliers=[-1,1,-1]

lgdates,difflgs=qf.levels_to_log_returns(cdates, \
    ratematrix,multipliers)
```

```python
#Mean vector and covariance matrix are inputs \
    to efficient frontier calculations
d=np.array(difflgs)
m=np.mean(d,axis=0)
c=np.cov(d.T)


#Show histogram of equal-weighted
#CHF-GBP-JPY log-changes
w=np.array([1/3]*3).T
#apply transform to get returns at portfolio level
portfolio=np.log(1+np.dot(np.exp(difflgs)-1,w))


#portfolio now contains the equal-weighted portfolio's
#log-returns. Create buckets - hist function doesn't
#seem to have "x or less" or "x or more" buckets
bucketnames=[]
bucketcounts=[]
#Bucket the end percentiles
low1=np.percentile(portfolio,1)
high1=np.percentile(portfolio,99)
bucketnames.append('<=%7.4f' % low1)
bucketcounts.append(sum(1 for x in portfolio if \
        low1 >= x))
#Count 20 even buckets in between low and high
nbucket=20
bucketwidth=(high1-low1)/nbucket
for i in range(20):
    attach=low1+i*bucketwidth
    detach=attach+bucketwidth
    mid=(attach+detach)/2
    bucketnames.append('%7.4f' % mid)
    bucketcounts.append(sum(1 for x in portfolio if \
     (x>=attach and x<=detach)))


#last bucket
bucketnames.append('>=%7.4f' % high1)
bucketcounts.append(sum(1 for x in portfolio \
    if x >= high1))


width=.5
plt.bar(range(nbucket+2),bucketcounts,width)
plt.xticks(range(nbucket+2),bucketnames, \
    rotation='vertical')
plt.grid()
```

```
plt.xlabel('Log-change')
plt.ylabel('Day count')
plt.title('Figure 8.1: Histogram of equal-weighted \
          CHF+GBP+JPY\n daily log-changes, '+ \
          lgdates[0][:4]+'-'+lastday[:4])
plt.show();


statnames,metrics,table=qf.StatsTable(np.exp(portfolio)-1)
headers=['Statistic','Value']
print(tabulate(table, headers, tablefmt='fancy_grid'))


port_log_ret=0
for t in range(len(d)):
    port_log_ret+=np.log(np.mean(np.exp(d[t,:])))
print('Portfolio cumulative return:', \
      np.exp(port_log_ret)-1)
print('Portfolio annual return:',np.exp(port_log_ \
    ret/int(len(d)/252))-1)
```

#Code Segment 8.2:

```
# get count
count=metrics[0]
#Transform logs to return space
x_returns=np.array(np.exp(difflgs)-1)
m_returns=np.mean(x_returns,axis=0)
c_returns=np.cov(x_returns.T)
# compute mean and std deviation directly from m and c
port_mean=np.dot(m_returns,w)
port_std=np.sqrt(np.matmul(np.matmul(w,c_returns),w))


#Redo histogram with normal assumption

bucketcounts=[]
bucketnames=[]
#Bucket the end percentiles
low1=port_mean+port_std*spst.norm.ppf(.01)
high1=port_mean+port_std*spst.norm.ppf(.99)
bucketwidth=(high1-low1)/nbucket
bucketcounts.append(spst.norm.cdf((low1-port_mean)/
      port_std)*count)
bucketnames.append('<=%7.4f' % low1)
for i in range(nbucket):
```

```python
        attach=low1+i*bucketwidth
        detach=attach+bucketwidth
        mid=(attach+detach)/2
        bucketnames.append('%7.4f' % mid)
        bucketcounts.append(spst.norm.pdf((mid-port_mean)/
            port_std)*count)


#last bucket
bucketcounts.append((1-spst.norm.cdf((high1-port_mean)/
        port_std))*count)
bucketnames.append('>=%8.4f' % high1)


width=.5
plt.bar(range(nbucket+2),bucketcounts,width)
plt.xticks(range(nbucket+2),bucketnames, \
    rotation='vertical')
plt.grid()
plt.xlabel('Log-change')
plt.ylabel('Day count')
plt.title('Figure 8.2: Histogram, delta-normal')
plt.show();


#Delta-normal calculations - redo the stats table
table_norm=np.copy(table)
table_norm[1][1]=str(port_mean+spst. \
    norm.ppf(1/(count+1))*port_std)      #min
table_norm[2][1]=str(port_mean+spst. \
    norm.ppf(count/(count+1))*port_std)      #max
table_norm[3][1]='%7.7f' % port_mean    #mean - should \
    be the same
table_norm[4][1]=table_norm[3][1]     #median - make it \
    equal the mean because normal
table_norm[5][1]=str(port_std)      #standard \
    deviation - use sqrt(w'Cw)
table_norm[6][1]="0"    #skewness - zero because normal
table_norm[7][1]="0"    #skewness - zero because normal
table_norm[8][1]="0"    #Jarque-Bera - zero because normal
table_norm[9][1]="1"    #Chi-squared - one because normal
table_norm[10][1]="0"    #Serial correlation - zero \
    by assumption
p=.99
norm_VaR=-(port_mean+spst.norm.ppf(1-p)*port_std)
table_norm[11][1]=str(norm_VaR)     #99% VaR - from formula
```

```
norm_cVaR=port_std*np.exp(-.5*(norm_VaR/port_std)**2)
norm_cVaR/=(1-p)*np.sqrt(2*np.pi)
norm_cVaR=-port_mean+norm_cVaR
table_norm[12][1]=str(norm_cVaR)      #99% cVar - from \
    formula
print(tabulate(table_norm, headers, \
    tablefmt='fancy_grid'))
```

#Code Segment 8.3:

```
#Compute gradient
port_gradient=np.matmul(c_returns,w)/port_std
print('Gradient (bps/day):',port_gradient)
print('Contributions to Std Dev:',port_gradient*w)
```

#Code Segment 8.4:

```
#Draw Cornish-Fisher admissability graph
stepsize=12*(np.sqrt(2)-1)/100
x=np.arange(-50*stepsize+.0001,
            50*stepsize,stepsize)
y1=[4*(1+11*(x/6)**2+np.sqrt((x/6)**4-6*(x/6)**2+1))][0]
y2=[4*(1+11*(x/6)**2-np.sqrt((x/6)**4-6*(x/6)**2+1))][0]
x=np.append(x,50*stepsize)
y1=np.append(y1,4*(1+11*(x[100]/6)**2))
y2=np.append(y2,4*(1+11*(x[100]/6)**2))
plt.plot(x,y1)
plt.plot(x,y2)
plt.fill_between(x,y1,y2,facecolor='green')
plt.xlabel('Skewness')
plt.ylabel('Excess Kurtosis')
plt.title('Figure 8.3: Allowed parameter combinations \
    for Cornish-Fisher')
plt.grid()
plt.show();
```

#Code Segment 8.5:

```
#Compute new z-score using 8.4
z=spst.norm.ppf(p)
znew=z-(1/6)*(z**2-1)*spst.skew(portfolio)
znew+=(z/24)*(z**2-3)*spst.kurtosis(portfolio)
```

```
znew-=(z/36)*(2*z**2-5)*spst.skew(portfolio)**2
print_str='Normal %2.f pct' % np.multiply(p,100.)
print_str+=" z: %8.5f" % z
print(print_str)
print('Cornish-Fisher: %8.5f' % znew)
#Compare with historical
hs_99VaR=-np.percentile(portfolio,1)
zhist=(hs_99VaR+port_mean)/port_std
print('Historical: %8.5f' % zhist)

#Show comparisons of VaRs
print_str='\nNormal %2.f pct' % np.multiply(p,100.)
print_str+=" VaR: %8.5f" % norm_VaR
print(print_str)
cf_99VaR=-port_mean+znew*port_std
print('Cornish-Fisher VaR: %8.5f' % cf_99VaR)
print('Historical VaR: %8.5f' % hs_99VaR)
```

#Code Segment 8.6:

```
#Show the Cholesky decomposition
#of the CHF-GPB-JPY covariance matrix
chol=np.linalg.cholesky(c)
print('(8.8) Cholesky decomposition of 3-currency \
      sample'+' covariance matrix:\n',chol*100)
```

#Code Segment 8.7:

```
#Generate random draws; use fixed seed to be replicable
from numpy.random import default_rng
rng = default_rng(12345678)

s_trial=rng.normal(0,1,size=[count,3])
logr_trial=np.matmul(chol,s_trial.T).T+m

#logr_trial has Monte Carlo log-returns; transform \
    to returns
r_trial=np.exp(logr_trial)-1

#Get trial portfolio returns
r_ptrial=np.matmul(r_trial,w)
print("Monte Carlo with simple normal draws")
statnames,mettrial,tabtrial=qf.StatsTable(r_ptrial)
print(tabulate(tabtrial, headers, tablefmt='fancy_grid'))
```

#Code Segment 8.8:

```
#Three-currency Monte Carlo with separate mixtures \
    of normals
import random

def mixparams(d_in):
    #Find mixture-of-2-normals parameters w1, r, and \
    sigma2 (7.20)
    sigma_mix=np.std(d_in)
    k_mix=spst.kurtosis(d_in)   #default is Fisher \
    (normal=0)
    k=k_mix/3.+1
    w_1=min(.05,.9/k)   #Avoid negative denominator in r
    r=(k*(1-w_1)*w_1+np.sqrt(w_1*(1.-w_1)*(k-1.)))/
        (w_1*(1-k*w_1))
    sigma_2=sigma_mix/np.sqrt(w_1*r+1.-w_1)
    return(w_1,r,sigma_2)
#Done with mixparams

rng = default_rng(33550336)    #5th perfect number
s_mix=[]
#Generate mix for each asset separately
for asset in range(len(d.T)):
    w1,r,s2=mixparams(d[:,asset])
    count_1=int(count*w1)
    count_2=count-count_1
    s_1=rng.normal(0,np.sqrt(r)*s2,size=count_1)
    s_2=rng.normal(0,s2,size=count_2)
    s_mix.append(random.sample(list(np.append(s_1,s_2)), \
    k=count))

#Cholesky factor of correlation matrix
corr_chol = np.linalg.inv(np.diag(np.sqrt \
    (np.diagonal(c)))) @ chol

#introduce covariance structure and translate
logr_mix=(corr_chol @ s_mix).T+m

#logr_mix has Monte Carlo log-returns; transform \
    to returns
ret_mix=np.exp(logr_mix)-1
```

```
#Get trial portfolio returns
ret_pmix=np.matmul(ret_mix,w)
print("Monte Carlo with leptokurtic mixtures of normals")
statnames,mettrial,tabtrial=qf.StatsTable(ret_pmix)
print(tabulate(tabtrial, headers, tablefmt='fancy_grid'))
```

#Code Segment 8.9:

```
#MCMC on 3x3 state transition matrix
import numpy as np
import matplotlib.pyplot as plt
from numpy.random import default_rng

rng = default_rng(138064852)   #Boltzmann

def tent(i,j):
    #Tent proposal distribution
    if j==i:
        return(2./3.)
    else:
        return(1./6.)

def transition(i,j):
    #Transition probability
    T=[[.6,.3,.1],[.3,.5,.2],[.1,.2,.7]]
    if i<0 or i>2 or j<0 or j>2 or (not \
    isinstance(i,int)) or (not isinstance(j,int)):
    return(0)
    return(T[i][j])

def picktent(x):
    #Pick a random state given previous state is x
    movers=[0,0,0,0,1,2]
    choose=rng.integers(0,6)
    pick=int(x+movers[choose])
    return(pick % 3)

n=1000   #Arbitrary
burnin=int(.2*n)

#Step 1
x=[0 for i in range(n)]
x[0]=1   #Start in middle state
```

```
for t in range(n-1):
    #Step 2
    s_t=picktent(x[t])
    #Step 3
    trans_ratio=transition(s_t,x[t])/transition(x[t],s_t)
    prop_ratio=tent(x[t],s_t)/tent(s_t,x[t])
    accept_ratio=trans_ratio*prop_ratio
    #Step 4
    u_t=rng.uniform()
    if accept_ratio >= u_t:
        x[t+1]=s_t
    else:
        x[t+1]=x[t]


for state in range(3):
    this_pct=sum([1 for samp in x[burnin:] if \
        samp==state])/(n-burnin)
    print_str="    State: %d" % state
    print_str+=" MCMC: %5.3f" % this_pct
    print_str+=" Theoretical: %5.3f" % float(1./3.)
    print(print_str)
```

#Code Segment 8.10:

```
#MCMC Gibbs Sampling to fill in missing data

need_data=True    #Indicator to make sure we got \
    previous year's data
lastday=qf.LastYearEnd()

while need_data:    #Get most recent year available
    firstday_e=str(int(lastday[:4])-10)+'-10-01' \
        #Go back 10 years (quarterly)
    #Quarterly economic data US, Euro, Japan
    seriesnames=['GDP','EUNNGDP','JPNNGDP']
    cdates,ratematrix=qf.GetFREDMatrix(seriesnames, \
        startdate=firstday_e, enddate=lastday)
    if not any(np.isnan(ratematrix[-1])):        #See if \
        we got desired data
        need_data=False
    else:    #go back a year
        lastday=str(int(lastday[:4])-1)+lastday[-6:]
```

```python
#Get log-changes of GDP data
lgdates_e,difflgs_e=qf.levels_to_log_returns(cdates, \
    ratematrix,[1,1,1])


#Monthly stock market data US, Euro, Japan
firstday_m=str(int(lastday[:4])-10)+'-09-01'  #Go back \
    10 years with quarter offset
seriesnames=['SPASTT01USM661N','SPASTT01EZM661N', \
    'SPASTT01JPM661N',]
cdates,ratematrix=qf.GetFREDMatrix(seriesnames, \
    startdate=firstday_m, enddate=lastday)
lgdates_m,difflgs_m=qf.levels_to_log_returns(cdates, \
    ratematrix,[1,1,1])


#Compute parameters explained in text
n_m=len(difflgs_m[0])                                       \
    #Number of monthly series
n_e=len(difflgs_e[0])                                       \
    #Number of quarterly series
T_m=len(difflgs_m)-3                                        \
    #Number of months in monthly series
T_e=len(difflgs_e)                                          \
    #Number of quarters in quarterly series
D_m=np.array(difflgs_m[:-3])                                \
    #Monthly data (n_m x T_m) (offset by a quarter)
D_e=np.array(difflgs_e)                                     \
    #Quarterly data (n_e x T_e)
mu_m=np.mean(D_m,axis=0)                                    \
    #Mean vector of monthly data
C_m=np.cov(D_m.T)                                           \
    #Covariance matrix of monthly data
mu_e=np.mean(D_e,axis=0)/3.                                 \
    #Month-ized mean vector of quarterly data
C_e=np.cov(D_e.T)/3.                                        \
    #Month-ized covariance matrix of quarterly data


#Monthly data quarter-ized and de-meaned
QD_m=[D_m[t]+D_m[t+1]+D_m[t+2]-3.*mu_m for t in \
    range(0,T_m,3)]


#Market/economic covariance matrix
C_me=(list(zip(*QD_m)) @ (D_e-np.tile(3.*mu_e,(T_e,1))))/ \
    (3.*T_e)
```

```
#Conditional distribution covariance matrix
C_e_bar_m=C_e-((C_me.T @ np.linalg.inv(C_m)) @ C_me)

#Set up for Gibbs sampler
y=np.zeroes((T_m,n_e))     #Output: pseudo-monthly \
    economic series
z=np.zeroes((T_m,n_e))     #pre-adjusted pseudo-monthly \
    economic series

#Step 1
x_t=mu_e
t=1
done=False
while not done:
    #Step 2 (python indexing convention off one from text)
    z[t-1]=rng.multivariate_normal(x_t,C_e_bar_m)
    #Step 3
    if t % 3 == 0: # This is a quarter-end
        adjust = (D_e[int(t/3)-1]-(z[t-1]+z[t-2]+ \
            z[t-3]))/3.
        for q in range(1,4):
            y[t-q]=z[t-q]+adjust
    #Step 4
    x_t=mu_e+((C_me.T @ np.linalg.inv(C_m)) @ \
    (D_m[t-1]-mu_m))
    t+=1
    done = (t > T_m)

#Plot quarterly economic series vs. monthly as \
    index values
names=['US','Europe','Japan']
for e in range(n_e):
    yy=np.exp(np.cumsum(y[:,e]))
    dd=[[D_e[i][e]/3]*3 for i in range(T_e)] \
        #straight-line interpolate quarterly to monthly
    DD=np.exp(np.cumsum(dd))
    plt.plot(range(T_m),yy)
    plt.plot(range(T_m),DD)
    plt.ylabel('Index')
    plt.xticks(range(0,T_m,12),lgdates_m[3:] \
    [::12],rotation=45)
    str_title='Figure 8.%d:' % (e+4)
```

```
        str_title+=seriesnames[e]+' ('+names[e]+'}'
        plt.title(str_title)
        plt.grid()
        plt.show();
```

#Code Segment 8.11:

```
#Sum last 3 conditional means
x_t=0
for t in range(-1,-4,-1):
    x_t+=mu_e+((C_me.T @ np.linalg.inv(C_m)) @ \
        (difflgs_m[-t]-mu_m))

print(f'Final quarterly mean vector for GDP log-changes,\
    quarter ending {lastday}')
for e in range(n_e):
    print('{:9}: {:8.5}'.format(names[e],x_t[e]))


#Display conditional covariance matrix
print('\nConditional covariance matrix:')
for e in range(n_e):
    print('{:9.6} {:9.6} {:9.6}'.format(C_e_bar_m[e][0], \
        C_e_bar_m[e][1],C_e_bar_m[e][2]))


#See if subsequent 1Q GDPs available
newday=str(int(lastday[:4])+1)+'-01-01'
seriesnames=['GDP','EUNNGDP','JPNNGDP']
cdates,ratematrix=qf.GetFREDMatrix(seriesnames, \
    startdate=lastday,enddate=newday)


#Show actual log-changes if available
print(f'\nActual log-changes of GDPs, first quarter  \
    {newday[:4]}')
for e in range(n_e):
    if not(np.isnan(ratematrix[-1][e])):
        lrt=np.log(ratematrix[-1][e]/ratematrix[0][e])
        print('{:9}: {:8.5}'.format(names[e],lrt))
    else:
        print('{:9}: Not available'.format(names[e]))
```

#Code Segment 9.1:

```
%matplotlib inline
import qrpm_funcs as qf
import numpy as np
#Find long-term standard deviation of US stock market
#Uses Ken French's website

#Cut off at last yearend
lastday=qf.LastYearEnd()
ld_yyyymm=int(lastday[:4]+lastday[5:7])
Date,market_minus_rf,SMB,HML,RF=qf.getFamaFrench3 \
    (enddate=ld_yyyymm)

ActualReality=qf.LogReturnConvert(market_minus_rf,RF)

#Compute overall monthly standard deviation
targetsd=np.std(ActualReality)

tstr='Annualized standard deviation of US stock market,\n'
tstr+=str(Date[0])[:6]+'-'+str(Date[len(Date)-1])[:6]
tstr+="(%.1f years)" % float(len(market_minus_rf)/12)
tstr+=': %.2f%%' % float(targetsd*np.sqrt(12))
print(tstr)
```

#Code Segment 9.2:

```
#Generate virtual reality with random normal draws with \
    targetsd
import random

random.seed(3.14159265)
VirtualReality=[random.gauss(0,targetsd) for i in \
    range(len(ActualReality))]

#Generate sample standard deviations for 3 lookback \
    periodicities
lookbacks=[12,36,60]
SampleSd=qf.GenSampleSd(VirtualReality,lookbacks)

#Draw the graph with 3 lines for the 3 periodicities
colors=['y-','b-','r-']
```

```
tstr='Figure 9.1, Virtual US Stocks '+str(Date[0])[:6]
tstr+='-'+str(Date[len(Date)-1])[:6]
tstr+=', annual sigma=%.2f' % float(targetsd*np.sqrt(12))
qf.PlotSampleSd(tstr,Date,SampleSd,lookbacks,colors)
```

#Code Segment 9.3:

```
#Generate sample standard deviations
lookbacks=[12,36,60]
SampleSd=qf.GenSampleSd(ActualReality,lookbacks)

#Graph
colors=['y-','b-','r-']
tstr='Figure 9.2, Actual US Stocks Sample Std Dev ' \
    +str(Date[0])[:6]
tstr+='-'+str(Date[len(Date)-1])[:6]
qf.PlotSampleSd(tstr,Date,SampleSd,lookbacks,colors)
```

#Code Segment 9.4:

```
import matplotlib.pyplot as plt
#Draw graph showing payoff pattern of put,
#call and straddle

underprices=np.arange(80,121,1)

strike=100
cost=5
putprices=np.maximum(strike-underprices,0)-cost
callprices=np.maximum(underprices-strike,0)-cost
straddleprices=putprices+callprices

plt.plot(underprices,putprices,label='Put',linestyle=':')
plt.plot(underprices,callprices,label='Call', \
    linestyle=':')
plt.plot(underprices,straddleprices,label='Straddle')
plt.title('Figure 9.3 - Put, call, straddle payoffs')
plt.legend()
plt.grid()
plt.show()
```

#Code Segment 9.5:

```
import pandas as pd
#Get VXO and VIX from Fred and
#graph them.

lastday=qf.LastYearEnd()
seriesnames=['VXOCLS','VIXCLS']
cdates,ratematrix=qf.GetFREDMatrix(seriesnames,
            enddate=lastday)

#Get rid of double nan's
vols=[ratematrix[i] for i in range(len(ratematrix)) if \
    pd.notna(ratematrix[i]).any()]
vdates=[cdates[i] for i in range(len(ratematrix)) if \
    pd.notna(ratematrix[i]).any()]

#vols now has VXO and VIX data where at least
#one of them is present.
x=range(len(vdates))
vxo=[row[0] for row in vols]
vix=[row[1] for row in vols]
plt.plot(x,vxo,label='VXO')
plt.plot(x,vix,label='VIX')
plt.title('Figure 9.4: Implied Volatilities '+ \
    vdates[0][:4]+'-'+vdates[len(vdates)-1][:4])

xskip=np.arange(0,len(vdates),1600)
tikskip=[vdates[x][:7] for x in xskip]
plt.xticks(xskip,tikskip)
plt.ylabel('Annual Implied Vol')
plt.legend()
plt.grid()
plt.show;

#10 largest dates
import heapq
print("Dates of 10 largest")
print([vdates[x] for x in heapq.nlargest(10, \
    range(len(vxo)), key=vxo.__getitem__)])
#Yearend VIX
print("Yearend VIX",vix[-1])
```

#Code Segment 9.6:

```
#Draw implied vols on two dates by moneyness
#Use downloaded file YYYY-12-31 from CBOE with all \
    option prices on that day
#The full file takes a LONG time to read in.
#Separate code needs to be run once a year before this \
    code segment; it
#is in Process_CBOE_file.ipynb and reads in file from \
    CBOE datashop and
#outputs SPX_UnderlyingOptionsEODCalcs_YYYY1231.xlsx.

import pandas as pd
import numpy as np
import datetime
import matplotlib.pyplot as plt
%matplotlib inline

#Get all SPX options on CBOE as of December 31 of \
    last year
yearend_string=str(datetime.datetime.now().
        year-1)+"-12-31"
df_opts=pd.read_excel(r"SPX_UnderlyingOptionsEODCalcs_" \
                    +yearend_string+".xlsx", \
                    engine="openpyxl")

#Subset the S&P 500 options with underlying SPX \
    (eliminate SPXW, weekly expirations)
df_spx = df_opts[(df_opts.underlying_symbol == "^SPX") & \
    (df_opts.root == "SPX")]

#Get S&P 500 price and quote date
spx_price = df_spx.active_underlying_price_1545. \
    unique()[0]
quote_date = df_spx.quote_date.unique()[0]
stqd = str(quote_date)[:10]    #Display version YYYY-MM-DD

#Look between 80% of the money and 120% of the money
df_spx=df_spx[(df_spx.strike > .8*spx_price) & \
    (df_spx.strike < 1.2*spx_price)]

#Eliminate expirations less than a week
df_spx=df_spx[df_spx.expiration>quote_date+np. \
    timedelta64(6,'D')]
```

```
#Show strike skew of March options
df_60to90=df_spx[(df_spx.expiration>quote_date+np. \
                timedelta64(60,'D')) & \
                (df_spx.expiration<quote_date+np. \
                timedelta64(90,'D'))]

strikes=[strike/spx_price for strike in df_60to90. \
    strike.unique()]
implieds=[np.average(df_60to90[df_60to90. \
        strike==strike].implied_volatility_1545) \
        for strike in df_60to90.strike.unique()]
sm1=[abs(str-1.) for str in strikes]
spx_ATM_60to90_implied = implieds[sm1.index(min(sm1))]

str_exp=df_60to90.expiration.iloc[0].strftime('%Y-%m-%d')
plt.plot(strikes,implieds,label=stqd)

#Add December 2008 graph
moneyness=[.8,.9,1.,1.1,1.2]
imp2008=[0.510000164, 0.437931821, \
        0.368329438,0.31789782,0.30067243]
plt.plot(moneyness,imp2008,label='2008-12-31')

plt.xlabel("Fraction of money")
plt.ylabel("Annualized implied volatility")
plt.legend()
plt.grid()
str_title="Figure 9.5: Moneyness skew SPX options:\n \
    Expiry "+str_exp+", Quoted "+stqd
str_title+="\nCompared with 2008-12-31 quotes"
plt.title(str_title)
plt.show()
```

#Code Segment 9.7:

```
#Get time skew of ATM options
#Find closest to the money
min_to_money = min(abs(df_spx.strike.unique()-spx_price))
df_ATM=df_spx[abs(df_spx.strike-spx_price) \
    <=min_to_money+5]
```

```python
times=[int((time-quote_date)/np.timedelta64(1,"D")) \
    for time in df_ATM.expiration.unique()]
implieds=[np.average(df_ATM[df_ATM.expiration==time]. \
        implied_volatility_1545) \
        for time in df_ATM.expiration.unique()]

#plt.plot(range(len(times)),implieds,label=stqd)
plt.plot(times,implieds,label=stqd)

#Add 2008-12-31 data
expiry=[7,31,91,182,365,730,1095]
imp2008=[.3612,.3683,.3819,.3750, \
        .3651,.3558,.3555]
plt.plot(expiry,imp2008,label='2008-12-31')

plt.xlabel("Time to maturity (days)")
plt.ylabel("Annualized implied volatility")
plt.grid()
plt.legend()
str_strike=str(df_ATM.strike.iloc[0])
str_title="Figure 9.6: Maturity skew ATM SPX options:\n \
    Strike "+str_strike
str_title+=", Money "+str(spx_price)+", Quoted "+stqd
str_title+="\n Compared with 2008-12-31 quotes"
plt.title(str_title)
plt.show();
```

```python
#Code Segment 9.8:
```

```python
import pandas as pd
import matplotlib.pyplot as plt
#Read time series of implied vol skews
#from csv file and graph them (time and
#moneyness skews)

df_skew=pd.read_csv('IV_skews.csv')
#skip daily info
stride=504
x=range(len(df_skew))

#Graph time and money skews side by side
plt.figure(figsize=(12,4))
```

```
#Time skew
#correct error
df_skew.loc[df_skew.index[df_skew.Time_skew>.4][0], \
    "Time_skew"]=float("nan")


plt.subplot(1,2,1)
plt.plot(x,df_skew.Time_skew)
plt.xticks(range(0,len(df_skew),stride), \
    df_skew.iloc[::stride].Date,rotation=45)
plt.grid()
plt.title('Figure 9.7a: Time skews')


#Moneyness skew
#Moneyness skew was determined by taking all options \
    with maturities
#between 90 and 360 days, and moneyness between \
    (.7 and .9) on the low
#side, and (1.1 and 1.3) on the high side. Then implied \
    volatilities were
#weighted by a metric that gives more weight to options \
    closer to the targets
#(.8,180) and (1.2, 180), and averaged.
plt.subplot(1,2,2)
plt.plot(x,df_skew.Money_skew)
plt.xticks(range(0,len(df_skew),stride), \
    df_skew.iloc[::stride].Date,rotation=45)
plt.grid()
plt.title('Figure 9.7b: Money skews')


plt.show();


n_time_pos=len(df_skew[df_skew.Time_skew>0])
print("Percent time skew positive: {:.2f}%". \
    format(100.*n_time_pos/len(df_skew)))
print("Source: Cboe Exchange, Inc. (Cboe)")
```

#Code Segment 9.9:

```
#Draw two smiles illustrating problem
#with LVM vs Market

strikes=np.arange(1,20)
original=[(s-10)**2/10+8 for s in strikes]
```

```
mktshift=[(s-.5-10)**2/10+8 for s in strikes]
modelshift=[(s+.5-10)**2/10+8 for s in strikes]

plt.plot(strikes,original,label='Original')
plt.plot(strikes,mktshift,label='Market Shift')
plt.plot(strikes,modelshift,label='Model Shift')

plt.ylabel('Implied Vol '+r'$sigma(x0;x,t)$')
plt.xlabel('Strike price x (moneyness)')
plt.grid()
plt.legend()
plt.title('Figure 9.8: LVM does not shift the way the \
    market shifts')
plt.show()
```

#Code Segment 9.10:

```
#compute pseudo-VIX at different underlying prices
import scipy.stats as spst

def black_scholes_call(under,strike,time,rfree,vol):
    #Formula 9.3 - returns price of call
    if under<=0 or strike<=0 or time<=0 or vol<0:
        return(0)
    d_1=(np.log(under/strike)+(rfree+vol**2/2)*time)/
      (vol*np.sqrt(time))
    d_2=d_1-vol*np.sqrt(time)
    call_val=under*spst.norm.cdf(d_1)-strike*np. \
     exp(-rfree*time)*spst.norm.cdf(d_2)
    return(call_val)
#done with black_scholes_call

def black_scholes_put(under,strike,time,rfree,vol):
    #use put-call parity (9.1)
    return(black_scholes_call(under,strike,time,rfree, \
          vol)-under+np.exp(-rfree*time)*strike)
#done with black_scholes_put

r=0; T=.25; sigma=.2; delta_K=1
X_list=np.arange(20,180,1)
K_list=np.arange(20,180,delta_K)
z=[]
for X in X_list:
```

```
    K_0=np.exp(r*T)*X     #use forward price as divider \
                            between puts and calls
                          #so no adjustment needed
    yy=0
    for K in K_list:
        if K<=K_0: #Puts are used below the divider
            y=black_scholes_put(X,K,T,r,sigma)
        else: #Calls are used above the divider
            y=black_scholes_call(X,K,T,r,sigma)
        yy=yy+delta_K*y/K**2   #one over strike-squared \
                                weighting
    #y contains portfolio valued at X
    z.append(2*np.exp(r*T)*yy/T)

plt.plot(X_list,z)
plt.title("Figure 9.9: Virtual VIX calculations")
plt.xlabel("$X_T$")
plt.grid()
plt.show()
```

#Code Segment 9.11:

```
#fit GARCH(1,1) model
initparams=[.12,.85,.6]
a,b,c=qf.Garch11Fit(initparams,ActualReality)

#Display results
print("a=%.3f" % a)
print("b=%.3f" % b)
print("c=%.3f" % c)

#Draw graph
t=len(ActualReality)
minimal=10**(-20)
stdgarch=np.zeroes(t)
stdgarch[0]=np.std(ActualReality)
overallmean=np.mean(ActualReality)
degarched=np.zeroes(t)   #series to hold de-garched \
    series y[t]/sigma[t]
degarched[0]=(ActualReality[0]-overallmean)/stdgarch[0]
#Compute GARCH(1,1) stddev's from data given parameters
for i in range(1,t):
    #Note offset - i-1 observation of data
```

```
    #is used for i estimate of std deviation
    previous=stdgarch[i-1]**2
    var=c+b*previous+\
        a*(ActualReality[i-1]-overallmean)**2
    stdgarch[i]=np.sqrt(var)
    degarched[i]=(ActualReality[i]-overallmean)/
        stdgarch[i]


#Annualize
stdgarch*=np.sqrt(12)

#Just show years
Year=[d/100 for d in Date]

plt.plot(Year,stdgarch)
plt.grid()
plt.title('Figure 9.10: GARCH(1,1) fit to US stock \
    market data')
plt.ylabel('GARCH Sample SDs')
plt.axis([min(Year),max(Year),0,70])
plt.show();

print("Annual sample std dev",targetsd*np.sqrt(12), \
    "= monthly variance of",targetsd**2,"bps")
print("Stationary check (a+b less than one): ",a+b)
print("Monthly target variance",c/(1-a-b),"bps")
print("Target annualized standard deviation: ", \
    np.sqrt(12*c/(1-a-b)))
```

#Code Segment 9.12:

```
#Compute before and after excess kurtosis
from scipy import stats
kurt_orig=stats.kurtosis(ActualReality,fisher=True)
kurt_degarch=stats.kurtosis(degarched,fisher=True)
print("Excess kurtois before and after deGarching:", \
    kurt_orig,kurt_degarch)
```

#Code Segment 9.13:

```
#Draw graph of pseudo-delta functions
xs=np.arange(-5,5.1,.1)
```

```python
for k in [1,2,4]:
    ys=[1/(1+np.exp(k*x)) for x in xs]
    plt.plot(xs,ys,label='k='+str(k))

plt.legend()
plt.title('Figure 9.12: Pseudo-delta functions')
plt.grid()
plt.show()
```

#Code Segment 10.1:

```python
#Show Fisher z-transform
import numpy as np
import matplotlib.pyplot as plt
%matplotlib inline

def fisherz(rho):
    #Fisher z-transform
    return(.5*np.log((1+rho)/(1-rho)))

x=np.arange(-.99,.9999,.01)
plt.plot(x,fisherz(x),label="transform")

fzeq1=(np.exp(2)-1)/(np.exp(2)+1)   #argument where \
    z-transform equals one
plt.plot(x,x/fzeq1,label="linear to z=1")
plt.title("Figure 10.1: Fisher z-transform")
plt.xlabel("Correlation")
plt.ylabel("Fisher Z")
plt.legend()
plt.grid()
plt.show();
```

#Code Segment 10.2:

```python
import scipy.stats as spst
#Form ranks from Pearson example
x=[1,-.1,1.5,1.7,-1,5]
y=[1,-.1,1.5,1.7,-1,-2]

print("X data:",x)
xr=7-spst.rankdata(x)
print("X ranks:",xr)
```

```
print("Y data:",y)
yr=7-spst.rankdata(y)
print("Y ranks:",yr)

pearson,psig=spst.pearsonr(x,y)
#Compute Spearman by doing Pearson on ranks
spearman,ssig=spst.pearsonr(xr,yr)
#Direct call to Spearmsn
spear_scipy,sspsig=spst.spearmanr(x,y)

print("Pearson correlation:",pearson)
print("Spearman correlation from Pearson ranks:",spearman)
print("Spearman from scipy:",spear_scipy)
```

#Code Segment 10.3:

```
import pandas as pd
#Get regional stock market index data from Ken French's \
    website.
#Convert daily to Wednesday-Wednesday weekly.

ff_head='http://mba.tuck.dartmouth.edu/pages/faculty/ken.
      french/ftp/'
ff_foot="_3_Factors_Daily_CSV.zip"
ff_names=["Europe","North_America","Japan"]

for name_index in range(len(ff_names)):
    print("Inputting ",ff_names[name_index])
    ffurl=ff_head+ff_names[name_index]+ff_foot
    #Skip the header rows
    df_region = pd.read_csv(ffurl, skiprows=6)
    #Standardize name of Date column and market return \
        column
    col0=df_region.columns[0]
    df_region.rename(columns={col0:'Date'},inplace=True)
    df_region.rename(columns={"Mkt-RF": \
        ff_names[name_index]},inplace=True)
    #Merge into aggregate
    if name_index == 0:
        df_returns=df_region[df_region.columns[0:2]]
```

```
        else:
            df_returns = df_returns.merge \
                (df_region[df_region.columns[0:2]], \
            left_on='Date', right_on='Date')


#Convert to log-returns
df_logs_day=np.log(1+df_returns \
    [df_returns.columns[1:]]/100)


#Convert dates to datetime format
df_logs_day.insert(0,"Date",df_returns["Date"],True)
df_logs_day["Date"] = pd.to_datetime \
    (df_logs_day["Date"], format='%Y%m%d')


#Convert log-returns to weekly (Wednesday-Wednesday)
#to avoid asynchronous trading effects
df_logs_day = df_logs_day.set_index("Date")
df_logs=df_logs_day.resample('W-Wed').sum()
#(Will include some holidays like July 4 and \
    December 25, so a little off)


#Remove the partial year at the end
lastyear=df_logs.index[-1].year
df_logs.drop(df_logs.index[df_logs.index. \
    year==lastyear],axis=0,inplace=True)


periodicity=52    #For use in later code segments


nobs=len(df_logs)
print(nobs," weekly observations starting",df_logs. \
    index[0].strftime("%Y-%m-%d"), \
      "ending",df_logs.index[-1].strftime("%Y-%m-%d"))
```

#Code Segment 10.4:

```
#Get and show correlation matrix and
#standard deviations
corr_matrix=df_logs[df_logs.columns].corr()
cov_matrix=df_logs[df_logs.columns].cov()
std_devs=[]
for i in range(len(ff_names)):
```

```
    #Annualize weekly data
    std_devs.append(np.sqrt(periodicity*cov_matrix. \
    iloc[i,i]))

print("Correlation matrix and standard deviations \
    (10.8):")
print(corr_matrix)
print('Annualized standard deviations:\n',std_devs)
zsig=np.sqrt(1/(nobs-3))
rsig=(np.exp(2*zsig)-1)/(np.exp(2*zsig)+1)
print('Correlation significance:',rsig)
```

#Code Segment 10.5:

```
#Compute minimum variance portfolio of three \
    regions (4.8)
cov_matrix_inverse=pd.DataFrame(np.linalg.pinv \
    (cov_matrix.values),cov_matrix.columns,cov_matrix. \
    index)
u=pd.Series([1]*len(cov_matrix_inverse),index=cov_ \
    matrix_ inverse.index)
minvport=cov_matrix_inverse.dot(u)
minvar=1/minvport.dot(u)   #This is second part of \
    formula (4.8)
minvport*=minvar     #This is first part of formula (4.8)
print('Minimum variance portfolio:')
print(minvport.to_string())

#Annualized standard deviation
annminstd=np.sqrt(minvar*periodicity)
print('Minimum variance portfolio annualized std \
    deviation:',annminstd)
#Find minimum component standard deviation
compminstd=min(std_devs)
comp_index=std_devs.index(compminstd)
print("Lowest component annualized std
        deviation",compminstd,"(",df_logs.columns \
    [comp_index],")")
```

#Code Segment 10.6:

```
#Generate graph of either simulated or historical sample \
    correlation
#from df_logs

def make_corr_plot(df_logs, rtrial, samplesize, \
    title_str, simulate):
#Generate a multivariate normal distribution using the \
    data in df_logs
#compute sample correlations of size samplesize and \
    graph them
#simulate: False, use historical data in df_logs
#          True, use simulated data in rtrial
    nobs=len(df_logs)
    corr_matrix=df_logs[df_logs.columns].corr()

    #Get sample correlations
    if simulate:
        samplecorrs=[np.corrcoef(rtrial[i-samplesize:i]. \
        transpose())for i in range(samplesize,nobs+1)]
    else:
        samplecorrs=[df_logs.iloc[i-samplesize:i] \
        [df_logs.columns].corr().values \
                    for i in range(samplesize,nobs+1)]
    sccol=['r','g','b']
    stride=int((nobs-periodicity+1)/
        (4*periodicity))*periodicity

    dates=df_logs.index[samplesize-1:]
    plot_corrs(dates,samplecorrs,corr_matrix,sccol, \
     stride,title_str+str(samplesize)+'-week sample \
     correlations')
#Done with make_corr_plot

def plot_corrs(dates,corrs,corr_matrix,sccol,stride, \
    title_str):
    #dates and corrs have same length
    #dates in datetime format
    #corrs is a list of correlation matrices
    #corr_matrix has the target correlations
    #names of securities are the column names of \
        corr_matrix
    #sccol is colors for lines
```

```python
    #stride is how many dates to skip between ticks \
        on x-axis
    #title_str is title string

    nobs=len(corrs)
    nsecs=len(corrs[0])

    #plot correlations in corrs, nsec per time period
    ncorrs=nsecs*(nsecs-1)/2
    z=0
    #Go through each pair
    for j in range(nsecs-1):
        for k in range(j+1,nsecs):
            #form time series of sample correlations
            #for this pair of securities
            cs=[corrs[i][j,k] for i in range(nobs)]
            plt.plot(range(nobs),cs, \
                    label=corr_matrix.columns[j]+'/'+ \
                    corr_matrix.columns[k], \
                    color=sccol[z])
            #Show target correlation in same color
            line=[corr_matrix.iloc[j,k]]*(nobs)
            plt.plot(range(nobs),line,color=sccol[z])
            z+=1

    plt.legend()
    tix=[x.strftime("%Y-%m-%d") for x in \
        dates[0:nobs+1:stride]]
    plt.xticks(range(0,nobs+1,stride),tix,rotation=45)
    plt.ylabel("Correlation")
    plt.title(title_str)
    plt.grid()
    plt.show();
#Done with plot_corrs

#Generate a simulation
#Show the Cholesky decomposition of the matrix
chol=np.linalg.cholesky(corr_matrix)
print('Cholesky:\n',chol)

#Generate random draws
nobs=len(df_logs)
nsecs=len(df_logs.columns)
strial=np.random.normal(0,1,size=[nobs,nsecs])
```

```
rtrial=np.matmul(chol,strial.T).T

samplesize=periodicity
title_str="Figure 10.2: Simulated "
simulate=True
import matplotlib.pyplot as plt
make_corr_plot(df_logs, rtrial, samplesize, title_str, \
    simulate)
print("Standard Error = ",np.tanh(1/np.sqrt \
    (periodicity-3)))
```

#Code Segment 10.7:

```
#Get sample 3-year simulated correlations
samplesize=156
title_str="Figure 10.3: Simulated "
simulate=True
make_corr_plot(df_logs, rtrial, samplesize, title_str, \
    simulate)
print("Standard Error = ",np.tanh(1/np.sqrt(156-3)))
```

#Code Segment 10.8:

```
#Get sample 3-year historical correlations
samplesize=156
title_str="Figure 10.4: Historical "
simulate=False
make_corr_plot(df_logs, rtrial, samplesize, title_str, \
    simulate)
```

#Code Segment 10.9:

```
#Get FHFA house price index and graph it
df_fhfa=pd.read_excel("https://www.fhfa.gov/DataTools/
    Downloads/Documents/HPI/HPI_PO_summary.xls", \
    skiprows=1)

#Plot seasonally adjusted index
seasonal_index="Seasonally-Adjusted Purchase-Only Index \
    \n(1991Q1=100)"
plt.plot(df_fhfa["Year"],df_fhfa[seasonal_index])
```

```
str_title="Figure 10.5: Seasonally Adjusted US House \
    Price Index\n"
str_title+=str(df_fhfa.iloc[0]["Year"])+"Q"+ \
    str(df_fhfa.iloc[0]["Quarter"])+"-"
str_title+=str(df_fhfa.iloc[-1]["Year"])+"Q"+ \
    str(df_fhfa.iloc[-1]["Quarter"])
plt.ylabel("HPI")
plt.title(str_title)
plt.grid()
plt.show();
```

#Code Segment 10.10:

```
import pandas as pd
import qrpm_funcs as qf
import datetime as dt
from datetime import datetime
import scipy.stats as spst
import numpy as np
import matplotlib.pyplot as plt

firstday="1970-12-31"
lastday=qf.LastYearEnd()
seriesnames=['WILL5000IND','DGS10']
cdates,ratematrix=qf.GetFREDMatrix(seriesnames,
                startdate=firstday,enddate=lastday)

#Put in dataframe - no na's, only monthends
df_stockbond=pd.DataFrame(ratematrix,index=[datetime. \
                strptime(cd,"%Y-%m-%d") \
                for cd in cdates]).dropna(). \
                resample('M').last()

#Convert to log-returns
#Assume Treasury rates given are for 10-year par bond
#paying semiannually
stock_logs=[]
bond_logs=[]
idx_stock=0
idx_tsy=1
T20=20.    #Number of semiannual periods in the 10-year \
    bond
```

```
oldrate=df_stockbond.iloc[0][idx_tsy]/200     #Semiannual \
    rate
for i in range(len(df_stockbond)-1):
    stock_logs.append(np.log(df_stockbond.iloc[i+1] \
                             [idx_stock]/df_stockbond. \
                             iloc[i][idx_stock]))
    #Use Formula 3.7 to get the duration of the par bond \
        in semiannual periods
    duration=qf.formula3p7(oldrate*100.,oldrate*100.,T20)
    newrate=df_stockbond.iloc[i+1][idx_tsy]/200
    #Return for the month: carry plus principal change
    bond_return=oldrate/6-duration*(newrate-oldrate)
    bond_logs.append(np.log(1+bond_return))
    oldrate=newrate


#bring dates back to strings
dates=[datetime.strftime(df_stockbond.index[i], \
        "%Y-%m-%d") \
        for i in range(1,len(df_stockbond))]

corrs=[]
stride=36
for i in range(len(stock_logs)-stride):
    rho,p=spst.pearsonr(stock_logs[i:i+stride], \
        bond_logs[i:i+stride])
    corrs.append(rho)

plt.plot(dates[stride:],corrs)
nobs=len(corrs)
stride_ticks=120
plt.xticks(range(0,nobs+1,stride_ticks), \
            dates[stride:-1:stride_ticks], \
            rotation=45)

#Shade insignificant area
fsig=1/np.sqrt(stride-3)
rsig=(np.exp(2*fsig)-1)/(np.exp(2*fsig)+1)

low_sig=[-np.abs(rsig)]*nobs
high_sig=[np.abs(rsig)]*nobs

plt.fill_between(range(nobs), low_sig, high_sig, \
                facecolor='gray', alpha=0.5,
        interpolate=True)
```

```
str_title="Figure 10.6: US Stock/Bond "+str(stride)+ \
        "-month correlations\n"
str_title+=dates[stride]+" to "+dates[-1]
str_title+="   (Gray=insignificant)"
plt.title(str_title)
plt.grid()
plt.show();
```

#Code Segment 10.11:

```
#Read current holdings of SPY Exchange-Traded-Fund (ETF)
#This is very close to the actual S&P 500 index
#There is a time mismatch - this is current while \
    options information is from
#yearend, so implied correlations will be off a little
import pandas as pd
import time
import datetime
import numpy as np

#Function used below to get implied volatilities
def find_implieds(df_ATM,quote_date,day_target):
    #find options in dataframe df_ATM having maturities \
        close to
    #day_target days from quote_date. Return average \
        implieds of those
    #options and a string giving one of the expiration \
        dates used.
    this_implied=0
    num_implied=0
    #Keep increasing the number of days interval
    #around day_target until some options are found
    for interval in range(16,86,10):
        for i_ATM in range(len(df_ATM)):
            if abs( int( \
              (df_ATM.iloc[i_ATM].expiration-quote_date) \
              /np.timedelta64(1, 'D'))-day_target)
                <interval:this_implied+=df_ATM.
                iloc[i_ATM].implied_volatility_1545
                num_implied+=1
                str_exp = str(df_ATM.iloc[i_ATM].
                expiration)[:10]
```

```
        if num_implied != 0:
            break

    return(this_implied/num_implied,str_exp)
#Done with find_implieds

#
# Step 1 - get SPY tickers
#
start_time = time.perf_counter()
url="https://www.ssga.com/us/en/individual/etfs/ \
        library-content/"+\
    "products/fund-data/etfs/us/holdings-daily-us-en- \
        spy.xlsx"
df_spy=pd.read_excel(url,skiprows=4,engine="openpyxl")
df_spy.dropna(thresh=3,inplace=True)    #Clean up junk at \
    the end
#Extract tickers and weights
orig_spy_tickers=[df_spy["Ticker"].iloc(0)[i].upper() \
    for i in range(len(df_spy))]
weights=[df_spy["Weight"].iloc(0)[i] for i in \
    range(len(df_spy))]
weights/=sum(weights)     #force weights to add to 1
end_time = time.perf_counter()
print("%d SPY tickers input, %7.3f seconds" % \
    (len(weights),end_time-start_time))


#
# Step 2 - get options on the tickers in SPY
# and compute ATM volatility about 75 days out
#
yearend_string=str(datetime.datetime.now().year-1)
df_spy_options=pd.
        read_excel(r"SPY_UnderlyingOptionsEODCalcs_"+ \
                yearend_string+"-12-31.xlsx", \
                engine="openpyxl")
end_time, start_time = time.perf_counter(), end_time
print("%d SPY options input, %7.3f seconds" % \
    (len(df_spy_options), end_time-start_time))

#Match up stock tickers with options
spy_tickers=[]
implieds=[]
```

```python
vis=[]    #vi's as in (10.16)
for i in range(len(orig_spy_tickers)):
    df_target=df_spy_options[df_spy_options. \
    underlying_symbol == orig_spy_tickers[i]]
    if len(df_target)>0:    #Did we find any options on \
    this ticker?
        spy_tickers.append(orig_spy_tickers[i])
        this_price = df_target.active_underlying_price_ \
        1545.unique()[0]
        quote_date = df_target.quote_date.unique()[0]
        #Find closest to the money
        min_to_money = min(abs(df_target.strike. \
        unique()-this_price))
        df_ATM=df_target[abs(df_target.strike- \
        this_price)==min_to_money]

        this_avg, str_exp = find_implieds \
        (df_ATM,quote_date,75)
        implieds.append(this_avg)
        vis.append(implieds[-1]*weights[i])

end_time, start_time = time.perf_counter(), end_time
print("%d SPY tickers matched with options, \
    %7.3f seconds" % (len(spy_tickers), \
    end_time-start_time))


#
# Step 3: Get SPX implied volatility about 75 days out
#
df_spx_options=pd. \
      read_excel(r"SPX_UnderlyingOptionsEODCalcs_"+ \
                yearend_string+"-12-31.xlsx", \
                engine="openpyxl")
end_time, start_time = time.perf_counter(), end_time
print("%d SPX options input, %7.3f seconds" % \
     (len(df_spx_options),end_time-start_time))
#Get SPX ATM volatility
this_price = df_spx_options.active_underlying_price_ \
    1545.unique()[0]
#Find closest to the money
min_to_money = min(abs(df_spx_options.strike.unique() \
    -this_price))
```

```python
df_ATM=df_spx_options[abs(df_spx_options.strike- \
    this_price)==min_to_money]

spx_ATM_60to90_implied, str_exp = find_implieds \
    (df_ATM,quote_date,75)

#Make histogram of implieds

n, bins, patches = plt.hist(implieds,bins=50)
plt.axvline(spx_ATM_60to90_implied, color='k',
        linestyle='dashed', linewidth=1)
plt.annotate('S&P 500 implied vol',
            xy=(spx_ATM_60to90_implied, .9*max(n)),
            xytext=(np.average(implieds)*1.5, .9*max(n)),
            va='center',color='k', arrowprops=
            dict(color='k',width=1,headwidth=4))
plt.annotate('Average implied vol',
            xy=(np.average(implieds), .7*max(n)),
            xytext=(np.average(implieds)*1.5, .7*max(n)),
            va='center',color='r', arrowprops=
            dict(color='r',width=1,headwidth=4))

plt.axvline(np.average(implieds), color='r', \
    linestyle='dashed', linewidth=1)
plt.xlabel("Annualized Implied Vol")
plt.ylabel("Count ("+str(len(implieds))+" total)")
plt.title("Figure 10.7: Histogram of ATM implied vols of \
        SPY components\n Expiring " \
        +str_exp+", Quoted "+str(quote_date)[:10])
plt.grid()
plt.show()

#Show number greater than SPX implied
n_greater = sum(iv > spx_ATM_60to90_implied for iv in \
    implieds)
print("SPX implied:",spx_ATM_60to90_implied)
print("Number greater:",n_greater)
print("Average implied:",np.average(implieds))

#Do calculation for formula 10.16
var_port=spx_ATM_60to90_implied**2
sum_vi2=sum([vi**2 for vi in vis])
sum_vi_2=sum(vis)**2
```

```
implied_corr=(var_port-sum_vi2)/(sum_vi_2-sum_vi2)
print("Implied correlation per formula (10.16):", \
    implied_corr)
```

#Code Segment 10.12:

```
## Graph CBOE COR3N series
## https://www.cboe.com/us/indices/dashboard/cor3m/
## Captured February 26, 2022
import pandas as pd

df_cor3m=pd.read_excel("cboe_cor3m.
    xlsx",engine="openpyxl")
plt.plot(range(len(df_cor3m)),df_cor3m["COR3M"])
plt.grid()
plt.title('Figure 10.8: CBOE implied correlations COR3M')
nobs=len(df_cor3m)
stride=36
plt.xticks(range(0,nobs,stride),df_cor3m["Date"]. \
    iloc[0:nobs:stride])
plt.xlim(0,nobs)
#plt.ylim(25,90)
plt.show()
```

#Code Segment 10.13:

```
import scipy.stats as spst
from scipy.optimize import minimize_scalar

#CHEAT! - get overall mean and standard deviation vectors
#In practice, would need to do everything out of sample -
#start with a learning sample, e.g.
overallmean=np.mean(df_logs.axis)
overallstd=np.std(df_logs)
tickerlist=df_logs.columns

#Get GARCH params for each ticker
initparams=[.12,.85,.6]
gparams=[qf.Garch11Fit(initparams,df_logs[ticker]) for \
    ticker in tickerlist]

minimal=10**(-20)
stgs=[] #Save the running garch sigmas
```

```
for it,ticker in enumerate(tickerlist):
    a,b,c=gparams[it]

    #Create time series of sigmas
    t=len(df_logs[ticker])
    stdgarch=np.zeroes(t)
    stdgarch[0]=overallstd[ticker]
    #Compute GARCH(1,1) stddev's from data given \
    parameters
    for i in range(1,t):
        #Note offset - i-1 observation of data
        #is used for i estimate of std deviation
        previous=stdgarch[i-1]**2
        var=c+b*previous+ \
            a*(df_logs[ticker][i-1]-overallmean[ticker])**2
        stdgarch[i]=np.sqrt(var)

    #Save for later de-GARCHing
    stgs.append(stdgarch)
    stdgarch=100*np.sqrt(periodicity)*stgs[it]   #Annualize
    plt.plot(range(len(stdgarch)),stdgarch,label=ticker)

plt.grid()
plt.title('Figure 10.9: GARCH(1,1) annualized standard \
        deviations '+ \
        min(df_logs.index.strftime("%Y%m"))+'-'+ \
        str(max(df_logs.index.strftime("%Y%m"))))
plt.ylabel('GARCH SDs')
plt.legend()
stride=5*periodicity
tix=[x.strftime("%Y-%m-%d") for x in df_logs. \
    index[0:len(df_logs)-1:stride]]
plt.xticks(range(0,len(df_logs),stride),tix,rotation=45)
plt.show()

for it,ticker in enumerate(tickerlist):
    print(ticker,'a=%1.4f' % gparams[it][0], \
            'b=%1.4f' % gparams[it][1], \
            'c=%1.8f' % gparams[it][2], \
            'AnnEquilibStd=%1.4f' % \
            np.sqrt(periodicity*gparams[it][2]/ \
                (1-gparams[it][0]-gparams[it][1])))
```

#Code Segment 10.14:

```
#Display before and after deGARCHing statistics

#Demeaned, DeGARCHed series go in dfeps
dfeps=df_logs.sort_values(by="Date").copy()
for it,ticker in enumerate(tickerlist):
    dfeps[ticker]-=overallmean[ticker]
    for i in range(len(dfeps)):
        dfeps[ticker].iloc[i]/=stgs[it][i]
    print(ticker)
    print('    DeGARCHed Mean:',np.mean(dfeps[ticker]))

    print('    Raw annualized Std Dev:',np.sqrt \
            (periodicity)*overallstd[ticker])
    print('    DeGARCHed Std Dev:',np.std(dfeps[ticker]))

    print('    Raw excess kurtosis:',spst.kurtosis \
            (df_logs[ticker]))
    print('    DeGARCHed Excess Kurtosis:',spst.kurtosis \
            (dfeps[ticker]))
```

#Code Segment 10.15:

```
#Get sample 156-month de-GARCHED correlations
samplesize=3*periodicity
title_str="Figure 10.10: Historical de-GARCHed "
simulate=False
make_corr_plot(dfeps, rtrial, samplesize, title_str, \
    simulate)
```

#Code Segment 10.16:

```
#Compute integrated correlations

InData=np.array(dfeps[tickerlist])

def IntegratedCorrObj(s):
    #Compute time series of quasi-correlation
    #matrices from InData using integrated parameter
    #xlam=exp(s)/(1+exp(s)); note this format removes
    #the need to enforce bounds of xlam being between
    #0 and 1. This is applied to formula 10.29.
```

```python
        #Standardize Q's and apply formula 10.34.
        #Returns scalar 10.34
        xlam=np.exp(s)
        xlam/=1+xlam
        obj10p34=0.
        previousq=np.identity(len(InData[0]))
        #Form new shock matrix
        for i in range(len(InData)):
            #standardize previous q matrix
            #and compute contribution to objective
            #function
            stdmtrx=np.diag([1/np.sqrt(previousq[s,s]) \
            for s in range(len(previousq))])
            previousr=stdmtrx @ (previousq @ stdmtrx)
            #objective function
            obj10p34+=np.log(np.linalg.det(previousr))
            shockvec=np.array(InData[i])
            vec1=shockvec @ np.linalg.inv(previousr)
            #This makes obj10p34 into a 1,1 matrix
            obj10p34+=vec1 @ shockvec

            #Update q matrix
            shockvec=np.mat(shockvec)
            shockmat=np.matmul(shockvec.T,shockvec)
            previousq=xlam*shockmat+(1-xlam)*previousq
        return(obj10p34[0,0])
#Done with IntegratedCorrObj

result=minimize_scalar(IntegratedCorrObj)

xlamopt=np.exp(result.x)
xlamopt/=1+xlamopt
print('Optimal lambda:',xlamopt)
print('Optimal objective function:',result.fun)
if xlamopt>=1 or xlamopt==0:
    halflife=0
else:
    halflife=-np.log(2)/np.log(1-xlamopt)
print('Half-life (years):',halflife/periodicity)

#Compute integrated correlations
nobs=len(InData)
nsecs=len(InData[0])
#Start quasi-correlation matrix series with identity
```

```
previousq=np.identity(nsecs)
rmatrices=[]
for i in range(nobs):
    stdmtrx=np.diag([1/np.sqrt(previousq[s,s]) \
        for s in range(nsecs)])
    rmatrices.append(np.matmul(stdmtrx,np.matmul \
        (previousq,stdmtrx)))
    shockvec=np.mat(np.array(InData[i]))
    #Update q matrix
    shockmat=np.matmul(shockvec.T,shockvec)
    previousq=xlamopt*shockmat+(1-xlamopt)*previousq

#Plot integrated correlations
iccol=['r','g','b']
xtitle='Figure 10.11: Integrated correlations λ=%1.5f' % \
    xlamopt
xtitle+=', '+min(df_logs.index.strftime("%Y-%m-%d"))+':'\
        +max(df_logs.index.strftime("%Y-%m-%d"))
dates=df_logs.index
stride=5*periodicity
plot_corrs(dates,rmatrices,corr_matrix,iccol,stride,xtitle)
```

#Code Segment 10.17:

```
#Map of objective with respect to half-life

halflife=int(halflife)
delta_halflife=int(halflife/2)

x=np.arange(halflife-delta_halflife,halflife+ \
    delta_halflife)
y=[IntegratedCorrObj(np.log((.5)**(-1/h)-1)) for h in x]

plt.plot(x/periodicity,y)
plt.title("Figure 10.12: Objective function as \
    half-life changes")
plt.xlabel("Halflife in years")
plt.ylabel("Objective")
plt.grid()
plt.show();
```

#Code Segment 10.18:

```python
def MeanRevCorrObj(params):
    #Compute time series of quasi-correlation
    #matrices from InData using mean reverting
    #formula 10.30. Standardize them and apply
    #formula 10.34. Returns scalar 10.34

    #Extract parameters
    alpha,beta=params
    #Enforce bounds
    if alpha<0 or beta<0:
        return(10**20)
    elif (alpha+beta)>.999:
        return(10**20)
    obj10p34=0
    #Initial omega is obtained through correlation
      targeting
    Rlong=np.corrcoef(InData.T)
    previousq=np.identity(len(InData[0]))
    #Form new shock matrix
    for i in range(len(InData)):
        #standardize previous q matrix
        #and compute contribution to objective
        #function
        stdmtrx=np.diag([1/np.sqrt(previousq[s,s]) \
                        for s in range(len(previousq))])
        previousr=np.matmul(stdmtrx,np.matmul \
            (previousq,stdmtrx))
        #objective function
        obj10p34+=np.log(np.linalg.det(previousr))
        shockvec=np.array(InData[i])
        vec1=np.matmul(shockvec,np.linalg.inv(previousr))
        #This makes obj10p34 into a 1,1 matrix
        obj10p34+=np.matmul(vec1,shockvec)

        #Update q matrix
        shockvec=np.mat(shockvec)
        shockmat=np.matmul(shockvec.T,shockvec)
        previousq=(1-alpha-beta)*Rlong+alpha*shockmat+ \
            beta*previousq
    return(obj10p34[0,0])
#Done with MeanRevCorrObj
```

```python
import scipy.optimize as scpo
#alpha and beta positive
corr_bounds = scpo.Bounds([0,0],[np.inf,np.inf])
#Sum of alpha and beta is less than 1
corr_linear_constraint = \
    scpo.LinearConstraint([[1, 1]],[0],[.999])

initparams=[.02,.93]

results = scpo.minimize(MeanRevCorrObj, \
        initparams, \
        method='trust-constr', \
        jac='2-point', \
        hess=scpo.SR1(), \
        bounds=corr_bounds, \
        constraints=corr_linear_constraint)

alpha,beta=results.x
print('Optimal alpha, beta:',alpha,beta)
print('Optimal objective function:',results.fun)
halflife=-np.log(2)/np.log(beta)
print('Half-life (years):',halflife/periodicity)

#Compute mean reverting correlations
nobs=len(InData)
nsecs=len(InData[0])
previousq=np.identity(nsecs)
Rlong=np.corrcoef(InData.T)
rmatrices=[]
for i in range(nobs):
    stdmtrx=np.diag([1/np.sqrt(previousq[s,s]) \
        for s in range(nsecs)])
    rmatrices.append(np.matmul(stdmtrx,np.matmul \
        (previousq,stdmtrx)))
    shockvec=np.mat(np.array(InData[i]))
    #Update q matrix
    shockmat=np.matmul(shockvec.T,shockvec)
    previousq=(1-alpha-beta)*Rlong+alpha*shockmat+ \
        beta*previousq

#Plot mean-reverting correlations
iccol=['r','g','b']
xtitle='Figure 10.13: Mean reverting correlations \
        α=%1.5f' % alpha
```

```
xtitle+=', β=%1.5f' % beta
xtitle+=',\n'+min(df_logs.index.strftime("%Y-%m-%d"))+ \
           ':'+max(df_logs.index.strftime("%Y-%m-%d"))
dates=df_logs.index
stride=5*periodicity
plot_corrs(dates,rmatrices,corr_matrix,iccol,stride,xtitle)
```

#Code Segment 10.19:

```
#MacGyver method - pairwise integrated
minimal=10**(-20)
xlams=[]
for it in range(len(tickerlist)-1):
    tick1=tickerlist[it]
    for jt in range(it+1,len(tickerlist)):
        tick2=tickerlist[jt]
        InData=np.array(dfeps[[tick1,tick2]])
        result=minimize_scalar(IntegratedCorrObj)
        xlamopt=np.exp(result.x)/(1+np.exp(result.x))
        print(tick1,tick2)
        print('    Optimal lambda:',xlamopt)
        print('    Optimal objective function:', \
            result.fun)
        if np.absolute(xlamopt)<minimal or xlamopt>=1:
            halflife=0
        else:
            halflife=-np.log(2)/np.log(1-xlamopt)
        print('    Half-life (years):',halflife/ \
            periodicity)
        xlams.append(xlamopt)

print('\nMedian MacGyver lambda:',np.median(xlams))
```

#Code Segment 11.1:

```
## Display financial metrics Table 11.2
## Source: Appendix A, median ratios
## https://www.moodys.com/research/Corporates-Global- \
    Moodys-Financial-Metrics-key-ratios-by-rating- \
    and--PBC_1261065
import pandas as pd
import numpy as np
metrics_filename="Moodys Key Metrics 2021.xlsx"
```

```
financial_metrics = pd.read_excel(metrics_filename, \
    sheet_name='Financial Metrics', engine="openpyxl")

print("Table 11.2: Moody's financial metrics")
print("Key ratios by rating for global nonfinancial \
    companies, 2021 update")
financial_metrics
```

#Code Segment 11.2:

```
#Display bar charts with investment grade and speculative
#grade defaults year by year
#Data from Moody's Corporate Default and Recovery \
    Rates, 1920-2021, Exhibit 37
#(File Default Reports - Annual-default-study-After-a- \
    sharp-decline-in-2021- defaults-will-rise-modest... \
    - 31Mar22.xlsx)
#Acquired from https://www.moodys.com/research/Annual- \
    default-study-After-a-sharp-decline-in-2021- \
    defaults--PBC_1323378
import pandas as pd
import numpy as np
import matplotlib.pyplot as plt
%matplotlib inline

moodys_default_filename='Default Reports - Annual- \
    default-study-After-a-sharp-decline-in-2021- \
    defaults-will-rise-modest... - 31Mar22.xlsx'
default_rates = pd.read_excel(moodys_default_filename, \
    sheet_name='Ex37', skiprows=2, \
        usecols = ['Year', 'Aaa', 'Aa', 'A', 'Baa', \
    'Ba', 'B', 'Caa-C', 'IG', 'SG', 'All'], \
    engine="openpyxl")

#Find number of actual years
n_years=default_rates.loc[default_rates['Year']== \
    'Mean'].index.values[0]
#Lop off the summary information after years
default_rates.drop(np.arange \
    (n_years,len(default_rates)),inplace=True)
#Change scale so that 1=1%
default_rates.IG=default_rates.IG.mul(100.)
```

```python
default_rates.SG=default_rates.SG.mul(100.)

fig=plt.figure() # Create matplotlib figure

#Set up two axes because of different orders of
#magnitude between IG and HY
ax = fig.add_subplot(111)
ax2 = ax.twinx() # Create another axis that shares the \
    same x-axis as ax.

width = 0.4

default_rates.IG.plot(kind='bar', color='blue', ax=ax, \
    width=width, position=1)
default_rates.SG.plot(kind='bar', color='red', ax=ax2, \
    width=width, position=0)

ax.set_ylabel('Investment Grade', color='blue')
ax2.set_ylabel('Speculative', color='red')

stride=10   #Label every decade
plt.xticks(range(0,n_years,stride),default_rates \
    ["Year"].iloc[::stride],rotation=45)

default_date_range="1920-"+str(default_rates['Year']. \
    iloc[n_years-1])
plt.title("Figure 11.1: Moody's corporate default \
    rates, "+default_date_range)
plt.show();

#Show averages, mins, maxes
print('Investment grade:')
print('    Min: ',min(default_rates.IG))
ig_default_rate_since_1983 = default_rates \
    [default_rates.Year>=1983].IG.mean()
print('    Avg: %1.3f' % np.average(default_rates.IG) + \
    ". Since 1983: %1.3f"% ig_default_rate_since_1983)
print('    Max: ',max(default_rates.IG)," Year: ", \
    list(default_rates.loc[default_rates. \
    IG==max(default_rates.IG)].Year)[0])
print('    Percentage of years with no defaults: ', \
    default_rates.IG.value_counts().iloc[0]*100./ \
    len(default_rates.IG))
```

```
print('Speculative:')
print('    Min: ',min(default_rates.SG))
sg_default_rate_since_1983 = default_rates \
    [default_rates.Year>=1983].SG.mean()
print('    Avg: %1.3f' % np.average(default_rates.SG)+". \
    Since 1983: %1.3f"% sg_default_rate_since_1983)
print('    Max: ',max(default_rates.SG)," Year: ", \
    list(default_rates.loc[default_rates. \
    SG==max(default_rates.SG)].Year)[0])
print('    Percentage of years with no defaults: ', \
    default_rates.SG.value_counts(). \
    iloc[0]*100./len(default_rates.SG))
```

#Code Segment 11.3:

```
#Produce Table 11.3
#Data from Moody's Corporate Default and Recovery  \
    Rates, 1920-2021, Exhibit 41
#Get restricted date range
date_range = pd.read_excel(moodys_default_filename,  \
    sheet_name='Ex41', nrows=2, engine="openpyxl")
recent_date_range = date_range.columns[0][-9:]

#Get table and transpose it
cumulative_rates = pd.read_excel(moodys_default_filename,\
    sheet_name='Ex41', skiprows=2, engine="openpyxl"). \
    transpose(copy=True)

idx_names = cumulative_rates.iloc[0]    #Put ratings in \
    column names
cumulative_rates.rename(columns = idx_names, \
    inplace = True)
cumulative_rates.index.rename(cumulative_rates.index[0], \
    inplace = True)    #Put "Rating\Horizon as index name"
cumulative_rates.drop([idx_names.name], inplace = True) \
    #Drop redundant ratings labels

print("Table 11.3: Moody's average corporate cumulative \
    default rates\n"+"(Percents, 1.0=1%) by letter \
    rating, "+recent_date_range)
pd.options.display.float_format="{:,.2f}".format
cumulative_rates*100.
```

#Code Segment 11.4:

```
#Source: https://www.spglobal.com/ratings/en/research/
#articles/220413-default-transition-and-recovery-2021-
#annual-global-corporate-default-and-rating-transition-
        study-12336975


sandp_default_filename = "SandP global credit 2021.xlsx"

sandp_date_range = pd.read_excel(sandp_default_filename, \
    sheet_name='Table 24', nrows=1, engine="openpyxl")
sandp_recent_date_range = sandp_date_range.iloc[0][0] \
    [-10:-1]


#Get table
sandp_cumulative_rates = pd.read_excel \
    (sandp_default_filename, sheet_name='Table 24', \
    skiprows=2, engine="openpyxl")


#Display table
print("Table 11.4: Standard & Poor's average global \
    corporate","\ncumulative default rates (percents,\
    1.0=1%) by letter rating, "+sandp_recent_date_range)
sandp_cumulative_rates
```

#Code Segment 11.5:

```
#Data from Moody's Corporate Default and Recovery Rates,
#1920-2021 Exhibit 33 (1-year)
#and Barclays Capital,
#"The Corporate Default Probability Model," April 2009
#ratings=['AAA','AA','A','BBB','BB','B','≤CCC']
edf2009=[.0093,.0264,.1198,.4393,1.852,10.22,33.904]
indices = [1,2,3,4,5,6,7]
#Calculate optimal width
width = np.min(np.diff(indices))/3

migrations=pd.read_excel(moodys_default_filename, \
    sheet_name = 'Ex33', skiprows = 2, engine = \
    "openpyxl")

ratings=list(migrations.columns[1:-3])    #Labels for \
    ratings
```

```
moodys=np.array(migrations["Def"].iloc[:-1])
#average C's
moodys[-1]=(moodys[-1]+migrations["Def"].iloc[-1])/2.
ratings[-1]="≤"+ratings[-1]
moodys=np.multiply(moodys,100.)   #scale so that 1 means 1%

fig = plt.figure()
ax = fig.add_subplot(111)
ax.bar(indices-width,moodys,width,color='b', \
    label='Moodys')
ax.bar(indices,edf2009,width,color='r',label='Barclays')
plt.grid()
plt.xticks(indices,ratings)
plt.yscale('log')
plt.ylabel('Percentage freq. of default, log-scale')
plt.legend()
str_title="Figure 11.2: Default rates, Moody's \
    historical "+ default_date_range
str_title+="\n and Barclays model 2009, log-scale"
plt.title(str_title)
plt.show()
```

#Code Segment 11.6:

```
#Source: https://www.spglobal.com/ratings/en/research/
#articles/220504-default-transition-and-recovery-2021-
#annual-global-sovereign-default-and-rating-transition- \
    study-12350530
#Table 17
import pandas as pd
sandp_default_filename = "SandP global credit 2021.xlsx"

sandp_date_range = pd.read_excel(sandp_default_filename, \
    sheet_name='Sov Table 17', nrows=1, engine="openpyxl")

sandp_recent_date_range = sandp_date_range.iloc[0][0] \
    [-10:-1]

#Get table
sandp_cumulative_rates = pd.read_excel(sandp_default_ \
    filename,sheet_name='Sov Table 17', skiprows=2, \
    engine="openpyxl")
```

```
#Display table
print("Table 11.6: Standard & Poor's average sovereign \
    foreign currency", \
      "\n cumulative default rates (percents, 1.0=1%) \
    by letter rating, "+sandp_recent_date_range)
sandp_cumulative_rates
```

#Code Segment 11.7:

```
%matplotlib inline
import qrpm_funcs as qf
import matplotlib.pyplot as plt
#Get European rates - show spreads

lastday=qf.LastYearEnd()

seriesnames=['IRLTLT01DEM156N','IRLTLT01FRM156N', \
    'IRLTLT01PTM156N','IRLTLT01GRM156N']
shortnames=['France','Portugal','Greece']
cdates,ratematrix=qf.GetFREDMatrix(seriesnames, \
    startdate='1997-12-31', enddate=lastday)
nobs=len(cdates)
x=range(nobs)
for i in range(len(shortnames)):
    plt.plot(x,[(y[i+1]-y[0])*100 for y in ratematrix], \
        label=shortnames[i])

plt.ylabel("Annual spread (bps)")
stride=24
plt.xticks(range(0,nobs,stride),[dt[:7] for dt in \
    cdates[::stride]],rotation=45)
plt.legend()
plt.grid()
plt.title("Figure 11.3: European spreads over Germany, \
    10-year rates")
plt.show();

print("Ending values ("+lastday+") of spreads over \
    Germany in bps/year")
for i in range(len(shortnames)):
    diff=np.multiply(ratematrix[-1][i+1]- \
      ratematrix[-1][0],100.)
    print(shortnames[i]," %4.1f" % diff)
```

#Code Segment 11.8:

```
#Data from Moody's Corporate Default and Recovery Rates,
#1920-2021 Exhibit 29 (5-year)
recoveries=pd.read_excel(moodys_default_filename, \
    sheet_name = 'Ex29', engine = "openpyxl")
first_column_name = recoveries.columns[0]
recovery_date_range = first_column_name[-10:-1] \
    #Extract this table's date range
ig_recovery = np.multiply(100.float \
    (recoveries[recoveries[first_column_name]=="IG"] \
    ["Unnamed: 5"].iloc[0]))
print(recovery_date_range+" Investment-Grade Average \
    5-Year Recovery: %.2f percent" % ig_recovery)
sg_recovery = np.multiply(100.float \
    (recoveries[recoveries[first_column_name] =="SG"] \
    ["Unnamed: 5"].iloc[0]))
print(recovery_date_range+" Speculative-Grade Average \
    5-Year Recovery: %.2f percent" % sg_recovery)
```

#Code Segment 11.9:

```
#Rough calculation of loss rates. Note slightly \
    different time periods.
ig_rough_loss_rate = (100. - ig_recovery) \
    * ig_default_rate_since_1983
print(recovery_date_range+" Investment-Grade Rough \
    Annual Loss Rate: %.2f basis points per year" \
    %ig_rough_loss_rate)
sg_rough_loss_rate = (100. - sg_recovery) \
    * sg_default_rate_since_1983
print(recovery_date_range+" Speculative-Grade Rough \
    Annual Loss Rate: %.2f basis points per year" \
    % sg_rough_loss_rate)
```

#Code Segment 11.10:

```
loss_rates = pd.read_excel(moodys_default_filename, \
    sheet_name = 'Ex30', skiprows = 2, \
    engine = "openpyxl")
ig_average_loss_rate = np.multiply(loss_rates["IG"]. \
    mean(),10000.)
```

```
print(recovery_date_range+" Investment-Grade Average \
    Annual Loss Rate: %.2f basis points per year" % \
    ig_average_loss_rate)
sg_average_loss_rate = np.multiply(loss_rates["SG"]. \
    mean(),10000.)
print(recovery_date_range+" Speculative-Grade Average \
    Annual Loss Rate: %.2f basis points per year" \
    % sg_average_loss_rate)
```

#Code Segment 11.11:

```
import matplotlib.pyplot as plt
import numpy as np
import scipy.stats
import pandas as pd
import qrpm_funcs as qf
#Get Moody's AAA and BBB yields from FRED.
#Splice together long-term US Treasury rate series,
#and subtract them off to form credit spreads.
#Display and correlate with VIX

def smooth_series(series,back):
#Smooth a time series by averaging "back" observations
    cum_series=np.cumsum(series)
    #Take averages
    smoo=(cum_series[back:]-cum_series[:-back])/back
    #Tack on stub at end
    return(np.concatenate((smoo, series[-back:]), axis=0))

lastday=qf.LastYearEnd()
seriesnames=['AAA','BAA','M1333AUSM156NNBR', \
          'LTGOVTBD','IRLTCT01USM156N']
cdates,ratematrix=qf.GetFREDMatrix(seriesnames,
          enddate=lastday)

#Splice together the three overlapping long-term
#Treasury series. They agree where they overlap
longterm=[]
for t in range(len(ratematrix)):
    #Take average of non-nan values of the overlapping \
        series
```

```
    num_non_nan=np.count_nonzero(~np.isnan(ratematrix[t] \
        [2:5]))
    if num_non_nan==0:
        longterm.append(longterm[-1])    #propagate the \
            previous value
    else:
        longterm.append(np.nansum(ratematrix[t][2:5])/ \
            num_non_nan)

n=len(longterm)

#time series of differences is rough - smooth it
#Roughness probably comes from different timings of
#observations of corporate yields and Treasurys
back=5  #Will take rolling back-month averages
aaa=[x[0]-y for (x,y) in zip(ratematrix,longterm)]
aaamean=np.mean(aaa)
aaa=smooth_series(aaa, back)

bbb=[x[1]-y for (x,y) in zip(ratematrix,longterm)]
bbbmean=np.mean(bbb)
bbb=smooth_series(bbb, back)

#Apply same transform to Treasurys for correlation
tsy=smooth_series(longterm, back)

#Show spread time series and straight line for averages
alabel='Aaa (avg=%1.2f' % aaamean
alabel+=')'
plt.plot(range(n),aaa,label=alabel,color='blue')
plt.plot(range(n),[aaamean]*n,color='blue')
blabel='Baa (avg=%1.2f' % bbbmean
blabel+=')'
plt.plot(range(n),bbb,label=blabel,color='orange')
plt.plot(range(n),[bbbmean]*n,color='orange')

plt.legend()
plt.grid()
stride=int((n+1)/4)
places=np.arange(0,n+stride,stride)
places[len(places)-1]=n-1
displaydates=[cdates[j][:7] for j in places]
plt.ylabel("Percentage spread")
plt.xticks(places,displaydates)
```

```
plt.title("Figure 11.4: Moody's smoothed yield spreads \
    over Treasurys")
plt.show();

ab_level=scipy.stats.pearsonr(aaa,bbb)[0]
at_diff=scipy.stats.pearsonr(np.diff(aaa),np.diff(tsy))[0]
bt_diff=scipy.stats.pearsonr(np.diff(bbb),np.diff(tsy))[0]
ab_diff=scipy.stats.pearsonr(np.diff(aaa),np.diff(bbb))[0]
print("Spread and Treasury data starts",cdates[0][:7])
print("Aaa/Baa level correlation: %.5f" % ab_level)
print("Aaa/Tsy difference correlation: %.5f" % at_diff)
print("Baa/Tsy difference correlation: %.5f" % bt_diff)
print("Aaa/Baa difference correlation: %.5f" % ab_diff)

print("\nAaa mean since 1983:", \
    np.mean(aaa[cdates.index("1983-01-01"):]))
print("Baa mean since 1983:", \
    np.mean(bbb[cdates.index("1983-01-01"):]))
```

#Code Segment 11.12:

```
#Get total returns on IG, HY, and Treasury indices \
    from FRED
from datetime import datetime, timedelta

seriesnames=['BAMLHYH0A0HYM2TRIV','BAMLCC0A0CMTRIV','DGS10']
xdates,xratematrix=qf.GetFREDMatrix(seriesnames, \
    enddate=lastday)

#Put in dataframe
df_spreads = pd.DataFrame({'Date': pd.to_datetime \
                          (xdates),'HY': [row[0] for \
                          row in xratematrix],'IG':\
                          [row[1] for row in \
                          xratematrix],'Tsy': [row[2] \
                          for row in xratematrix]})
#Change to monthly and get rid of NAs
df_spreads=df_spreads.resample('M', on='Date').last(). \
    dropna()

#Convert Treasury rates to index levels. Only need final \
    value of bond_idx
#Assume rates given are for 10-year par bond paying \
    semiannually
```

```python
bond_idx=[100.]*len(df_spreads)
T20=20    #20 semiannual periods

oldrate=df_spreads['Tsy'].iloc[0]/200.    #Semiannual rate
for i in range(len(df_spreads)-1):
    #Use formula (3.8) to get duration of par bond
    #Coupon and discount rate are from the old period
    y=1/(1+oldrate)
    #Duration is in half-years
    duration=(oldrate*y/(1-y)**2)*(1-y**T20-T20* \
        (1-y)*y**T20)+T20*y**T20
    newrate=df_spreads['Tsy'].iloc[i+1]/200.
    #Return for the month
    bond_return=oldrate/6-duration*(newrate-oldrate)
    #Compute index levels for compatibility
    bond_idx[i+1]=bond_idx[i]*(1.+bond_return)
    oldrate=newrate

df_spreads['BondIndex'] = bond_idx    #Tack on the \
    index-ized 10-year rates

#Format start and end dates and get elapsed time in years
dt_start = datetime.strftime(df_spreads['Date'].iloc[0], \
    "%Y-%m-%d")
dt_end = datetime.strftime(df_spreads['Date'].iloc[-1], \
    "%Y-%m-%d")
years=(df_spreads['Date'].iloc[-1]-df_spreads['Date']. \
    iloc[0])/(timedelta(days=1)*365.25)

#Get annualized rates of return
tsy_annual=(df_spreads['BondIndex'].iloc[-1]/ \
    df_spreads['BondIndex'].iloc[0])**(1/years)-1.
ig_annual=(df_spreads['IG'].iloc[-1]/df_spreads['IG']. \
    iloc[0])**(1/years)-1.
hy_annual=(df_spreads['HY'].iloc[-1]/df_spreads['HY']. \
    iloc[0])**(1/years)-1.

#Get vols of log-returns of Tsy, IG, and HY
df_spreads['tsy_log_ret'] = np.log(df_spreads \
    ['BondIndex']).diff()
df_spreads['IG_log_ret'] = np.log(df_spreads['IG']).diff()
df_spreads['HY_log_ret'] = np.log(df_spreads['HY']).diff()
```

```
str_range="Annualized rates of return from "
str_range+=dt_start + " to " + dt_end + " (%4.1f" % \
    years + " years)"

print(str_range)
print("US Treasury 10-year: %5.4f, Vol: %5.4f" % \
      (tsy_annual,np.sqrt(12.)*df_spreads \
      ['tsy_log_ret'].std()))
print("US Corp Master (IG): %5.4f, Vol: %5.4f" % \
      (ig_annual,np.sqrt(12.)*df_spreads['IG_log_ret']. \
      std()))
print("  (spread over Tsy): %5.4f" % (ig_annual- \
      tsy_annual))
print("US HY Master 2     : %5.4f, Vol: %5.4f" % \
      (hy_annual,np.sqrt(12.)*df_spreads['HY_log_ret']. \
      std()))
print("  (spread over Tsy): %5.4f" %  (hy_annual- \
      tsy_annual))
```

#Code Segment 11.13:

```
import scipy.stats as spst
#Graph sample term structure of credit spreads

def bsm_d1_2var(sig_sqrttime,dratio):
    #Black-Scholes-Merton d1
    return((-np.log(dratio)+(sig_sqrttime**2/2))/ \
        sig_sqrttime)
#End bsm_d1_2var


def bsm_d2_2var(sig_sqrttime,dratio):
    #Black-Scholes-Merton d2
    return(bsm_d1_2var(sig_sqrttime,dratio)-sig_sqrttime)
#End bsm_d2_2var


def merton_credit_spread(sigma,T,dratio):
    #Merton credit spread (see 11.13, equivalent to \
        Merton (14))
    sigsqt=sigma*np.sqrt(T)
    d_1=bsm_d1_2var(sigsqt,dratio)
    d_2=bsm_d2_2var(sigsqt,dratio)
    log_arg=spst.norm.cdf(-d_1)/dratio+spst.norm.cdf(d_2)
    return(-np.log(log_arg)/T)
#End merton_credit_spread
```

```
sigma=np.sqrt(.2)
x=np.arange(.001,6.,.001)
for dratio in [.7,.8,.9,1.0,1.2]:
    y=[merton_credit_spread(sigma,t,dratio) for t in x]
    y2 = np.ma.masked_greater_equal(y, 0.4)
    plt.plot(x,y2,label=dratio)

plt.legend()
plt.grid()
plt.xlabel("Time (years)")
plt.ylabel("Spread over Treasury: .1 = 10%")
plt.title("Figure 11.5: Term structure of Merton credit \
    spreads, +"n sigma_V^2=sv2:.2f".format(sv2=sigma**2)")
plt.show();
```

#Code Segment 11.14:

```
#Draw capital stack for JNJ

def show_capital_stack(ticker,title,stock,par_debt):
    labels = [ticker]
    bottom_tranche = [stock]
    top_tranche = [par_debt]
    width = 0.35

    plt.bar(labels, bottom_tranche, width, label='Stock')
    plt.bar(labels, top_tranche, width, \
        bottom=bottom_tranche, label='Debt')

    plt.ylabel('Billions of dollars')
    plt.title(title)
    plt.legend()

    plt.show();

#Fourth quarter 2021
date_JNJ="2021Q3"
S_JNJ=449.737
D_par_JNJ=34.751-31.608
title="Figure 11.6: JNJ capital stack "+date_JNJ
show_capital_stack('JNJ',title,S_JNJ,D_par_JNJ)
```

#Code Segment 11.15:

```python
#Distance to default, d1, and black-scholes calculation
#For JNJ

def bsm_d1(underlying,strike,time,rfrate,sigma):
    #Black-Scholes-Merton d1
    return(bsm_d1_2var(sigma*np.sqrt(time), \
        strike*np.exp(-rfrate*time)/underlying))
#End bsm_d1

def bsm_d2(underlying,strike,time,rfrate,sigma):
    #Black-Scholes-Merton d2=d_def
    return(bsm_d2_2var(sigma*np.sqrt(time), \
        strike*np.exp(-rfrate*time)/underlying))
#End bsm_d2

def bsm(underlying,strike,time,rfrate,sigma):
    #Black-Scholes-Merton call price
    d_1=bsm_d1(underlying,strike,time,rfrate,sigma)
    d_2=bsm_d2(underlying,strike,time,rfrate,sigma)
    call_price=underlying*spst.norm.cdf(d_1)- \
        np.exp(-rfrate*time)*strike*spst.norm.cdf(d_2)
    return(call_price)
#End bsm

def show_merton_computations(name,S,D_par,sigma_S,r,T):
    #Rough calculation for enterprise value - see text \
        below for
    #better estimate
    V=S+D_par

    print('Ratios for %s:'% name)
    print('      D/V:',D_par/V)
    print('      D/S:',D_par/S)
    print('      S/V:',S/V)
    print(' ln(V/D):',np.log(V/D_par))

    #rough calculation for enterprise volatility - \
        scale stock
    #volatility by S/V
    sigma_V = (S/V)*sigma_S
    print('\nComputations for %s:'% name)
    print('      S/V-scaled enterprise vol:',sigma_V)
```

```
    print('Risk-neutral growth rate r-sig^2/2:', \
        r-sigma_V**2/2)

    #Risk-neutral distance to default
    d_def=bsm_d2(V,D_par,T,r,sigma_V)
    print("Risk-neutral distance to default:",d_def)
    print("   Default probability N(-d_def):", \
        spst.norm.cdf(-d_def))

    #Black-Scholes
    Call_V=bsm(V,D_par,T,r,sigma_V)
    Put_V = np.exp(-r*T)*D_par-V+Call_V
    print("\nDebt components for %s:"% name)
    print("              Par value of debt:",D_par)
    print("       Time value of par debt:", \
        D_par*(1-np.exp(-r*T)))
    print("          Value of default put:",Put_V)
    print(" Current market value of debt:",V-Call_V)
#End show_merton_computations

## Get 10-year Treasury rate at yearend
lastday=qf.LastYearEnd()
seriesnames=['DGS10']
tydates,tymatrix=qf.GetFREDMatrix(seriesnames, \
    startdate=lastday,enddate= lastday)
ten_year_tsy=tymatrix[0][0]/100.

#Data for JNJ; assume (counterfactually) 10-year debt \
    for illustrative purposes
#2021Q4 data from Bloomberg EV
#From 2021-12-31 Bloomberg HIVG
sigma_S_JNJ=.17255
show_merton_computations('JNJ',S_JNJ,D_par_JNJ, \
    sigma_S_JNJ, ten_year_tsy,10)

print("\nTable 11.3 10-year Aaa default  * \
    (1-IG-recovery) * D_par:",cumulative_rates \
    ["Aaa"][10]*(100.-ig_recovery)*D_par_JNJ/100.)
```

#Code Segment 11.16:

```python
#Iterative solution of sigma-v and V for JNJ
#Using (11.7) and (11.16)
import numpy as np
import scipy.stats as spst

def form11_16(stock,value,sigma_stock,d_1):
    #Formula 11.16 for enterprise volatility
    return(stock*sigma_stock/(spst.norm.cdf(d_1)*value))

def iter_enterprise(name,stock,d_par,sigma_stock, \
    rfree,time):
    #Search for V that solves S(=observed stock \
        price)=bsm(V, sigmaV)
    #where sigmaV is according to 11.11
    #Bracket solution for binary search
    V0=d_par+stock/2 #Starting guess
    Vsmall, Vbig = 0, 2*V0
    threshhold = 10**(-8)
    count = 0
    while count < 200:
        #Try enterprise value in brackets
        V=(Vsmall+Vbig)/2
        d1=bsm_d1(V,d_par,time,rfree,sigma_stock)
        sigma_V=form11_16(stock,V,sigma_stock,d1)
        new_S=bsm(V,d_par,time,rfree,sigma_V)
        #Which way to go for binary search?
        if new_S-stock > threshhold:
            Vbig = V
        elif stock-new_S > threshhold:
            Vsmall = V
        else:
            break
        count+=1

    print('%s enterprise value at par:     %5.3f' \
        % (name,stock+d_par))
    print('%s enterprise value at market:  %5.3f' \
        % (name,V))
    print('%s enterprise volatility:       %5.3f' \
        % (name,sigma_V))
```

```
    print('\n                            D_par:', \
        d_par)
    print('  Market value of debt (D_par-Put=V-S):', \
        V-stock)
    print('                Time value of par debt:', \
        d_par*(1-np.exp(-rfree*time)))
    print('              Implied default put value:', \
        d_par*np.exp(-rfree*time)-V+stock)
    print('Default put value as a fraction of par:', \
        np.exp(-rfree*time)-(V-stock)/d_par)
    print('                        d_1 at solution:', \
        d1)
    print('(%d iterations for accuracy %e' % \
        (count,threshhold)+')')
#Done with iter_enterprise

#For JNJ
iter_enterprise('JNJ',S_JNJ,D_par_JNJ,sigma_S_JNJ, \
    ten_year_tsy,10)
```

#Code Segment 11.17:

```
#Fourth quarter 2021
date_CHTR="2021Q4"
S_CHTR=112.622
D_par_CHTR=204.942-S_CHTR
title="Figure 11.7: CHTR capital stack"
show_capital_stack('CHTR',title,S_CHTR,D_par_CHTR)
```

#Code Segment 11.18:

```
#Data for CHTR; assume (counterfactually) 10-year debt \
    for illustrative purposes
sigma_S_CHTR=.29561    #From Bloomberg HIVG
iter_enterprise('CHTR',S_CHTR, \
    D_par_CHTR,sigma_S_CHTR, ten_year_tsy,10)
#Bonds used for YAS: 4.75 of 2/1/32 on February 24, \
    2022: OAS of 351

print("\nTable 11.3 10-year Ba default \
    * (1-SG-recovery) * D_par:",cumulative_rates \
    ["Ba"][10]*(100.-sg_recovery)*D_par_CHTR/100.)
```

#Code Segment 11.19:

```python
#Get VIX index (which is daily)
vxnames=['VXOCLS','VIXCLS']
vxdates,vxmatrix=qf.GetFREDMatrix(vxnames,enddate=lastday)

#Drop double nans
combined_dates=[]
combined_vix=[]
for i in range(len(vxdates)):
    if not all(np.isnan(vxmatrix[i])):
        combined_dates.append(vxdates[i])
        combined_vix.append(vxmatrix[i][1]) \
            #Use VIX but switch to VXO if not available
        if np.isnan(combined_vix[-1]): combined_vix[-1] \
            =vxmatrix[i][0]

#Find monthends
monthend_dates=[]
monthend_vix=[]
for i in range(1,len(combined_dates)+1):
    usenextguy = (i==len(combined_dates))   #last \
        datapoint is a monthend
    if not usenextguy:
        usenextguy = (combined_dates[i-1].split('-') \
            [1]!=combined_dates[i].split('-')[1])
    if usenextguy:
        monthend_dates.append(combined_dates[i-1])
        monthend_vix.append(combined_vix[i-1])

#cdates and ratematrix from Figure 11.4
#find out start of VIX data in bond yield data
#Monthly dates for bond yields look like
#YYYY-MM-01 but they're really the last business day
vixstart=cdates.index(vxdates[0][:8]+'01')
rates_and_vix=[ratematrix[vixstart+i]+[monthend_vix[i]] \
    for i in range(len(monthend_vix))]

#Smooth VIX
vix=[x[5] for x in rates_and_vix]
vix2=np.cumsum(vix)
vix3=(vix2[back:]-vix2[:-back])/back
vix=np.concatenate((vix3, vix[-back:]), axis=0)
```

```python
#Correlate smoothed spreads with VIX
av_level,av_pvalue=scipy.stats. \
    pearsonr(vix,aaa[vixstart:])
bv_level,bv_pvalue=scipy.stats. \
    pearsonr(vix,bbb[vixstart:])
av_diff,avd_pvalue=scipy.stats. \
    pearsonr(np.diff(vix),np.diff(aaa[vixstart:]))
bv_diff,bvd_pvalue=scipy.stats. \
    pearsonr(np.diff(vix),np.diff(bbb[vixstart:]))
print("VIX data starts",cdates[vixstart][:7], \
    "ends",cdates[-1][:7]+";",len(vix),"periods")
print("Aaa/VIX level correlation: %.5f" % av_level)
print("Baa/VIX level correlation: %.5f" % bv_level)
print("Aaa/VIX difference correlation: %.5f" % av_diff)
print("Baa/VIX difference correlation: %.5f" % bv_diff)
high_pvalue=max(av_pvalue,bv_pvalue,avd_pvalue,bvd_pvalue)
print("Reject null hypothesis of zero correlation \
        with\n"+ \
        "    probability at least one minus:",high_pvalue)
```

#Code Segment 11.20:

```python
#Show correlations by decade rates/spreads

lastdecade=int(lastday[:3])
lastdecade*=10
decades=np.arange(1920,lastdecade+1,10)

decade_starts=[]
for d in decades:
    decade_string=str(d)+'-01-01'
    decade_starts.append(cdates.index(decade_string))

#Close out most recent decade
decade_starts.append(len(cdates))

decade_correlations=[]
for i,d in enumerate(decades):
    avgspd_decade=( \
        aaa[decade_starts[i]:decade_starts[i+1]]+ \
        bbb[decade_starts[i]:decade_starts[i+1]])/2
```

```
      tsy_decade=tsy[decade_starts[i]:decade_starts[i+1]]
      avgt_diff=scipy.stats.pearsonr \
          (np.diff(avgspd_decade),np.diff(tsy_decade))[0]
      decade_correlations.append(avgt_diff)

#Display bar chart
indices=np.arange(len(decades))
width = 0.4
plt.bar(indices,decade_correlations,width,color='black')
plt.grid()
plt.xticks(indices,decades)
plt.ylabel("Correlation")
plt.title("Figure 11.8: Correlations by decade:\n  \
    AAA/BBB average spd chgs versus Treasury rate chgs")
plt.show();

at_diff,at_pvalue=scipy.stats.pearsonr(np.diff(aaa), \
    np.diff(tsy))
bt_diff,bt_pvalue=scipy.stats.pearsonr(np.diff(bbb), \
    np.diff(tsy))

print("Spread and Treasury data starts",cdates[0][:7], \
    "ends",cdates[-1][:7]+";","periods:",len(cdates))
print("AAA/Tsy difference correlation: %.5f" %at_diff, \
        "p-value:",at_pvalue)
print("BBB/Tsy difference correlation: %.5f" %bt_diff, \
        "p-value:",bt_pvalue)
```

#Code Segment 12.1:

```
import pandas as pd
import qrpm_funcs as qf
import numpy as np
from datetime import datetime
import ssl
#Get exchange rates and US riskfree rates
lastday=qf.LastYearEnd()
seriesnames=['DEXUSEU','DGS1']
while True:
    cdates,ratematrix=qf.GetFREDMatrix(seriesnames, \
      enddate=lastday)
    usd_per_euro=ratematrix[-1][0]
    rt1_us=ratematrix[-1][1]
```

```python
    if not np.isnan(usd_per_euro): break
    lastday=lastday[:8]+str(int(lastday[-2:])-1)   #Back\
        up over holidays

print("As of:",cdates[-1])
usd_per_euro=ratematrix[-1][0]
rt1_us=ratematrix[-1][1]
print("    Spot dollars per euro (f/d) %.4f" \
    % usd_per_euro)
print("    US 1-year rate rf %.4f" % rt1_us)

#Put end-of-month exchange rates in dataframe for \
    later use
df_fx_d = pd.DataFrame(np.array(ratematrix)[:,0], \
                index=[datetime.strptime \
                (cd,"%Y-%m-%d") for cd in cdates], \
                columns=[seriesnames[0]])
#Drop NaNs and save only monthends
df_fx=df_fx_d.dropna().resample('M').last()
#Form log-returns; negative means dollar strengthened
#so it is ln((f/d)1/(f/d)0) where f is dollar d is euro
df_fx=np.log(df_fx).diff().dropna()

#Problem with Bundesbank's certificate - drop verification
try:
    _create_unverified_https_context = ssl._create_ \
        unverified_context
except AttributeError:
    # Legacy Python that doesn't verify HTTPS \
        certificates by default
    pass
else:
    # Handle target environment that doesn't support \
        HTTPS verification
    ssl._create_default_https_context = _create_ \
        unverified_https_context

#Read one-year rates from Bundesbank
bundesbank_url = "https://www.bundesbank.de/statistic-rmi/
        StatisticDownload?tsId="
bundesbank_url += "BBSIS.M.I.ZST.ZI.EUR.S1311.B.A604. \
    R01XX.R.A.A._Z._Z.A&"
```

```
bundesbank_url += "its_csvFormat=en&its_ \
    fileFormat=csv&mode=its"
df_csv = pd.read_csv(bundesbank_url,skiprows=4)
df_german = df_csv.rename(index=str, \
        columns={df_csv.columns[0]: "Date", \
        df_csv.columns[1]: "Rate"})
#Check latest
bundesbank_lastdate=df_german['Date'].iloc[-1]
if bundesbank_lastdate >= lastday[:7]:
    rt1_german=df_german.loc[df_german['Date'] == \
        lastday[:7]]["Rate"].iloc[0]
    bundesbank_lastdate = lastday[:7]
else: #Bundesbank hasn't yet updated rates to last day \
    of previous year. Mach Schnell!
    rt1_german=df_german["Rate"].iloc[-1]

print("    German 1-year rate rd %.4f" % rt1_german, \
    "as of",bundesbank_lastdate)

#Calculate currency forward price per (12.2)
time=1
fwd_price=usd_per_euro*np.exp((rt1_us-rt1_german)* \
    time/100.)
print("\n    1yr forward dollars per euro %.4f" \
    %fwd_price)
```

#Code Segment 12.2:

```
euro_invested=10000.
euro_forward=euro_invested*np.exp(rt1_german/100*time)
usd_invested=euro_invested*usd_per_euro
usd_forward=usd_invested*np.exp(rt1_us/100*time)

def show_currency_forward_table(title):

    print(title)
    print("Item         |         Dollars (USD=f)         |
        Euros (EUR=d)    |       Ratio")
    print("-"*90)
    print("Time 0     |", \
        "         {:8,.1f}".format(usd_invested), \
        "         |       {:8,.1f}".
    format(euro_invested), \
```

```
          "          |  Spot USD/EUR {:6,.4f}".
       format(usd_per_euro))
    print("1yr rfree |", \
          "              {:8,.3f}".format(rt1_us), \
          "           |          {:8,.3f}".
       format(rt1_german), \
          "          |")
    print("Time 1    |", \
          "              {:8,.1f}".format(usd_forward), \
          "           |          {:8,.1f}".
       format(euro_forward), \
          "          |  Fwd USD/EUR {:6,.4f}".
       format(fwd_price))

show_currency_forward_table("Table 12.1: Hedging \
    EUR 10,000")
```

#Code Segment 12.3:

```
show_currency_forward_table("Table 12.2: Hedging plus \
    gain")

#Calculations for Philippe's investment in TSLA
#under dollar-crash/TSLA up scenario
underlying_dollar_appreciation=.2
new_usd_per_euro=5
new_tsla_value=usd_invested*(1+underlying_dollar_ \
    appreciation)
unhedged_tsla_gain_usd=new_tsla_value-usd_forward
unhedged_tsla_gain_euro=unhedged_tsla_gain_usd/
     new_usd_per_euro
final_euro_total=euro_forward+unhedged_tsla_gain_euro

print("T=1 TSLA  |", \
      "              {:8,.1f}".format(new_tsla_value), \
      "           |                        ", \
      "|              {:6,.4f}". \
    format(underlying_dollar_appreciation))
print("T=1 Unhdgd|", \
      "              {:8,.1f}". \
    format(unhedged_tsla_gain_usd), \
      "           |          {:8,.1f}". \
    format(unhedged_tsla_gain_euro), \
```

```
        "        |Crash USD/EUR {:6,.4f}". \
     format(new_usd_per_euro))
print("Final amt |", \
        "                    ", \
        "           |          {:8,.1f}". \
     format(final_euro_total), \
        "        | Final return {:6,.4f}". \
     format(final_euro_total/euro_invested-1.))
print("No hedge  |", \
        "           {:8,.1f}".format(new_tsla_value), \
        "           |          {:8,.1f}".format(new_tsla_ \
     value/new_usd_per_euro), \
        "        |Final no hdg {:6,.4f}".format( \
                      (new_tsla_value/new_usd_per_ \
     euro)/euro_invested-1.))
```

#Code Segment 12.4:

```
#Parameter calculations for dollar/euro TSLA quanto
import yfinance as yf
#https://github.com/ranaroussi/yfinance

tsla = yf.Ticker("TSLA")
df_tsla=tsla.history(period="max")    #Prices are adjusted
df_tsla=df_tsla.resample('M').last()
#Form log-returns
df_tsla=pd.DataFrame(np.log(df_tsla["Close"]).diff(). \
    dropna())

# Join underlying and currency
df_join=df_tsla.join(df_fx).dropna()

print("Data from",df_join.index[0]. \
    strftime("%Y-%m-%d"),"to", \
    df_join.index[-1].strftime("%Y-%m-%d"))
#Current price of underlying in foreign currency
X_0=usd_invested
print("           Current price of underlying X_0: \
    %.2f" % X_0)
print("                            Time horizon T: \
    %f" % time)
print("           Domestic riskfree rate r_d: \
    %.4f" % rt1_german)
```

```
print("                    Foreign riskfree rate r_f: \
    %.4f" % rt1_us)
print("         Foreign currency strike price K_f: \
    %.2f" % usd_forward)


#Annualized standard deviations
sigma_X=df_join.std()["Close"]*np.sqrt(12.)
sigma_R=df_join.std()[df_fx.columns[0]]*np.sqrt(12.)
print("Annualized volatility of underlying sigma_X: \
    %.4f" % sigma_X)
print(" Annualized volatility of f/x rate sigma_R: \
    %.4f" % sigma_R)
#Correlation
rho=df_join.corr().iloc[0,1]
print("    Correlation between underlying and f/x: \
    %.4f" % rho)
```

#Code Segment 12.5:

```
import scipy.stats as spst

#Prices of quanto call and quanto put
def quanto_call(X_0,T,r_f,r_d,K_f,sigma_X,sigma_R,rho):
    #returns price of quanto call from (12.23)
    #Variables have to be positive
    if X_0<=0 or T<=0 or K_f<=0 or sigma_X<0 or sigma_R<0:
        return(0)
    q=r_d-r_f-rho*sigma_X*sigma_R
    d_plus=(np.log(X_0/K_f)+(r_d-q+sigma_X**2/2)*T)/ \
        (sigma_X*np.sqrt(T))
    d_minus=d_plus-sigma_X*np.sqrt(T)
    #Get cumulative normals
    n_of_d_plus=spst.norm.cdf(d_plus)
    n_of_d_minus=spst.norm.cdf(d_minus)
    qc=X_0*np.exp(-q*T)*n_of_d_plus-K_f*np. \
        exp(-r_d*T)*n_of_d_minus
    return(qc)

def quanto_put(X_0,T,r_f,r_d,K_f,sigma_X,sigma_R,rho):
    #compute price of quanto put from (12.25)
    #calls quanto_call and uses put-call parity
```

```python
    qc=quanto_call(X_0,T,r_f,r_d,K_f,sigma_X,sigma_R,rho)
    qp=qc-X_0+np.exp(-r_d*T)*K_f

    return(qp)

#Compute example quanto call value
q_c = quanto_call(X_0, time, rt1_us/100., \
            rt1_german/100., usd_forward,sigma_X, \
            sigma_R, rho)
#Scale by 1/fwd
q_c/=fwd_price
print("              Buy Quanto call: %.2f" % q_c)

#Compute example plain vanilla call value
bs_c = quanto_call(X_0, time, rt1_us/100.,  \
            rt1_us/100., usd_forward,sigma_X, 0., 0.)
print("       Write Dollar-only call: %.2f" % bs_c)

up_cost=q_c-bs_c
print("  Cost of hedging TSLA upside: %.2f" % up_cost)

#Compute example quanto put value
q_p = quanto_put(X_0, time, rt1_us/100., \
            rt1_german/100., usd_forward,sigma_X,  \
            sigma_R, rho)
#Scale by 1/fwd
q_p/=fwd_price
print("\n              Write Quanto put: %.2f" % q_p)

#Compute example plain vanilla put value
bs_p = quanto_put(X_0, time, rt1_us/100., rt1_us/100., \
            usd_forward,sigma_X, 0., 0.)
print("          Buy Dollar-only put: %.2f" % bs_p)

down_cost=bs_p-q_p
print("Cost of hedging TSLA downside: %.2f "% down_cost)
total_cost=up_cost+down_cost
print("\n        Total cost of hedging: %.2f" \
    % total_cost)
```

#Code Segment 12.6:

```
pwc_french_euro_budget=20000000.
french_bottle_cost=10.
us_bottle_cost=french_bottle_cost*usd_per_euro
french_bottle_sales_price=french_bottle_cost*1.1
pwc_num_imported=pwc_french_euro_budget/french_bottle_cost

print("Table 12.3: Philippe Wine Company summary")
print("Location      |       France")
print("CEO           |       Philippe")
print("Import budget| EUR {:12,.1f}". \
    format(pwc_french_euro_budget))
print("Cost/bottle   |    USD {:7.4f}". \
    format(us_bottle_cost))
print("Sales price   |    EUR {:7.4f}". \
    format(french_bottle_sales_price))
print("Num imported  |     {:12,.1f}". \
    format(pwc_num_imported))

print("\nT=0 USD/EUR  |    USD {:7.4f}".
      format(usd_per_euro))
print("Cost/bot, lcl|    EUR {:7.4f}". \
    format(french_bottle_cost))
print("Profit        |    EUR {:12,.1f}". \
    format(pwc_num_imported*(french_bottle_sales_ \
    price-french_ bottle_cost)))

fx_bad=us_bottle_cost/french_bottle_sales_price
print("\nBad USD/EUR  |    USD {:7.4f}".format(fx_bad))
print("Cost/bot, lcl|    EUR {:7.4f}". \
    format(us_bottle_cost/fx_bad))
print("Profit        |    EUR {:12,.1f}".format(0))
```

#Code Segment 12.7:

```
#Calculations for Philippe-Ken Wine Company

def display_company_stats(new_rate,title):

    french_euro_budget=10000000.
    french_bottle_cost=10.
    us_bottle_cost=french_bottle_cost*usd_per_euro
```

```
us_usd_budget=french_euro_budget*usd_per_euro
french_bottle_sales_price=french_bottle_cost*1.1
us_bottle_sales_price=us_bottle_cost*1.1

print(title)
print("Location        |       France       |       USA \
        |     Total")
print("CEO             |       Philippe     |       Ken \
        |")
print("Import budget| EUR {:12,.1f}". \
      format(french_euro_budget), \
      " | USD {:12,.1f}".format(us_usd_budget),"|")
print("Cost/bottle  |     USD {:7.4f}". \
      format(us_bottle_cost), \
      "    |     EUR {:7.4f}". \
      format(french_bottle_cost),"  |")
print("Sales price  |     EUR %.4f" % \
      french_bottle_sales_price, \
      "   |     USD %.4f" % us_bottle_sales_price,"  |")

print("\n")
local_french_cost=us_bottle_cost/new_rate
local_us_cost=french_bottle_cost*new_rate
french_bottles=french_euro_budget*new_rate/ \
      us_bottle_cost
us_bottles=us_usd_budget/new_rate/french_bottle_cost
total_bottles=french_bottles+us_bottles
french_pandl=french_bottles*(11-us_bottle_cost/ \
      new_rate)
us_pandl=us_bottles*(us_bottle_sales_price-french_ \
      bottle_cost*new_rate)
total_pandl=french_pandl+us_pandl/new_rate

print("USD/EUR         |     %.4f" % new_rate,"        | \
                |")

print("Cost/bot lcl |     EUR {:7.4f}". \
      format(local_french_cost), "   |        \
      USD {:7.4f}".format(local_us_cost),"  |")
print("Num imported |     {:12,.1f}". \
      format(french_bottles), \
      " |     {:12,.1f}".format(us_bottles), \
      "|     {:12,.1f}".format(total_bottles))
```

```
    print("Profit         |   EUR{:12,.1f}". \
        format(french_pandl), \
        " |   USD{:12,.1f}".format(us_pandl), \
        "|  EUR{:12,.1f}".format(total_pandl))


#Show table at current exchange rate
display_company_stats(usd_per_euro, \
                "Table 12.4: Philippe-Ken Wine Company: \
                unchanged f/x")
```

#Code Segment 12.8:

```
display_company_stats(1.0,"Table 12.5: Philippe-Ken Wine \
    Company: strong dollar")
```

#Code Segment 12.9:

```
display_company_stats(1.5,"Table 12.6: Philippe-Ken Wine \
    Company: weak dollar")
```

#Code Segment 12.10:

```
#Show number-of-bottles curve for Siegel's paradox
%matplotlib inline
import matplotlib.pyplot as plt

x=np.arange(usd_per_euro-.3,usd_per_euro+.3+.01,.01)
z=x/usd_per_euro
y=z+1/z

i=np.arange(len(x))
plt.plot(i,y,color='red')
plt.xticks(i[::10],[str(round(float(label), 3)) \
    for label in x[::10]])
plt.xlabel("Dollars per euro")
plt.ylabel("Millions of bottles")
plt.title("Figure 12.1 Total bottle volume of \
    Philippe-Ken Wine Company")
plt.grid()
plt.show()
```

#Code Segment 12.11:

```python
#More Siegel's Paradox calculations
#Roots of quadratic in (12.12)
a_poly=11
b_poly=-1
c_poly=-11
discriminant=b_poly**2-4*a_poly*c_poly

low_root=(-b_poly-np.sqrt(discriminant))/(2*a_poly)
high_root=(-b_poly+np.sqrt(discriminant))/(2*a_poly)
print("Roots of (12.12) polynomial:",low_root,1,high_root)

print("Profit less than original between (f/d)=", \
      usd_per_euro,"and",high_root*usd_per_euro)

#minimum profit location
min_root=(4+np.sqrt(158/3))/11
print("Minimum profit at z=",min_root, \
      "(f/d)=",min_root*usd_per_euro)

#minimum profit amount
min_profit=1000000*(min_root+1)* \
    (11-21*min_root+11*min_ root**2)/min_root**2
print("Minimum hedged profit",min_profit)
profit_giveup_percent=100.-min_profit/20000.
print("Percentage profit giveup at minimum:  \
    %.2f" % profit_giveup_percent)
#Compute unhedged profit at that point
print("Unhedged (PWC) profit at minimum hedged profit:", \
    20000000*(1.1*min_root-1))
```

#Code Segment 12.12:

```python
#Show profitability graphs for Siegel's paradox -
#Philippe-Ken Wine Company

#Broad range and narrow range
x=np.arange(.5,2.01,.01)
title_str="Figure 12.2: Philippe-Ken Wine Company profit"

for graph_no in [1,2]:

    z=x/usd_per_euro
```

```python
    y_hedged=[(zz+1)*(11-21*zz+11*zz**2)/zz**2 \
        for zz in z]   #(12.29)
    y_unhedged=20*(1.1*z-1)
    y_constant=[2]*len(y_hedged)

    i=np.arange(len(x))
    plt.plot(i,y_hedged,color='red', \
        label='US/France PKWC')
    if graph_no==1:
        plt.plot(i,y_unhedged,color='blue', \
            label='France only PWC')
    plt.plot(i,y_constant,color='green', \
        label='Unchanged rates')
    plt.xticks(i[::20],[str(round(float(label), 3)) \
        for label in x[::20]])
    plt.xlabel("Dollars per euro")
    plt.ylabel("Millions of euros")
    plt.legend(loc='lower right')
    plt.title(title_str)
    plt.grid()
    plt.show()

    #next iteration
    x=np.arange(usd_per_euro,high_root* \
        usd_per_euro+.001,.001)
    title_str="Figure 12.3: Philippe-Ken Wine company \
        profit: neighborhood"
```

```python
#Code Segment 12.13:
```

```python
#Get Treasury rates; compare them to SOFR rates from \
    IHS Markit
import pandas as pd
import numpy as np
import qrpm_funcs as qf
import matplotlib.pyplot as plt
%matplotlib inline

fname="USD SOFR"
df_out = pd.read_excel(fname+".xlsx",engine="openpyxl")
#Drop unused old index column
df_out = df_out.drop(df_out.columns[0], axis=1)
```

```python
seriesnames = ['DGS3MO','DGS1','DGS5','DGS10','DGS20', \
    'DGS30']
tenors = [3.,12.,60.,120.,240.,360.]
firstday = df_out["Reference Date"].iloc[0]. \
    strftime('%Y-%m-%d')
lastday = qf.LastYearEnd()

cdates,ratematrix = qf.GetFREDMatrix(seriesnames, \
    startdate=firstday,enddate=lastday)

df_tsys = pd.DataFrame(ratematrix,columns=seriesnames)
df_tsys["Date"] = cdates

df_tsys.dropna(inplace=True)      #Drop NaNs
df_tsys.set_index("Date",inplace=True) \
        #Make the date the index

#Combine Treasurys and SOFR so spreads can be computed
df_both = df_tsys.copy()
for t,m in enumerate(tenors):
    #Form dataframe with SOFR rates
    df_m = pd.DataFrame(list(df_out["Interest Rate"] \
                 [df_out["Int Months"]==m]), \
                 columns=["X"+seriesnames[t]])
    df_m["Date"] = list(df_out["Reference Date"] \
                 [df_out["Int Months"]==m].dt. \
                 strftime('%Y-%m-%d'))
    df_m.set_index("Date",inplace=True)
    df_both = df_both.join(df_m, how = 'inner')

#Form spread series
for series in seriesnames:
    df_both["S"+series[3:]]=df_both["X"+series]- \
        df_both[series]
    #Drop components
    df_both = df_both.drop(columns=["X"+series,series])

figtitle="Figure 12.4: US swap spreads over Treasurys"+ \
    "(by maturity)\nSource:IHS Markit"
df_both.plot(title=figtitle,ylabel="pct",grid=True,rot=45)
```

#Code Segment 12.14:

```
spread_profit = - 10**8 * df_both["S30"].iloc[-1] * \
    10**(-2)
print("Profit from $100Mn 30-year spread: ${:,}". \
    format(spread_profit),"as of",df_both.index[-1])
```

#Code Segment 12.15:

```
#Show put buying

#Graphing code used in all subsequent distribution \
    shaping figures
def dual_dist_hedge_graph(x,y,y_norm,leg_trade, \
    title1,title2):
    plt.figure(figsize=(12,4))
    #Payoff graph
    plt.subplot(1,2,1)
    plt.plot(x,x,label='Underlying')
    plt.plot(x,y,label=leg_trade)
    plt.xlabel("Underlying at maturity")
    plt.ylabel("Value at maturity")
    plt.grid()
    plt.legend()
    plt.title(title1)
    #Distribution graph
    plt.subplot(1,2,2)
    plt.xlabel("Underlying")
    plt.ylabel("Probability density")
    plt.plot(x,y_norm,label='Original')
    plt.plot(y,y_norm,label=leg_trade)
    plt.grid()
    plt.legend()
    plt.title(title2)

    plt.show()

#Front ends for quanto_call and quanto_put routines above
#Simplifies them to Black-Scholes (same as formula 9.3)
def black_scholes_call(X,K,T,r,sigma):
    return(quanto_call(X,T,r,r,K,sigma,0.,1.))
def black_scholes_put(X,K,T,r,sigma):
    return(quanto_put(X,T,r,r,K,sigma,0.,1.))
```

```
#Common parameters used in all subsequent distribution \
    shaping figures
money=100
time=1
rfree=.02
sigma=.2
x=np.arange(50.,150.,1.)
y_norm=spst.norm.pdf(np.log(x),np.log(money)+ \
    rfree*time,sigma)

#Buy-put trade
put_strike=90
put_cost=black_scholes_put(money,put_strike,time, \
    rfree,sigma)

under_with_trade=[max(put_strike-put_cost,u-put_cost) \
    for u in x]
title_1="Figure 12.6a: Payoff of put plus underlying: \
    \nstrike=%3.f" % put_strike
title_1+=", cost=%2.2f" % put_cost
title_2="Figure 12.6b: Density function with and \
    w/out put"
legend="W/put"

dual_dist_hedge_graph(x,under_with_trade,y_norm,legend, \
    title_1,title_2)
```

```
#Code Segment 12.16:
```

```
#Show selling call

call_strike=110
call_cost=black_scholes_call(money,call_strike,time, \
    rfree, sigma)

under_with_trade=[min(call_strike+call_cost,u+call_cost) \
    for u in x]
title_1="Figure 12.7a: Payoff of underlying minus call: \
    \nstrike=%3.f" % call_strike
```

```
title_1+=", Cost=%2.2f" % call_cost
title_2="Figure 12.7b: Density function with and w/out \
    written call"
legend="W/call"


dual_dist_hedge_graph(x,under_with_trade,y_norm,legend, \
    title_1,title_2)
```

#Code Segment 12.17:

```
#Show put spread

low_put_strike=80
high_put_strike=90
low_put_cost=black_scholes_put(money,low_put_strike, \
    time,rfree,sigma)
high_put_cost=black_scholes_put(money,high_put_strike, \
    time,rfree,sigma)

under_with_trade=np.concatenate(( \
    [u+high_put_strike-low_put_strike for u in x if \
        u<=low_put_strike], \
    [high_put_strike for u in x if \
        low_put_strike<u<high_put_strike], \
    [u for u in x if u>=high_put_strike]))
under_with_trade-=(high_put_cost-low_put_cost)

title_1="Figure 12.8a: Payoff of put spread plus \
    underlying:\nHighStrk=%3.f"% high_put_strike
title_1+=", HighCst=%2.2f" % high_put_cost
title_1+=";\nLowStrk=%3.f" % low_put_strike
title_1+=", LowCst=%2.2f" %low_put_cost
title_2="Figure 12.8b: Density function with and w/out \
    put spread"
legend="W/put spread"

dual_dist_hedge_graph(x,under_with_trade,y_norm,legend, \
    title_1,title_2)
```

#Code Segment 12.18:

```
#Show (bear) call spread

low_call_strike=110
high_call_strike=120
low_call_cost=black_scholes_call(money,low_call_strike, \
    time,rfree,sigma)
high_call_cost=black_scholes_call(money, \
    high_call_strike,time,rfree,sigma)

under_with_trade=np.concatenate(( \
    [u for u in x if \ u<=low_call_strike], \
    [low_call_strike for u in x if
        low_call_strike<u<high_call_strike], \
    [u+low_call_strike-high_call_strike for u in x if
        u>=high_call_strike]))
under_with_trade+=(low_call_cost-high_call_cost)

title_1="Figure 12.9a: Payoff of call spread plus\
    underlying:\nHighStrk=%3.f" \
    % high_call_strike
title_1+=", HighCst=%2.2f" % high_call_cost
title_1+=";\nLowStrk=%3.f" % low_call_strike
title_1+=", LowCst=%2.2f" %low_call_cost
title_2="Figure 12.9b: Density function with and w/out \
    call spread"
legend="W/call spread"

dual_dist_hedge_graph(x,under_with_trade,y_norm,legend, \
    title_1,title_2)
```

#Code Segment 12.19:

```
#Show a long straddle

call_cost=black_scholes_call(money,money,time,rfree,sigma)
put_cost=black_scholes_put(money,money,time,rfree,sigma)

under_with_trade=np.concatenate(\
    ([money-call_cost-put_cost for u in x if \
        u<=money], \
```

12 Appendix: Code Segments585

```
        [u+(u-money)-call_cost-put_cost for u in x if \
            u>money]))

title_1="Figure 12.10a: Payoff of underlying plus \
    straddle:"+"\nCall Strike=Put Strike=%3.f" % money
title_1+=",\nCall Cost=%2.2f" % call_cost
title_1+=", Put Cost=%2.2f" % put_cost
title_2="Figure 12.10b: Density function with and w/out \
    +straddle"
legend="W/+straddle"

dual_dist_hedge_graph(x,under_with_trade,y_norm,legend, \
    title_1,title_2)
```

#Code Segment 12.20:

```
#Show a short straddle

under_with_trade=np.concatenate(\
    ([u+(u-money)+call_cost+put_cost for u in x if \
    u<=money],[money+call_cost+put_cost for u in x if \
    u>money]))

title_1="Figure 12.11a: Payoff of underlying minus \
    straddle:"+"\nCall Strike=Put Strike=%3.f" % money
title_1+=",\nCall Cost=%2.2f" % call_cost
title_1+=", Put Cost=%2.2f" % put_cost
title_2="Figure 12.11b: Density function with and w/o \
    -straddle"
legend="W/-straddle"

dual_dist_hedge_graph(x,under_with_trade,y_norm,legend, \
    title_1,title_2)
```

#Code Segment 12.21:

```
#Show a (short) strangle

put_strike=90
call_strike=110

put_cost=black_scholes_put(money,put_strike,time, \
    rfree,sigma)
```

```
call_cost=black_scholes_call(money,call_strike,time, \
    rfree, sigma)

under_with_trade=np.concatenate(\
    ([u+(u-put_strike) for u in x if u<=put_strike], \
    [u for u in x if put_strike<u<call_strike], \
    [call_strike for u in x if u>=call_strike]))
under_with_trade+=call_cost+put_cost

title_1="Figure 12.12a: Payoff of underlying with \
    strangle:\nCall Strike=%3.f" % call_strike
title_1+=", Call Cost=%2.2f" % call_cost
title_1+=";\nPut Strike=%3.f" % put_strike
title_1+=", Put Cost=%2.2f" % put_cost
title_2="Figure 12.12b: Density function with and \
    w/out strangle"
legend="W/strangle"

dual_dist_hedge_graph(x,under_with_trade,y_norm, \
    legend, title_1,title_2)
```

#Code Segment 12.22:

```
#Show payoff pattern of a butterfly spread

low_strike=80
mid_strike=100
high_strike=120

low_call_cost=black_scholes_call(money,low_strike,time, \
    rfree,sigma)
mid_call_cost=black_scholes_call(money,mid_strike,time, \
    rfree,sigma)
high_call_cost=black_scholes_call(money,high_strike, \
    time,rfree,sigma)

under_with_trade=np.concatenate(\
    ([u for u in x if u<=low_strike], \
    [u+(u-low_strike) for u in x if \
    low_strike<u<=mid_strike], \
    [u+ (high_strike-u)*(mid_strike-low_strike)/ \
    (high_strike-mid_strike) \
     for u in x if mid_strike<u<=high_strike], \
    [u for u in x if u>high_strike]))
```

```
trade_cost=low_call_cost-2*mid_call_cost+high_call_cost
under_with_trade-=trade_cost

title_1="Figure 12.13a: Payoff of underlying w/butterfly \
    spread:\nLow=%3.f"% low_strike
title_1+="; Mid=%3.f" % mid_strike
title_1+="; High=%3.f" % high_strike
title_1+="; Trade cost=%2.2f" % trade_cost
title_2="Figure 12.13b: Density function w/ and w/out \
    butterfly"
legend="W/butterfly"

dual_dist_hedge_graph(x,under_with_trade,y_norm,legend, \
    title_1,title_2)
```

#Code Segment 12.23:

```
#Show payoff pattern of a zero cost collar

put_strike=90
call_strike=117.50468    #just did trial and error to \
    find strike that matches prices

put_cost=black_scholes_put(money,put_strike,time,rfree, \
    sigma)
call_cost=black_scholes_call(money,call_strike,time, \
    rfree,sigma)

under_with_trade=np.concatenate(\
    ([put_strike for u in x if u<=put_strike], \
    [u for u in x if put_strike<u<=call_strike], \
    [call_strike for u in x if call_strike<u]))

title_1="Figure 12.14a: Payoff of underlying with ZC \
    collar:\nPut Strike=%3.f"% put_strike
title_1+="; Call Strike=%3.f" % call_strike
title_1+="; Option costs=%2.2f" % put_cost
title_2="Figure 12.14b: Density function with and w/out \
    ZC collar"
legend="W/ZC collar"

dual_dist_hedge_graph(x,under_with_trade,y_norm,legend, \
    title_1,title_2)
```

#Code Segment 12.24:

```
#Simple delta example

def greeks(price,strike,r,time,sigma):
    #return a 6-vector of Black-Scholes Greeks:
    #BS price, delta, gamma, theta, vega, rho
    if price<=0 or strike<=0 or time<=0:
        return(6*[0])
    #Black-Scholes price
    d1=(np.log(price/strike)+(r+sigma**2/2)*time)/ \
        (sigma*np.sqrt(time))
    d2=d1-sigma*np.sqrt(time)
    n_of_d1=spst.norm.cdf(d1)
    n_of_d2=spst.norm.cdf(d2)
    bs_call=price*n_of_d1-np.exp(-r*time)*strike*n_of_d2
    #Greeks
    delta=n_of_d1
    gamma=np.exp(-d1**2/2)/(price*sigma*np. \
        sqrt(2*np.pi*time))
    vega=time*gamma*sigma*(price**2)
    rho=strike*n_of_d2*time*np.exp(-r*time)
    theta=.5*((price*sigma)**2)*gamma+r*rho/time
    gr_vec=[bs_call,delta,gamma,theta,vega,rho]
    return(gr_vec)

sigma=.2
rf=.02
X0=K=100
T=.25

Orig_price,delta,gamma,theta,vega,rho=greeks(X0,K,rf,T,sigma)

X0_new=100.1
New_price,new_d,new_g,new_t,new_v,new_r=greeks(X0_new,K, \
    rf,T,sigma)
diff_delta=(New_price-Orig_price)/(X0_new-X0)

print("      Original X0: %.2f" % X0)
print("   Original Price: %.4f" % Orig_price)
print("            Delta: %.4f" % delta)
print("\n          New X0: %.2f" % X0_new)
print("        New Price: %.4f" % New_price)
print("Difference delta: %.4f" % diff_delta)
```

#Code Segment 12.25:

```python
#Graph theta from previous example as a function of strike

strikes=np.arange(50,151,1)

plt.plot(strikes,[greeks(X0,k,rf,T,sigma)[3] \
                for k in strikes],label="Call")
plt.plot(strikes,[greeks(X0,k,rf,T,sigma)[3]+ \
                rf*k*np.exp(-rf*T)for k in \
                strikes],label="Put")
plt.xlabel("Strike price")
plt.ylabel("Theta")
plt.legend()
plt.grid()
str_title="Figure 12.15: Theta as a function of strike \
    price\n"
str_title+="Price=%3.f" % X0
str_title+=", r=%3.2f" % rf
str_title+=", T=%3.2f" % T
str_title+=", sigma=%3.2f" % sigma
plt.title(str_title)
plt.show();

print("ATM call theta",greeks(X0,X0,rf,T,sigma)[3])
print("ATM put theta",greeks(X0,X0,rf,T,sigma)[3]+ \
        rf*X0*np.exp(-rf*T))
```

#Code Segment 12.26:

```python
#Gamma and vega

fig=plt.figure() # Create matplotlib figure

#Set up two axes because of different orders of
#magnitude between gamma and vega
ax = fig.add_subplot(111)
ax2 = ax.twinx() # Create another axis that shares \
    the same x-axis as ax.

ax.plot(strikes,[greeks(X0,k,rf,T,sigma)[2] \
                for k in strikes], \
                color='black')
```

```python
ax2.plot(strikes,[greeks(X0,k,rf,T,sigma)[4] \
                for k in strikes], label="Vega", \
                color='black')

ax.set_ylabel('Gamma', color='blue')
ax.yaxis.label.set_color('blue')
ax.tick_params(axis='y', colors='blue')

ax2.set_ylabel('Vega', color='red')
ax2.yaxis.label.set_color('red')
ax2.tick_params(axis='y', colors='red')

#ax.set_xlabel("Strike price")
ax.grid(axis="x")
plt.grid()

str_title="Figure 12.16: Gamma, vega as a function of \
    strike price\n"
str_title+="Price=%3.f" % X0
str_title+=", r=%3.2f" % rf
str_title+=", T=%3.2f" % T
str_title+=", sigma=%3.2f" % sigma
plt.title(str_title)
plt.show();

print("ATM delta",greeks(X0,X0,rf,T,sigma)[1])
print("ATM gamma ",greeks(X0,X0,rf,T,sigma)[2])
print("ATM vega ",greeks(X0,X0,rf,T,sigma)[4])
print("Vega/gamma ratio ",X0**2*T*sigma)
```

References

[Acerbi 2002] Carlo Acerbi, "Spectral Measures of Risk: A Coherent Representation of Subjective Risk Aversion," *Journal of Banking & Finance*, Volume 26, Issue 7, July 2002, pp. 1505–1518. `http://dx.doi.org/10.1016/S0378-4266(02)00281-9`.

[Acerbi and Tasche 2001] Carlo Acerbi and Dick Tasche, "Expected Shortfall: a natural coherent alternative to Value at Risk," Bank for International Settlements White Paper, May 9, 2001. `bis.org/bcbs/ca/acertasc.pdf`.

[Adam and Fernando 2006] Tim R. Adam and Chitru S. Fernando, "Hedging, speculation, and shareholder value," *Journal of Financial Economics*, Volume 81, Issue 2, August 2006, pp. 283–309. `https://doi.org/10.1016/j.jfineco.2005.03.014`.

[Aldasoro and Ehlers 2018] Iñaki Aldasoro and Torsten Ehlers, "The Credit Default Swap Market: What a Difference a Decade Makes," *BIS Quarterly Review*, June 2018. `www.bis.org/publ/qtrpdf/r_qt1806b.htm`.

[Alessi and McBride 2015] Christopher Alessi and James McBride, "The Eurozone in Crisis," Council on Foreign Relations, February 11, 2015. `https://www.cfr.org/backgrounder/eurozone-crisis`.

[Ali, Mikhail, and Haq 1978] Mir M. Ali, N. N. Mikhail, and M. Safiul Haq, "A Class of Bivariate Distributions Including the Bivariate Logistic," *Journal of Multivariate Analysis*, Volume 8, Issue 3, 1978, pp. 405–412. `https://doi.org/10.1016/0047-259X(78)90063-5`.

[Allais 1953] Maurice Allais, "Le comportement de l'homme rationnel devant le risque: critique des postulats et axiomes de l'Ecole Americaine," *Econometrica*, Volume 21, Issue 4, October 1953, pp. 503–546. `https://doi.org/10.2307/1907921`.

[Allayannis and Weston 2001] George Allayannis and James P. Weston, "The Use of Foreign Currency Derivatives and Firm Market Value," *The Review of Financial Studies*, Volume 14, Issue 1, January 2001, pp. 243–276. `https://doi.org/10.1093/rfs/14.1.243`.

[Allen, Litov, and Mei 2006] Franklin Allen, Lubomir Litov and Jianping Mei, "Large Investors, Price Manipulation, and Limits to Arbitrage: An Anatomy of Market Corners," *Review of Finance*, Volume 10, Issue 4, 2006, pp. 682–683. `https://doi.org/10.1007/s10679-006-9008-5`.

[Altman 1968] Edward I. Altman, "Financial Ratios, Discriminant Analysis and the Prediction of Corporate Bankruptcy," *The Journal of Finance*, Volume 23, Issue 4, September 1968, pp. 589–609. `https://doi.org/10.1111/j.1540-6261.1968.tb00843.x`.

[Amadeo 2020] Kimberly Amadeo, "AIG Bailout, Cost, Timeline, Bonuses, Causes, Effects," *The Balance*, November 16, 2020. `www.thebalance.com/aig-bailout-cost-timeline-bonuses-causes-effects-3305693`. Downloaded April 15, 2022.

[Ang and Timmerman 2011] Andrew Ang and Allan Timmermann, "Regime Changes and Financial Markets," NBER Working Paper 17182, June 2011. https://doi.org/10.3386/w17182.

[Araújo and Issler 2011] Fabio Araújo and João Victor Issler, "A Stochastic Discount Factor Approach to Asset Pricing Using Panel Data Asymptotics," Getulio Vargas Foundation, 2011. http://bibliotecadigital.fgv.br/dspace/bitstream/10438/8234/5/A-Stochastic-discount-factor-approach-to-asset-pricing-using-panel-data-asymptotics.pdf.

[ADEH 2001] Philippe Artzner, Freddy Delbaen, Jean-Marc Eber, and David Heath, "Coherent Measures of Risk," *Mathematical Finance*, Volume 9, Issue 3, 2001, pp. 203–228. https://doi.org/10.1111/1467-9965.00068.

[Audrino, Huitema, and Ludwig 2015] Francesco Audrino, Robert Huitema, and Markus Ludwig, "An Empirical Analysis of the Ross Recovery Theorem," 2015. Available at SSRN. https://dx.doi.org/10.2139/ssrn.2433170.

[Bachelier 1900] Louis Bachelier, *Theory of Speculation: The Origins of Modern Finance* (Mark Davis and Alison Etheridge, translators). Princeton University Press, 1900 original, 2011 translation. https://books.google.com/books?id=XcZwuHGRxsgC.

[Backus, Gregory, and Zin 1989] David K. Backus, Allan W. Gregory, and Stanley E. Zin, "Risk Premiums in the Term Structure: Evidence from Artificial Economies," *Journal of Monetary Economics*, Volume 24, Issue 3, November 1989, pp. 371–399. https://doi.org/10.1016/0304-3932(89)90027-5.

[Bai, Goldstein, and Yang 2018] Jenny Bai, Robert S. Goldstein, and Fan Yang, "Is the Credit Spread Puzzle a Myth?," October 22, 2018 (revised October 29, 2020). Georgetown McDonough School of Business Research Paper; University of Connecticut School of Business Research Paper No. 18–28. Available at SSRN. https://dx.doi.org/10.2139/ssrn.3262310.

[Banz 1981] Rolf W. Banz, "The Relationship between Return and Market Value of Common Stocks," *Journal of Financial Economics*, Volume 9, Issue 1, March 1981, pp. 3–18. https://doi.org/10.1016/0304-405X(81)90018-0.

[Basel 2011] Basel Committee on Banking Supervision, "Messages from the Academic Literature on Risk Measurement for the Trading Book," Working Paper Number 19, 2011. www.bis.org/publ/bcbs_wp19.pdf.

[Behrens, Woolrich, Walton, et al. 2007] T. Behrens, M. Woolrich, M. Walton, et al., "Learning the Value of Information in an Uncertain World." *Nature Neuroscience*, Vol. 10, 2007, pp. 1214–1221. https://doi.org/10.1038/nn1954

[Berg et al. 2018] Tobias Berg, Valentin Burg, Ana Gombović, and Manju Puri, "On the Rise of the FinTechs – Credit Scoring Using Digital Footprints," FDIC CFR WP 2018-04, September 2018. www.fdic.gov/bank/analytical/cfr/2018/wp2018/cfr-wp2018-04.pdf.

[Bernoulli 1738] Daniel Bernoulli, "Exposition of a New Theory on the Measurement of Risk," *Econometrica*, Vol. 22, Issue 1, January 1954, pp. 23–36. English translation of the 1738 Latin original. https://dx.doi.org/10.2307/1909829.

[Bertsekas 1996] Dmitri Bertsekas, *Constrained Optimization and Lagrange Multiplier Methods*, Athena Scientific, Belmont, Mass., 1996. www.mit.edu/~dimitrib/Constrained-Opt.pdf.

[Black 1976] Fischer Black, "The Pricing of Commodity Contracts," *Journal of Financial Economics*, Volume 3, Issues 1–2, January–March 1976, pp. 167–179. https://doi.org/10.1016/0304-405X(76)90024-6.

[Black, Derman, and Toy 1990] Fischer Black, Emanuel Derman and William Toy, "A One-Factor Model of Interest Rates and Its Application to Treasury Bond Options," *Financial Analysts Journal*, Volume 46, Issue 1, January–February 1990, pp. 33–39. www.jstor.org/stable/4479294.

[Black and Karasinski 1991] Fischer Black and Piotr Karasinski, "Bond and Option Pricing When Short Rates Are Lognormal," *Financial Analysts Journal*, Volume 47, Issue 4, July–August 1991, pp. 52–59. www.jstor.org/stable/4479456.

[Black and Litterman 1991] Fischer Black and Robert B. Litterman, "Asset Allocation: Combining Investor Views with Market Equilibrium," *The Journal of Fixed Income*, Volume 1, Issue 2, Fall 1991, pp. 7–18. https://doi.org/10.3905/jfi.1991.408013.

[Black and Perold 1992] Fischer Black and André F. Perold, "Theory of Constant Proportion Portfolio Insurance," *Journal of Economic Dynamics and Control*, Volume 16, Issues 3–4, July–October 1992, pp. 403–426. https://doi.org/10.1016/0165-1889(92)90043-E.

[Black and Scholes 1973] Fischer Black and Myron Scholes, "The Pricing of Options and Corporate Liabilities," *Journal of Political Economy*, Volume 81, Issue 3, May–June 1973, pp. 637–654. https://doi.org/10.1086/260062.

[Bollerslev 1986] Tim Bollerslev, "Generalized Autoregressive Conditional Heteroskedasticity," *Journal of Econometrics*, Volume 31, Issue 3, April 1986, pp. 307–327. https://doi.org/10.1016/0304-4076(86)90063-1.

[Bollerslev 1990] Tim Bollerslev, "Modelling the Coherence in Short-Run Nominal Exchange Rates: A Multivariate Generalized Arch Model," *The Review of Economics and Statistics*, Volume 72, Issue 3, August 1990, pp. 498–505. https://doi.org/10.2307/2109358.

[Bolster, Lindsey, and Mitrusi 1988] Paul Bolster, Lawrence Lindsey, and Andrew Mitrusi, "Tax Induced Trading: The Effect of the 1986 Tax Reform Act on Stock Market Activity," NBER Working Paper 2659, July 1988. www.nber.org/papers/w2659.pdf.

[Bossaerts 2018] Peter Bossaerts, "Formalizing the Function of Anterior Insula in Rapid Adaptation," *Frontiers in Integrative Neuroscience*, December 4, 2018. https://doi.org/10.3389/fnint.2018.00061.

[Bouchaud, Potters, and Aguilar 1997] Jean-Philippe Bouchaud, Marc Potters, and Jean-Pierre Aguilar, "Missing Information and Asset Allocation," 1997. https://arxiv.org/abs/cond-mat/9707042.

[Box 1949] George E. P. Box, "A General Distribution Theory for a Class of Likelihood Criteria," *Biometrika*, Volume 36, Issue 3–4, December 1949, pp. 317–346. https://doi.org/10.1093/biomet/36.3-4.317.

[Box 1976] George E. P. Box, "Science and Statistics," *Journal of the American Statistical Association*, Volume 71, 1976. pp. 791–799. https://doi.org/10.1080/01621459.1976.10480949.

[Boyarchenko et al. 2018] Nina Boyarchenko, Pooja Gupta, Nick Steele, and Jacqueline Yen, "Negative Swap Spreads," *Economic Policy Review*, Federal Reserve Bank of New York, Volume 24, Issue 2, October 2018. www.newyorkfed.org/research/epr/2018/epr_2018_negative-swap-spreads_boyarchenko.html.

[Boyd and Vandenberghe 2004] Stephen Boyd and Lieven Vandenberghe, *Convex Optimization*, Cambridge University Press, 2004. https://web.stanford.edu/~boyd/cvxbook/.

[Braudel 1992] Fernand Braudel, *Civilization and Capitalism 15th–18th Century. Volume II: The Wheels of Commerce* (Reynold Siân, translator). University of California Press, 1992, pp. 97–99. www.ucpress.edu/book/9780520081154/civilization-and-capitalism-15th-18th-century-vol-ii.

[Breeden and Litzenberger 1978] Douglas T. Breeden and Robert H. Litzenberger, "Prices of State-Contingent Claims Implicit in Option Prices," *The Journal of Business*, Volume 51, Issue 4, October 1978, pp. 621–651. www.jstor.org/stable/2352653.

[Buss, Schönleber, and Vilkov 2019] Adrian Buss, Lorenzo Schönleber, and Grigory Vilkov, "Expected Correlation and Future Market Returns," July 2019. Available at SSRN. https://dx.doi.org/10.2139/ssrn.3114063.

[Cain 2015] Fraser Cain, "Is the Universe Finite or Infinite?," *Universe Today*, March 27, 2015. https://phys.org/news/2015-03-universe-finite-infinite.html.

[Carhart 1997] Mark M. Carhart, "On Persistence in Mutual Fund Performance," *The Journal of Finance*, Volume 52, Issue 1, March 1997, pp. 57–82. https://doi.org/10.2307/2329556.

[Carlson 2007] Mark Carlson, "A Brief History of the 1987 Stock Market Crash with a Discussion of the Federal Reserve Response." Federal Reserve Board, Washington, D.C. 2007, p. 17. www.federalreserve.gov/pubs/feds/2007/200713/200713pap.pdf.

[Charras-Garrido and Lezaud 2013] Myriam Charras-Garrido and Pascal Lezaud. "Extreme Value Analysis: An Introduction." *Journal de la Societe Française de Statistique*, Volume 154, Issue 2, 2013, pp. 67–97. https://hal-enac.archives-ouvertes.fr/hal-00917995.

[Chen, Lakshminarayanan, and Santos 2006] M. Keith Chen, Venkat Lakshminarayanan, and Laurie Santos, "How Basic Are Behavioral Biases? Evidence from Capuchin Monkey Trading Behavior," *Journal of Political Economy*, Volume 114, June 2006, pp. 517–537. https://papers.ssrn.com/sol3/papers.cfm?abstract_id=911244.

[Chen, Roll, and Ross 1986] Nai-Fu Chen, Richard Roll and Stephen A. Ross, "Economic Forces and the Stock Market," *The Journal of Business*, Volume 59, Issue 3, July 1986, pp. 383–403. www.jstor.org/stable/2352710.

[Clayton 1978] David G. Clayton, "A Model for Association in Bivariate Life Tables and Its Application in Epidemiological Studies of Familial Tendency in Chronic Disease Incidence." *Biometrika*, Volume 65, Issue 1, 1978, pp. 141–151. https://doi.org/10.1093/biomet/65.1.141.

[Cornish and Fisher 1938] E. A. Cornish and R. A. Fisher, "Specification of Distributions," *Revue de l'Institut International de Statistique / Review of the International Statistical Institute*, Volume 5, Issue 4, January 1938, pp. 307–320. https://doi.org/10.2307/1400905.

[Cox, Ross, and Rubenstein 1979] John C. Cox, Stephen A. Ross, and Mark Rubinstein, "Option Pricing: A Simplified Approach," *Journal of Financial Economics*, Volume 7, Issue 3, September 1979, pp. 229–263. https://doi.org/10.1016/0304-405X(79)90015-1.

[Cox, Ingersoll, and Ross 1985] John C. Cox, Jonathan E. Ingersoll, Jr. and Stephen A. Ross, "A Theory of the Term Structure of Interest Rates," *Econometrica*, Volume 53, Issue 2, March 1985, pp. 385–407. https://doi.org/10.2307/1911242.

[Cramer 1728] Gabriel Cramer, Letter to N. Bernoulli, May 21, 1728, cited in https://plato.stanford.edu/entries/paradox-stpetersburg/#HistStPetePara.

[Crosbie and Bohn 2003] Peter Crosbie and Jeffrey Bohn, "Modeling Default Risk," KMV White Paper 2003. In *World Scientific Reference on Contingent Claims Analysis in Corporate Finance. Volume 2: Corporate Debt Valuation with CCA* (Crouhy, Galai, and Wiener, eds.), 2019, pp. 471–506. https://doi.org/10.1142/9789814759595_0020.

[Cunliffe 2017] Sir Jon Cunliffe, "Ten Years On: Lessons from Northern Rock," Bank of England Speech, September 29, 2017. www.bankofengland.co.uk/-/media/boe/files/speech/2017/ten-years-on-lessons-from-northern-rock.pdf.

[Czasonis, Kritzman, and Turkington 2022] Megan Czasonis, Mark Kritzman, and David Turkington, "Relevance," *Journal of Investment Management*, Volume 20, Issue 1, 2022. https://dx.doi.org/10.2139/ssrn.3803440.

[Daníelsson 2002] Jón Daníelsson, "The Emperor Has No clothes: Limits to Risk Modelling," *Journal of Banking & Finance*, Volume 26, Issue 7, July 2002, pp. 1273–1296. https://doi.org/10.1016/S0378-4266(02)00263-7.

[Demeterfi, Derman, Kamal, and Zou 1999a] Kresimir Demeterfi, Emanuel Derman, Michael Kamal and Joseph Zou, "More Than You Ever Wanted to Know about Volatility Swaps," March 1999. www.semanticscholar.org/paper/More-than-You-ever-Wanted-to-Know-about-Volatility-Demeterfi-Derman/3d9cfbe5ff32fd805f79c85b1e48fa9ac84e9128.

[Demeterfi, Derman, Kamal, and Zou 1999b] Kresimir Demeterfi, Emanuel Derman, Michael Kamal and Joseph Zou, "A Guide to Volatility and Variance Swaps," *The Journal of Derivatives*, Volume 6, Issue 4, Summer 1999, pp. 9–32. https://doi.org/10.3905/jod.1999.319129.

[DeMiguel, Garlappi, and Uppal 2009] Victor DeMiguel, Lorenzo Garlappi, and Raman Uppal, "Optimal Versus Naive Diversification: How Inefficient Is the 1/N Portfolio Strategy?," *The Review of Financial Studies*, Volume 22, Issue 5, May 2009, pp. 1915–1953. https://doi.org/10.1093/rfs/hhm075.

[Diamond and Dybvig 1983] Douglas W. Diamond and Philip H. Dybvig, "Bank Runs, Deposit Insurance, and Liquidity," *Journal of Political Economy*, Volume 91, Issue 3, 1983, pp. 401–419. https://doi.org/10.1086/261155.

[Diebold and Li 2006] Francis X. Diebold and Canlin Li, "Forecasting the Term Structure of Government Bond Yields," *Journal of Econometrics*, Volume 130, Issue 2, February 2006, pp. 337–364. https://doi.org/10.1016/j.jeconom.2005.03.005.

[Dupire 1994] Bruno Dupire, "Pricing with a Smile," *Risk*, Volume 7, Issue 1, 1994, pp. 18–20. http://citeseerx.ist.psu.edu/viewdoc/download?doi=10.1.1.320.5063&rep=rep1&type=pdf.

[Durrett 2013] Rick Durrett, *Probability: Theory and Examples*, Edition, Cambridge University Press, 2013. https://services.math.duke.edu/~rtd/PTE/PTE4_1.pdf).

[Eidan 2012] Gal Eidan, "Copulas in Machine Learning," in Jaworski et al., *Copulae in Mathematical and Quantitative Finance: Proceedings of the Workshop Held in Cracow, 10–11 July 2012*, Springer, 2012. http://rentals.springer.com/product/9783642354076.

[Ellis 2021] Diane Ellis, "Designated Reserve Ratio for 2022," Memo, Federal Deposit Insurance Corp., December 14, 2021. www.fdic.gov/news/board-matters/2021/2021-12-14-notice-sum-c-mem.pdf.

[Elton, Gruber, and Padberg 1978] Edwin J. Elton, Martin J. Gruber, and Manfred W. Padberg, "Simple Criteria for Optimal Portfolio Selection: Tracing out the Efficient Frontier," *The Journal of Finance*, Volume 33, Issue 1, 1978, pp. 296–302. https://doi.org/10.1111/j.1540-6261.1978.tb03407.x.

[Engle 1982] Robert F. Engle, "Autoregressive Conditional Heteroscedasticity with Estimates of the Variance of United Kingdom Inflation," *Econometrica*, Volume 50, Issue 4, July 1982, pp. 987–1007. https://doi.org/10.2307/1912773.

[Engle 2002] Robert Engle, "Dynamic Conditional Correlation: A Simple Class of Multivariate Generalized Autoregressive Conditional Heteroskedasticity Models," *Journal of Business & Economic Statistics*, Volume 20, Issue 3, 2002. https://doi.org/10.1198/073500102288618487.

[Engle 2009] Robert Engle, *Anticipating Correlations: A New Paradigm for Risk Management*, Princeton University Press, 2009. www.jstor.org/stable/j.ctt7sb6w.

[Engle and Ng 1993] Robert F. Engle and Victor K. Ng, "Measuring and Testing the Impact of News on Volatility," *The Journal of Finance*, Volume 48, Issue 5, December 1993, pp. 1749–1778. https://doi.org/10.1111/j.1540-6261.1993.tb05127.x.

[Engleberg, Reed, and Ringgenberg 2018] Joseph Engleberg, Adam Reed and Matthew Ringgenberg, "Short-Selling Risk," *Journal of Finance*, Volume 73, Issue 2, 2018, pp. 755–786. https://doi.org/10.1111/jofi.12601.

[Fama 1970] Eugene F. Fama, "Efficient Capital Markets: A Review of Theory and Empirical Work, *The Journal of Finance*, Volume 25, Issue 2, May 1970, pp. 383–417. https://doi.org/10.2307/2325486.

[Fama and French 1992] Eugene F. Fama and Kenneth R. French, "The Cross-Section of Expected Stock Returns," *The Journal of Finance*, Volume 47, Issue 2, June 1992, pp. 427–465. https://doi.org/10.1111/j.1540-6261.1992.tb04398.x.

[Fama and French 2015] Eugene F. Fama and Kenneth R. French, "A Five-Factor Asset Pricing Model," *Journal of Financial Economics*, Volume 116, Issue 1, April 2015, pp. 1–22. https://doi.org/10.1016/j.jfineco.2014.10.010.

[Feldhütter and Schaefer 2018] Peter Feldhütter and Steven Schaefer, "The Myth of the Credit Spread Puzzle," *Review of Financial Studies*, Volume 31, Issue 8, August 2018, pp. 2897–2942. https://doi.org/10.1093/rfs/hhy032.

[Fiacco and McCormick 1968] A. V. Fiacco and G. P. McCormick, *Nonlinear Programming: Sequential Unconstrained Minimization Techniques*, Wiley, 1968. 1990 reprinting at https://books.google.com/books?id=icWjpwgigkAC.

[Foster 2018] Joe Foster, "Gold Hedging: A Precious Lesson Learned," Van Eck Monthly Gold Commentary, November 2018. www.vaneck.com/ucits/literature/gold-commentaries/vaneck-gold-commentary-2018-11_english.pdf.

[Frazzini and Pedersen 2014] Andrea Frazzini and Lasse Heje Pedersen, "Betting against Beta," *Journal of Financial Economics*, Volume 111, Issue 1, January 2014, pp. 1–25. `https://doi.org/10.1016/j.jfineco.2013.10.005`.

[Frye 2005] Jon Frye, "Principals of Risk: Finding Value-at-Risk through Factor-Based Interest Rate Scenarios," 2005. `www.semanticscholar.org/paper/ Principals-of-Risk-:-Finding-Value-at-Risk-Through-Frye/ c0cabab4aebf9d04e58a3084e4f35ea4d57045aa`.

[Furletti 2022] Mark Furletti, "An Overview of Credit Card Asset-Backed Securities," Federal Reserve Bank of Philadelphia Discussion Paper, December 2002. `www .philadelphiafed.org/-/media/frbp/assets/consumer-finance/ conference-summaries/CreditCardSecuritization_012002.pdf`.

[GARP 2017] GARP Buy Side Risk Managers Forum, "Liquidity Risk Principles for Asset Managers," October 2017. `www.garp.org/media/a1Z1W0000031yWQUAY`.

[Gastwirth, Gel, and Miao 2009] Joseph L. Gastwirth, Yulia R. Gel, and Weiwen Miao, "The Impact of Levene's Test of Equality of Variances on Statistical Theory and Practice," *Statistical Science*, Volume 24, Issue 3, August 2009, pp. 343–360. `https://doi .org/10.1214/09-STS301`.

[Gasull, Jolis, and Utzet 2015] Armengol Gasull, Maria Jolis, and Frederic Utzet, "On the Norming Constants for Normal Maxima," *Journal of Mathematical Analysis and Applications*, Volume 422, Issue 1, 2015, pp. 376–396. `https://doi.org/ 10.1016/j.jmaa.2014.08.025`.

[Gentle 1998] James E. Gentle, *Numerical Linear Algebra for Applications in Statistics*, Springer Statistics and Computing, 1998, p. 93. `https://doi.org/10.1007/ 978-1-4612-0623-1`.

[George 1879] Henry George, *Progress and Poverty*, D. Appleton & Co. 1879. `www .henrygeorge.org/pchp2.htm`.

[Geyer-Klingeberg et al. 2018] J. Geyer-Klingeberg, M. Hang, A. W. Rathgeber, et al., "What Do We Really Know about Corporate Hedging? A Meta-Analytical Study." *Business Research*, Volume 11, 2018, pp. 1–31. `https://doi.org/10.1007/s40685- 017-0052-0`.

[Gikhman 2011] Ilya I. Gikhman, "A Short Remark on Feller's Square Root Condition," 2011. Available at SSRN. `https://papers.ssrn.com/sol3/papers.cfm? abstract_id=1756450`.

[Gilbert and Sullivan 1885] W. S. Gilbert and Arthur Sullivan, *The Mikado*, 1885. `www .gsarchive.net/mikado/webopera/mk208d.html`.

[Glasserman and Li, 2005] Paul Glasserman and Jingyi Li, "Importance Sampling for Portfolio Credit Risk," *Management Science*, Volume 59, Issue 11, November 2005, pp. 1643–1656. `https://doi.org/10.1287/mnsc.1050.0415`.

[Glosten, Jagannathan, and Runkle 1993] Lawrence R. Glosten, Ravi Jagannathan and David E. Runkle, "On the Relation between the Expected Value and the Volatility of the Nominal Excess Return on Stocks," *The Journal of Finance*, Volume 48, Issue 5, December 1993, pp. 1779–1801. `https://doi.org/10.2307/2329067`.

[Goldberg and Giesecke 2004] Lisa R. Goldberg and Kay Giesecke, "Forecasting Extreme Financial Risk," 2004. Available at SSRN. `https://papers.ssrn.com/sol3/ papers.cfm?abstract_id=624766`.

[Graham 1949] Benjamin Graham, *The Intelligent Investor* (Jason Zweig, ed.). HarperCollins, 1949 (2005 Edition). `www.harperbusiness.com/book/9780060752613/ Intelligent-Investor-Benjamin-Graham/`.

[Hagan et al. 2002] Patrick S. Hagan, Deep Kumar, Andrew S. Lesniewski, and Diana E. Woodward, "Managing Smile Risk," *Wilmott Magazine*, July 2002, pp. 84–108. https://web.archive.org/web/20150329204211/http://www.wilmott.com/pdfs/021118_smile.pdf.

[Hájek 2022] Hájek, Alan, "Pascal's Wager," in *The Stanford Encyclopedia of Philosophy* (Fall 2022 Edition) (Edward N. Zalta, ed.). https://plato.stanford.edu/archives/fall2022/entries/pascal-wager/.

[Hall and Maingi 2019] Arden Hall and Raman Quinn Maingi, "The Mortgage Prepayment Decision: Are There Other Motivations Beyond Refinance and Move?," Working Paper 19–39, Philadelphia Federal Reserve. https://www.philadelphiafed.org/consumer-finance/mortgage-markets/the-mortgage-prepayment-decision-are-there-other-motivations-beyond-refinance-and-move.

[Halmos 1963] P. R. Halmos, "What Does the Spectral Theorem Say?," *The American Mathematical Monthly*, Volume 70, Issue 3, March 1963, pp. 241–247. https://doi.org/10.2307/2313117.

[Hansen and Jagannathan 1991] Lars Peter Hansen and Ravi Jagannathan, "Implications of Security Market Data for Models of Dynamic Economies," *Journal of Political Economy*, Volume 99, Issue 2, April 1991, p. 225. https://doi.org/10.1086/261749.

[Harvey 1988] Campbell R. Harvey, "The Real Term Structure and Consumption Growth," *Journal of Financial Economics*, Volume 22, Issue 2, December 1988, pp. 305–333. https://doi.org/10.1016/0304-405X(88)90073-6.

[Hastings 1970] W. K. Hastings, "Monte Carlo Sampling Methods Using Markov Chains and Their Applications," *Biometrika*, Volume 57, Issue 1, 1970, pp. 97–109. https://doi.org/10.1093/biomet/57.1.97.

[Hayek 1945] F. A. Hayek, "The Use of Knowledge in Society," *The American Economic Review*, Volume 35, Issue 4, September 1945, pp. 519–530. www.jstor.org/stable/1809376.

[Heston 1993] Steven L. Heston, "A Closed-Form Solution for Options with Stochastic Volatility with Applications to Bond and Currency Options," *The Review of Financial Studies*, Volume 6, Issue 2, April 1993, pp. 327–343. https://doi.org/10.1093/rfs/6.2.327.

[Hirschman 1964] Albert O. Hirschman, "The Paternity of an Index," *The American Economic Review*, Volume 54, Issue 5, September 1964, p. 761. www.jstor.org/stable/1818582.

[Ho and Lee 1986] Thomas S. Y. Ho and Sang-Bin Lee, "Term Structure Movements and Pricing Interest Rate Contingent Claims," *The Journal of Finance*, Volume 41, Issue 5, December 1986, pp. 1011–1029. https://doi.org/10.2307/2328161.

[Hobbes 1651] Thomas Hobbes, *Leviathan, or the Matter, Forme, & Power of a Commonwealth Ecclesiastical and Civil*, Andrew Crooke, 1651. www.gutenberg.org/files/3207/3207-h/3207-h.htm.

[Hoffman, Postel-Vinay, and Rosenthal 2019] Phillip Hoffman, Gilles Postel-Vinay, and Jean-Laurent Rosenthal. *Dark Matter Credit*, Princeton University Press, 2019. https://press.princeton.edu/books/hardcover/9780691182179/dark-matter-credit.

[Homer and Sylla 2005] Sidney Homer and Richard Sylla, *A History of Interest Rates*, Fourth Edition, Wiley, 2005. www.wiley.com/en-us/A+History+of+Interest+Rates,+4th+Edition-p-9780471732839.

[Hotelling 1931] Harold Hotelling, "The Generalization of Student's Ratio," *Annals of Mathematical Statistics*, Volume 2, Issue 3, August 1931, pp. 360–378. https://doi.org/10.1214/aoms/1177732979.

[Huberman 1982] Gur Huberman, "A Simple Approach to Arbitrage Pricing Theory," *Journal of Economic Theory*, Volume 28, Issue 1, October 1982, pp. 183–191. https://doi.org/10.1016/0022-0531(82)90098-9.

[Hull and White 1990] John Hull and Alan White, "Pricing Interest-Rate-Derivative Securities," *The Review of Financial Studies*, Volume 3, Issue 4, 1990, pp. 573–592. www.jstor.org/stable/2962116.

[Idzorek 2006] Thomas M. Idzorek, "Developing Robust Asset Allocations," Working Paper, Ibbotson Associates, 2006. http://citeseerx.ist.psu.edu/viewdoc/summary?doi=10.1.1.600.2083.

[Jackwerth and Menner 2020] Jens Carsten Jackwerth and Marco Menner, "Does the Ross Recovery Theorem Work Empirically?" *Journal of Financial Economics*, Volume 137, Issue 3, September 2020, pp. 723–739. https://doi.org/10.1016/j.jfineco.2020.03.006.

[James and Stein 1961] W. James and C. M. Stein, "Estimation with Quadratic Loss," *Proceedings of the Fourth Berkeley Symposium on Mathematical Statistics and Probability*, Volume 1, 1961, pp. 361–379. https://doi.org/10.1007/978-1-4612-0919-5_30.

[Jarosik, Bennett, Dunkley, et al. 2011] N. Jarosik, C. L. Bennett, J. Dunkley, et al., "Seven-Year Wilkinson Microwave Anisotropy Probe (WMAP) Observations: Sky Maps, Systematic Errors, and Basic Results," *The Astrophysical Journal Supplement Series*, Volume 192, Issue 2, 2011. https://dx.doi.org/10.1088/0067-0049/192/2/14.

[Jarque and Bera 1980] Carlos M. Jarque and Anil K. Bera, "Efficient Tests for Normality, Homoscedasticity and Serial Independence of Regression Residuals," *Economics Letters*, Volume 6, Issue 3, 1980, pp. 255–259. https://doi.org/10.1016/0165-1765(80)90024-5.

[Jegadeesh and Titman 1993] Narasimhan Jegadeesh and Sheridan Titman, "Returns to Buying Winners and Selling Losers: Implications for Stock Market Efficiency," *The Journal of Finance*, Volume 48, Issue 1, March 1993, pp. 65–91. https://doi.org/10.2307/2328882.

[Jensen 1906] J. L. W. V. Jensen, "Sur les fonctions convexes et les inégalités entre les valeurs moyennes," *Acta Mathematica*, Volume 30, 1906, pp. 175–193. https://doi.org//10.1007/BF02418571.

[Jensen 1967] Michael C. Jensen, "The Performance of Mutual Funds in the Period 1945–1964," *Journal of Finance*, Volume 23, Issue 2, 1967, pp. 389–416. https://doi.org/10.1111/j.1540-6261.1968.tb00815.x.

[Jin and Jorion 2006] Yanbo Jin and Philippe Jorion, "Firm Value and Hedging: Evidence from U.S. Oil and Gas Producers," *The Journal of Finance*, Volume 61, Issue 2, 2006, pp. 893–919. https://doi.org/10.1111/j.1540-6261.2006.00858.x.

[Jones, Mason, and Rosenfeld 1984] E. Philip Jones, Scott P. Mason and Eric Rosenfeld, "Contingent Claims Analysis of Corporate Capital Structures: An Empirical Investigation," *The Journal of Finance*, Volume 39, Issue 3, Papers and Proceedings, Forty-Second

Annual Meeting, American Finance Association, San Francisco, CA, December 28–30, 1983 (July 1984), pp. 611–625. https://doi.org/10.2307/2327919.

[Jorion 1986] Philippe Jorion, "Bayes-Stein Estimation for Portfolio Analysis," *The Journal of Financial and Quantitative Analysis*, Volume 21, Issue 3, September 1986, pp. 279–292. https://doi.org/10.2307/2331042.

[Jorion 1992] Philippe Jorion, "Portfolio Optimization in Practice," *Financial Analysts Journal*, Volume 48, Issue 1, January–February 1992, pp. 68–74. https://www.jstor.org/stable/4479507.

[Kahneman 2011] Daniel Kahneman, *Thinking, Fast and Slow*, Farrar, Straus, and Giroux, 2011. https://us.macmillan.com/books/9780374533557/thinkingfastandslow.

[Kahneman and Tversky 1979] Daniel Kahneman and Amos Tversky, "Prospect Theory: An Analysis of Decision under Risk," *Econometrica*, Volume 47, Issue 2, March 1979, pp. 263–292. https://doi.org/10.2307/1914185.

[Karush 1939] William Karush, "Minima of Functions of Several Variables with Inequalities as Side Conditions," Master's thesis, University of Chicago, 1939. https://catalog.lib.uchicago.edu/vufind/Record/4111654.

[Kealhofer 2003a] Stephen Kealhofer, "Quantifying Credit Risk I: Default Prediction," *Financial Analysts Journal*, Volume 59, Issue 1, January–February 2003, pp. 30–44. www.jstor.org/stable/4480449.

[Kealhofer 2003b] Stephen Kealhofer, "Quantifying Credit Risk II: Debt Valuation," *Financial Analysts Journal*, Volume 59, Issue 3, May–June 2003, pp. 78–92. www.jstor.com/stable/4480485.

[Keating and Shadwick 2002] Con Keating and William Shadwick, "A Universal Performance Measure," 2002. https://pdfs.semanticscholar.org/a63b/0a002c6cf2d4085f7ad80cbfd92fe3520521.pdf.

[Kessel 1971] Reuben A. Kessel, "The Cyclical Behavior of the Term Structure of Interest Rates," in *Essays on Interest Rates, Volume 2*, NBER, 1971. www.nber.org/books-and-chapters/cyclical-behavior-term-structure-interest-rates.

[Keynes 1929] John Maynard Keynes, *A Tract on Monetary Reform*, MacMillan and Co., 1929. https://ia903007.us.archive.org/15/items/tractonmonetaryr0000keyn/tractonmonetaryr0000keyn.pdf.

[Keynes 1937] John Maynard Keynes, "The General Theory of Unemployment," *The Quarterly Journal of Economics*, Volume 51, Issue 2, February 1937, pp. 209–223. https://doi.org/10.2307/1882087.

[Khanna 2021] U.S. Representative Ro Khanna, "Statement: Rep. Khanna on Gamestop Trades," January 28, 2021. https://khanna.house.gov/media/press-releases/statement-rep-khanna-gamestop-trades.

[Kim and Pittel 2000] Jeong Han Kim and Boris Pittel, "Confirming the Kleitman-Winston Conjecture on the Largest Coefficient in a q-Catalan Number," *Journal of Combinatorial Theory Series A*, Volume 92, Issue 2, November 2000, pp. 197–206. https://doi.org/10.1006/jcta.1999.3054.

[Kjeldsen 2000] Tinne Hoff Kjeldsen, "A Contextualized Historical Analysis of the Kuhn–Tucker Theorem in Nonlinear Programming: The Impact of World War II," *Historia Mathematica*, Volume 27, Issue 4, November 2000, pp. 331–361. https://doi.org/10.1006/hmat.2000.2289.

[Knight 1921] Frank H. Knight, *Risk, Uncertainty, and Profit*. Houghton Mifflin Co., The Riverside Press, 1921. `www.econlib.org/library/Knight/knRUP.html`.

[Krainer 2004] John Krainer, "What Determines the Credit Spread?," FRBSF Economic Letter, Federal Reserve Bank of San Francisco, December 10, 2004. `https://ideas.repec.org/a/fip/fedfel/y2004idec10n2004-36.html`.

[Kritzman 2000] Mark Kritzman, *Puzzles of Finance*, John Wiley & Sons, 2000. `www.wiley.com/en-us/Puzzles+of+Finance:+Six+Practical+Problems+and+Their+Remarkable+Solutions-p-9780471246572`.

[Kroll, Levy, and Markowitz 1984] Yoram Kroll, Haim Levy, and Harry M. Markowitz, "Mean-Variance Versus Direct Utility Maximization," *The Journal of Finance*, Volume 39, Issue 1, March 1984, pp. 47–61. `https://doi.org/10.1111/j.1540-6261.1984.tb03859.x`.

[Kuhn and Tucker 1951] H. W. Kuhn and A. W. Tucker, "Nonlinear Programming," in *Berkeley Symposium on Mathematical Statistics and Probability*, 1951, pp. 481–492. `https://projecteuclid.org/euclid.bsmsp/1200500249`.

[Ledoit and Wolf 2003] Olivier Ledoit and Michael Wolf, "Honey, I Shrunk the Sample Covariance Matrix," UPF Economics and Business Working Paper No. 691, 2003. `http://dx.doi.org/10.2139/ssrn.433840`.

[Ledoit and Wolf 2004] Olivier Ledoit and Michael Wolf, "A Well-Conditioned Estimator for Large-Dimensional Covariance Matrices," *Journal of Multivariate Analysis*, Volume 88, Issue 2, February 2004, pp. 365–411. `https://doi.org/10.1016/S0047-259X(03)00096-4`.

[Lee 2018] Paul L. Lee, "A Retrospective on the Demise of Long-Term Capital Management," blog post, 2018. `https://clsbluesky.law.columbia.edu/2018/09/10/a-retrospective-on-the-demise-of-long-term-capital-management/`.

[Li 2000] David X. Li, "On Default Correlation: A Copula Function Approach," *The Journal of Fixed Income*, Volume 9, Issue 4, Spring 2000, pp. 43–54. `https://doi.org/10.3905/jfi.2000.319253`.

[Lindley 1980] D. V. Lindley, "L. J. Savage – His Work in Probability and Statistics," *The Annals of Statistics*, Volume 8, Issue 1, January 1980, pp. 1–24. `www.jstor.org/stable/2240741`.

[Litterman and Scheinkman 1991] Robert B. Litterman and José Scheinkman, "Common Factors Affecting Bond Returns," *The Journal of Fixed Income*, Volume 1, Issue 1, Summer 1991, pp. 54–61. `https://doi.org/10.3905/jfi.1991.692347`.

[Lockett and Leng 2022] Hudson Lockett and Cheng Leng, "China's 'Dim Sum' Bond Sales Surge on Demand from Domestic Investors," *Financial Times*, July 30, 2022. `www.ft.com/content/ac31d244-33b7-4375-8b0d-696140d1bda0`.

[López de Prado 2020] Marcos López de Prado, *Machine Learning for Asset Managers*, Cambridge Elements, Quantitative Finance, April 2020. `www.cambridge.org/core/elements/abs/machine-learning-for-asset-managers/6D9211305EA2E425D33A9F38D0AE3545`.

[Lucas 1976] Robert E. Lucas, "Econometric Policy Evaluation: A Critique," *Carnegie-Rochester Conference Series on Public Policy*, Volume 1, 1976, pp. 19–46. `https://doi.org/10.1016/S0167-2231(76)80003-6`.

[Lyashenko and Mercurio 2019] Andrei Lyashenko and Fabio Mercurio, "Looking Forward to Backward-Looking Rates: Completing the Generalized Forward Market Model,"

November 6, 2019. Available at SSRN. `https://papers.ssrn.com/sol3/papers.cfm?abstract_id=3482132`.

[Macaulay 1938] Frederick R. Macaulay, *Some Theoretical Problems Suggested by the Movements of Interest Rates, Bond Yields and Stock Prices in the United States since 1856*, NBER, 1938. p. 44. `www.nber.org/chapters/c6342`.

[Mahalanobis 1936] Mahalanobis, P. C. "On the Generalized Distance in Statistics," *Proceedings of National Institute of Sciences (India)*, Volume 2, Issue 1, 1936, pp. 49–55. `https://doi.org/10.1007/s13171-019-00164-5`.

[Maillard 2012] Didier Maillard, "A User's Guide to the Cornish Fisher Expansion," 2012 (revised 2018). Available at SSRN. `https://papers.ssrn.com/sol3/papers.cfm?abstract_id=1997178`.

[Mandelbrot 1963] Benoit Mandelbrot, "The Variation of Certain Speculative Prices," *The Journal of Business*, Volume 36, Issue 4, October 1963, pp. 394–419. `www.jstor.org/stable/2350970`.

[Mander and Wigglesworth 2017] Benedict Mander and Robin Wigglesworth, "How Did Argentina Pull Off a 100-Year Bond Sale?," *The Financial Times*, June 20, 2017. `www.ft.com/content/5ac33abc-551b-11e7-9fed-c19e2700005f`.

[Marchenko and Pastur 1967] V. A. Marchenko and L. A. Pastur, "Distribution of Eigenvalues for Some Sets of Random Matrices," *Mathematics of the USSR Sbornik*, Volume 1, 1967, p. 457. English translation `https://iopscience.iop.org/article/10.1070/SM1967v001n04ABEH001994/meta`.

[Markowitz 1952] Harry Markowitz, "Portfolio Selection," *The Journal of Finance*, Volume 7, Issue 1, March 1952, pp. 77–91. `https://doi.org/10.2307/2975974`.

[Markowitz 1959] Harry M. Markowitz, *Portfolio Selection: Efficient Diversification of Investments*, Yale University Press, 1959. `www.jstor.org/stable/j.ctt1bh4c8h`.

[Martin and Ross 2019] Ian Martin and Stephen Ross, "Notes on the Yield Curve," *Journal of Financial Economics*, Volume 134, Issue 3, September 2019, pp. 689–702. `https://doi.org/10.1016/j.jfineco.2019.04.014`.

[McDonald and Paulson 2015] Robert McDonald and Anna Paulson, "AIG in Hindsight," *Journal of Economic Perspectives*, Volume 29, Issue 2, Spring 2015, pp. 81–106. `https://dx.doi.org/10.1257/jep.29.2.81`.

[Merton 1974] Robert C. Merton, "On the Pricing of Corporate Debt: The Risk Structure of Interest Rates," *The Journal of Finance*, Volume 29, Issue 2, May 1974, pp. 449–470. `https://doi.org/10.1111/j.1540-6261.1974.tb03058.x`.

[Metropolis 1987] Nicholas Metropolis, "The Beginning of the Monte Carlo Method," *Los Alamos Science*, Special Issue 1987. `http://library.lanl.gov/cgi-bin/getfile?15-12.pdf`.

[Metropolis et al. 1953] Nicholas Metropolis, Arianna W. Rosenbluth, Marshall N. Rosenbluth, and Augusta H. Teller, "Equation of State Calculations by Fast Computing Machines," *Journal of Chemical Physics*, Volume 21, 1953, p. 1087. `https://doi.org/10.1063/1.1699114`.

[Meyer 2000] Carl Meyer, *Matrix Analysis and Applied Linear Algebra*, Society for Industrial and Applied Mathematics, 2000. `https://dl.acm.org/doi/10.5555/343374`.

[Michaud 1989] Richard O. Michaud, "The Markowitz Optimization Enigma: Is 'Optimized' Optimal?," *Financial Analysts Journal*, Volume 45, Issue 1, January–February 1989, pp. 31–42. `www.jstor.org/stable/4479185`.

[Michaud, Esch, and Michaud 2013] Richard Michaud, David Esch, and Robert Michaud, "Deconstructing Black-Litterman: How to Get the Portfolio You Already Knew You Wanted," 2013. Available at SSRN. https://dx.doi.org/10.2139/ssrn.2641893.

[Michaud and Michaud 1998] Richard Michaud and Robert Michaud, *Efficient Asset Management: A Practical Guide to Stock Portfolio Optimization and Asset Allocation*, Oxford University Press 1998 (Second Edition, 2008) www.newfrontieradvisors.com/media/2155/efficient-asset-management-book.pdf.

[Mishkin 2006] Frederic S. Mishkin, "Globalization: A Force for Good?" Speech, October 12, 2006. https://fraser.stlouisfed.org/title/statements-speeches-frederic-s-mishkin-919/globalization-a-force-good-35638.

[Mitchener and Weidenmier 2008] Kris James Mitchener and Marc D. Weidenmier, "The Baring Crisis and the Great Latin American Meltdown of the 1890s," *The Journal of Economic History*, Volume 68, Issue 2, June, 2008, pp. 462–500. www.jstor.org/stable/40056382.

[Modigliani and Miller 1958] Franco Modigliani and Merton H. Miller, "The Cost of Capital, Corporation Finance and the Theory of Investment," *The American Economic Review*, Volume 48, Issue 3, June 1958, pp. 261–297. www.jstor.org/stable/1809766.

[Modigliani and Modigliani 1997] Franco Modigliani and Leah Modigliani, "Risk-Adjusted Performance," *The Journal of Portfolio Management*, Volume 23, Issue 2, Winter 1997, pp. 45–54. https://doi.org/10.3905/jpm.23.2.45.

[Modukuri et al. 2003] Srinivas Modukuri, Vikas Reddy, David Rashty, and Marianna Fassinotti. "Mortgage Convexity Risk," Lehman Brothers Fixed Income Research, June 30, 2003.

[Morini 2011] Massimo Morini, *Understanding and Managing Model Risk*, Wiley Finance, 2011. www.wiley.com/en-us/Understanding+and+Managing+Model+Risk:+A+Practical+Guide+for+Quants,+Traders+and+Validators-p-9780470977613

[Murphy et al. 2021] Sherry L. Murphy, Kenneth D. Kochanek, Jiaquan Xu, and Elizabeth Arias, "Mortality in the United States." NCHS Data Brief No. 427, December 2021. Centers for Disease Control and Prevention National Center for Health Statistics. www.cdc.gov/nchs/products/databriefs/db427.htm.

[Musk 2021] Elon Musk, Tweet, posted January 28, 2021. https://twitter.com/elonmusk/status/1354890601649610753?lang=en.

[Nair, Wierman, and Zwart 2020] Jayakrishnan Nair, Adam Wierman, and Bert Zwart, *Fundamentals of Heavy Tails*, 2020 (prepublication). Cambridge University Press, 2022. https://docs.google.com/forms/d/e/1FAIpQLSdd4YH248k0yKMHVsKG3syGZXwnREF-1k7LTd7iU01Y_nfWlQ/viewform?usp=sf_link.

[Nelson 1991] Daniel B. Nelson, "Conditional Heteroskedasticity in Asset Returns: A New Approach," *Econometrica*, Volume 59, Issue 2, March 1991, pp. 347–370. https://doi.org/10.2307/2938260.

[Nelson and Siegel 1987] Charles R. Nelson and Andrew F. Siegel, "Parsimonious Modeling of Yield Curves," *The Journal of Business*, Volume 60, Issue 4, October 1987, pp. 473–489. www.jstor.org/stable/2352957.

[Nicholas and Preble 2016] Tom Nicholas and Matthew G. Preble, "Michael Milken: The Junk Bond King," Harvard Business School Case Collection, March 2016 (Revised May 2021). www.hbs.edu/faculty/Pages/item.aspx?num=50852.

[Niederhoffer and Osborne 1966] Victor Niederhoffer and M. F. M. Osborne, "Market Making and Reversal on the Stock Exchange," *Journal of the American Statistical Association*, Volume 61, Issue 316, December 1966, pp. 897–916. `https://doi.org/10.2307/2283188`.

[Nolan 2020] John P. Nolan, *Univariate Stable Distributions: Models for Heavy-Tailed Data*, Springer Series in Operations Research and Financial Engineering, 2020. `https://doi.org/10.1007/978-3-030-52915-4_1`.

[O'Cinneade 2012] Colm O'Cinneade, "Bayesian Methods in Investing," in *The Oxford Handbook of Quantitative Asset Management* (Scherer and Winston, eds.). Oxford University Press, 2012, pp. 87–115. `https://global.oup.com/academic/product/the-oxford-handbook-of-quantitative-asset-manage ment-9780199685059?lang=en&cc=is`.

[Olick 2020] Diana Olick, "Weekly Mortgage Refinances Spike 26% as Interest Rates Tank on Coronavirus Fears," CNBC, March 4, 2020. `www.cnbc.com/2020/03/04/weekly-mortgage-refinances-spike-26percent-with-help-from-coronavirus.html`.

[Orr 2019] Leanna Orr, "Jack Meyer's Convexity Shutting Down," Institutional Investor, July 18, 2019. `www.institutionalinvestor.com/article/b1gbjbdmkpx8j2/Jack-Meyer-s-Convexity-Shutting-Down`.

[Pan and Statman 2012] Carrie H. Pan and Meir Statman, "Questionnaires of Risk Tolerance, Regret, Overconfidence, and Other Investor Propensities," *Journal of Investment Consulting*, Volume 13, Issue 1, 2012, pp. 54–63. `https://papers.ssrn.com/sol3/papers.cfm?abstract_id=2144481#`.

[Petram 2014] Lodewijk Petram, *The World's First Stock Exchange* (Lynne Richards, translator). Columbia Business School Publishing, 2014. `https://cup.columbia.edu/book/the-worlds-first-stock-exchange/9780231163781`.

[Petroff 2015] Alanna Petroff, "Sleepy Switzerland Jolts Currency Markets," *CNN Business*, January 15, 2015. `http://money.cnn.com/2015/01/15/investing/switzerland-euro-currency-ceiling/`. Downloaded April 15, 2022.

[Pitts and Selby 1983] C. G. C. Pitts and M. J. P. Selby, "The Pricing of Corporate Debt: A Further Note," *The Journal of Finance*, Volume 38, Issue 4, September 1983, pp. 1311–1313. `https://doi.org/10.1111/j.1540-6261.1983.tb02301.x`.

[Pomatto, Strack, and Tamuz 2020] Luciano Pomatto, Philipp Strack, and Omer Tamuz, "Stochastic Dominance under Independent Noise," *Journal of Political Economy*, Volume 128, Issue 5, 2020, pp. 1877–1900. `https://doi.org/10.1086/705555`.

[Popper 1962] Karl Popper, *Conjectures and Refutations: The Growth of Scientific Knowledge*, Routledge, 1962 (Taylor & Francis 2014 edition). `www.google.com/books/edition/Conjectures_and_Refutations/zXh9AwAAQBAJ?hl=en&gbpv=0`

[Pratt 1964] John W. Pratt, "Risk Aversion in the Small and in the Large," *Econometrica*, Volume 32, Issue 1/2, January–April 1964, pp. 122–136. `https://doi.org/10.2307/1913738`.

[Pringle 2021] Kenneth G. Pringle, "The GameStop Phenomenon Is Hardly New. Here's How a Similar Squeeze Played Out in 1923," *Barron's*, February 3, 2021 (updated February 7, 2021). `https://www.barrons.com/articles/the-gamestop-pheno menon-is-hardly-new-heres-how-a-similar-squeeze-played-out -in-1923-51612361822`

[Protter 2005] Phillip Protter, *Stochastic Integration and Differential Equations*, Second Edition, Version 2.1. Springer, 2005. https://doi.org/10.1007/978-3-662-10061-5.

[Pukthuanthong and Roll 2015] Kuntara Pukthuanthong and Richard Roll, "Agnostic Tests of Stochastic Discount Factor Theory," 2015. Available at SSRN. https://papers.ssrn.com/sol3/papers.cfm?abstract_id=2595740.

[Pulley 1983] Lawrence B. Pulley, "Mean-Variance Approximations to Expected Logarithmic Utility," *Operations Research*, Volume 31, Issue 4, July–August 1983, pp. 685–696. www.jstor.org/stable/170783.

[Qin, Linetsky, and Lie 2018] Likuan Qin, Vadim Linetsky, and Yutian Nie, "Long Forward Probabilities, Recovery, and the Term Structure of Bond Risk Premiums," *The Review of Financial Studies*, Volume 31, Issue 12, December 2018, pp. 4863–4883. https://doi.org/10.1093/rfs/hhy042.

[Rabin 2000] Matthew Rabin. "Risk Aversion and Expected-Utility Theory: A Calibration Theorem." *Econometrica*, Volume 68, Issue 5, 2000, pp. 1281–1292. www.jstor.org/stable/2999450.

[Reinganum 1981] Marc R. Reinganum, "Abnormal Returns in Small Firm Portfolios," *Financial Analysts Journal*, Volume 37, Issue 2, March–April 1981, pp. 52–56. www.jstor.org/stable/4478439.

[Reinhart and Rogoff 2009] Carmen Reinhart and Kenneth Rogoff, *This Time Is Different: Eight Centuries of Financial Folly*, Princeton University Press, 2009. https://press.princeton.edu/titles/8973.html.

[Rendleman and Bartter 1980] Richard J. Rendleman, Jr. and Brit J. Bartter, "The Pricing of Options on Debt Securities," *The Journal of Financial and Quantitative Analysis*, Volume 15, Issue 1, March 1980, pp. 11–24. https://doi.org/10.2307/2979016.

[Roberts and Varberg 1973] A. Wayne Roberts and Dale E. Varberg, *Convex Functions*, New York: Academic Press, 1973.

[Robinson 2013] Kenneth J. Robinson, "Savings and Loan Crisis 1980–1989," Federal Reserve History, November 22, 2013. www.federalreservehistory.org/essays/savings-and-loan-crisis.

[Rockafellar and Uryasev 2000] R. Tyrrell Rockafellar and Stanislav Uryasev, "Optimization of Conditional Value-at-risk," *Journal of Risk*, Volume 2, Issue 3, Spring 2000, pp. 21–41. https://doi.org/10.21314/JOR.2000.038.

[Roll 1977] Richard Roll, "A Critique of the Asset Pricing Theory's Tests Part I: On Past and Potential Testability of the Theory," *Journal of Financial Economics*, Volume 4, Issue 2, March 1977, pp. 129–176. https://doi.org/10.1016/0304-405X(77)90009-5.

[Rönsberg 2011] Andrea Rönsberg, "S&P Warning Puts Damper on Eurogroup Plans," *Deutsche Welle*, May 7, 2011. www.dw.com/en/sp-warning-puts-damper-on-eurogroup-plans/a-15212433.

[Rosenberg and Marathe 1976] Barr Rosenberg and Vinay Marathe, "Common Factors in Security Returns: Microeconomic Determinants and Macroeconomic Correlates," No. 44, Research Program in Finance Working Papers from University of California at Berkeley, 1976. https://econpapers.repec.org/paper/ucbcalbrf/44.htm.

[Ross 1976] Stephen A. Ross, "The Arbitrage Theory of Capital Asset Pricing," *Journal of Economic Theory*, Volume 13, Issue 3, December 1976, pp. 341–360. `https://doi.org/10.1016/0022-0531(76)90046-6`.

[Ross 2013] Stephen A. Ross, "The Recovery Theorem," *Journal of Finance*, Volume 70, Issue 2, 2013. pp. 615–648. `https://doi.org/10.1111/jofi.12092`.

[Rovelli 2018] Carlo Rovelli, *The Order of Time*, Riverhead Books, 2018. `www.penguinrandomhouse.com/books/551483/the-order-of-time-by-carlo-rovelli/`.

[Rubinstein and Leland 1981] Mark Rubinstein and Hayne E. Leland, "Replicating Options with Positions in Stock and Cash," *Financial Analysts Journal*, Volume 37, Issue 4, 1981, pp. 63–72. `https://doi.org/10.2469/faj.v37.n4.63`.

[Ruder 1988] David S. Ruder, "The October Market Break: A Stimulant to United States-Japanese Cooperative Securities Regulation," Speech delivered February 18, 1988. `www.sec.gov/news/speech/1988/021888ruder.pdf`.

[Salmon 2009] Felix Salmon, "Recipe for Disaster: The Formula That Killed Wall Street," *Wired*, February 23, 2009. `www.wired.com/2009/02/wp-quant/`.

[Samouilhan 2021] Nick Samouilhan and Alex Muir, "Chinese Government Bonds: How Do They Measure Up in a Multi-asset Framework?," Wellington Management, September 2021. `www.wellington.com/en/insights/chinese-government-bonds-cgb-measure`.

[Scherer 2002] Bernd Scherer, "Portfolio Resampling: Review and Critique," *Financial Analysts Journal*, Volume 58, Issue 6, 2002, pp. 98–109. `https://doi.org/10.2469/faj.v58.n6.2489`.

[Securities and Exchange Commission 2010] U.S. Securities and Exchange Commission, "SEC Approves Short Selling Restrictions," February 24, 2010. `www.sec.gov/news/press/2010/2010-26.htm`.

[Shakespeare 1597] William Shakespeare, *Romeo and Juliet*. `http://shakespeare.mit.edu/romeo_juliet/full.html`.

[Shannon 1948] C. E. Shannon, "A Mathematical Theory of Communication," *The Bell System Technical Journal*, Volume 27, Issue 3, July 1948, pp. 379–423. `https://doi.org/10.1002/j.1538-7305.1948.tb01338.x`.

[Sharpe 1964] William F. Sharpe, "Capital Asset Prices: A Theory of Market Equilibrium under Conditions of Risk," *The Journal of Finance*, Volume 19, Issue 3, September 1964, pp. 425–442. `https://doi.org/10.2307/2977928`.

[Sharpe 1994] William F. Sharpe, "The Sharpe Ratio," *The Journal of Portfolio Management*, Volume 21, Issue 1, Fall 1994, pp. 49–58. `https://doi.org/10.3905/jpm.1994.409501`.

[Shevtsova 2010] Irina Shevtsova, "An Improvement of Convergence Rate Estimates in the Lyapunov Theorem," *Doklady Mathematics*, Volume 82, 2010, pp. 862–864. `https://doi.org/10.1134/S1064562410060062`.

[Shleifer and Vishny 2012] Andrei Shleifer and Robert W. Vishny, "The Limits of Arbitrage," *The Journal of Finance*, Volume 52, Issue 1, 2012. pp. 35–55. `https://doi.org/10.1111/j.1540-6261.1997.tb03807.x`.

[Shumway and Stoffer 2017] Robert H. Shumway and David S. Stoffer, *Time Series Analysis and Its Applications (With R Examples)*, Springer Texts in Statistics, 2017.

[Siegel 1972] Jeremy J. Siegel, "Risk, Interest Rates and the Forward Exchange," *The Quarterly Journal of Economics*, Volume 86, Issue 2, May 1972, pp. 303–309. `https://doi.org/10.2307/1880565`.

[Sortino and Price 1994] Frank A. Sortino and Lee N. Price, "Performance Measurement in a Downside Risk Framework," *The Journal of Investing*, Volume 3, Issue 3, Fall 1994, pp. 59–64. https://doi.org/10.3905/joi.3.3.59.

[Stanley 1997] Richard P. Stanley, *Enumerative Combinatorics, Vol. 2*, Cambridge Studies in Advanced Mathematics, 62, Cambridge University Press, 1997.

[Strathern 1997] Marilyn Strathern, "Improving Ratings: Audit in the British University System," *European Review*, Volume 5, Issue 3, 1997, p. 308. https://doi.org/10.1002/(SICI)1234-981X(199707)5:3<305::AID-EURO184>3.0.CO;2-4.

[Student 1908] Student (William Gosset), "The Probable Error of a Mean," *Biometrika*, Volume 6, Issue 1, March 1908, pp. 1–25. https://doi.org/10.2307/2331554.

[Stulz 2007] René M. Stulz, "Hedge Funds: Past, Present, and Future." *Journal of Economic Perspectives*, Volume 21, Issue 2, 2006, pp. 175–194. https://doi.org/10.1257/jep.21.2.175.

[Tainter 1990] Joseph Tainter, *The Collapse of Complex Societies*, Cambridge University Press, 1990. www.cambridge.org/us/academic/subjects/archaeology/archaeological-theory-and-methods/collapse-complex-societies?format=PB&isbn=9780521386739.

[Teng, Ehrhardt, and Günther 2015] Long Teng, Matthias Ehrhardt, and Michael Günther, "The Pricing of Quanto Options under Dynamic Correlation," *Journal of Computational and Applied Mathematics*, Volume 275, 2015, pp. 304–310. https://doi.org/10.1016/j.cam.2014.07.017.

[Tett 2009] Gillian Tett, *Fool's Gold: How the Bold Dream of a Small Tribe at J.P. Morgan Was Corrupted by Wall Street Greed and Unleashed a Catastrophe*, Simon & Schuster, 2009. www.simonandschuster.com/books/Fools-Gold/Gillian-Tett/9781439100134.

[TMPG 2021] Treasury Market Practices Group, "Convexity Hedging during the 2021 Rate Sell Off," TMPG Meeting, March 23, 2021. www.newyorkfed.org/medialibrary/Microsites/tmpg/files/TMPG_Convexity_Hedging_presentation_03_23_21.pdf.

[Tödter 2008] Karl-Heinz Tödter, "Estimating the uncertainty of relative risk aversion," *Applied Financial Economics Letters*, Volume 4, Issue 1, 2008, pp. 25–27. https://doi.org/10.1080/17446540701335474.

[Treynor 1965] Jack L. Treynor, "How to Rate Management of Investment Funds," *Harvard Business Review*, Volume 43, Issue 1, January–February 1965, pp. 63–75. https://web-s-ebscohost-com.proxy.library.nyu.edu/ehost/detail/detail?vid=2&sid=1987b375-0f73-45cd-84ab-3affcac596be%40redis&bdata=JnNpdGU9ZWhvc3QtbGl2ZQ==#AN=3866364&db=bth.

[Trzcinka 1986] Charles Trzcinka, "On the Number of Factors in the Arbitrage Pricing Model," *The Journal of Finance*, Volume 41, Issue 2, June 1986, pp. 347–368. https://doi.org/10.2307/2328440.

[U.S. EIA 2020] U.S. Energy Information Administration, "WTI Crude Oil Futures Prices Fell Below Zero because of Low Liquidity and Limited Available Storage," *This Week in Petroleum*, April 22, 2020. www.eia.gov/petroleum/weekly/archive/2020/200422/includes/analysis_print.php.

[Vasicek 1977] Oldrich Vasicek, "An equilibrium characterization of the term structure," *Journal of Financial Economics*, Volume 5, Issue 2, November 1977, pp. 177–188. https://doi.org/10.1016/0304-405X(77)90016-2.

[VNM 1953] John von Neumann and Oskar Morgenstern, *Theory of Games and Economic Behavior*, Princeton University Press, 1953. https://archive.org/details/in.ernet.dli.2015.215284/page/n5

[Wallace 1980] Anise Wallace, "Is Beta Dead?," *Institutional Investor*, July 1980, pp. 23–30.

[Wasserstein and Lazar 2016] Ronald L. Wasserstein and Nicole A. Lazar, "The ASA Statement on p-Values: Context, Process, and Purpose," *The American Statistician*, Volume 70, Issue 2, 2016, pp. 129–133. https://doi.org/10.1080/00031305.2016.1154108.

[Wearden 2011] Graeme Wearden, "Swiss Bid to Peg 'Safe Haven' Franc to the Euro Stuns Currency Traders," *The Guardian*, September 6, 2011. www.theguardian.com/business/2011/sep/06/switzerland-pegs-swiss-franc-euro.

[Welch 2000] Ivo Welch, "Views of Financial Economists on the Equity Premium and on Professional Controversies," *Journal of Business*, Volume 73, Issue 4, October 2000, pp. 501–537. https://doi.org/10.1086/209653.

[White 2009] Lawrence J. White, "A Brief History of Credit Rating Agencies: How Financial Regulation Entrenched this Industry's Role in the Subprime Mortgage Debacle of 2007–2008," Mercatus Center, George Mason University, October 2009. www.mercatus.org/publications/monetary-policy/brief-history-credit-rating-agencies-how-financial-regulation#end4.

[Wigner 1960] Eugene P. Wigner, "The Unreasonable Effectiveness of Mathematics in the Natural Sciences," *Communications on Pure and Applied Mathematics*, Volume 13, Issue 1, 1960, pp. 1–14. https://doi.org/10.1002/cpa.3160130102.

[Willkens 2005] Sascha Willkens, "Option Pricing Based on Mixtures of Distributions: Evidence from the Eurex Index and Interest Rate Futures Options Market," *Derivatives Use, Trading, and Regulation*, Volume 11, 2005, pp. 213–231. https://doi.org/10.1057/palgrave.dutr.1840020.

[Wise and Bhansali 2010] Mark Wise and Vineer Bhansali, *Fixed Income Finance: A Quantitative Approach*, McGraw-Hill Finance & Investing, 2010. www.mhprofessional.com/fixed-income-finance-a-quantitative-approach-9780071763417-usa.

[Yeats 1919] William Butler Yeats, "The Second Coming," 1919. www.poetryfoundation.org/poems/43290/the-second-coming.

Index